Sociology

And The Human Experience

THE TREE OF LIFE

This sculpture is permanently located in the Town Plaza, and has become the graphic symbol of Columbia, Maryland. The sculptor is Pierre duFayet. The sculpture is composed of Fiberglas overlaid with gold leaf. The Tree of Life is a modern representation of people celebrating life, symbolizing people joined together in community, dependent on each other for their growth and well-being. It is also known as the People Tree.

Sociology 3 ed.

And The Human Experience

DONALD A. HOBBS
STUART J. BLANK
Both of Catonsville Community College

1807 1982
175 YEARS OF PUBLISHING

JOHN WILEY & SONS, INC.
New York
Chichester
Brisbane
Toronto
Singapore

Cover: Mobile "The Red Ear" by Alexander Calder, 1957,
          Collection Neuberger Museum, State University of
          New York, College at Purchase; gift of Roy R. Neuberger.
          Photo by Terry Lennon

Photo Research by Teri Leigh Stratford
Photo Editor, Stella Kupferberg

Library of Congress Cataloging in Publication Data:

Hobbs, Donald A., 1926–
    Sociology and the human experience.

    Bibliography: p.
    Includes indexes.
    1. Sociology.   I. Blank, Stuart J., 1942–
II. Title.
HM51.H59   1982   301   81-13126
ISBN 0-471-08281-3   AACR2

Printed in the United States of America

10 9 8 7 6 5 4 3 2

We dedicate this book to
those whom we especially love:

MIRIAM E. AND JOSEPH J. BLANK

DANIEL, JONATHAN AND MARY LOU HOBBS

Preface

Purpose of the Book

Human experience is a social experience. Ever since people first gathered together, some have clung to the earth and old ways while others have reached for the stars and new ways. Whatever their desires, their goals, or their dreams, however, people have also reached for and clung to each other. This shared dependence of human beings upon one another through all the events and activities of life, through both social stability and social change, is the essence of sociology and comprises the major theme of our book.

Sociology and the Human Experience introduces college students to the study of sociology. We hope that in learning sociology students will also acquire a sociological perspective of the human experience—an understanding and appreciation of the fact that, above all, people are social beings. We have therefore attempted not only to teach sociology but also to encourage students to use the sociological perspective to examine American society and their personal relation to it.

Changes in the Third Edition

The third edition of *Sociology and the Human Experience* has been revised extensively. First, we have tried to make the text more readable and thus more accessible to today's students. We have also dramatically increased the number of illustrations.

Substantial changes have been made in the organization of the book. There are now 12 chapters instead of 10 units, and the sequence in which various subjects are presented has been improved. This new organization has allowed us to increase the emphasis on certain important topics. For instance, racism and sexism are now discussed after stratification under social inequality. The subject of bureaucracy is now covered in a chapter called "Working and Work Organizations." Another new chapter is "Collective Behavior and Social Change." It discusses the different types of collective behavior and the theory behind them as well as social movements and social change.

In addition to revising and updating the information that appeared in the previous edition, we have added a significant amount of new material. There are three entirely new sections: "The Aging Syndrome in America," "Humans as Unique Primates," and "Sociobiology." There are also many other additions throughout the text. For instance, treatment of ethnic and minority groups has been expanded; a description of the collapse of the ancient Mayan ecosystem has been added to the discussion of ecology; coverage of the structural-functionalist, conflict, and symbolic-interactionist theories of social interaction has been included in the section on the sociological perspective; and a discussion of assimilation versus pluralism in America has been added to the section on minority status.

We have also provided additional learning aids for the students. For each of the 36 sections, we have included a list of the key terms and important names that appear in that section. Furthermore, an itemized summary is given at the end of each chapter.

Organization of the Book

Sociology and the Human Experience is divided into 12 chapters, each of which contains three sections. Although the sections within a chapter are interrelated, every section has been designed as an independent lesson. Each section begins with a list of objectives for the students, followed by the text itself. At the end of the section there is a list of key names and sociological terms, a study guide for review, and a practice test with an accompanying answer key. Following the third section of each chapter, there is also a summary of the entire chapter and a list of suggestions for further reading. In the back of the book, we have provided a glossary, a list of all the references cited in the text, and indexes of important names and subjects.

How to Use the Book

The organization of *Sociology and the Human Experience* is intended to encourage students to complete one section at a time. We believe that students learn better when they study manageable amounts of material and do not try to accomplish too much in one sitting. Of course, the way in which any textbook is ultimately used depends upon the instructor and the students. Time restrictions and personal preferences almost always mean that not all of the material included in a book can be covered in class. With this in mind, we have provided the study guides, practice tests, chapter summaries, and other aids to learning to help students more readily acquire information for which they may be held responsible.

Especially to the Student

We hope you find this book both educational and enjoyable. Our desire has been to make sociology interesting and even exciting, which is how we find it. Let us know what you may have particularly liked about the book as well as what you feel we might improve.

Donald A. Hobbs
Stuart J. Blank

ACKNOWLEDGMENTS, THIRD EDITION

We offer our special gratitude to our editor, Carol Luitjens. Her ideas, encouragement, and pursuit of excellence inspired us to produce a significantly improved edition of *Sociology and the Human Experience*. We also thank all the staff at Wiley for their care and help.

The following people helped us shape the new edition and should be recognized:

Barbara Bolaños, College of the Desert; Thomas Cravens, Meramec Community College; Loren Dow, Emory-Henry College; Vera FitzGerald, Cypress College; Eleanor Hall, Rend Lake College; John Henderson, Scottsdale Community College; Joe Jioia, Moraine Valley Community College; Joseph Long, Plymouth State College; Michael McCloskey, Truman College; Bill Mullin, Lane Community College; Norman Thu, College of the Desert; Robert Trotter, Pan American University; Howell Watkins, Midland College; Franklin Watson, Central Connecticut State College; David Yaukey, University of Massachusetts; George Yelagotes, Millersville State College.

Finally, for reading and criticizing the manuscript, we are sincerely grateful to:

Norman Culbertson, Yakima Valley Community College; Vincent Davis, Mt. Hood Community College; Elias Nigem, University of Toledo; Herbert Shellans, Phoenix College; and Laura Valvatne, Community College of Denver.

D.A.H.
S.J.B.

Contents

Chapter 1
Sociology as a Discipline, a Science, and a Perspective

SECTION 1 SOCIOLOGY AS AN ACADEMIC DISCIPLINE
- THE HUMAN SEARCH FOR KNOWLEDGE
- THE PERSISTENT HUMAN PREDICAMENT
- THE SOCIOLOGICAL SEARCH FOR KNOWLEDGE
- ABOUT SOCIOLOGY AND SOCIOLOGISTS
- SOCIOLOGY AS A DISCIPLINE WITH SPECIALIZED AREAS

Objectives

After completing this section, the student should be able to:
1. Define and explain the purpose of cosmogonies.
2. Identify experiences that contribute to the persistent human predicament.
3. Explain why sociology appeared in 19th-century Europe.
4. Describe the differences between social statics and social dynamics.
5. Identify the content and the method of sociology.
6. Give examples of social interaction.
7. Name at least four specialized areas of sociology.

If we were to divide only the past 50,000 years of human existence into lifetimes of about 62 years, there would have been about 800 such lifetimes. Humans spent at least 650 of these lifetimes in caves.

For only the past 70 lifetimes have people been able to communicate from one generation to another through writing. Only during the past six lifetimes have many people seen printed language. The vast majority of all the material goods that we use in our day-to-day lives was developed during the present century.

(Toffler, 1970)

THE HUMAN
SEARCH FOR
KNOWLEDGE

Humans are one of the species of life on the planet Earth, namely *Homo sapiens*. The poet Wallace Stevens said that humankind has a "rage for order." It may be this rage for order that drives humanity to seek explanations for the beginning of the world and of what life is all about. Since ancient times, groups of people have created colorful and similar explanations of how it all began. Such attempts to explain the beginnings of time are called cosmogonies. A cosmogony is a theory about the creation of the world and of humans by some great god or gods.

There have been many attempts to describe the beginnings of the world. Witch doctors, wizards, mystics, priests, scholars, and scientists have tried to answer questions about the origins of the universe and the origins of human beings.

Almost every ancient tribe had a cosmogony. In *The People's Almanac* there are stories of creation (cosmogonies) cited from the following sources: African (Efik-Ibibio), Biblical (Old Testament), Chinese, Egyptian, Greek, Gypsy, Hindu, Mayan, Navajo, Norse, plus a scientific theory that also can be considered a type of cosmogony (Wallechinsky and Wallace, 1975). Even the modern nations of the world attempt to provide answers about how everything began. Without knowing from where they came, people tend to feel anxious and lost. The words to the song "Lost in the Stars" by Kurt Weill and Maxwell Anderson capture some of these feelings of anxiety and fear of being lost. The following song also offers an explanation of how the world began—a cosmogony.

Before Lord God made the sea or the land
He held all the stars in the palm of His hand
And they ran through His fingers like grains of sand
And one little star fell alone.
Then the Lord God hunted through the wide night air
For the little dark star in the wind down there
And He stated and promised He'd take special care
So it wouldn't get lost no more.
Now a man don't mind if the stars get dim
And the clouds blow over and darken him
So long as the Lord God's watching over him
Keeping track how it all goes on.
But I've been walking through the night and day
Till my eyes get weary and my head turns gray,
And sometimes it seems maybe God's gone away
Forgetting His promise and the words He'd say,
And we're lost out here in the stars—
Little stars, big stars,
Glowing through the night,
And we're lost out here in the stars.
(ANDERSON AND WEILL, 1946)

Are we lost out here in the stars? Our Earth is one lonely lump of matter that circles a minor star that we call the Sun. People use words like *infinity* (space without beginning and ending) and *eternity* (time without beginning and ending). How much can these words really mean to us? Humans do have beginnings, and humans have endings. It is a very sobering experience to see ourselves located in an infinite and eternal universe. So, as the poet suggests, humanity lives with a rage for order—a need to know. We humans have always sought knowledge in order to feel that we have some control over the world and our lives. Humankind wants to shake off the fear that we *are* lost out here in the stars. All across the Earth and through the ages of time, people have tried to put into order the mysteries of the universe and of human behavior. This is the human search for knowledge.

THE PERSISTENT HUMAN PREDICAMENT

We all share the human predicament. Birth we do not ask for, yet we are born. Death we seldom hope for, yet we do die. We are children of humans. Most of us become parents of humans. Each generation is born into a world that it did not make. We are social beings. We cannot survive without other people. As infants,

Lost in the stars?

we are helpless. We survive only because of what others do for us. Being social means being dependent upon others and having others dependent upon us. Because we are social beings, we care about what others do and about what others think. This is part of the human predicament.

But there is more to the human predicament. While being social, each of us is also a unique individual. Born a child of the universe, we each find ourself imprisoned within time and space and the group. We are also imprisoned within our single savage selves. As *Homo sapiens*, we are limited to our five senses. Our thinking is limited to the way our brains are made. With the predicament of these limitations, our species has persisted in seeking knowledge. We seek to put into order the mysteries of the universe and the complexities of human behavior.

Despite our search for knowledge and our rage for order, the human predicament remains with us. We never seem to find that final satisfying explanation about the world and the human experience. When we believe that we have made some sense of the ways of the world, something completely unexpected takes place. Again we are puzzled. Whether we are foolish or wise, careful or reckless, learned or ignorant, religious or sacrilegious, disaster can strike without warning. Misfortunes such as floods, earthquakes, droughts, murder, and war occur again and again without logical reasons. Because of the human predicament, some philosophers have said that "life is absurd, that the universe is a cosmic joke, and that Sisyphus best symbolizes man—endlessly pushing a huge stone uphill, only to see it roll down again, and so he must begin again his pointless action" (Bensman and Rosenberg, 1963).

THE SOCIOLOGICAL SEARCH FOR KNOWLEDGE

We have said that a need to know or a rage for order is the cause of the human search for knowledge. Sociology, a fairly recent attempt to add to human knowledge about human behavior, is the scientific study of the social lives of human beings. When experiences that people take for granted begin to undergo change, people begin to ask questions about what is happening. They wonder about the world around them and about their place in the world. This is what happened in 19th-century Europe. Great social changes began to occur as a result of the Industrial Revolution. Peasants whose families had worked on farms for generations moved to cities. Here they became industrial workers. Small towns became large cities. Rural people became urban. Working in industry and living in cities greatly changed the ordinary lives of many people who came from rural areas. The old values and old behaviors simply did not fit into the new way of life. At the same time, people could not feel secure about a future that seemed to promise even more changes in their lives. Once the old people had been the guides for the younger people. Now, with so much change, the past seemed to have nothing to do with the present. The old could not tell the young what the

Search for knowledge.

ever-changing future would hold in store for them. Sociology—the scientific study of society—came into existence as an attempt to provide orderly explanations for what seemed to be very disorderly changes occurring in 19th-century European societies.

The term *sociology* was coined by French social philosopher Auguste Comte (1798–1857). Comte was interested in the debates held by educated people about the changing times. He especially wanted to know whether people could experience dramatic social changes without suffering certain hardships. Comte believed that a *science of society* was both possible and desirable. He believed that the scientific methods of the physical sciences could be used to study society. Once a science of society was established, Comte thought, sociology could provide means for improving the human condition. Since such a science did not exist, Auguste Comte set about creating it and naming it "sociology" (Timasheff, 1967).

Comte divided the new science of sociology into two main areas. He called these two areas *social statics* and *social dynamics*. Social statics would be the study of the social structure that undergoes very little change and a study of the relationships between various parts of society. Social dynamics would be the study of how societies develop and change through the passing of time. Comte was convinced that people had profited by using scientific methods in studying the physical world. Therefore, he concluded, people could also gain by developing a science of society, using the same procedures used in the physical sciences—experimentation, observation, and comparison.

Some of Comte's ideas and theories about the nature of human beings and about society as a whole are not taken too seriously by modern sociologists. Still, he remains an extremely important figure in the history of sociology. While there were many others who contributed to early sociological thinking, we have to regard Comte as the founder of sociology. It was Comte who got other scholars in the 19th century to accept the idea of a science of society and it was his pioneering efforts that established sociology as one more tool to be used in the human search for knowledge.

ABOUT SOCIOLOGY AND SOCIOLOGISTS

Not everyone knows what sociology is nor what sociologists do. Some people believe that sociologists are one type of socialist. Others believe that sociology is what one should study to become a social worker. Let us try to answer the questions "What is sociology?" and "What is a sociologist?"

What Is Sociology?

There are different opinions regarding how to answer the question "What is sociology?" To a certain extent, there are as many sociologies as there are sociologists. Despite the differences of opinion among individual sociologists, we believe the following definition will be helpful and accurate. Sociology is the scientific study of *social interaction* among human beings. Since the next two sections of this chapter deal in more detail with the basic parts of this definition, our treatment here is brief.

Look at it this way. Content is *what* one studies. Method is *how* one studies. The *method* of science is the same for astronomy, chemistry, biology, psychology, and sociology. Each of these disciplines deals with a different subject matter or content. Still, each of these disciplines depends on the scientific method for arriving at answers.

The method of sociology is scientific investigation and analysis. The *content* of sociology is social interaction. Stated simply, "social" implies the involvement of others. To influence others or to be influenced by others is social interaction. Almost all of our experiences come from our involvement with others—our thoughts, feelings, hopes, and fears. A person's biography is a social biography.

The word *interaction* further reveals the content of sociology. "Inter" indicates that we are concerned with whatever takes place between and among people. "Action" indicates that we are concerned with what people do—their behavior (Vernon, 1965). Social interaction occurs when people take each other into account and influence one another.

Finally, since bees and ants and monkeys and other species besides humans engage in social interaction, sociologists often use the term *human interaction* in exactly the same way as the term *social interaction*. Whether we call it social interaction or human interaction, that is the focal point of sociological inquiry.

What Are Sociologists?

Sociologists are men and women who carefully study human societies. They focus on any human behavior that involves two or more people. In a book that has been popular with both teachers and students of sociology, Peter Berger (1929–   ) presents various images that people have of sociologists. Our answers to the question "What are sociologists?" are based upon Berger's observations.

Sociologists are people who are overwhelmingly interested in the behaviors of people. They will go anywhere that people gather together. Sociologists are interested in people, in people's history, in people's institutions, and in people's passions. Tell the sociologist of the people's moments of tragedy and grandeur and ecstasy. Lead the sociologist to people acting out their everyday, commonplace lives. The sociologist seeks out the *action* that takes place between and among people. To find the action, sociologists will go to the most respected or to the most despised places. For the sociologist, nothing is too sacred nor too distasteful. Whether the behavior be that of priest or prostitute, the sociologist will have questions and will seek answers. Whether the action involves great intellectual discoveries, employment in a restaurant, or childen playing on skateboards, the sociologist is interested in the action. Sociologists are professional social scientists. Their main focus of attention is the *action* that occurs between two or more people (Berger, 1963).

Sociologists are individuals who share in common an interest in the diverse behaviors of the human race within social situations. No two sociologists may have any more than that in common.

SOCIOLOGY AS A DISCIPLINE WITH SPECIALIZED AREAS

The term *Academe* is used to describe the world of colleges and universities. Academe is the place where scholars, teachers, and students consider the knowledge collected by those in the past while investigating what they might add to this vast collection of information and ideas. In Academe people move from room to room, from building to building, and, sometimes, from campus to campus. People in Academe also move from academic discipline to academic discipline.

Most academic institutions are composed of departments or divisions of knowledge. These can be seen as neatly piled packages of knowledge that are labeled with titles such as biology, chemistry, literature, history, philosophy, sociology, and so on. The student who has enrolled in an introductory sociology course is about to open one of these packages of knowledge.

In Academe the phrase *academic discipline* refers to any number of courses grouped together because they share in a major area of study and a common body of knowledge. A course in introductory sociology is merely a beginning look at the discipline of sociology. Most colleges and universities offer many other sociology courses that treat in more detail some of the subjects touched upon in an introductory course. Specialized areas of sociology include criminology, demography, marriage and family, medical sociology, race and ethnic relations, social problems, social stratification, urban sociology, and many others. One can become a specialist in just about any aspect of sociological inquiry.

Each of the specialized areas of sociology has *social interaction* as its focal point. Whether considering marriage, crime, or race relations, the sociologist must investigate, describe, and analyze the patterns of social interaction. The sociologist will observe the patterns of interaction between a husband and a wife, between a criminal and a police officer, and between two people of different races. Social interaction occurs when human beings take each other into account and exert a mutual influence upon one another (Weber, 1947). As people, sociologists participate in the human experience. As social scientists, sociologists seek to describe and to understand the human experience.

KEY TERMS AND NAMES FROM SECTION 1

Homo sapiens

cosmogony

rage for order

science of society

social statics

social dynamics

social interaction

persistent human predicament

Academe

Auguste Comte

STUDY GUIDE FOR SECTION 1

1. For a very long time people did not have written language to communicate from one generation to another. DURING HOW MANY LIFETIMES HAVE HUMANS COMMUNICATED THROUGH WRITTEN LANGUAGE?

2. Human beings have been classified by scientists as one of the species on Earth. WHAT NAME HAS BEEN GIVEN TO THE SPECIES HUMANKIND?

3. Through the years people have created stories about how the universe and humankind came into existence. WHAT TERM IS USED TO DESCRIBE THESE ATTEMPTS TO EXPLAIN THE BEGINNING OF TIME?

4. All people share in the persistent human predicament. IDENTIFY SOME HUMAN CHARACTERISTICS AND EXPERIENCES THAT CONTRIBUTE TO WHAT WE ARE CALLING THE PERSISTENT HUMAN PREDICAMENT.

5. When things that people take for granted begin to undergo change, people begin to ask questions about what is happening. DESCRIBE THIS PROCESS AS IT OCCURRED DURING THE 19TH CENTURY IN EUROPE.

6. Auguste Comte, seeking to establish a science of society, coined the term *sociology*. NAME AND DESCRIBE THE TWO AREAS OF STUDY THAT COMTE EXPECTED SOCIOLOGY TO INVESTIGATE.

7. We have described both the content and the methods of sociology. HOW ARE THE METHODS OF SOCIOLOGY SIMILAR TO THOSE USED IN ASTRONOMY, CHEMISTRY, BIOLOGY, AND PSYCHOLOGY?

8. The content of sociology is social interaction. EXPLAIN WHAT OCCURS WHEN SOCIAL INTERACTION TAKES PLACE.

9. TO WHAT DOES "ACADEME" REFER?

10. The phrase *academic discipline* refers to any number of courses grouped together because they share in a major area of study and a common body of knowledge. NAME AT LEAST FOUR SPECIALIZED AREAS OF SOCIOLOGY.

PRACTICE TEST FOR SECTION 1

Select the best answer.

1. Communication through written language has existed for about
A.   70 lifetimes.
B.   5 lifetimes.
C.   50 lifetimes.
D.   90 lifetimes.
E.   Always.

2. Cosmogonies are explanations of
A.   The concepts of eternity and infinity.
B.   The persistent human predicament.
C.   The origins of the universe and humans.
D.   The human search for knowledge.
E.   None of the above.

3. The term *Homo sapiens* refers to
A.   The animal kingdom.
B.   All living things.
C.   All thinking life forms.
D.   Human beings.

4. Sociology came into being as a result of
A.   Many social changes occurring in 19th-century America.
B.   Many social changes resulting from the Industrial Revolution.
C.   Many social changes resulting from the Reformation.
D.   The need for social workers in 19th-century Europe.

5. The term *sociology* was coined by
A.   Toffler.
B.   Timasheff.
C.   Comte.
D.   Berger.

6. The study of the social structure that undergoes little change and the study of relationships between various parts of society is known as

A.   Social statics.
B.   Social interaction.
C.   Socialization.
D.   Social dynamics.

7. Two areas that Comte said should be studied by sociology are
A.   Industrialization and urbanization.
B.   Social interaction and symbolic interaction.
C.   Social statics and social dynamics.
D.   Cosmogonies and science.

8. The method of sociology is
A.   Based upon inspiration and faith.
B.   Scientific investigation and analysis.
C.   Different from the methods of other sciences.
D.   Both B and C.

9. What occurs when people take each other into account and have a mutual influence upon one another?
A.   Social interaction.
B.   The persistent human predicament.
C.   Human interaction.
D.   Scientific investigation.
E.   Both A and C.

10. The word *social* suggests that sociology is concerned with human beings as
A.   Independent beings.
B.   Interacting beings.
C.   Isolated beings.
D.   Biological beings.
E.   None of the above.

Answer Key

1.	A	**6.**	A
2.	C	**7.**	C
3.	D	**8.**	B
4.	B	**9.**	E
5.	C	**10.**	B

SECTION 2   SOCIOLOGY AS A SCIENCE
- INTERPRETATIONS OF REALITY
- THE SCIENTIFIC METHOD
- TECHNIQUES OF SOCIOLOGICAL RESEARCH
- THE PRINCIPLE OF CAUSATION
- OBJECTIVITY AS A SOCIOLOGICAL GOAL
- SOCIOLOGY AS ONE OF THE SOCIAL SCIENCES

Objectives
After completing this section, the student should be able to:
1. Recognize how human views of reality affect human behavior.
2. Give examples of personal, social, and objective reality.
3. Describe the five major steps in the scientific method.
4. Explain the purposes of experimental and control groups in planned experiments.
5. Explain how the Hawthorne effect can reduce the value of some planned experiments.
6. Describe how sample surveys are done by using terms such as *random sample, population*, and *response bias*.
7. Indicate how case studies can be made of a person, a group, and an event.
8. Cite some examples of participant observation studies.
9. Recognize guidelines for behavior that make up the ASA's Code of Ethics.
10. Describe the principle of causation by using such terms as *independent* and *dependent variables*.
11. Explain why objectivity is difficult to maintain when observing human behavior.

Why did the American government assist in bringing peace between Egypt and Israel through the 1979 Camp David Accords? Did the Americans do this to aid their own best political interests, as some claim? Or did the Americans help to establish peace for humanitarian reasons, as others claim? Did the 900 members of the People's Temple in Guyana willingly commit suicide or were they unknowingly fooled by the Reverend Jim Jones? Are we in the midst of a sexual revolution, or is the present generation merely talking more openly about sexual behavior? Were the assassinations of John F. Kennedy, Martin Luther King, Jr., and Robert F. Kennedy committed by individuals acting on their own? Or were those assassinations part of a conspiracy? What are the right or *real* answers to such questions? What is reality? Actually, one person's reality can be very different from another person's reality about the same subject. Interpretations of reality are very important, because they can influence the ways in which people behave.

INTERPRE-TATIONS OF REALITY

In the 1920s the American sociologist W. I. Thomas (1863–1947) considered the nature of reality. Thomas coined the phrase "definition of the situation." He said that if people define certain situations as real, those situations are real in their consequences. Thomas was convinced that the way in which people perceive or define reality determines the way in which they behave (Volkart, 1951). To *perceive* means to understand and to be aware of something. So, for example, if one perceives the American political system as having little influence on one's life, one will probably not participate in the political process. The person's definition of the situation would be that voting is meaningless; therefore, the person would not vote.

The idea that behavior results from perception can be applied to a number of social situations. The way in which one perceives religion will determine the way in which one behaves in regard to religion. The way in which one perceives sex will determine one's sexual behavior. The way in which one perceives marriage will determine the way in which one behaves as a husband or a wife or even whether one considers getting married at all. Thus, according to the definition of the situation, a person's reality is how that person defines it.

Sociologists identify three ways in which we can perceive ourselves and all the things and events in the world around us. According to this view, reality can be perceived as follows.

Personal and Unique Reality

Personal and unique reality consists of ideas and beliefs that an individual believes to be true. It has been said that, in certain respects, every person is like all other persons, like some other persons, and like no other person (Kluckhohn and Murray, 1956). Personal reality coincides with the idea that each individual is like no other. Given the uniqueness of a person's capacities and experiences, it is reasonable to assume that, to some extent, reality is how one defines it.

Social and Shared Reality

If, however, the personal reality is reinforced through the opinions of others (every person is like some other person), the social and shared reality emerges. When this occurs, each person's unique reality is supported by the consensus of others who see things in the same way. This reality exists within a cultural context.

Objective and Scientific Reality

Scientific reality is considerably different from either personal or social reality because it does not depend on how a person or people claim they feel about the world. Objective reality is the version of reality that can be discovered and verified through science and the scientific method.

There can be disagreements about reality among people who rely on personal or social interpretations and other people who rely on interpretations based on scientific findings. As an example, for a long time people believed that the Earth was flat. This view of the Earth was based on personal and socially shared interpretations of reality. Science, using an objective interpretation, has proved that the Earth is not flat but that it is shaped like a spheroid. As another example, some people say that one race of humans is superior or inferior to another. Those who believe this depend on their personal and social perceptions. Science, using an objective interpretation of reality, tells us that all races of humans belong to the same species—*homo sapiens*— and that black, red, white, yellow, and all mixtures of people have a similar range of inherited abilities (Montagu, 1965).

THE SCIENTIFIC METHOD

The poet has said that humankind has a rage for order. Throughout history there has been evidence of the human search for knowledge. Seemingly lost out here in the stars, humans use various means to discover the reality of the human predicament. Modern science attempts to achieve an objective view of reality in

Sociologist collecting data.

any area studied. The *scientific method* is one procedure used by people to answer questions about the human experience and about the universe at large. The scientific method can be described as having five steps:

1. Formulate a hypothesis.
2. Develop a research design.
3. Collect data.
4. Analyze data.
5. Draw conclusions.

The hypothesis is a statement specifying a particular relationship between two or more variables. A hypothesis is an educated guess. For example, we might hypothesize that interracial marriages are more "successful" than racially homogeneous marriages. We might state the hypothesis this way: "The incidence of marital dissastisfaction among interracial marriages is significantly less frequent and less severe than among racially homogeneous marriages." In this case, our variables are racial background and marital success. A research design is a plan that must be developed in order to verify our hypothesis. For example, we might go to the Marriage License Bureau and gather lists of interracial couples and racially homogeneous couples who were married within the past five years. From both lists we might select every *n*th (any number) couple and proceed to interview them in an attempt to discover the degree of dissatisfaction with the marriage. This would be the process of collecting data. We would then analyze the data by comparing the degree of dissatisfaction expressed by our interviewees. Finally, we would draw conclusions based on the previous four steps used in our scientific method. The conclusions will reflect back to the hypothesis, and on the basis of conclusions, we either accept the hypothesis or reject it. In fact, we might suggest some type of modification in the study and start over again. Each step is related to every other step, which makes the scientific method a compact, logical unit of investigation.

TECHNIQUES OF SOCIOLOGICAL RESEARCH

Despite obvious differences between the physical and social sciences, all sciences have in common the use of the scientific method. However, each science must develop its own techniques, because each science considers different subject matter. Sociologists do not use telescopes, microscopes, test tubes, and beakers when they study human social behavior. Let us describe four techniques that are used in sociological research (Berelson and Steiner, 1967).

Planned Experiments

Suppose we want to find out whether there is a relationship between propaganda and prejudice (our two variables). To be more exact, we want to find out whether a propagandistic film favoring the ideas of humanism and equality can have any influence upon prejudicial attitudes. One way to find out is to use a planned experiment. The purpose of the experiment is to manipulate one variable (film) and test its influence on another variable (prejudicial attitudes).

We could select a group of children and measure the amount of prejudicial feelings they have toward group X. Let's say that the group of children we have selected all exhibit similar prejudicial feelings toward group X, according to our testing.

After a period of time, we would meet with the children again. This time we would show half of the children the film on humanism and equality. Those children who see the film would be called the "experimental group" because the variable (film) is shown to them. The other half of the children who do *not* see the film would be called the "control group." The function of the control group is to make sure that if a change in attitudes is found in the experimental group, the change results from seeing the film and not from some other factor such as the simple passing of time, for example.

When we give the retest to both groups of children, we measure the degree of change in attitudes. If we find a significant difference between the experimental group and the control group on the retest, we can assume that the film on humanism and equality did have an effect on prejudicial attitudes.

There are certain problems that can occur when using planned experiments involving people. For one thing, if an experiment involves many people, it can be costly in terms of money and time. It could take years to conduct an experiment. Another thing is that our values forbid us from using people in experiments that might harm them in some way. Also, people might be unwilling to take part in an experiment. Sociologists certainly cannot force people to cooperate. Finally, people are likely to behave differently when they know that they are part of an experiment, and this tendency could ruin the experiment.

It is a fact that any experiment in which people know they are being studied seems to cause them to behave in misleading ways. This is called the *Hawthorne effect*. This term comes from some experiments done in the 1930s at the Hawthorne branch of Western Electric Company outside of Chicago. The purpose of the experiments was to discover what factors might cause workers at the branch to increase their productivity. A particular group of workers was isolated from the other workers. Then their working conditions were changed in various ways at different times. Changes were made for the experimental group in reference to such things as temperature, humidity, rest periods, lighting, lunch times, and methods of getting paid. It was discovered that *any* change in working conditions could bring about temporary increases in production. This was misleading. Actually, it was not the changes that increased productivity. Instead, it was because the workers enjoyed being part of the experiment. They wanted to please those who were giving them so much attention!

The Hawthorne effect shows how the findings of some experiments may be due only to the attention given to the people in the study, not to the factors being tested. Because of this and other drawbacks involving the use of people in planned experiments, the social sciences depend more on other techniques for research (Roethlisberger and Dickson, 1939).

Sample Surveys

A technique used more often by sociologists is the survey. Survey research includes the use of questionnaires or interviews and sometimes a combination of both. The purpose of surveys is to gather information about large numbers of people. Americans have been taking surveys for over 150 years, beginning with a survey on political opinion about the presidential election in 1824 (Gergen and Schambra, 1979).

The group of people whose attitudes or behavior interests the sociologist is called the *population*. A population could consist of *all* college students, *all* married women, *all* voters, *all* baseball fans, or *all* people who listen to radio. It is very hard to interview *all* the people from any particular grouping. There isn't the time. And who would have the opportunity to survey an entire population of millions? Instead, a portion of any population is surveyed. That portion is called a *sample*. A sample consists of a small number of individuals drawn from the population. The researcher should be sure that a sample accurately represents the population. If it does not, then conclusions drawn from the survey are limited only to those who are the sample and cannot be applied to the population. There is a way to be sure that a sample does truly represent a population. Let us explain further.

The usual method of making sure that a sample is representative is to make a random selection of subjects. A *random sample* means that every member of a population has an equal chance of being selected. A certain number of names could be pulled out of a box filled with names. A list of random digits could be an alternative. Also, a population could be divided into categories such as age, race, religion, or sex. Then a random sample could be drawn from each of those categories. This technique is called *stratified random sampling*. The categories in the sample should be represented in the same proportion as they exist in the population from which the sample is drawn.

Contrasted with modern standards, early surveys were crude and unreliable. Over the years surveys have become more reliable. Modern public opinion polls (surveys) conducted by Gallup, Harris, Yankelovich, and Roper have proved themselves to be highly accurate. "Working with the laws of probability, statisticians have determined that, 95 percent of the time, a random survey of 1500 persons will produce results that have a margin of error of plus or minus 3 percent." For example, a survey of 1500 people that shows 55 percent favor passing the Equal Rights Amendment (ERA) can be considered reliable. If the same poll were to be repeated 20 times, in 19 times support for the ERA would equal between 52 and 58 percent. In the one other time—the 20th—the support would be above or below those figures (Gergen and Schambra, 1979).

The survey is a valuable source of information about people's attitudes and behavior. It has limitations, however. People will sometimes express opinions on subjects about which they know little or nothing. In surveys that depend upon questionnaires mailed out, response rates of less than 50 percent are common. Furthermore, at least 10 percent of American adults are not literate enough to complete a questionnaire without help. Another limitation is the fact that false information may be given, particularly in face-to-face interviews. People will respond differently depending upon who is conducting the interviews. This is called *response bias*. It suggests that people responding to surveys can be influenced by *who* is doing the questioning as much as by *what* is being asked (Selltiz et al., 1962). Whether one is old or young, man or woman, black or white, native born or naturalized citizen, such characteristics can be significant factors in the surveying process.

Case Studies

Only some of the human experience can be studied by observing people in action or by surveying for attitudes and behavior. Using another technique, we make exhaustive studies of people or groups. Such studies are called *case studies* or *case histories*. Making a case study is an attempt to do research in depth. A case study can be made of a person, a group, a social institution, or a community. Case studies, or case histories, can be made even of *events*, such as riots, wars, and religious movements. Accumulating information for an exhaustive case study requires much research. Sociologists should make use of documents such as diaries, letters, public records, eyewitness accounts, and autobiographies. *One* case study by itself cannot prove much of anything. But if there are many case studies that tend to agree and that tend to provide insights to more general conditions, then sociologists are on the road to a generalization that could prove significant. Because the case-study technique examines human behavior in specific, precise detail, it has been called the "social microscope" (Young, 1966).

Participant Observation Studies

Some sociologists become active participants in the human experience that they are observing. Sociologists have been known to join religious cults, to live in the Bowery in New York City with alcoholic bottle gangs, and to join groups who hang around such places as poolrooms, carry-out shops, and street corners. To gain special insights to human behavior, sociologists have also lived in communes and joined militant political groups.

One sociologist spent time as an observer in a mental hospital. His findings indicated that the patients were treated more like prisoners than like people needing help and support. In fact, being in the mental hospital seemed to cause more harm than offer help to the patients (Goffman, 1961). Another such study was made by spending many hours with poolroom sharks. They earned their money by pretending to be not-so-good at first and then proving to be good enough to win regularly as the money stakes were raised in the betting. This study provided insights into the codes of morality by which many pool hustlers survive (Polsky, 1967).

One anthropologist associated with a group of black men who hung around a corner in Washington, D.C., during 1962 and 1963. By befriending these men and participating in their lives, he was able to record their daily activities as they "frequented the street corner, the alleys, hallways, poolrooms, beer joints, and private houses in the immediate neighborhood." The experience led him to observe the lives of these men in places outside their neighborhood as well. He found himself joining them as they appeared in courtrooms, jails, hospitals, dance halls, and various other places in Washington, Maryland, and Virginia. By winning the confidence of these men, the anthropologist was able to participate in their lives and to provide us with a better understanding of a life-style unknown to the majority of Americans (Liebow, 1967).

One kind of religious cult is the doomsday group. Such a group was joined by some social scientists acting as participant observers. A woman who said she heard voices predicting that the United States would suffer a devastating flood encouraged her followers to give up everything and prepare for the end at a given hour. When the hour came and passed, the woman said that God had postponed the disaster because the believers had been so faithful. This explanation was accepted by the believers who remained members of the religious cult. This study indicated that people can remain devoted to a cause and a group even when there is a dramatic change in predictions and plans (Festinger, Schachter, and Back, 1950).

Another doomsday group infiltrated by social scientists was a cult in which members believed that the world was coming to an end very soon. This cult believed that a limited number of people would be saved by travelers in flying saucers from outer space. These friendly aliens were supposedly going to take the believers to another planet. This study revealed that people can accept the most outlandish beliefs while receiving support for their beliefs from one another (Festinger, Riecken, and Schachter, 1956).

Participant observation requires the sociologist to participate in a situation being studied. The sociologist should be sure to keep in mind that he or she is in the situation to gather knowledge. Some governmental agencies have used this technique to gain information about groups thought to be dangerous to the nation's welfare. Sociologists use this technique as a means of research, not as a means to prevent or to change the behavior of the group being observed.

One participant observation study has caused much controversy. In a book by Laud Humphreys entitled *Tearoom Trade: Impersonal Sex in Public Places*, he describes one kind of social setting for homosexual behavior among men. After learning of several locations for sexual "kicks without commitment" (called tearooms by those involved), Humphreys observed hundreds of acts of fellatio. He wrote:

Fortunately the very fear and suspicion of tearoom participants produces a mechanism that makes such observations possible; a third man (generally one who obtains voyeuristic pleasure from his duties) serves as a lookout, moving back and forth from door to window. Such a "watchqueen," as he is labeled in the homosexual argot, coughs when a police car stops nearby or when a stranger approaches. Having been taught the watchqueen role by a cooperating respondent, I played the part faithfully while observing hundreds of acts of fellatio.

(Humphreys, 1970)

Humphreys' opportunity for participant observation contributed to knowledge about *one* kind of homosexual behavior that occurs in modern society. Using this technique, the goal is to get knowledge about human behavior without changing the behavior being observed. If Humphreys had informed the men of his intentions, their behavior would probably have been altered. This would have misrepresented the reality that such research seeks to discover. Participant observation is useful because it provides information that ordinary observation probably cannot provide.

As we have said, this study caused considerable controversy—less for its content than for its technique. Participant observation has been defined as a technique in which the observer participates in the daily life of people being studied, either with or without the knowledge of those whose behavior is being studied. Controversy about such studies occurs because "masquerading" and deceiving others is thought to be unethical by some critics (Becker and Geer, 1957).

There have been many critics of Humphreys' methodology. Others have said that while this approach was undesirable, it was necessary to gather the desired information. One such critic, Nicholas Von Hoffman, a staff writer for the *Washington Post*, said that "if a straight male were to hang around a tearoom, he wouldn't see anything out of the ordinary, so that if you're going to find out what's happening, you must give the impression that you're one of the gang." Participant observation is the only method by which this type of insight can be achieved.

Here are some ethical points that have been made in criticisms of Humphreys' study:

1. In studying the sexual behavior of men in restrooms, Humphreys violated their rights to intimacy and privacy.

2. The participants in impersonal sex were and still remain unaware of the actual purpose of Humphreys' presence as a watchqueen.

3. Although Humphreys' intent may have been above reproach, his methods chipped away at the essential rights of individuals. The ends, the goals, however noble, do not justify the means that undermine personal liberties (Von Hoffman, Horowitz, and Rainwater, 1970).

As a profession, sociology has an ethical commitment to the pursuit of knowledge. There is a special responsibility for sociologists to respect the integrity and dignity of individuals, not only as research subjects but as individual citizens as well. Recently the American Sociological Association adopted certain guidelines for behavior that make up the ASA's Code of Ethics. According to the ASA, sociologists are expected to:

1. Maintain objectivity and integrity in conducting research.

2. Respect the research subjects' rights to privacy and dignity.

3. Preserve the confidentiality of research data.

4. Protect research subjects from personal harm.

No research technique should have even a potential chance for harming people. Any scientific and social benefits to be gained from research procedures must not be at the cost of human rights (Erikson, 1965). The problem of ethics in research centers upon a choice between two values—the right to privacy and the right to know. Eventually, it should be the value system of society that determines the balance between the right of an individual to privacy and the right of the public to know and understand some or all of the human experience.

THE PRINCIPLE OF CAUSATION

A basic belief of the sciences is that all events have causes. Whether the event is the hijacking of an airplane or the failure of a student to pass a test, the principle of causation applies. The *principle of causation* suggests that each and every event has a cause or causes. In the social sciences, there are often many causes of an event rather than a single cause. This is referred to as *multiple causation*.

Juvenile delinquency is a serious problem in the United States. People want to understand why young people commit crimes. Instead of searching for a single cause, sociologists try to identify factors associated with becoming delinquent. Factors said to be linked with delinquent behavior include family background, poverty, peer group pressure, and easy opportunities to commit crime. This is an example of recognizing multiple causation for a condition in society.

Sociologists study cause and effect by studying how various variables can influence one another. A *variable* can be an attitude, behavior pattern, or condition that is subject to change. Put another way, a variable is a characteristic that can vary. Age, race, religion, sex, and social class are variables. So is intelligence. Causation occurs when one variable influences another variable. For example, frustration or being prevented from achieving goals can lead to aggression. In this case there is a relationship between the two variables of frustration and aggression. The variable that causes the effect is known as the *independent variable* (in this case, frustration). The variable that is the effect is known as the *dependent variable* (in this case, aggression). Many traffic accidents occur after drivers have consumed much beer or wine or liquor. The two variables would be too much drinking and traffic accidents. Too much drinking of alcohol would be the independent variable and the traffic accidents would be the dependent variable.

We discuss the subject of causation further in Section Thirty, Social and Cultural Change.

OBJECTIVITY AS A SOCIOLOGICAL GOAL

The scientific method requires one to remain uninfluenced by personal opinions and feelings when doing research. Objectivity exists when an observation is not influenced by one's personal prejudices, beliefs, or values. Scientists should describe what is, not what they think should be. In mathematics, objectivity is easy to achieve: 2 plus 2 equals 4. Being objective is harder when one must consider oneself, one's family and friends, and one's whole style of life. Studies indicate that people tend to see what they want to see or what they expect to see. The ethical code of sociology expects the sociologist to be intellectually honest. Remaining honest is a very important part of being objective about human behavior. Objectivity is an attitude that is more difficult to maintain when dealing with human behavior than when observing, for example, other life forms through a microscope. Nevertheless, objectivity is one of the goals of sociologists. Conclusions drawn should not be considered absolute and final. Sociology is a self-correcting discipline. Nothing in sociology is so sacred that it cannot be challenged. There are no truths so absolute that they cannot be subject to change when new evidence comes to our attention.

SOCIOLOGY AS ONE OF THE SOCIAL SCIENCES

Throughout this section we have said that sociology is a science. It depends on the scientific method and on scientific research techniques. To be more exact now, sociology is one of the social sciences. All of the social sciences have the same general interest—the human experience. The differences among anthropology, psychology, sociology, and all the other social sciences are academic. The lines of division are somewhat blurred. The basic difference among the social sciences is in the angles of vision or the emphasis on particulars. All the social sciences must be aware of the relationships between individuals, groups, and societies. This is equally true for anthropology, economics, political science, psychology, and sociology. Again, all of the social sciences are concerned with the human experience.

Anthropology as a social science originally concentrated on the study of preliterate folk societies. With the spread of mass society, anthropologists also have studied the human experience within urban, industrial societies. Anthropologists are concerned with many of the same social matters that concern sociologists. In addition, anthropologists direct their attention to a people's language, legends, and history. Economics is especially concerned with the ways in which people produce, distribute, and consume goods and services. Political science concentrates on the ways in which people establish and recognize authority through various forms of government. As for psychology, its main focus is on the individual's development. Psychologists direct their attention to the human nervous system, to human intelligence, mental health, and mental disorders. Together, all of the social sciences are comrades in their search to understand and to describe the human experience.

KEY TERMS AND NAMES FROM SECTION 2

definition of the situation

personal and unique reality

social and shared reality

objective and scientific reality

the scientific method

hypothesis

research design

planned experiments

dependent and independent variables

experimental group

control group

Hawthorne effect

sample survey

population

random sample

case study

participant observation

doomsday group

principle of causation

multiple causation

objectivity

the social sciences

W. I. Thomas

Laud Humphreys

STUDY GUIDE FOR SECTION 2

1. W. I. Thomas introduced the concept "definition of the situation." HOW DOES THIS CONCEPT RELATE TO PEOPLE'S PERCEPTION OF REALITY?

2. Sociologists say there are three ways in which people might perceive reality: personal, social, and objective. EXPLAIN THE BASIS FOR EACH OF THESE PERCEPTIONS OF REALITY.

3. The scientific method is one procedure used to answer questions about the human experience and the universe at large. LIST THE FIVE STEPS OF THE SCIENTIFIC METHOD AS DESCRIBED IN THE TEXT.

4. The planned experiment is one technique of sociological research. DESCRIBE THE FUNCTIONS OF THE EXPERIMENTAL AND CONTROL GROUPS.

5. WHAT IS THE HAWTHORNE EFFECT? EXPLAIN THE ORIGINS OF THIS TERM.

6. Another type of sociological research is the sample survey. EXPLAIN HOW THIS TECHNIQUE WORKS BY REFERRING TO SUCH TERMS AS *POPULATION, SAMPLE*, AND *RANDOM SAMPLE*.

7. Working with the laws of probability, statisticians have determined that a random survey of a certain number of people will produce results that have a certain margin of error. WHAT NUMBER OF PEOPLE IS CONSIDERED RELIABLE, AND WHAT IS THE MARGIN OF ERROR?

8. The survey is a valuable source of information about people. EXPLAIN WHY IT HAS CERTAIN LIMITATIONS. WHAT IS RESPONSE BIAS?

9. Making a case study is an attempt to do research in depth. WHAT ARE SOME EXAMPLES OF TYPES OF CASE STUDIES?

10. To accumulate information for case studies, WHAT KIND OF DOCUMENTS CAN SOCIOLOGISTS USE?

11. Participant observations also provide sociologists with information about human behavior. DESCRIBE THE BEHAVIOR OF A SOCIOLOGIST INVOLVED IN A PARTICIPANT OBSERVATION.

12. BRIEFLY DESCRIBE AT LEAST THREE CASES OF PARTICIPANT OBSERVATION CITED IN THE TEXT. WHAT KNOWLEDGE WAS GAINED FROM EACH CASE?

13. Humphreys' study of one kind of homosexual behavior did provide knowledge. WHAT ARE SOME ETHICAL POINTS THAT HAVE BEEN MADE IN CRITICISMS OF HUMPHREYS' PARTICIPANT OBSERVATION?

14. The sociologist studies cause and effect by studying how various variables influence one another. EXPLAIN THE RELATIONSHIP THAT EXISTS BETWEEN INDEPENDENT AND DEPENDENT VARIABLES. MAKE UP AN EXAMPLE IN WHICH SUCH VARIABLES ARE USED.

15. Sociologists should be objective when doing research. DEFINE OBJECTIVITY AND EXPLAIN ITS IMPORTANCE IN SOCIOLOGICAL RESEARCH.

16. All the social sciences have the same general interest in common. WITH WHAT ARE ALL THE SOCIAL SCIENCES CONCERNED?

PRACTICE TEST FOR SECTION 2

Select the best answer.

1. Which type of relationship exists between perception and behavior?
A. Perception and behavior are not related.
B. Behavior results from perception.
C. Perception results from behavior.
D. None of the above statements is correct.

2. Which of the following is *not* a way in which people might perceive reality?
A. Personally objective.
B. Personally.
C. Socially.
D. Scientifically.

3. The first step in the scientific method is to
A. Create a research design.
B. Collect the data.
C. Formulate a hypothesis.
D. Draw conclusions.

4. The research technique that uses a control group and an experimental group is the
A. Planned experiment.
B. Sample survey.
C. Case study.
D. Participant observation.

5. The Hawthorne effect occurs when
A. Scientists attempt to fool people.
B. People behave differently because they know they are being studied.
C. Scientists use the case study technique.
D. People resist attempts of scientists to discover facts.

6. Important parts of the survey technique are
A. Control group and experimental group.
B. Participation and observation of the researcher.
C. Control group and non-control group.
D. Population and sample.

7. Modern opinion polls and surveys are most accurate if a random survey is made of at least how many people?
A. 500
B. 1000

C.   1500
D.   2500

8.   Statisticians say that a reliable random survey will produce results that have a margin of error of plus or minus
A.   3 percent
B.   5 percent
C.   10 percent
D.   15 percent

9.   Which of the following correctly describes "response bias"?
A.   People do not exhibit prejudice in answering surveys.
B.   People are influenced by who is doing the questioning.
C.   Researchers fail to ask questions of enough people.
D.   Researchers select only their kind of people for study.

10.   Detailed study of events such as riots, wars, and revolutions can best be made by
A.   Planned experiments.
B.   Sample surveys.
C.   Case studies.
D.   Participant observations.

11.   Which sociological research technique has been called the "social microscope"?
A.   Planned experiments.
B.   Sample surveys.
C.   Case studies.
D.   Participant observations.

12.   In which technique of sociological research does the sociologist become actively involved in the situation being studied?

A.   Planned experiments.
B.   Sample surveys.
C.   Case studies.
D.   Participant observations.

13.   Which of the following is not a criticism made of Laud Humphreys' participant observation study?
A.   He violated the men's rights to privacy.
B.   He failed to identify his reason to the men for being present.
C.   His research is useless without pictures.
D.   Both A and B.

14.   Causation occurs when
A.   One variable remains isolated.
B.   An independent variable causes a dependent variable.
C.   A dependent variable causes an independent variable.
D.   Both B and C are correct.

15.   Objectivity exists when an observation is
A.   Uninfluenced by one's personal beliefs.
B.   Consistent with the scientific method.
C.   Not based on a person's prejudices.
D.   All of the above.

16.   Which of the following is not one of the social sciences?
A.   Economics.
B.   Zoology.
C.   Anthropology.
D.   Both A and B.

Answer Key

1.	B	7.	C	12.	D
2.	A	8.	A	13.	C
3.	C	9.	B	14.	B
4.	A	10.	C	15.	D
5.	B	11.	C	16.	B
6.	D				

SECTION 3 THE SOCIOLOGICAL PERSPECTIVE
- "NO MAN IS AN ISLAND"
- THE RELATIONSHIP OF THE INDIVIDUAL TO SOCIETY
- SOCIAL INTERACTION
- THREE WAYS TO VIEW SOCIETY: SOCIOLOGICAL THEORIES
- THE SOCIOLOGICAL IMAGINATION
- THE SOCIOLOGICAL PERSPECTIVE: A SUMMARY

Objectives

After completing this section, the student should be able to:

1. Explain in what way most human behavior involves other people.
2. Describe the views of individual determinists and social determinists.
3. Give examples of sociological theories.
4. Describe the structural–functional view of society.
5. Describe the conflict view of society.
6. Describe the symbolic interactionist view of society.
7. Define and give examples of human interaction.
8. Explain how the term *dysfunctional* is used in the structural–functional view of society.
9. Give examples of personal troubles and public issues.
10. Describe the microworld and the macroworld.

For many years, in the rural areas of Europe, church bells would be rung to inform people that someone in the community had died. In a 1623 essay, the poet John Donne wrote the following lines that are well known and much loved:

No man is an island, entire of itself; every man is a piece of the continent, a part of the main. If a clod be washed away by the sea, Europe is the less, as well as if a promontory were, as well as if a manor of thy friend's or of thine own were. Any man's death diminishes me, because I am involved in mankind; and therefore never send to know for whom the bell tolls; it tolls for thee.

(John Donne, 1623)

"NO MAN IS AN ISLAND"

We are all involved in humankind. From birth to death each person participates in society. Neither an individual nor any human experience can be understood independently of the individual's involvement with other humans. We cannot exaggerate the importance of people to people. Imagine completely removing yourself from the ties of family, friends, and all other people too. Alone and isolated, imagine what your thoughts, feelings, and actions might be. No one has ever existed totally independent of society. But some people have experienced different degrees of independence. The famous explorer of the Antarctic, Admiral Byrd, voluntarily isolated himself for several months in a polar region. In that isolation, he experienced what we consider to be a basic sociological truth. In his diary Byrd wrote that solitude is an excellent state in which to observe how much our behavior is influenced by others. He said that much of what we take for granted through contacts with others becomes painfully apparent in isolation. According to Byrd, even laughter no longer is apt to occur when one is so isolated: ". . . now when I laugh, I laugh inside; for I seem to have forgotten how to do it out loud." He wrote that laughing aloud is mostly a way to *share* pleasure. In our everyday relations with other people, great importance is attached to physical appearance. In isolation, Byrd wrote, physical appearance seems to have little significance: "Looking in the mirror . . . I decided that a man without women around him is a man without vanity . . . how I look is no longer of the least importance; all that matters is how I feel" (Byrd, 1938).

The sociological perspective is a point of view that most, if not all, human behavior involves others either directly or indirectly. In fact, most of our individual behavior is not purely individualistic. Humans, as social beings, do not live in a social vacuum. In order even to think, we need a language of some kind. And how do we learn language to use in our thought process? From others. We are what we are because of the influence of others that may have occurred yesterday, last week, last year, or last decade. No human is an island. We are each a piece of the continent of humankind.

THE RELATIONSHIP OF THE INDIVIDUAL TO SOCIETY

For a long time scholars have debated over different views about the relationship between an individual and society. Does a person control the conditions of society? Or do the conditions of society control the person? Does an individual have free will? Is a person free to become what he or she chooses? Or is a person more controlled by society—even a rubber stamp of society? These are the kinds of questions that the scholars have debated. Those who see the person as an independent being who makes decisions and acts freely are called *individual determinists*. Those who see the person as acting always under the influence and control of society are called *social determinists* (Vernon, 1965).

The views of people presented by individual determinists and by social determinists seem to conflict. However, sociologists would say that both are somewhat correct, but neither is entirely correct. It makes no sense to separate the individual and society: one does not—cannot—exist without the other. The sociological perspective is that each person is part of society. Society is made up of people who influence one another in many ways. We know that individuals make choices and decisions. But the kinds of choices and decisions they make are limited by their experiences and involvement in society.

Consider the relationships within a family unit consisting of a husband, a wife, and a child. A husband influences his wife and his child. A wife influences her husband and her child. The child influences its mother and its father. Add another child. A grandparent. Another grandparent. Add an aunt. And an uncle. Add a cousin. Another cousin. A neighbor. Friends. Co-workers. If we were to expand this list we would end up with an entire society. A society is a network of relationships among individuals. Each will influence others, and each will be influenced by others. This is social interaction. Social interaction is at the very heart of the human experience.

SOCIAL INTERACTION

The unique perspective that sociology has is that the most basic and significant of all human behavior is social interaction. People need people. This is the supreme fact of the human experience. Human beings are social beings. What we love and hope for or hate and fear are experienced because of our involvement with others.

Social interaction occurs when people take each other into account and influence one another. Checking out at the supermarket requires social interaction. Playing baseball is social interaction. What happens at school, at work, and at home all involve social interaction if two or more people have influences upon the others involved in the activity. In day-to-day life, a person meets people, competes with them or cooperates with them, agrees or disagrees with them, laughs with them or at them. In all such cases, social interaction takes place. Some social bonds are strong and lasting. Others are weak and here today, gone tomor-

Social interaction.

row. Some social relationships, such as marriage or friendship, can last all through one's life. All kinds of social bonds are based upon social interaction.

We simply cannot avoid the fact that each of us is bound in some degree to other people. Despite our single savage selves, despite our unique individualism, despite the idea of individual determinism, each person feels, thinks, and acts as a result of social interaction with other human beings.

THREE WAYS TO VIEW SOCIETY: SOCIOLOGICAL THEORIES

The general view of the sociological perspective is that people are social beings and that human behavior results from human interaction. Almost all sociologists agree on this general sociological perspective. Still, there are several ways to emphasize *how* society is organized and *why* people behave as they do. These are theories. A sociological theory is an attempt to organize facts and ideas so that we are able to explain certain patterns of social structure and behavior. Now let us briefly describe each of the three major viewpoints of the way society is structured and the way people behave in society.

The Structural-Functional Viewpoint

This point of view suggests that society should be seen as a living thing with parts that assist one another to keep the system alive and functioning. Each activity in some way helps to maintain a stable social system. These parts and activities have useful functions that meet the basic needs of the population. Things remain as they are—stable—because the government, economy, educational system, religion, and family life all contribute functions that maintain order. Social order is necessary for human survival, it is said. Social cooperation is more desirable than conflict.

Within the structural-functional viewpoint is the belief that there are both latent and manifest functions. *Manifest functions* are intended to occur and are easily recognized by those who participate in the system. *Latent functions* are the results of the structure that were neither intended nor are easily recognized. It should be understood that not all parts of and activities in society can be considered functional. Some events can upset the social balance and are considered *dysfunctional*—harmful (Merton, 1968). For example, American business and industry have the manifest function of providing goods and services upon which our lives depend. They can also be seen as dysfunctional because business and industry exhibit the latent function of polluting the environment.

The structural-functional view of society has been criticized as being too conservative. The emphasis is on social order and the desirability of stability. Thus, structural-functionalism tends to ignore the value of social change (Blau, 1972). This criticism can be criticized itself. We can assume that a "stable" society can have as one of its values that of progress. The society can have built within its structure certain functions that can achieve progress through social change. The civil rights movement sought social change in the structure of American society.

Through the passing of laws during the 1954–1965 "decade of progress," the structure of the American government helped to bring about necessary and beneficial social changes.

The Conflict Viewpoint

This point of view suggests that society should be seen as a social experience of constant struggle and change. Society is viewed as a population of individuals and groups, and of activities that are constantly in conflict. Since there is a limited amount of wealth and resources to be distributed, conflict and competition occur among groups for what is available. There are sociologists who believe that conflict makes a society more vital and responsive to the population in general. Disagreements and competition among groups of people and among parts of the social structure result in social changes that promote progress (Coser, 1957).

Those who believe that social conflict is not necessarily harmful emphasize positive results. Conflict can bring people together as they pursue common interests. When groups compete with one another, attention is brought to bear on social problems. Such attention, turning into concern, can lead to helpful changes that may not have occurred otherwise. In recent years the civil rights movement and the women's liberation movement are examples of social conflicts that have caused important changes. Changes resulting from such conflicts prevent society from becoming stagnant (Robertson, 1977).

The Symbolic Interaction Viewpoint

This point of view suggests that society should be seen as a process of interaction among people by means of symbols. Social structure is created as people interact with one another. There is the belief that the "reality" of society exists in the personal and shared perceptions of its population. Society has no objective existence. The symbolic interaction viewpoint emphasizes the feelings, thoughts, and actions of individuals. And, it is said, individuals acquire "acceptable" ways of being by adjusting to the expectations of others. By agreeing upon the meanings of certain gestures, facial expressions, movements, and language, people share experiences that contribute to the existence of society. The major difference between this viewpoint and the views of structural functionalism and of conflict is that this view does not emphasize large sections of society. Instead, symbolic interaction is concerned with the day-to-day interpretations that people make of the social interaction they experience with others. Thus, society exists as a shared system of symbols and agreed-upon definitions of those symbols.

THREE WAYS TO VIEW A SOCIOLOGY CLASS

Sociologist Judson R. Landis provides us with an excellent example of how to apply each of the sociological points of view to a sociology class. The following closely follows what he has written, although we have altered it somewhat.

Structural–Functional View.   Why does the sociology class exist? Its functions are to present knowledge about and interpretations of the human experience. It also functions to provide the instructor with a job. The structure of the class consists of an instructor, students, and a syllabus. Attending class regularly is functional if the student expects to receive a passing grade. Cutting class regularly could be dysfunctional. Giving tests is functional because test results help the instructor to know how well the students are learning. When the instructor gives assignments and when students listen, read, memorize, and give back on tests what is expected of them, manifest functions are occurring. Landis points out that a latent function of this whole procedure might be that students are being trained to do what is expected of them, as they must do when they hold jobs in large organizations.

Conflict View.   From the conflict point of view, the testing and grading system creates a situation in which the instructor is dominant and the students are subordinate. Competing for scarce resources (A's) leads to certain types of behavior. Cheating to get good grades, memorizing soon-to-be-forgotten information, and rivalries with other students might occur. Some antagonism may exist between the instructor and some of the students who believe the instructor is unfair, too hard, or a bad teacher. Or the instructor may interpret low test grades as indicating that the students do not like the sociology course or are not trying hard enough to pass. Any of the above circumstances have an element of conflict within them.

Symbolic Interaction View.   Using this approach, we examine the interaction that takes place between the instructor and students. We would look for verbal and nonverbal signals that pass back and forth. Perhaps a difficult subject is being discussed in class. The instructor attempts to judge how well the students understand the subject. What is covered and how it is covered may be adjusted according to the instructor's interpretation of the students' understanding. Picture a student who is completely disgusted with the instructor and the subject of sociology. Notice the hostility that is communicated through the student's gestures, tone of voice, body language, and remarks made to other students. The symbolic interactionist would be interested in any actions, reactions, or changes in behavior exhibited by either instructor or students that occur as a result of social interaction within the sociology class (Landis, 1980).

THE SOCIOLOGICAL IMAGINATION

Further insights into the sociological perspective are to be found in *The Sociological Imagination* and other works by C. Wright Mills (1916–1962). Mills emphasized the differences between *personal troubles* and *public issues*. Troubles, he said, occur within the character of the individual and that individual's immediate social setting. To solve personal troubles, we must look to the individual. Issues, he said, occur within the larger social experiences of humankind. To solve public issues, we must look to the social structure of society.

For example, a husband and wife may have problems in their marriage. To seek solutions to their problems, we must look at the individuals involved. We must examine how they feel, what they expect, and how compatible they are. To resolve the troubles of the married couple would require concentrating on *their* personal problems. On the other hand, if the divorce rate in society is very high, we then must look at the social structure. We must examine the institutions of marriage and family. To resolve the troubles associated with marriage and family would require concentrating on the desirability or undesirability of such relationships.

As another example, consider unemployment. Mills said that if in a city of 100,000 only one person is unemployed, that is a personal trouble. For its relief we would look to the character of the person, the person's skills, and immediate opportunities. But if in a nation of 50 million employees, 15 million are unemployed, that is an issue. Then we could not hope to find its solution in the same way with which we would deal with one individual. In this case, the very structure of opportunities has changed. To understand correctly and state the problem would require us to consider the functioning of the economic and political institutions of the social structure. An extremely high rate of unemployment is not a matter of personal troubles for a scattering of individuals. It is, instead, an example of a public issue (Mills, 1959).

The world of personal troubles and personal celebrations is called the *microworld*. It consists of our immediate experiences with others in face-to-face interaction. It is a familiar and personal world. Whatever meaning life has for us is discovered and maintained in the microworld. We learn early in childhood that this familiar and personal world is located within a much larger, impersonal, and unfamiliar world. This world is called the *macroworld*. It is the world of public issues. The microworld and what occurs within it can make sense only if it is seen as part of the larger macroworld in which it is located. And the macroworld can have little meaning to us unless we experience it through the face-to-face interactions in our microworld (Berger and Berger, 1972).

THE SOCIOLOGICAL PERSPECTIVE: A SUMMARY

In conclusion, the sociological perspective is an approach to studying human beings as social beings. The emphasis is on the ties that bind us together through space and time. Just as the tree and the forest are related, so are biography and history, and so are a human and society. Each one of us *is* involved in humankind.

It should be apparent that sociology has a point of view that places social structure and human interaction in the foreground. Sociology concentrates on the social structures and collective life of humanity, not on the psychological nor biological aspects of people. We believe that humanity can achieve something greater through a better understanding of itself. It has been said that each person is a problem in search of a solution. Through the intelligent and creative use of the sociological perspective, we believe that we might perceive the problems and discover the solutions.

KEY TERMS AND NAMES FROM SECTION 3

the sociological perspective

"No man is an island"

individual determinists

social determinists

social interaction

structural–functional view of society

conflict view of society

social change

symbolic interaction view of society

personal troubles

public issues

microworld

macroworld

C. Wright Mills

STUDY GUIDE FOR SECTION 3

1. Opinions differ in reference to the relationship between an individual and society. HOW DO SOCIAL DETERMINISTS AND INDIVIDUAL DETERMINISTS VIEW THE RELATIONSHIP?

2. The most signifcant of all human behavior is social interaction. DEFINE SOCIAL INTERACTION AND GIVE EXAMPLES OF IT.

3. There are several ways to emphasize how society is organized and why people behave as they do. These are theories. HOW IS THE TERM *SOCIOLOGICAL THEORY* DEFINED IN THE CHAPTER?

4. The structural–functional viewpoint suggests that each part of and each activity in society has a useful function. HOW IS SOCIETY AND THE HUMAN EXPERIENCE DESCRIBED IN THIS VIEW?

5. Within the structural–functional viewpoint is the belief that there are latent and manifest functions. EXPLAIN WHAT LATENT AND MANIFEST FUNCTIONS ARE AND GIVE EXAMPLES OF EACH.

6. HOW DOES THE TERM *DYSFUNCTIONAL* APPLY TO THE STRUCTURAL–FUNCTIONAL VIEWPOINT OF SOCIETY?

7. Another view of how society is organized and why people behave as they do is the conflict viewpoint. HOW ARE SOCIETY AND THE HUMAN EXPERIENCE DESCRIBED IN THIS VIEW?

8. Still another view of how society is organized and why people behave as they do is the symbolic interaction viewpoint. HOW ARE SOCIETY AND THE HUMAN EXPERIENCE DESCRIBED IN THIS VIEW?

9. Sociologist Judson R. Landis applied each of the sociological points of view to a sociology class. EXPLAIN HOW THE STRUCTURAL–FUNCTIONAL, CONFLICT, AND SYMBOLIC INTERACTION VIEWS CAN EACH BE APPLIED TO THE CLASSROOM SETTING.

10. C. Wright Mills makes a distinction between personal troubles and public issues. HOW DO THEY DIFFER? HOW DOES MILLS SAY EACH CAN BE RESOLVED?

11. Each of us is involved in a microworld and a macroworld. WHAT IS THE DIFFERENCE BETWEEN THE TWO AND HOW ARE THEY RELATED TO ONE ANOTHER IN REFERENCE TO A PERSON'S LIFE?

12. The sociological perspective is an approach to studying human beings as social beings. WHAT *TWO* ASPECTS OF THE HUMAN EXPERIENCE ARE PLACED IN THE FOREGROUND FOR STUDY?

PRACTICE TEST FOR SECTION 3

Select the best answer.

1. The belief that people have free will and act independently of one another is associated with
A. Social determinism.
B. The sociological perspective.
C. Individual determinism.
D. Biological determinism.

2. Which is an example of social interaction?
A. Playing solitaire.
B. Arguing with a friend.
C. Jogging.
D. Wondering which answer is correct.

3. An attempt to organize facts and ideas to explain cetain patterns of social structure and human behavior is
A. Called a theory.
B. An example of individual determinism.

C. An example of social determinism.
D. Called a public issue.

4. Studying society by emphasizing constant struggle and change is using the
A. Structural–functional approach.
B. Conflict approach.
C. Symbolic interaction approach.

5. Studying society by emphasizing stability, social order, and social cooperation is using the
A. Structural–functional approach.
B. Conflict approach.
C. Symbolic interaction approach.

6. Studying society by emphasizing how the "reality" of a society exists in the personal and shared perceptions of the population is using the
A. Structural–functional approach.

B. Conflict approach.

C. Symbolic interaction approach.

7. Manifest functions are

A. Not intended.

B. Easily recognized.

C. Intended to occur.

D. Not easily recognized.

E. Both B and C.

8. According to C. Wright Mills, to solve public issues we must

A. Look at specific individuals.

B. Look at solutions to other problems.

C. Examine the social structure.

D. Concentrate on what is desirable for each person.

9. The world of our immediate experiences with others is called the

A. Fantasy world.

B. Unfamiliar world.

C. Microworld.

D. Macroworld.

E. Both A and D.

10. The author of *The Sociological Imagination* is

A. John Donne.

B. C. Wright Mills.

C. Patrick G. Bailey.

D. Auguste Comte.

11. The Sociological perspective

A. Studies human beings as social beings.

B. Places social structure in the foreground.

C. Places human interaction in the foreground.

D. Emphasizes the ties binding people together.

E. All of the above.

Answer Key

1.	C	**7.**	E
2.	B	**8.**	C
3.	A	**9.**	C
4.	B	**10.**	B
5.	A	**11.**	E
6.	C		

CHAPTER SUMMARY

1. The term *sociology* was coined by French social philosopher Auguste Comte. Comte believed that the scientific study of society could explain the disorderly changes occurring in 19th-century Europe. Comte divided the new science of sociology into two main areas called social statics and social dynamics.

2. In the 1920s American sociologist W. I. Thomas coined the phrase "definition of the situation." He said that if people define certain situations as real, those situations are real in their consequences. Thomas believed that the way people perceive reality determines how they behave.

3. Sociologists identify three ways in which we can perceive the world around us. Personal and unique reality consists of ideas and beliefs that a person believes to be true. If the personal reality is reinforced by opinions of others, a social and shared reality emerges. Objective and scientific reality is the version of reality that is discovered by the scientific method.

4. The scientific method is a procedure used to answer questions about the human experience and about the physical world. All sciences have in common the

use of the scientific method. The five steps used in the scientific method are: formulate a hypothesis; develop a research design; collect data; analyze data; and draw conclusions.

5.   Each science must develop its own techniques of investigation. Four techniques used by sociologists are planned experiments, sample surveys, case studies, and participant observations.

6.   Scientists believe that all events have causes. The principle of causation suggests that every event has a cause or causes. When there are many causes of an event, this is referred to as multiple causation.

7.   Objectivity exists when an observation is not influenced by one's personal prejudices, beliefs, or values. The ethical code of sociology expects sociologists to be intellectually honest. Sociology is a self-correcting discipline. There are no truths not subject to change if new evidence becomes available.

8.   The basic differences among the social sciences are in the angles of vision or the emphasis on particulars. Anthropology, economics, political science, psychology, and sociology all seek to understand and to describe the human experience.

9.   The sociological perspective is the view that most, if not all, human behavior involves other people. The most significant human behavior is social interaction. Social interaction occurs when people take each other into account and influence one another.

10.   A sociological theory is an attempt to explain patterns of social structure and human behavior. Three major sociological theories are structural functionalism, conflict theory, and symbolic interaction.

SUGGESTIONS FOR FURTHER READING RELATING TO CHAPTER 1

Bates, Alan B., *The Sociological Enterprise* (Boston: Houghton Mifflin, 1967). Chapters 5 and 6 contain especially good descriptions of careers in sociology and how sociologists are trained.

Berger, Peter L., *Invitation to Sociology: A Humanistic Perspective* (New York: Doubleday Anchor Books, 1963). While acknowledging the importance of scientific procedures in sociology, the philosophical orientation of the book is stimulating and profound.

Cole, Stephen, *The Sociological Method: An Introduction to the Science of Sociology*, 3rd ed. (Chicago: Rand McNally, 1980).

Cuzzort, R. P., *Humanity and Modern Sociological Thought* (New York: Holt, Rinehart and Winston, 1969). The essay entitled "The Use of Sociological Thought" explains how sociology can be utilized.

Goffman, Erving, *Interaction Ritual: Essays in Face-to-Face Behavior* (New York: Doubleday Anchor Books, 1967). Goffman comments on the significance of glances, gestures, positions, and remarks that influence participants in social interaction.

Homans, George C., *Social Behavior: Its Elementary Forms* (New York: Harcourt, Brace and World, 1961). Homans offers a set of general propositions on social behavior as an exchange of activities between two or more individuals.

Inkeles, Alex, *What Is Sociology?* (Englewood Cliffs, N.J.: Prentice-Hall, 1964). This is an excellent and concise introduction to the discipline and profession of sociology.

Madge, John H., *The Origins of Scientific Sociology* (New York: The Free Press, 1962). Madge describes and analyzes some of the major empirical studies con- ducted by social scientists.

Miller, Delbert C., *Handbook of Research Design and Social Measurement* (New York: David McKay, 1970). Part I provides a guide for conducting sociological research.

Syzmanski, Albert, "Toward a Radical Sociology," *Sociological Inquiry*, Vol. 40 (Winter, 1970), pp. 3–11. Syzmanski calls for a radicalization of sociology, ar- guing that sociologists should side with the exploited members of society.

Von Hoffman, Nicholas, Irving Horowitz, and Lee Rainwater, "Sociological Snoopers and Journalistic Moralizers," *Transaction*, Vol. 7, No. 7 (May 1970), pp. 4–8. This is a provocative dialogue between a journalist and two sociolo- gists about the research activities of Laud Humphreys in the study "Impersonal Sex in Public Places."

Chapter 2
Socialization: Human Beings as Social Beings

SECTION 4   THE NEED TO EXPERIENCE SOCIALIZATION

- HUMAN NATURE AND HUMAN NURTURE
- YOU CAN'T BE HUMAN ALL BY YOURSELF
- PRECONDITIONS FOR SOCIALIZATION
- "THERE WAS A CHILD WENT FORTH"
- AIMS OF SOCIALIZATION
- DELIBERATE AND UNCONSCIOUS SOCIALIZATION

Objectives

After completing this section, the student should be able to:

1. Recognize the influence of socialization on human personality and behavior.
2. Explain the sociological views on heredity versus environment.
3. Identify two preconditions for successful socialization to occur.
4. Describe four particular aims of socialization.
5. Explain how socialization can be both deliberate and unconscious.

O bserve an infant. It is helplessly dependent for survival upon the constant care and attention it receives from others, but the infant is neither grateful nor ungrateful for its existence. The infant does not think, reason, plan, nor hope as we ordinarily define such behaviors. It has no pride, no shame, no conscience. The infant is merely an organism with the potential for becoming human. Only time and the efforts of others can transform this creature into a complex, social being.

HUMAN NATURE
AND HUMAN
NURTURE

People are not born human. We become human through the process of social interaction. Over 60 years ago two influential American sociologists wrote that "It is only slowly and laboriously, in fruitful contact, co-operation, and conflict with his fellows, that one attains the distinctive qualities of human nature" (Park and Burgess, 1921).

Each society has a culture. *Culture* refers to all those ways of thinking, feeling, and behaving that are passed on from one generation to the next. Cultures contain certain knowledge, beliefs, morals, customs, skills, and laws. In order for an individual to participate in a society's culture, the person must experience the process of socialization. It is socialization that transforms the organism into a social being. It is through socialization that one learns the content of one's culture. Without socialization, human cultures could not be passed on from one generation to another.

Ashley Montagu (1905–   ), an anthropologist, has written many essays and books on the human experience. He has said that each person becomes bound to the group into which the person has been socialized. So, Montagu says, the "individual" is a myth. Apart from social groups, a person acquires no personality. On the other hand, a member of a social group acquires a personality that is formed from the social interaction that occurs within the group. Montagu says that the child soon learns that in order to be loved and satisfied, the child must satisfy the requirements of others. The child must cooperate and give up or at least postpone the satisfaction of certain desires. The child must behave in a socially acceptable manner in order to receive the love and approval of others (Montagu, 1966).

For many years a controversy has existed having to do with human nature and human nurture. Human nurture has to do with one's environment and socialization. Human nature has to do with one's heredity. Which is more important—environment or heredity? We believe that the question itself can mislead the way we think about human development. Consider the following: Which is more important to water—hydrogen or oxygen? Water is a combination of both hydrogen and oxygen, so if either element were missing, water would be nonexistent. Just as hydrogen and oxygen combine to produce water, so do the factors of heredity and environment combine to produce human beings.

Sociologists tend to play down the significance of heredity (human nature) and to emphasize the significance of environment and socialization (human nurture). As a consequence, throughout this book the impact of environment and socialization—the human *experience*—is emphasized far more than the importance of heredity. Sociologists study human nurture, not human nature. Nevertheless, biological and hereditary influences also must be considered if one seeks to understand human behavior.

YOU CAN'T BE HUMAN ALL BY YOURSELF

We have said that the infant comes into the world as an organism and becomes fully human only as a result of the socialization process. By stating "You can't be human all by yourself," we are proposing that an isolated individual does not have enough biological traits to produce human characteristics. Our physical selves give us the ability to become human, but unless we can interact with others, our potential to become human cannot be fulfilled. There is evidence to support this view. Through the years cases of extremely isolated children have come to the attention of social scientists. The nonhuman condition of these *social isolates*, as such children are called, supports the idea that one must experience social interaction in order to become fully human.

In 1970 a 13-year old girl, Susan Wiley, was discovered in Arcadia, California. The girl had been kept all her life in almost complete isolation. Officials who investigated the case said that although Susan had the normal capacity for learning, she had the mind of an infant. Doctors placed her mental development at that of an infant 12 to 18 months old (*The Sun*, 1970). Sociologist Kingsley Davis offers a more detailed account of another social isolate in two 1940s articles in the *American Journal of Sociology* (Davis, 1940, 1947).

PRECONDITIONS FOR SOCIALIZATION

Successful socialization occurs when one acquires the ways of thinking, feeling, and behaving of the group to which one belongs. The family is usually the first agent of socialization. It is the parents of the child who set examples for the child to follow. And the parental examples are supposed to represent behavior that is socially approved. Parents act as agents of socialization when they express approval and disapproval of the child's behavior. Actually, for successful socialization to occur, at least the following two preconditions must exist.

The Child Must Have an Adequate Biological Inheritance.

Socialization is a matter of learning how to think, feel, and behave. In order to learn, the child must have adequate biological equipment. If a child is born with brain damage or deaf or blind or with any serious hereditary disadvantage, the process of socialization becomes more difficult, although not impossible. Our heredity provides us with the potential ability to experience socialization. Then it is the society in which we live that provides us with the cultural content of socialization.

There Must Be an Ongoing Society from Which the Child Learns

Society was here before we were born. It will probably be here long after we are gone. In order for a child to learn anything, there must be a society whose culture is there to be learned by the child. Society's influence on each person is something that cannot be denied. When we speak of society, we are referring to all the people who surround us and who affect us and have impact upon us. Each of us is located in some certain section of the social system. Our social location affects almost everything that we learn and do. Our location within society will influence the way we use language. It will affect our religious beliefs. Speaking of society's impact on us, Peter Berger has said that "It is there, something that cannot be denied and that must be reckoned with. . . . In sum, society is the walls of our imprisonment in history" (Berger, 1963).

"THERE WAS A CHILD WENT FORTH"

The term *socialization* is a modern term, but the *fact* of socialization is as old as humankind. Years before sociology became a respected social science, American poet Walt Whitman described the process of socialization in a poem published in 1855. Here are excerpts from "There Was a Child Went Forth" by Walt Whitman:

There was a child went forth every day;
And the first object he look'd upon, that object he became;
And that object became part of him for the day, or a certain part of the day, or for many
  years, or stretching cycles of years. . . .

. . . the old drunkard staggering home from the outhouse of the tavern, whence he had late-
    ly risen.
And the school-mistress that passed—and the quarrelsome boys,
And the tidy and fresh-cheek'd girls—and the barefoot negro boy and girl,
And all the changes of city and country, wherever he went.
His own parents,
He that had father'd him, and she that had conceiv'd him in her womb, and birth'd him,
They gave this child more of themselves than that;
They gave him afterward everyday—they became part of him.
Men and women crowding fast in the streets . . .
The streets themselves, and the facades of houses, and goods in the windows . . .
The horizon's edge, the flying sea-crow, the fragrance of salt marsh and shore mud;
These became part of that child who went forth every day, and who now goes, and will
    always go forth every day.

Walt Whitman was not a sociologist. He was a poet. But his poem certainly shows that he was aware of how each person is shaped and influenced by moment-to-moment experiences. In his poem, Whitman captured what we mean when we refer to the process of socialization.

AIMS OF SOCIALIZATION

Each generation must become "civilized" according to the culture of the adults who make up their society at that time in history. This is true whether we are thinking of a rural tribal society or an urban industrial society. It is nothing less than foolish to believe that "everyone should be able to do one's own thing." One would have no "thing" to do without first experiencing socialization. As human beings we are social beings. To survive we must learn how to interact successfully with those who provide us with the means to survive. Consider the four following particular aims of socialization.

The Teaching of Basic Disciplines

Through socialization the child learns how to discipline itself in reference to matters considered important by society. For example, the child is disciplined to eat and to reject certain kinds of food. The child is disciplined as to when and where body wastes are to be eliminated. And, according to the way in which sexuality is defined in society, the child is disciplined to experience sexuality in that particular way. At birth the infant demands complete and immediate fulfillment of its desires. Through discipline, the maturing person gradually learns to control physical and emotional behavior. By doing so, the individual becomes an accepted member of society. Thus, the socialization process should encourage one to act in ways that are considered proper by society.

The Creation of Goals and Ambitions

Through socialization children learn what is thought to be worth achieving. They learn what must be done to acquire self-respect and the respect of others. Depending upon the values of the society, the children's attitudes and behaviors will reflect those values if socialization is successful. Imagine a society in which the most important values are based upon religious beliefs. Then one should expect to find a number of people very much involved in religious behavior. Some, no doubt, would eagerly seek to hold some special position within the religious organization. On the other hand, imagine a society in which the most important values are based upon progress in technology and science. Then many people would likely seek to become engineers and scientists. All societies encourage their people to seek certain goals, to have certain ambitions, and to perform certain tasks.

The Teaching of Special Skills

While encouraging certain goals and ambitions within its members, a society must also provide the means by which the goals can be reached. Ambitions learned through socialization can be realized by acquiring the necessary skills. In small tribal societies, traditional skills are passed on from one generation to another. There is little or no change in the skills. The young learn from the old through imitation and continual practice. Such is not the case in large industrial societies, which are continually seeking new ways of doing things. The concept

Teaching special skills.

of progress complicates learning special skills because the skills change so rapidly. Industrial societies rely upon formal and very specialized education in order to teach special skills. Nevertheless, whether it be through imitation and practice or through formal and specialized education, an important aim of socialization is to teach special skills.

The Definition of Social Roles

All societies require people to play social roles. Robert Ezra Park (1864–1944) said that "everyone is always and everywhere more or less consciously playing a role. . . . It is in these roles that we know each other; it is in these roles that we know ourselves" (Park, 1950). All human interaction takes place through the playing of social roles. At various times during one day, a woman might play the roles of daughter, sister, mother, student, employer, customer, and wife. As she moves from one situation to another during the day, she must play the role appropriate for each situation. Her ability to play the various social roles was developed through the process of socialization.

Each of the four aims of socialization mentioned above could apply to any type of society. These are the general functions that the process of socialization should perform. As a result, life should have some pattern and meaning for those who participate in their society's culture (Broom and Selznick, 1968).

DELIBERATE AND UNCONSCIOUS SOCIALIZATION

People need to experience socialization. It shapes one's life-style and even one's personality. It is a continuing process in each person's life. W. I. Thomas described the early years of life thus:

As soon as the child has free motion and begins to pull, tear, pry, meddle, and prowl, the parents begin to define the situation through speech and other signs and pressures: "Be quiet," "Sit up straight," "Blow your nose," "Wash your face," "Mind your mother," "Be kind to sister," etc. . . . His wishes and activities begin to be inhibited and gradually, by definitions within the family, by playmates, in the school, in the Sunday School, through reading, by formal instruction, by informal signs of approval and disapproval, the growing member learns the code of society.

(Thomas, 1967).

The formal instruction mentioned by Thomas is all those bits of advice and reactions to a child's behavior within the family circle. But formal instruction also includes all the specialized training and education that one receives in modern society. All of these are examples of deliberate and intended socialization.

Thomas mentions the informal signs of approval and disapproval that also help one to learn the "code of society." These informal signs can be very subtle. For example, the man at work in the shipyard may not work as hard as his co-workers think he should. Or he may work so hard that he makes the production of the other workers look bad. In either case he could receive some kind of disapproval from his co-workers. In some way they will express their contempt for him. This is not because they are interested in "socializing" him. Their disapproval occurs because they do not want his working habits to interfere with their own established routines and reputations.

There are many informal and unconscious means of socialization. In recent years, racial friction in American cities has caused some adults to lock the doors of their cars as they enter neighborhoods populated mostly by another race. Children riding in the cars can pick up this cautious behavior as a pattern. The children might conclude that people of another race are some kind of threat or danger to be locked out. Thus, adults can unconsciously contribute to the racial attitudes of their children without either the adults or the children being aware of it at the time.

Formal socialization accomplishes much. We learn to seek goals and to have ambitions. We are formally taught basic disciplines, special skills, and social roles. But we must not overlook how much of our socialization occurs informally and unconsciously. We learn attitudes, skills, and social roles without even realizing that we are being influenced. Parents have been known to say, "Do as I say, not as I do," but more than most of us know, the *doing* has more effect than the *saying*.

KEY TERMS AND NAMES FROM SECTION 4

culture

human nature and human nurture

process of socialization

social isolates

biological inheritance

basic disciplines

goals and ambitions

special skills

social roles

deliberate and unconscious socialization

formal and informal socialization

society and our imprisonment in history

Robert Ezra Park

W. I. Thomas

Peter Berger

Ashley Montagu

STUDY GUIDE FOR SECTION 4

1. The infant is helplessly dependent upon others for survival. WHY DO SOCI-OLOGISTS CONSIDER HUMAN NURTURE AND HUMAN NATURE TO BE IM-PORTANT? WHICH DO SOCIOLOGISTS EMPHASIZE?

2. Ashley Montagu has said that in a sense the "individual" is a myth. WHAT DOES HE MEAN BY THIS, AND HOW DOES THE PROCESS OF SOCIALIZA-TION RELATE TO WHAT MONTAGU MEANS?

3. One can't be human all by oneself. WHAT EVIDENCE DOES THE CASE OF THE SOCIAL ISOLATE NAMED SUSAN PROVIDE TO SUPPORT THIS STATE-MENT?

4. So that successful socialization can occur for an individual, at least two pre-conditions must exist. WHAT ARE TWO NECESSARY PRECONDITIONS FOR SUCCESSFUL SOCIALIZATION? WHY?

5. You have read excerpts from Walt Whitman's poem entitled "There Was a Child Went Forth." WHICH IMPORTANT SOCIOLOGICAL CONCEPT DOES THIS POEM DEMONSTRATE?

6. We have said that it is pure foolishness to say that everyone should be able to do one's own thing. WHAT DO SURVIVAL AND SOCIALIZATION HAVE TO DO WITH OUR STATEMENT?

7. LIST FOUR AIMS OF SOCIALIZATION THAT HAVE BEEN PRESENT IN ALL HUMAN SOCIETIES.

8. In small tribal societies, skills are learned through imitation and practice. WHAT COMPLICATES THE LEARNING OF SKILLS IN LARGE URBAN INDUS-TRIALIZED SOCIETIES?

9. Children experience both deliberate (formal) and unconscious (informal) so-cialization. GIVE TWO EXAMPLES OF BOTH FORMAL AND INFORMAL SO-CIALIZATION.

PRACTICE TEST FOR SECTION 4

Select the best answer.

1. The means by which a person ac-quires ways of thinking, feeling, and behaving in order to participate in soci-ety is called

A. Naturalization.
B. Socialization.
C. Generalization.
D. Human nature.

2. Which of the following would be incorrect?

A. To be human is to be involved in a network of social relationships.
B. Heredity alone is enough to make human beings social beings.
C. Human nature is necessary but not enough by itself to develop social characteristics.
D. One is socially bound to the group or groups in which one has been socialized.

3. Heredity is to environment just as
A. Human nature is to human nurture.
B. Socialization is to culture.
C. Human nurture is to human nature.
D. Social interaction is to human interaction.

4. Which of the following is not a basic aim of socialization?
A. To develop basic disciplines.
B. To create goals and ambitions.
C. To define social roles.
D. To encourage nonconformity to social norms.

5. In all human groupings, people interact
A. Through playing social roles.
B. By inheriting social behavior.
C. Without emotional involvement.
D. None of the above.

6. Who said that society is the "walls of our imprisonment in history"?
A. James Oates.
B. Ashley Montagu.
C. Peter Berger.
D. W. I. Thomas.

7. The poem "There Was a Child Went Forth" reflects the importance of
A. Sociology.
B. Socialization.
C. Human nature.
D. Adequate biological inheritance.

8. "Everyone is always and everywhere more or less consciously playing a role. . . . It is in these roles that we know each other; it is in these roles that we know ourselves." Who said this?
A. Robert Ezra Park.
B. Ashley Montagu.
C. Donald O'Sullivan.
D. W. I. Thomas.

9. Socialization is fundamentally what type of process?
A. Behavioral.
B. Attitudinal.
C. Learning.
D. Inherited.

Answer Key

1.	B	6.	C
2.	B	7.	B
3.	A	8.	A
4.	D	9.	C
5.	A		

SECTION 5 SOCIALIZATION DURING THE FORMATIVE YEARS

- FAMILY AS A SOCIALIZING AGENT
- UNIQUE EXPERIENCES AND SOCIALIZATION
- PEER GROUP AS A SOCIALIZING AGENT
- SCHOOL AS A SOCIALIZING AGENT
- MASS MEDIA AS A SOCIALIZING AGENT
- THE FREUDIAN THEORY OF PERSONALITY
- COOLEY'S LOOKING-GLASS SELF
- MEAD'S SIGNIFICANT OTHERS AND GENERALIZED OTHER
- CONCLUDING REMARKS

Objectives

After completing this section, the student should be able to:

1. Explain in what ways the family is the first agent of socialization.
2. Explain why children raised in the same family during the same years are different from one another.
3. Describe the influence of the peer group in socialization.
4. Identify how schools and mass media contribute to socialization.
5. Describe behavior associated with the id, ego, and superego.
6. Recognize the importance of identification and repression.
7. Describe the looking-glass self.
8. Explain how taking the role of the other applies to socialization.
9. Describe the functions of significant others and the Generalized Other in socialization.

The most important period in the socialization process is those early years when the self-concept comes into being. These years are called the *formative years*. A human *self-concept* consists of two ingredients:

1. A sense of identity answering the question"Who am I?"

2. A sense of self-esteem answering the question "What am I worth?"

At birth the infant has no sense of identity nor any sense of self-esteem. It is only from interacting with others that we acquire a sense of who we are and what we are worth.

If we were to ask a three-year-old girl whether she is an ectomorph or a mesomorph, the girl would not know what to answer. Since no one has told her what she is, the child can attach no meaning to such words. However, ask the same child whether she is a boy or a girl and she will be positive in her response. By age three, people already will have informed the child of her gender, and they will have been treating her accordingly. Sexual identity is learned very early in life. Being labeled either "boy" or "girl" helps the child to establish a self-image and even to exhibit certain behaviors. Why? Because other people expect the child to behave in particular ways. Over a short period of time, the child makes such expectations the basis for his or her attitudes and behavior. This is early socialization.

FAMILY AS A SOCIALIZING AGENT

While the child depends upon others for its identity, it also relies on others for the fulfillment of its basic needs. In order to receive these, the child must consider and respond to its parents' wishes and expectations. The child begins the transition from egocentrism to sociocentrism (see Glossary for definitions). Gradually the child realizes that its parents can grant or withhold affection, approval, and any number of other things the child wants and needs. Being dependent on others requires the child to become a social being. It can no longer afford to be what one writer has called "an unthinking, demanding little tyrant" (Hodges, 1971). Parents express disapproval and displeasure as well as approval and pleasure. To receive what it wants and needs, the child must act according to its parents' expectations. Usually, this means that the child has begun to act according to the expectations also of society at large. In this way, the family should be seen as the *first* agent of socialization. Society's attitudes, beliefs, and behavior expectations are introduced to the child within the family circle.

Within the family circle the child learns that power and authority must be considered. The child learns social rules about such things as property. The differences among one's personal property, another's personal property, and collective property are learned. And the first experiences of love, generosity, greed, hope, and disappointment occur within the family. Socialization occurs when the child realizes that the way it acts influences how others in turn react. Approval can make the child happy and hopeful. Disapproval can make the child sad and fearful. We discuss the family as a social institution in more detail in Section 23. For now we want to emphasize how important the family's function is in socialization. The personality of an adult is mostly formed during childhood years. How the individual will respond to various situations later in life depends very much upon how the child comes to experience life and to see itself in these early years within the family.

UNIQUE EXPERIENCES AND SOCIALIZATION

Everybody has a story. Everybody lives a life that has not been, is not being, and will not be exactly duplicated. No one has a double because no two people have lived identical moment-to-moment lives. Children raised in the same family, house, and neighborhood during the same years will be different. They will be different because they will have *unique experiences* that will help to create their personalities. Two sociologists have touched upon this subject of unique experiences and socialization in the following passage:

Why is it that children in the same family are so different from one another, even though they have had the same experiences? The point is that they have not had the same experiences; they have had social experiences which are similar in some respects and different in others. Each child enters a different family unit. One is the firstborn; he is the only child until the arrival of the second, who has an older brother or sister to fight with, and so on. Parents change, and do not treat all their children exactly alike. Children enter different peer groups, may have different teachers and survive different incidents.

(Horton and Hunt, 1972)

PEER GROUP AS A SOCIALIZING AGENT

For every child there comes a time when children their own age become important socializing influences. Brothers and sisters—siblings—and cousins and neighborhood children all become factors in each other's socialization. A peer group is a group made up of individuals who are near the same age and who have approximately equal status. Peer influence comes from equals. On the other hand, parents are figures of authority. For many children, early socialization can result from a mixture of influences from adults and peers at the same time. Let us explain further.

Many youngsters experience their earliest peer contacts under the supervision of parents or older brothers and sisters. Or such early peer contacts may occur under the watchful eyes of those in charge of nursery schools, playgrounds, or day-care centers. Under these circumstances, peer-group socialization is little more than learning basic social skills. During this period, children become aware of the presence and wishes of others of their same age and status. They learn how to defend themselves or how to get others of the same age to help them defend themselves. As the children play, they advance in their abilities to interact socially.

Children in elementary and junior high schools use similar reasons for rating their peers. Social class does not seem to matter. For example, characteristics of boys chosen as leaders show little difference between working-class and middle-class groups. Both groups expect the boys to be good at sports, to appear daring, self-confident, enthusiastic, and to have a good sense of humor. Popularity in peer groups seems to be related to leadership. Being friendly and good-looking also are highly rated characteristics. The youngster who is attractive and self-confident has the easiest road to peer acceptance.

Children know and care about what is expected of them by their peers. This knowledge influences their attitudes and behavior. Some studies reveal that less popular children have lower self-esteem than their more popular peers. In fact, if lack of popularity is something they can do something about, they do. Many children make conscious efforts to change, whether the change involves attitudes, appearance, or behavior (Clausen, 1968).

Some writers say that the peer group is anti-family. They suggest that the peer group will encourage conformity to the wishes of the group rather than of parents. The term *youth culture* has been used in recent years. This suggests that there is a style of life that excludes adult values. It is true that children and their parents tend to decrease their shared activities in the later years of elementary school. At the same time, peer group activities tend to increase. Still, there need not necessarily be conflict between family loyalty and peer-group loyalty. This is true especially if the parents continue to keep the family together through common interests, mutual respect, and expressions of affection. Dorothy Barclay, a child expert of *The New York Times*, observed that:

So much has been written and said in recent years of the child's need for the company and influence of his "age-mates," his "peers," that adults might almost be considered superfluous. Some schools of thought suggest, for instance, that the good teacher is the one who keeps her own thoughts and ideas to herself, serving only as a catalyst. Mothers and fathers could easily assume from some of the speeches beamed their way that the less they "did"—in the old parental sense— the better, the more "up-to-date" parents they would be. As a result, many adults, quite understandably, are confused about children. It follows as a corollary that many children are also confused about adults.

(Bensman and Rosenberg, 1963)

Children coming from unstable homes in which parents offer little guidance or support turn to the peer group. Such children will use the peer group as their source of values and behaviors. In neighborhoods where juvenile delinquency is widespread, children from unstable homes will be more influenced by peer group than by family. This should not mislead us to conclude that most peer groups are in fact anti-family. Most peer groups in the United States continue to reflect the dominant values of society at large. Most young people exhibit behavior that is socially acceptable. Finally, it is common for young people to seek emotional support from their families even after adolescence. We should not overlook this fact, since the generation gap tends to be overplayed in mass media.

SCHOOL AS A SOCIALIZING AGENT

Throughout the United States there are state laws that require children to attend school. State governments dictate the number of hours, days, and weeks per year that children must be in school. Since attendance is compulsory, most American children do attend regularly, whether they want to or not. Youngsters receive various types of socialization in school. They receive instruction in reading, writing, arithmetic, sports, and many skills relating to different occupational specialties. This is the *acknowledged curriculum*. There is also what has been called the *hidden curriculum*. To survive academically and socially, youngsters must learn to follow directions and to respond to commands. They must learn to line up, to be quiet, to wait, to act interested even when they are not, and to please teachers without being condemned as a teacher's pet. What all this hidden curriculum amounts to is that the teacher is the child's first boss. Learning to do what the boss wants is an important part of the hidden curriculum.

With few exceptions, schooling in the United States is a kind of training and preparation for adult participation in the large organizations of business, industry, and government. Sociologist Kenneth Neubeck says that students should have more say in the policies and decisions affecting them. He says that schools should be opened up to the outside world so that young people can learn about the realities they will face when they are adults. In his critical approach to schooling as an agent of socialization, Neubeck writes:

Rather than only reading about the world of work, students should be out talking to workers, union organizers, managers, and professionals. Instead of discussing current events, students should be creating or participating in political campaigns and social-change movements. Any gap between the school and the real world is an artificial one, and there is no reason to permit it to exist.

Finally, Neubeck says,

Rich educational opportunities from cradle to grave can be made available to all — but only if we are willing to press for change rather than moan about the existing system.

(Neubeck, 1979)

MASS MEDIA AS A SOCIALIZING AGENT

Americans own more television and radio sets than the people of any other nation on Earth. Other media that influence young people during the formative years include books, comics, magazines, movies, newspapers, and records and tapes. Although these agents of socialization do not allow people to interact with them very much, their influence on both young and old is tremendous. From mass media we are informed of the news of the hour. We are entertained. Children are especially influenced by television, but we must not underestimate the influences of the other media. In addition to television and radio, magazines, newspapers, movies, and other media all contribute to making us more like each other in our views and expectations. This is socialization.

THE FREUDIAN THEORY OF PERSONALITY

Sigmund Freud (1856–1939) believed that biological drives are the basis for all human activity. According to Freud, the biological drives, although sexual in origin, are blind, so to speak. Freud described these drives as vague strivings without any specific aims or objectives. In other words, these are unconscious drives. This

Mass media as a socialization agent.

unconscious self is what Freud called the *id*. The id consists of biological drives that release energy. The id is activated by what Freud called the *pleasure principle*—the demand for immediate and complete gratification. Without undergoing socialization, people would be without morals, violent, and antisocial. In Freudian theory, the process of socialization occurs when the biological selfishness of the id is repressed and its energy directed toward socially acceptable goals and objectives. There is more to Freud's theory than this. Let us continue.

According to Freud, the human personality is made up of three parts—the id, the ego, and the superego. We have described the id as the unconscious self that is activated by the pleasure principle. The *ego* is the conscious self. Its function is to identify opportunities and goals that are available to the person. The ego tries to see the reality of a situation. The ego tries to restrain and check the id's demands for immediate and complete satisfaction. Thus, Freud said, the ego operates on the *reality principle*. The ego deals in terms of what is possible. The reality principle allows the ego to limit and direct the id's dedication to the pleasure principle. What the ego has to do is to engage in reality testing. The ego must explore and evaluate the world's reactions to certain behaviors. The ego, operating on the reality principle, can give up immediate gratifications in order to achieve long-range objectives. For example, a person might postpone achieving certain goals right now in order to achieve something else later.

The third part of the human personality Freud called the *superego*. The superego is the part of a person's personality that is created through socialization during the formative years. The superego comes into being when a child accepts the attitudes of parents as correct and when the child recognizes the authority of the parents. Actually, the superego is made up of the values and attitudes of society as they have been taught to the child by the parents. It is the superego—the conscience—that keeps the ego from giving in to the pleasure-seeking demands of the id. The superego encourages the ego to direct energies toward socially acceptable goals.

One could picture the ego as the battleground of the personality. The id and the superego fight to gain control of the ego. Any drive-in threatre on a Saturday night embodies more battles in the parked cars than those appearing on the screen in front of the parked cars! Many an ego finds itself under siege as ids and superegos collide in the forms of kisses, caresses, and whispered "no's." Sometimes the id wins. Sometimes the superego wins. And whether the id or the superego wins, the ego is going to receive *some kind* of gratification. Ironic, isn't it?

When Freud considered the human experience of socialization, he identified two major means by which socialization takes place. Freud used the terms *identification* and *repression*. He said that socialization occurs most directly through parental repression of a child's antisocial drives. Then, Freud said, by identifying with its parents, a child learns to behave in socially acceptable ways. The formation of one's personality occurs as a result of the experiences of repression and identification.

Since socialization and the formation of personality depend so much upon repression and identification, the way in which repression happens is very important. Children learn what is and is not acceptable by noting what their parents allow or deny them. Wanting to become like their seemingly all-powerful parents, the children observe how their parents behave. Parents, in turn, project their images by the kinds of demands they make on their children. If the child is ignored and neglected by receiving no limitations nor guides for behavior, identification will not occur. This means that the child's superego will have little or no opportunity to develop. As a result, the child is likely to be dominated by biological drives. The child will not be prepared to postpone gratification nor use its energies for socially approved activities. Later, the child-turned-adult will likely come into conflict with the laws and social expectations of society at large. This would be the result of *underrepression*.

On the other hand, *overrepression* can also be harmful to one's development. Too strong a repression of biological impulses can produce an overly strong superego. When the superego becomes this powerful, the ego feels pressure to deny all of the id's impulses. Then the ego is troubled by conflict. An extraordinarily strong superego can lead to feelings of guilt and anxiety about pleasure.

The ideal socialization would allow for a balance between the influences of the id and the superego. From the Freudian theory of personality, ideal socialization transfers the "unthinking, demanding little tyrant" into a healthy, functioning human being. Thus, through identification and proper repression, socialization turns human beings into social beings who can make helpful contributions to their society (Bensman and Rosenberg, 1963).

COOLEY'S LOOKING-GLASS SELF

In 1902 Charles Horton Cooley (1864–1929) used the example of one's reflection in a mirror to explain how others can influence the way in which one sees oneself. Cooley wrote:

> *Each to each a looking glass*
> *Reflects the other that doth pass.*
>
> *As we see our face, figure, and dress in the glass, and are interested in them because they are ours, and pleased or otherwise with them according as they do or do not answer to what we should like them to be; so in imagination we perceive in another's mind some thought of our appearance, manners, aims, deeds, character, friends, and so on, and are variously affected by it.*

(Cooley, 1964)

Cooley said that we each receive an impression of ourselves by imagining how others regard us. He believed that there are three major elements in this sort of "self idea":

1. Our perception of how we appear to others.
2. Our perception of how others judge our appearance.
3. How we feel about those judgments.

The looking-glass self means that we learn who we are by imagining how others perceive us. A real mirror reflects an image of our physical self. Our perception of others' reactions toward us reflects our social self. Keep in mind that Cooley's emphasis was not so much upon the real responses of others toward us. His emphasis was upon our *interpretations* of others' responses toward us. People could be laughing at us or laughing with us. Whatever the fact may be, it is our *interpretation* of the laughter that makes us feel happy or insecure.

Differences can exist between how one views oneself, how one thinks others view oneself, and how others actually do view oneself. If parents and peers continually criticize, reject, and neglect a child, the child will come to question its own worth. As a result of others' negative responses, the child acquires a negative self-image. But we can also mistake how others feel about us. We could interact with people who really like us, but if we have come to think of ourselves negatively, we will probably interpret even positive feelings toward us as being negative.

Cooley emphasized the deep impressions made on people by early childhood experiences. Nevertheless, one's self-concept can be changed later in life. We can redefine ourselves. Once having a negative self-image from the looking-glass self, we still can acquire a positive image. This is the basis of therapeutic endeavors. For example, the World Community of Al-Islam in the West (Black Muslims) have had some success in rehabilitating criminals, alcoholics, and drug addicts by replacing negative with positive self-images. This can be accomplished by having an individual identify strongly with a successful group with a positive self-image.

MEAD'S SIGNIFICANT OTHERS AND GENERALIZED OTHER

George Herbert Mead (1863–1931) taught for many years at the University of Chicago as a professor of philosophy. He did not publish his ideas, but after his death his students edited books based upon stenographic transcripts of his lectures and upon some of his unpublished writings. Like Freud and Cooley, Mead also believed that social interaction is the basic factor in socializing an individual. Mead introduced the concept of symbolic interaction. As we indicated earlier, symbolic interaction occurs through symbols such as language, gestures, and facial expressions. He believed that one must be able to step outside oneself and see oneself from the view of others. Mead called this "taking the role of the other"—seeing ourselves as others see us.

Mead believed that *self* develops as the child accepts the values of society. All those around us who participate in the customs of our society can be thought of as the *Generalized Other*, Mead said. The Generalized Other also consists of people we have never met and probably never will meet. It even consists of people who have been dead for a long time but who once contributed to and participated in the beliefs and customs of our society. When we do accept the values and customs of the Generalized Other, it can be said that we have experienced successful socialization.

Within the Generalized Other are people who are especially important to us. Parents, siblings, and close friends make vital contributions to the development of our personalities. Such people are our *significant others*, as Mead described them. Usually a significant other is someone with whom we share an intimate relationship. Such relationships include expectations for permanency. However, a significant other can also be a person who touches our life for a short time. If the relationship leaves a lasting influence on one's behavior and outlook on life, the other person has to be considered a significant other. Everyone has significant others within the Generalized Other. It is usually the significant others who have the most influence on us during the formative years.

Mead also introduced the concepts of the *I* and *me* to sociological literature. He used the term *I* to describe the part of an individual's self that, in this book, we call the single savage self—a spontaneous and self-constructing self. On the other hand, Mead used *me* to refer to that part of an individual's self that has been forged by the internalization of society's values and behavior expectations. The Generalized Other and significant others can be seen as creators of the *me*. For all that we know, the *I* may be the ghost in the machine of the human organism. It is a mystical and poetic concept that corresponds to the concept of the true self.

CONCLUDING REMARKS

The formative years do form the basic personality that each person will exhibit throughout life. Still, socialization does not cease when one is accepted as an adult by society. People continue to participate in new experiences that will further affect their personalities. Although members of a society share common values and behaviors, they also experience different episodes in life. Each individual will encounter different people, places, and situations. Within the same society, people will belong to different religions, will live in different regions, will be subject to different controls, and will be granted or denied different opportunities. All these factors contribute to lifelong socialization, our subject for the next section of this chapter.

KEY TERMS AND NAMES FROM SECTION 5

formative years

egocentrism

sociocentrism

family as socialization agent

siblings

peer group as socialization agent

school as socialization agent

acknowledged and hidden curricula in schools

unique experiences in socialization

id, ego, superego

pleasure principle

reality principle

identification and repression

the looking-glass self

Generalized Other

significant others

I and me

Sigmund Freud

Charles Horton Cooley

George Herbert Mead

STUDY GUIDE FOR SECTION 5

1. A human *self* concept consists of two ingredients. WHAT ARE THEY, AND WHAT QUESTIONS ABOUT THE SELF DO THEY ANSWER?

2. A child depends on others for self-identity and for fulfillment of basic needs. EXPLAIN HOW THE CHILD EXPERIENCES THE TRANSITION FROM EGOCENTRISM TO SOCIOCENTRISM.

3. Society's attitudes, beliefs, and behavior expectations must be introduced to the child. WHAT IS THE FIRST AGENT OF SOCIALIZATION?

4. Children raised in the same family, house, and neighborhood during the same years can still be very different from one another. WHY AREN'T SUCH CHILDREN EXACTLY ALIKE?

5. The peer group is an important factor in socialization. DEFINE THE TERM *PEER GROUP*.

6. Being accepted by one's peers is important to most children. IDENTIFY SOME CHARACTERISTICS THAT ARE RELATED TO PEER-GROUP POPULARITY.

7. Some writers say that the peer group is anti-family. DOES THERE HAVE TO BE CONFLICT BETWEEN FAMILY AND PEER GROUP?

8. WHICH CHILDREN ARE MORE LIKELY TO USE THE PEER GROUP AS THEIR SOURCE FOR VALUES AND BEHAVIORS?

9. The book refers to American schools having both an *acknowledged* curriculum and a *hidden* curriculum. HOW ARE THEY DIFFERENT? HOW DOES EACH TYPE OF CURRICULUM CONTRIBUTE TO SOCIALIZATION?

10. Kenneth Neubeck says that students should have more say in educational policies and decisions affecting them. CITE ACTIVITIES THAT NEUBECK BELIEVES WOULD MAKE THE SCHOOLS BETTER AGENTS OF SOCIALIZATION.

11. Mass media are socializing agents in American society. IDENTIFY TYPES OF MASS MEDIA. HOW DO MEDIA AFFECT OUR BEHAVIOR?

12. The Freudian theory of personality includes references to special terms. DESCRIBE FREUD'S THEORY BY REFERRING TO THE FOLLOWING: ID, EGO, SUPEREGO, PLEASURE PRINCIPLE, AND REALITY PRINCIPLE.

13. Freud believed that socialization and personality formation depend on both identification and repression. EXPLAIN.

14. The manner in which repression occurs affects personality greatly. WHAT ARE THE PROBABLE RESULTS OF "UNDERREPRESSION" AND "OVERREPRESSION"?

15. A real mirror reflects an image of our physical self. ACCORDING TO COOLEY'S LOOKING-GLASS SELF THEORY, WHAT THREE ELEMENTS CONTRIBUTE TO ONE'S IDEA OF SELF?

16. According to Cooley, differences can exist between how one thinks others view oneself and how others actually do view oneself. EXPLAIN HOW THIS CAN OCCUR.

17. Mead believed that one must be able to step outside oneself and see oneself from the view of others. WHAT PHRASE DID MEAD USE TO DESCRIBE THIS BEHAVIOR?

18. Mead said that there are people whom we have never met who contribute to our socialization. WHAT TERM DID HE USE FOR THIS?

19. In our socialization experiences, we interact with people who are especially important to the development of our personalities. WHAT DID MEAD CALL THESE PEOPLE?

PRACTICE TEST FOR SECTION 5

Select the best answer.

1. Having a sense of identity and self-esteem are ingredients of the
  A. Generalized Other.
  B. Self-concept.
  C. Significant others.
  D. Id.

2. The phrase "an unthinking, demanding little tyrant" is associated with
A.   Sociocentrism.
B.   Egocentrism.
C.   Superego.
D.   Ego.

3. For most people, the first agent of socialization is the
A.   Peer group.
B.   School.
C.   Family.
D.   None of the above.

4. Children raised in the same family and neighborhood during the same years will likely have what type of experience?
A.   Identical.
B.   Completely different.
C.   Similar.
D.   It could be any of the above.

5. Children become aware of the presence and wishes of others of their same age and status
A.   Through mass media.
B.   When they reach junior high school.
C.   In the peer group.
D.   In the family.

6. When the family offers little guidance or support, children are apt to seek such things from
A.   Mass media.
B.   The peer group.
C.   School.
D.   The generation gap.

7. Most peer groups in the United States
A.   Are anti-family.
B.   Exhibit behavior that is socially acceptable.
C.   Exhibit behavior that is not socially acceptable.
D.   Both A and C.

8. Characteristics of the "hidden curriculum" in schools include learning
A.   Participation in sports.
B.   Reading and writing.
C.   History.
D.   None of the above.

9. Viewing the teacher as the child's first boss is part of
A.   Peer group pressures.
B.   Acknowledged curriculum.
C.   Hidden curriculum.
D.   All of the above.

10. Various forms of mass media include
A.   Television.
B.   Radio.
C.   The classroom.
D.   Only A and B.

11. Mass media contribute to making Americans
A.   Happy and independent of others.
B.   More willing to pay taxes.
C.   Eager to use libraries.
D.   More like each other.

12. According to Freud, the major means by which socialization occurs are through
A.   Identification and repression.
B.   Generalized Other and significant others.
C.   Underrepression and overrepression.
D.   The schools and mass media.

13. Regarding the id, which of the following is incorrect?
A.   It operates on the reality principle.
B.   It is activated by the pleasure principle.
C.   It consists of unconscious drives.
D.   It consists of biological drives.

14. Accepting parental values and authority is characteristic of the
A.   Id.

B.   I.
C.   Ego.
D.   Superego.

15. Who developed the concept known as the looking-glass self?
A.   Sigmund Freud.
B.   Charles Horton Cooley.
C.   George Herbert Mead.
D.   George Eliopoulos.

16. The part of human personality that demands immediate and complete gratification is the
A.   Id.
B.   Ego.
C.   Superego.
D.   Looking-glass self.

17. If a child is ignored and neglected by receiving no limitations or guides for behavior, which of the following would *not* occur? The child will
A.   Develop a strong superego.
B.   Be motivated by the pleasure principle.
C.   Come into conflict with society's laws.
D.   Be dominated by biological drives.

18. Cooley said that our perception of others' reactions toward us reflects our

A.   True self.
B.   Physical self.
C.   Actualized self.
D.   Social self.

19. Mead believed that one must be able to step outside oneself and see oneself from the view of others. Mead called this
A.   Taking the role of the other.
B.   The looking-glass self.
C.   The reality principle.
D.   The Generalized Other.

20. According to Freud, overrepression can lead to all of the following except one. Which one?
A.   Weakening of the superego.
B.   Denial of biological impulses.
C.   Anxiety and guilt concerning id impulses.
D.   Development of an overly strong superego.

21. Those people who have an especially important influence on our personalities are known as
A.   Primary others.
B.   Generalized Other.
C.   Significant others.
D.   Important others.

Answer Key

1.	B	**8.**	D	**15.**	B
2.	B	**9.**	C	**16.**	A
3.	C	**10.**	D	**17.**	A
4.	C	**11.**	D	**18.**	D
5.	C	**12.**	A	**19.**	A
6.	B	**13.**	A	**20.**	A
7.	B	**14.**	D	**21.**	C

SECTION 6   SOCIALIZATION AS A LIFELONG PROCESS
- THE TRUE SELF
- SOCIALIZATION THROUGH ROLES
- ROLE CONFLICTS
- SOCIAL CONTROLS AS FACTORS IN SOCIALIZATION
- SOCIAL LOCATION AS A FACTOR IN SOCIALIZATION
- RITES OF PASSAGE FROM BIRTH TO DEATH

Objectives
After completing this section, the student should be able to:
1. Discuss the philosophical and sociological views of the *true self*.
2. Identify various social roles.
3. Explain how role playing contributes to socialization.
4. Give examples of role expectancy, role performance, and role conflict.
5. Define positive and negative sanctions.
6. Explain how social location both grants and denies certain life chances.
7. Describe in what way rites of passage are part of the socialization process.
8. Give examples of rites of passage.

*N*o person crosses the same river twice, because the river has changed, and so has the person.

Heraclitus (540–470 B.C.)

During the 1960s, books of Hermann Hesse became popular among young people in the United States. Hesse had written and published the books earlier in the 20th century. *Siddartha* (1922) and *Steppenwolf* (1927) were probably the two Hesse books most read during the 1960s, but a third book, *Demian* (1919), also received its share of attention. On a separate page in the front of the novel, Hesse wrote the following: "All I wanted to do was live according to the promptings of my true self. Why was that so hard to do?" These words convey a sense of profound importance and mystery about the true self. Young people tend to think in terms of finding their true selves. Mature philosophers and poets in many cultures have sought to know and understand their true selves. Let us consider the concept of true self from a sociological perspective.

THE TRUE SELF   Sociologists can be young, philosophical, and poetic, but when they reach into their sociological bag and try to pull forth a *true self*, they come away with empty hands. Where is the true self that youth seeks and about which philosophers and poets have spoken for so many years? Perhaps the question must be answered like this: Here today, gone tomorrow. Or: Here this moment, gone next moment. Unquestionably the concept of a true self is reassuring, but the validity of the concept, when examined from the sociological perspective, becomes doubtful, to say the very least.

At any given moment in life an individual is a self that totals all the experiences of all one's preceding moments. The agents of socialization work upon each individual from the moment of birth to the moment of death. Each of us is a product of one's time and place and personal experiences. Socialization is an ongoing process. Therefore, the self is ongoing and is constantly influencing and being influenced through relationships with other selves. Consequently, because socialization is a lifelong process, we can search high and low through space and time without discovering one constant true self among all the human beings who have inhabited Earth.

SOCIALIZATION THROUGH ROLES

Earlier we quoted a famous sociologist as having said that "everyone is always and everywhere, more or less consciously playing a role." It is wrong to suggest that people who play roles are not being true to themselves or that they are being deceitful. Social roles are part and parcel of an individual's behavior when interacting with other people in various situations. Every social situation has a *role expectancy* for us to fulfill.

Most of William Shakespeare's plays were produced in the New Globe Theater, and the motto of that theatre was "the whole world plays the actor." In his play *As You Like It*, Shakespeare's words in Act Two, Scene Seven also capture the content of sociological role theory:

All the world's a stage,
And all the men and women merely players.
They have their exits and their entrances,
And one man in his time plays many parts . . .

All the men and women are merely players on the stage of society. Each social situation is like a scene in which we make our appearance and our exit. This is continuous throughout one's lifetime. By participating in a continuous chain of social situations that require us to play social roles, we are experiencing a continuous process of socialization. By fulfilling the role expectancies in each situation, we become more integrated within our society.

Even though the early formative years do have a tremendous impact on what we will be like in the following years, socialization is a lifelong process. In the previous section, we mentioned a woman who might, during one day, play various social roles. We said that she could play the roles of daughter, mother, sister, student, employee, customer, and wife. We said then that her ability to play the various roles was developed through the process of socialization. Now, to add to that statement, we are saying that the very fact that she plays the roles is also part of the socialization process.

"And one man in his time plays many parts."

There is a difference between *role expectation* and *role performance*. Role expectations are the ways of behaving that society stresses as being proper in given situations. Role performance refers to how well a person fulfills the expectations of society for given situations. Obviously, all people do not and probably cannot fulfill all the role expectations encountered throughout a lifetime.

ROLE CONFLICTS W. I. Thomas was mentioned in Chapter 1 as having introduced the term *definition of the situation*. Thomas asserted that every social situation in which one participates has been predefined as far as role expectancy is concerned. The behavior has been predetermined by the group who make up the social situation. An individual entering a social situation is expected to observe the appropriate behavior for the situation.

Role performance refers to how well a person fulfills the expectations for role playing in a given situation. The matter is not, however, as simple as it might seem to be. It is entirely possible for a person to be in two situations at the same time. We could use the word *status* in place of *situation*. Most social situations do require us to occupy a certain status or position. We are then expected to play the role appropriate to that status or position. Status can be the rank or the position of a person in a group. A role is the behavior expected of one who occupies the status. Since each person can occupy a number of statuses and be expected to perform the roles appropriate to each status, role conflict can result. Occupying two statuses or being in two situations at the same time can bring about role conflict for an individual. Let us cite an example.

In Baltimore some years ago, the term *stealing* was used by both taxicab drivers and their employers to describe a practice of cab drivers that involved withholding money from employers. Everyone in the cab business knew that stealing occurred. They also knew that it was against the law. Still, stealing was common. Few cab drivers could make a decent day's wage if they depended only on money collected during regular passenger trips during which the meter flag was down and the meter clicked off the expense of the trip. Thus, most drivers, when they could, would double up on passengers—a technique in which the taxi would carry more than one fare at a time to more than one destination. The meter would register for only one fare's trip, but both passengers would pay the cab driver. The driver's legitimate income for this trip would be 40 percent of the one fare, with 60 pecent of it going to the taxicab company. However, the money received from the other fare would be pocketed in full by the driver. This was one kind of stealing. Another type was the practice of "high-flagging" while carrying passengers. To do this, the driver would not allow the meter to register at all (leaving the meter flag in the "up" position), thus collecting all the money paid for the trip. In a sense, this kind of behavior was the unofficial definition of the cab-driving situation, but some role conflict could occur for some cab drivers.

Imagine a cab driver who believed that this accepted procedure of stealing was wrong. Suppose, however, that he was a man who had a wife and five children completely dependent on his income. This would be an example of a citizen who had respect for the law, yet who was in a job situation in which the unofficial rules included stealing, without which he would be unable adequately to fulfill his role as breadwinner for his family. Here would be a man desiring to play the role of law-abiding citizen while at the same time desiring to play the role of adequate provider for his family. This would be an example of a man occupying two different statuses or positions with conflicting role expectancies. The result would be a role conflict.

Role conflict can occur in many social situations. The college professor who wants to concentrate on teaching may be required by the college to exhibit evidence of research and scholarship. A college student entrusted to supervise a test given to a class may encounter role conflict upon seeing a friend who is cheating. A store manager whose daughter works in the same store and who consistently comes to work late could encounter role conflict. A police officer who has been trained to exhibit restraint in the face of provocation could experience role conflict when being taunted with insults and showered with debris. It can be difficult for an individual to integrate successfully all the social roles expected by society. A society that can minimize role conflicts offers its people potential stability and tranquility.

SOCIAL CONTROLS AS FACTORS IN SOCIALIZATION

Societies seek to instill within their populations the desire and willingness to behave in accordance with the expectations of the Generalized Other. To guarantee that most people observe most rules most of the time, societies develop sanctions that encourage conformity and discourage nonconformity. *Positive sanctions* are rewards received by people acting in accordance with social expectations (or at least who seem to be doing so). Such rewards range from approving smiles to increases in pay, promotion in status, or even special awards banquets which celebrate how good a person has been for the community and country. *Negative sanctions* are threats of punishment that are intended to keep people in line. When a person is punished, the society assumes that the punishment will deter that person from misbehaving again. Society also assumes that such punishment will set an example for others not to step out of line.

There are formal and informal rewards that act as positive sanctions in the United States. The young man who scores a touchdown for his team will probably be patted on his rear by his teammates. This would be an informal award. The young woman who graduates from college will be honored by commencement exercises and the granting of a college degree. This is an example of a formal reward. Some psychologists believe that positive sanctions (rewards) are a better means of convincing both children and adults to conform to society's expectations than are negative sanctions (punishments). We believe that a combination of positive and negative sanctions is necessary for encouraging conformity.

Positive and negative sanctions are types of social controls. The promises of rewards are intended to keep people pursuing socially acceptable roles. The threats of punishments are intended to prevent people from pursuing socially unacceptable roles. At the very least, sanctions make people *appear* to do what is condoned and appear *not* to do what is condemned. This may be all that is necessary to maintain most social orders.

During the past quarter of a century there has been considerable discussion about parents being too permissive with children and about society at large being too permissive in general. Some social critics contend that crimes and riots and other antisocial behavior occur because society fails to demand that people conform to the rules.

In a novel by Joseph Wambaugh entitled *The New Centurions*, the function of police in contemporary society is treated with insight and sensitivity. One of the policemen in the novel is Kilvinsky. Kilvinsky is a philosopher in a patrol car—not an uncommon phenomenon. At one point in the novel Kilvinsky contrasts today with the days of the early Christians in Rome:

It's the great myth—the myth whatever it happens to be that breaks civil authority. I wonder if a couple of centurions might've sat around like you and me one hot dry evening talking about the myth of Christianity that was defeating them. They would have been afraid, I bet, but the new myth was loaded with "don'ts" so one kind of authority was just being substituted for another. Civilization was never in jeopardy.

But today the "don'ts" are dying or being murdered in the name of freedom and we policemen can't save them. Once the people become accustomed to the death of a "don't," well then, the other "don'ts" die much easier. Usually all the vice laws die first because people are generally vice-ridden anyway. Then the ordinary misdemeanors and some felonies become unenforceable until freedom prevails. Then later the free people have to organize an army of their own to find order because they learn that freedom is horrifying and ugly and only small doses of it can be tolerated.

(Wambaugh, 1970)

Kilvinsky is particularly concerned with what he interprets as an erosion of the "don'ts" that are necessary for maintaining social order.

Sociologist Peter Berger has said that "No society can exist without social controls." The following social controls that Berger describes are, for the most part, threats of punishment (negative sanctions) that society can inflict on individuals who refuse to play socially approved roles (Berger, 1963).

Physical Violence

Berger says that physical violence is the ultimate and probably the oldest means of social control. He says that "In the savage society of children it is still the major one." All societies have some form of police that are used to maintain order by threat of force if everything else fails. Even the most democratic and free society will produce force as a means of control if all else should fail as a means of persuasion. Berger says that "Violence is the ultimate foundation of any political order." In any society that is dedicated to some concept of justice, use of force is generally restricted to situations where the *threat* of violence has failed to prevent or to guarantee certain behavior.

Economic Pressure

All people must have access to certain basic needs such as food, clothing and shelter—not to mention all the goods and services associated with modern industrial societies. Inappropriate behavior can lead to loss of economic incomes that, in turn, can lead to various hardships. When alarm clocks ring early in the morning, people get up and go to work because they have to make ends meet, not because going to the factory or school or store or office is necessarily what one wants to do at that moment.

Group Persuasion

Individuals tend to alter their original opinions so that their thinking conforms more closely to the group with which they identify. Berger offers the following example of how group dynamics include the ability to change an individual's opinion:

. . . if you have a group of twenty cannibals arguing over cannibalism with one noncannibal, the chances are that in the end he will come to see their point, and, with just a few face-saving reservations (concerning, say, the consumption of close relatives), will go over completely to the majority's point of view. But if you have a group discussion between ten cannibals who regard human flesh aged over sixty years as too tough for cultivated palates and ten other cannibals who fastidiously draw the line at fifty, the chances are that the group will eventually agree on fifty-five as the age that divided . . . when it comes to sorting out prisoners. What lies at the bottom of this apparently inevitable pressure towards consensus is probably a profound human desire to be accepted, presumably by whatever group is around to do the accepting.

(Berger, 1963)

Both young and old people in any group can be pressured into conforming to group expectations. Group persuasion can be the motivation for an individual's first sexual experience, initial consumption of alcohol or marijuana, or conversion to a religion. Because we care about what the members of our group think about us, we often adjust our thinking and our behavior to coincide more with that of the group.

Ridicule and Gossip

The threat of ridicule is a potent instrument of social control over both children and adults. Children often conform in order to escape being laughed at. Adults also try to avoid appearing foolish. Most people have experienced the "freezing fear of making oneself ridiculous in some social situation."

Gossip about a person occurs when that person is not present. All gossip need not be bad, but most people attempt to avoid being gossiped about for fear that some misrepresentation of self will occur. The threats of ridicule and gossip are especially effective in small communities and organizations where most people know each other. People care about what others say and think about them. That is why ridicule and gossip are effective social controls.

Ostracism

Banishment or removal from established social contacts is called *ostracism*. For example, failing to conform to the dogma and rituals of a religion can result in excommunication, one form of ostracism. Another example would be that used by the Amish Mennonites—shunning. Should one of the Amish become sexually involved with an outsider, that person is ignored and, although the individual may remain in the community, no one will speak to the offender. Still another example of ostracism is the political practice of exile. The book *Man Without a Country* tells of a man who said "God damn the United States of America. I never want to hear anything about this country again!" The judge then convicts him to a lifetime aboard a ship under conditions that allow all comforts except any mention of his native land. The story conveys the tragedy of an ostracized individual cut adrift from familiar places and people. Even informal ostracism can be practiced by small children when one child is rejected and no longer welcomed by its former playmates. As a threat, ostracism is a very powerful social control.

SOCIAL LOCATION AS A FACTOR IN SOCIALIZATION

Certainly the nation into which one is born and in which one lives throughout a lifetime will have considerable effect on the individual. One learns to appreciate and to observe the customs and values of one's culture. One learns to worship the gods of one's people, to appreciate the art, to speak the language, and generally to become a participating member of the nation in which one matures. Whether one is born in Nigeria or in the United States is a matter of *geographic* location. Whether one is born in New England or in the American South is also a matter of geographic location. *Social location* is something else. One could be a New Englander and still have the same social location as one who is a Southerner. By social location, we mean social class.

Every society has a ranking system of levels in which people are said to be located. The concept of social location is of particular interest to sociologists, but one need not be a sociologist to have heard of the upper class, middle class, and lower class. A system of social levels or strata is called *social stratification*. The subject of social stratification is treated in detail in Chapter 6, but it must be mentioned here because social class has a profound impact on the socialization experience of any individual in society. Each social class is characterized by a general life-style that differs from the life-style of the other social classes in the same society.

Max Weber (1864–1920), a German sociologist and scholar, said that one's social location allows for certain *life chances* and grants or denies certain privileges, power, and prestige to the individual. Access to or denial of privileges, power, and prestige contributes to different experiences of socialization for people within the same society or even within the same city or town.

To illustrate this thesis, let us imagine two infants who were born 50 years ago at the same hour on the same day in the same hospital. One infant was the son of a migrant worker (lower-lower class) while the other was the son of a stockbroker (upper-middle class). With startling accuracy, we might have predicted at that very hour what kind of human beings would develop from these "prehuman" infants.

Lying in the crib of the broker was a boy who would have access to privileges that would enhance his life chances. He would live in a fine home in an attractive and stable neighborhood. The broker's son would grow up eating a carefully planned diet that would contribute to his good health and to a sense of well-being. He would have access to the finest schools that would prepare him to succeed in the finest colleges in the country. He would develop a taste for fine music and paintings, travel first-class to Europe during the summers, use a correct vocabulary, make regular visits to the dentist, and receive the finest medical care available throughout his life. He would join prestige organizations and would associate with peers enjoying the same advantages. Based on statistics, he would probably live longer than the infant who was in the crib next to him. Today, 50 years after his birth, the broker's son is probably an executive in a powerful corporation.

Lying in the next crib was the migrant worker's boy, who would have access to none of the privileges accorded to the broker's son. Living in shacks throughout the rural farming areas of America, moving from place to place with his family, the migrant worker's son would grow up with a meager diet lacking protein. He would attend school sporadically, finally terminating his education without having learned very much beyond basic abilities in reading and writing. His only exposure to music would come from hearing songs sung by other workers in the fields. The walls of the shacks would be devoid of anything artistic. His language, while earthy, would be sparse and inadequate for expressing himself in society at large. He might never see a dentist, and medical care would be restricted to the bare essentials required by law or by emergencies called to the attention of employers or public agencies and clinics. Today, 50 years after birth, the migrant worker's son is probably a migrant worker himself, sometimes working, sometimes unemployed.

Such circumstances—life chances—would occur because these two people were born into families with different social locations, thus causing them to have entirely different socialization experiences. One might be applauded for his accomplishments while the other might be blamed for his lack of accomplishments. We wonder what would have happened to these two people if, when no one was looking, someone had quickly switched infants from one crib to another!

RITES OF PASSAGE FROM BIRTH TO DEATH

Every society attempts to reinforce the stability of its established structure and behavior patterns. To do this, society provides its members with rituals and ceremonies that observe important changes in individuals' lives. Such rituals and ceremonies are called *rites of passage*. The term *rites of passage* was first used by the Flemish anthropologist A. Van Gennep (1873–1957) in his book *Les Rites de Passage* published in 1908. Van Gennep demonstrated that all societies observe rituals of transition as significant changes occur.

Whenever the status of an individual undergoes change, whenever community affairs undergo change, and whenever nature itself changes from season to season, such changes are acknowledged by ceremonies. These ceremonies—rites of passage—act as continuing socialization experiences throughout the lifetimes of society's members. By participating in these shared experiences, people recognize how much they belong to their groups, their community, and their nation.

Rites of passage support and intensify people's loyalties and devotion to the established social order. This is part of lifelong socialization (Van Gennep, 1960).

Almost all societies observe important occasions such as birth, puberty, marriage, and death as part of the lifelong process of socialization. Certain rituals are shared so that society at large recognizes that a significant event has taken place. Rites of passage are observations of transition (passage) from one condition or status to another. Few human societies would totally ignore such important experiences, but there are also less significant occasions that are acknowledged by rites of passage. Robert Bierstedt says that there is no natural reason why a student who has earned the required credits, paid all tuition, and passed final exams should not receive a college degree through the mail. Nevertheless, enough people believe that the transition from undergraduate to graduate status is important. Being important, it deserves public recognition and public reward. The graduation commencement consists of the rites that observe the individual's change in status (Bierstedt, 1970). This is part of lifelong socialization.

From birth to death the rites of passage carry us through the years on the carpet of our culture. We share with our fellow travelers in society the socializing experiences that make us what we are. Two modern poets have touched on the first and the final rites of passage, birth and death, in the following poems.

*Recapitulations**

I was born downtown on a wintry day
   And under the roof where Poe expired;
Tended by nuns my mother lay
   Dark-haired and beautiful and tired.

Doctors and cousins paid their call,
   The rabbi and my father helped.
A crucifix burned on the wall
   Of the bright room where I was whelped.

At one week all my family prayed,
   Stuffed wine and cotton in my craw;
The rabbi blessed me with a blade
   According to the Mosaic Law.

The white steps blazed in Baltimore
   And cannas and white statuary.
I went home voluble and sore
   Influenced by Abraham and Mary.
               KARL SHAPIRO

Passage†

What have we done to death? I, less American than most,
Still must speak stiffly to say "the body," "the corpse," "the remains."
The thought dries my mouth. I jeer at Forest Lawn, detest cosmetic
Youth, and yet if I can I ignore death's awkward bulk.

In the Slovenian village where my uncle's father died
They coffined him and took him out under the pale sky.
The villagers formed a procession two hundred meters long,
Flags first, with black (no cross—he had left the church).

Then the village band, slow marching to brass and beat,
Then our family carrying cedar wreaths, then the coffin on a cart,
And then the villagers by twos and threes on down the road.
I marched too and dropped my pinch of dust into the grave.

I know that this is better than our thin American way.
And yet . . . I look around me and see forming clouds so dense
That I feel that when our village bears a child we should bring him
In his basket home from the hostel and his mother's side.

Flags draped, brass band at slow march, green wreaths, and
Mourning villagers following him down the single street.

CARL BODE

KEY TERMS AND NAMES FROM SECTION 6

the true self

socialization through role playing

role expectation

role performance

role conflict

definition of the situation

social controls

positive sanctions

negative sanctions

ostracism

physical violence

economic pressures

social stratification

social location

life chances

social class

rites of passage

W. I. Thomas

Peter Berger

Max Weber

A. Van Gennep

STUDY GUIDE FOR SECTION 6

1. Herman Hesse wrote: "All I wanted to do was live according to the promptings of my true self. Why was that so hard to do?" HOW COULD YOU RESPOND TO HIS QUESTION FROM THE SOCIOLOGICAL PERSPECTIVE?

2. Every social situation has a role expectancy for us to fulfill. ARE PEOPLE WHO PLAY ROLES BEING DECEITFUL? WHY?

3. Sociologists say that each person plays many roles. LIST AT LEAST FOUR SOCIAL ROLES THAT *YOU* PLAY FROM DAY TO DAY.

4. BRIEFLY DEFINE THE TERMS *ROLE EXPECTATION* AND *ROLE PERFORM-ANCE*.

5. If a person is in two social situations at the same time that require different behaviors, WHAT SOCIOLOGICAL TERM APPLIES?

6. Both status and role are related to social interaction. NOTE THE DIFFERENCE BETWEEN THESE TERMS BY WRITING DEFINITIONS FOR EACH.

7. Role conflict can occur in many social situations. GIVE TWO EXAMPLES OF ROLE CONFLICT.

8. To guarantee that most people observe most behavior expectations most of the time, there are sanctions that encourage conformity and discourage nonconformity. WHAT IS THE DIFFERENCE BETWEEN POSITIVE AND NEGATIVE SANCTIONS?

9. GIVE EXAMPLES OF BOTH FORMAL AND INFORMAL POSITIVE SANCTIONS.

10. Both positive and negative sanctions are social controls used to maintain conformity to social expectations. WHICH DO *YOU* BELIEVE ARE MORE EFFECTIVE? WHY?

11. Peter Berger has said that no society can exist without social controls. WHICH SOCIAL CONTROLS DOES BERGER DESCRIBE?

12. Both geographic and social locations are factors in socialization. The concept of social location especially interests sociologists. WHAT IS THE DIFFERENCE BETWEEN GEOGRAPHIC AND SOCIAL LOCATION?

13. Max Weber said that one's social location allows for certain life chances. EXACTLY WHAT DID WEBER SAY IS GRANTED OR DENIED TO AN INDIVIDUAL BECAUSE OF SOCIAL LOCATION?

14. In the text we describe two infants. One was born the son of a migrant worker. The other was born the son of a stockbroker. We wondered what would happen if, when no one was looking, someone had switched infants from one crib to another. WHAT DIFFERENCE DO *YOU* THINK IT WOULD HAVE MADE IN THEIR LIVES? WHY?

15. Societies observe rituals and ceremonies whenever the status of an individual undergoes important change. WHAT DO ANTHROPOLOGISTS AND SOCIOLOGISTS CALL THESE RITUALS?

16. Rituals and ceremonies serve as reinforcements for socializing members of society throughout their lives. EXPLAIN WHY THIS IS SO.

PRACTICE TEST FOR SECTION 6

Select the best answer.

1. One who fulfills the expectations of society according to a situation's definition exhibits
A. Role expectation.
B. Peer expectation.
C. Role performance.
D. Only A and B.

2. Social role playing
A. Does not occur in personal relationships.
B. Requires people to deceive people.
C. Requires one to adapt to the definition of the situation.

D. Is especially important outside the family.

3. Rewards received by people who conform with social expectations are known as
A. Rites of passage.
B. Positive sanctions.
C. Status sanctions.
D. Negative sanctions.

4. The oldest and ultimate means of social control is
A. Ostracism.
B. Economic pressure.
C. Physical violence.
D. Ridicule and gossip.

5. Social controls are
A. Positive sanctions.
B. Negative sanctions.
C. Factors in socialization.
D. All of the above.

6. Which of the following is *not* correct? Social location
A. Is a function of geographical location.
B. Grants or denies privileges, power, and prestige.
C. Allows for certain life chances.
D. Both B and C.

7. Rituals that observe significant changes in people's lives are known as
A. Roles of passage.
B. Rites of passage.
C. Role performance.
D. Role expectation.

8. Role conflict occurs when

A. Two people try to achieve the same goal.
B. A person plays contradictory roles at the same time.
C. An individual plays more than one role in a day.
D. All of the above.

9. Shunning, as practiced by the Amish Mennonites, is an example of
A. Ostracism.
B. Ridicule.
C. A positive sanction.
D. Rites of passage.

10. An instructor who achieves all course objectives is exhibiting
A. Role performance.
B. Role conflict.
C. Role expectation.
D. Only A and C.

11. Every social situation in which one participates
A. Has been predefined in reference to role expectation.
B. Has behavior predetermined by the group.
C. Requires people to occupy a position or status.
D. All of the above.

12. Who said that one's social location allows for certain life chances?
A. Peter Berger.
B. A. Van Gennep.
C. Max Weber.
D. W. I. Thomas

Answer Key

1.	C	7.	B
2.	C	8.	B
3.	B	9.	A
4.	C	10.	A
5.	D	11.	D
6.	A	12.	C

CHAPTER
SUMMARY

1. Culture refers to all those ways of thinking, feeling, and behaving that are passed on from one generation to the next. To participate in society's culture, one must experience the process of socialization. Through socialization, one learns the content of one's culture.

2. For many years a controversy has existed regarding human nature and human nurture. Human nature has to do with one's heredity. Human nurture has to do with one's environment and socialization. Sociologists tend to play down the significance of human nature and to emphasize the importance of environment and socialization.

3. Cases of extremely isolated children have come to the attention of social scientists. The nonhuman condition of these social isolates supports the contention that one must experience socialization through social interaction in order to become fully human.

4. For successful socialization to occur, at least two preconditions must exist: The child must have an adequate biological inheritance and there must be an ongoing society from which the child can learn.

5. There are four universal aims of socialization: The teaching of basic disciplines, the creation of goals and ambitions, the teaching of special skills, and the definition of social roles. Socialization helps give life meaning for those who participate in their society's culture.

6. The most important period for socialization is during the early, formative years. This is when the self-concept comes into being. One acquires a sense of identify and self-esteem. Through social interaction people acquire a sense of who they are and what they are worth.

7. The family is the first agent of socialization. A child acquires beliefs and attitudes and learns how to behave. The first experiences of love, hope, and disappointment occur within the family.

8. Children raised in the same family, house, and neighborhood and during the same years will not be exactly alike. They have unique experiences that will contribute to their unique personalities.

9. For every child there comes a time when other children become important socialization influences. A peer group is made up of youngsters who are near the same age and who have about equal status. Children know and care about what their peers expect from them. This has an influence on each child's values, attitudes, and behavior.

10. The mass media constitute another agent of socialization. Television, radio, books, comics, magazines, movies, newspapers, and records and tapes all influence both adults and children.

11. Schools and the educational system also serve as agents of socialization. Schools teach basic skills like reading, writing, and arithmetic. Children also acquire skills in sports and in different occupational specialties. The hidden curriculum requires young people to learn to follow directions and how to respond to commands. The teacher is the child's first boss.

12.   The Freudian theory of personality emphasizes biological drives as the basis for human activity. According to Freud, human personality is made up of id, ego, and superego. The pleasure principle motivates the id. The reality principle motivates the ego. Two major means by which socialization takes place are identification and repression.

13.   Cooley's looking-glass self offers further insights into human personality and formation of self-concept. The looking-glass self means that we learn who we are by imagining how others perceive us. Our perception of others' reactions toward us reflects our social self.

14.   Like Freud and Cooley, George Herbert Mead also believed that social interaction is the basic factor in socialization. He used terms such as the I and the me, the Generalized Other, and significant others. His theory also was about the formation of human personality and self-concept.

15.   Socialization also occurs through the playing of social roles. A social role is behavior expected of one who occupies a given status. Role performance refers to how well a person fulfills the role expectation. Role conflict can occur.

16.   To guarantee that most people observe most rules most of the time, societies develop negative and positive sanctions. Positive sanctions are rewards. Negative sanctions are threats of punishment. Both act as social controls that maintain a high degree of conformity.

17.   Every society has a ranking system of levels in which people are said to be located. This is called social stratification. Each level has a life-style that is different from the life-styles of other levels. Max Weber said that these different social locations allow for certain life chances.

18.   Rituals and ceremonies that observe important changes in people's lives are called rites of passage. Rites of passage encourage people's loyalties and devotion to the established social order. By participating in these shared experiences, people recognize how much they belong to their groups, their community, and their nation. Birth, reaching maturity, marriage, and death are universal experiences that occur during the lifelong process of socialization.

SUGGESTIONS FOR FURTHER READING RELATING TO CHAPTER 2

Benedict, Ruth, *Patterns of Culture* (Baltimore: Penguin Books, 1946). This book shows how socialization develops behavior patterns and personality types that are appropriate for various cultures.

Clausen, John A., editor, *Socialization and Society* (Boston: Little, Brown, 1968). This is a collection of eight theoretical papers on the relationship between individuals and society and the process of socialization.

Davis, Kingsley, "Extreme Social Isolation of a Child," *American Journal of Sociology*, Vol. 45 (January 1940), pp. 554–565; and "Final Note on a Case of Extreme Isolation," *American Journal of Sociology*, Vol. 52 (March 1947), pp.

423–437. Articles on social isolates that demonstrate the significance of socialization.

Elkin, Frederick, *The Child and Society* (New York: Random House, 1965). This is a good, readable paperback that focuses on preconditions for socialization and discusses the major agencies of socialization.

Goffman, Erving, *The Presentation of Self in Everyday Life* (New York: Doubleday Anchor Books, 1959). Goffman analyzes social interaction in terms of a theatrical performance. Considerable attention is devoted to the concepts of role expectation and role performance.

Goslin, David A., editor, *Handbook of Socialization Theory and Research* (Chicago: Rand McNally, 1969). This is a comprehensive review of socialization presented in a collection of essays on childhood, adolescence, middle age, and old age.

Kett, Joseph F., *Rites of Passage: Adolescence in America, 1790 to the Present* (New York: Basic Books, 1977). This book argues that changes in young people and their roles in society are the result of economic factors and the rise of the new middle class.

Mead, Margaret, *Male and Female: A Study of the Sexes in a Changing World* (New York: William Morrow & Co., 1949). Roles of men and women in various societies are examined. Mead stresses that socially ascribed statuses and roles account for most behavior, not biology.

Montagu, Ashley, *On Being Human* (New York: Hawthorne Books, 1966). In this work Montagu considers many of the significant findings of scientists as they relate to our species' nature and nurture aspects.

Riesman, David, Nathan Glazer, Reuel Denney, *The Lonely Crowd: A Study of the Changing American Character* (New Haven: Yale University Press, 1962. Abridged edition with a new foreward). This is a discussion of how socialization can produce personalities identified as tradition-directed, inner-directed, and other-directed.

Rose, Peter I., editor, Socialization and the Life Cycle (New York: St. Martin's Press, 1979). This book has a variety of articles that treat the socialization process as it occurs throughout people's lives.

Rosenberg, Bernard, *The Province of Sociology* (New York: Thomas Y. Crowell Co., 1972). Chapter 4 offers an excellent description of the emergence of the human self.

Winn, Marie, *The Plug-in Drug* (New York: Bantam Books, 1978). This is an analysis of the impact of television on children. Among other conclusions, it is suggested that television viewing discourages creativity in children.

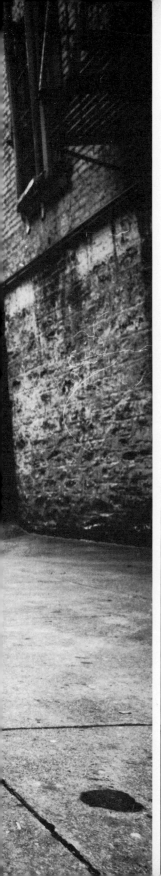

Chapter 3
Culture as the Fabric of Human Society

SECTION 7   CULTURE AS HUMAN EXPERIENCE
- THREE WAYS TO DESCRIBE CULTURE
- THREE COMPONENTS OF CULTURE
- ETHICAL ABSOLUTISM
- CULTURAL RELATIVISM
- "A HINT OF HUMAN GOODNESS"
- IDEAL AND REAL CULTURE
- THE AMERICAN WAY OF LIFE

Objectives

After completing this section, the student should be able to:

1.   Give both a popular and a sociological definition of culture.
2.   Recognize ideology, technology, and social organization as parts of human cultures.
3.   Describe the views of ethical absolutists.
4.   Describe the views of cultural relativists.
5.   Explain the difference between ideal and real culture.
6.   Identify both humanistic and production values of American culture.

Most of us can remember how, as children, the word *culture* was used to describe those things that seemed unimportant to us and our young friends. Culture had something to do with having good manners. Culture was opera, symphonies, ballet, using the right fork, and appreciating exhibits in art museums. This is still the *popular* interpretation of the word. Even most adults probably think of such things when they refer to culture. From the popular point of view, being cultured would mean preferring Beethoven to the Beatles, leg of lamb to hamburger, symphonies to rock concerts, and brandy to beer. The fact is that all of these are part of our culture. And much more. Every society has a culture. The sociological view of culture would include all the material things used by the people and all the patterns of behavior exhibited by the people. Culture includes "knowledge, belief, art, morals, laws, custom and any other habits and capabilities acquired by members of society" (Tylor, 1872).

THREE WAYS
TO DESCRIBE
CULTURE

We believe that Robert Bierstedt's treatment of the meaning of culture in *The Social Order* is especially helpful. The three following descriptions of culture are based on his writing (Bierstedt, 1970).

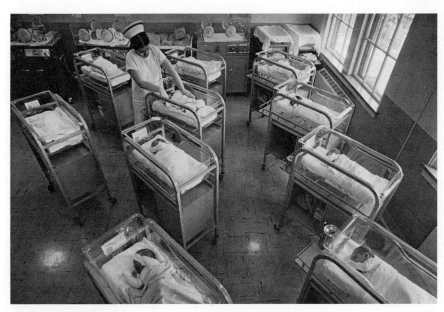

We've only just begun.

Culture as Learned Behavior

In the previous chapter on socialization, we describe the human being as a social being. At birth the infant is neither social nor antisocial. The infant is socially neutral (asocial). The infant is born into a society that has cultural expectations. The society will expect the infant to grow into an adult with particular ways of thinking, feeling, and behaving. To participate in society's culture, the individual must *internalize* appropriate behavior. To internalize means to make something so much a part of oneself that it seems to be natural. Unlike other species, humans must *learn* to do most of the things they do. To learn, one must have an adequate biological inheritance and one must be exposed to a culture. Most behavioral patterns are cultural in origin.

Observe a room full of newborn babies squirming and squalling behind a hospital window. See how many sizes and shapes and colors in which infants are born. If we were allowed behind that window, no examination of the babies themselves would reveal which would be Protestant and which would be Catholic. We could not tell which would learn English and which would learn Spanish. No physical examination could reveal which baby would salute which flag. However, if we could know the culture to which these babies would be exposed, we could predict such matters with impressive accuracy. Again, what we call human behavior is more often culturally acquired behavior than it is biologically required behavior. The fact that we must eat and drink is explained by physical needs. What, when, how, and where we eat is explained by cultural expectations. Culture, not physical heredity, accounts for the observable differences among human groupings.

Culture as Social Heritage

One's social heritage is that which comes to or belongs to a person by reason of social location. Culture is passed on from one generation to another through socialization. A culture tends to accumulate certain skills, values, behaviors, and material things. A visit to the Smithsonian Institute or, for that matter, most museums, reveals how American culture has continued to accumulate through the years.

A kind of culture shock

There is a curious fact about the social heritage—culture tends to be both static (remains the same) and dynamic (changing). Once having internalized culture at a given time, people are reluctant to change their established way of life. Through most of recorded history, people seem to have believed change to be undesirable and stability as desirable (LaPiere, 1965). The prospect of change can seem threatening. Still, every human culture is subject to and does experience change. Those who speak of a *generation gap* picture two generations at odds with one another. According to this view, the parent generation favors the established ways while the youth generation favors dynamic change. If a generation gap does exist in modern societies, we believe that the differences are of degree and not of substance. Let us explain.

Part of the social heritage of almost every modern society is the high value placed on progress. Parents encourage young people to seek progress, and progress is a form of social change. Debates between generations are seldom about whether *any* change should occur. Instead, the debates are usually about how much change, how fast it should occur, and which methods shoud be used for bringing change. During the United States presidential campaign in 1972, a reporter for the *Village Voice* wrote:

> . . . *One woman, in her early 50's was eager to talk: she was about to do something she had never done before—vote Republican. She saw McGovern as running with the kids, he wanted changes that "were too fast, too sudden." It was not his direction but his pace she complained about, a feeling expressed by many . . . who are conservative by instinct and only slowly accept the new and the different.*
>
> (Smith, 1972)

This is what we mean by saying the differences are of degree and not so much of substance. Modern societies do seek progress through change. Still, both the parent and youth generations continue to support, for the most part, the established values and behavioral expectations of their social heritage.

Culture as a Way of Life

The great differences in human behavior become obvious when we study people in different cultures. As a design or blueprint for living, each culture represents a unique way of life. Each culture has a unique combination of values, rules, roles, and relationships. These provide the people in each society with guides for appropriate behavior. For example, the American way of life is significantly different from the Chinese way of life. The life-style of the Amish is very different from that of the Hopi Indians.

Perhaps the experience of *culture shock* is proof enough of how unique each culture or life-style is. Culture shock occurs when a person is placed into a culture that is very different from what the person is accustomed to. The Peace Corps volunteer, the foreign diplomat, the world traveler, and the anthropologist have all experienced culture shock. For example, culture shock occurs when an American suddenly finds him- or herself

... in a place where yes may mean no, where a "fixed price" is negotiable, where to be kept waiting in an outer office is no cause for insult, where laughter may signify anger. . . . The culture shock phenomenon accounts for much of the bewilderment, frustration, and disorientation that plagues Americans in their dealings with other societies.

(Toffler, 1970)

In conclusion, these three descriptions of culture emphasize different ways to look at culture. Culture does require the learning of behavior. Culture does consist of a social heritage. Culture is a way of life. As Robert Bierstedt has said, we simply cannot exaggerate the importance of culture in human life. Without our referring to culture, we cannot begin to understand an individual, a particular social group, nor an entire society (Bierstedt, 1970).

THREE COMPONENTS OF CULTURE

We have said that there are many differences among the cultures created by humankind. We also must recognize that cultures have certain similarities. Let us explain. It is true that people worship different gods in different ways, but it is more significant that all cultures have a religion. It is true that people have different political and family structures, but it is more significant that all cultures have some form of government and some form of family.

A contemporary social scientist identified three components (parts) of culture that can be found in every society. They are ideology, technology, and social organization (LaPiere, 1965). Combined, these three components make up the fabric of human society—culture.

Ideology

An ideology is made up of ideas, beliefs, and values that are shared by a human grouping. An ideology can include scientific facts as well as myths, religious beliefs as well as legends, and superstitions as well as folklore. All cherished values

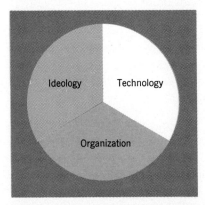

Diagram No. 1   Universal Components of Culture

that touch upon definitions of worth, beauty, and achievement are part of an ideology. A society's ideology justifies why the people act as they do. Ideology justifies particular social, moral, economic, and political interests of society.

Technology

This component of culture consists of all the material items that members of a society have and use. If we tried to list the material culture of American society, it would take us a long time. "Neither the Sears Roebuck catalogue by itself nor all the catalogues together would exhaust the material possessions of the American people" (Bierstedt, 1970).

Technology also refers to nonmaterial assets such as skills, crafts, and arts that enable people to produce material goods. All societies must find the means to meet basic human needs for food, clothing, and shelter. These needs for survival are met by the technology of a society.

Social Organization

Every culture has a network of rules, roles, and relationships that create a patterned, regulated social order. The basis of any social order depends upon each person's ability and willingness to cooperate with others. Without the ability of people to cooperate, no college, commune, nor corporation could function for very long. Haven't we all heard someone say at one time or another, "We've got to get organized"?

Rules and expectations for behavior established by society are called *social norms*. Observing social norms helps to organize the social interaction of society's members. The fact that all societies have social norms indicates the vital relationship between social life and social organization. Robert Bierstedt made the following observations:

By and large, whatever we do, whenever and wherever we do it, falls into certain patterns that are set for us by our society. There are norms for meeting people and norms for taking leave of them, norms for writing and norms for speaking, norms for eating and drinking, norms for playing and working, norms for dating and dancing, norms in classrooms and in cafeterias, norms in hospitals and hotels, and so for every conceivable activity in almost every conceivable situation.

(Bierstedt, 1970)

Because of the important position they occupy in human society and in the discipline of sociology, the variety and significance of social norms are treated in greater detail in the next section of this chapter.

Now let us briefly summarize what we have said about culture so far. We have said that each society has a unique culture. This means that each society has a culture different from those of other societies. We have also said that every society's culture has the components of ideology, technology, and social organization. Consider this curious conclusion: Cultures are *similar* because of their efforts to meet the recurring needs of people. Cultures are *different* because of their efforts to meet the recurring needs of people. Think about that for a while!

ETHICAL ABSOLUTISM

The term *ethics* refers to moral principles that guide the behavior of a person or an entire society. Every society interprets some behavior as moral and other behavior as immoral. What is thought to be moral in one society may be considered immoral in another society. Nevertheless, there are philosophers and religious people who believe that there are behaviors that are always right and other behaviors that are always wrong for human beings. In other words, there is an absolute good and bad. There is absolute justice and injustice. People who think like this can be called *ethical absolutists*. They believe that what is right and wrong is always right and wrong. Ethical principles do not change from time to time or from place to place. A person does not have to *know* what is absolutely right and wrong to be an ethical absolutist. The person can simply believe that there are absolute rights and wrongs in reference to the human condition. Of course, many philosophers and religious people believe that they do know what is good and bad for all people. To be absolute means to be without doubt or limitation. Ethical absolutists have no doubt that there are universal circumstances that are always good and always bad for the human condition. For example, Martin Luther King, Jr. (1929–1968) wrote that:

> . . . *there are two types of laws: just and unjust. I would be the first to advocate obeying just laws. One has not only a legal but a moral responsibility to obey just laws. Conversely, one has a moral responsibility to disobey unjust laws. I would agree with St. Augustine that "an unjust law is no law at all."*
> . . . *Any law that uplifts human personality is just. Any law that degrades human personality is unjust.*
>
> (King, 1964)

Finally, we can say that ethical absolutists believe that there is an *optimum human condition*. This means that there is a best condition for humankind that never has changed nor ever will change. The idea of an optimum human condition is discussed in much more detail in Section 36.

CULTURAL RELATIVISM

Societies' cultures differ from one another because of their efforts to meet the recurring needs of their particular peoples. As we said earlier, behavior considered moral, desirable, justifiable, and appropriate in one society can be considered the opposite in another society. Any society's culture is the result of that society's experience in history. Some anthropologists say that there is little evidence, if any, to prove that certain social norms prevail in every society. What is right in one place and time can be wrong in another place and time. Thus, right and wrong, they would say, must be relative to each particular culture. People who

Martin Luther King, Jr.

think like this can be called *cultural relativists*. Cultural relativism is based on the following principles:

1. Every cultural trait has meaning within its own cultural context.

2. Every culture should be judged by its own ethical principles.

3. Standards of right and wrong and of good and bad are defined by the culture of the society in which they appear.

Put more simply, a cultural relativist would say that we should not judge the beliefs and behavior of other cultures by what we consider to be right and wrong in the culture of our own society. Many social scientists claim that to argue that one life-style or culture is superior or inferior to another is foolish. Such an argument would ignore the more open-minded views of cultural relativism, they would say. Let us explain our point of view on cultural relativism.

So long as an attempt is being made to describe the *idea* of cultural relativism, we have no complaints. Recognizing that right and wrong and good and bad are interpreted differently in different cultures provides valuable insights to the human experience. Understanding the idea of cultural relativism helps us to see how certain cultural norms can serve the purposes of certain societies. Like the respected anthropologist Robert Redfield (1897–1958), we understand that

Cultural relativism means that the values expressed in any culture are to be both understood and themselves valued only according to the way the people who carry that culture see things.

(Redfield, 1953)

Also like Robert Redfield, we believe that it is desirable to look further. We should examine the *purposes* that the values and behavior serve. Simply because cultural traits serve a society's purposes does not make those traits good for the human condition. A specific culture may *not* serve to further the interests and welfare of the people. We cannot say who is to judge the "goodness" or the "badness" of a society's social structure. We do say that making such judgments is as appropriate as saying that everything is relative to a time and place.

It seems to us that cultural relativists deny themselves the opportunity to consider the fascinating possibility that there *is* an optimum human condition. Consider this: If moral judgements are to be related to human needs, and if there are basic needs common to all human beings, it seems to follow that there are standards that apply to all human beings (whether we know what they are or not). This, of course, is the view of ethical absolutism, and not that of cultural relativism.

"A HINT OF HUMAN GOODNESS"

Robert Redfield described an ancient custom of a band of Pawnee in which each year a captive was sacrificed to Venus, Morning Star, to ensure abundant crops. Each year a victim was fattened and kept uninformed of what lay ahead. Then, on the proper day, the captive was bound to a scaffold, tomahawked, and shot with arrows. In the year 1818, in what is now Nebraska, a young girl from another tribe was bound and prepared to be sacrificed. Suddenly a young Pawnee named Petalesharoo stepped forward and firmly declared that the sacrifice was wrong and should be abolished. Furthermore, he said that he was prepared to die unless the victim were released. Cutting the girl's cords, Petalesharoo put her on a horse, mounted another, and escorted the intended victim to safety. Redfield referred to Petalesharoo's act as "a hint of human goodness." Here is a case of a distinguished anthropologist placing a positive value of conduct that flew in the face of the Pawnee culture. From a cultural relativist's point of view, sacrificing a victim each year in order to ensure good crops was moral and appropriate within the context of Pawnee culture. Redfield said,

Perhaps Petalesharoo is one of those . . . who caught the great idea in history . . . of man's humanity to man, and acted out that idea to his own danger and against his

own people and his own compelling tradition. . . . So Petalesharoo gets my praise on that account.

Redfield called Petalesharoo's act a "hint of human goodness," not a hint of Pawnee goodness or American goodness. When Redfield spoke of *human goodness,* he left behind his commitment to the theory of cultural relativity. He was addressing himself to the human condition. To aspire to "man's humanity to man" is to commit oneself to a form of ethical absolutism (Redfield, 1953).

By presenting the prevailing points of view of both cultural relativists and ethical absolutists, we have tried to show that the subject of cultural relativism is not beyond challenge. However, even if one subscribed to ethical absolutism or to the possibility of an optimum human condition, the *concept* of cultural relativity is still useful when studying the structure and functions of culture.

IDEAL AND REAL CULTURE

Ideal culture consists of those patterns of behavior that are formally approved and that members of a society are encouraged to observe. Real culture consists of those patterns of behavior that members of society actually do observe. In the United States the ideal culture consists of stated beliefs in such things as monogamy (see Glossary), reverence for a god, and respect for the government. In ideal American culture people are honest, loyal, and productive workers. Some Americans come close to fulfilling these cultural expectations most of the time. Some Americans fulfill these expectations some of the time. Some Americans avoid most of the cultural expectations most of the time. A person learns about both the ideal culture and the real culture through the socialization process.

THE AMERICAN WAY OF LIFE

In a nation as large as the United States we have a society composed of many strands that together make up the fabric of the American culture. At any moment, in any place where there is a person, something is involving that person in some strand of that fabric. Babies who cry are tended to. Automatic transmissions break and require repair. Roofs and faucets leak, a taxi discharges a passenger, two people kiss, people laugh, fight, and die. The radio blares, the television picture blurs, while people react to this situation and to that situation with frustration, despair, glee, and celebration. No two people and no two situations are exactly alike. People are unique because lives are unique. In one sense we are isolated. In another sense we experience certain ties that bind us together. Separated by miles, social class, race, ethnic group, religion, sex, occupation, and value orientations, we still share a moment in the history of our people.

American society is complex and dynamic. American history has been much involved with democracy, industrialism, and capitalism. American culture has been very influenced by two sets of values. They are production values and humanistic values. On one hand, American culture has emphasized the *production values* of doing, achieving, producing, efficiency, and success. On the other hand, Americans have endorsed the *humanistic values* of knowing, caring, loving, and being known, cared for, and loved. These two sets of values do not have to conflict. Still, if production values are given more attention than humanistic values, people lose an important sense of community and common concerns (Saxton, 1979).

The American way of life has been created by threading together various strands that we call values. Together, they make up the fabric of American culture. On the day following the assassination of Martin Luther King, Jr., and only 60 days before his own assassination was to occur, Robert F. Kennedy emphasized the humanistic values of American culture while also mentioning the production values. Kennedy said:

. . . *whenever we tear at the fabric of life which another man has painfully and clumsily woven for himself and his children, the whole nation is degraded. . . .*

We must recognize that this short life can neither be ennobled or enriched by hatred or revenge. Our lives on this planet are too short and the work to be done too great to let this spirit flourish any longer in our land.

Of course we cannot vanquish it with a program, nor with a resolution. But we can perhaps remember . . . that those who live with us are our brothers, that they share with us the same short moment of life, that they seek — as we do — nothing but the chance to live out their lives, in purpose and happiness, winning what satisfaction and fulfillment they can. Surely this bond of common faith, this bond of common goal, can begin to teach us something. Surely we can learn, at least, to look at those around us as fellow men and surely we can begin to work a little harder to bind the wounds among us to become in our own hearts brothers and countrymen once again.

(quoted in Newfield, 1969)

American life has been dedicated to progress and the future. Within the fabric of American culture has been a democratic strand emphasizing the dignity of the individual and the responsible judgment of the masses. This is the ideal culture of the American experience. Sometimes it has been in the forefront of America's real culture. Sometimes it has been neglected, allowing the special interests of the few to be fulfilled at the expense of the general well-being of the many.

KEY TERMS AND NAMES FROM SECTION 7

popular view of culture	generation gap
sociological view of culture	culture shock
asocial	ideology
to internalize	technology
static and dynamic	social organization

social norms

ethical absolutism

optimum human condition

cultural relativism

"a hint of human goodness"

ideal and real culture

production values

humanistic values

Martin Luther King, Jr.

Robert Redfield

Petalesharoo

STUDY GUIDE FOR SECTION 7

1. EXPLAIN HOW THE POPULAR AND SOCIOLOGICAL INTERPRETATIONS OF THE TERM *CULTURE* ARE DIFFERENT.

2. To learn, one must have an adequate biological inheritance and one must be exposed to a culture. WHICH INFLUENCES BEHAVIOR MORE?

3. Part of the social heritage of modern societies is the high value placed on progress. HOW DOES THIS FACT RELATE TO THE CONCEPT OF A GENERATION GAP?

4. Each culture has its own unique design for living. DESCRIBE THE EXPERIENCE OF CULTURE SHOCK.

5. Although the cultures of the world are different from one another, they all have three components. They are ideology, technology, and social organization. DESCRIBE HOW EACH COMPONENT CONTRIBUTES TO THE HUMAN EXPERIENCE.

6. Cultures are similar and cultures are different because of their efforts to meet the recurring needs of people. EXPLAIN.

7. The term *ethics* refers to moral principles that guide the behavior of a person or an entire society. EXPLAIN WHAT IS MEANT BY ETHICAL ABSOLUTISM. WHAT ARE ETHICAL ABSOLUTISTS?

8. Cultural relativists believe that right and wrong are relative to each particular culture. WHAT DOES THIS MEAN?

9. Robert Redfield referred to Petalesharoo's behavior as a "hint of human goodness." WHAT DO YOU THINK OF PETALESHAROO'S BEHAVIOR? WAS HE RIGHT OR WRONG IN WHAT HE DID? ARE YOU ANSWERING AS A CULTURAL RELATIVIST OR AS AN ETHICAL ABSOLUTIST?

10. All societies can be said to have ideal and real cultures. DESCRIBE HOW THEY DIFFER FROM ONE ANOTHER.

11. Both production values and humanistic values have influenced Americans. DESCRIBE EACH OF THESE TWO SETS OF VALUES. WHICH DO YOU BELIEVE HAS CONTRIBUTED MORE TO MAKING AMERICAN SOCIETY WHAT IT IS TODAY?

PRACTICE TEST FOR SECTION 7

Select the best answer.

1. Most behavioral patterns
A. Result from physical heredity.
B. Are cultural in origin.
C. Result from id influences.
D. Are antisocial.

2. In modern American society, the established values and behavioral expectations are observed, for the most part, by
A. The parent generation.
B. Only native-born citizens.
C. The parent and youth generations.
D. People who favor progress.

3. The component of culture that consists of material items, skills, crafts, and arts is the
A. Ideological component.
B. Organizational component.
C. Technological component.

4. The component of culture that consists of the most important beliefs of the people is
A. Ideology.
B. Social organization.
C. Technology.

5. The component of culture that includes rules, regulations, and roles is
A. Ideology.
B. Social organization.
C. Technology.

6. The component of culture that meets the basic human needs of food, shelter, and clothing is
A. Ideology.
B. Social organization.
C. Technology.

7. The confusion that an unprepared visitor might experience when placed in a society with an unfamiliar culture is called

A. Cultural relativism.
B. Ethical shock.
C. Ethical relativism.
D. Cultural shock.

8. Behavior that is moral in one society is immoral in another society. This is the view of
A. Cultural relativism.
B. Ethical absolutism.

9. There is an optimum human condition. This is a view of
A. Cultural relativism.
B. Ethical absolutism.

10. If moral judgments are to be related to human needs, and if there are basic needs common to all human beings, it follows that there are standards that apply to all human beings. This is a view of
A. Cultural relativism.
B. Ethical absolutism.

11. The term *culture* refers to all of the following except which one?
A. Learned ways of behaving.
B. The social heritage.
C. A way of life.
D. Basic physical needs.

12. Patterns of behavior that members of society actually do observe are an example of
A. Real culture.
B. Culture ethicalism.
C. Ideal culture.
D. Social culture.

13. Production values are concerned with
A. Achieving.
B. Efficiency.
C. Success.
D. All of the above.

Answer Key

1.	B	**8.**	A
2.	C	**9.**	B
3.	C	**10.**	B
4.	A	**11.**	D
5.	B	**12.**	A
6.	C	**13.**	D
7.	D		

SECTION 8 CULTURE AS A SYSTEM OF SOCIAL NORMS

- THE ORIGINS OF SOCIAL NORMS
- THREE TYPES OF SOCIAL NORMS: FOLKWAYS, MORES, AND LAWS
- WHY PEOPLE CONFORM TO SOCIAL NORMS

Objectives

After completing this section, the student should be able to:

1. Relate normative behavior to social relationships.
2. Describe what occurs when a normative structure collapses.
3. Distinguish between folkways and mores.
4. Explain what can occur when new laws contradict social mores.
5. Recognize how laws can change people's attitudes and behavior.
6. Explain what causes most people to observe most of the norms most of the time.

Like other species, humans are born with specific needs. People must eat, drink, sleep, excrete, maintain adequate health, and interact with others. How people engage in these activities is controlled by social norms. *Social norms* are rules and regulations that apply to *expectations* for human behavior. They serve as guideposts specifying what one should, ought to, and must do, as well as what one should not, ought not, and must not do (Vander Zanden, 1966). Social norms approve and condemn various behaviors.

There is a great variety of norms to which a person is expected to conform in modern societies. Most people belong to many groups. Both formal and informal groups expect certain behavior from their members. Social norms may reduce the freedom of people, but they also make life more predictable and less complicated. Without social norms, groups and society at large could hardly exist. With social norms, people know what to expect of others and what others expect of them. Observing the social norms is called *normative behavior*. Normative behavior contributes order and stability to social interaction.

THE ORIGINS OF SOCIAL NORMS

William Graham Sumner (1840–1910) had a significant impact on the sociological view of social norms. In his book published in 1906, entitled *Folkways*, Sumner said that social norms are the product of a people's history. He said that norms represent human efforts to deal with basic and recurring human needs.

Humankind has sought the means to survive through lengthy and often painful trial-and-error efforts. If, in the past, an attempt to meet a particular need was successful, it was adopted. In time, that way of behavior became the accepted and expected way for people to behave. This trial-and-error process produced habits for the individual and customs for the group. In this way, normative behavior would come into being. Sumner pointed out that the creation of social norms was "never conscious, and never foreseen or intended." He said that norms are "unconsciously set in operation" and "handed down by tradition" (Sumner, 1906). Thus, through trial and error or by simple accident, groups have arrived at a pattern of behavior. Most norms arise in this haphazard and unintentional manner. However, some norms are created purposely and consciously. In the United States, for example, laws are one kind of social norm. Laws are intentionally enacted to deal with specific matters.

Social norms are products of human experiences both from long ago and from recent history. Each generation is born into a society where the accumulated norms have become part of the established social order. In some cases, norms outlive the situations in which they originated. The so-called *blue laws* are an example of this. These laws originated in the New Haven Colony in Connecticut. They were bound in blue paper and dealt with matters of morality. One law demanded the strict observance of the Sabbath. Throughout the colonies such laws were passed that prohibited sports, travel, and work on Sundays. All such laws became known as blue laws. Most such laws have since been repealed. Still, many local governments still prohibit the sale of retail goods on Sunday (Seligman, 1957).

Like other cultural elements, social norms are both static and dynamic. Still, a normative structure persists. Discussing the psychology of norms, Muzafer Sherif points out that a normative structure can collapse but that another normative structure will take its place.

People cannot eat and drink norms. The norms cannot give life, if nothing else is left in life. But friction may increase to such a pitch that the whole superstructure of norms collapses; the individual, with countless others like himself, frees himself from his prescribed role, crushes the role of the privileged one, and with this the oppressor himself. We find many illustrations of this as we look at the history of the revolutions. The end result is not chaos, but the formation of a new superstructure of norms.

(Sherif, 1966)

Despite social change—even revolution—a normative structure persists.

THREE TYPES OF SOCIAL NORMS: FOLKWAYS, MORES, AND LAWS

Sociologists classify social norms in various ways. We have selected *folkways, mores,* and *laws* as three broad classifications of social norms. Although different from one another, these three types of norms are all behavioral expectations. All three influence the feeling, thinking, and behavior of individuals and groups. To one degree or another, they all approve or disapprove of certain behaviors.

Folkways

Folkways are social norms that guide us through the ordinary social encounters of everyday life. Literally, folkways are the ways of the folk. They are simply the customary ways in which people of a particular group behave. Folkways indicate what is proper in such areas as etiquette, clothes, use of language, food, and many other routine matters that have become established customs. Folkways *are* customs. Most people expect most other people to observe most of the folkways most of the time.

In modern societies changes occur very rapidly. Fads and fashions are adopted by people and then discarded before they can have existed long enough to be called customs. The most popular song of last month is a "golden oldie" this month. So it is with hair styles, clothing styles, games, dances, and slang. Such here-today-gone-tomorrow behaviors should not be confused with folkways. They could, instead, be called pseudocustoms (Ogburn and Nimkoff, 1964).

The United States consists of many different groups. Many of the same folkways are observed by the majority of Americans. There are also folkways that belong only to certain parts of the country, only to certain *ethnic groups* (see Glossary), certain occupations, and certain social classes. The general American population observes such folkways as eating three meals a day, shaking hands, standing in lines, arriving on time for appointments, and celebrating birthdays. But, as we have said, people respond not only to the folkways of society at large but to the folkways of special groups as well. Some years ago the following remarks were made by a 19-year-old youth. His remarks indicate that he was responding to the customs or folkways of his street gang:

When I was twelve, thirteen, we used to think it was smart to walk past a newsstand and when the guy turned his back we'd snatch a bunch of papers. . . . We just did it to be ornery. You did just what the others did.

Now, a guy don't have to be a good fighter to belong to our gang. . . . I don't care if he's a sissy, so long as he minds his own business. If trouble starts, he don't have to be a Joe Louis, but he sure as hell can't run off. I myself, I like to go out with a guy that isn't going to run from it . . . because if it's your fight, you don't want to chicken out.

David Dressler, from whose tape recording the above excerpt was taken, writes that this same boy also observed folkways more generally accepted in American society. He did not steal from department stores; he paid for items he wanted. He courted a young woman in a conventional way. In fact, some years after the tape recording was made, the youth married a young woman in a civil ceremony. Thereafter, he supported his wife, and a daughter when she was born, to the best of his ability. Here was a case of a person observing the customs of a special group while also observing the norms of general American society concerning the marketplace, courtship, and family life (Dressler, 1969).

We have tried to make the point that there are general folkways that apply to a society's general population and that there are specific group folkways that

We all shake hands.

can apply to such groupings as a baseball team, a brokerage house, a local PTA, a local barbershop, and the young crowd that hangs around the fountains in a shopping mall. Either type of folkway is to be seen as simply the customary, normal, and habitual way people behave in groups. Folkways are expectations for behavior that are based on mutual understandings within the group.

If an individual ignores a folkway, no severe punishment will result. Other members of the group may be annoyed, but they probably won't react with extreme displeasure. Eating peculiar combinations of food, using obscene language at the wrong time, or wearing blue jeans to a formal affair could make a person seem a little odd or not in the know. Gossip might occur. People might ridicule the person. The group may even decide to ostracize the individual for not behaving "properly." But these reactions are mild contrasted to the reactions of a group when an individual violates social norms that have to do with strong moral convictions.

Mores

A society or group expects its members to observe folkways. Members are *required* to observe *mores* (pronounced mor'āz). Folkways and mores are both social norms. One can tell them apart in two ways:

1. By how much importance people attach to them.
2. By how severe the punishment is for violators.

People attach far more importance to mores than to folkways. Violations of mores can bring far more severe punishment than can violations of folkways.

"The mores can make anything right and prevent condemnations of anything" (Sumner, 1906). In other words, right and wrong are defined according to what members of society believe to be helpful or harmful for the people of their society. Behavior encouraged in one society can be defined as immoral and criminal in another society. In some cultures it has been moral to have more than one wife or husband. It has been moral to kill unwanted babies and helpless old people. In some cultures it has been moral to hold people in slavery, to steal, to eat human flesh, and to torture heretics. At this time in American history, each of those acts is considered immoral. American mores forbid such behavior.

Unlike folkways, mores apply to everyone in the United States. They have become part of the legal system and religious beliefs of American society. In fact, the Ten Commandments and the Bill of Rights might be thought of as being the basic mores of American ideal culture. Remembering that mores approve and condemn, consider this: American mores approve monogamy and condemn polygamy; approve using drugs for medical treatment and condemn using drugs for pleasure; approve killing during war and condemn killing for personal reasons; approve political radicals and condemn political revolutionaries; approve religious dedication and condemn religious intolerance; approve disciplining children and condemn child abuse; approve a state of law and order and condemn repressive government. This list could be much longer, but these examples should indicate matters with which American mores are concerned.

Earlier in this section, we said that no *severe* punishment results from not observing folkways. To be considered unusual or to be the victim of gossip and ridicule are informal negative sanctions. They cannot be called really severe reactions. Sanctions that support mores, however, have more emotional content than those supporting folkways. People who observe mores (or who at least *seem* to observe them) are respected and praised in public. This positive recognition contributes to their own self-esteem. But those who violate mores are subject to formal negative sanctions such as loss of privileges and prestige, imprisonment, and physical punishment. When it becomes known that one has violated mores or when one fears being found out, personal guilt and anxiety can hurt one's self-esteem. Society *does* hold people accountable for what they do and for what they fail to do.

We do believe that people must be held responsible for their behavior. We believe that a combination of rewards and punishments is necessary for encouraging conformity. Both positive and negative sanctions can encourage people to observe the social norms. At the very least, such sanctions cause people to *appear* to conform. That, it would seem, is enough to maintain most social orders.

Laws

Laws are social norms that are intended to deal with specific circumstances. Some laws are concerned with mundane (common and ordinary) matters. What we have in mind are such things as traffic control, zoning practices, building permits, and the type of trash can one must use. Laws that deal with these matters are mundane and have little to do with morality. This kind of law seeks to establish dependable procedures for keeping society functioning. Such laws have been called "morally neutral" (Horton and Hunt, 1972).

There are also many laws that are concerned with morality. Laws exist to reinforce mores. Some people do not accept or observe the mores of society. It is to protect society from such people that laws are passed in order to enforce the mores. People who refuse to conform to mores reinforced by laws are subject to formal negative sanctions. Actually, threats of legal punishment act as a social control for many people. Violations of laws can result in fines, penalties, imprisonment, and execution.

Henry David Thoreau (1817–1862) said that no one "with a genius for legislation has appeared in America. They are rare in the history of the world" (Thoreau, 1849). There have been occasions when laws have been passed that contradict the mores about which people feel so strongly. When laws clash with mores, people are most likely to observe the mores and avoid obeying the laws. Let us cite some examples from American history.

Thoreau and many other Americans objected to the Fugitive Slave Act of 1850. That law declared that all citizens must turn in to the authorities any people who were classified as fugitive slaves. The Fugitive Slave Act was ignored by those Americans who believed slavery to be immoral. Instead, they assisted people classified as fugitive slaves to escape capture. Much of this effort against the law was known as the Underground Railroad. By the time the Civil War began, runaways were being helped in every northern state of the Union.

The Eighteenth Amendment to the Constitution was passed in 1919. This made the manufacture and sale of alcoholic beverages illegal. Many Americans objected. They believed that they had the right to decide on such a matter for themselves. Thus, prohibition was a failure during the 1920s. Too many people refused to consider the consumption of liquor as being immoral.

During the Second World War, many restrictions and controls were enacted by the government. Price controls and rationing were intended to help the war effort. Again, many Americans chose to violate the law. They believed that the government had no right to prevent free trade and to trample individual rights. The law seemed more immoral than the acts that were declared unlawful.

In more recent years, laws forbidding the possession, marketing, or consumption of marijuana have been ignored by unknown numbers of people. There are people who say that marijuana has no connection with immorality. In fact, because of social pressures, many local laws have become less demanding in reference to marijuana.

We should like to make one final point about the significance of laws as social norms. It has often been said that "You can't legislate morality." Considering the examples we have cited, this statement seems to be accurate. However, we should recognize that laws can and do influence the behavior of people. In some cases, a law can be thought of as an instrument of education. Once passed, it announces to the citizenry that such-and-such behavior is correct, right, and moral. Most people usually obey most laws. Life requires much of each individual. Happily or sadly, most people find little time to dispute a law. The symbols of government are powerful enough in the minds of most citizens. When new laws are enacted, they are obeyed. A kind of social conditioning can take place. Continued observance of a law lends dignity to the law and to the actions it requires or forbids. Time passes. Then, if the law has stayed in effect and been generally observed, a new generation grows up accepting the law. It represents the normal, usual, expected, and *right* way for people to behave (Horton and Hunt, 1972). Probably the best examples of laws changing both behavior and attitudes are provided in modern nations. Total social revolutions have altered cultural patterns from marketing economies to command economies and from religious orientation to atheistic orientation. We have in mind such nations as the Soviet Union and China. In the United States, the laws motivated by the Civil Rights Movement of the 1960s have already made an impact on American mores in reference to racial equality.

WHY PEOPLE CONFORM TO SOCIAL NORMS

Social norms indicate what people in a society should or should not think, say, or do under certain circumstances. Of course, few individuals conform to each and every social norm all the time. There is a range of permissible behavior in reference to role performance and in reference to normative behavior. As we have said before, some people come very close to conforming to most of the norms, some conform to some of the norms, and some attempt to avoid conforming to any of the norms of society at large. But we repeat: most people conform to most of the norms most of the time. Let us identify three reasons for this.

Indoctrination

When we are born, we immediately reside in a social location. The group that shares this location with us has already established definitions of situations and role expectations. Without any serious questioning we tend to accept the cultural fabric of our immediate surroundings and the norms of our significant others. All this occurs through the process of socialization. We have internalized most social norms of our group before we are aware that there might be other behavior and beliefs. Our personalities and our self-concepts are developed by the internalization of social norms. Such matters as what we eat, how we eat, the language we speak, the gods we worship, and what we expect of others become, for us, the proper and, perhaps, the *only* way of doing things. This process of indoctrination begins immediately. It is a constant process throughout the lives of most individuals. Indoctrination is one reason why most of the people conform to most of the norms most of the time.

Habituation

We are creatures of habit. If we have learned to eat our food with forks, spoons, and knives, it is with these utensils that we are most comfortable even when eating Chinese food, which hundreds of millions of other people eat with chopsticks. Customs of speech and customs of etiquette become second nature to us, which is simply a way of saying that they have become habits. We might say "please" and "thank you" or "shut up" and "get lost." Standing in line and holding doors open for other people are as much habits as they are expressions of fair play or kindness. Once having become habituated to certain behaviors, we tend to observe them automatically. It is more difficult to reject folkways and mores than it is to conform to them. We become accustomed to the comforts of the "habit cage" (Cuber and Harroff, 1965).

Practicality

Another reason why most people conform to most of the norms most of the time is because we can see that norms are useful in that they provide us with the means to interact with a minimum of confusion and disorder. Where people work together on an assembly line, it would not be very practical if some should take a break from work for coffee and doughnuts at 10:00 A.M. while others walk away from the assembly line for a break at 11:00 A.M. An assembly line requires workers to perform as a team, since the total of their efforts produces a completed product. When the work break occurs, the line stops moving, and all people stop work, conforming to the work norm of the plant. Also, most people observe the practice of waiting their turn whether it be outside a ticket booth in the cold of winter or inside a heated lobby. It is both reasonable and practical to wait in lines on such occasions. By conforming in such cases, the individual avoids the anger of others who also are waiting and who arrived on the scene earlier. Most norms *are* useful and practical, and most people recognize this to be true.

KEY TERMS AND NAMES FROM SECTION 8

normative behavior

origins of social norms

folkways: general and specific

blue laws

mores

laws versus mores

indoctrination

habituation

habit cage

practicality

revolution and normative structure

pseudocustoms

legislation and morality

William Graham Sumner

STUDY GUIDE FOR SECTION 8

1. It can be said that social norms reduce the freedom of *individuals*. HOW DOES NORMATIVE BEHAVIOR CONTRIBUTE TO SOCIAL ORDER?

2. Most social norms do not originate as a result of carefully planned meetings. WHEN AND HOW DO SOCIAL NORMS ORIGINATE?

3. In some cases, social norms outlive the situation of their origin. EXPLAIN WHY THE BLUE LAWS ARE AN EXAMPLE OF THIS.

4. Muzafer Sherif says that a normative structure can collapse as a result of revolution. WHAT FOLLOWS SUCH A COLLAPSE?

5. NAME THREE TYPES OF SOCIAL NORMS. IN WHAT WAY ARE THEY SIMILAR?

6. Folkways guide us through the ordinary social encounters of everyday life. IDENTIFY AT LEAST THREE FOLKWAYS OF AMERICAN CULTURE.

7. Some social behavior is here today and gone tomorrow. GIVE SOME EXAMPLES. WHAT TERM IS USED TO DESCRIBE SUCH FADS AND FASHIONS?

8. There are folkways that are observed only by certain groups in American culture. CITE EXAMPLES OF FOLKWAYS THAT ARE LIMITED TO ONLY PARTS OF THE GENERAL AMERICAN CULTURE.

9. Folkways and mores are not of equal importance. EXPLAIN WHY. HOW DO REACTIONS DIFFER TO VIOLATIONS OF FOLKWAYS AND VIOLATIONS OF MORES?

10. IDENTIFY THE TWO DOCUMENTS THAT MIGHT BE THOUGHT OF AS REPRESENTING THE BASIC MORES OF AMERICAN IDEAL CULTURE.

11. Sumner said that "The mores can make anything right and prevent condemnations of anything." EXPLAIN THIS STATEMENT. DO YOU AGREE?

12. Social mores both approve and condemn various behaviors. CITE EXAMPLES OF AMERICAN MORES THAT APPROVE AND THOSE THAT CONDEMN.

13. Both positive and negative sanctions help to enforce social mores. EXPLAIN HOW REWARDS AND PUNISHMENTS AFFECT PEOPLE'S SELF-ESTEEM.

14. Laws are social norms intended to deal with specific circumstances. Some laws are concerned with morality. Some are concerned with mundane matters. EXPLAIN THE DIFFERENCE AND GIVE EXAMPLES OF BOTH.

15. Sometimes laws contradict mores. The likelihood is that people will observe the mores rather than the laws. CITE FOUR EXAMPLES OF THIS IN AMERICAN HISTORY.

16. It has often been said that "You can't legislate morality." EXPLAIN WHY THIS STATEMENT IS NOT ENTIRELY TRUE. HOW CAN LAWS INFLUENCE THE BELIEFS AND BEHAVIOR OF PEOPLE?

17. Most people conform to most of the norms most of the time. IDENTIFY THREE REASONS FOR THIS THAT WE DISCUSS AT THE END OF THIS SEC-

TION. EXPLAIN HOW EACH FACTOR ENCOURAGES THE OBSERVANCE OF SOCIAL NORMS.

PRACTICE TEST FOR SECTION 8

Select the best answer.

1. The best definition of social norms is
A. Behavior that follows socially approved standards.
B. The most frequently observed behavior.
C. Expectations for behavior.
D. Normative behavior.

2. When normative structures collapse, the final result is
A. Chaos and disorder.
B. A new normative structure.
C. Increased freedom.
D. Revolution.

3. Examples of behavioral expectations are
A. Folkways.
B. Mores.
C. Laws.
D. All of the above.

4. Norms whose violation brings formal punishments are
A. Folkways.
B. Mores.
C. Laws.
D. All of the above.

5. The degree of importance and the severity of punishment show the difference between
A. Laws and social norms.
B. Mores and social norms.
C. Folkways and mores.
D. Folkways and social norms.

6. Fads and fashions are examples of
A. Folkways.
B. Mores.
C. Social norms.
D. Pseudocustoms.

7. If a person ignores a folkway

A. Mores go into effect.
B. No severe punishment occurs.
C. Members of the group may be annoyed.
D. Both B and C.

8. Laws that deal with mundane matters could be based upon
A. Folkways.
B. Mores.
C. Pseudocustoms.
D. All of the above.

9. When laws clash with mores, people are most likely to
A. Observe the mores.
B. Substitute folkways for the laws.
C. Observe the laws.
D. Ignore both the laws and the mores.

10. Most people conform to
A. Laws more than folkways or mores.
B. Most of the norms some of the time.
C. Most of the norms most of the time.
D. All of the norms all of the time.

11. To say that people are accustomed to the comforts of the "habit cage" is evidence of
A. Indoctrination.
B. Practicality.
C. Habituation.
D. An ideal culture.

12. Most social norms
A. Have little to do with social order.
B. Are useful and practical.
C. Are based upon important laws.
D. None of the above.

Answer Key

1. C
2. B
3. D
4. C
5. C
6. D
7. D
8. A
9. A
10. C
11. C
12. B

SECTION 9   VARIETIES OF SUBCULTURES
- ETHNIC SUBCULTURES
- TWO BLACK-AMERICAN LIFE-STYLES
- REGIONAL SUBCULTURES
- OCCUPATIONAL SUBCULTURES
- RELIGIOUS SUBCULTURES
- AGE SUBCULTURES
- SOCIAL CLASS SUBCULTURES
- CONTRACULTURES
- ALL IN THE FAMILY

Objectives
After completing this section, the student should be able to:

1.   Recognize subcultures as specific life-styles that contribute to the total culture.

2.   Give examples of ethnicity crossing political boundaries.

3.   Identify three factors that have affected the status of ethnic groups in the United States.

4.   Contrast the life-styles of the internally acculturated and the externally adapted.

5.   Explain in what ways religions, age groups, social classes, occupations, and regions of the country are subcultures.

6.   Describe values and behaviors associated with contracultures.

We have described culture as the fabric of human society, providing the people of each society with a design for living. In this section we will examine culture as a fabric held together also by threads called *subcultures*. These are life-styles *within* the total culture. Each subculture is part of the total culture, but each subculture also has unique characteristics. There are many types of subcultures within the total culture of American society. Each of us participates in a number of subcultures. Now let us describe some of these types of American subcultures.

ETHNIC
SUBCULTURES   An ethnic group consists of people who share common cultural characteristics. Members of an ethnic group have historical ties of ancestry, nationality, language, religion, and race. People of the same ethnicity can live in different countries. In that case, all members of an ethnic group need not have the same nationality. Jews, who live in many countries, are an ethnic group. Germans also live in

many countries and are an ethnic group. At this time in history, Germans may have a *political nationality* of West Germany, East Germany, Poland, France, Czechoslovakia, Austria, or the Soviet Union. Members of an ethnic group may be separated by political boundaries. Still, they retain a consciousness of kind based on such factors as language, legends, customs, and religion.

Many modern societies are ethnically heterogeneous. This means that there are many ethnic groups in such countries as the United States, the Soviet Union, Yugoslavia, Canada, and various other countries. In the Soviet Union, there are more than a hundred ethnic groups. Many of them continue to use their own languages and to follow their own customs and religions. Such groups are part of the total Soviet culture, but they also belong to ethnic groups that are one kind of *subculture*. Usually, the term *ethnic group* refers to a minority group whose values and behavior are somewhat different from those of the majority population. Ethnic groups as minority groups come into existence for a number of reasons. Migrations, wars that change national boundaries, and slavery are historical events that have created ethnic minorities in various countries.

In the United States today, people are not as conscious of their ethnic origins as their ancestors were. In earlier American history a person's ethnic identity had more influence. Many different kinds of people came to the United States as immigrants. In the 19th century and during the early years of the 20th century, ethnic differences were very noticeable in the United States. Each ethnic subculture was characterized by certain attitudes and behavior relating to diet, styles of clothes, child-raising techniques, religions, and occupations. The people of each ethnic group tended to believe that their group was superior to other ethnic groups.

Ralph Waldo Emerson (1803–1882) was a devoted advocate of the American democratic experiment. He welcomed the increasing heterogeneity (differences) of the American population. About the many immigrants who were establishing new ethnic subcultures he wrote:

The energy of Irish, Germans, Swedes, Poles, and Cossacks, and all the European tribes—and of the Africans, and of the Polynesians—will construct a new race, a new religion, a new state, a new literature, which will be as vigorous as the new Europe which came out of the smelting-pot of the Dark Ages. . . .

(Quoted in Gabriel, 1940)

But Emerson's optimism was not shared by all Americans. Instead, many resented and feared the increasing number of foreign immigrants. Confronted with this hostility from native Americans, most immigrants segregated themselves into ethnic neighborhoods in American cities. Within the Little Italys, Germantowns, and Polish neighborhoods, the ethnic groups shared their consciousness of kind and subcultural life-styles within the general American culture. Ethnic organizations such as the Irish Hibernian Society, the German-American Bund, and the Sons of Italy provided their members with a sense of belonging. In time, each group contributed its own values and customs to the general American culture.

In the United States, the status (position in relation to others) of an ethnic group depended on such factors as:

1. The length of time its members had been present in the population in substantial numbers.

2. The ability to *avoid* being too visible. Visibility could apply to style of clothes, foreign accents, and customs.

3. The extent to which immigrants had become Americanized.

In a speech delivered on July 4, 1915, Louis Dembitz Brandeis defined the cure for visibility and what was necessary for *Americanization*:

What is Americanization? It manifests itself, in a superficial way, when the immigrant adopts the clothes, the manners, and the customs generally prevailing here. Far more important is the manifestation presented when he substitutes for his mother tongue the English language as the common medium of speech. But the adoption of our language, manners and customs is only a small part of the process. To become Americanized the change wrought must be fundamental. However great his outward conformity, the immigrant is not Americanized unless his interests and affections have become deeply rooted here. And we properly demand of the immigrant even more than this — he must be brought into complete harmony with our ideals and aspirations and cooperate with us for their attainment. Only when this has been done will he possess the national consciousness of an American.

(Quoted in Miller, 1954)

Brandeis was the son of immigrants himself. He had had to struggle to win his own Americanization by adopting the general American culture's manners, customs, and attitudes. He spoke of the need to "possess the national consciousness of an American." His speech exhibited his own fading visibility plus his own consciousness of kind with the general American population.

Ethnic group subcultures are not as recognizable in the United States as they once were. This is because of intermarriage among the various groups and because of what Judge Brandeis called Americanization. The most visible ethnic subcultures today are those now called minority groups. This would include American Indians, black-Americans, Mexican-Americans, and Puerto Ricans. Many people in these minority groups experience social disadvantages. They suffer oppression, neglect, poverty and the results of continuing visibility. Our next subtopic deals with two subcultural life-styles that were identified in the black-American population by sociologist Jessie Bernard in the 1960s.

TWO BLACK-AMERICAN LIFE-STYLES

Bernard said that the two life-styles she was describing were almost exactly the opposite from each other. The important difference between the two seemed to be based upon the values and behavior of the people involved. In fact, she quoted Hylan Lewis who described the "respectable" and "nonrespectable" people:

. . . In general, the respectable persons are defined by what they do not do. They are people who are careful of their public conduct and reputation: they don't drink whisky in public or get drunk in public; they don't frequent the taverns; they don't get in trouble; and they are proud of their lack of contact with the law and the courts . . . ; their sex life lacks the frank, open and . . . promiscuous character of the relations among their opposites.

(Bernard, 1966)

Bernard thought this to be too simplified a way of interpreting the two life-styles. She preferred to accentuate what she saw as being positive in both life-styles. Those people who tried to conform to the standards of ideal American culture she called the *internally acculturated.* By this she meant that they were people who had internalized the social norms so that the norms were part of their personalities. Those people who did not internalize the social norms and lived outside the mainstream of American culture she called the *externally adapted.* We shall describe each life-style separately. Then we show the significance of the kinds of work that attract the people of each life-style.

The Internally Acculturated

Bernard said that those black-Americans whom she described as internally acculturated are conventional and conservative. When an acculturated person violates norms, there are feelings of guilt, conflict, and anxiety. The internally acculturated black-Americans are like internally acculturated white-Americans. They are dedicated to the concept of progress. They seek to prove themselves capable and conscientious members of the community. To them, it is important to appear to be productive and respectable within the limits of the general American culture. If we were to use Freudian terms, we could say that they are guided by the reality principle.

The Externally Adapted

Bernard said that those black-Americans whom she described as externally adapted did not really internalize the norms of the general American culture. On the surface, however, they can adapt themselves to society's demands when necessary. Bernard said that this subculture is especially pleasure-seeking. They are people who have learned to live outside the mainstream of American life. They are dedicated to a kind of fun morality and seek immediate gratification for their desires. Bernard said that to those who live the externally adapted life "the prospect of a modest job and a stable family life has little appeal." For them, she said, there is much more prestige and real material reward forthcoming from illegal behavior. *Hustling* is both more satisfying and less demanding than the low-paying job and the little pleasure that accompanies legitimate efforts. If we were to use Freudian terms, we could say that the externally adapted are guided by the pleasure principle.

The Ethos of Work: Two Points of View

Nothing distinguishes these life-styles more dramatically than in the kinds of work they are attracted to. The members of both can be equally industrious, but in quite different ways. The internally acculturated seek types of work characterized by stability, steadiness, and security. The externally adapted seek the adventures and risks of hustling. Those who spend their talents in illegal activities often exhibit the same level of imagination and enterprise as those engaged in legitimate activities.

Jessie Bernard cites a National Educational Television program in which certain attitudes were revealed about work by a group of teenage boys. Two of the youths were black, with one voicing opinions of the internally acculturated and the other expressing the views of the externally adapted. One youth was a Puerto Rican. The other three youths were white and also voiced opinions consistent with the social norms of conventional society. The following excerpt from that program is based on notes taken by Jessie Bernard. The black youth is involved in the life-style of the externally adapted, and the Puerto Rican youth has experienced much the same kind of background. Both were school dropouts, and the Puerto Rican youth was married and a father.

Moderator: How do you get money?
Black youth: Oh, you can always find some way.
Moderator: How?
Black youth: Well, I go out on the street and hustle . . .
Moderator: What's that?
Black youth: (somewhat taken aback) Hustle . . .
Moderator: Yes, but what is it?
Black youth: Well, you have to make it seem as though she's doing something for you . . .
Moderator: What else do you do?
Black youth: Well, you walk down the street and ask people if they want you to do something. And here's a man wants a package delivered. That's fifty dollars . . .
Moderator: What kind of package would pay that much to be delivered?
Black youth: (smiling knowingly) I never ask. It's none of my business. I never know what's in the package.
Moderator: Wouldn't you rather have a steady job?
Black youth: If it paid and you didn't have to work so hard.
Moderator: Did you ever have a job?
Black youth: I used to work for the Neighborhood House. But it was too hard.
Moderator: What kind of work was it?
Black youth: Taking care of those kids. They kept asking questions.
Moderator: How old were they?
Black youth: Seven to thirteen.
Moderator: How much pay would you want?
Puerto Rican: I used to work and got only $45 a week so I quit.

Black youth: You can't go far on $45.
Puerto Rican: Not with a family.
Black youth: You can do better than that by mugging. You could get that in one night.
Puerto Rican: It depends on who you mug. . . .

The Puerto Rican and the black youth then engaged in a brief, matter-of-fact discussion of mugging. They viewed it simply as one of several ways to get money, better than some, not as good as others. Neither youth considered mugging or any other form of hustling to be a disgrace of any kind. These two young men did not seem to be rebels against a world that had done them wrong. They did not seem to be seeking revenge in their illegal acts. They did not see themselves as criminals. They simply took it for granted that there were certain ways to get money with a minimum of effort and that not to jump at such opportunities was foolish.

On the other hand, the other youths in the group—the three whites and the other black youth—kept bringing into the discussion references to the values of honesty, work, and waiting for what you want. "Thus," says Jessie Bernard, "two totally different approaches to life and its problems were reflected, and the two groups talked past—rather than to—one another" (Bernard, 1966).

One final thought: neither we, the authors, nor Jessie Bernard, our source, are suggesting that those two life-styles are characteristic only of America's black population and other minorities. Certainly, evidence abounds that the white majority population also has its externally adapted segment involved in deviant behavior. We chose to cite this study by Jessie Bernard because it offers insight into subcultures (or life-styles).

REGIONAL SUBCULTURES

Some countries (societies) have geographic regions populated by people who share and emphasize certain values and behaviors that differ in some ways from other regions of the same country. These differences, while usually not very profound, produce people who have special tastes in food, recreation, modes of dress, or styles of architecture and who speak in different dialects of the same language. Topography, climate, economic factors, and historic events can affect regional populations so that they participate in a regional subculture as well as in the society's total culture. In the United States we recognize regional differences in those who come from the East, the Middle West, the South, and the Far West. We can recognize a New England accent as opposed to a Southern accent. There are even variations in American sign language among the deaf, depending on the region of the country. For example, graduates of the Maryland School for the Deaf claim they invented the signs for the terms "gulp" and "zap." These signs have since come to be used by other deaf people in the Middle Atlantic region (Frank, 1981). We associate boiled lobsters with Maine, steamed crabs with Maryland, and fried chicken wth Kentucky. The rodeo is popular in the Southwest while lacrosse is especially popular in the Middle Atlantic states. Because of mass communications and rapid transportation, the regional differences are no longer as pronounced as they once were. Still, the various geographic regions of the United States continue to represent one other type of American subculture.

OCCUPATIONAL SUBCULTURES

Occupations are very influential subcultures. People who work at the same kind of job certainly have much in common. They receive about the same income. They probably live in the same kind of neighborhood. And they will speak the same specialized language that is associated with their kind of work. Finally, they will probably belong to the same union or association. Consequently, each occupation or profession lays the groundwork for an entire subcultural life-style. There are role expectations and social norms to be observed within each occupational subculture.

On a day-to-day basis, the interests and problems associated with one's work and with one's co-workers are very important. In fact, general strikes, slowdowns, and sick-ins are good examples of how people can place the interests and welfare of their occupational subcultures before the interests and welfare of society at large. Most people internalize the norms and observe the roles associated with their occupational subcultures.

People who share the same occupational subcultures tend to view the world similarly. For example, American industrial workers are more likely to be Democrats than Republicans. Executives in large businesses are more likely to be Republicans than Democrats. Successful business people usually find the established system more to their liking than do people who work for hourly wages. Small-business owners are less sympathetic toward large chain stores than are manual laborers. Civil servants become more alarmed than do farmers about inflation. The point we are making by citing these examples is this: one's occupation has as much affect on one's likes and dislikes as it does on one's skills and productivity. This offers further evidence of occupations as subcultural life-styles (Bensman and Rosenberg, 1963).

RELIGIOUS SUBCULTURES

Religious differences within a society create religious subcultures. In American society there is a multitude of various religious cults, denominations, and organized religions. Catholics, Jews, Mormons, Muslims, and various Protestant denominations all offer special subcultural experiences to those who practice their customs and hold their views.

AGE SUBCULTURES

All societies have role expectations for members who fall into certain age brackets. Because of this, a society's population can be seen as a collection of age-conscious subcultures. In most tribal societies, the very young are expected to be carefree together and respectful toward those in the older age brackets. Certain rites and rituals observe the changing age status as the very young move into ad-

Viewing the world similarly.

olescence, then into young adulthood, then into mature adulthood, and then into the age of the elders. Each age group occupies itself with its own interests, concerns, and accomplishments.

In large industrial societies, it is more difficult to identify when one enters and leaves each age subculture, but we think it is safe to make the following generalizations. The concerns and activities of the very young differ from those of the teenage years. The concerns and activities of young adults differ from those of the middle-aged, just as the middle-aged differ from the elderly. From one age group to another, there are obvious differences in reference to diet, clothes, recreation, and family roles. There are subcultural life-styles associated with these age groups. No doubt about it. Nor can there be any doubt about each age group being convinced that its life-style makes more sense than those of the younger and older generations. Henry David Thoreau said that "Every generation laughs at the old fashions, but follows religiously the new" (Thoreau, 1854). Robert Bierstedt used the term *temporocentrism* to describe this "unexamined and largely unconscious acceptance of one's . . . own era, one's own lifetime, as the center of sociological significance" (Bierstedt, 1948). When a person is temporocentric, he or she believes in the superiority of his or her own age group and subcultural life-style.

SOCIAL CLASS SUBCULTURES

When we refer to social class, we refer to a person's social location within a society. We discussed the importance of social class origins in Chapter 2. Remember that Max Weber said that one's social location grants or denies certain privileges, power, and prestige. We explained then that one's social class location determines the life-styles of people throughout their lives. This means that social class is one more type of subculture within the general American culture. Values, attitudes, and behavior are quite different from one social class to another. We discuss the significance of social class in much more detail in Chapter 6.

CONTRA-CULTURES

Most subcultures support the society's total culture even though each subculture has its own particular values and behaviors. A subculture is a group that shares cultural patterns that are distinct but not in conflict with the general culture. A *contraculture* is a special type of subculture. It *is* a subculture, but its values and behavioral norms oppose those of society at large. Nonconformity to the norms of society is typical of those who belong to a contraculture (Yinger, 1960). However, members of contracultures do conform to the social norms of their own group. Some sociologists have used the term *counterculture* in the same way that J. Milton Yinger first used *contraculture*.

One example of a contraculture would be a street-corner gang with a life-style including drug addiction and various forms of hustling such as mugging, pimping, and assisting the various agencies of the criminal underworld. In fact, the criminal underworld, sometimes called organized crime, can be defined as a powerful contraculture that clashes with the ideal culture of American society. Those whom we earlier described as the externally adapted are involved in contracultural activities. Recall the matter-of-fact discussion on mugging.

Another example of a contraculture would be some of the counterculture communes, both urban and rural, that reject conventional jobs, avoid marriage, and consider the consumption and accumulation of material goods to be of little value.

Still another example would be the homosexual communities that exist in large cities. Homosexuals refer to their life-style as the "gay world." In recent years there has been mounting evidence that many homosexuals want to become accepted as an ordinary sexual subculture and not as a contraculture in conflict with society at large. The Gay Liberation Movement has staged demonstrations in which homosexuals publicly demanded that they be accepted within the mainstream of American society. We believe that there are signs of homosexuality becoming less controversial. Indeed, in the not-too-distant future, legalized homosexual marriages may be acceptable. After all, homosexuals have been pairing off with lasting success for centuries in many cultures of the world. Even now, while such marriages are not recognized as legal, "homosexual marriages are sometimes quite enduring . . . despite the forces of society—religious, social, legal, economic—that combine to drive the couple apart" (Saxton, 1979). Here, then is an example of a contraculture that may in time qualify as merely another of the various subcultures that combine to create the fabric of American culture. In time, homosexuality may not be defined as behavior that clashes with or contradicts the patterns of society's total culture.

ALL IN THE FAMILY

In the early 1970s, Archie Bunker became television's most popular leading man in the successful television series *All in the Family*. Perhaps Archie Bunker never heard of terms such as *subcultures* and *contracultures*, but he certainly had an exceptional consciousness of kind. He saw himself menaced by a "rising tide of spades, spics, spooks, schwartzes, coons, colored, chinks, chosen people, Commies, and their commie crapola, jungle bunnies, jigs, pinkos, pansies, hebes, yids, bleeding hearts, tamale eaters, yentas, atheists, weirdos, dumb Polacks, dingbats, meatheads, fairies, fruits, fags and four eyes" (*Newsweek*, 1971). The Archie Bunkers of the United States come in all colors, all religions, from all occupations and all regions, and of all ages. The population of American society totals over 225 million people who have both very little in common and very much in common. In our complex society, each person belongs to various subcultures just as each person must play various roles.

Near the horizon

To the rest of the world, the diversity of the United States does not seem so significant (Feldman and Thielbar, 1972). Americans make up less than six percent of the Earth's population. New Yorkers may make a distinction between Brooklynites and Manhattanites, and Minnesotans might distinguish between Minneapolitans and Saint Paulites. However, Europeans see little or no difference between a New Yorker and a Midwesterner—they are all Americans. From the outsiders' perspectives, there is a recognizable American character type based on a common life-style.

Like it or not, we are "all in the family."

KEY TERMS AND NAMES FROM SECTION 9

subcultures as life-styles

ethnic subcultures

visibility

Americanization

minority groups

the internally acculturated

the externally adapted

regional subcultures

occupational subcultures

religious subcultures

age subcultures

temporocentrism

social class subcultures

contracultures

Gay Liberation Movement

all in the family

Jessie Bernard

Robert Bierstedt

STUDY GUIDE FOR SECTION 9

1. In this section we discuss the concept of subcultures and cite examples of them. DESCRIBE THE RELATIONSHIP BETWEEN A SOCIETY'S TOTAL CULTURE AND ITS VARIOUS SUBCULTURES.

2. Members of an ethnic group may be separated by political boundaries. WHAT FACTORS ENCOURAGE THEM TO RETAIN A CONSCIOUSNESS OF KIND?

3. In earlier American history, a person's ethnic identity was more influential than it is today. WHAT KIND OF DIFFERENCES EXISTED IN REFERENCE TO ATTITUDES AND BEHAVIORS?

4. In earlier American history, the status of an ethnic group depended upon three factors. IDENTIFY THOSE THREE FACTORS.

5. Judge Brandeis spoke of steps that ethnic groups would have to take in order to possess "the national consciousness of Americans." WHAT DID BRANDEIS CONSIDER NECESSARY FOR WHAT HE CALLED "AMERICANIZATION"?

6. WHICH ETHNIC GROUPS IN THE UNITED STATES ARE MOST VISIBLE TODAY? WHY?

7. Jessie Bernard described two black-American life-styles in the 1960s. WHAT TERMS DID SHE USE FOR EACH LIFE-STYLE? DESCRIBE THE VALUES AND BEHAVIORS OF THE TWO LIFE-STYLES.

8. Certain parts of the United States can be seen as subcultures. CITE SOME CULTURAL DIFFERENCES IN THE REGIONAL SUBCULTURES.

9. Occupations are very influential subcultures within the United States. EXPLAIN WHY OCCUPATIONAL SUBCULTURES ARE IMPORTANT TO PEOPLE.

10. A society's population can be seen as a collection of age-conscious subcultures. IDENTIFY SUCH SUBCULTURES AND EXPLAIN WHY THEY EXIST.

11. WHAT DOES THE TERM *TEMPOROCENTRISM* MEAN?

12. Social class refers to a person's social location. WHY IS A SOCIAL CLASS A TYPE OF SUBCULTURE?

13. Each subculture has its own values and expectations for behavior, but most subcultures support the society's total culture. WHAT ARE CONTRACULTURES? WHAT IS CHARACTERISTIC OF THEIR VALUES AND BEHAVIORS?

14. NAME THREE CONTRACULTURES MENTIONED IN THE TEXT. ADD ANY OTHER EXAMPLES OF CONTRACULTURES THAT YOU CAN IDENTIFY.

PRACTICE TEST FOR SECTION 9

Select the best answer.

1. The relationship between a society's total culture and its subcultures
A. Is based on hostility.
B. Has subcultures as part of the total culture.
C. Requires people to give up old beliefs.
D. All of the above.

2. Which of the following is not an ethnic group?
A. Black-Americans.
B. German-Americans.
C. Jewish-Americans.
D. Female-Americans.

3. The visibility of an ethnic group refers to its
A. Sensitivity.
B. Identifiability.
C. Hostility.
D. Ability to see what is right and wrong.

4. Nonconformity to the norms of society at large is characteristic of those who belong to
A. A subculture.
B. A contraculture.
C. An internally acculturated subculture.
D. An age-conscious subculture.

5. Teaching as a profession lays the groundwork for an entire life-style. What type of subculture does this describe?
A. Regional.
B. Ethnic.
C. Contracultural.
D. Occupational.

6. Every generation laughs at the old fashions but follows religiously the new. This statement is an example of
A. Temporocentrism.
B. Transitionism.

C. Cultural lag.

D. None of the above.

7. Jessie Bernard said that people who tried to conform to the standards of ideal American culture are

A. Externally adapted.

B. Internally acculturated.

C. Concerned with respectability.

D. Both B and C.

8. We could say that the externally adapted are guided by

A. The norms of ideal American culture.

B. The pleasure principle.

C. The reality principle.

D. Fear and depression.

9. Which of the following is not a subculture?

A. Religious group.

B. Ethnic group.

C. Multinational corporation.

D. All are subcultures.

10. A contraculture

A. Supports the total culture.

B. Is a subculture.

C. Is based on seniority.

D. All of the above.

Answer Key

1.	B	**6.**	A
2.	D	**7.**	D
3.	B	**8.**	B
4.	B	**9.**	C
5.	D	**10.**	B

CHAPTER SUMMARY

1. The sociological view of culture includes all material things used by people and all patterns of behavior exhibited by people. Culture includes "knowledge, belief, art, morals, laws, custom and any other habits . . . acquired by members of society." Culture requires the learning of behavior. Culture consists of a social heritage. Culture is a way of life that is learned through the socialization process.

2. An ideology is made up of ideas, beliefs, and values that are shared by a human grouping. Technology consists of material items and skills, crafts, and arts. Social organization refers to the rules, roles, and relationships that create a patterned and regulated social order. Every society's culture has these components of ideology, technology, and social organization.

3. Ethical absolutism and cultural relativism are two ways to view human behavior. Some say that moral judgments should be related to human needs. They say that there are basic needs common to all humans. Therefore, they say, it seems to follow that there are standards that apply to all human beings. This is the view of ethical absolutism. Cultural relativists say that right and wrong are relative to time and place and to each particular culture. They say that the behavior of people in one culture should not be judged by the values and standards of another culture.

4. Ideal culture consists of those patterns of behavior that are formally approved and that members of society are encouraged to observe. Real culture consists of those patterns of behavior that members of society actually do ob-

serve. A person learns about both the ideal and real cultures through the socialization process.

5.   American culture has been influenced by production values and humanistic values. Production values include an emphasis upon achieving, producing, efficiency, and success. Humanistic values emphasize caring, loving, knowing, and being known.

6.   Social norms are rules and regulations that apply to expectations for human behavior. Norms approve and condemn various behaviors. With social norms, people know what to expect of others and what others expect of them. Observing the social norms is called normative behavior. Normative behavior contributes order and stability to social interaction.

7.   Three broad classifications of social norms are folkways, mores, and laws. All three influence the feeling, thinking, and behavior of individuals and groups. To one degree or another, each approves or disapproves of certain behaviors.

8.   In 1906, WIlliam Graham Sumner published his book about social norms, entitled *Folkways*. Folkways are customs. Society expects people to observe folkways. Society demands that people observe mores. Mores have to do with strong moral convictions. Laws are social norms that are intended to deal with specific circumstances. Society demands that people obey laws.

9.   Most people conform to most of the norms most of the time. Reasons for such conformity include indoctrination, habituation, and practicality. We are indoctrinated very early. We are creatures of habit. Most norms *are* useful and practical, and most people recognize this to be true.

10.   Subcultures are life-styles that exist within the total culture of society. Each subculture is part of the total culture, but each also has unique characteristics. There are many types of subcultures within the total culture of the United States.

11.   Each member of society participates in a number of subcultures. Types of subcultures in the United States include ethnic, regional, occupational, religious, age, and social class. A contraculture is a deviant subculture that contradicts the prevailing norms of society at large.

SUGGESTIONS FOR FURTHER READING RELATED TO CHAPTER 3

Clarke, M., "On the Concept of Subculture," *British Journal of Sociology*, Vol. 25 (1974), pp. 428–441. Clarke raises a number of significant questions about existence of subcultures.

Downs, James F., *Cultures in Crisis* (California: Glencoe Press, 1971). This paperback discusses cultural relativism stressing that one's culture determines one's view of the world.

Feldman, Saul D., and Gerald Thielbar, *Lifestyles: Diversity in American Society* (Boston: Little, Brown, 1972). This is a collection of essays defining the phenomenon of life-styles, including social class, regional, sexual, ethnic, and deviant.

Handlin, Oscar, *Children of the Uprooted* (New York: Grosset & Dunlap, 1971). Handlin, a noted historian, writes about the cultural interactions between ethnic groups that have contributed so much to the American experience.

Hostetler, John, *Amish Society* (Baltimore: John Hopkins Press, 1963). Hostetler describes a "cultural island" within American society that leads to a better understanding of the significance of subcultures.

Hunt, Robert, editor, *Personalities and Cultures* (Austin, Texas: University of Texas Press, 1967). This is a wide-ranging collection of articles about personalities and cultures as seen from the viewpoint of psychological anthropology.

Mead, Margaret, *Culture and Commitment: A Study of the Generation Gap* (New York: Doubleday, 1970). Mead associates the generation gap with current crises in American society.

Miner, Horace, "Body Ritual Among the Nacirema," *American Anthropologist*, Vol. 58 (June 1956), pp. 503–507. As a review of the strange customs of a North American culture, this essay could be used as an antidote for ethnocentrism.

Perry, Troy, *The Lord Is My Shepherd and He Knows I'm Gay* (New York: Bantam Books, 1972). Reverend Perry, a male homosexual, provides a sensitive insight into the homosexual subculture, emphasizing the religious experiences of those in the gay world.

Vogt, Evon, and Ethel Albert, editors, *People of Rimrock: A Study of Values in Five Cultures* (New York: Atheneum, 1966). This work deals with the role of values among human groupings in close proximity, including the Zuni, Navaho, Spanish-Americans, Mormons, and Texas homesteaders.

Yinger, J. Milton, "Contraculture and Subculture," *American Sociological Review*, Vol. 25 (October 1960), pp. 625–635. This article describes normative systems that have as their basic theme conflicting values opposed to the values of the larger society.

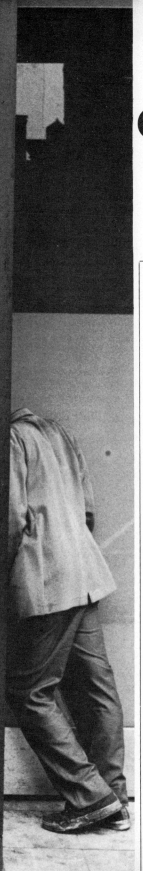

Chapter 4
Social Deviance

SECTION 10   CONFORMITY AND DEVIANCE
- WHAT IS CONFORMITY?
- WHAT IS DEVIANCE?
- VARIOUS VIEWS OF DEVIANCE

Objectives
After completing this section, the student should be able to:
1. Explain in what ways both conformists and nonconformists have been viewed favorably in the United States.
2. Describe in what way society reacts to deviants identified as freaks, sinners, boat-rockers, sick, alienated, and simply as human beings.

If a man does not keep pace with his companions, perhaps it is because he hears a different drummer. Let him step to the music which he hears, however measured or far away.

(Henry David Thoreau)

In the previous chapter, we pointed out that each society's culture has expectations for behavior. These behavioral expectations are called social norms. We have said that most people observe most of the social norms most of the time. This is conformity. Social deviance occurs when a person ignores or rejects social norms.

WHAT IS
CONFORMITY?

In Chapter 2 on the socialization process, we said that all societies seek to instill within their populations the desire and willingness to conform to societal expectations. As we have said, most people conform to most of the norms most of the time. In order to discourage noncomformity and to encourage conformity, human groupings develop positive and negative sanctions (see Glossary).

The terms *conformist* and *nonconformist* have meanings other than their definitions. We mean that many individuals prefer to be thought of as noncomformists. That term has become associated with something "good" much as the term individualist is a "good" label. For example, a conformist can be seen as one who submits to external demands, and one who, at times, violates conscience in the pursuit of the rewards and comforts of the herd. Consider some similar words that convey quite different meanings. We could substitute the phrase *team player* for the word *conformist*. We could substitute the word *deviant* for the words *individualist* and *nonconformist*. Suddenly the individualist labeled a "deviant" and the conformist labeled a "team player" evoke different images simply because of the substituted terms (Aronson, 1972).

In the United States, the nonconformist usually is *not* held in high esteem by those who are sharing the situation in which the person refuses to conform to group expectations. On the other hand, the nonconformist is likely to be praised by historians and pictured as a hero by historians, writers, and filmmakers long after the fact of the nonconforming behavior. As one contemporary social scientist has written:

When we look a little closer, we see an inconsistency in the way our society seems to feel about conformity [team playing] and nonconformity [deviance]. For example, one of the great best sellers of the 1950s was a book by John F. Kennedy called Profiles in Courage, *wherein the author praised several politicians for their courage in resisting great pressure and refusing to conform. To put it another way, Kennedy was praising people who refused to be good team players, people who refused to vote or act as their parties or constituents expected them to. Although their actions earned Kennedy's praise long after the deeds were done, the immediate reactions of their colleagues were generally far from positive.*

(Aronson, 1972)

Complete deviancy and total conformity are each extreme, ideal-type behaviors in a society. There is always some kind of deviant behavior within society. Deviancy is implicit in the very idea of society, a point made by Emile Durkheim many years ago and accepted by sociologists ever since (Bell, 1971). Durkheim wrote:

Imagine a society of saints, a perfect cloister of exemplary individuals. Crimes, properly so called, will there be unknown; but faults which appear minor to the laymen will create there the same scandal that the ordinary offense does in the ordinary consciousness.

(Durkheim, 1938)

To conclude this subtopic, we offer the following simple definition of social conformity. Conformity exists where a person's opinions and behavior coincide with the prevailing values and behavior of the social units with which the person identifies.

WHAT IS DEVIANCE?

It is far more difficult to define "deviancy" and "deviant behavior" than it is to define "conformity." Cultures and subcultures differ in their definitions of what is deviant. However, all cultures and subcultures have rules and behavioral expectations whose violations evoke disapproval, anger, or indignation. Where there are rules, there is deviance (Cohen, 1966). Thus, deviant behavior is behavior representing a departure from social norms.

Deviant behavior can be relative to circumstances. For example, in the United States public nudity is a behavior condoned (approved) in the infant but condemned in the adult. Drinking alcohol is condoned for those over the legal age and condemned for those under the legal age. Killing people is condoned in war and condemned when done for personal reasons. Drug consumption is condoned for research and for medical treatment and condemned for enjoyment. Copulation is condoned in marriage and condemned when it is extramarital.

Deviant behavior can also depend on the period of time within any one society. Styles, fashions, and fads come and go depending upon the times. The people seen as sinners, rebels, misfits, and criminals in the past may be thought of as heroes and heroines in the future. The "straights" who conformed to the norms of yesteryear may be thought of as deviants by later generations. History, legends, and literature can reinterpret their behavior (Dinitz et al., 1969). Bonnie and Clyde were a pair of robbers and killers in the 1930s. Thirty years later they were pictured as romantic figures in a movie bearing their names. This is not to say that robbing and killing were condoned by society in the 1960s. It does say something about how attitudes can change toward people from one period to another within the same society.

There really is no one behavior that is always called deviant and no one behavior that is always called desirable. Therefore, we have to be careful when we attempt to define deviancy. Let us say that deviance is behavior that is considered undesirable by the majority of people at a certain time. Deviance represents some form of undesirable difference in the view of the majority of people. This difference can be viewed in various ways, as the following discussion of deviation from the norms indicates.

VARIOUS VIEWS OF DEVIANCE

The Deviant as Freak

There are those who say that deviation should be used in a precise and literal sense. In this view, most people behave normally, while those who exhibit deviant behavior deviate from the average or norm. This definition of deviance stresses the statistical exception. In other words, the deviant person is a "freak." Behavior is seen, for example, as being either criminal or law-abiding, as loyal or disloyal, and as hallucinatory or rational. This is not a very satisfactory way to define deviant behavior. It encourages us to deal only with extremes and not with real human beings (Dinitz et al., 1969). When we discussed ideal and real culture in Chapter 3 we said then that probably everyone deviates from the norms of a society's ideal culture.

The Deviant as "Sinner"

The religious-ideological definition of deviance centers on concepts originating in religious terminology: sinner, heretic, and apostate. A sinner is one who violates the expected or "proper" ways of thinking and acting. Viewing the deviant as a sinner is believing that this individual is violating doctrines and norms that the sinner *has accepted* but simply does not live up to. A heretic, unlike the sinner, is considered a deviant because the heretic *rejects* some or all of the "proper" ways of thinking and acting. An apostate is one who not only rejects the

New Wave conformity.

dogma and faith but who also accepts an entirely different set of principles, norms, and traditions. This kind of deviant behavior is thought to be more threatening to the maintenance of social solidarity than the behavior of sinners or heretics. The apostate is a renegade and a defector. In the secular world, this same kind of definition of deviance is applied to those who are judged to be traitors to or deserters from The Cause, whatever it might be (Dinitz et al., 1969).

The Deviant as Boat-Rocker

In this view, deviance is seen as behavior that *interferes* with the smooth running of the group or institution or society as a whole. Deviance is seen as behavior that creates stress and strain and threatens the well-being of the whole. As one writer has said:

This is the view most widely held and applied by schoolteachers, wardens, mental hospital attendants, policemen, social workers, parole officers, military officers, and others charged with keeping peace and order. . . .

This boat-rocking image is also implied in most psychological definitions of "normal," "adjusted," and "mature." The healthy and well-integrated person is defined as the one who happily complies with social expectations, who is a productive cog in society's machine, who wants to do what he "ought" to do.

(Simmons, 1969)

Close inspection of this view should reveal the bias in favor of the status quo. The boat-rocking image of deviance is ideologically conservative, since it holds the continuance of the existing social order to be in the interests of the entire group.

The Deviant as Sick Person

From this view, the deviant is seen as not being responsible for his or her behavior. The deviant, being "sick," is viewed as being partly or completely irrational. At the very least, the deviant is confused and needs help more than an application of negative sanctions. In this view, just as human organs are subject to infection, disease, and impaired functioning, so also are psychic and social behavior subject to unhealthy or impaired functioning (Dinitz et al., 1969). Actually, the concept of mental pathology is more a synonym for deviance than an explanation of it. In order to explain why some members of a group deviate while others do not, the deviants are defined as pathological. But this involves a kind of circular reasoning. Look at it this way: people violate norms because they are psychopaths, and we know that they *are* psychopaths because of their norm-violating behavior. Deviant behavior is explained by internal disturbance and internal disturbance is inferred from the deviant behavior. Thus, as stated above, the term "psychopath" is simply a synonym for norm-violator or deviant. It is not a very satisfactory explanation (Simmons, 1969).

The Deviant as Alienated Person

We discuss the concept of alienation (see Glossary) in Section 15. People become alienated as a result of the structure of modern mass society. In large industrial societies, people feel a certain sense of powerlessness. They feel they have little control over the events around them or even over their own lives. This view sees modern humans as trapped and being at the mercy of decisions made at levels beyond their reach. There is the feeling that nothing is certain and predictable even in one's day-to-day existence. With the strings controlled by distant others in power, people feel like puppets. Then they become out of touch with the values and social norms of their own society. Gradually alienation sets in.

The alienated are deviants cut off from the society in which they live. "They are *in* the society but not *of* the society since they do not accept most of the norms used as standards" for behavior by society at large (Dinitz et al., 1969). Alienation is said to be responsible for many suicides because suicide often involves people who feel they have lost the meaning of life. Alienation is said to be the cause of various mass movements with beliefs that do not conform to the values of society at large. Various religious cults and extremist political movements are said to result from feelings of alienation. Some segments of the population expect such mass movements to give new meanings to their lives (Dinitz et al., 1969).

The Deviant as Human Being

Finally, there is the view of the deviant as simply another human being who has a few quirks and some particular problems that make him or her different. This calm and accepting view of the deviant is sometimes found in small towns and in stable urban neighborhoods. People come to know the local "characters" so well that the nonconformist and deviant are recognized first as human beings and only secondarily as deviants. One social psychologist gives us a good example of this view of deviants as human beings when he describes a small town with which he is familiar.

I spent some time in a small Midwestern town where virtually everyone knew that one of the high school teachers was lesbian, that one of the prominent lawyers was homosexual, that one of the dentists was strung out on drugs, that one of the leading doctors sometimes performed abortions. But these people were also productive members of the community and well-known coffee break companions, so the townspeople tolerated and even protected them.

(Simmons, 1969)

In Conclusion

We said earlier that there is no precise, universal behavior that can be called deviant behavior as opposed to normal behavior. We have suggested that deviance is behavior that represents some form of undesirable difference. When we consider what it is to be human—the human condition—it is not difficult to accept the probability that all human beings are a little deviant in one way or another. In each of us there is a bit of the freak, the sinner, the boat-rocker, the sick, or alienated person. More important, there is most certainly in each of us the single savage self that we call human being.

KEY TERMS AND
NAMES FROM
SECTION 10

conformity

nonconformity

deviance

deviant as freak

deviant as sinner

heretic

apostate

deviant as boat-rocker

deviant as sick person

deviant as alienated person

deviant as human being

Emile Durkheim

STUDY GUIDE FOR SECTION 10

1. All human groupings encourage conformity and discourage nonconformity. WHAT IS CONFORMITY?

2. The terms *conformist* and *nonconformist* have acquired meanings that are not part of their literal definitions. EXPLAIN HOW THESE TERMS CAN BE INTERPRETED BEYOND THEIR ACTUAL DEFINITIONS.

3. Deviant behavior can be relative to circumstances. CITE SOME EXAMPLES IN WHICH CIRCUMSTANCES DETERMINE WHETHER BEHAVIOR IS CONDONED OR CONDEMNED IN THE UNITED STATES.

4. Deviant behavior can also be relative to periods of time within any one society. HOW CAN THE EVALUATION OF A NONCONFORMIST DIFFER WHEN BEING MADE BY CONTEMPORARIES AND BY LATER HISTORIANS?

5. Where there are rules, there is deviance. Emile Durkheim said that deviancy is implicit in the very idea of society, meaning that there is always some kinds of deviant behavior within society. HOW COULD THIS APPLY EVEN TO DURKHEIM's "SOCIETY OF SAINTS, A PERFECT CLOISTER OF EXEMPLARY INDIVIDUALS"?

6. There is no specific behavior that is universally called deviant behavior as opposed to normal behavior. HOW DO WE DEFINE DEVIANCE IN THE TEXT?

7. One view of deviancy suggests that most people behave normally and that a deviant person is a "freak." WHY IS THIS NOT A VERY SATISFACTORY WAY TO DEFINE DEVIANT BEHAVIOR?

8. The religious-ideological definition of deviance centers on concepts originating in religious terminology. USING THE RELIGIOUS TERMS, HOW DO SINNERS, HERETICS, AND APOSTATES DIFFER IN THE WAYS IN WHICH THEY EXPRESS THEIR DEVIANCES?

9. In viewing the deviant as a "boat-rocker," deviant behavior is said to create stress and strain that threaten the well-being of the group. WHY IS THE BOAT-ROCKING IMAGE OF DEVIANCE IDEOLOGICALLY CONSERVATIVE?

10. In order to explain why some members of a group deviate while others do not, the deviants are defined as sick or pathological. IN WHAT WAY DOES THIS INTERPRETATION OF DEVIANCY INVOLVE A KIND OF CIRCULAR REASONING?

11. One interpretation of deviancy sees the deviants as being alienated from the values and norms of their own society. WHAT IS SUPPOSED TO HAVE CAUSED THIS ALIENATION OF THE INDIVIDUAL?

12. One way to view a deviant is simply to see him or her as another human being. EXPLAIN WHAT ONE'S REACTION TO A DEVIANT WOULD BE IF THIS IS THE VIEW TAKEN.

PRACTICE TEST FOR SECTION 10

Select the best answer.

1. Deviance is implicit in the very idea of society. This statement is associated with
A. Emile Durkheim.
B. Henry David Thoreau.
C. Albert K. Cohen.
D. Thomas Robert Malthus.

2. The process by which people adapt themselves to behavioral expectations is termed
A. Aberrant behavior.
B. Deviance.
C. Nonconformist behavior.
D. Conformity.

3. Deviant behavior is behavior that violates
A. Social norms.
B. Institutions.
C. Values.
D. Social roles.

4. The view of the deviant as a statistical exception is that of a
A. Boat-rocker.
B. Sinner.
C. Heretic.
D. Freak.

5. According to the religious-ideological view of deviance, one who not only rejects the dogma and faith but who also accepts an entirely different set of principles and traditions is a(n)
A. Freak.
B. Sinner.
C. Heretic.
D. Apostate.

6. From the religious conceptions of deviance, the most threatening type of deviant is the
A. Sinner.
B. Heretic.
C. Apostate.

7. When deviance is seen as behavior that creates stress and strain which threatens the well-being of the whole, the deviant is viewed as a
A. Heretic.
B. Boat-rocker.
C. Freak.
D. Sick person.

8. The most ideologically conservative image of deviance is that of the
A. Boat-rocker.
B. Sinner.
C. Apostate.
D. Alienated.

9. Central to the image of the deviant as sick is the concept of
A. Alienation.
B. Anomie.
C. Mental pathology.
D. Sin.

10. This view of deviance includes the belief that the emergence of mass society has vitally affected the lives of those who live in it. Which view of deviance is implied? The deviant as
A. Alienated person.
B. Freak.
C. Boat-rocker.
D. Human being.

Answer Key

1.	A	**6.**	C
2.	D	**7.**	B
3.	A	**8.**	A
4.	D	**9.**	C
5.	D	**10.**	A

SECTION 11   THREE SOCIOLOGICAL THEORIES OF DEVIANCE
- THE ANOMIE THEORY OF DEVIANCE
- THE LABELING THEORY OF DEVIANCE
- THE GROUP-SUPPORT THEORY OF DEVIANCE

Objectives

After completing this section, the student should be able to:

1. Describe innovation, retreatism, rebellion, and ritualism as forms of deviant behavior.
2. Identify the most important variable used to define deviant behavior according to the labeling theory.
3. Explain why people commit deviant acts, according to the group-support theory.

In the previous section of this chapter we discussed the various views that people have of those who deviate from the social norms of society. We said that deviance is behavior that is considered undesirable by the majority of people. Now we must attempt to offer explanations (theories) about why people exhibit deviant behavior. We have selected three sociological theories of deviance that do provide us with some insights into why people violate social norms.

THE ANOMIE THEORY OF DEVIANCE

Anomie is a French word that means "normlessness." It is a condition in society in which there is an absence of or confusion about social norms. Picture a society that has failed to provide some individuals opportunities to achieve goals that have been said to be worth seeking. We are thinking of goals that have been set and honored by the majority of the population. What happens is that those people denied the opportunity to reach the goals legitimately exhibit anomie. They are apt to behave in one of four ways: innovation, retreatism, rebellion, or ritualism. Any one of these four behaviors is considered deviant. In American history, various minority groups have experienced great disadvantages in achieving the generally agreed upon goals of American society. It has been such subgroups who have exhibited higher rates of deviance then the general population (Merton, 1968).

The American design for living has encouraged people to think in terms of progress and the future. The accumulation of wealth has been a success symbol in American society. Americans have emphasized the production values of doing, achieving, producing, efficiency, and success. Yet, as we indicated above, there are Americans whose income, social class, or racial and ethnic status make it difficult to achieve the success goals through legitimate means. It is often people from these subgroups who resort to illegitimate means or deviant behavior to attain the goals. The anomie theory assumes that rates of deviant behavior vary considerably by income, social class, and ethnic and racial status. The highest rate and the most pressure for deviation occur among lower socioeconomic groups. The people in these groups have less opportunity to acquire material goods. Their educational levels are very much below the statistical norm for the society (Clinard, 1968).

When a person is prevented from legitimately reaching cultural goals, there are four possible ways for the person to react or adapt. Each of the four following adaptations are forms of deviant behavior, according to Robert K. Merton's anomie theory (Merton, 1968).

Innovation as Deviation

Innovation is a form of deviance when a person uses illegitimate methods to achieve a certain cultural goal. Delinquent behavior of juveniles and criminal behavior of adults are examples of acquiring wealth by deviant behavior. As we have said, the accumulation of wealth is a generally accepted goal in the United States. In the lower socioeconomic groups there are few opportunities for legitimate realization of this goal. Consequently, innovative but illegitimate means are frequently used by the lower-lower class to get money and be "successful." According to the anomie theory, there are people who have internalized (come to believe in) the cultural emphasis upon material success but who have no legitimate means to succeed. Theft, burglary, robbery, playing the numbers, and prostitution are all examples of innovation. To innovate in these ways is to use unconventional means for achieving socially approved ends. People who engage in these activities conform to the value of success but deviate from the norms for acquiring success.

One sociologist has illustrated innovative adaptation by considering the goals and means in Academe (Cuzzort, 1969). One of the legitimate goals of students in higher education is achieving a high grade-point average. We can recognize study, hard work, and taking tests and examinations as legitimate means to high grades. Students who pursue these means to academic success are conformists within the educational system. However, other students might seek the goal of good grades but reject the means for attaining them. Such students could innovate different means to achieve the same goals. Such students might cheat by using cribs or by having other students take their exams for them. In rare instances, students have been known to gain access to the institution's office of records and to alter grades. This illustration of innovative adaptation to the norms also shows that individuals can accept socially approved goals while deviating from the norms in order to achieve the goals.

Retreatism as Deviation

Retreatism is a form of deviance because the individual abandons *both* cultural goals and the means for attaining them. Suppose that an individual has internalized success goals but then finds that he or she cannot achieve them through legitimate means. Such an individual then stops trying to be successful and even rejects the value of the goals that had previously been internalized. Sociologically, such individuals become "true aliens." "Defeatism, quietism and resignation are manifested in escape mechanisms which ultimately lead him to 'escape' from the requirements of the society" (Merton, 1968). Suicide is the ultimate form of retreatism. Other forms of retreatism manifested in American society include alcoholism, drug addiction, and some forms of mental illness. The retreatist in Academe would be a student who has ceased to care about grades and who sees little value in studying or in taking examinations. This individual becomes a nonstudent, a dropout (Cuzzort, 1969). According to the anomie theory, retreatism is a form of deviance in which the socially disinherited neither seek the conventional rewards held out by society nor suffer the frustrations that ordinarily accompany the striving for socially defined success.

Rebellion as Deviation

Rebellion is a form of deviance in which the individual rejects conventional cultural goals. Those who rebel hope to establish a new social structure. They seek to change the standards of success. Many observers of history and social movements have noted that "it is typically members of a rising class rather than the most depressed strata who organize the resentful and the rebellious [individuals] into a revolutionary group" (Merton, 1968). Much of the social unrest of the late 1960s was started by college students. The students were much better off than the minorities whose plight was part of the students' reasons for rebellion against the status quo. As we look back on those explosive years of the late 1960s, we can see how differently today's students behave. With some exceptions, the majority of college students today are mostly concerned with success in college as a means to occupational success. Still, one cannot be sure how long this attitude will prevail.

In the *Merry Month of May*, a novel by James Jones that centers on the French student rebellion of 1968, the theme of anomie expressed through rebellion is treated candidly. In one scene in the novel, a young man responds to his liberal father's remark about being proud of his son's participation in the student rebellion. His response provides insight into the reasoning of the rebellious young man who had rejected the conventional cultural goals and who now hoped to establish a new social structure.

"You're proud of me!" the boy cried. "What do I care whether you're proud of me! You, with your money, rich, and writing all those crappy films you write! Look at you, all of you: sitting there boozing it up! Boozers! Lushheads! Getting fat in the

Retreatism.

belly and fat in the mind! With your old Louis Treize and your ritzy apartment! You're proud of me! After what your generation did to the world?" . . .

"Hypocrites! Absolute hypocrites, all of you! Well, we're going to pull you down. Pull the whole damn society down. Down around your ears. We haven't got anything to put in its place yet, but something good—something better than what exists—has got to happen." He caught a breath. "Oh, what's the use of trying to explain anything to you? Old phonies like you?"

(Jones, 1970)

Ritualism as Deviation

Many people seem to accept things just as they are without making any real effort to pursue cultural goals described as desirable. Ritualism is behavior characterized by people simply going through the motions on a day-to-day basis. Life becomes routine. The person observes the social norms without seeking the cultural goals. Are such people deviants or are they simply conformists? Merton defined ritualism as a form of deviant behavior, but he acknowledged that ritualists are often not labeled as deviant. Imagine a person who appears on the job on time every working day. The person occupies a desk and shuffles through papers, following all the rules and regulations. But the person does not care about advancement or even how well the job is done. This is ritualism. More recently the term *burnout* has been used to describe what Merton calls ritualism.

THE LABELING THEORY OF DEVIANCE

According to this theory of deviance, a social group or a society creates deviance by making the rules which, when broken, define the breaker of the rules as a deviant. The group or society applies these rules to particular people and then labels them as outsiders. Deviant behavior is behavior that people so label (Becker, 1963). Consistent with the labeling theory of deviance are the following observations.

Deviance is not a property inherent in certain forms of behavior; it is a property conferred upon these forms by the audiences which directly or indirectly witness them. Sociologically, then, the critical variable is the social audience . . . since it is the audience which eventually decides whether or not any given action or actions will become a visible case of deviation.

(Erikson, 1962)

It should be clear, then, that whether or not an act is considered deviant depends upon how other people react to it. It depends on how people label the act. One writer has pictured what might happen in a classroom situation if a student were to admit publicly that he had stolen a car or committed a burglary without anyone ever knowing that he had done so. His classmates would probably respond without much ado over this admission of a past crime of which he was never officially accused. Suppose the same student had admitted to the act and added that he had been imprisoned as a result of being caught and found guilty. The reaction of his classmates could be different. The *act* would have been the same, but society's labeling of the person as a guilty criminal could cause the classmates to see other undesirable characteristics not noticed previously (Clinard, 1968).

We have said that according to the labeling theory of deviance a deviant is one to whom that label has successfully been applied. Accepting this interpretation of deviance is to accept the following two points:

1. The only thing that we can be sure people who have been labeled deviant share in common is the experience of being so labeled. Beyond that we cannot be certain. (This is not an attempt to deny that most people convicted of larceny have, in all probability, stolen something. But so have all of us. The key question is why some thieves become known as criminals and others—the rest of us—do not.)

2. This being the case, whether a given act is deviant depends not upon the nature of the act but upon how other people react to it (McGee, 1973).

This labeling approach brings with it a different conception of deviant behavior than the more traditional approaches, which focused on the deviant behavior itself. The labeling theory places the spotlight on the actors and the way in which they perceive one another (Gibbs, 1966). People are continually rating, scaling, and labeling those around them. Some statuses override all other statuses and are given certain priorities. In the United States, race has been a special status. To be a black American has been given more attention when considering an individual than have other statuses of the same individual such as social class, occupation, education, or sex. "The fact that one is a physician or middle class or female will not protect one from being treated as [black-American] first and any of these other things second" (Becker, 1963). And so it is with the status of deviant. Howard S. Becker (1928–   ) describes the significance of deviant status as follows.

One receives the status as a result of breaking a rule, and the identification proves to be more important than most others. One will be identified as a deviant first, before other identifications are made. The question is raised: "What kind of person would break such an important rule?" And the answer is given: "One who is different from the rest of us, who cannot or will not act as a moral human being and therefore might break other important rules." The deviant identification becomes the controlling one.

Once an individual's social status becomes that of deviant first, human being second, changes are likely to occur in the individual's self-image. The deviant comes to think of self as deviant and finds it increasingly difficult to return to a conventional status. Some sociologists have compared the labeling experience with that of the self-fulfilling prophecy, a situation in which a person or a group is described to have certain characteristics and then begins to display the characteristics that were said to exist.

(Becker, 1963)

At the front of Howard S. Becker's *Outsiders: Studies in the Sociology of Deviance* appears a selection from William Faulkner's *As I Lay Dying*, and it may be the perfect literary explanation of what Becker and other sociologists are saying when they discuss what is called the labeling theory of deviance:

Sometimes I ain't so sho who's got ere a right to say when a man is crazy and when he ain't. Sometimes I think it ain't none of us pure crazy and ain't none of us pure sane until the balance of us talks him that-a-way. It's like it ain't so much what a fellow does, but it's the way the majority of folks is looking at him when he does it.

THE GROUP-SUPPORT THEORY OF DEVIANCE

We refer to a special type of subculture in Section 9 that is called contraculture. Contracultures are subcultures that clash with and contradict the attitudinal and behavioral norms of society at large. Nonconformity to the norms of society at large is typical of those individuals belonging to contracultures. (Some sociologists use the term *counterculture* in the same way in which we are using the term *contraculture*.) Contracultures encourage their members to behave in ways that are interpreted as deviant by society at large.

According to the group-support theory of deviance, individuals commit deviant acts because they have learned supporting beliefs and values from a contraculture. This is the same way that people learn to conform to conventional beliefs and values from subcultures that support the total society. Individuals also are encouraged in their deviant behavior by agreement with and approval of fellow members of the contraculture. A contraculture is essentially a "community of deviants" who have in common attitudes and behaviors that are subject to penalty by the larger society (Cohen, 1966).

For a contraculture to develop and survive within the total society, it is necessary for individuals to interact with one another and to discover that they do have common values and interests. These common values and interests deviate in ways that are not acceptable to the total society. The deviant individual must rationalize in some meaningful way his or her willingness to accept the deviant norms rather than the norms of the total society (Bell, 1971). As one authority put it:

The acquisition of status within the new group is accompanied by a loss of status outside the group. To the extent that the esteem of outsiders is of value to the members of the group a new problem is engendered. To this problem the typical solution is to devalue the good will and respect of those whose good will and respect are forfeit anyway.

(Cohen, 1955)

Realizing and accepting the fact that one has become a member of a recognizable deviant *group* has a powerful impact on one's conception of oneself. For example, a drug addict revealed that the moment she felt she was really "hooked" was when she realized that she no longer had friends who were not drug addicts (Becker, 1963).

According to the group-support theory of deviance, the individual receives support for his or her deviant behavior from fellow members of the deviant group—the contraculture. Moving into the deviant group provides one with the means to carry on deviant activity with a minimum of trouble. Problems to be faced in evading the total society's social controls have been faced before by others in the deviant group. The means to deal with threats from society at large have been found. For example, young thieves meet older thieves who have had enough experience so that they can explain how to get rid of stolen merchandise while avoiding the risk of being caught. "Every deviant group has a great stock of lore on such subjects and the new recruit learns it quickly" (Becker, 1963).

KEY TERMS AND NAMES FROM SECTION 11

anomie

anomie theory of deviance

innovation

retreatism

rebellion

ritualism

labeling theory of deviance

act, actor, and social audience

self-fulfilling prophecy

group-support theory of deviance

contraculture

counterculture

Robert K. Merton

Howard S. Becker

STUDY GUIDE FOR SECTION 11

1. NAME THE THREE SOCIOLOGICAL THEORIES OF DEVIANCE MEN-TIONED IN THE TEXT.

2. Particular subgroups in American society have higher rates of deviance than the general population. EXPLAIN WHY THIS IS SO.

3. In the text we selected four possible types of individual adaptations to culturally defined goals when legitimate means to cultural goals are blocked. Each type of adaptation is a form of deviant behavior according to the anomie theory. NAME THE FOUR TYPES.

4. According to the anomie theory, retreatism is a form of deviance in which an individual abandons both the cultural goals and the means for attaining them. CITE AT LEAST TWO EXAMPLES OF INDIVIDUAL RETREATISM.

5. The anomie theory includes rebellion as a form of deviance. EXPLAIN HOW INDIVIDUAL REBELLION CAN BE INTERPRETED TO BE A TYPE OF ADAPTA-TION TO CULTURALLY DEFINED GOALS WHEN LEGITIMATE MEANS TO CULTURAL GOALS ARE BLOCKED.

6. According to the labeling theory of deviance, behavior is considered deviant depending upon how others react to it. Deviant behavior is behavior that people so label. WHAT REACTIONS ARE APT TO OCCUR WITHIN AN INDIVIDUAL WHO HAS BEEN LABELED A DEVIANT?

7. The labeling approach to studying deviance allows for a different conception of deviant behavior than the more traditional approaches. HOW DOES HOWARD S. BECKER DESCRIBE THE SIGNIFICANCE OF DEVIANT STATUS FROM THE VIEWPOINT OF THOSE WHO DO THE LABELING?

8. Nonconformity to the norms of society at large is typical of individuals belonging to contracultures. ACCORDING TO THE GROUP-SUPPORT THEORY OF DEVIANCE, WHY DO INDIVIDUALS COMMIT DEVIANT ACTS?

9. The group-support theory of deviance contends that individuals receive support for their deviant behavior from fellow members of the deviant group. EXPLAIN HOW THIS AFFECTS ONE'S CONCEPTION OF SELF AND HOW THE DEVIANT GROUP SUPPORTS THE DEVIANT INDIVIDUAL.

PRACTICE TEST FOR SECTION 11

Select the best answer.

1. Anomie is a French word that means
A. Despair.
B. Fulfillment.
C. Normlessness.
D. Conformity.

2. Deviance results from an absence of or confusion about social norms according to the
A. Anomie theory.
B. Group-support theory.
C. Labeling theory.
D. All of the above.

3. A person who accepts both the cultural goals of society and the socially approved means for achieving those goals is exhibiting
A. Innovation.
B. Retreatism.
C. Conformity.
D. Rebellion.

4. Using unconventional means for achieving socially approved goals is an example of
A. Conformity.
B. Innovation.
C. Ritualism.
D. Retreatism.

5. A student who uses illegitimate means to achieve high grades is exhibiting
A. Conformity.
B. Innovation.
C. Ritualism.
D. Rebellion.

6. The ultimate form of retreatism is
A. Suicide.
B. Alcoholism.
C. Drug addiction.
D. Mental illness.

7. A student who sees little value in studying and has stopped caring about grades is
A. An innovator.
B. A conformist.
C. A ritualist.
D. A retreatist.

8. One who rejects cultural goals and seeks to establish a new social structure is exhibiting
A. Innovation.
B. Ritualism.
C. Rebellion.
D. Retreatism.

9. Whether or not an act is considered deviant depends upon how other people react to it. This is according to the
A. Anomie theory.
B. Labeling theory.
C. Group-support theory.

10. Who of the following is associated with the anomie theory?
A. Robert Merton.
B. Howard S. Becker.
C. Max Weber.
D. Carol Kilgus.

11. Who of the following is associated with the labeling theory?
A. Robert Merton.

B. Howard S. Becker
C. Max Weber.
D. All of the above.

12. The most important variable in the labeling process is the
A. Act.
B. Actor.
C. Audience.
D. Behavior of the deviant.

13. A contraculture is a community of

A. Deviants
B. Individualists.
C. Conformists.
D. Both A and C.

14. A person commits deviant acts because such behavior was learned within a contraculture. This view is consistent with the
A. Anomie theory.
B. Labeling theory.
C. Group-support theory.

Answer Key

1.	C	**8.**	C
2.	A	**9.**	B
3.	C	**10.**	A
4.	B	**11.**	B
5.	B	**12.**	C
6.	A	**13.**	D
7.	D	**14.**	C

SECTION 12   TWO DEVIANT SUBCULTURES
- PIMPING AND PROSTITUTION
- SKID ROW
- APPLYING THE THREE SOCIOLOGICAL THEORIES OF DEVIANCE

Objectives

After completing this section, the student should be able to:

1. Describe the life-style of pimps and prostitutes.
2. Describe the life-style of Skid Row.
3. Apply the anomie, labeling, and group-support theories to the pimping and prostitution life-style.
4. Apply the anomie, labeling, and group-support theories to the Skid Row life-style.

When discussing the varieties of subcultures in Section 9, we described two black-American life-styles identified by sociologist Jessie Bernard. One is called the "internally acculturated," and the other is called the "externally adapted." The externally adapted are described as people who have not really internalized the social norms of the total American culture. However, they can and do adapt themselves to society's demands when necessary. At the time we discussed these two black-American life-styles, we said that the white majority also has its externally adapted segment that is involved in deviant behavior. In this section we describe two deviant subcultures that approximate the characteristics of those whom Bernard defined as the externally adapted. People who participate in the subcultures of pimps and prostitutes and of Skid Row can and do adapt themselves to some of the conventional values and behavior patterns of the total American culture. In fact, a case can be made that these deviant subcultures are as much "threads" of the American culture fabric as any other types of subcultures making up the total American culture. The people described in this section are not eager to overthrow the established social order. They are simply people who have chosen life-styles that deviate from the social norms of society at large.

PIMPING AND
PROSTITUTION   People who visit or who live in large cities catch fleeting glimpses of flashy men in ornate cars and of women on street corners offering sexual activities for money. What is to most people a mysterious and private world of a pimp and his women is graphically described in a photojournalistic study by Susan Hall and Bob Adelman entitled *Gentleman of Leisure: A Year in the Life of a Pimp.* (All quoted passages in this subsection are reprinted by permission of the New

American Library, Inc.) In an "Author's Note" at the beginning of their book, Hall and Adelman write:

Gentleman of Leisure *documents the private life of a pimp and his prostitutes. The people who appear in the photographs are not models. Only names have been changed to protect the "guilty."*

To our knowledge, this clandestine world has never before been penetrated by camera and tape recorder. . . .

Our central concern was the bond that joins a pimp and his women: why a girl voluntarily selects a pimp and stays with him after she has chosen. We wondered what this pimp had that made prostitutes, who are so shrewd with men in their work, give up all their money and dedicate themselves to him.

We agree with Hall and Adelman when they claim that the values and attitudes revealed in this study "are widely shared by pimps and whores and are representative of this way of life." Pimps and prostitutes participate in a life-style that is unquestionably an alternative to what they would call the "straight world."

A pimp is a man to whom prostitutes give their earnings. A pimp's women are called his "wives," and the relationship of one pimp's woman to another of his women is described as "wife-in-law." The customers of the prostitutes are called "tricks," "Johns," "dates," or simply "customers." A successful pimp has a "bottom woman," who is the woman who has been with him for the longest time, who has earned special status and privileges, and who is entrusted with certain responsibilities. When a woman decides she will work for a particular pimp, the decision is called "choosing," Each pimp is said to have a "game," which is the pimp's strategy in manipulating his women. The "game" can be sexual prowess, romantic emphasis, threats of physical violence, maintaining a woman's drug addiction, or any variety of such "games."

Hall and Adelman's study of a year in the life of a pimp named Silky offers a specific documentary that is representative of an alternate life-style engaged in by pimps and their prostitutes. The average pimp has two women, but Silky has seven or eight working for him during the year covered in the study. His women pick up customers in bars and on the streets. A successful pimp does not have to keep a close watch on his women, says Silky:

"I used to drive around and watch the girls. A lot of fellows try to keep their girls in check. Occasionally, I'll drive around to see if there's an unhappy lady who belongs to another fellow. You can get girls that way. You invite them to breakfast, and if they're impressed or sad, they might even say yes. But checking my own — I have too much respect for them. I know they give me all their money. My girls would not stash. Money's not that important. It's just necessary and part of living in the world as well as we do."

Silky is a successful pimp by his own admission, and by the evaluations made of him by the women who work for him:

"Silky puts all his time into being a ladies' man. Another guy has to go to work. Silky dedicates his energies to pleasing us. Whatever he does, it's for us. Him and us together. If I was really unhappy, he'd try and get me happy."

"The term is pimp, but I don't use it," says Silky. "I'm a professional gentleman of leisure. I have absolutely nothing to do. I stay in bed and take showers. I'm just a connoisseur of resting and a television freak. I do make more money than the President of the United States. If I were in another way of life, I'd have to hustle more. As a black man, I've never had alternatives anyway. I could have played first base, run the mile, or become an entertainer, but I was a natural pimp, so I just pursued my talents."

". . . He had six white women and his Eldorado and he'd been making very good money. He's certainly one of New York's biggest pimps. Maybe the most successful. But that didn't impress me. I was only going to stay for a weekend.

"I stayed for two weeks and we went out every single night — to clubs and after-hours spots. Silky didn't get me through sex. We spent time together, we had fun. That's why I began to like him. Then I chose."

This life-style of the pimp–prostitute world appears to be crass and strictly materialistic to most outsiders. However, there does seem to be evidence that unconventional primary relationships do develop between the pimp and his women and between the women who work together for the same pimp.

Silky says that the relationship between a pimp and a whore is also a personal relationship between a man and a woman and that money is only part of the reason why they continue their relationship. In fact, Silky says that "Our personal relationship is number one. Money is a part of that relationship because money is a rule and a law of life." Some insights to these personal relationships are provided in the following remarks made by Silky and by some of his women:

"If a girl is interested in building a life with me, then I can make an investment in her and give her a foundation. She gets an apartment and presents on her birthday, Christmas, and our anniversary. The relationship builds. . . .

After we've been together for a year or so, a dedication is built. Loyalty and understanding creates a kind of love in me. It becomes complete man-woman."

"My devotion makes Silky stick to me. I've earned that. It may not be love on his part, but it's loyalty and a closeness that comes from being through a lot . . . together.

"Recently, there've been weeks and months when I haven't seen Silky. . . . Still I talk to him every day — sometimes for hours. We stay close and personal. Of course, we don't have much sex. But sex with Silky isn't personal, because you know he's having sex with all the other girls. In this business, sex becomes unimportant. It's just there. You have to do a lot of growing up to realize this."

"I sincerely try to have a personal relationship with every girl. If we continue to be together, we progress. I try to make ladies out of women. I train them, I give them my style. They're to please me. I never have to speak more than once. . . . I emphasize the emotional aspect and the development of our personal and social relationship."

"Silky's other girls are my wives-in-law. They refer to me as 'Mother.' I've been with Silky the longest, and they discuss their problems with me when Silky's busy. I try to help them understand him. I want to help him by making the girls stick. You

might think I'd be jealous—me being in love with Silky and his having other women. I'm not. I accept the fact that he's a pimp. That automatically means he has other women."

Silky says that he can provide a woman with a "foundation." He cites how he provides apartments and presents for his women. He pays their telephone bills, and he bails them out of jail when that is necessary. The personal relationships that exist between Silky and his women provide a day-to-day feeling of security for the women. Silky even speaks of a potential future for the women who work for him. The women also allude to this future time when the personal aspects of the relationships will remain, while the present-day occupational roles change. One of Silky's women says:

"When I leave him after a fight, I might have four hundred dollars. I check into a hotel. Less the money I pay for the hotel, I buy a few things and when my money runs out, I call Silky. I'm basically lazy. I have to have a pimp to make money. If I'm by myself, I make just enough to get by. I don't have nothing. If I go to jail, I don't get out. If I get sick for a couple of weeks and my rent's due, I can't pay it. With Silky, I have financial security. He takes care of these expenses. . . . I feel very dependent on Silky. I feel helpless. I'm scared that I might be so totally dependent on him I won't be able to do things for myself. . . . He puts it in my head that I can't make it without him. I'm really believing him."

Silky is 25 years old. Most of his women are younger than he is, although one—his "bottom woman"—is 27. Evidence of this future orientation of togetherness is expressed by the 27-year-old prostitute:

"I won't be working much longer—a year or a couple of years. Then Silky will get me a beauty parlor. That's what I want. I could make good money and I'm so tired of tricks. Silky won't be in this forever. Old pimps are really ridiculous. But I'll continue to support him, even when he stops, and I don't care how many women he has or who's his favorite for the moment. I have a place in his life.

"Silky and me trust each other. We have the most mature relationship either of us has ever had. . . .

"I'm trying to get Silky organized. He's always lived for today, but he's beginning to think about tomorrow. Last year, he ran through over three hundred thousand dollars. I can't say where it went. It's not his style to think about saving and investing in business."

About the future, Silky says:

"Most people in the life don't plan. They think they can always pimp and always be a prostitute. Suddenly it's all over and they have to get a job. I plan to buy businesses and get out in ten years. If not sooner.

"If Sandy's by my side to help me, she'll come right along. I plan to buy her a large beauty salon. Something she would enjoy. If she continued in the business, she'd keep her phone and give her dates to the other little girls I had. She'd madam *on the side. Girls who get older and stay in the life become madams; others get their own businesses."*

Silky and his women live in New York. Their life-style is hardly typical of the total American culture, so we call it a deviant subculture. Still, by reading the excerpts from *Gentleman of Leisure*, it should be apparent that Silky and his women are participant members of American society. Their interests in consuming goods and services produced by the total culture are not unlike those of the majority of Americans. Their preoccupation with relationships with their significant others—in this case the significant others are other pimps and prostitutes—are not unlike the preoccupations of the majority of Americans. They think and speak of love, loyalty, work, and rewards. As Silky says, "I'm also a human being. I bleed. I sweat. I feel." As we said in our discussion of Jessie Bernard's externally adapted life-style, those who spend their talents in illegal activities often exhibit the same level of imagination and enterprise as those engaged in legitimate activities. Their imaginations and their energies lead them into activities and provoke feelings that are both similar to and dissimilar from those of other Americans who do not occupy themselves with pimping and prostitution. As we have said previously, the American design for living has been created by threading together diverse strands that we call values. Together, these diverse strands make up the real culture. Silky and his women and those who share "the life" with them are engaging in a deviant life-style. At the same time, they are contributing to the cultural fabric that is the American design for living.

SKID ROW

The term *Skid Row* is used to describe a certain area of any large city in the United States that attracts homeless men who have no commitment to the work ethic. The men are involved in a life-style in which drinking alcohol is the major motivation for living from one day to the next. Originally, the term used was *Skid Road*, a name that originated in Seattle, Washington. It was used to describe a street down which logs were skidded to the sawmill. It was a street lined with flophouses, taverns, and gambling houses (Spradley, 1970). Skid Road attracted transients, criminals, and chronic alcoholics. Today "Skid Row" represents not only a specific area in any large city but also a way of life. Various terms have been used by both sociologists and lay people to describe those who participate in the life-style of Skid Row. They have been called bums, winos, lushes, smokehounds, vagrants, tramps, drunks, hobos, panhandlers, and down-and-outers. The following paragraph is based on a passage written by James P. Spradley in an article entitled "Down and Out on Skid Road" (Spradley, 1972). Anyone who has been near the center of any large American city is apt to have seen such a man and to have asked such questions of oneself.

Picture a man moving slowly down the street. Everything about him suggests to the world that he is down and out. His poorly fitting clothes cover a hollow chest and sagging muscles. He wears a faded hat, shoes cracked with age and exposure to weather. His face is lined so that he seems older than he actually is. A half-empty bottle bulges in his topcoat pocket. His sports jacket and trousers are wrinkled and dirty and probably were purchased from a secondhand clothing store. His walk is unsteady, his face unshaven, and those who pass him detect the odor of cheap wine. From time to time he stretches out his hand toward the people passing by—those who have entered his world this morning from distant suburbs. Those to whom the hand is stretched and those who smell the odor of cheap wine wonder about the man. Who is he? Should he he pitied? Should he be jailed? Is he a homeless man in need of rehabilitation? Is he an alcoholic in need of medical treatment? From the outsider's point of view the man is obviously down on his luck and adrift at the bottom of society.

A closer look at this man and the thousands like him who can be found in large American cities reveals a life-style focused upon obtaining and consuming alcohol. The man is not a loner nor a social isolate. He and those with whom he associates live as social beings within a subculture of their own. It is a subculture that

prescribes and provides mutual aid in meeting the problems of survival: food, drink, shelter, illness, and protection. But more than that it is a society that also provides the emotional support found in the acceptance by, and the companionship of, fellow human beings.

(Peterson and Maxwell, 1958).

On Skid Row heavy drinking is a group experience. Skid Rowers place strong emphasis on group drinking, and the completely acculturated drunk is by definition a conformist. The drunk on Skid Row has rejected the established values of the total culture and conforms to the basic values of the Skid Row subculture. The group's need for alcohol is more important than matters relating to food, shelter, clothing, employment, and health. Because Skid Row is the drunk's total social world, it alone grants him any status, acceptance, and security that he may possess. The condemnation of the community at large and the approval of his drinking companions on Skid Row combine with his habituated desire for drinking to structure the Skid Rower's life-style around alcohol. "In his own eyes as well as in the eyes of others, Skid Rowers and nonskid rowers alike, he has become a totally committed member of a deviant group" (Wallace, 1965).

One excerpt in Samuel E. Wallace's *Skid Row as a Way of Life* describes the behavior of a small bottle gang who provide each other with emotional support and companionship that is not unusual among members of Skid Row. Wallace describes a group of men who sit on the ground and discuss such things as the merits of wine and the dependability or generosity of certain members of the group. Systematically they consume at least six bottles of wine. While killing off a bottle each man would take a swallow, hold the bottle, and then pass it on when another would hold out his hand. They would praise each other for not taking too much from the bottle at one swallow, and they would especially praise a member of the group who would get up and stagger off to buy another bottle of wine. That bottle gang was a primary group (See Glossary).

Skid Row.

Walking through or along the fringes of Skid Row, an outsider can see individual men standing in doorways of deserted stores or buildings, sitting with backs against walls, or lying on the sidewalk in full view of everyone in drunken sleep. An outsider is apt to conclude that here is one human being who is completely out of touch with the rest of the human race, but such is not usually the case. Most Skid Rowers are known to most of their kind in the area. They speak when they pass one another. They argue with one another, and they help one another. The fear of being picked up as vagrants is ever present, and the Skid Rower who has not spent some time in jail is a rarity. In cold weather, Skid Rowers try to accumulate enough money to sleep on a narrow cot in one of the flophouses in the area. When the weather is mild and the police are not cracking down, the Skid Rower prefers to find a doorway and a piece of cardboard for sleeping accommodations. Money is obtained by Skid Rowers by means of begging, collecting wastepaper in pushcarts for local rag and paper dealers, and by taking other odd jobs that might appear on a day-to-day basis. The writers of this text have given money to Bowery "residents" who have cleaned our windshields when our cars were stopped at traffic lights in New York City. We have also given away coins to Skid Rowers who hang around the waterfront section of Baltimore City. Some Skid Rowers steal, and they say that they have little difficulty peddling on the street the things they have stolen. Tools, transistor radios, shirts, and other clothing are all said to be items that can be sold fast on the street (Spradley, 1972).

Because the life-style of the Skid Row subculture is offensive to most Americans, the inhabitants of Skid Row have developed their own plans for survival. "They have adopted a nomadic style of life—moving from one urban center to another to maximize their freedom. In spite of their efforts, sooner or later, most tramps find themselves arrested. . . ." (Spradley and McCurdy, 1971). This aspect of the Skid Row life-style is especially well documented and described in James P. Spradley's *You Owe Yourself a Drunk: An Ethnography of Urban Nomads*. In jail or on the street, the participants in the life-style of Skid Row are unquestionably a deviant subculture in the view of the total American culture.

In the summer of 1980 an unusual reaction to this life-style occurred in San Francisco. *Newsweek* described the occasion:

A band played, there was speechmaking and food—and several of the honored guests stood by, guzzling cheap wine from the bottle. It was the opening last week of "Wino Park," a 5,000-square-foot sanctuary specially designed for about 400 neighborhood alcoholics in San Francisco's sleazy South of Market district. The idea was fostered by a community-oriented Methodist church, Glide Memorial, which consulted the winos themselves before turning a vacant lot into a park featuring galvanized-steel "sleeping tubes" and wide-body benches for cozy reclining. "It's ours, we'll keep it clean," vows habitué Robert (Bird) Yarborough. Some problems, however, were evident on opening day: a false rumor of a stabbing in the park buzzed through the ceremonies, and the loungers felt betrayed when police arrested two of them for drinking. Yet most people seem to like the idea. Says area resident Bill McGee: "I feel safer with them in there than when they're jammin' me for a penny every time I walk down the street."

(*Newsweek*, July 7, 1980)

APPLYING THE THREE SOCIOLOGICAL THEORIES OF DEVIANCE

Recall the three sociological theories of deviance discussed in the previous section. The anomie theory's innovation, the labeling theory, and the group-support theory can each be used to account for the life-style of pimping and prostitution. The anomie theory's retreatism, the labeling theory, and the group-support theory can each be used to account for the life-style of Skid Row. Do you see how these theories can be applied to deviant subcultures?

KEY TERMS
FROM
SECTION 12

pimp

prostitute

wife-in-law

bottom woman

choosing

a deviant life-style

Skid Road

Skid Row

group drinking

bottle gang

primary group

STUDY GUIDE FOR SECTION 12

1. The life-style of the pimp–prostitute world appears crass and strictly materialistic to most outsiders. Silky claims that money is only part of the reason a pimp and whore work together. WHAT OTHER REASONS FOR STAYING TOGETHER IN "THE LIFE" ARE GIVEN BY SILKY AND THE PROSTITUTES WHO WORK FOR HIM?

2. Silky says that he provides a woman with a "foundation." EXACTLY WHAT DOES SILKY PROVIDE ON A DAY-TO-DAY BASIS?

3. Silky and his women speak of a potential future which they will have when they have left "the life." WHAT DO THEY PLAN FOR THE FUTURE?

4. Silky and his women live in New York City. Their life-style is hardly typical of the total American culture. We call it a contraculture or a deviant subculture. DESPITE THIS, WHAT EVIDENCES ARE THERE THAT SILKY AND HIS WOMEN DO PARTICIPATE IN SPECIFIC ASPECTS OF AMERICAN CULTURE?

5. Skid Row is an area of any large city in the United States that attracts a certain type of man. DESCRIBE THE ATTITUDES AND MAJOR MOTIVATION FOR THOSE WHO RESIDE IN SKID ROW.

6. Various terms have been used to describe those who participate in the life-style of Skid Row. LIST AT LEAST FIVE SUCH TERMS.

7. From an outsider's point of view, a man of Skid Row is down on his luck and adrift at the bottom of society. EXPLAIN WHY THIS VIEW DOES NOT ADEQUATELY DESCRIBE THE SOCIAL CIRCUMSTANCES OF LIFE ON SKID ROW. REFER TO THE GROUP-SUPPORT THEORY.

8. On Skid Row heavy drinking is a group experience, and the completely acculturated drunk is by definition a conformist. IF SKID ROW IS A DEVIANT SUBCULTURE, WHY IS IT CORRECT TO CALL THE DRUNK A CONFORMIST?

9. Even those who participate in the life-style of Skid Row need money. HOW IS MONEY OBTAINED BY SKID ROWERS? WHAT IS MONEY USED FOR?

10. In the previous section we described three sociological theories of deviance. APPLY EACH OF THESE THEORIES TO THE LIFE-STYLES OF PIMPING AND PROSTITUTION AND OF SKID ROW.

PRACTICE TEST FOR SECTION 12

Select the best answer.

1. The book *Gentleman of Leisure* is associated with which deviant subculture?
A. Pimping and prostitution.
B. Counterculture.
C. Skid Row.
D. Contraculture.

2. Skid row as a deviant subculture represents which adaptation according to the anomie theory?
A. Retreatism.
B. Rebellion.
C. Innovation.
D. Ritualism.

3. The woman who has been with a pimp for the longest time and who has earned special status and privileges is known as a
A. Wife.
B. Common-law-wife.
C. Wife-in-law.
D. Bottom woman.

4. An area of a city that attracts homeless men who are involved in a life-style in which drinking alcohol is a major motivation is known as
A. The Bowery.
B. Ghetto.
C. Skid Row.
D. Flophouse.

5. According to anomie theory, pimping and prostitution represent which type of adaptation?
A. Ritualism.
B. Retreatism.
C. Innovation.
D. Rebellion.

6. According to Silky, a preferable term for "pimp" is
A. Raconteur.
B. Gentleman of leisure.
C. Connoisseur.
D. Masseur.

7. The relationship between Silky and his women provides a day-to-day feeling of security for the women. Sociologically, this type of relationship may be described as
A. Primary.
B. Secondary.
C. Tertiary.

8. It was said of the Skid Row lifestyle that it is a subculture that "prescribes and provides mutual aid in meeting the problems of survival: food, drink, shelter, illness, and protection ... it is a society that also provides the emotional support found in the acceptance by, and the companionship of, fellow human beings." Which theory of deviance best incorporates these ideas?

A. Anomie theory.

B. Labeling theory.

C. Group-support theory.

Answer Key

1.	A	5.	C
2.	A	6.	B
3.	D	7.	A
4.	C	8.	C

CHAPTER SUMMARY

1. Complete deviancy or total conformity is each an ideal-type situation in society. There is always some kind of deviant behavior within society. Conformity exists where a person's opinions and behavior coincide with prevailing values and behavior of social units with which the person identifies.

2. Deviant behavior represents a departure from social norms. Since deviance is relative there is no one behavior that is always considered to be deviant. Deviance represents some form of undesirable difference from the viewpoint of the majority of people within society.

3. Deviants can be seen in the following ways by the majority: as freak, as sinner, as boat-rocker, as sick or alienated person, and simply as a human being.

4. Three sociological theories of deviance provide insights into why people violate social norms. The anomie theory identifies innovation, retreatism, rebellion, and ritualism as patterns of deviancy. The labeling theory contends that a deviant is one to whom the label of deviant has been applied by the social audience. The group-support theory suggests that individuals commit deviant acts because they have learned the supporting beliefs and values from a contraculture.

5. Examples of contracultures cited in the book are the deviant subcultures of pimps and prostitutes and of Skid Row. Although deviants, people in these contracultures can and do adapt themselves to some of the conventional values of the total American culture.

6. The anomie theory's innovation, the labeling theory, and the group-support theory can each be used to account for the life-style of pimping and prostitution. The anomie theory's retreatism, the labeling theory, and the group-support theory can each be used to account for the life-style of Skid Row.

SUGGESTIONS FOR FURTHER READING RELATING TO CHAPTER 4

Aronson, Elliot, *The Social Animal* (San Francisco: W. H. Freeman, 1972). In Chapter 2, "Conformity," Aronson identifies variables that increase or decrease the likelihood of conformity. This chapter also summarizes findings of important empirical studies on conformity.

Becker, Howard S., editor, *The Other Side* (New York: The Free Press, 1967). Various sociologists discuss the relationship between deviant behavior and society. This is a good source for understanding the labeling theory of deviant behavior.

Cohen, Albert K., *Deviance and Control* (Englewood Cliffs, N.J.: Prentice-Hall, 1966). We especially recommend Chapter 7, "Introduction to Anomie Theory," and Chapter 8, "Group Support: What Are the Others Doing?"

Gibbs, Jack P., "Conceptions of Deviant Behavior: The Old and the New," *Pacific Sociological Review*, Vol. 9 (Spring 1966), pp. 9–14. This article summarizes two conceptions of deviance, giving concise descriptions and critiques of both approaches.

Glaser, Daniel, *Social Deviance* (Chicago: Markham, 1971). This work focuses on the variety of activity that has been directed toward social control of deviance. Glaser cites the six "R's" of social control: revenge, rejection, repression, restraint, rehabilitation, and reintegration.

Spiegel, Don, and Patricia Keith-Spiegel, editors, *Outsiders USA: Original Essays on 24 Outgroups in American Society* (San Francisco: Rinehart Press, 1973). This is a collection of essays classifying outsiders based on age, physical status, socioeconomic status, deviant behavior patterns, ethnicity, and occupational roles. The essays are refreshingly opinionated and well documented. The outsiders include such categories as the fetus, the physically disabled, the consumer, the homosexual, the black-American, the woman, the policeman, and others.

Chapter 5
Social Organization: Gemeinschaft and Gesellschaft

SECTION 13   TYPOLOGIES AS SOCIOLOGICAL TOOLS
- WHAT TYPOLOGIES ARE NOT
- WHY TYPOLOGIES ARE USEFUL
- IDEAL CONSTRUCTS, TYPOLOGIES, AND POLAR EXTREMES
- TYPOLOGIES OF TRADITIONAL AND MODERN SOCIETIES

Objectives
After completing this section, the student should be able to:
1. Explain why typologies are useful as sociological tools.
2. Draw an ideal construct and name the three parts.
3. Identify the typologies associated with Howard P. Becker, Robert Redfield, Emile Durkheim, and Ferdinand Tonnies.

*G*emeinschaft and *Gesellschaft* are two types of societies. In this section we show how societies can be classified and studied by using a tool of sociology called a *typology*. This tool is known by other terms such as *ideal type, pure type, constructed type, model, ideal construct*, and *mental construct*. All these terms refer to the same sociological tool. Sociologists might use any of the terms, depending on individual preference.

WHAT
TYPOLOGIES
ARE NOT

Typologies are not real. They are abstractions. An abstraction is an idea about an object or behavior. It is not a real object or a real behavior. When sociologists use typologies, they are not considering exact reality. Max Weber defined typologies as ideal (pure) types of social behavior that do not actually exist in reality. They are exaggerations of social reality (Weber, 1947, 1958). When we speak of traditional, folk societies, we speak only of exaggerations of societies that do not exist in reality. Likewise, when we speak of modern, mass societies, we speak only of exaggerations of societies that do not exist in reality. Nevertheless, keep this in mind: typologies *are* useful sociological tools.

WHY
TYPOLOGIES
ARE USEFUL

Typologies or ideal constructs help us to understand social circumstances. Physicists use a system of weights and measurements to understand and describe the physical world. If a physicist thinks of one horsepower in terms of raising 33,000 pounds one foot per minute or 550 pounds one foot per second, that is an example of using abstractions to understand physical things (Defleur et al., 1971). One cannot hold a horsepower, or pound, or foot, second, or minute in one's hand. They are abstractions created by minds to study reality. This is how sociologists use typologies. Typologies are useful because they help sociologists gain insights into real social circumstances and human relationships. To exaggerate is to magnify. To magnify is to see things more clearly. To see things more clearly is to be better informed. This is exactly why typologies are useful.

IDEAL CONSTRUCTS, TYPOLOGIES, AND POLAR EXTREMES

Sociologists have made many attempts to create typologies that can help us understand society and human relationships. It was Max Weber who developed the concept of the ideal type as a way to accentuate and exaggerate reality. Be sure that you understand that *ideal* does not mean *best* when it is used this way. When we speak of an ideal type (typology), we mean "idea in the mind." To create an ideal type, we should accentuate reality rather than describe it accurately. Again, typologies are abstractions of reality and not reality itself. A typology is a model used to examine real situations. In other words, "Here is the perfect model. Now let us see how close real-life situations come to the perfect model." That is what a sociologist could say when creating a typology.

One valuable use of typologies is to contrast two circumstances that are extremely different. Both of the two typologies are called polar extremes in this case. It was Sir Henry S. Maine (1822–1888) who first used ideal types as polar opposites or extremes (Maine, 1911). Our Diagram No. 2 is a drawing of an *ideal construct* that has not yet been put to use. Note that the ideal construct is made up of three parts. There are two *polar extremes* and one line that is called a *continuum*. A little further on, we shall use an ideal construct that treats actual social circumstances.

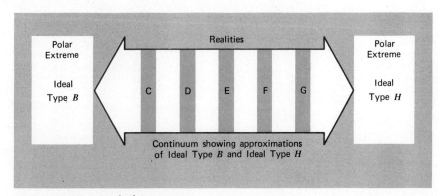

Diagram No. 2　An Ideal Construct

Diagram No. 2 shows two ideal types identified as *B* and *H*. They are the two polar extremes. Along the line called the continuum are other letters that come close to either "ideal" letter *B* or to "ideal" letter *H*. Of course, this diagram does not provide any information that makes sense. The letters of the alphabet are used only to complete the appearance of an ideal construct. The letters *B* and *H* represents typologies. The letters on the continuum represent situations of reality that fall between the two polar extremes. Now let us try to make clearer how typologies can be used in this way by discussing a real social practice, that of mate selection.

Methods of mate selection leading to marriage vary from one society to the next. We can identify two polar extremes of an ideal construct that represent two methods of selecting mates. The actual practice of these two extremes is rarely found in any society. Reality tends to alter the methods that are supposedly practiced in a society. The two polar extremes in reference to mate selection are:

1. Mate selection by mutual choice.

2. Mate selection by parental choice.

Mate selection.

The first, mate selection by mutual choice, suggests that a couple is completely free of outside influences when they decide to marry. It suggests that their selection of one another as mates results from their own reasonable (or unreasonable—romantic love being what it is) decision. The second, mate selection by parental choice, suggests that a couple is matched for marriage as a result of deliberations and decisions of their parents.

Let us consider five human groupings whose methods of mate selection can be placed on a continuum between the two polar extremes we have identified above. We are referring to practices of mate selection that have occurred during the 20th century. The ideal construct would look like Diagram No. 3.

Many Americans believe that the emphasis placed on compatibility and romantic attraction just about eliminates factors in mate selection other than mutual choice. However, whether conscious or unconscious, the attitudes and values learned from the family and the immediate pressure from the family continue to assert themselves as factors influencing mate selection in the United States. This is why we placed the Anglo-Americans near the pole of Mutual Choice but not at the pole. Moving across the continuum, we find that the rural Irish have had more opportunity for mutual choice than the Apache Americans. The Apache have had more freedom in mate selection than the Japanese and Indians. However, again note that no society is located at the other polar extreme of mate selection by Parental Choice. "In most such societies, the couple are at least consulted about the arrangement; and their own inclinations are, to some extent, respected—that is, they may exercise some veto power if their parents' choice is totally unacceptable to them." And this is why we placed no particular group at the pole of Parental Choice (Burgess et al., 1963; Saxton, 1979).

We hope that we have not confused anyone by this brief treatment of mate selection methods among various human groupings. Our purpose has been merely to cite an example of how an ideal construct can be used in reference to some real social phenomenon. We simply happened to choose mate selection as the subject to use with the poles and the continuum. Think of all the typologies we could consider as polar extremes and then of all the real types that could fit upon the continuum: patriot and traitor; upper class and lower class; rural and urban; saint and sinner; introvert and extrovert; radical and reactionary; Charlie Brown and Superman.

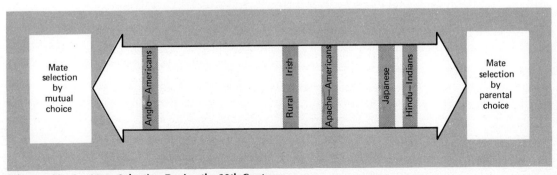

Diagram No. 3   Mate Selection During the 20th Century

TYPOLOGIES OF TRADITIONAL AND MODERN SOCIETIES

In this subtopic we describe some of the typologies created to examine the historic trend from small, traditional, rural societies to large, modern, industrial societies (McKinney and Loomis, 1963). We want to show the changes that have taken place in both social structure and human relationships. All of the following examples are not exactly alike, but they do have something in common. They all refer to dramatic differences that exist between traditional and modern societies. These typologies are exaggerations placed at polar extremes in each study. We could establish a continuum from each study upon which we could locate real societies.

Howard P. Becker's Sacred and Secular Societies

Becker (1899–1960) makes it clear that sacred and secular societies are typologies representing polar extremes. The sacred society is isolated from the rest of the world. It seeks to avoid contacts with the outside world. The in-group and out-group feelings are very strong (see Glossary). People emphasize specifics rather than generalities. Within the sacred community social contacts are characterized by intimacy. Tradition and rituals play an important part in the people's lives. Kinship ties are strong. Socialization through social controls occurs more through sacred sanctions than through threats of violence. Fear of gossip and ridicule are also effective social controls. Science is nonexistent. Superstition prevails.

At the opposite pole of Becker's continuum is the secular society. Tradition and rituals are at a minimum. Science is used as a powerful force to accomplish progress through change. In fact the very idea of progress dominates thinking. Sacred sanctions and informal social controls such as gossip and ridicule are not very effective. Formal laws act as social controls. Still, when someone breaks a law, the people usually do not react with strong social disapproval. Legal contracts are often the basis for agreements. Kinship ties are weak. A high value is placed upon individual achievements and individual rights.

Robert Redfield's Folk–Urban Continuum

Redfield's study emphasizes the characteristics of the ideal traditional folk society. His folk society is the polar opposite of modern industrial societies. Redfield says that his folk society is a typology and that no real society is exactly like it:

The type is an imagined entity, created only because through it we may hope to understand reality. Its function is to suggest aspects of real societies which deserve study, and [what] may be generally true about society.

(Redfield, 1947)

The folk society described by Redfield is small in population, containing no more people than can come to know each other well. Both culturally and physically it is isolated, preliterate, and homogeneous. The economy is independent of the outside world and does not tend to grow beyond the ability to maintain a subsistence level for the population. Technology is uncomplicated; sex and age are criteria for the division of labor. Traditional patterns of belief and behavior are subscribed to without question. Kinship ties are strong, and the family is the central unit of action. When people help each other, it is because family and community ties require it to such a degree that helping seems to be the natural thing to do. In a folk society people accept existing conditions as the way things should be. Stability and predictability are characteristic of life. Based on tradition, human interaction is spontaneous and personal. People are not motivated to be reflective, critical, or experimental. Redfield writes:

What is done in the ideal folk society is done not because somebody or some people decided, at once, that it should be done, but because it seems "necessarily" to flow from the very nature of things. There is, moreover, no disposition to reflect upon traditional acts and consider them objectively and critically. In short, behavior in the folk society is traditional, spontaneous, and uncritical.

(Redfield, 1947)

Redfield does not present a detailed description of the polar exteme of folk society, although he implies that it is urban life, composed of characteristics opposite of those of folk society. For example, whereas people of folk society would reject new ways by saying, "It has never been done thus," people of industrial society would be more likely to ask, "Does it work?" and then try the new way without further ado (Lerner, 1958).

Emile Durkheim's Mechanical Solidarity and Organic Solidarity

Emile Durkheim (1858–1917) studied the differences between traditional and modern societies just as Becker and Redfield and other social scientists have done. The term *solidarity* refers to a group's sense of unity and togetherness. Durkheim believed that the *division of labor* in a society influences the type of solidarity experienced by people. The term *mechanical solidarity* applies to a traditional society. The term *organic solidarity* applies to a modern society. These terms are unusual, but Durkheim's description of these two typologies is very similar to Becker's and Redfield's works.

Mechanical solidarity exists in a traditional society. There is little doubt about with whom an individual belongs. The division of labor is simple. Each man plays the same roles in about the same way as every other man. The same situation applies for women. The people are mentally and morally homogeneous. They share beliefs and values in common. There is an intense feeling of unity. This type of society is one pole of Durkheim's ideal construct.

The other polar extreme is modern society with its organic solidarity. Here people do not have strong feelings of unity. Instead of sharing bonds of kinship, the people merely function for one another's needs. Durkheim believed that industrialization had created specialists who depend on one another in only impersonal ways. Business people, for example, relate to each other as business associates only. This is true of private industry and also the large bureaucracies of modern governments. Relationships among people are limited to special interests and, therefore, are easily broken. Such relationships are interdependent only because each person functions as a specialist within an "organic system" that requires cooperation (Durkheim, 1933).

Ferdinand Tonnies' Gemeinschaft and Gesellschaft

Since the next two sections of this chapter describe both *Gemeinschaft* and *Gesellschaft* in detail, we will not do so here. Tonnies (1855–1936) used *Gemeinschaft* as the term for traditional society and *Gesellschaft* as the term for modern society. The terms apply to two types of social structures and to two types of human interaction. They are typologies that are also polar extremes.

There is a distinct contrast between social structure and human relationships in traditional societies and modern societies. Of all the terms used in sociology to contrast these two typologies, we prefer *Gemeinschaft* and *Gesellschaft*. These German words cannot be perfectly translated into English. Some sociologists do substitute the word *community* for *Gemeinschaft* and the word *society* for *Gesellschaft* (Loomis, 1963). As we describe *Gemeinschaft* in Section 14 and *Gesellschaft* in Section 15, we will draw upon the works of Becker, Redfield, Durkheim, Tonnies, and other writers who have contributed to the study of the changing human experience.

KEY TERMS AND NAMES FROM SECTION 13

typology	mechanical solidarity
abstraction	organic solidarity
polar extremes	*Gemeinschaft*
continuum	*Gesellschaft*
mate selection by mutual choice	Max Weber
mate selection by parental choice	Howard P. Becker
sacred and secular societies	Robert Redfield
folk–urban continuum	Emile Durkheim
division of labor	Ferdinand Tonnies

STUDY GUIDE FOR SECTION 13

1. Typologies are not real. They are exaggerations of social reality. EXPLAIN WHY AND HOW TYPOLOGIES ARE USEFUL TO SOCIOLOGISTS.

2. Sir Henry S. Maine first used ideal types as polar opposites. DRAW AN IDEAL CONSTRUCT AND IDENTIFY THE THREE PARTS.

3.   We refer to two practices of mate selection used by five groups during the 20th century. The five human groupings represent five different procedures for mate selection. WHY DID WE NOT PLACE ANY ONE GROUP EXACTLY IN ONE OF THE CATEGORIES OF MATE SELECTION?

4.   Howard P. Becker created two typologies representing two polar extremes of traditional and modern societies. NAME THE TWO TYPOLOGIES. IDENTIFY AT LEAST TWO DIFFERENCES THAT PLACE BECKER'S TYPOLOGIES AT POLAR EXTREMES.

5.   Robert Redfield focused his attention on traditional society. WHAT DID HE NAME TRADITIONAL SOCIETY? LIST AT LEAST FOUR CHARACTERISTICS OF REDFIELD'S FOLK SOCIETY.

6.   Emile Durkheim also wrote about how traditional and modern societies are different. WHAT TERMS DID HE USE? WHAT ONE FACTOR DID DURKHEIM BELIEVE INFLUENCED THE TYPE OF SOLIDARITY EXPERIENCED BY PEOPLE? WHAT DOES SOLIDARITY MEAN?

7.   Becker, Redfield, Durkheim, and Tonnies all used typologies to describe the trend from traditional to modern societies. IN YOUR OWN WORDS, DESCRIBE THE TWO POLAR EXTREMES THAT WE CALL TRADITIONAL AND MODERN SOCIETIES.

PRACTICE TEST FOR SECTION 13

Select the best answer.

1.   A typology is

A.   An exaggeration of a real social circumstance.

B.   An actual description of reality.

C.   A polar extreme that exists in reality.

D.   Only A and C.

2.   In an ideal construct, the line on which there are approximations of reality is called

A.   An ideal type.

B.   A continuum.

C.   A model.

D.   A mental construct.

3.   The phrases *mechanical* and *organic solidarity* are associated with

A.   Howard P. Becker.

B.   Robert Redfield.

C.   Emile Durkheim.

D.   Ferdinand Tonnies.

4.   The term *folk society* is associated with

A.   Howard P. Becker.

B.   Robert Redfield.

C.   Emile Durkheim.

D.   Ferdinand Tonnies.

5.   The terms *Gemeinschaft* and *Gesellschaft* are associated with

A.   Sir Henry S. Maine.

B.   Emile Durkheim.

C.   Ferdinand Tonnies.

D.   Max Weber.

6.   The phrases *sacred* and *secular societies* are associated with

A.   Howard P. Becker.

B.   Sir Henry S. Maine.

C. Robert Redfield.
D. None of the above.
7. Which of the following terms is associated with traditional societies?
A. Mechanical solidarity.
B. Organic solidarity.
C. Secular.
D. *Gesellschaft.*

8. According to Emile Durkheim, the factor that determines the type of solidarity in human societies is the
A. Strength of kinship ties.
B. Division of labor.
C. Level of literacy.
D. Types of social controls.

Answer Key

1. A
2. B
3. C
4. B
5. C
6. A
7. A
8. B

SECTION 14   GEMEINSCHAFT: TRADITIONAL, RURAL SOCIETY

- ASIMOV'S FICTIONAL PLANET OF ROSSEM
- SOCIAL STRUCTURE OF *GEMEINSCHAFT*
- HUMAN RELATIONSHIPS IN *GEMEINSCHAFT*

Objectives

After completing this section, the student should be able to:

1. Describe the importance of the family in the social structure of *Gemeinschaft.*
2. Describe how religion and education are experienced in *Gemeinschaft.*
3. Describe the social organization of economics in *Gemeinschaft.*
4. Explain how government activies occur within *Gemeinschaft.*
5. Define and give examples of primary groups.
6. Explain how a caste system creates ascribed statuses.
7. Describe human relationships within *Gemeinschaft.*

Through the years of human existence, there have been many different cultures among the societies of humankind. Still, these various cultures have also had certain similarities. Each society has had to meet human needs within the framework of a social structure. And, it seems, there is a relationship between the kind of social structure and the way human interaction occurs within a society.

In this section we describe both the social structure and the human relationships typical of *Gemeinschaft*, the traditional society. A traditional society is one in which legends, beliefs, and customs are handed down from one generation to another with little or no changes. Because things have been done the same way for so long, the folkways and mores have a sacred quality about them. Life moves on generation after generation without living standards or technology or values changing.

ASIMOV'S FICTIONAL PLANET OF ROSSEM

Gemeinschaft is a typology not to be found in pure form in reality. Such a society is approximated in science fiction by Isaac Asimov's description of a simple, rural planet of a galaxy existing far in the future. The following passage is from Asimov's *Second Foundation:*

Rossem is one of those marginal worlds usually neglected in Galactic history and scarcely ever obtruding itself upon the notice of men of the myriad happier planets. . . .

Along the chilly wastes of Rossem, villages huddled. Its sun was a small ruddy niggard that clutched its dribble of heat to itself, while snow beat thinly down for nine months of the year. The tough native grain lay dormant in the soil those snow-filled months, then grew and ripened in almost panic speed, when the sun's reluctant radiation brought the temperature to fifty.

Small, goatlike animals cropped the grasslands, kicking the thin snow aside with tiny, tri-hooved feet.

The men of Rossem had, thus, their bread and their milk—and when they could spare an animal—even their meat. The darkly ominous forests that gnarled their way over half of the equatorial region of the planet supplied a tough, fine-grained wood for housing. . . .

. . .Galactic history glided past peacefully enough, and the peasants scrabbled life out of the hard soil.

(Asimov, 1964)

We cite this brief selection from Asimov's fiction in order to set a mood or present a picture of what an isolated traditional society might be like.

SOCIAL STRUCTURE OF *GEMEINSCHAFT*

The ideal traditional society is small, both in the size of its population and in the amount of territory it occupies. Because it is isolated from other societies, little social change occurs from one generation to the next. The population is homogeneous in a genetic and in a cultural sense. Throughout their activities a profound sense of community is shared by the people. This can be seen in their uncritical and nonaggressive ways of social interaction. There is little evidence of social disorganization. There is little friction and conflict. Instead, there is much cooperation among the people and between the people and their social institutions. We have selected the following structural characteristics of *Gemeinschaft* to provide a picture of this polar extreme in human societies (Redfield, 1947; Bensman and Rosenberg, 1963; Hodges, 1971).

Family

The family is so important that it occupies the central place in the social structure of a traditional society. Families are dominated by the men—usually the eldest man if the family is extended to include adult brothers and sisters and cousins and their offspring too. Marriages are arranged by the family. Marriages are stable and last throughout the lifetimes of those so joined. Individuals receive social recognition from their family membership. On the other hand, the family can be shamed and sometimes punished for the misbehavior of a member. Most important, within traditional societies it is the family that is responsible for performing functions that maintain the existence of the community. Within the family circle, children are protected from bodily harm and provided with their basic needs. The family cares for the children in times of injury and illness.

Religious rituals and beliefs are introduced to the children within the family. And, of course, the family is the first agent of socialization. It must educate the children so that they can participate in the culture of *Gemeinschaft*. Finally, the family provides both the young and the old with a sense of identity. Each family has a fixed position that it known by all other members of the society. Men and women know who they are and how they are seen by others because of their age, sex, and birth order in their families.

Economics

In *Gemeinschaft* there is a simple level of technology. Economic skills are learned through imitation and practice. They are handed down from generation to generation with little or no change. The concept of progress is meaningless. Any surplus of food or any other supplies simply does not occur. Instead, a *subsistence economy* exists. This means that the economy provides only what is needed for survival at the moment. This is adequate much of the time, but droughts and pestilence can bring disaster. *Gemeinschaft* is nonindustrial. The main occupation is likely to be food gathering, hunting and fishing, flock-tending, or agriculture. Since the level of techology is low, the division of labor is simple, as Durkheim described it. Each man plays the same roles in about the same way as every other man, with the same being true for women. There is little or no economic competition, and mutual assistance is common. The one likely division of labor would be that based on sex roles, although that would not necessarily be true in societies whose economies depend upon agriculture for economic survival.

Religion

Gemeinschaft emphasizes the importance of tradition. The folkways and mores are expectations for behavior and are based upon sacred beliefs. The religion of *Gemeinschaft* is somehow present in all other areas of life. Religion is expressed through chants, oaths, dances, and elaborate ceremonies that are performed to bring good fortune. Religious observances are expected to provide more abundant game, better crops, good health, victory in war, long life, and fertility. To be fully alive in *Gemeinschaft* is to be part of an ancient and sacred way of life. This religious experience must be more important than any individual's interest and welfare.

Education

History, folklore, myths, and traditions are taught by word of mouth. *Gemeinschaft* is a preliterate society. This means that the people have no written language. Therefore, all social skills are learned through imitation and practice. They too are handed down from generation to generation with very little change. The only "source book" for *Gemeinschaft* is the memory of an elder. As the old

In Gemeinschaft youth depends on the memory of an elder.

wise man of the Gambia said in Alex Haley's *Roots*, " 'How else could you know of the great deeds of the ancient kings, holy men, hunters, and warriors who came hundreds of rains before us? . . . The history of our people is carried to the future in here.' And he tapped his gray head" (Haley, 1976).

Government

We have said that the family occupies the central place in the social structure of *Gemeinschaft*. Family heads known as elders are responsible for disciplining the few individuals who violate the customs of the group. Actually, what we think of as government activities cannot be separated from nongovernment activities in *Gemeinschaft*. This is so because the population is so culturally homogeneous. Social controls are in operation in the forms of informal community pressures, threats of gossip, and ostracism. Laws are not arranged in some systematic order. Instead, behavior is regulated by the people's internalization of sacred values. Behavior is regulated by customs that are not questioned because the customs are also sacred.

Social Stratification

All societies have means by which the population is divided into positions of privilege, power, and prestige. This is called *social stratification*. One's social location depends on the status (position) of one's family in *Gemeinschaft*. This is typical of a *caste system*. A caste system is one in which a person cannot improve or lose one's adult status in society. Factors such as age and sex also contribute to one's status. Individual efforts and achievements do not affect one's status within a caste system. Individuals accept their place in the social order without question or criticism. These fixed positions, occupied as a result of being born into a certain family and of a certain sex, are called *ascribed statuses*.

HUMAN RELATIONSHIPS IN *GEMEINSCHAFT*

A *Gemeinschaft* is a society in which the population shares a strong feeling of to-getherness. They believe that they are all the same kind of people—good people. Those who live in *Gemeinschaft* experience strong emotional ties with their neighbors. They may not admire and love everyone individually, but they *know* everyone in the community. Max Weber used the term "communal" to describe relationships of people in *Gemeinschaft* (Weber, 1958).

In this kind of society an individual can see a person and recall that person's parents, brothers and sisters, place of residence, and even certain events in that person's life. Frequent face-to-face contacts enable people to become involved with one another in many ways. Their lives mesh in so many ways that they are entangled or embraced collectively, depending upon the point of view one wants to take.

There is a simplicity about human relationships in *Gemeinschaft*. The way in which they communicate with each other is easily understood by all. There is lit-tle confusion about who meant to say what because there are few misunder-stood messages. "A handshake, a smile, or a frown convey messages which are clearly understood by all." The way in which they interact is personal, emotional, and spontaneous. People are regarded as people, not as functionaries who will serve a specific need of the moment (Hodges, 1971).

As we have said, a traditional society is isolated and small in population. Peo-ple come to depend upon their fellows for approval, support, and affection. Charles Horton Cooley introduced the term *primary group* to sociology. People who make up a primary group share very intimate and emotional relationships. Cooley said that people become so close "that one's very self, for many purposes at least, is the common life and purpose of the group" (Cooley, 1909). Primary groups are groups of people who share close, personal relationships. Cooley cited examples of primary groups in modern society such as the family, the children's play group, and the neighborhood or community group of elders. The description Cooley gave of primary groups resembles the circumstances of *Ge-meinschaft*. We can say, then, that an outstanding characteristic of human rela-tionships in *Gemeinschaft* is that they are primary relationships. *Gemeinschaft* re-lationships are very similar to those of primary groups.

Members of *Gemeinschaft* care about each other's well-being. They will lend a helping hand to a neighbor without expecting repayment or personal gain. The *Gemeinschaft* relationship involves trusting one another. It involves being concerned about one another. Cooperation is typical. "The *Gemeinschaft*, in short, welds people into a common unity. It is in this sense that the term means community" (Defleur et al., 1971). Within this sense of community is the conviction that whatever is good or bad for the community is good or bad for the individual. Those who live in *Gemeinschaft* are very conservative. Traditions are all-important. Therefore, the population seeks to conserve the social structure and type of relationships that have been passed down by the ancestors of the present generation.

This concludes our description of *Gemeinschaft*. Remember that we have been describing an ideal type of society, not one that exists in reality. *Gemeinschaft* is a typology of a pure traditional society. There have been many societies in human history that have closely resembled the typology we have presented here.

KEY TERMS AND
NAMES FROM
SECTION 14
        traditional society

homogeneous population

meaninglessness of concept of progress

subsistence economy

preliterate society

elders

caste system

ascribed status

communal relationships

primary groups

primary relationships

Alex Haley

Charles Horton Cooley

Max Weber

STUDY GUIDE FOR SECTION 14

1. The family occupies the central place in the social structure of *Gemeinschaft*. EXPLAIN WHAT IS MEANT BY THIS STATEMENT.

2. The religion of *Gemeinschaft* pervades all other aspects of life. Religion is expressed through chants, oaths, dances, folklore, and magic, along with elaborate rites and ceremonies. WHAT REWARDS ARE EXPECTED BY THOSE WHO FOLLOW THE RITUALS AND BELIEFS OF THEIR RELIGION?

3. In *Gemeinschaft* economic skills are learned through imitation and practice, and they are passed down from one generation to another without significant change. DESCRIBE THE ECONOMY OF *GEMEINSCHAFT* BY CITING SUCH FACTORS AS THE CONCEPT OF PROGRESS, THE ACCEPTANCE OF A SUBSISTENCE ECONOMY, TYPES OF OCCUPATIONS, AND THE DIVISION OF LABOR.

4. A *Gemeinschaft* is a preliterate society, so education is not based on written materials. HOW IS EDUCATION PRESENTED, AND WHAT IS THE "SOURCE BOOK" FOR FOLK SOCIETIES?

5. In the text, we have said that governmental activities cannot really be separated from nongovernmental activities in *Gemeinschaft*. EXPLAIN WHY THIS IS SO.

6. All societies have means by which an individual is rated and scaled in reference to the rest of the population. In *Gemeinschaft* one's privileges, power, and prestige are directly related to one's ascribed status. EXPLAIN HOW THIS WORKS, AND DESCRIBE THE REACTION OF THOSE WHO EXPERIENCE THIS FORM OF SOCIAL STRATIFICATION.

7. Charles Horton Cooley introduced the term *primary group* to sociology. WHAT ARE PRIMARY GROUPS? CITE THREE EXAMPLES.

8. Recall that Max Weber used the term *communal* to describe relationships in *Gemeinschaft*. Also, since *Gemeinschaft* relationships are similar to those that exist in primary groups, we can say that human relationships in *Gemeinschaft* are primary relationships. IN YOUR OWN WORDS, DESCRIBE HUMAN RELATIONSHIPS WITHIN *GEMEINSCHAFT*.

PRACTICE TEST FOR SECTION 14

Select the best answer.

1. Which of the following words is used as a synonym for *Gemeinschaft*?
A. Society.
B. Community.
C. Culture.
D. City.

2. The institution that occupies the central place in the social structure of *Gemeinschaft* is the
A. Economy.
B. Government.
C. Religion.
D. Family.

3. The population of *Gemeinschaft* is
A. Homogeneous.
B. Diverse.
C. Heterogeneous.
D. Large.

4. In *Gemeinschaft*, economic skills are learned through
A. Formal education.
B. Imitation and practice.
C. Specialized training.
D. Individual initiative.

5. The type of economy that prevails in *Gemeinschaft* is a

A. Surplus economy.
B. Command economy.
C. Subsistence economy.
D. Market economy.

6. The only source book in *Gemeinschaft* is
A. The Bible.
B. The national constitution.
C. A prayer book.
D. The memory of an elder.

7. Fixed positions occupied as a result of birth are called
A. Ascribed statuses.
B. Genetic statuses.
C. Inherited statuses.
D. Achieved statuses.

8. The term *primary group* was introduced into the sociological literature by
A. Charles Horton Cooley.
B. Max Weber.
C. Isaac Asimov.
D. Erich Fromm.

9. The type of interaction that prevails in primary relations is
A. Superficial.
B. Formal.
C. Intimate.
D. Role-oriented.

Answer Key

1.	B	**6.**	D
2.	D	**7.**	A
3.	A	**8.**	A
4.	B	**9.**	C
5.	C		

SECTION 15   GESELLSCHAFT: MASS, URBAN SOCIETY
- ASIMOV'S FICTIONAL PLANET OF TRANTOR
- SOCIAL STRUCTURE OF *GESELLSCHAFT*
- HUMAN RELATIONSHIPS IN *GESELLSCHAFT*
- THE TREND FROM *GEMEINSCHAFT* TO *GESELLSCHAFT*
- BEYOND *GEMEINSCHAFT* AND *GESELLSCHAFT*

Objectives

After completing this section, the student should be able to:

1. Describe the characteristics of family, religion, economics, education, government, and social stratification in *Gesellschaft.*
2. Contrast the attitudes and behaviors of people in *Gemeinschaft* and *Gesellschaft.*
3. Define and give examples of secondary groups.
4. Define and give examples of pseudo-*Gemeinschaft* behavior.
5. Explain how a social-class system creates achieved statuses.
6. Apply the term *alienation* to the human experience in *Gesellschaft.*
7. Describe human relationships within *Gesellschaft.*

As we said at the beginning of the previous section about *Gemeinschaft*, the cultures of humankind have been both very different and very similar. In this section we describe both the social structure and the human relationships typical of *Gesellschaft*, the modern, mass society. Both the structure and the relationships in *Gesellschaft* are affected very much by the concept of progress. The people of modern, mass societies are heterogeneous and more competitive than cooperative. Indeed, *Gesellschaft* is a typology at the polar extreme from *Gemeinschaft.*

ASIMOV'S FICTIONAL PLANET OF TRANTOR

In the previous section we included a description of a fictional planet. It was a simple, rural planet named Rossem. In the following passage, Asimov describes a totally urban planet of the same galaxy existing far in the future:

This was Trantor. . . . As the center of the Imperial Government for unbroken hundreds of generations and located, as it was, in the central regions of the Galaxy among the most densely populated and industrially advanced worlds of the system it could scarcely help being the densest and richest clot of humanity the Race had ever seen.

Its urbanization, progressing steadily, had finally reached the ultimate. All the land surface of Trantor, 75,000,000 square miles in extent, was a single city. The population, at its height, was well in excess of forty billions. This enormous popu-

lation was devoted almost entirely to the administrative necessities of Empire, and found themselves all too few for the complications of the task. Daily, fleets of ships in the tens of thousands brought the produce of twenty agricultural worlds to the dinner tables of Trantor. . . .

There was no green to be seen; no green, no soil. . . . The entire world was one functional distortion. There was no living object on its surface but man, his pets, and his parasites.

(Asimov, 1966)

As we said before, we cite a passage of Asimov's fiction to set a mood. In this case it is the mood and picture of a totally urbanized, mass society. Now we shall describe the social structure and human relationships typical of *Gesellschaft*. Following that, we consider the trend from traditional to modern societies and the possible effects upon the human experience.

SOCIAL STRUCTURE OF *GESELLSCHAFT*

The ideal modern society is densely populated. It can be large or small in territory, but the people are crowded together. *Gesellschaft* is ever-changing, very urban, and industrialized. The values of productivity, efficiency, and progress are emphasized. Modern society does seek progress, but debates occur among the population as to which change represents real progress. The population of *Gesellschaft* is heterogeneous in a genetic and in a cultural sense. There is no strong sense of community in *Gesellschaft* as there would be in *Gemeinschaft*. Instead, *Gesellschaft* is characterized by friction and conflict between individuals and between groups. As we did for *Gemeinschaft* in the previous section, we have selected the following structural characteristics for *Gesellschaft* to provide a picture of this other polar extreme in human societies.

Family

Although the family remains the basic unit of society in *Gesellschaft*, it no longer is the central instrument for individual activity. Families are not dominated by men, although the husband-father continues to occupy a privileged position. Marriages are formed as a result of a couple's mutual choice, based on romantic attraction and compatibility. Married couples tend to have fewer children than those in *Gemeinschaft*. The ability to obtain divorce is relatively easy, resulting in increasing numbers of marital breakups. Traditional functions of the family have, to a great extent, been assumed by political, educational, economic, and religious institutions. (We discuss "Family as a Social Institution" in Section 23.)

Economics

Mass, urban, industrial society is characterized by a complex economic system in which the division of labor is elaborate and specialized. Competition for positions within the economy requires people to seek occupations and professions that they think they can master and that are available. Success within the economic system depends on individual achievement. Few specific positions are ascribed on the basis of family membership. The technology of mass society is complicated and sophisticated. It requires special training that far exceeds the simple imitation and practice techniques used for learning skills in a folk society. Formal and specialized education are important to industrial societies. The concept of progress complicates the learning of economic skills because of continual change. The production of goods and services in *Gesellschaft* far exceeds the subsistence economy of *Gemeinschaft*. So does the ever-increasing consumption of goods and services. These economic characteristics of *Gesellschaft* are found in both capitalistic and socialistic economies. (We discuss "Economics as a Social Institution" in Section 24.)

Religion

To a certain degree, religion's function in *Gesellschaft* is to support other various sectors of society. Mass society is more secular than sacred in almost all its activities. Religion persists as a special experience for some individuals and as one of the competing agencies in mass society as a whole. The concept of sacredness does not pervade most of the social activities in mass society as it does in folk society. In fact, the separation of the secular and the sacred is expected in *Gesellschaft*. The sacred is consigned to a position of lesser importance and influence. Science dominates the supernatural aspects of religion, yet religion does persist. (We discuss "Religion as a Social Institution" in Section 24.)

Education

For a long time formal education was a luxury enjoyed only by the wealthy and privileged upper classes. When the Industrial Revolution and the trend toward urbanization occurred, more people required more education. Modern society has a literate population. There is a commitment to recorded history instead of the oral history, folklore, legends, and traditions of *Gemeinschaft*. Inability to read and write is a great disadvantage in modern society. Formal and specialized education is necessary to maintain the bureaucracies of industry and government. In fact, almost any occupational role in *Gesellschaft* requires some literacy and specialized education. Furthermore, formal education is used as a tool to socialize the population of modern, mass societies. It has replaced the family, to some extent, in reference to teaching people what is expected of them. (We discuss "Education as a Social Institution" in Section 24.)

Government

The folkways and mores of mass society are not associated with the sacred. They are not deeply internalized by a population believing that this is the way to do it because this is the way it has always been done. Various mores and folkways are weakened and redefined. Rapid social change requires the government of

Gesellschaft to substitute legal, written codes. These too are subject to redefinition and change as time goes by. All mass societies have highly organized, bureaucratic governments. However, the governments of dynamic, urban, industrial societies do not possess a sacred quality. Whether totalitarian or democratic, no government can rule indefinitely without at least the tacit consent of the governed. (We discuss "Politics as a Social Institution" in Section 24.)

Social Stratification

All societies have means by which an individual is rated and scaled in reference to the rest of the population. *Gesellschaft* contains a form of social stratification composed of multiple life-styles. Each differs in its capacity to provide and to deny certain opportunities. One's social location in *Gesellschaft* is not necessarily fixed at birth. But there is a relationship between one's social class and one's access to privileges, power, and prestige in society. Recall our example of the two infants in Chapter 2. One was born the son of a stockbroker (upper-middle class) while the other was born the son of a migrant worker (lower-lower class). We indicated then how differently the lives of the two infants probably would unfold.

There is less rigidity in *Gesellschaft* than in *Gemeinschaft* regarding social status. Individual efforts and achievements *are* far more significant in *Gesellschaft* than in *Gemeinschaft*. One of the dominant values of *Gesellschaft* is that which encourages the individual to strive for status and success in material and nonmaterial areas. One's social location and social roles are not *ascribed* but are *achieved* in the ideal mass society. (Chapter 6 presents a detailed explanation of the significance of social stratification.)

HUMAN RELATIONSHIPS IN *GESELLSCHAFT*

A *Gesellschaft* is a society in which the population is large and heterogeneous. The relationships among people are very different from those of *Gemeinschaft*. Recall that Max Weber used the term *communal* to describe relationships among people in *Gemeinschaft*. To describe relationships in *Gesellschaft*, Weber used the term *associative*. Merely to associate with people is not the same as sharing a feeling of community. Associative relationships are not characterized by strong emotional ties. People in associative relationships do not interact as intimately as those who interact in primary relationships that are typical of *Gemeinschaft*. In modern mass societies, people engage in *secondary relationships* more often than in primary relationships. Secondary relationships are impersonal and exist to get things done. Each person functions in some way for the other person. For example, the dentist interacts with the patient. This is a secondary relationship. The dentist and the patient each plays a role that complements the other's role. Neither is a significant other. The dentist and patient need know little more about

Urban dwellers become blasé.

each other than what they see during scheduled appointments. They have no reasons to care about each other as whole human beings.

Ferdinand Tonnies, author of *Gemeinschaft* and *Gesellschaft*, described those in *Gesellschaft* as being isolated from one another. In secondary relationships, people are interested only in their own individual welfare and not in the circumstances of others. Tonnies said that a condition of tension often exists among those who interact in *Gesellschaft*. When one interferes in another's personal life, it's looked upon as a hostile act, not as evidence of one's caring about another's welfare. Tonnies said:

Nobody wants to grant and produce anything for another individual, nor will he be inclined to give ungrudgingly to another individual, if it be not in exchange for a gift or labor equivalent that he considers at least equal to what he has given.

For everything pleasant which someone does for someone else, he expects, even demands, at least an equivalent. He weighs exactly his services, flatteries, presents, and so on, to determine whether they will bring about the desired results.

(Tonnies, 1963)

Let us consider how density (being tightly packed) in *Gesellschaft* affects human relationships. Each person in mass society daily comes into contact with many people. It is actually impossible to become involved with most of the people one encounters each day. Think of a college student who travels from home to college and back home five days a week. Each day the student is apt to encounter thousands of people (by seeing, by hearing, and even through social interaction). In a way, then, most people become no more important than decorations in the student's environment. They are seen or heard or dealt with in some small way. Then they are gone and probably forgotten.

Members of Gemeinschaft are concerned about each other's well-being. Members of *Gesellschaft* often pretend to be concerned. For example, perhaps an insurance agent comes to discuss one's life and death and loved ones. He or she could pretend to feel some personal concern about the insured and the insured's family. The real reason the agent is there is to sell insurance. For the agent, selling insurance is a means to provide his or her income. Robert Merton used the term pseudo-*Gemeinschaft* to describe behavior in which one acts concerned without really feeling concerned (Merton, 1946). One businessman said, "In my business, I can see how a lot of people in their business deals will make some kind of gesture of friendliness, sincerity and so forth, most of which is phony" (Merton, 1968). Again, pseudo-*Gemeinschaft* is behavior in which one pretends concern in order to get the other person to do what helps oneself.

Secondary relationships in *Gesellschaft* are transitory (here today, gone tomorrow). People do not quickly reveal very much about themselves to others. They let only a little of themselves show till their relationship develops more, if that happens. Still, people in modern, urban societies are not overly suspicious of outsiders. Such suspicion about outsiders is typical of traditional, folk societies. People in urban settings come into contact with people from many different backgrounds. In urban, mass societies, people tend to be tolerant of differences. Living in densely populated cities, urban dwellers became blasé (indifferent) about things different and unusual. Long-time residents of large cities have learned to ignore those around them. It would be too emotionally exhausting always to react to helpless derelicts, prostrate alcoholics, blind beggars, and other people in distress (Bensman and Rosenberg, 1963). In much the same way, members of *Gesellschaft* learn to ignore the ethnic, religious, racial, occupational, and social-class differences of those with whom they must associate. They may not approve of or be happy about those differences. But, liking them or not, their blasé attitudes allow them to interact with those who are not what they think of as "our kind of people."

We have summarized the contrasting characteristics of *Gemeinschaft* and *Gesellschaft* in Diagram No. 4.

THE TREND FROM *GEMEINSCHAFT* TO *GESELLSCHAFT*

Human societies have been undergoing a global transition from *Gemeinschaft* to *Gesellschaft*. It is important to remember that these two terms refer to two polar extremes. There is no pure *Gemeinschaft* with only primary relationships. There is no pure *Gesellschaft* with only secondary relationships. But real societies do come close to being one way or the other. The trend is away from small rural, traditional societies and toward large, urban, modern societies. This is the reality of the human experience in recent centuries. "The whole habitable globe is quaking from the effects of . . . industrialization and urbanization. And the folk society has, in fact, ceased to exist" (Bensman and Rosenberg, 1963).

GEMEINSCHAFT ⟷ GESELLSCHAFT	
Small population	Large, dense population
Homogeneous population	Heterogeneous population
Concept of progress meaningless	Progress oriented
Profound sense of community	Friction and conflict
Cooperation and mutual assistance	Competition
Subsistence economy	Consumption economy
Sacred orientation	Secular orientation
Laws are not codified	Legal, written codes subject to change
Ascribed status stressed	Achieved status stressed
Skills through imitation and practice	Formal and specialized education
Traditional	Dynamic
Communal relationships	Associative relationships
Primary relations and groups	Secondary relations and groups
People relate to others as people	People are functionaries for others
Genuine concern for others	Pseudo–Gemeinschaft
A limited number of contacts	A multiplicity of contacts
Very ethnocentric	Cosmopolitan and blasé
Alienation	Spontaneity
Informal promise	Legal contract
Solidarity and togetherness	Bureaucratic organization and individualism

Diagram No. 4   Contrasting Gemeinschaft and Gesellschaft

It would be incorrect to label either *Gemeinschaft* or *Gesellschaft* as necessarily good or bad. Both *Gemeinschaft* and *Gesellschaft* are better interpreted as neutral terms (Nisbet, 1970). The Earth's human population has been increasing dramatically. At the same time, urbanization and industrialization of societies have increased. People who live in urban societies have a multitude of social contacts and belong to many different groups. The old feelings of kinship among people has declined. The trend has been toward human relations that are more formal, impersonal, and transitory. The legal contract has replaced the informal promise (Maine, 1911). The cooperation and togetherness typical of human interaction in *Gemeinschaft* has been replaced with secondary relationships. Now people more often look after their own individual, special interests. When it seems to be necessary, people compete with the special interests of other people. Nevertheless, primary relationships remain part of and very important to the people of modern society. Let us explain.

The Persistence of Primary Groups

In our daily lives we all experience secondary relationships and belong to secondary groups. This fact, however, does not mean that primary relationships and primary groups are not *also* part of our experiences. People seem to need people in their lives who are more than only furnishings or functionaries. People need people who care about them and people to care about, it seems. Families, friendships, and love affairs provide primary relationships. In sociological thinking, a *group* can consist of two or more people who are socially interacting. So those involved in families, friendships, and love affairs are participating in primary groups. In *Gesellschaft*, primary relationships meet the human needs for sharing, caring, concern, and love. Even *cliques* (small groups of people who work together with special bonds of loyalty) provide people with primary settings within large, bureaucratic organizations. The loss of kinship feelings and the growth of secondary settings has not left us without opportunities to continue to experience meaningful human relationships. Primary groups within the secondary environment of *Gesellschaft* provide us with opportunities to express love and loyalty.

Technology and the Concept of Progress

Part of the social heritage of almost every modern society is the high value placed on progress. In the trend from *Gemeinschaft* to *Gesellschaft*, humankind has enlarged its horizons. Technological progress has brought cures for diseases, an expectation for longer life, and more leisure for many people. Once humans dared to cross the next hill. Now they dare to cross the space between planets. A poet declares that we have promises to keep and miles to go before we sleep. The promises of modern, mass industrial societies are somehow linked with the modern dedication to the concept of progress. Alvin M. Weinberg, former director of the Federal Energy Administration's Office for Energy Research and Development, has said that ". . . we ought to remember that in the pretechnical age, life, even though in harmony with nature, was short and brutal" (Weinberg, 1980). Within the huge organizations of *Gesellschaft* are the technological skills and the ideological potential for improving the human experience.

The Experience of Alienation

Karl Marx (1818–1883), C. Wright Mills (1916–1962), Erich Fromm (1900–1980), and many other critics of modern society have suggested that the trend from *Gemeinschaft* to *Gesellschaft* has caused people to suffer from alienation. What does *alienation* mean? It means feeling cut off from or out of touch with one's immediate surroundings. To feel like a useless small cog in a gigantic machine is to feel alienated. Feeling alienated causes one not to care about other people. One can even become alienated from oneself and experience extremely low self-esteem. Alienation can be characterized by feelings of anxiety and despair. Feeling that one does not belong, feeling lonely and powerless, and feeling that life is meaningless are all symptoms of alienation (Josephson and Josephson, 1962).

The alienation of people from themselves and from any sense of productivity is a fact of daily life. It does not matter *which* modern society one considers. "What difference does it make, as far as work itself goes, whether a person is monitoring a set of dials in a Soviet state-managed oil refinery or a Standard Oil of America refinery?" People in modern industrial societies will be alienated from their labor as long as their work is so specialized that they need act little more than like robots (Anderson, 1971). Although machines could free humans from meaningless work, the division of labor in industry has, according to Marx, alienated rather than freed the individual. Marx said, "The laborer exists for the process of production, and not the process of production for the laborer" (Marx, 1961).

Erich Fromm said that many people have misunderstood what Marx meant in the preceding statement. Marx was not speaking primarily of the economic misuse of the working class, nor of the equalization of income, in that statement. Instead, Marx was concerned about the liberation of people from a certain kind of work. Marx believed that industrialization was destroying human individuality. Marx feared that people were being turned into parts of the very machines on which they worked. And people were becoming the slaves of things (Fromm, 1961). In other words, society has placed more importance on production values than on the humanistic values. This can cause people to become dehumanized and alienated from the people around them. Even more important, too much emphasis on technology and production can cause people to become alienated from themselves.

BEYOND
GEMEINSCHAFT
AND
GESELLSCHAFT

We have promises to keep and miles to go before we sleep. There is little time for sleep. We want to progress in technology *and* in human compassion. Erich Fromm said that we are usually half-asleep. We are only enough awake to go about our business. We are not awake enough to go about living and caring (Fromm, 1962). We have promises to keep, miles to travel, and no time at all to sleep. The trend from *Gemeinschaft* to *Gesellschaft* could continue on *beyond Gesellschaft*. Fromm and many others have anticipated a social trend away from the impersonal and alienated conditions of modern times. In 1962 Erich Fromm wrote:

I believe that the development of man in the last four thousand years of history is truly awe-inspiring. . . .

I believe that the One World which is emerging can come into existence only if a New Man comes into being—a man who has emerged from the archaic ties of blood and soil, and who feels himself to be the son of man, a citizen of the world whose loyalty is to the human race and to life, rather than to any exclusive part of it; a man who loves his country because he loves mankind, and whose judgment is not warped by tribal loyalties.

(Fromm, 1962)

Sacred and secular societies are typologies. Rural and urban societies are typologies. Mechanical solidarity and organic solidarity are typologies. Folk and mass societies are typologies. *Gemeinschaft* and *Gesellschaft* are typologies. Society is an abstraction. People are real, located in time and space. Time past, time present, and, hopefully, time future. Space here and space there. Time and space are abstractions. People are real.

You do what you must—
   this world and then the next—
   one world at a time . . .
And you take hold of a handle
   by one hand or the other
   by the better or worse hand
   and you never know
   maybe till long afterward
   which was the better hand . . .
In the darkness with a bundle of grief
   the people march.
In the night, and overhead a shovel of stars
   for keeps, the people march;
Where to? what next?*

(SANDBURG, 1936)

KEY TERMS AND NAMES FROM SECTION 15

mass, urban society	production and consumption economy
heterogeneous population	specialized economy
technological progress	literacy

*From *The People, Yes* by Carl Sandburg, copyright © 1936 by Harcourt Brace Jovanovich, Inc.; copyright © 1964 by Carl Sandburg. Reprinted by permission of the publishers.

multiple life-styles	cliques
rapid social change	persistence of primary groups
achieved status	alienation
associative relationships	Karl Marx
secondary relationships	Erich Fromm
secondary groups	Max Weber
population density	Ferdinand Tonnies
pseudo-*Gemeinschaft*	Robert K. Merton
blasé attitudes	Carl Sandburg

STUDY GUIDE FOR SECTION 15

1. The family in *Gesellschaft* has differences from the family in *Gemeinschaft*. DESCRIBE THESE DIFFERENCES.

2. The economy of *Gesellschaft* far exceeds the subsistence economy of *Gemeinschaft*. DESCRIBE THE ECONOMY OF *GESELLSCHAFT*. CITE SUCH FACTORS AS CONCEPT OF PROGRESS, INDIVIDUAL ACHIEVEMENT, AND THE RELATIONSHIP BETWEEN TECHNOLOGY AND EDUCATION.

3. Religion and the sacred do not appear in most events. EXPLAIN THE RELATIVE POSITIONS OF THE SACRED AND SECULAR IN *GESELLSCHAFT*.

4. *Gesellschaft* is characterized by a literate population. WHAT EVIDENCE OF AND REASONS FOR LITERACY ARE CITED IN THE TEXT?

5. Folkways and mores in *Gesellschaft* are not associated with the sacred traditions of ancestors. HOW DOES THIS AFFECT THE BEHAVIOR OF GOVERNMENTS OF *GESELLSCHAFT*?

6. There is less rigidity in *Gesellschaft* than in *Gemeinschaft* regarding social location, ascribed status, and achieved status. DEFINE THESE TERMS AND EXPLAIN HOW THEY APPLY TO *GESELLSCHAFT*.

7. *Gesellschaft* is characterized by secondary relationships. Weber used the term *associative* to describe human relations. DESCRIBE HOW PEOPLE RELATE TO ONE ANOTHER IN SUCH RELATIONSHIPS.

8. WHAT IS PSEUDO-*GEMEINSCHAFT* BEHAVIOR? GIVE AN EXAMPLE.

9. In urban, mass societies, people tend to be tolerant of differences, even blasé. EXPLAIN WHY THIS IS TRUE FOR *GESELLSCHAFT* AND NOT FOR *GEMEINSCHAFT*.

10. In the trend from *Gemeinschaft* to *Gesellschaft*, the legal contract has replaced the informal promise. EXPLAIN WHY THIS IS SO.

11. Primary groups and relationships persist in *Gesellschaft*. EXPLAIN WHY THIS IS TRUE AND GIVE EXAMPLES OF PRIMARY GROUPS IN SECONDARY SETTINGS.

12. Many social critics have said that the trend from traditional to modern societies has caused people to suffer from alienation. DESCRIBE THE DIFFERENT WAYS IN WHICH PEOPLE CAN FEEL ALIENATED.

13. Marx said that "The laborer exists for the process of production, and not the process of production for the laborer." HOW DID ERICH FROMM EXPLAIN MARX'S VIEWS IN THAT STATEMENT?

14. Erich Fromm believed that "The One World which is emerging can come into existence only if a New Man comes into being." DESCRIBE WHAT THIS "NEW MAN" WOULD BE LIKE.

PRACTICE TEST FOR SECTION 15

Select the best answer.

1. What type of orientation is characteristic of *Gesellschaft*?
A. Progress.
B. Subsistence.
C. Sacred.
D. Tradition.

2. It was stated in the text that within the *Gesellschaft* is the unique separation of the
A. Rational and the scientific.
B. Secular and the sacred.
C. Sound and the fury.
D. Supernatural and the religious.

3. According to Max Weber, the term used to describe the relationships of people in *Gesellschaft* is
A. Associative.
B. Communal.
C. Pseudo-*Gemeinschaft*.
D. Primary.

4. Which of the following is correct?
A. Secondary relations are to *Gemeinschaft* as primary relations are to *Gesellschaft*.
B. Primary relations are to *Gemeinschaft* as secondary relations are to *Gesellschaft*.

5. "In my business, I can see how a lot of people in their business deals will make some kind of gesture of friendliness, sincerity and so forth, most of which is phony." These types of business deals are examples of
A. Pseudo-*Gemeinschaft* relations.
B. *Gemeinschaft* relations.
C. Primary relations.
D. Pseudo-*Gesellschaft* relations.

6. The global transition from *Gemeinschaft* to *Gesellschaft* has been accompanied by
A. The replacement of the legal contract with the informal promise.
B. A decline in feelings of kinship.
C. A trend toward more informal, personal, and enduring relations.
D. A decrease in alienating processes.

7. What is characterized by feelings of anxiety, apathy, meaninglessness, and despair?
A. Loneliness.
B. Poverty.
C. Unrequited love.
D. Alienation.

8. According to Karl Marx, what has alienated rather than freed the individual in contemporary societies?
A. Democracy.
B. Egalitarianism.
C. Industrialism.
D. Class consciousness.

9. "The laborer exists for the process of production, and not the process of production for the laborer." This statement is attributed to
A. Erich Fromm.
B. Karl Marx.
C. C. Wright Mills.
D. Ferdinand Tonnies.

10. Which of the following is *not* associated with *Gesellschaft?*
A. Progress-oriented.
B. Industrial.
C. Heterogeneous population.
D. Communal feelings.

11. The technology of mass society is
A. Based on age and sex.
B. Sophisticated.
C. Complex.
D. Based on ascribed status.
E. Both B and C.

12. Which of the following is necessary to maintain the bureaucracies of mass society?
A. Large families.
B. Heterogeneous population.
C. Formal and specialized education.
D. Secular religion.

13. In mass society, social location and social roles are
A. Ascribed.
B. Biologically transmitted.
C. Achieved.
D. Fixed and unchanging.

14. Secondary relations are
A. Person-oriented.
B. Durable.
C. Intimate.
D. Role and goal-oriented.

15. Human societies are undergoing a transition from
A. Secular to sacred.
B. *Gemeinschaft* to *Gesellschaft.*
C. Urban to folk.
D. Organic solidarity to mechanical solidarity.

16. Which of the following is an example of a secondary relationship?
A. Clique.
B. Friends.
C. Classmates.
D. Family.

17. Which of the following is *not* a characteristic feeling of alienation?
A. Security.
B. Despair.
C. Isolation.
D. Self-estrangement.

Answer Key

1.	A	**7.**	D	**13.**	C
2.	B	**8.**	C	**14.**	D
3.	A	**9.**	B	**15.**	B
4.	B	**10.**	D	**16.**	C
5.	A	**11.**	E	**17.**	A
6.	B	**12.**	C		

CHAPTER SUMMARY

1. Max Weber defined typologies as ideal (pure) types of social behavior that do not actually exist in reality. They are exaggerations of reality. Traditional folk society and modern mass society are exaggerations that do not exist in pure form in reality.

2.   Sociological typologies can be used to study the historic trend from small, traditional, rural society to large, modern, urban society. Prominent typologies that treat this trend include: Howard P. Becker's sacred and secular societies; Robert Redfield's folk–urban continuum; Emile Durkheim's mechanical and organic solidarity; and Ferdinand Tonnies' *Gemeinschaft* and *Gesellschaft*.

3.   The ideal traditional society is small both in the size of its population and in the amount of territory it occupies. Because it is isolated from other societies, little social change occurs from one generation to the next. The population is homogeneous in a genetic and in a cultural sense.

4.   The family occupies the central place in the social structure of traditional society. The level of technology is simple. Economic skills are learned through imitation and practice. To be fully alive in *Gemeinschaft* is to be part of an ancient and sacred way of life.

5.   *Gemeinschaft* is a preliterate society. One's social location depends on the status of one's family. This is typical of a caste system. Born into a family, one has ascribed status.

6.   A *Gemeinschaft* is a society in which people share a strong feeling of togetherness and experience meaningful emotional ties with their neighbors. Max Weber used the term *communal* to describe the relationships of people in *Gemeinschaft*. The description of primary groups by Cooley resembles the type of relationships in traditional societies.

7.   The ideal modern society is densely populated. It can be large or small in territory. *Gesellschaft* is ever-changing, very urban, and industrialized. The values of productivity, efficiency, and progress are emphasized.

8.   The population of *Gesellschaft* is heterogeneous in a genetic and in a cultural sense. The family remains the basic unit of society; however, it no longer is at the center of most individual activity. The division of labor is elaborate and specialized. The technology of mass society requires special training. The concept of progress complicates the learning of skills because of continual changes in most areas of life.

9.   The concept of the sacred does not influence many social activities in mass society as it does in folk society. Religion continues to exist. Still, science dominates the secular activities of the population of the literate, modern society.

10.   Mass society requires formal education to maintain the bureaucracies of industry and government. Social stratification in *Gesellschaft* is characterized by achieved status rather than ascribed status.

11.   *Gesellschaft* has a large and heterogeneous population. Max Weber described relationships in *Gesellschaft* as associative. Secondary relationships occur more often than primary. Most social interaction is impersonal, transitory, and superficial. The term pseudo-*Gemeinschaft* has been used to describe behavior in which one pretends to be concerned without really feeling any concern at all.

12.   Human societies have been undergoing a global transition from *Gemeinschaft* to *Gesellschaft*. The trend has been away from small, rural societies and toward large, urban societies. Industrialization and urbanization seem to be pushing the folk society off the edge of the Earth.

13. The trend from *Gemeinschaft* to *Gesellschaft* has caused people to experience alienation. Alienation means feeling cut off from or out of touch with one's immediate surroundings. Alienation is characterized by feelings of anxiety, despair, loneliness, powerlessness, and meaninglessness. To feel like a useless small cog in a gigantic machine is to feel alienated.

SUGGESTIONS
FOR FURTHER
READING
RELATING TO
CHAPTER 5

Blau, Peter M., *Bureaucracy in Modern Society* (New York: Random House, 1956). Blau sets forth the theory and actual operation of bureaucratic organizations.

Gans, Herbert J., *The Urban Villagers* (New York: Free Press, 1962). This study of an Italian working-class neighborhood in Boston reveals a pocket of *Gemeinschaft* within *Gesellschaft*.

Gordon, Mitchell, *Sick Cities: Psychology and Pathology of American Urban Life* (Baltimore: Penguin Books, 1969). Gordon discusses the nature of metropolitanization, warning that it will cause problems endangering the health, safety, and human spirit of urban dwellers.

Josephson, Eric, and Mary Josephson, editors, *Man Alone: Alienation in Modern Society* (New York: Dell, 1962). This is a superb collection of writings addressing themselves to the following questions: Who are the alienated? What are the conditions that lead to alienation? What are the possibilities of restoring and/or securing a greater integration of individual and group?

Kroeber, Theodora, *Ishi in Two Worlds* (Berkeley: University of California Press, 1961). Kroeber has written a remarkable biography. She has done more than that, however. Ishi is the lone survivor from a folk society that had existed since the Age of Pericles. One day this Stone-Age man walked into San Francisco and mass, urban society. It is a true and fascinating tale.

Lenski, Gerhard, *Human Societies: A Macrolevel Introduction to Sociology* (New York: McGraw-Hill, 1970). This is an evolutionary approach to the study of human societies. Part II, "Preindustrial Societies," is of special interest, considering hunting and gathering societies, horticultural societies, agrarian societies, and specialized societal types.

Morain, Lloyd L., *The Human Cougar* (Buffalo: Prometheus Books, 1976). "The lives of more and more of us are captured by governmental, corporate, and other institutional pressures. What a marvelous time for Lloyd Morain to show us how to save the 'human cougar' in each of us!"—Nicholas Johnson.

Nisbet, Robert, *History of the Idea of Progress* (New York: Basic Books, 1980). Nisbet insists that the idea of progress has been the most important idea of the past 3000 years of Western history.

Vidich, Arthur J., and Joseph Bensman, *Small Town in Mass Society*, rev. ed. (Princeton: Princeton University Press, 1968). This work indicates that mass urban society dominates the form and focus of life in seemingly provincial small towns.

Whyte, William H., Jr., *The Organization Man* (New York: Simon & Schuster, A Clarion Book, 1972). Whyte describes the impact that large organizations have upon individual lives. He shows a relationship between the bureaucratic ethic and the social ethic in modern American life.

Wirth, Louis, *On Cities and Social Life*, selected papers edited by Albert J. Reiss, Jr. (Chicago: University of Chicago Press, Phoenix Books, 1964). We especially recommend the reading of these two essays: "Urbanism as a Way of Life" and "World Community, World Society, and World Government: An Attempt at a Clarification of Terms."

Chapter 6
Social Stratification as a Form of Social Inequality

SECTION 16 METHODS USED FOR IDENTIFYING SOCIAL STRATA

- THE OBJECTIVE APPROACH
- THE REPUTATIONAL APPROACH
- THE SUBJECTIVE APPROACH
- A BRIEF CRITIQUE OF CLASS ANALYSIS

Objectives

After completing this section, the student should be able to:

1. Recognize that people classify themselves into strata above and below one another.
2. Describe the objective method for studying social stratification.
3. Describe the reputational method for studying social stratification.
4. Describe the subjective method for studying social stratification.
5. Describe W. Lloyd Warner's six-strata social class system.
6. Recognize that social classes are typologies.

In this chapter we discuss social stratification. The word *stratification* was first used by geologists. Stratification refers to the formation of layers of the Earth's crust. *Social stratification* refers to the formation of a society's population into levels based upon privilege, power, and prestige. Sociologists did not make up the concept of social stratification. People everywhere have classified themselves and those around them into categories above and below one another. People have created levels of superiority, equality, and inferiority. The process of social stratification places families and individuals into a social system of unequals.

Over two thousand years ago Aristotle referred to the very rich, the very poor, and all those people in between. In the early years of the American Republic, James Madison observed that some citizens had more status than others. The word *status* is of Latin origin, meaning "standing." In *The Federalist*, Madison wrote about "those who are creditors and those who are debtors." He said that the American population was divided into "different classes" and that each class held different values and views.

Sociologists recognize two kinds of social stratification. There can be a social caste system or a social class system. A *social caste system* refers to levels of society in which people remain for their lifetimes. Social barriers in a caste system are rigid and strictly observed. Because of socialization, people do not even consider changing their social levels. Caste systems are rare today, but they have existed in various societies. The most famous caste system in history was the one that existed in India. Elaborate rules of etiquette and the Hindu religion strongly supported India's caste system. Now, it is illegal, although not eliminated.

A *social class system* does provide some opportunities for people to improve their social standing. Moving from one level of society to another is called *social mobility*. Our treatment of social stratification in this chapter emphasizes the characteristics of social class and not those of social caste. People are very interested in their social positions. Sociologists are very interested in the way people behave. Therefore, the subjects of social status and social stratification are of particular interest to sociologists. Three general approaches to or methods for studying social stratification have been used by sociologists. They are:

1. The objective approach
2. The subjective approach
3. The reputational approach

Let us now describe each of these approaches in some detail.

THE OBJECTIVE APPROACH

Aristotle said that there were three strata (levels) of society. He referred to the very rich, the very poor, and all those in between. What he did was to stratify Greek society by using wealth, property, and income as his criteria (standards). Although Aristotle was not a sociologist, he had used the objective approach to identify different strata of society. The objective approach allows an individual to decide what to use as a basis for assigning individuals or families to various strata in society. This approach to studying social stratification depends upon careful and detailed observations being made by the sociologist. It is the sociologist who decides who is where based on what. Stratification is based on criteria set by the sociologist. It should be understood that there is nothing definite or guaranteed about the results of an objective study of social class. Different sociologists have used different criteria in their studies to decide how a community or society is stratified. The same population might end up being divided very differently into social classes according to which criteria are used by various sociologists.

In the 19th century, Karl Marx observed that Western capitalist society was stratified into only two classes. He used only one criterion—the ownership of the means of production. Marx wrote:

Society as a whole is more and more splitting up into two great hostile camps, into two great classes directly facing each other: Bourgeoisie and Proletariat.

(Marx and Engels, 1848)

The *bourgeoisie*, Marx said, was the capitalist class that owned the means of production such as coal mines and factories. The *proletariat* was the working class that survived only by working for those who owned the means of production. Marx was an economic determinist. This means that he believed that all cultures developed into what they were as a result of their economic activities. In order to understand the social structure and human relationships in a society, Marx believed that it is necessary first to understand the economic system.

Board meeting.

Karl Marx was a great scholar in the 19th century and has had a great impact on 20th-century thinking. He has been recognized as a sociologist, an economist, a historian, a philosopher, and a journalist. For students interested in knowing more about Karl Marx's sociological thought, we include two excellent sources in the "Suggestions for Further Reading" at the conclusion of this chapter.

The objective approach is one of the methods used by modern sociologists to study social stratification. They do not all choose the same criteria for judging who is in which social class. There is a great volume of statistics available in modern societies that can be interpreted and used to identify social classes. For example, a sociologist may identify a society's stratification based on an annual income of a family by using the following scale:

Class One	Income above $100,000
Class Two	Income between $50,000 and $99,999
Class Three	Income between $25,000 and $49,999
Class Four	Income between $10,000 and $24,999
Class Five	Income between $5000 and $9999
Class Six	Income below $5000

This, then, is an example of a sociologist using income as the criterion and choosing to divide a population accordingly. If this were done, it is probably true that each of the classes would participate in a life-style quite unlike the others. However, it should be apparent that a family in Class Two with an income of $99,000 is not really going to be different from the family in Class One with an income of $100,000. Strata simply are not that clearly identifiable. In a sense, these classes are typologies, and each tends to fade into the other.

Let us cite just one more example of using the objective approach in an attempt to identify social strata. This time we shall use education as the criterion for social class, creating the following scale:

Class One	College graduate with doctorate degree
Class Two	College graduate with master's degree
Class Three	College graduate with bachelor's degree
Class Four	High school graduate with diploma
Class Five	High school attendance without graduating
Class Six	Dropped out of school before ninth grade

Once again we have created a pattern of social stratification based on one criterion—educational achievement. Again, it is probably true that each of the classes would participate in a life-style unlike the others. However, we know that education is never an absolute criterion for placing people on a scale of privilege, power, and prestige just as annual income is inadequate in itself.

Using one criterion for identifying social strata can be useful. Still, most modern sociologists choose to work with multiple criteria. Criteria most often used by contemporary sociologists are *income, occupation, education,* and *family background.* In the second section of this chapter we consider these determinants of social class plus several other important indicators of social strata.

THE REPUTATIONAL APPROACH

Sociologists did not make up the concept of social stratification, nor did they coin the term *social class.* People classify themselves and others into categories and were doing so long before sociologists were ever heard of. The reputational approach to studying social stratification proves this point. This approach is based on the way in which people rate each other. The reputational approach is especially effective in small communities. This approach is called reputational because the members of a community are placed in a class depending upon their *reputations* in the community. People in a community know who does and who does not have special privileges. They know who does and does not have access to power. They know who has prestige and who does not. Using the reputational approach, sociologists find out what the people in a community already know.

This is how it works: The sociologist goes into a small community and selects a sample of long-term residents. Using in-depth interviews, the sociologist asks the long-term residents to rate other community members on a scale from highest to lowest. The people who work with the sociologists and who make judgments about the standings of community members are called *judges* or *raters.* In order to discover what criteria the judges use to place people in different levels, the sociologist asks them to explain why they rated specific people or families as they did.

The most influential series of studies of social stratification in which the reputational approach was used was done by W. Lloyd Warner and his associates (Warner, 1963). Totaling at least ten different books, the "Yankee City Series" investigated the stratification of several small communities in the United States during the 1930s and 1940s. "Yankee City" was really Newburyport, Massachusetts, a town of about 17,000 people. "Old City" was really Natchez, Mississippi, a town with a population of about 10,000 people. "Jonesville" was really Morris, Illinois, a town of about 6000 people. The three towns had in common their relatively small size. The fact that each town was located in a different region of the United States encouraged sociologists to conclude that the social-class structures found in each town—similar to one another—existed in a general way throughout the United States. The six-class structure identified by Warner and his associates remains the most popular description of social classes in the United States today. The six classes are referred to as upper-upper, lower-upper, upper-middle, lower-middle, upper-lower, and lower-lower (Warner, 1960). Although they are not very descriptive terms, most sociologists are comfortable with using this six-class terminology.

The following descriptions of the six-class stratification of American small towns are based on information gathered and interpreted by W. Lloyd Warner and his associates, who carefully interviewed a wide range of people. In the interviews it became apparent that people used certain terms for those who were their equals and other terms to designate individuals whom they believed to be above or below them in status. Diagram No. 5, showing the social perspectives of social classes in Old City, contains phrases actually used by people being interviewed—"old aristocracy," "no 'count lot," "shiftless people," "po' whites," "old families," and so forth.

In Yankee City phrases such as "Hill Streeters," "Riverbrookers," and "lowdown Yankees who live in the clam flats" were used to indicate high and low social standing. People were asked to comment on a wide array of human activities within the towns:

. . . with the aid of . . . testimony such as the area lived in, the type of house, kind of education, manners, and other symbols of class it was possible to determine very quickly the approximate place of any individual in the society.

In the final analysis, however, individuals were placed by the evaluations of the members of Yankee City itself, e.g., by such explicit statements as "she does not belong" or "they belong to our club."

(Warner and Lunt, 1941)

Although the studies that make up the "Yankee City Series" were done during the 1930s and 1940s, we believe that the social stratification of American towns is similar today, with some differences because of general changes within American society as a whole. We have estimated the percentage of people in each class level.

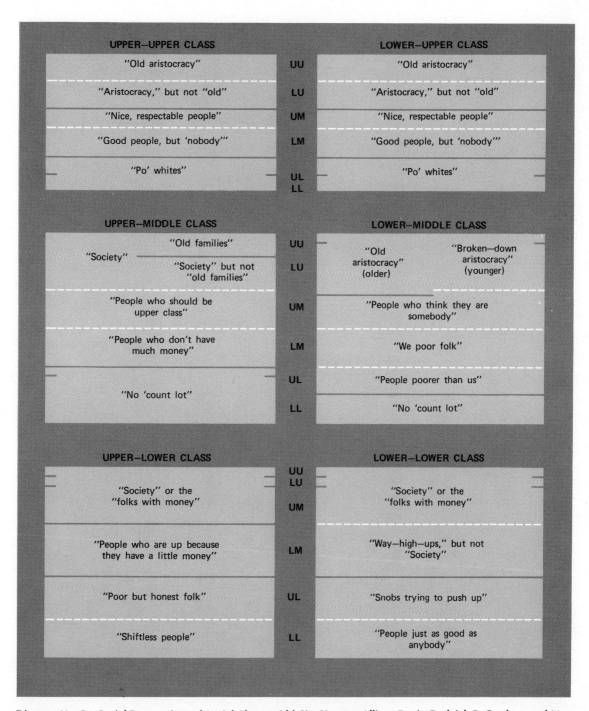

Diagram No. 5   Social Perspectives of Social Classes, Old City [Source: Allison Davis, Burleigh B. Gardner, and Mary R. Gardner, Deep South (Chicago: University of Chicago Press, 1941), p. 65.]

The Upper-Upper Class (One Percent)

These are the *old families*, meaning that they have lived in the community and have been at the top of the class structure for many generations. "Present members of the class were born into it: the families into which they were born can trace their lineage through many generations participating in a way of life characteristic of the upper class back to a generation marking the lowly beginnings out of which their family came" (Warner, 1960). Such families tend to intermarry within their own class. Exceptions are made for their children to marry the wealthy sons and daughters of the newly rich in the class level below. They have sufficient wealth, power, and social prestige to maintain a life-style without anxieties about status. The adults hold membership in exclusive clubs and are active in charitable organizations. Their children attend exclusive prep schools and prestige universities. These people are the social aristocracy of small-town America. They are aware of this, and all the rest of the people in the community accept the fact (Reissman, 1959).

The Lower-Upper Class (Two Percent)

The lower-upper class does not lack the money to qualify for top social status. They are often wealthier than those at the top of the class structure, but they do lack a long line of distinguished ancestors. Actually, these families have a life-style very similar to that of the old family class. They too have access to some exclusive clubs and are active in charitable organizations. As W. Lloyd Warner put it:

On the average, the new families, socially inferior to the old ones, have more money, better houses, more expensive automobiles, and other material goods that are superior in dollars and cents to those of their social superiors. But if the success of the new families is due to wealth, their money is felt to be too new; if due to occupational triumph, their achievement is too recent; if the source of their new social power is educational attainment, what they have learned, while highly valued, is too newly learned and insufficient.

(Warner, 1962)

These are the *nouveaux riches* (newly rich). While they hope to enter the top class of old families, they must wait their turn in time. Eventually their children or their children's children may be accepted by the social elite. Until then, "they must learn how to act, fill their lives with good deeds, spend their money on approved philanthropy (charity) and reduce their arrogance to manageable proportions" (Warner, 1960).

The Upper-Middle Class (11 Percent)

The upper-middle class is composed of "college-educated professionals, scientists, managers, highly-skilled technicians, businessmen, and their families" (Vanfossen, 1979). They are active leaders in the community. They belong to associations that are well-known to the public and that are well-received in mass media. Belonging to associations such as the Rotary, Lions, Elks, and Kiwanis, they are organization people with career orientations. Although they live in comfortable homes in better residential sections of town, their incomes and house values do not equal those of the upper classes. Some of the upper-middle class are new-comers to town, having relocated because of their occupations or professions. These new people are not as conscious of the class structure and are not particu-larly anxious to move up socially. However, those upper-middle families that are native to the town are more aware of being socially inferior to the upper classes. They are apt to experience frustrations and anxieties as they anticpate the possi-bilities of moving up the class ladder into the lower-upper class (Warner, 1962). Almost all upper-middle class people are exposed to some college education.

The Lower-Middle Class (33 Percent)

Warner and his associates described the people in the lower-middle class during the 1930s and 1940s. They were said to be extremely proper and conservative, careful with their money, frugal, farsighted, and forever anxious about what their neighbors thought of them. The children of the lower-middle class families would sometimes finish high school, but college education was not one of their objec-tives in life. In the small towns and in the cities of America at that time, the low-er-middle class was composed economically of small businessmen, a small per-centage of highly skilled workmen and supervisors, and a large number of clerks, salespeople, and workers in similar categories (Warner, 1962).

Two somewhat radical changes have occurred in the lower-middle class since the days of the early studies. Today the lower-middle class may still be thought of as being proper and conservative. But, they, like most Americans, are not care-ful with their money in the sense that they save it and struggle to remain out of debt. Once they boasted that they owed no money to anyone. Today they boast that they have good credit. The second somewhat radical change in the lower-middle class can be seen in the educational level. It is now common for lower-middle class people to attend community colleges and state colleges. Their edu-cation enables the lower-middle class to fill occupational positions that have higher status than clerk, salesperson, or industrial worker. However, we do not want to suggest that the lower-middle class does not continue to provide the economy with clerks, salespeople, and industrial workers. It does. Many of the courses offered in community and state colleges are intended to upgrade the status of such positions and to improve the ability of those who fill such occupa-tional roles.

The Upper-Lower Class (33 Percent)

This class is often called the *working class*. There is now an increase in the per-centage of upper-lower class people who complete high school. Many continue to drop out before graduation, taking occupational positions in industry as blue-collar workers doing semiskilled labor. The American labor movement has raised the standard of living considerably for the working class since the 1930s. Many such families have higher incomes than those who are ranked in the white-collar, lower-middle class. This class has been described as "counting among their virtues cleanliness, honesty, and respectablility, all of which are important for them to maintain" (Reissman, 1959). More and more working-class people are attending night classes in adult education programs or in community colleges. They attend, not to obtain a college degree, but to further their preparation for jobs that require the learning of new skills periodically.

The Lower-Lower Class (20 Percent)

When Warner's study of Yankee City was made, he wrote:

The lower-lower class, referred to as "Riverbrookers" or the "low-down Yankees who live in the clam flats," have a "bad reputation" among those who are socially above them. This evaluation includes beliefs that they are lazy, shiftless, and won't work, all opposites of the good middle-class virtues. . . . They are sometimes said to "live like animals" because it is believed that their sexual mores are not too exacting and that pre-marital intercourse, post-marital infidelity, and high rates of illegitimacy, sometimes too publicly mixed with incest, characterize their personal and family lives.

(Warner, 1960)

This description of the lower-lower class in Yankee City during the 1930s does not differ very much from the *reputation* of the lower-lower class population in the United States today. In Warner's time and in our own time, those who live in poverty deserve only part of this reputation. Research by social scientists has revealed that many such people are "guilty" of little more than being poor. If many of them lack the desire to get ahead, it could very well be because there is little or no real opportunity to alter their present status.

Michael Harrington described those in the lower-lower class as *the other America*. Harrington wrote:

. . . tens of millions of Americans are, at this very moment, maimed in body and spirit, existing at levels beneath those necessary for human decency. If these people are not starving, they are hungry, and sometimes fat with hunger, for that is what cheap foods do. They are without adequate housing and education and medical care. . . . The American poor are pessimistic and defeated, and they are victimized by mental suffering to a degree unknown in Suburbia.

These people are the rejects of the affluent society. They never had the right skills in the first place, or they lost them when the rest of the economy advanced.

(Harrington, 1963)

The lower-lower class lives in the worst sections of small towns and large cities. Many of the families are on some kind of public relief. Often work is nonexistent. Many, like migrant workers, are involved in some type of menial seasonal work. These are the misfits of society—the lifelong disadvantaged. Few escapes are provided within the present American social system that allow the children born into poverty to escape their lower-lower class location. Poverty is produced anew in each generation.

The Levels of the Common and Uncommon Americans

W. Lloyd Warner called the three top classes the *level above the common people*. The lower-middle class and the upper-lower class (working class) are called the *level of the common people*, while the lower-lower class is the *level beneath the common people*. The status structure of the United States as revealed by the reputational studies of Warner and his associates consists of class typologies. Each class tends to merge into the one below it and the one above it as far as attitudes and behavior are concerned. All individuals and families reputed to be located in any given class do not exactly resemble one another. There are variations. Furthermore, there are regional and cultural differences in various communities throughout the United States that cause differences between the characteristics of families reputed to be in the same social class. Nevertheless, W. Lloyd Warner claims that the social classes throughout the United States and the kinds of people in them show far greater similarities than differences. "A good test of this statement is that people who move from one region to another recognize their own and other levels in the new community and know how to adjust themselves" (Warner, 1962). To a certain degree, the six-class system discovered in Yankee City exists across the entire United States. We believe that Warner's six-class structure is a very useful way to view social stratification in the United States. See Diagram No. 6.

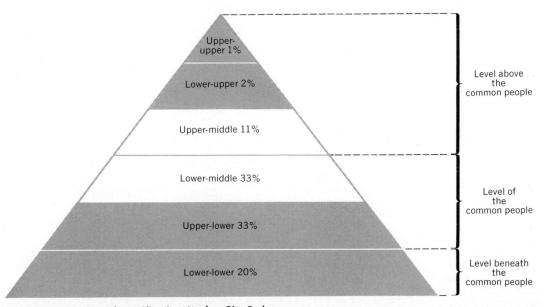

Upper-upper 1%

Lower-upper 2%

Upper-middle 11%

Lower-middle 33%

Upper-lower 33%

Lower-lower 20%

Level above the common people

Level of the common people

Level beneath the common people

Diagram No. 6   Social Stratification: Yankee City Series

THE SUBJECTIVE
APPROACH

Another way to identify social stratification within a society or community is to ask people how they classify *themselves*. Using the subjective approach, the sociologist depends on the self-identification of those being interviewed or surveyed. During the years the "Yankee City Series" was being compiled by using the reputational approach, other attempts to identify class consciousness in the United States used the subjective approach. Let us cite three classic examples of the subjective method used during the 1940s.

The Gallup Poll's Approach to Class Consciousness

For many years, Americans liked to think of the United States as a democracy that had no classes. Prior to World War II, Americans, if they *had* to speak of themselves in terms of social class, would most often simply claim to be middle class. In 1940 the Gallup Poll surveyed a nationwide sample of Americans, asking them the following question: "To what social class in this country do you think you belong—the middle class, the upper, or the lower?" (Gallup and Rae, 1940). The response was:

Upper class	6%
Middle class	88%
Lower class	6%

That early Gallup Poll study seemed to indicate that Americans were simply not class conscious: only 12 percent believed themselves to be anything other than middle class. Having been limited only to three terms (upper, middle, lower), most chose to place themselves in the middle. They probably chose "middle" because of the American emphasis on everyone being "equal" in the 1940s. Also, the term "lower class" is not something people can identify with comfortably.

Richard Centers' Approach to Class Consciousness

Richard Centers, an American social scientist, set out to prove that Americans are more class conscious than it might seem. He also proved that Americans are somewhat word conscious. In 1945 Centers used the same approach as the Gallup Poll with some small but significant alterations. The question asked by Centers was: "If you were asked to use one of these four names for your social class, which would you say you belonged in: the middle class, lower class, working class, or upper class?" (Centers, 1949). Those surveyed responded as follows:

Upper class	3%
Middle class	43%
Working class	51%
Lower class	1%
Don't know	1%
Don't believe in class	1%

If nothing else, the results of Centers' study indicate that Americans considered the term *working class* to be respectable. The term *lower class* was just about ignored.

Other surveys in omitting "working class" as an alternative thereby left "middle class" as the only possible response for many. Both "upper" and "lower" class choices carried such negative connotations within American values that most people rejected both in favor of the "middle" class alternative.

(Reissman, 1959)

Fortune **Magazine's Approach to Class Consciousness**

Most subjective studies of social stratification supply the class terms. People merely choose from the terms provided them. In a survey done by *Fortune* magazine, people were given some class terms from which to choose. They were also invited to supply their own terms for identifying their social standings. In this study Americans identified themselves by such terms as best, highest, above average, better, in between, moderate, normal, poor, poorest, pauper, third rate, underclass, American class, freethinker class, good-citizen class, foreign class, and Negro class. Furthermore, over 25 percent of those who participated in the survey did not use *any* term to describe their class position. They simply selected the category of "Don't know," which was offered them by those conducting the survey.

A BRIEF CRITIQUE OF CLASS ANALYSIS

Students who are introduced to sociology should know that there are sociologists who discount the reliability of viewing society and human interaction within a system of social stratification. The concept of social class is too murky and indefinite to be useful, they say. "The last word," says Robert Bierstedt,

has clearly not been said on this interesting and indeed intriguing subject. Problems of . . . social stratification . . . will continue to engage the best attention and effort of sociologists in the decades to come. Only after much more research, and after refinement of concepts too, will it be possible to arrive at safe conclusions.

(Bierstedt, 1970)

Still, like Aristotle, James Madison, Karl Marx, W. Lloyd Warner, and so many other viewers of the social scene, we are convinced that social class is a concept that is not only useful but also valid.

KEY TERMS AND NAMES FROM SECTION 16

social stratification

social caste and social class systems

social mobility

objective approach

ownership of the means of production

bourgeoisie

proletariat

economic determinism

criterion and criteria

determinants of social class

reputational approach

privileges, power, and prestige

judges or raters of status

Yankee City Series

Warner's six-class structure

old families

nouveaux riches

working class

subjective approach

Gallup Poll

Karl Marx

W. Lloyd Warner

Michael Harrington

Richard Centers

STUDY GUIDE FOR SECTION 16

1. Three broad approaches or methods for studying social stratification have been used by sociologists. NAME EACH OF THE THREE APPROACHES.

2. EXPLAIN HOW THE OBJECTIVE METHOD FOR STUDYING SOCIAL STRATIFICATION IS USED.

3. In the 19th century, Karl Marx used the objective approach in describing the social stratification that existed in Western capitalist society. WHAT CRITERION DID MARX USE? WHICH SOCIAL CLASSES DID MARX SAY EXISTED?

4. Modern sociologists do not all choose exactly the same criterion or criteria for identifying social class. WHICH CRITERIA OR VARIABLES ARE MOST OFTEN USED BY CONTEMPORARY SOCIOLOGISTS? (NAME FOUR.)

5. In the text we point out that social classes should be seen as typologies. EXPLAIN WHY THIS SEEMS TO BE A REASONABLE VIEW OF SOCIAL CLASSES.

6. EXPLAIN HOW THE REPUTATIONAL METHOD FOR STUDYING SOCIAL STRATIFICATION IS USED. WHY IS IT MOST EFFECTIVE IN SMALL COMMUNITIES?

7. W. Lloyd Warner and his associates produced reputational studies of several small communities in the United States during the 1930s and 1940s. BY WHAT NAME HAVE THE BOOKS CONCERNED WITH THESE STUDIES BECOME KNOWN?

8. The class structure identified by Warner and his associates remains the most popular description of social classes in the United States today. NAME THE SIX CLASSES; CITE EACH ONE'S PERCENTAGE OF THE TOTAL UNITED STATES POPULATION.

9. BRIEFLY DESCRIBE THE TOP LEVEL OF WARNER'S SIX-CLASS SYSTEM.

10. BRIEFLY DESCRIBE THE SECOND LEVEL OF WARNER'S SIX-CLASS SYSTEM.

11. BRIEFLY DESCRIBE THE THIRD LEVEL OF WARNER'S SIX-CLASS SYSTEM.

12. BRIEFLY DESCRIBE THE FOURTH LEVEL OF WARNER'S SIX-CLASS SYSTEM.

13. BRIEFLY DESCRIBE THE FIFTH LEVEL OF WARNER'S SIX-CLASS SYSTEM.

14. BRIEFLY DESCRIBE THE BOTTOM LEVEL OF WARNER'S SIX-CLASS SYSTEM.

15. Using the term *common people*, W. Lloyd Warner designated three levels onto which the six classes could be placed. NAME THE THREE LEVELS. IDENTIFY THE CLASSES THAT WARNER SAID ARE LOCATED ON EACH OF THE THREE LEVELS.

16. EXPLAIN HOW THE SUBJECTIVE METHOD FOR STUDYING SOCIAL STRATIFICATION IS USED.

17. In a 1940 Gallup Poll the results of a subjective study on social class showed that only 12 percent of Americans believed themselves to be anything other than middle class. WHAT PROBABLE REASONS CAN BE CITED FOR EXPLAINING THE RESULTS OF THAT SURVEY?

18. In 1945 Richard Centers used the same approach as the Gallup Poll with some small but significant changes. HOW AND WHY DID THE RESULTS OF THE CENTERS STUDY DIFFER FROM THOSE OF THE GALLUP POLL'S STUDY?

19. *Fortune* magazine's subjective study of social class asked Americans to supply their own terms and indicate their social standing. WHAT RESULTED FROM THIS STUDY OF AMERICAN CLASS CONSCIOUSNESS?

PRACTICE TEST FOR SECTION 16

Select the best answer.

1. What exists when a population is ranked into strata or levels according to the distribution of privilege, power, and prestige?
A. Social institutions.
B. Capitalism.
C. Social stratification.
D. Communism.

2. Unequal rewards and privileges, as well as unequal distributions of rights and duties, characterize
A. All stratification systems.
B. Some stratification systems.
C. Caste systems exclusively.
D. Class systems exclusively.

3. A system in which levels of people have statuses fixed for their lifetimes is known as a
A. Stratification system.
B. Class system.
C. Status system.
D. Caste system.

4. Which of the following is *not* a method for studying social stratification?
A. Reputational approach.
B. Humanistic approach.
C. Subjective approach.
D. Objective approach.

5. A system that denies opportunities for upward social mobility is a(n)
A. Communistic system.

B. Class system.

C. Caste system.

D. Open system.

6. The objective approach to the study of social stratification

A. Allows an investigator to decide which criteria to use as a basis for assigning individuals or families into various strata of society.

B. Relies on income as the sole criterion to differentiate social classes from one another.

C. Places emphasis on the appraisals of those being stratified.

D. Is based on the way in which members of a community appraise others.

7. Karl Marx

A. Differentiated capitalist societies into the "level above the common people," and the "level of the common people," and the "level beneath the common people."

B. Observed that capitalist societies were stratified into six social strata not unlike Warner's studies.

C. Stratified capitalist societies on the basis of the ownership of the means of production.

8. Variables frequently used by sociologists for identifying social classes include all of the following but one. Which one?

A. Income.

B. Education.

C. Ethnic origins.

D. Occupation.

9. The reputational approach is especially effective in

A. Small communities.

B. Large communities.

C. Transient communities.

10. "People in a community know who does and who does not have spe-cial privileges. They know who does and does not have access to power. They know who has prestige and who does not." Assuming the truth of these statements, which approach to study-ing social stratification would be most effective?

A. Reputational approach.

B. Subjective approach.

C. Objective approach.

11. The most influential series of studies of social stratification in which the reputational approach was used was done by W. Lloyd Warner. This se-ries was called the

A. Old City Series.

B. Yankee City Series.

C. Jonesville Series.

D. Class Consciousness Series.

12. It is said that these people have sufficient wealth, power, and social prestige to maintain a life-style devoid of anxieties about status. Who are they?

A. The upper-upper class.

B. The lower-upper class.

C. The upper-lower class.

D. The upper-middle class.

13. This class does not lack the mon-ey to qualify for top social status. They are often wealthier than those at the top of the class structure. They do lack a long line of distinguished ancestors. Who are they?

A. The upper-middle class.

B. The lower-upper class.

C. The upper-upper class.

D. The lower-middle class.

14. The upper-lower class has been referred to as

A. The other America.

B. The *nouveaux riches*.

C. The working class.

D. The level beneath the common people.

15. Which of the following is not categorized as a level above the common people?
A. Upper-upper class.
B. Upper-middle class.
C. Lower-upper class.
D. Lower-middle class.
16. Self-identification is synonymous with the
A. Subjective approach.
B. Objective approach.
C. Reputational approach.

17. In 1940 the Gallup Poll surveyed a nationwide sample of Americans. It asked them the following question: "To what social class do you think you belong—the middle class, the upper, or the lower?" The overwhelming majority of responses stated the
A. Upper.
B. Middle.
C. Lower.

Answer Key

1. C	**7.** C	**13.** B
2. A	**8.** C	**14.** C
3. D	**9.** A	**15.** D
4. B	**10.** A	**16.** A
5. C	**11.** B	**17.** B
6. A	**12.** A	

SECTION 17 DETERMINANTS AND INDICATORS OF SOCIAL STRATA

- WEALTH, PROPERTY, AND INCOME RELATED TO STATUS
- OCCUPATION RELATED TO STATUS
- EDUCATION RELATED TO STATUS
- PERSONAL ACHIEVEMENT RELATED TO STATUS
- FAMILY BACKGROUND RELATED TO STATUS
- RESIDENCE RELATED TO STATUS
- LEISURE TIME RELATED TO STATUS
- IN CONCLUSION

Objectives

After completing this section, the student should be able to:

1. Explain why no *one* criterion is in itself a reliable yardstick to measure an individual's social status.

2. Explain how corporate wealth affects the distribution of power in the United States.

3. Explain why occupation is both a good indicator and a good determinant of one's social class.

4. Describe how formal education is related to social status.

5. Determine how family background can affect one's social status.

6. Contrast personal achievement that brings lasting recognition with celebrity status.

7. Explain how place of residence can be an indicator of social status.

8. Recognize that leisure time is especially related to the highest and the lowest social statuses.

We concluded the previous section by stating that we believe that social class is a valid and useful concept. It helps us to understand and describe why people behave as they do. In this section on social stratification we identify and describe what circumstances determine social location. Most modern American sociologists choose to work with more than one criterion for determining social class. We have selected seven indicators of social status that we believe determine the privileges, power, and prestige available to the American population. We must emphasize that no *one* of these criteria is in itself a reliable yardstick. No one criterion is completely dependable in measuring an individual's or a family's standing either in a small community or in the nation as a whole.

WEALTH, PROPERTY, AND INCOME RELATED TO STATUS

Most Americans own little more than their clothes, household goods, automobiles, small amounts of cash, and a fraction of the value of a house that is on a 20- or 30-year mortgage (Lundberg, 1968). The vast majority of Americans depend upon annual salaries, hourly wages, or personal fees for their incomes. Generally, only salaries and professional fees can provide what Americans think of as the "good life." People with fairly high positions in business or government depend upon more than their salaries. Many such people receive expense accounts and other special privileges that go along with their occupational positions. As one's salary moves above the average income, one's income from expense accounts and special privileges also increase. Executives in the business world have access to expensive automobiles, small aircraft, the best restaurants, entertainment, and vacations around the world. They can afford such life-styles because of certain "fringe" benefits that add greatly to their actual incomes. Certainly these people can afford to enjoy more than clothing, household goods, and other essentials. While they remain employed, they can enjoy the good life (Anderson, 1971). These people are in the upper-middle class.

The people mentioned above are not the real holders of wealth and power in the United States. Salaries, professional fees, and fringe benefits simply are not the real source of upper-class position. Corporate wealth is the main source of all large money incomes and great family fortunes in the United States. Let us explain. The American economic system is basically capitalistic. Businesses and industries are privately owned. The largest and most important businesses are owned through shares of corporate stock. Such stock ownership is concentrated in the hands of a very small percentage of the population. This is a fact not widely advertised. Consider the following.

During the last quarter of a century there was a tendency for some Americans to conclude that a kind of "people's capitalism" exists in the United States. In 1952 there were 6,500,000 shareholders; in 1956, 8,600,000; in 1959, 12,500,000; in 1962, 17,000,000; in 1965, 20,100,000; and in 1970, the peak of 30,800,000 American shareholders was reached (Annual Report, 1975). The President of the New York Stock Exchange wrote in a 1972 message to members and allied members of the Exchange that

. . . while it is true that 106 million individuals have an indirect stake in the market through their participation in pension funds, insurance companies and other institutions, we have repeatedly pointed out that we not only want the individual investor in his own right—we need him.

(Haack, 1971)

In the same month, the President of the American Stock Exchange wrote in his annual report that the volume increase in the buying and selling of stocks and bonds "reflects a broader public base" and efforts being made "to encourage sound investing practices on the part of public customers" (Kolton, 1971).

These figures and remarks are deceiving, since "1.6 percent of the population owns more than 80 percent of all stock, 100 percent of state and local bonds, and 88.5 percent of corporate bonds" (Lundberg, 1968). We are talking about wealth here. Wealth is unquestionably a significant determinant of social class. Wealth provides the means to pursue a life-style unattainable by those without wealth. Wealth is necessary for upper-class position with only the rarest exceptions being families that retain reputations of high prestige and social standing along with limited finances. It is the upper class that possesses most of the wealth of the United States. The upper class has most of the power to decide how the nation's resources will be allocated from decade to decade and from generation to generation, political administrations notwithstanding. .

A few years ago *Town and Country* magazine described the concentration of wealth in America in an article entitled "The Wealthiest Americans." The article referred to the United States as "the last bastion of free enterprise." It was estimated that there are about 200,000 millionaires in the United States. The article featured "74 individuals and families who, with assets of $200 million or more, comprise the very summit of American wealth." At the top of this "summit" of American wealth are "oillionaires and cattle barons, investment bankers and industrialists." Also noted among the richest Americans are those who make greeting cards, pet food, and baby shampoo. *Town and Country* asks "And where else in the world . . . could such fabulous riches be mined from such comforting products as these?" (Rottenberg, 1978). We wonder how such wealth associated with such products can be so "comforting." Greeting cards, pet foods, and baby shampoo must seem very unimportant to the hundreds of millions of desperately poor people around the world.

Here are the top eight families identified by *Town and Country*:

The du Ponts of Wilmington, Delaware worth $3 to $5 billion;

The Mellons of Pittsburgh, Pennsylvania worth $3 to $5 billion;

The Gettys of Los Angeles, California worth $2 to $3 billion;

The Rockefellers of New York worth $1 to $2 billion;

The Fords of Detroit worth $600 million to $1 billion;

The Hunts of Dallas worth $600 million to $1 billion;

The Pews of Philadelphia worth $600 million to $1 billion;

The Pritzkers of Chicago worth $600 million to $1 billion.

Keep in mind that there are 60 other families whose assets are worth from $200 to $400 million (Rottenberg, 1978). Most of these people do not know exactly what they are worth from one day to the next. They *do know* they are very wealthy!

There are many more people in the United States who *do know* they are very poor. Through the years, governmental agencies, private foundations, and indi-

Affluence!

vidual social investigators have attempted to define poverty. Who is poor in the United States? Ferdinand Lundberg provides us with a challenging definition of being poor in his book entitled *The Rich and the Super-Rich*:

For my part, I would say that anyone who does not own a fairly substantial amount of income-producing property or does not receive an earned income sufficiently large to make substantial regular savings or does not hold a well-paid securely tenured job is poor. He may be healthy, handsome and a delight to his friends — but he is poor. By this standard at least 70 percent of Americans are certainly poor, although not all of these by any means are destitute or poverty stricken.

(Lundberg, 1968)

Lundberg recalls the depression of the 1930s when so many Americans became destitute overnight simply because their jobs no longer existed. He reminds us that even executives can find themselves losing well-paid jobs for such impersonal reasons as job discontinuance, company mergers, technical innovations, or plant relocation. Even these executives can suddenly find, to their amazement, that they too are really poor once the salary and fringe benefits disappear. Then, too, Lundberg points out, there are people who may not lose their jobs but who do suffer economic setbacks from medical and other emergencies that occur. Lundberg says that people with such experiences can become "as helpless as wandering beggars. They are, in fact, poor. In such eventualities the man of property is evidently in a different position. He is definitely not poor." (Lundberg, 1968).

It should be obvious to what extent wealth and property can influence the class position of an individual or family in the United States. We have said that no *one* criterion is in itself a reliable yardstick by which to measure with certainty one's social class. Still, it should be apparent to the reader that nothing can count as heavily as the possession of or lack of wealth, property, and income. Economic inequality underlies most of the class differences relating to other matters such as occupation, education, personal achievement, use of leisure time, and access to power. Now let us consider these and other determinants and indicators of social strata.

OCCUPATION RELATED TO STATUS

It seems that when humans develop specialized types of work they also begin to ascribe certain prestige to each occupation. A society located within a forest near a river might produce an occupational hierarchy in which social status was highest among warriors, then high among the boat builders, and low among the fishermen. To a certain extent, this is also true in mass, urban, industrial societies. There is no absolute answer as to why one occupation would carry more prestige and honor than another. In modern society, a high-prestige occupation usually is more financially rewarding, although there are exceptions to this. One sociological study of esteem that people held for various occupations in the United States indicated that Supreme Court justices have far more prestige than do building contractors, yet many building contractors' incomes far exceed the salaries of Supreme Court justices (Hodge, 1964).

Occupation plays a major role in shaping the life-style of an individual. It also enables sociologists to draw fairly accurate conclusions about other aspects of the individual's life. Connections can be made between one's occupation and one's education, cultural tastes, recreational and leisure-time activities, and political affiliation. If we know nothing else about an individual, simply knowing his or her occupation can provide us with insights to that person's social class. To a certain extent, occupation can determine one's social class. At the same time, occupation can indicate into which social class an individual was born. In other words, people tend to be "assigned" a class status according to their occupations. The irony is that many people find a limited variety of occupations open to them because of their social locations at birth. Depending on one's family status, socialization within the family and peer group tends to develop attitudes and expectations within an individual that prepare the person for a certain type or level of occupation. The reputation an occupation has in the eyes of the populace both indicates and determines an individual's social status.

EDUCATION RELATED TO STATUS

Many people in the United States have come to associate formal education with the means to elevate one's social status and economic welfare. This has been characteristic of modern, bureaucratic, industrial societies. The recent trend in the United States has been one in which just about *everyone* is encouraged to get in touch with the college or university of his or her choice. The high esteem formerly granted people with college educations may disappear, resulting in a *deemphasis* on the importance of college credits and even of college degrees. Nevertheless, for the moment, college is the place where everyone is supposed to be. College classes are held in government buildings, churches, business plants, hospitals, mental institutions, and prisons.

In the United States a person's life-style is vitally affected by whether he or she has not completed high school or has a high school diploma, a college degree, or an advanced college degree. Because of the bureaucratization of modern society, the vast majority of jobs have educational requirements. The individual who lacks the expected educational qualifications is almost automatically ineligible. This affects one's chances for being both hired and promoted. The higher bureaucratic strata are reserved for people with more education. The influence that educational attainment has on income is indicated in Diagram No. 7, which shows the percentages of employed American men between ages 45 and 54, the peak earning years, who earned $15,000 or more during 1971 (Current Population Reports, 1972). At present, the amount of formal education an individual can obtain will affect that person's occupation, occupational level, income, reputation, and power and influence in the community and even in the nation at large.

Not high school graduates	High school graduates		
	No years of college	1–3 years of college	4 years of college or more
5.6%	12.5%	21.4%	43.3%

Diagram No. 7   Education and Earnings for Men, Ages 45–54

Even views held on important matters are different according to the amount of education people receive. For example, 70 percent of Americans with five or more years of college believe pregnant women should be able to get legal abortions simply if they choose to. Only 45 percent of high school graduates and 33 percent of those who did not finish high school agreed. Adultery was called "always wrong" by less than 50 percent of those with five or more years of college. Of those people with less than a high school education, 81 percent called adultery "always wrong" (Ladd, 1979).

PERSONAL ACHIEVEMENT RELATED TO STATUS

The concept of the "self-made man" played an important part in shaping the thinking of 19th-century Americans. Americans liked the idea of a rugged individualist who could overcome all obstacles and win public esteem through individual achievement. Abraham Lincoln's humble origins and his study by the light of the fireplace became an American legend. Now, in the latter part of the 20th century, the emphasis is not so much on humble origins as it is on someone who is exceptional in some way. Military generals, artists, scientists, politicians, clergy, entertainers, and sport figures are held in high public esteem because of their personal achievements in the eyes of both the masses and the elite. Rock and roll entertainers are welcomed in the posh surroundings of the upper class as long as they remain popular. The high status of such people does not come so much from their incomes, occupations, education, or family backgrounds. It comes from their *having made it.* They acquire *celebrity status.*

Personal achievement can bring about lasting recognition and prestige. An individual can enjoy certain privileges and even power for many years to follow. However, it is also true that celebrities are just as apt to fade rapidly from public esteem as they rose to the having-made-it status. The rise and fall of celebrities is a theme that substitutes modern pathos in mass culture for Shakespearean tragedy in Elizabethan England. The "Whatever Became Of . . ." and "Where Are They Now?" features in mass media is evidence of the fragile quality of personal achievement as a determinant of social status.

FAMILY BACKGROUND RELATED TO STATUS

One's status and one's access to privileges, power, and prestige can be closely linked with the achievements and status of one's parents, grandparents, and remote ancestors. The significance of family background has never been as dramatic in America as in societies with nobility and aristocracy. Still, it has been a factor in American society. Newly established communities do not place as much importance on this factor as do older communities. Family background is of more importance in small towns than in large cities. The small towns of New England have been considerably preoccupied with family background. Although the Civil War was a very disruptive influence on old families, family background continues to be a means of judging people's worth in the South. Generally, family background is given less attention as one moves westward across the United States. However, some of the older Western communities continue to stress the importance of one's origins and ancestry (Rose and Rose, 1969).

Considering the American population as a whole, we can easily recognize that family background is decreasingly important in determining the status of individuals. This is particularly true if we are thinking of the importance of an individual's family *name* and *reputation*. Remember, however, the importance of wealth and property in conferring privileges, power, and prestige. The individual whose ancestors accumulated a vast fortune that has been handed down through the generations has a distinct advantage and high status in any community. In these cases, there can be no questioning the importance of family background.

RESIDENCE RELATED TO STATUS

If we knew nothing else about an individual other than his or her location of residence, this one fact could probably serve as a reliable indicator of that individual's social status. Although there are exceptions, such factors as money, neighborhood reputations, and people's consciousness of kind do tend to bring together families with similar incomes, attitudes, and behavior. This means that many neighborhoods and residential developments throughout the United States are composed of families sharing distinctive social class life-styles. We have come a long way from that time when Americans spoke of people living on the "wrong side of the tracks," but residential location does continue to influence how an individual or family is evaluated by others.

In some communities, the length of time in which a family has had residence determines the status conferred upon members of the family. For example, a medical director of a famous hospital in Boston is said to have complained that, although his distinguished career lent him some prestige, he was still not accepted as a Bostonian simply because he had not been born in Boston. Hoping for acceptance in the highest class, this successful professional man, without a trace of humor, celebrated the fact that at least his children would be accepted because they had been born in Boston. It is difficult to say why prestige should be attached to how long people have lived in an area. Nevertheless, this is the case in many communities.

LEISURE TIME RELATED TO STATUS

In 1899 Thorstein Veblen published a classic American sociological work entitled *The Theory of the Leisure Class*. Veblen described the upper-upper class as the leisure class. To be part of the "upper crust" was to be a member of a family that could live off the accumulated wealth of its ancestors. Inherited wealth automatically provided and demanded that one follow a high life-style of leisure and gentility. To *work* at anything other than efforts for charity or as members of boards of trustees for great institutions was enough to destroy a family's reputation among their fellow elite. Charity and decision making at high levels were acceptable because they were polite or genteel ways in which one might use one's leisure time (Veblen, 1899). Part of the genteel tradition within the upper classes of the late 19th century included membership in exclusive clubs. In Gerald Carson's *The Polite Americans*, he writes: "The clubs whose members represent a fair cross section of the Establishment . . . are well financed and . . . are conservators of the outlook of the Frightfully Nice People" (Carson, 1966). A popular novelist of the late 19th century had a middle-class man voice his contempt for such clubs and for what they represented, saying:

Oh, I know it's none of my business; but I don't like the principle. I like to see a man act like a man. I don't like to see him taken care of like a young lady. Now, I suppose that fellow belongs to two or three clubs, and hangs around them all day, looking out the windows — I've seen 'em — instead of trying to hunt up something to do for an honest livin'.

(Howells, 1928)

As we have said, Thorstein Veblen wrote about the very rich. These were people who were described as being very concerned about *conspicuous consumption*. They were people anxious to prove their high status by obviously consuming the "good things" of life. For example, the way in which summer vacations were spent would indicate how well-to-do a family was in the late 19th century. The longer and farther the vacation, the more prestige associated with it. Among Bostonians, the Old Families of the upper class would prefer to go to Bar Harbor, a fashionable summer resort off the coast of Maine. Nantasket, a famous beach on the south shore of Boston Harbor, was popular too. However, Nantasket was not considered to have as much prestige as a vacation spot as the farther-away Bar Harbor. Such things mattered a great deal to the powerful families of the upper classes, said Veblen.

Times have changed. Contemporary sociologists no longer emphasize the gentility, taste preferences, and recreation of the upper class. Veblen's views now seem to be too limited. The characteristics of the upper class described by Veblen were only a small part of the importance of the upper class. It is more realistic to recognize how much the power of the upper class affects the entire population of the country. As we have said, the families at the top of the social-class system decide how the nation's resources are used from decade to decade and from generation to generation. Furthermore, the wealthy upper class can afford to run for and to serve in high political positions. And they do. In recent years, *this* is the way in which many in the upper class have increasingly used their leisure time.

One more point about the possession and use of leisure time should be made. People who occupy the lower stratum of American society also possess leisure time. This leisure time exists for reasons quite unlike those that provide the upper class with leisure time. There is little for the lower class to do in a society that usually demands formal qualifications for jobs. These are the unemployed, the seasonal workers, the semi-employed. Elliot Liebow's study of black street-corner men entitled *Tally's Corner* treats this aspect of the possession and use of leisure time. In his introduction to the book Liebow writes:

The great bulk of the material is drawn from two dozen Negro men who share a corner in Washington's Second Precinct as a base of operations. These men are un-skilled construction workers, casual day laborers, menial workers in retailing . . . or are unemployed.

The main body of the data comprises a record of the day-by-day routines of these men as they frequented the streetcorner, the alleys, hallways, poolrooms, beer joints and private houses in the immediate neighborhood. Frequently, how-ever, associations which began on the streetcorner led . . . out of the neighborhood to courtrooms, jails, hospitals, dance halls, beaches and private houses elsewhere in Washington and in Maryland and Virginia.

(Liebow, 1967)

Seeing leisure time as time spent as one chooses to spend it (whether one wants it that way or not), it would seem that the people with the most leisure time at this point in American history are those who are located at the *top* and at the *bottom* of the American class system.

IN CONCLUSION

In Section 16 of this chapter we described the objective approach as one way to identify social strata. We said then that modern sociologists who use the objective approach do not all choose exactly the same criteria for judging who has what status. The seven criteria we have discussed in this section do provide sociologists with insights into the different life-styles of the various American social classes. In the next section we look at the consequences of one's social location, and we consider what the likelihood is for Americans to move upward and downward within the American social class structure.

KEY TERMS AND NAMES FROM SECTION 17

corporate wealth

people's capitalism

top eight families, U.S.A.

economic inequality

occupational hierarchy

self-made man

celebrity status

conspicuous consumption

leisure time

Ferdinand Lundberg

Thorstein Veblen

Elliot Liebow

STUDY GUIDE FOR SECTION 17

1. Most Americans own little more than their clothes, household goods, auto-mobiles, small amounts of cash, and some residential equity in 20- or 30-year mortgages. Some have access to additional fringe benefits. These sources of wealth are not the prime source of upper-class position. WHAT IS THE REAL SOURCE OF GREAT FAMILY FORTUNES IN THE UNITED STATES?

2. In 1972 the President of the New York Stock Exchange referred to 106 million Americans who have a stake in the stock market. CITE FIGURES THAT REVEAL THE ABOVE REMARK TO BE MISLEADING IN REFERENCE TO POSSESSION OF WEALTH IN THE UNITED STATES.

3. We have said that no *one* criterion is in itself a reliable yardstick by which to measure with certainty one's social class. STILL, WHAT ONE TYPE OF INEQUALITY UNDERLIES MOST OF THE CLASS DIFFERENCES REGARDING LIFE CHANCES AND LIFE-STYLES IN AMERICA?

4. If we know nothing else about an individual, simply knowing his or her occupation can provide us with insights to that person's social class. EXPLAIN WHY OCCUPATION IS A GOOD INDICATOR AND DETERMINANT OF ONE'S SOCIAL CLASS.

5. The current trend in the United States is one in which just about everyone is encouraged to go to college. HOW ARE AN AMERICAN'S LIFE-STYLE AND VIEWS VITALLY AFFECTED BY THE QUANTITY AND QUALITY OF FORMAL EDUCATIONAL EXPERIENCES?

6. One's status and one's access to privileges, power, and prestige can be closely linked with the achievements and status of one's parents, grandparents, and remote ancestors. EXPLAIN WHY THIS IS SO. WHERE DOES FAMILY BACKGROUND CONTINUE TO BE A SIGNIFICANT FACTOR FOR JUDGING PEOPLE'S STATUS?

7. Some people in American society can achieve high status which need not be associated with wealth, occupation, education, or family background. DESCRIBE THE SPECIAL CIRCUMSTANCES ASSOCIATED WITH "CELEBRITY STATUS."

8. If we knew nothing else about an individual other than his or her location of residence, this one fact could serve as a reliable indicator of the individual's social status. EXPLAIN WHY PLACE OF RESIDENCE IS A FACTOR IN INDICATING ONE'S SOCIAL STATUS.

9. Thorstein Veblen's *The Theory of the Leisure Class* presented a view of the upper-upper class as one preoccupied with displaying a high life-style of leisure and gentility, involving charitable acts, membership in exclusive clubs, and prestigious vacations. We believe that these superficial characteristics of the upper-upper class have been overstressed. WHAT IS A MORE CONTEMPORARY VIEW OF THE ROLE OF THE UPPER-UPPER CLASS IN AMERICAN POLITICAL AND ECONOMIC LIFE?

10. People with the least status in American society—those in the lower-lower class—also possess considerable leisure time. EXPLAIN WHY THIS IS SO AND HOW THEIR TIME IS LIKELY TO BE SPENT.

11. WHAT ARE *YOUR* SOCIAL-CLASS ORIGINS? WHAT CRITERIA ARE YOU USING TO MAKE A JUDGMENT ABOUT YOURSELF?

PRACTICE TEST FOR SECTION 17

Select the best answer.

1. For their incomes, the majority of Americans depend upon
A. Annual salaries or hourly wages.
B. Professional fees.
C. Corporate wealth.
D. Only A and B.

2. According to Ferdinand Lundberg, what percentage of Americans is poor?
A. 70 percent.
B. 40 percent.
C. 25 percent.
D. 15 percent.

3. Which of the following most affects life chances and life-styles in the United States?
A. Politics.
B. Education.
C. Economics.
D. Occupations.

4. The majority of corporate stocks, state and local bonds, and corporate bonds are owned by what percentage of Americans?
A. 66 percent.
B. 46 percent.
C. 16.6 percent.
D. 1.6 percent.

5. *Town and Country* magazine estimated that there are about how many millionaires in the United States?
A. 200
B. 2,000.
C. 20,000.
D. 200,000.

6. In the United States, people tend to be "assigned" a class status according to their
A. Religion.
B. Occupation.
C. Geographic location.
D. None of the above.

7. A factor *not* very important in determining the status of many Americans today is
A. Personal achievement.
B. Education.
C. Family background.
D. Occupation.

8. High social status that comes from one's "having made it" is called
A. Status achievement.
B. Celebrity status.
C. Status ascription.
D. Social climbing.

9. According to the amount of education people receive
A. Views on important matters are different.
B. People's life-styles are vitally affected.
C. Jobs are granted or denied.
D. All of the above.

10. *The Theory of the Leisure Class* was written by
A. Gerald Carson.
B. Elliot Liebow.
C. Thorstein Veblen.
D. Ferdinand Lundberg.

11. The phrase "wrong side of the tracks" refers to which determinant of social status?

A. Wealth.
B. Residence.
C. Race.
D. All of the above.

12. Leisure time is most available to those in the

A. Upper class.
B. Middle class.
C. Lower class.
D. Both A and C.

Answer Key

1.	D	**7.**	C
2.	A	**8.**	B
3.	C	**9.**	D
4.	D	**10.**	C
5.	D	**11.**	B
6.	B	**12.**	D

SECTION 18   THE SIGNIFICANCE OF SOCIAL LOCATION AND SOCIAL MOBILITY

- SOCIAL SEGREGATION WITHIN SOCIAL LOCATIONS
- LIFE CHANCES WITHIN SOCIAL LOCATIONS
- LIFE-STYLES WITHIN SOCIAL LOCATIONS
- SOCIAL MOBILITY BETWEEN SOCIAL LOCATIONS

Objectives

After completing this section, the student should be able to:

1.   Recognize that much social segregation is voluntary and give examples of where this occurs.
2.   Describe how social location can affect life chances relating to health, life expectancy, education, and occupation.
3.   Explain why the life-styles of Workton and Stylton are very different.
4.   Explain why rising living standards do not always mean that upward social mobility has occurred.

Just as there are geographic locations where people are born, live, and sometimes leave, so are there social locations in which people are born, live, and sometimes leave. Not all sociologists agree on the number of social classes in America or on what determines social class, but most contemporary sociologists do accept the validity of the concept of social class as an individual's social location. The authors of this text recognize that any social class can be seen as a typology placed on a continuum ranging from the upper-upper class pole to the lower-lower class pole. We also can recognize that an individual's access to privilege, power, and prestige is very definitely affected by social location at birth. Still, an individual's experiences *can* bring about a movement from one social location to another, either up or down the social ladder. In this section we examine the consequences of one's social location. We then attempt to determine the extent of social mobility in the United States and what factors affect the rate of social mobility.

SOCIAL SEGREGATION WITHIN SOCIAL LOCATIONS

More often than not, there is a self-imposed social segregation among both children and adults. Sociosexual mores and dating vary considerably by social class. Young people reflect the values and expectations of parents and peers (Saxton, 1979). As a consequence, most dating and courtship takes place between people with similar social status. Most marriages occur between couples with similar social backgrounds.

One contemporary sociologist makes the shrewd observation that lunch hour during a workday is probably the most conspicuously segregated hour of each day (Rose, 1971). He points out that business and government organizations may require people of different classes to *work* closely together. At lunchtime they tend to separate by social class. Occupation is an important determinant of social class. One finds secretaries and clerks meeting for lunch hour while executives meet with executives. Furthermore, in hospital or factory cafeterias catering to all classes, there are usually particular areas staked off either officially or unoffically as separate eating territories for doctors, nurses, and nonprofessional workers, just as workers on the line are apt to segregate themselves from the supervisors who eat in the same cafeteria.

Both private and public social gatherings are usually attended by people from the same social class. This form of social segregation has been explained as a result of there being a spirit of sociability expected of people at a party that requires them to treat each other as social equals. This is difficult to achieve if there is much discrepancy in class status of the guests. In fact, many people are uncomfortable at annual office parties simply because such occasions throw together people of various statuses (Rose, 1971).

It has been said that social location largely determines which parts of the total American culture an individual is apt to experience: "opera, country club, and cotillion, or jukebox, tavern, and brawl" (Horton and Hunt, 1980).

LIFE CHANCES WITHIN SOCIAL LOCATIONS

We have cited Max Weber as having said that one's social location allows for certain life chances. Weber said that one's social location grants or denies certain privileges, power, and prestige. Recall the two infants, one born the son of a migrant worker (lower-lower class) and the other born the son of a stockbroker (upper-middle class). In that section we explain how social location at birth can determine the life-styles of individuals throughout their lifetimes. We contend that the existence of social class in America is a reality that affects the ideal of equal opportunity. From birth to death, the opportunities and rewards available to an individual are affected by the person's social location. Life chances and social location are closely linked.

Mortality and Health

Earlier we said that education is a good indicator of social status. One study shows the dramatic relation between education and mortality (the frequency of death in a certain group or category of people). There is grim evidence of the difference of life chances according to social location. Consider this: men between ages 25 and 64 with less than five years of education had a mortality rate 49 percent higher than that of men with some college. Women with less than five years of education had a mortality rate 98 percent higher than that of women college

Most social gatherings are attended by the same social class.

graduates. It seems that the higher social classes not only have better life chances, they even have a better chance for *life* itself! Studies also indicate that the higher one's social class the less chance there is for a person to become a casualty in time of war (Horton and Hunt, 1980).

We have also said that occupation is a good indicator of social status. One study revealed a relationship between occupation and mortality. It suggested that executives, professionals, and proprietors are much less likely to die from various diseases than are service workers and laborers (Tuckman et al., 1965). Blue-collar workers are hurt more often on the job than white-collar workers, in addition to suffering more from occupational diseases (Metropolitan Life, 1975).

Mental Health and Illness

Dozens of studies show that the lower class suffers from mental illness much more than do the higher classes. In fact, the rate of illness increases as one views the classes from top to bottom. One study was based on a representative sample in midtown New York. It revealed an obvious relationship between social location and mental health (Srole et al., 1962). See Diagram No. 8. Here is an important point to be made about social location and mental illness: there is a great difference between the kind of treatment given the mentally ill in the upper classes and the mentally ill in the lower classes. Often the so-called treatment received by the lower class person is simply removal from society into a mental institution. The upper-class mentally ill are much more likely to receive complete medical care that can help them.

Mental Health Categories	Highest Stratum	Lowest Stratum
Well	30.0%	4.6%
Mild symptom formation	37.5	25.0
Moderate symptom formation	20.0	23.1
Marked symptom formation	6.7	16.7
Severe symptom formation	5.8	21.3
Incapacitated	0.0	9.3

Diagram No. 8   Relationship Between Mental Health and Social Location

Quantity and Quality of Education

We have said that a person's life-style is very influenced by the education acquired. People need education to qualify for jobs in business, industry, and government. The amount of education acquired can affect a person's occupational opportunities and income. A person's reputation in the community can also be affected by the amount and type of educational background he or she has. One who is born into a low social location will not receive the quantity or quality of education available to those born into a higher social location. For many years there has been an unintended tradition in the United States: we have provided the poorest classes with the poorest educations and the richest classes with the richest educations. This has prevented us from providing real equality of opportunity to our children.

Even in the lower grades, the quality of a school is very much determined by the attitudes and expectations of adults in the neighborhood. If the neighborhood adults have failed to "make it" and there is a feeling of failure all around, the school is apt to be seen only as a place to supervise the children till they are old enough to quit. Drab surroundings with crowded housing and irregular family life contribute to a lack of desire in children to succeed in school.

In recent years the emphasis on racial pride among lower-class blacks has changed attitudes toward formal education in some lower-class black communities. It may be that lower-class blacks are presently placing more importance on formal education than are the traditionally disinterested lower-class whites. For many generations, lower-class Americans have sought to get out of school as soon as possible. Young men preferred to drop out and get jobs. Young women would drop out, have children, and stay at home. Traditionally, lower-class men might say, "You don't learn as much about life in schoolbooks as you do in the school of hard knocks." This would be part of the socialization process for youngsters with a lower social location. On the other hand, middle- and upper-class families have long emphasized the importance of formal education. Obviously, one's life chances are affected by the educational attitudes and opportunities present in one's social location. If we are to break with the old traditions of unequal educations, the original inequality of social class has to be changed (de Lone, 1979).

Occupational Opportunities

Most people are limited in the occupations open to them because of their social locations at birth. Once the lower-class youth looks for a job, he or she discovers that something is lacking. Perhaps we should say that the prospective employer finds that something is lacking. Most lower-class job applicants lack the education, work habits, and poise to command a job with an adequate income or with a promising future. Most middle-class job applicants have undergone a socialization that has led them to emphasize the importance of formal education. They have been led to believe that they should rise above their family origins, although we should point out that most middle-class people retain their social location throughout life.

As for the upper classes, they have no need to fear for their future in society. From the cradle, their social location has provided them with all the means to succeed in an established, orderly society. Their privileges, power, and prestige are assured at birth and continue to provide a life-style foreign to most Americans. Some, like the Roosevelts, Lodges, Rockefellers, and Kennedys elect to devote a major part of their lives to public service. Even this kind of behavior among the upper classes can be related to the facts of their social locations at birth. Opportunities were available to them that are unknown to the vast majority of Americans. Such public service on the part of the very wealthy upper class can be seen as commendable. It can also be interpreted as a class effort for preserving the special privileges associated with the upper classes.

LIFE-STYLES WITHIN SOCIAL LOCATIONS

Because of the social segregation of the various classes and because of the different life chances available to those with different social locations, we can observe various subcultural life-styles within the class system of the United States. In this subtopic we consider the life-style of the lower-lower class nationally and then contrast the life-styles of the upper-middle and the upper-lower classes in one large eastern city in the United States.

Poverty and the Lower-Lower Class

One of the authors of this text received a form letter from Janet Murrow (Mrs. Edward R. Murrow) in which she wrote on behalf of efforts being made by Planned Parenthood programs. Speaking of those Americans living in poverty, Murrow pleaded that we seek, in her words, "the means to equalize their life chances." Believing that portions of her letter describe the life-style of lower-lower class Americans as well as anything we have read, we should like to share the following quotations from her letter:

. . . At least 3 million men, women and children live in migrant camps in unalleviated misery, without sanitation, heat or running water. A tar paper shack rents for

$10 a week per worker and is paid for with backbreaking labor: the migrant bends 600 times an hour to cut celery (35¢ a crate); crawls in the dirt 10 to 12 hours picking potatoes (30¢ a barrel). Life expectancy is only 49 years—until then the migrant simply endures, going everywhere and getting nowhere, isolated from the mainstream of American life.

The children suffer the most, starting in the fields at the age of five, exposed to lethal pesticides and machines that can maim or kill. Of the 800,000 children under 16 who do migrant work, few get past the sixth grade. They go to school four to five months a year; take turns wearing shoes and clothes; watch other children eat lunch. In Mathis, Texas, 96% of the children had not had a glass of milk in six months and in Immokallee, Florida, there are children starving. And still more children are born—often by the side of the road—their feet placed on a treadmill forever.

Throughout America poverty and large numbers of children go hand in hand— not only in migrant camps, but in countless dirt farms and in the eroded centers of our cities, regions of misery, where 60% of the nation's poor live. Too many children too soon is a classic cause of poverty: a third of all five-child families are poor, living at the edge of disaster. Such families are breeding grounds for juvenile delinquency, crime, child abuse, alcoholism, mental deficiency. The children are never well because they never have enough to eat; are unequipped mentally or physically to improve their lot: problem children who will in turn produce problem families.

Contrasting Life-Styles of Upper-Middle and Upper-Lower Classes

In one large American city on the East Coast there are two neighborhoods located side by side, separated by one street with heavy traffic. What makes these two neighborhoods interesting to contrast is the fact that both have populations that are almost exclusively white, Anglo-Saxon, and Protestant. Whatever differences there are between the life-styles of each neighborhood cannot be accounted for by such factors as race or ethnic origins or religion or by location in the city. The neighborhoods are side by side and have populations almost identical in race, ethnic origin, and religion. Indeed, both neighborhoods have been in existence for at least 75 years without any dramatic change in population makeup.

The life-styles of the people in these two neighborhoods differ because each neighborhood has a different *social* location. One neighborhood, which we shall call "Workton," is an upper-lower class (working class) neighborhood. The other neighborhood, which we shall call "Stylton," is an upper-middle class neighborhood for the most part. Some families in Stylton consider themselves to be in the upper class because of the prestige associated with their old family names. By describing these two neighborhoods we are presenting what we believe to be two different life-styles that developed because of social location.

Migrant workers, U.S.A.

Workton: A Working-Class Neighborhood

The wealth and property of Workton families is limited to monies earned from wages and houses with 20- or 30-year mortgages. Most of the houses in Workton are either small-frame individual homes or row houses. The recently married couples usually rent apartments in the neighborhood until they can manage to make a down payment on their own mortgaged house. For generations, young people have grown up, courted, and married *within* the neighborhood. Two clothing mills located on the edge of Workton have provided employment for many of the men and some of the women for as long as the neighborhood has been in existence.

Few residents of Workton have any education beyond high school. Many dropped out of high school as soon as the 16-year-old age requirement was met. An elementary and junior high school are located in Workton. Those who attend high school must leave the neighborhood each day, usually aboard public buses. Most prefer not to bother.

Leisure-time recreation includes such activities as bowling, going to movies, and playing softball and football by informally choosing up teams on Saturday or Sunday mornings. A city-sponsored recreation field located in Workton provides Workton residents with a place for both adults and children to play. Neighborhood taverns are gathering places for adults, with television, dart boards, shuffle boards, and card tables providing sources of recreation. Beer and blended whiskey are the favored alcoholic drinks.

Workton residents do not worry about where their next meal is coming from. Their diets tend to stress starchy foods, and the Sunday dinner is often a chuck roast—well done—with potatoes, gravy, and one green vegetable. Going out to dinner is not a common routine for Workton families or for young people on dates, although the neighborhood restaurants do draw factory workers for breakfast and coffee. When Workton families do eat out, it is in the neighborhood restaurants, not in restaurants located in other parts of the city that are written about by columnists in the local newspapers.

Veterans' organizations such as the American Legion and Veterans of Foreign Wars provide Workton families with organization halls and bars that also serve as recreational facilities. Bull roasts, crab feasts, patriotic observations, and dances are sponsored by these organizations and by some of the churches in the neighborhood. Most families in Workton belong to the Democratic party, and the political clubs also provide a place for community gatherings.

Medical and dental care are within the means of Workton residents, but doctors and dentists are usually not consulted unless emergencies arise. Preventive dentistry and regular physical checkups are not part of the Workton life-style. Most residents fear dentists, respect doctors, and resent having to pay money to either.

The boys of Workton have a reputation outside the neighborhood as being tough and eager to prove it. The girls' reputations are best described by outsiders as "blooming early and fading fast." Many of the women are overweight by the time they are 25, although they are very conscious of their appeal to men before they get married. Men continue to stress their own physical prowess in adulthood.

In their day-to-day social contacts, Workton residents tend to be outgoing and friendly with one another but suspicious of outsiders. Marriages occur in the late teens or early twenties. After marriage the women usually stay at home to raise children, clean the house, and do the marketing. If a young Workton child misbehaves in public, it is not uncommon for a parent to slap and yell at the child. Misbehavior is more apt to occur in the presence of the mother than of the father. The father's main responsibility toward the children is to provide money for upkeep and to discipline if the mother's authority proves to be ineffective.

Stylton: An Above the Common People Neighborhood

The wealth and property of Stylton families has been accumulated through the years by inherited stocks and bonds, real estate, and other investments. The men earn substantial salaries in executive positions for private enterprise or as professionals working independently or with private enterprise. Most families in Stylton live in large houses which, although they are old both to the family and to the neighborhood, are in good repair and can be thought of as investments themselves. As in Workton, generations of young people have grown up, courted, and married within the neighborhood, but it should be pointed out that many marry people of their class from *outside* the neighborhood—people whom they meet at social events and at out-of-town colleges and universities.

Almost all the residents of Stylton finish high school and continue on through college. Many of the children attend private schools which are prep schools for the prestige institutions of higher education around the country. It is not uncommon to hear a youth from Stylton ask a stranger "Where do you go to school?", and the answer can reveal whether that person is "one of us or not." Although the residents of Stylton are not as loyal to their neighborhood as those of Workton, they are certainly loyal to and preoccupied with their social class, whether or not they call it that.

Leisure-time recreation for Stylton residents includes playing tennis, golf, and lacrosse and attending live theater. They also go to first-run movies outside the neighborhood. There are very few commercial establishments actually located in the neighborhood except for a pharmacy and some specialty shops for food and clothes and pet supplies. The young people are very much involved with social events associated with their private schools. Adults are usually members of a private club located on the edge of Stylton. The most popular drinks at the club are bourbon and scotch in the winter and gin and vodka in the summer.

Stylton residents eat well both in quality and in nutritional value of food. An eye roast, medium rare, with a variety of side dishes is a typical dinner, and wine is served at dinner more often than not. Going out for dinner is popular with Stylton families and with young people on dates. Stylton residents are familiar with most of the good restaurants in the metropolitan area. While Workton families eat dinner between five and six P.M., Stylton families have dinner between seven and eight P.M. at home and between eight and nine P.M. at the restaurants around town.

Veterans' organizations play a very small role in Stylton. The local private club both supplies recreational facilities and sponsors social events during the year. Men belong to exclusive professional and business organizations and many to the Masons. Women are actively involved with charitable organizations and various book and flower clubs. Most families in Stylton are registered Republicans, but they do not use their political affiliation as a focal point for community activities.

Stylton's residents receive excellent medical and dental care, which is predicated upon preventive maintenance rather than emergency treatment. It is common to see young children with braces, and regularly scheduled dental and doctor appointments are all part of the year's schedule for both children and adults in Stylton. Such activities are taken for granted and considered to be a necessary part of one's routine.

In their day-to-day social contacts the people of Stylton are extremely concerned about being polite. As one of our friends has said jokingly, "If you get within two feet of a Styltonite he or she is certain to say 'Excuse me.' " The ladies-and-gentlemen orientation is very strong in Stylton. Even the young are considered to be snobs by outsiders. Both boys and girls are preoccupied with being in style, knowing the right people, and going to the right places—which might be schools, theaters, clubs, dances, resorts, and a multitude of other "right" places.

Once the young are married, the men are expected to participate in the raising of the children more than the men of Workton are. The women of Stylton often have maids to assist them with the children and with housekeeping. The women do their own marketing. If a young Stylton child should misbehave while at the market with mother, the mother is apt to grit her teeth and refrain from any real show of annoyance or intimidation. Slapping and yelling are just not done in public by Stylton parents.

Life-Styles and Life Chances

Being born in Workton or in Stylton must certainly affect the life chances of the infant carried home from the hospital. Each neighborhood has an entirely different social location, even though they exist side by side in the city. A British sociologist has said that an accurate description of the social class system is:

to say that it operates, largely through the inheritance of property, to ensure that each individual maintains a certain social position, determined by his birth and irrespective of his particular abilities.

(Bottomore, 1966)

By describing Workton and Stylton we have tried to show how social location does provide for an inheritance of property and all that has come to be associated with property that we call life-style. The life-style inheritance of a Workton infant differs considerably from that of a Stylton infant. Those inherited life-styles will, more often than not, have a lifelong influence on the life chances of Workton and Stylton residents.

Still, there is *some* movement from one social location to another. This is called social mobility by sociologists. Let us turn our attention to what chances there are for Americans to move from one social location to another within the present American social-class system.

SOCIAL MOBILITY BETWEEN SOCIAL LOCATIONS

We have said that a person's life chances are very much affected by social location at birth. One sociologist has said that "One should be very careful how one chooses one's parents" (Berger and Berger, 1972). Most people remain in the social location in which they are born. Still, some upward social mobility occurs, as does downward mobility. Sociological studies indicate that upward social mobility increases with further economic development in industrial societies. This increase in upward mobility is due to the growth in numbers of white-collar and professional occupations and the decrease in the need for blue-collar workers (Bottomore, 1966). When people get higher-status jobs, it means they have gotten more education. It means they make more money, and they probably acquire more self-esteem. Education, income, and occupations are considered determinants of social location. Thus, sociologists interpret the increase in higher-status jobs as evidence of an increase in upward mobility. Perhaps there is more upward mobility than downward mobility in the United States today. One should remember, however, that most social mobility takes place between social levels that are close together. Few people can move from the working class to the upper class, for example, within their own lifetimes (Bottomore, 1966).

Sociological studies of social mobility have usually compared the social-class status of a father and his son. They seek to establish if the son's status is higher or lower than his father's status. In one study the percentage of sons who achieved professional or managerial positions was related to the occupations of their fathers. In the following table the terms refer to the status of fathers. The percentages refer to the percentages of sons who reach professional or managerial positions (Blau, 1965):

Professional:	55%
Managerial:	49%
Sales:	46%
Clerical:	38%
Skilled:	28%
Service:	21%
Semiskilled:	20%
Unskilled:	12%

The table clearly shows that chances for achieving economic security associated with professional and managerial positions steadily decline down the occupational status ladder.

The standard of living for Americans in the lower-middle class and the upper-lower class has improved considerably over the past 50 years, if we measure living standards by material possessions, education, access to medical care, and leisure time. Many people in the working- and lower-middle classes take these improvements as evidence of upward social mobility. We do not believe that this is the case at all. The living conditions of these classes have improved, but this is not in itself evidence of upward social mobility on the part of working- and lower-middle class families. The complexities of bureaucratic, industrial society have required these Americans to acquire more education and more training. This has led to better-paying jobs and more participation in the consumption-oriented society that America represents today. In the 1950s lower-middle class youth were *supposed* to finish high school according to their social-class norms. In the 1980s lower-middle class youth (and adults) are *supposed* to get some exposure to college.

To a lesser degree the working class has experienced somewhat the same changes in educational expectations for occupational fulfillment. On the other hand, the life-styles of the classes called the level above the common people have not really changed very much. The lives of the people of the lowest class have not undergone any dramatic shift for the better. Because of technological developments, the lower-lower class of unskilled workers have less chance for upward mobility today than 50 years ago. Indeed, a goodly portion of the working class also has experienced downward social mobility. The need for their manual work has decreased in proportion to the sophistication of the industrial complex.

Americans want to believe in the creed of equality. We want to believe that, even though we may not be economic equals, we are social equals with opportunities for upward mobility limited only by one's talents, aptitudes, and efforts.

The positions at the top are open to those who have the talents, aptitudes, and whatever else it takes to reach them. At the same time . . . we must be prepared to accept the corollary: those who do not reach the top do not deserve to. Americans of all classes have held to this belief and have made it legend. The honor roll is filled with the names of heroes who give substance to the legend, and in every period there is always a fresh example of someone who has gone from rags to riches.

(Reissman, 1959)

Despite what many Americans may want to believe about the equality of opportunity in the United States, barriers to upward mobility have been and still are part of American society. The very fact of social locations as subcultures is enough to perpetuate certain life-styles for the majority of people born into each social class. For the most part, children are prepared by their parents to participate in a life-style very similar to that of the class into which they are born. The process of socialization within each class and the power, privilege, and prestige of the upper classes tend to minimize any dramatic upward social mobility.

KEY TERMS AND NAMES FROM SECTION 18

self-segregation by social class

life chances

mortality

poverty

Workton

Stylton

inherited life-styles

social mobility

upward mobility

downward mobility

creed of equality

Max Weber

STUDY GUIDE FOR SECTION 18

1. More often than not there is a voluntary social segregation among both children and adults in American society. CITE SOME EXAMPLES OF BEHAVIOR THAT SUPPORTS THIS OBSERVATION.

2. Both private and public social gatherings are usually attended by people from the same social class. EXPLAIN WHY THIS FORM OF SOCIAL SEGREGATION OCCURS.

3. Both education and occupation have been cited as reliable indicators of social status. WITHOUT CITING STATISTICS, EXPLAIN HOW ONE'S EDUCATION AND OCCUPATION CAN BE LINKED WITH HEALTH AND LIFE EXPECTANCY.

4. When we speak of life chances we include the chances for mental health or mental illness. There seems to be a relationship between the rate of mental illness and social class. WHAT DO STUDIES REVEAL ABOUT THE RELATIONSHIP BETWEEN SOCIAL LOCATION AND MENTAL HEALTH?

5. WHAT DIFFERENCES EXIST BETWEEN THE TREATMENT GIVEN THE MENTALLY ILL IN THE UPPER CLASSES AND THE MENTALLY ILL IN THE LOWER CLASSES?

6. We have said that a person's life-style is affected by the education one acquires. IN WHAT WAYS CAN THE QUANTITY AND QUALITY OF EDUCATION AFFECT ONE'S LIFE CHANCES?

7. EXPLAIN HOW ONE'S LIFE CHANCES ARE AFFECTED BY EDUCATIONAL ATTITUDES WITHIN ONE'S SOCIAL LOCATION.

8. Most people in American society are limited in the occupations open to them because of their social locations at birth. CONTRAST THE DIFFERENT OCCUPATIONAL PROSPECTS THAT EXIST FOR THOSE WITH UPPER-, MIDDLE-, AND LOWER-CLASS ORIGINS.

9. Some of the very wealthy upper class choose to devote a major part of their lives to public service. On one hand, this can be seen as very commendable behavior. HOW ELSE MIGHT THE PARTICIPATION OF MEMBERS OF THE UPPER CLASS IN PUBLIC SERVICE BE INTERPRETED?

10. Speaking of Americans living in poverty today, Janet Murrow pleads that we seek, in her words, "the means to equalize their life chances." WHAT STEPS DO YOU THINK WOULD HAVE TO BE TAKEN IN ORDER TO PROVIDE THE LOWER-LOWER CLASS WITH OPPORTUNITIES "EQUAL" TO THE MAJORITY OF AMERICANS?

11. The neighborhoods of Workton and Stylton are described in the text because they offer examples of contrasting life-styles. WHAT FIVE FACTORS DO THESE TWO NEIGHBORHOODS HAVE IN COMMON? WHAT ONE FACTOR ACCOUNTS FOR THEIR DIFFERENT LIFE-STYLES?

12. The life-styles of Workton and Stylton are different in a number of ways. BRIEFLY INDICATE HOW THEY DIFFER.

13. Social mobility is the term used to describe movement from one social class to another, and it does occur in American society. However, one sociologist jokingly remarked that "One should be very careful how one chooses one's parents." WHAT DOES THIS REMARK SUGGEST ABOUT THE EXTENT OF SOCIAL MOBILITY IN THE UNITED STATES?

14. It would seem that upward social mobility increases in bureaucratic, industrial societies that experience increasing economic development. DESCRIBE THE CIRCUMSTANCES THAT MIGHT ACCOUNT FOR THIS INCREASE IN UPWARD MOBILITY.

15. Sociological studies of social mobility usually compare the social-class status of a father and his son. WHAT CONCLUSIONS CAN BE DRAWN FROM THE TABLE IN THE TEXT THAT SHOWS THE RELATIONSHIP BETWEEN A FATHER'S OCCUPATION AND THE LIKELIHOOD OF HIS SON REACHING PROFESSIONAL OR MANAGERIAL STATUS?

16. The standard of living for Americans at the level of the common people has improved considerably during the past 50 years. WHY IS THIS FACT NOT NECESSARILY EVIDENCE OF UPWARD SOCIAL MOBILITY AS FAR AS INDIVIDUAL FAMILIES ARE CONCERNED?

17. The life-styles of the classes above the level of the common people have not changed very much during the past 50 years. EXPLAIN WHY.

18. Americans want to believe that even though we may not be economic equals, we are social equals with opportunities for upward social mobility limited only by one's talents, aptitudes, and efforts. WHY IS THIS MORE A DESIRE THAN A FACT IN AMERICAN SOCIETY?

PRACTICE TEST FOR SECTION 18

Select the best answer.

1. Which of the following describes the relationship between social location and life expectancy?
A. The lower the social class, the higher the life expectancy.
B. Life expectancy is independent of social location.
C. The higher the social class, the lower the life expectancy.
D. The higher the social class, the higher the life expectancy.

2. Which of the following describes the relationship between social location and mental illness?

A. The higher the social class, the higher the rate of mental illness.
B. The lower the social class, the higher the rate of mental illness.
C. Rates of mental illness are independent of social location.
D. The lower the social class, the lower the rate of mental illness.

3. The majority of Americans
A. Have unlimited opportunities for upward social mobility.
B. Remain in the social location into which they were born.
C. Experience a change in social lo-

cation sometime during their lives.

4. Social mobility patterns in American society have been affected by all the following but one. Which one?

A. A change in the occupational structure.

B. The expansion of white-collar and professional occupations.

C. A technology that has reduced the need for unskilled labor.

D. A changing technology that has increased the need for unskilled labor.

5. The observable differences between Workton and Stylton are attributed to

A. The different ethnic origins of the respective communities.

B. The different geographic locations.

C. The different age structures of each community.

D. The different social locations.

6. Which of the following is correct?

A. For many generations, there has been an intended tradition in the United States to provide the poorest classes with the poorest education and the richest classes with the richest education.

B. A child born into a lower social location is not apt to receive the quantity nor the quality education available to those born into a higher social location.

C. The quality and quantity of education received is independent of the social location.

7. Which of the following is correct?

A. The quality of treatment received by the mentally ill is independent of social location.

B. The lower-class mentally ill are less likely to receive competent medical and psycotherapeutic care than the middle- or upper-class mentally ill.

C. The upper-class mentally ill tend to be treated in the same manner as are the middle- and lower-class mentally ill.

8. Which of the following is characteristic of Stylton?

A. Emergency dental and medical care is the rule.

B. Male preoccupation is with demonstrating physical prowess.

C. Neighborhood taverns function as gathering places for adults.

D. Local private clubs are sources for recreational and social events.

9. Studies of the comparative social-class status of fathers and their sons have found that the chances for achieving the economic security that accompanies professional and managerial positions

A. Steadily decline as one goes down the occupational status ladder.

B. Remain the same regardless of the social location.

C. Steadily increase as one goes down the occupational status ladder.

10. Many working class families have experienced downward social mobility because

A. The need for manual work has decreased.

B. Of the curtailment of governmental welfare programs.

C. Of their unwillingness to improve their lives.

D. Of the development of more stringent welfare rules.

11. Stylton is to the upper-middle class as Workton is to the

A. Upper-lower class.

B. Lower-middle class.
C. Lower-lower class.
D. Lower-upper class.
12. Social mobility is most likely to occur from the
A. Lower-lower class to the upper-middle class.
B. Lower-upper class to the upper-upper class.
C. Upper-lower class to the lower-upper class.

D. Lower-middle class to the lower-upper class.
13. Whether one experiences "opera, country club, and cotillion, or jukebox, tavern, and brawl" is a function of
A. Individual initiative.
B. Chance.
C. Social location.
D. Geographic location.

Answer Key

1.	D	**8.**	D
2.	B	**9.**	A
3.	B	**10.**	A
4.	D	**11.**	A
5.	D	**12.**	B
6.	B	**13.**	C
7.	B		

CHAPTER SUMMARY

1. Social stratification is the division of a population into levels based upon privileges, power, and prestige. Social stratification places individuals and families into a social system of unequals. Social caste systems and social class systems are two kinds of social stratification.

2. Three methods for studying social stratification are the objective approach, the subjective approach, and the reputational approach.

3. The objective approach allows sociologists to decide what criteria to use as a basis for assigning individuals and families to social strata. For example, Karl Marx used the ownership of the means of production to stratify 19th century Western capitalist society. Modern sociologists frequently use income, education, occupation, and family background as criteria for determining social location.

4. The reputational approach is based on the way in which people rate and scale one another. This approach is called reputational because people's status is determined by their reputations in a community. This approach will work well only in a small community where most people are known to one another. The most influential study was the "Yankee City Series" in which a six-class system was found by W. Lloyd Warner and his associates.

5. The subjective approach is used by asking people how they identify their own social status. This approach depends on the self-identification of those being interviewed. Studies made by the Gallup Poll, Richard Centers, and *Fortune* magazine are cited as examples of the subjective approach in the text.

6.   Modern sociologists prefer to use multiple criteria for determining social location. Seven indicators often used are as follows: wealth; occupation; education; personal achievement; family background; residence; amount of leisure time. No one of these criteria is in itself a reliable yardstick for identifying social location.

7.   One's social location grants and denies certain privileges, power, and prestige. From birth to death, the opportunities available to an individual are affected by the person's social location. In the United States, one's social location would be a social-class location.

8.   Life chances and social location are closely linked. Mortality, health, mental health, and illness are affected by one's class location. Also, the quantity and quality of education and any occupational opportunities are directly linked to social location.

9.   Workton is an upper-lower class neighborhood while Stylton is an upper-middle class neighborhood. The life-styles in these two neighborhoods are very different. The differences between Workton and Stylton are not due to factors such as race, ethnic origins, religion, or residential location in the city. The different values, attitudes, and behaviors between the people of Workton and of Stylton can be accounted for only by reference to their different social locations.

10.   Social mobility occurs when a person experiences movement from one social location to another. Most people remain in the social location into which they were born. Americans want to believe in the existence of equality of opportunity. Still, because social classes are subcultures with particular life-styles, the majority of people have opportunities limited for them by their social origins.

SUGGESTIONS FOR FURTHER READING RELATING TO CHAPTER 6

Baltzell, E. Digby, *The Protestant Establishment: Aristocracy and Caste in America* (New York: Random House, 1964). Baltzell, a sociologist who identifies himself with the upper class, presents an understanding but critical appraisal of the American social elite.

Bensman, Joseph, and Arthur J. Vidich, *The New American Society: The Revolution of the Middle Class* (Chicago: Quadrangle, 1971). Students should be especially interested in this updated look at social stratification in America. We recommend Part III, "Emerging Life Styles and the New Classes."

Brittain, John A., *The Inheritance of Economic Status* (New York: Brookings, 1977). Brittain's view is that family background is very significant in predicting one's chances for economic success.

Davis, Kingsley, and Wilbert Moore, "Some Principles of Stratification," *American Sociological Review*, Vol. 10 (April 1945). These writers maintain that social stratification is universal. They say that it functions to motivate people to occupy more responsible positions in society by offering greater rewards as one moves up.

Dollard, John, *Caste and Class in a Southern Town* (New York: Doubleday Anchor Book, 1957). This is a classic study conducted in a small town during the 1930s. It provides an excellent backdrop for contemporary American racial relations while offering insights to the relationship between social stratification and privilege and power.

Gordon, Milton, *Social Class in American Sociology* (New York: McGraw-Hill, 1963). This is a thorough critical analysis of major empirical studies of social stratification in the United States. Gordon examines the validity of the social-class concept, the theory of social class, and research in social class.

Hollingshead, August, *Elmtown's Youth* (New York: John Wiley, 1949). This study of a small, Midwestern community focuses on the relationship between adolescent behavior and family social location.

Jencks, Christopher et al., *Who Gets Ahead? The Determinants of Economic Success in America* (New York: Basic Books, 1979). This book explores how a combination of factors can explain career achievement.

Josephson, Matthew, *The Robber Barons* (New York: Harcourt, Brace & World, A Harvest Book, 1962). This is a fascinating account about the ways in which many present-day American upper-class families achieved their high statuses. Josephson writes about the 19th-century capitalists who boldly seized special privileges, powers, and prestige.

Lipset, Seymour M., and Reinhard Bendix, *Social Mobility in Industrial Society* (Berkeley: University of California Press, 1959). This is a good source for a further discussion of social mobility written by two respected sociologists.

Lefebvre, Henri, *The Sociology of Marx*, translated from the French by Norbert Guterman (New York: Random House, Vintage Books, 1969).

Marx, Karl, *Selected Writings in Sociology and Social Philosophy*, translated by T. B. Bottomore, edited by T. B. Bottomore and Maximilien Rubel with a forward by Erich Fromm (New York: McGraw-Hill, paperback edition, 1964). This and the preceding book provide excellent presentations of Karl Marx's sociological thought.

Rodman, Hyman, *Lower-Class Families: The Culture of Poverty in Negro Trinidad* (New York: Oxford University Press, 1971). This work is a very detailed description of lower-class family life and values within a community. It reveals the impact of poverty on culture and family organization.

Schoenbaum, David, *Hitler's Social Revolution* (New York: Doubleday Anchor Books, 1967). This book offers an in-depth look at social class and status in Nazi Germany, 1933 to 1939.

Shaw, Denis J. B., "Social Classes," *The Soviet Union* edited by R. W. Davis (London: George Allen & Unwin, 1978). Shaw's chapter on social class in the Soviet Union today is objective and well worth reading.

Chapter 7
Minority Status as a Form of Social Inequality

SECTION 19   WE AND THEY

- CONSCIOUSNESS OF KIND AND CONSCIOUSNESS OF DIFFERENCE
- ETHNOCENTRISM
- METHODS USED FOR MAINTAINING SOCIAL DISTANCE
- ASSIMILATION, PLURALISM, AND MINORITY-GROUP EXPERIENCES
- LATINO MINORITY GROUPS IN THE UNITED STATES
- AMERICAN INDIANS AS A MINORITY GROUP

Objectives

After completing this section, the student should be able to:

1.   Recognize the consequences of people experiencing a consciousness of kind and consciousness of difference.
2.   Define the term *ethnocentrism* and cite examples of ethnocentric attitudes and behavior.
3.   Explain how ethnocentrism can be both functional and dysfunctional.
4.   Describe how social distance is maintained between groups.
5.   Explain how assimilation and pluralism have been part of the American experience.
6.   Describe the circumstances of Latinos as a minority group.
7.   Describe the circumstances of American Indians as a minority group.

William Graham Sumner introduced the terms *in-group* and *out-group* to sociology. *We* are the in-group. *They* are the out-group (Sumner, 1906). Each of us belongs to various in-groups. Our families, our peer groups, our schools, our fraternities and sororities are our in-groups. Even broader groupings such as nation, religion, occupation, social class, and sex can be thought of as in-groups. All of those who do not belong to one of our in-groups are seen as members of the out-group. It is truly a matter of We and They. Chances are that we do not really know why we include ourselves and exclude the others. Chances are that they do not really know why they include themselves and exclude all of us. People are conscious of their own kind and of those they consider different. People choose to associate with those they consider to be their own kind and reject those who seem different. Let us look at this idea in more detail.

CONSCIOUSNESS OF KIND AND CONSCIOUSNESS OF DIFFERENCE

The concept consciousness of kind was introduced to sociology by Franklin H. Giddings (1855–1931). He said that similarities that people see in one another encourage them to join together. Some people seek out their own kind and form groups for the purpose of social interaction. This is done consciously. Those who are different in the eyes of the original in-group then come together themselves because they have been excluded from the original in-group. Each group then becomes an in-group and an out-group, depending on whose point of view is being considered. All of this, Giddings said, is based on consciousness of kind and consciousness of difference. When people become members of some groups, they then exclude themselves from other groups. By joining with those we consider our kind, we separate ourselves from the other kind. "We are always conscious of our kind and conscious too of those who are not our kind. And furthermore, it is always *they* who are different—*we* are always ourselves." (Bierstedt, 1970). People who belong to in-groups believe that their way of life is superior to any others. This is a form of ethnocentrism.

ETHNO-CENTRISM

William Graham Sumner introduced the term *ethnocentrism* in his 1906 classic *Folkways*. He defined it as a "view of things in which one's own group is the center of everything, and all others are scaled and rated with reference to it." Sumner said that each group boasts of its superiority and, with pride and vanity, looks upon all outsiders with disdain and contempt.

Citing examples of ethnocentrism, Sumner wrote:

The Jews divided all mankind into themselves and Gentiles. They were the "chosen people." The Greek and Romans called all outsiders "barbarians." . . . The Arabs regarded themselves as the noblest nation and all others as more or less barbarous.

The Greenland Eskimo think that Europeans have been sent to Greenland to learn virtue and good manners from Greenlanders.

(Sumner, 1906)

Perhaps nine-tenths of all the names given by . . . tribes to themselves mean "Men," "The Only Men," or "Men of Men," that is We are Men, the rest are something else. . . . This is the language of ethnocentrism; it may be read in the newspaper of any civilized country today.

(Keller and Davie, 1924)

Sumner said that all other groups are scaled and rated in reference to one's own group. This means that some of the groups of outsiders are considered to be more acceptable than others. Actually, the way ethnocentrism works is that those outside groups who more resemble one's own group are the ones found more acceptable.

Not all members of any group are *equally* ethnocentric. Some members of a group are entirely preoccupied with the virtues of their own group and the vices of the outsiders. Other members of the same group may evidence little interest in such matters. In fact, some individuals within a group may feel that their own group has certain shortcomings when compared with outsiders. Nevertheless, it is still safe to generalize and to describe ethnocentrism as one of the dominant characteristics of such human groups as races, religions, nationalities, social classes, fraternal orders, street-corner gangs, and even the sexes.

Belfast: ethnocentrism can cause conflict and suffering.

Is ethnocentrism good or bad for individuals and groups? This depends on one's point of view. On one hand, ethnocentrism can be seen as being *functional* (see Glossary). It can promote unity and stability within a group. As examples, patriotism and religious dedication strengthen the morale, faith, and fellowship of human groupings. For an individual, ethnocentrism allows one to feel a certain pride in the achievements of one's own group. This can increase the individual's own self-image. On the other hand, ethnocentrism can be seen as *dysfunctional* (see Glossary). Many conflicts have occurred between groups representing different religions or nationalities. Such conflicts have resulted in suffering and even destruction for some groups. Ethnocentrism can encourage intolerance of other groups. Human technology has reached the state where humanity could destroy itself. Extreme ethnocentrism can be self-destructive by limiting peaceful interaction between various types of human groupings. In such cases, ethnocentrism would certainly be dysfunctional.

METHODS USED FOR MAINTAINING SOCIAL DISTANCE

Members of groups do experience a consciousness of kind and a consciousness of difference based on ethnocentrism. As a result, social distance is maintained between a dominant group and a minority group. *Social distance* is a feeling of separation or actual social separation between or among groups. "The greater the social distance between two groups of different status or culture, the less

sympathy, understanding, intimacy, and interaction there is between them."
(Theodorson and Theodorson, 1969).

When one group dominates and exploits (uses) another group, the dominant
group finds a reason to justify its superior status. The dominant group uses methods to maintain social distance between itself and the minority group. Diagram
No. 9 illustrates the methods used to maintain social distance and the status quo.
Now let us describe five methods used for maintaining social distance between
groups.

Ethnic and Racial Slurs

An old folk saying is "sticks and stones may break my bones but names will
never hurt me." That is not entirely true. The use of ethnic and racial slurs is the
least harmful of the five methods for maintaining social distance, but slurs used
against any particular group *are* harmful. Slurs tend to dehumanize people. Slurs
can create hurtful ethnic and racial antagonisms within society. In one study of
racial and ethnic slurs, a high correlation was found between the intensity of prejudice felt toward a group and the number of slurs used for that group. The more
prejudice felt toward a group, the more numerous the insults about that group
(Palmore, 1967). We should note that minority groups also use ethnic and racial
slurs about other groups, including the dominant group.

Stereotypes

We do not treat everyone or everything as unique. We tend to lump together
things that seem alike, type them, place them in categories. A stereotype is an exaggerated idea, image, or belief associated with some group of people. When we

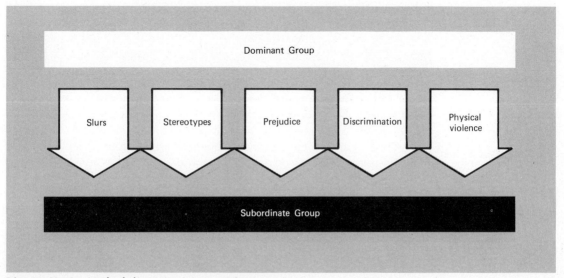

Diagram No. 9   Methods for Maintaining Social Distance

stereotype, we fail to recognize individual differences. "The 'typical' black, Jew, or Italian does not exist, except in the imagination, on the stage, and in fiction" (Berry and Tischler, 1978). Once a person has come to believe his or her stereotypes of others, the stereotypes tend to resist challenge. If one meets a person who does not behave like the stereotype, one sees that person as an exception to the rule. One does not easily give up one's stereotypes of other groups. Statements like "Some of my best friends are . . ." and "He's not like the rest of them." are examples of admitting exceptions while keeping the stereotype about the group. Television's Archie Bunker became famous for playing the game according to these rules. At its best, a stereotype is a partial truth. At its worst, it is a great distortion of reality.

Prejudice

Frequently, prejudice is seen as a hasty prejudgment of an individual or group. There have been those who believed that "if one only knew the facts and had some firsthand experience with the people who are disliked," the prejudice would disappear. Prejudice is far more complex than this. If prejudice were merely a prejudgment, then knowledge and experience would be all that is needed to get rid of prejudicial thinking (Vander Zanden, 1966). "More often, however, attitudes of hostility arise *after* groups have come into contact, and presumably know something about each other" (Berry and Tischler, 1978).

Prejudice is a state of mind. It is a set of negative attitudes and feelings. Prejudice involves "intensely held and strongly felt sentiments about an out-group. Most often, feelings about the out-group are negative, while those about one's own group are positive" (Hraba, 1979). People often think and feel on one level and act on another. There is a difference between attitudes and actions. Negative attitudes toward another group is prejudice. Negative actions against another group is discrimination.

Discrimination

Discrimination is an unfavorable treatment of people based on their minority-group status. Any practice, policy, or procedure that denies an individual or group equality of opportunity based on ethnic, racial, or sexual background is discriminatory. The United Nations gives the following definition: "Discrimination is any conduct based on a distinction made on the grounds of natural or social categories which have no relation to individual capacities or merits, or to the concrete behavior of the individual person" (Allport, 1958).

In recent years strong official efforts have been made to eliminate discriminatory behavior in the United States. As long ago as the 1940s Robert MacIver said that "It is more effective to challenge conditions [discrimination] than to challenge attitudes or feelings [prejudice]" (MacIver, 1948). Today, discriminatory practices in the United States are condemned by all the major social institutions. Discrimination no longer carries the authority of the legal system. Still, in reference to minority groups, both prejudice and discrimination persist in maintaining social distance between groups.

Physical Violence

The most severe and ultimate method of maintaining social distance is physical violence. Throughout American history, there have been countless examples of using the threat of violence or violence itself as a means to maintain social distance. Violence is always an outgrowth of milder states of mind. Although some people bark without biting, there is seldom a bite without previous barking (Allport, 1958). When other methods have failed to maintain social distance, the dominant group often decides to use its ultimate social control—physical violence.

ASSIMILATION, PLURALISM, AND MINORITY-GROUP EXPERIENCES

Recall our description of ethnic subcultures in Section 9. We said then that for many years each immigrant group in America either chose or was forced to remain apart from the general American culture. Many people believed this was how things should be. We also pointed out that another viewpoint was very influential during the same years. This was the view that all Americans should give up their old languages, customs, and identities. We quoted both Emerson and Brandeis as praising the idea of bringing all Americans together into one homogeneous culture. The first viewpoint mentioned above is that of *pluralism* (see Glossary). The other viewpoint is that of *assimilation* (see Glossary). These are conflicting views. Each point of view describes a way in which Americans might experience and participate in the American republic. Both points of view are the result of people being ethnocentric and of people observing a consciousness of kind and a consciousness of difference. Let us explain both the views and experiences that Americans have had regarding assimilation and pluralism.

Assimilation and Minority Groups

Assimilation occurs when a minority group gives up its separate identity and cultural traits and adopts those of the dominant group or general culture. Sociologists define the term *minority group* to mean a group that is discriminated against so that it experiences various types of social inequality. When we use the term we are not referring to numbers. From the sociological point of view, the minority group can be many or few in number. The important point is that the group is in a subordinate position because of prejudice and discrimination.

In United States history the view has been widely held that racial and cultural differences are undesirable. Many Americans believe that the entire population should be Americanized. This means getting rid of cultural traits that are not in line with the mainstream of culture. Assimilation would mix and merge minority characteristics into the dominant culture's characteristics. The dominant culture might be changed somewhat but the minority group's culture as a whole would disappear. As far as the United States is concerned, "Assimilation has been the unofficial doctrine" (Hraba, 1979). During the late 19th and early 20th centuries, this continued to be true. Fifty years ago American sociologists wrote that "The assimilation of immigrants, throughout the national life of America, has gone on with ease and unusual rapidity. . . . In so far as conditions are kept favorable and the process is not disturbed by official or patriotic impatience, it will continue as in the past" (Reuter and Hart, 1933). But assimilation has not continued as in the past. The winds have shifted. During the 1960s, 1970s, and 1980s there has been a renewed emphasis on ethnic and racial pride. The old melting-pot idea of assimilation appears to have been replaced with an emphasis on pluralism. American society may now be moving toward a condition in which various ethnic and racial groups will insist on maintaining their separate cultural identities. This is pluralism.

Pluralism and Minority Groups

Those people who favor pluralism believe that cultural variety within a nation is highly desirable. Pluralism is seen as a source of strength. It is believed to add color and interest to a society. Pluralists "dislike seeing a group lose its identity and uniqueness, discard its traditions, and permit its values, its folk dances, and its arts to perish from want of nourishment. They refer to the 'melting pot mistake' and the failure of the Americanization program" (Berry and Tischler, 1978).

In a pluralist society, language and other minority-group values and behaviors are maintained by various groupings. To a degree, the dominant or mainstream culture is acquired by minority-group members. However, consciousness of kind and of difference and ethnocentrism are definitely emphasized by minority-group members. Actually there would be no dominant or minority groups in a *genuine* pluralistic society. Ideally, all groups would coexist in a democratic atmosphere in which mutual respect would be enjoyed. But that is the ideal. It is not what the real American experience is at this time, although it does seem to be the trend.

LATINO MINORITY GROUPS IN THE UNITED STATES

The term *Latino* is used to identify the peoples of Latin America. In the United States it is used as a general term to include all citizens and noncitizens of Latin American descent. The Latinos have become a very large minority group in the United States during the past 25 years. The Census Bureau estimates that there are at least 12 million Latinos officially in the United States. It is not known how many illegal Latino aliens there are. Estimates have been made ranging from 4 million to 12 million. There are also 3.4 million Latinos on the island of Puerto Rico who are American citizens. Of the 12 million Latinos officially in the United States, there are 7.2 million Mexican Americans; 1.8 million Puerto Ricans; 850,000 Cubans; 900,000 Central and South Americans; and 1.5 million who claim "other Spanish" origin (Sandoval, 1980).

Population experts say it is too early to predict the impact on mainstream American culture of the rapidly increasing Latino population. Still, there is no doubt about their presence becoming more obvious, despite "a tendency to remain behind a formidable barrier to assimilation—the Spanish language" (Lindsey, 1979). Of the Latino population in the United States, 30 percent live in California, 22 percent in Texas, 13 percent in New York State, and 8 percent distributed through the states of Arizona, Colorado, and New Mexico. The remaining 27 percent are located throughout the United States. Latinos were once concentrated in the *rural* Southwest. Now 85 percent live in cities. The six American cities in which Latinos are concentrated are (Sandoval, 1980):

New York	1,907,600
Los Angeles	1,827,700
San Antonio	656,000
San Francisco	550,500
Miami	512,000
Chicago	420,000

Throughout American history the Latino minority groups have generally suffered from prejudice and discrimination. Most have traditionally been denied equal opportunity in most walks of life. In the year when the United States of America celebrated its 200th birthday, 67 percent of adult Americans of Mexican origin and 77 percent of adult Puerto Ricans living in the United States had not graduated from high school. Only 33.9 percent of the white adult population had not completed high school. At the same time, 23.7 percent of all Latinos in the United States were below the poverty level. Only 9.3 percent of the total population was below the poverty level (U.S. Bureau of the Census, 1977). An exception to this pattern would be the large Cuban community in Florida. Those who arrived in the United States in the 1960s were middle-class people who used their backgrounds to advantage in Miami. Over 100,000 more Cubans came to Florida in small boats during 1980.

Latinos are united by their Spanish language and by their dedication to Roman Catholicism, with, of course, some exceptions. But the different groups are often rivals in the same community. There is little general agreement, for example, about what those of Latino origin should be called. Many young urban Mexican-Americans call themselves *Chicanos*. Older Mexican-Americans dislike that term. The term *Hispanics* is preferred in many American communities. Around Washington, D.C., the term *Latinos* is preferred. In New Orleans the preferred term is *Latins* (Lindsey, 1979). Puerto Ricans generally prefer to be called Puerto Ricans.

The members of each Latino minority group are proud of their cultural origins and the accomplishments of some of their people here in the United States. Some individuals seek assimilation into the general American culture. But pluralism does seem to be making heavy inroads on the older goal of assimilation. Many Latinos are determined to maintain a certain social distance from those whom they call the *Anglos* (any persons from white American ethnic groups other than Latinos). Puerto Ricans, Mexicans, Cubans, and other Latinos in the United States experience a consciousness of kind and difference even among their own Latino groupings. This is additional evidence of pluralism in American culture.

AMERICAN INDIANS AS A MINORITY GROUP

There was a total of 600,000 American Indians in the year 1800. Because of superior numbers and military strength, the settlers from the American Republic moved ever westward against the will of the various Indian tribes. By 1850 there were only 250,000 American Indians. At this time there are close to 850,000 American Indians in the United States (U.S. Bureau of the Census, 1980).

Throughout American history the various tribes of American Indians have suffered from severe prejudice and discrimination. They have been described as a "population without hope and burdened with problems of unemployment, violence, and insecurity. Alcoholism has become a serious problem among Indians." Their suicide rate, especially among young people, is much higher than that of other groups. "While reservation life may be a means of preserving cultural pluralism, few Indian societies have prospered under the direction of a dominant society that has defined their role in narrow and negative terms" (Perrucci, Knudsen, and Hamby, 1977).

"There was a conflict between assimilationist and pluralistic policies for American Indians during the 1960s." Militant new Indian leaders challenged assimilationist views and demanded that Indians not become a forgotten minority. Such leaders were no doubt influenced and inspired by black activists of the times. "At a meeting in 1964, leaders of the National Indian Youth Council demanded red power [also called Indian power]. . . . Red power means retention of Indian lands and tribal identities, and a maximum control of their own development" (Davis, 1978).

To realize their new ambitions for independence from white control and to press their demands on the larger society, Indians are now increasingly organizing. Indian leadership is now adopting cultural principles from the larger society. "This means the acquisition of language skills, the reading of law, practical experience with bureaucracy, and so on. . . . The irony is that the more successful Indian leadership is," the more Americanized the Indian leaders will become (Hraba, 1979). Thus, we find that pluralism and assimilation can lead to a common result!

American Indians are increasingly organizing.

KEY TERMS AND
NAMES FROM
SECTION 19

in-group and out-group

consciousness of kind

consciousness of difference

ethnocentrism

functional and dysfunctional

social distance

dominant group

minority group

ethnic and racial slurs

stereotypes

prejudice and discrimination

physical violence

assimilation versus pluralism

Americanization

Latinos   American Indians

Chicanos   Franklin H. Giddings

Hispanics   William Graham Sumner

Anglos

STUDY GUIDE FOR SECTION 19

1. Giddings wrote about consciousness of kind and consciousness of difference. HOW DOES GIDDINGS' THINKING RELATE TO SUMNER'S IN-GROUPS, OUT-GROUPS, AND ETHNOCENTRISM?

2. Not all members of any group are equally ethnocentric. EXPLAIN HOW THIS CAN BE SO.

3. It seems that all societies are ethnocentric and that all groups are ethnocentric in reference to other groups. Whether this is good or bad depends on one's point of view. HOW CAN ETHNOCENTRISM BE FUNCTIONAL? GIVE EXAMPLES.

4. HOW CAN ETHNOCENTRISM BE DYSFUNCTIONAL? GIVE EXAMPLES.

5. Social distance is maintained between a dominant and a minority group. EXPLAIN HOW THIS WORKS.

6. There are five methods that can be used to maintain social distance. IDENTIFY AND DESCRIBE HOW EACH OPERATES TO MAINTAIN SOCIAL DISTANCE BETWEEN GROUPS.

7. There is a difference between people's attitudes and people's actions. EXPLAIN HOW THIS STATEMENT RELATES TO PREJUDICE AND DISCRIMINATION.

8. When sociologists use the term *minority group*, they do not mean to refer to numbers. HOW DO SOCIOLOGISTS USE THE TERM *MINORITY GROUP*?

9. EXPLAIN HOW ASSIMILATION AND AMERICANIZATION ARE RELATED.

10. Pluralism has been experienced by groups in the United States with minority status. HOW HAS THE EXPERIENCE OF AMERICAN MINORITY GROUPS BEEN DIFFERENT FROM *GENUINE* PLURALISM?

11. Latinos were once concentrated in the rural Southwest. WHAT PERCENTAGE OF LATINO AMERICANS NOW LIVE IN URBAN AREAS?

12. With reference to education and living standards, WHAT EVIDENCE IS THERE THAT LATINOS HAVE EXPERIENCED THE DISADVANTAGES OF MINORITY STATUS?

13. The various tribes of American Indians have suffered from severe prejudice and discrimination. WHAT HAVE BEEN THE RESULTS OF THEIR EXPERIENCES OF MINORITY STATUS?

PRACTICE TEST FOR SECTION 19

Select the best answer.

1. "We are the chosen people." This statement is an example of
A. Humanocentrism.
B. Assimilation.
C. Ethnocentrism.
D. Cultural pluralism.

2. That "view of things in which one's own group is the center of everything and all others are rated with reference to it" is the definition of
A. Cultural relativism.
B. The persistent human predicament.
C. Ethical absolutism.
D. Ethnocentrism.

3. Ethnocentrism promotes unity and stability within human groupings. This means that ethnocentrism is
A. Functional.
B. Institutionalized.
C. Dysfunctional.
D. A latent function.

4. Ethnocentrism can cause conflict among human groupings. This is to say that ethnocentrism is
A. Humanocentric.
B. Functional.
C. Illegal.
D. Dysfunctional.

5. In a study of racial and ethnic slurs, a high correlation was found to exist between the number of slurs for a minority group and the
A. Intensity of prejudice toward the group.
B. Amount of inequality toward the group.
C. Extent of discrimination against the group.
D. Intensity of violence toward the group.

6. An exaggerated idea, image, or belief associated with some group is a(n)
A. Discriminatory practice.
B. Assimilationist view.
C. Stereotype.
D. Pluralistic view.

7. When people stereotype, there is a failure to recognize
A. Group characteristics.
B. Similarities within human groupings.
C. Collective traits.
D. Individual differences.

8. Attitudes are to actions as prejudice is to
A. Stereotypes.
B. Discrimination.
C. Social distance.
D. None of the above.

9. All major American institutions attempt to eliminate
A. Prejudice.
B. Social distance.
C. Group differences.
D. Discrimination.

10. The idea of bringing all Americans, irrespective of racial and ethnic backgrounds, together into one homogeneous culture is known as
A. Assimilation.
B. Pluralism.
C. Collectivism.
D. Ethnocentrism.

11. When a minority group gives up its separate, unique identity and adopts the cultural traits of the dominant group, the process is known as
A. Pluralism.
B. Institutionalization.
C. Assimilation.
D. Cultural absolutism.

12. Any group that is discriminated against and experiences various types of social inequalities is a
A. Minority group.
B. Primary group.
C. Dominant group.
D. Secondary group.

13. The idea of a melting pot is consistent with which concept?
A. Collectivism.
B. Pluralism.
C. Segregation.
D. Assimilation.

14. According to *official* government statistics, the Latino population in the U.S. is
A. 6 million.
B. 12 million.
C. 18 million.
D. 24 million.

15. In American society, the largest segment of the Latino population is made up of
A. Puerto Ricans.
B. Cubans.
C. Central and South Americans.
D. Mexican Americans.

16. The state having the largest Latino population is
A. Texas.
B. New York.
C. California.

D. New Mexico.

17. The percentage of Latinos living in urban areas is
A. 25 percent.
B. 60 percent.
C. 85 percent.
D. 10 percent.

18. What percentage of the Latino population lives below the poverty level?
A. 23.7 percent.
B. 11.9 percent.
C. 42.8 percent.
D. 63.4 percent.

19. According to current estimates, how many American Indians are there in the U.S.?
A. 2 million.
B. 850,000.
C. 4 million.
D. 500,000.

20. These people have been described as a "population without hope and burdened with the problems of unemployment, violence, insecurity . . . alcoholism" and a high suicide rate. Who are they?
A. Mexican Americans.
B. Illegal aliens.
C. Migrant workers.
D. American Indians.

Answer Key

1.	C	**8.**	B	**15.**	D
2.	D	**9.**	D	**16.**	C
3.	A	**10.**	A	**17.**	C
4.	D	**11.**	C	**18.**	A
5.	A	**12.**	A	**19.**	B
6.	C	**13.**	D	**20.**	D
7.	D	**14.**	B		

SECTION 20   RACISM AS A FORM OF SOCIAL INEQUALITY

- RACISM AS A UNIQUE FORM OF ETHNOCENTRISM
- THE ORIGINS OF MODERN RACISM
- THE ETHNIC ANALOGY: "IF *WE* MADE IT, WHY CAN'T *THEY*?"
- THE AMERICAN DILEMMA
- THE MODERN SCIENTIFIC VIEW OF RACE
- "WHAT HAPPENS TO A DREAM DEFERRED?"

Objectives

After completing this section, the student should be able to:

1.   Define racism.
2.   Explain why racism is a unique form of ethnocentrism.
3.   Describe the origins of modern racism.
4.   Explain why black African immigrants have had more difficulty experiencing assimilation than white European immigrants.
5.   Describe the American dilemma in reference to race.

*T*o future generations it may seem unbelievable that a slight difference in the chemical composition of their skins has caused [people] to hate, despise, revile and persecute each other.

(Little, 1969)

RACISM AS A
UNIQUE FORM
OF ETHNO-
CENTRISM

In human history, many different "-isms" have shaped the human experience. People have been involved with Hinduism, Buddhism, Judaism, Islamism, Catholicism, Protestantism, nationalism, capitalism, socialism, fascism, and communism. Across the Earth, different peoples have clung to the beliefs of these various "-isms." There is one other "-ism" that has had a significant impact on the affairs of humankind. We are referring to *racism*.

   Racism is the belief that one racial group is superior or inferior to other races. It is a unique form of ethnocentrism. Only a few human groupings in history have considered themselves superior on the basis of race (Van den Berghe, 1967). Racists believe that intelligence, character, and personality traits are inherited from one generation to the next. They believe that a society develops the way it does because of the race of its people and not because of their experiences throughout their history (Montagu, 1965). Racists believe that heredity is much more important than socialization in developing personality and an entire society's culture. They believe that:

1. Human nature is determined by heredity.
2. Intelligence and character are genetically determined.
3. Races differ basically in morality and personality.
4. Intermarriage between races causes a degeneration of the species.
5. Races should remain "pure."

THE ORIGINS OF MODERN RACISM

Racism is a fairly recent kind of human behavior. Ashley Montagu claims that the modern conception of race developed during the 1700s. The growth of racism is associated with slavery and the establishing of colonies by white Europeans and Americans. Inhumanity of all kinds has existed since ancient times. But the persecutions and oppression of some groups by other groups in earlier times resulted from ethnocentrism *not* based on race. Conflicts occurred because of religious differences. Differences of culture or politics or social class brought about conflicts between peoples. People simply did not think in terms of superiority or inferiority based on race. "The objection to people on 'racial' or biological grounds is virtually a purely modern innovation. That is the basic sense in which modern group antagonism differs from that which prevailed in earlier periods" (Montagu, 1965).

THE ETHNIC ANALOGY: "IF *WE* MADE IT, WHY CAN'T *THEY?*"

Give me your tired, your poor,
Your huddled masses yearning to breathe free,
The wretched refuse of your teeming shore,
Send these, the homeless, tempest-tossed, to me,
I lift my lamp beside the golden door.
EMMA LAZARUS

The above inscription found on the Statue of Liberty has inspired millions who have come to the United States from other lands. America was supposed to be the haven for the oppressed and downtrodden of the world. Seeking a new life, some 42 million immigrants came to find political freedom, to escape religious persecution, and to find economic opportunities. Of course, these Anglo-Americans, German-Americans, Greek-Americans, Irish-Americans, Italian-Americans, Jewish-Americans, and Polish-Americans, plus the immigrants from many other countries all had obstacles and disadvantages to overcome. Assimilation did not come easily to any national group who emigrated to the United States. Neverthe-

European immigrants to U.S.A., 1902.

less, no one group had the tremendous obstacles and disadvantages of those that faced the Afro-Americans.

It has often been said that the European immigrant groups were successfully assimilated despite widespread hostility and discrimination used against them. Why have black-Americans not been able to accomplish what the European ethnic groups accomplished? James Baldwin has said that American blacks have had a unique experience in history (Baldwin, 1963). All oppressed groups share the common bonds of oppression and inequities. But, as Baldwin said, black-Americans have had to face circumstances much more complex than any encountered by European immigrants. Because of racial prejudice, black-Americans have been denied opportunities. The denial of opportunities resulted in a lower standard of living. The lower standard of living increased the prejudice of

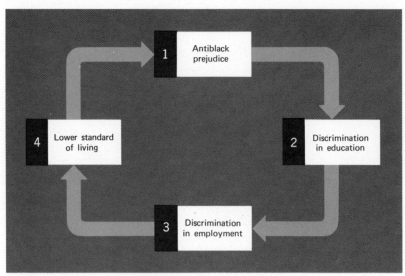

Diagram No. 10   American Blacks and the Vicious Cycle

whites. Around and around it went for a hundred years *after* the terrible centuries of slavery. Look at Diagram No. 10 to see how the vicious cycle has operated against blacks in American history.

For most Europeans, immigration involved choice and self-direction. Most Africans were forcibly transported into a hostile environment and stripped of their cultural heritage. The very nature of American slavery limited choices and self-direction. African men, women, and children were uprooted from their native lands, both physically and psychologically. As slaves they were regarded as property, as nonpersons.

Slavery and a body of law defining the status of slaves had become institutionalized by the time the English colonies in North America gained their independence. The laws defined not only the status and rights of slaves but of slaveholders as well. The masters maintained absolute power over their property. No options, choices, or alternatives were available to the slaves.

Unlike the European ethnics, blacks had no cultural cushion to sustain them. While the European ethnics encountered widespread hostility and discrimination, they had the comfort of their Old World cultures. These cultural heritages functioned to provide social and psychological support for the white immigrants. Black-Americans were systematically stripped of their cultures and their humanity. The Africans who arrived in North America were a diverse people, representing many cultures and speaking many languages. Through deliberate efforts, much of their Old World cultures failed to survive. Slaves were forbidden to practice their traditional religions and were required to practice the religion of the oppressor. They were forbidden to speak their native tongues and were required to speak the language of the oppressor, although denied formal instruction in that language (Pinkney, 1969). Again, we stress that there were no options, no choices, and no alternatives.

Another unique quality of the black-American experience has had to do with America's changing economy. When the European ethnics arrived in the United States, the economy was ready to accept large numbers of unskilled laborers into expanding industries. With increased specialization, the need for unskilled labor has diminished significantly. To make matters worse, the gap has been widening between the requirements of the labor market and the amount and quality of education being received by black-Americans. Traditionally in the United States, education has been the vehicle for upward mobility. Because of inadequate education, many black-Americans are virtually useless in today's labor market.

It is harder to escape poverty today than it was during the years the European ethnics arrived. John Kenneth Galbraith quipped that if you have to be poor, at least have the good sense to be born during a time when everybody is poor. According to Charles Silberman (1964), "The European ethnics showed this good judgment; they arrived at a time when the great majority of the population was poor. Everyone competed on more or less equal terms." Today, however, blacks are struggling in an already affluent society. The sense of deprivation among the immigrants was not nearly as accentuated as among blacks. The European ethnics came to the United States from much poorer countries, with a low standard of living and at a time when job aspirations were low. They sensed little deprivation in having to take the most menial jobs. On the other hand, black-Americans—engulfed by affluence—have experienced a heightened sense of deprivation.

Blacks are also distinguished from the European ethnics by the factor of visibility. The ethnics could resolve the problem of assimilation through *Americanization*. Silberman says that "The Irishman could lose his brogue and, if he so desired, change his name; and when his income permitted, he could move away from the slum and lose himself in a crowd" (Silberman, 1964). Black people can-

South Carolina plantation, 1862.

not lose themselves in a white crowd, regardless of their wealth or their education. They remain black and highly visible.

Silberman's statement raises another point. Immigrants settled in ethnic areas amid the slums of the central city. Once their incomes permitted, they could move away from the ghetto to less segregated neighborhoods. Because of residential segregation, however, blacks have been denied that option. Freedom of choice in residence has traditionally been based upon income and education. Kenneth Clark has said that "America has contributed to the concept of the ghetto the restriction of persons to a special area and the limiting of freedom of choice on the basis of skin color" (Clark, 1965).

Then, too, there is the element of time and nostalgia. Many immigrant groups and their descendants exaggerate the ease of escape from ghettos. When the European ethnics were immersed in poverty, they too exhibited the pathologies associated with poverty: high rate of alcoholism, family desertions, illegitimacy of births, juvenile delinquency, and adult criminality. No doubt many white groups exaggerate how easily and how quickly they escaped from poverty.

The white immigrants who worked long, hard hours had the hope of a better future, either for themselves or, at least, for their children. Through hard work and perseverance, one could make it to better times. For many black-Americans, however, a different vision emerges: despite hard work and perseverance, full assimilation seems remote.

"We made it, why can't they?" Perhaps the answer to that question is that the history of ethnic Americans and the history of black-Americans is so different that the question itself is meaningless.

THE AMERICAN DILEMMA

After years of thorough study, a major work in American race relations appeared in 1944 entitled *An American Dilemma*. Under the direction of Gunnar Myrdal, a Swedish social scientist, and supported by funds from the Carnegie Corporation, a group of scholars delved into the racial problems of American society. Their central thesis emerged as follows: despite all the economic, political, and social ramifications, the American race issue was basically an ideological issue, and the American dilemma was pictured as a moral dilemma featuring

> ... the ever raging conflict between, on the one hand, the valuations preserved on the general planes which we shall call the "American Creed," where the American thinks, talks and acts under the influence of high national and Christian precepts, and, on the other hand, the valuations on specific planes of individual and group living, where personal and local interests; economic, social and sexual jealousies; considerations of community prestige and conformity; group prejudices against particular persons or types of people; and all sorts of miscellaneous events, impulses, and habits dominate his outlook.

> (Rose, 1964)

Myrdal viewed the difference between the American *creed* of humanism, justice, and equality and the American *deed* of racism, prejudice, and discrimination as the cause of the American dilemma.

In his famous essay entitled "Letter from a Birmingham Jail," Martin Luther King, Jr., wrote: "We know through painful experience that freedom is never voluntarily given by the oppressor; it must be demanded by the oppressed." The protest of black-Americans has been an attempt to reconcile the difference between the American creed and the American deed, as identified by Gunnar Myrdal in *An American Dilemma.* As the Honorable John Conyers, Democratic Congressman from Michigan, has said, "All we want is for America to be what it says it is" (Biesanz and Biesanz, 1969).

THE MODERN SCIENTIFIC VIEW OF RACE

Modern science rejects the ideology of racism. The United Nations Educational, Scientific, and Cultural Organization (UNESCO) convened a group of experts in the fields of biology, genetics, and physical anthropology to discuss the scientific view of race. The following excerpts come from a statement published by UNESCO.

One: *Scientists are generally agreed that all [people] living today belong to a single species,* Homo sapiens, *and are derived from a common stock.*

Two: *Some of the physical differences between human groups are due to differences in hereditary constitution and some to differences in the environments in which they have been brought up. . . . Existing races are merely the results of the total effect of such processes (hereditary and environment) on the human species.*

Three: *National, religious, geographical, linguistic and cultural groups do not necessarily coincide with racial groups; and the cultural traits of such groups have no demonstrated connection with racial traits. Americans are not a race . . . Jews are not a race . . . nor are people who speak English. . . . The use of the term "race" in speaking of such groups may be a serious error, but it is one which is habitually committed.*

Four: *Human races can be, and have been, classified in different ways by different anthropologists. Most of them agree in classifying the greater part of existing [humankind] into at least three large units (Mongoloid, Negroid, Caucasoid). . . . Furthermore, the differences in physical structure which distinguish one major group from another give no support to popular notions of general "superiority" or "inferiority" which are sometimes implied in referring to these groups.*

Five: *Most anthropologists do not include mental characteristics in the classification of human races. Studies within a single race have shown that both innate capacity and environmental opportunity determine the results of tests of intelligence and temperament, though their relative importance is disputed. . . . It has been recorded that different groups of the same race . . . may yield considerable differences in intelligence tests. When, however, the two groups have been brought up from childhood in similar environments, the differences are very slight.*

Six: *The scientific material available to us at present does not justify the conclusions that inherited genetic differences are a major factor in producing the differences between the cultural achievements of different peoples or groups.*

Seven: *There is no evidence for the existence of so-called "pure" races. . . . In regard to race mixture, the evidence points to the fact that human hybridization has* *been going on for an indefinite, but considerable time. . . . As there is no reliable evidence that disadvantageous effects are produced thereby, no biological justification exists for prohibiting intermarriage between persons of different races.* *

Because of our rage for order we may very well classify *Homo sapiens* into this race and that race and yet another race or two, but modern science's message is clear: humankind is one.

"WHAT HAPPENS TO A DREAM DEFERRED?"

Langston Hughes was an internationally famous black poet and author. He was a gentle man, yet there was a prophetic warning in his poem entitled "What Happens to a Dream Deferred?"

Does it dry up
like a raisin in the sun?
Or fester like a sore—
And then run?
Does it stink like rotten meat?
Or crust and sugar over—
Like a syrupy sweet?
Maybe it just sags
Like a heavy load.
Or does it explode?*
                    LANGSTON HUGHES

Not all dreams are impossible dreams. We believe that it is becoming increasingly clear that the American dream of equality and social justice for all can be fulfilled through the dedicated efforts of the present generation of Americans. Like individuals, nations must struggle to live according to their best ideals. Because of human frailties, it *is* difficult to match the creed with the deed. Still, we believe that the American dream is one to be preferred and fulfilled rather than deferred and defiled.

KEY TERMS AND NAMES FROM SECTION 20

racism and racists

the vicious cycle

immigration

slavery in the United States

*From *Race and Science. The race question in modern science.* Reproduced by permission of UNESCO. Copyright © 1951, 1952, 1953, 1954, 1960, 1961.
*Reprinted by permission of Harold Ober Associates, Inc. Copyright © 1951 by Langston Hughes.

visibility

ghetto

residential segregation

American dilemma

American creed and American deed

scientific view of race: UNESCO

Mongoloid, Negroid, Caucasoid

James Baldwin

Gunnar Myrdal

Langston Hughes

STUDY GUIDE FOR SECTION 20

1. Human affairs have been dramatically affected by racism. DEFINE RACISM. EXPLAIN WHY IT IS CONSIDERED A UNIQUE FORM OF ETHNOCENTRISM.

2. Frequently, it has been said that although European immigrants encountered hostility and discrimination, they did manage to become assimilated despite the obstacles. WHY HAVE BLACK-AMERICANS HAD MORE DIFFICULTY IN REFERENCE TO ASSIMILATION?

3. No doubt white ethnic groups have exaggerated how easily and how quickly they escaped from poverty. WHEN EUROPEAN ETHNICS WERE CAUGHT UP IN POVERTY, WHAT PATHOLOGIES ASSOCIATED WITH POVERTY DID THEY EXHIBIT?

4. Privileged groups seldom give up their privileges voluntarily. WHAT DID MARTIN LUTHER KING, JR., SAY ABOUT OPPRESSORS, FREEDOM, AND THE OPPRESSED?

5. Congressman John Conyers is quoted as saying, "All we want is for America to be what it says it is." HOW DOES THIS RELATE TO THE MORAL PROBLEM IDENTIFIED BY GUNNAR MYRDAL IN *AN AMERICAN DILEMMA*?

6. Blacks are also distinguished from the white ethnics by the factor of visibility. WHAT IS MEANT BY THE TERM *VISIBILITY* AND HOW HAS IT AFFECTED ETHNICS AND BLACKS IN AMERICAN HISTORY?

7. Racism is a fairly recent kind of human behavior. HOW DOES ASHLEY MONTAGU DESCRIBE THE ORIGINS OF RACISM?

8. Describe how the vicious cycle has operated against blacks in American history.

9. Modern science rejects the ideology of racism in a statement published by UNESCO. CITE SOME POINTS MADE IN THE UNESCO STATEMENT.

PRACTICE TEST FOR SECTION 20

Select the best answer.

1. Racists believe that

A. Intelligence and character are socially determined.

B. Heredity is more important than socialization.

C. Human nurture is more important than human nature.

D. Differences between individuals are greater than differences between racial groups.

2. According to Montagu, modern group antagonisms differ from antagonisms in earlier periods of history because they are based on

A. Cultural differences.

B. Socioeconomic factors.

C. Religious differences.

D. Racial differences.

3. Which of the following is *not* caused by visibility?

A. Easy assimilation.

B. Identifiability.

C. Difficulty in assimilation.

D. All are caused by visibility.

4. According to Kenneth Clark, "America has contributed to the concept of the ghetto the restriction of persons to a special area and the limiting of freedom of choice on the basis of . . ."

A. Religious affiliation.

B. Socioeconomic status.

C. Ethnic background.

D. Skin color.

5. According to *An American Dilemma*, the cause of the racial issue is a gap between

A. Good people and bad people.

B. Humanistic values and production values.

C. Rich people and poor people.

D. The American creed and the American deed.

6. According to UNESCO, the Jewish people are classified by all of the following except one. Which one?

A. *Homo sapiens.*

B. Cultural group.

C. Racial group.

D. Ethnic group.

7. Because of racial prejudice, black-Americans have been denied opportunities. The denial of opportunities has resulted in a lower standard of living. The lower standard of living has increased the prejudice of whites. This process is known as the

A. Culture of poverty.

B. Ethnic analogy.

C. Definition of the situation.

D. Vicious cycle.

8. Racism is a form of ethnocentrism based upon a belief in the superiority of a group's

A. Cultural evolution.

B. Technological development.

C. Biological endowment.

D. Socioeconomic development.

9. According to Ashley Montagu, racism had its origins in the

A. 18th century.

B. 17th century.

C. 19th century.

D. 15th century.

10. According to *An American Dilemma*, the central issue in American race relations is

A. Political.

B. Economic.

C. Social.

D. Moral.

11. The European ethnics could resolve the problems associated with assimilation through a change in name or a change in accent. Racial minorities, however, cannot change their skin col-

or. This difference indicates the significance of
A. The vicious cycle.
B. The ethnic analogy.
C. Visibility.
D. Pluralism.
12. "We know through painful experience that freedom is never voluntarily given by the oppressor; it must be demanded by the oppressed." This statement is attributed to
A. Malcolm X.
B. The Supreme Court Decision of 1954.
C. Martin Luther King, Jr.
D. Rosa Parks.

Answer Key

1.	B	**7.**	D
2.	D	**8.**	C
3.	A	**9.**	A
4.	D	**10.**	D
5.	D	**11.**	C
6.	C	**12.**	C

SECTION 21   SEXISM AS A FORM OF SOCIAL INEQUALITY

- FEMININITY AND MASCULINITY:FROM NATURE OR NURTURE?
- PATRIARCHY AS A SOCIAL SYSTEM
- KNOW YOUR ENEMY: A SAMPLING OF SEXIST QUOTATIONS
- ANDROGYNY AS A SOCIAL SYSTEM
- IN CONCLUSION?

Objectives

After completing this section, the student should be able to:

1. Explain how femininity and masculinity are acquired.
2. Describe characteristics of patriarchy as a social system.
3. Recognize sexist remarks.
4. Describe characteristics of androgyny as a social system.

Throughout history, the cultures of most human societies have clearly defined specific social roles for women and other specific social roles for men. Closely linked to social roles are the social statuses that are available to men and women. Like social roles, social statuses are, more often than not, related to an individual's sex. Historically, in the United States and in other countries, women have experienced the types of social inequalities associated with minority group status.

In *Women, Society and Change*, Evelyne Sullerot writes: "It is clear that women are dissatisfied almost throughout the world and that a constant debate about their position is in progress. Almost every national constitution proclaims equality of rights and responsibilities for citizens of both sexes" (Sullerot, 1971). Nevertheless, women have minority status in almost all those nations. Sullerot says that resistance to *real* legal equality is extremely strong. The resistance comes not only from men. Many women continue to argue in favor of the old traditional male and female social roles.

FEMININITY AND MASCULINITY: FROM NATURE OR NURTURE?

Over and over we have written that people acquire their values, attitudes, and behaviors by exposure to the culture of their society. We acknowledge that there are biological factors at work in everyone's life too. But we believe that social influences have more to do with shaping personalities than does heredity. On the subject of femininity and masculinity, we must apply the same rule. Feminine and masculine characteristics are defined by culture and acquired by those who participate in a society's culture. What contributes more to what we call femininity and masculinity? Sociologists would say nurture, meaning the socialization process of any particular society, not human nature.

Margaret Mead published *Sex and Temperament in Three Primitive Societies* in 1935. She argued then that masculinity and femininity are, for the most part, culturally determined. Mead has described some remote cultures in which men are as tender with and as happy to care for children as are women. Simply because a woman's breast fills with milk does not mean that the woman suddenly also is filled with deep, selfless love and maternal instincts. If this seems to happen, the happening is not biological—it is a result of cultural conditioning.

What is feminine and how does one achieve femininity? What is masculine, and how does one achieve masculinity? Most sociologists agree with Margaret Mead. Masculinity and femininity are traits that are defined by society and then taught to male and female children through the socialization process.

PATRIARCHY AS A SOCIAL SYSTEM

What is patriarchalism? It is the authority, the rule, the dominion of the male as father. In marriage that is patriarchal, the husband is the head. If, as usually happens, it is also patrilineal, the children take their father's name. If it is also patrilocal, the son takes his bride into his father's home, which becomes her home also. . . .

Patriarchalism is the enthronement of man as father. As father he is the bearer of the torch of life. It is passed on, that precious torch, from generation to generation—through the medium of a womb. To have a womb you need a woman. A woman is, supremely, a womb, as a man is, supremely, the bearer of the seed of life. That is their destiny. Their destiny decides their function. Their function defines their relationship.

(Mace and Mace, 1960)

The above quotation describes both attitudes and behaviors that occur within marriage and family. These same attitudes and behaviors extend into the general cultural fabric of most societies. In patriarchal societies, men have access to far more privileges, power, and prestige than do women, with rare exceptions. In other words, a patriarchal social system is a system in which women are treated as a minority group. And, as we point out throughout this chapter, minority groups are the victims of social inequality in American society.

Patriarchy is a social system in which the man usually rules with unchallenged authority the lives of his women and children. It is a system in which adultery by women is considered unforgivable while adultery by men brings little or no sanctions. This is called the double standard. Women are required or encouraged to remain in domestic confinement, removed from most outside activities. Ownership of property is either denied women or is very limited. In a patriarchal system, most women remain at home, where it is thought they belong. Women have little to say about any economic or political matters of importance.

From just a housewife to just a typist.

American society continues to be patriarchal in many ways. There are some shifting attitudes. Women who go out to work are now often described approvingly as seeking self-fulfillment. Women who stay "at home" meet with subtle disapproval. Beatrice Buckler, editor of *Working Women*, said that once "a woman had to defend her position if she wanted to work. Now you have only to go out and ask the nearest housewife what she does and she'll answer, "Just a housewife." There's been a tremendous change in attitude" (*Newsweek*, 1976). See Diagram No. 11.

Increasing numbers of women seek to enter the labor market. Some are married. Some have children. Some are widowed, divorced, separated, or single. Whatever their status, most women earn considerably less than men. Women are overrepresented in low-status, low-paying jobs. This results from sexism—a form of social inequality. Sexism is the basis of any patriarchal social system. Sexism is a form of prejudice and discrimination. It has occurred in most societies. Consider the following sexist remarks from around the world.

KNOW YOUR
ENEMY: A
SAMPLING OF
SEXIST
QUOTATIONS

Robin Morgan's *Sisterhood Is Powerful* is an anthology of writings from the women's movement, published in 1970. We especially appreciate Robin Morgan's including in her book the following collection of sexist quotations. These quota-

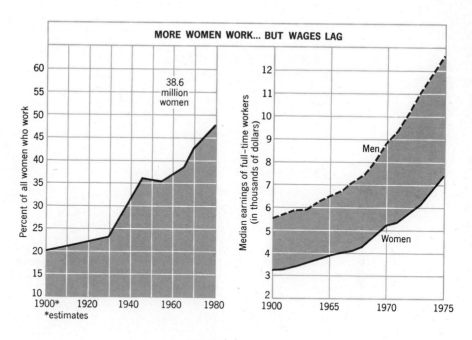

Diagram No. 11   Women, Working, and Wages

tions offer excellent examples of taken-for-granted attitudes held by men in nations from all over the world. Recall that slurs are one method for maintaining social distance so that one group is dominant and another is subordinate.

The glory of man is knowledge, but the glory of woman is to renounce knowledge.

Chinese proverb

Women are sisters nowhere.

West African proverb

Whenever a woman dies there is one quarrel less on earth.

German proverb

In childhood a woman must be subject to her father; in youth, to her husband; when her husband is dead, to her sons. A woman must never be free of subjugation.

The Hindu Code of Manu, V

And the rib, which the Lord God had taken from man, made he a woman and brought her unto the man. And Adam said, This is now bone of my bone, and flesh of my flesh; she shall be called Woman, because she was taken out of Man.

Genesis 2:22–23

Suffer women once to arrive at an equality with you, and they will from that moment become your superiors.

Cato the Elder, 195 b.c.

The five worst infirmities that afflict the female are indocility, discontent, slander, jealousy, and silliness. . . . Such is the stupidity of woman's character, that it is incumbent upon her, in every particular, to distrust herself and to obey her husband.

Confucian Marriage Manual

A man in general is better pleased when he has a good dinner than when his wife talks Greek.

Samuel Johnson

The whole education of women ought to be relative to men. To please them, to be useful to them, to make themselves loved and honored by them, to educate them when young, to care for them when grown, to counsel them, to console them, and to make life sweet and agreeable to them—these are the duties of women at all times and what should be taught them from infancy.

Jean Jacques Rousseau

Most women have no characters at all.

Alexander Pope

I never knew a tolerable woman to be fond of her own sex.

Jonathan Swift

Nature intended women to be our slaves . . . they are our property; we are not theirs. They belong to us, just as a tree that bears fruit belongs to a gardener. What a mad idea to demand equality for women! . . . Women are nothing but machines for producing children.

Napoleon Bonaparte

To man a man is but a mind. Who cares what face he carries or what he wears? But woman's body is the woman.

Ambrose Bierce

Regard the society of women as a necessary unpleasantness of social life, and avoid it as much as possible.

Count Leo Tolstoy

And a woman is only a woman but a good cigar is a smoke.

Rudyard Kipling

Woman have great talent, but no genius, for they always remain subjective.

Arthur Schopenhauer

The woman's fundamental status is that of her husband's wife, the mother of his children.

Talcott Parsons

Women should receive a higher education, not in order to become doctors, lawyers, or professors, but to rear their offspring to be valuable human beings.

Alexis Carell, MAN, THE UNKNOWN

Woman as a person enjoys a dignity equal with man, but she was given different tasks by God and by Nature which perfect and complete the work entrusted to man.

Pope John XXIII

It would be preposterously naive to suggest that a B.A. can be made as attractive to girls as a marriage license.

Dr. Grayson Kirk, former President, Columbia University

Women, in general, want to be loved for what they are and men for what they accomplish. The first for their looks and charm, the latter for their actions.

Theodor Reik

Women are usually more patient in working at unexciting, repetitive tasks. . . . Women on the average have more passivity in the inborn core of their personality. . . . I believe women are designed in their deeper instincts to get more pleasure out of life—not only sexually but socially, occupationally, maternally—when they are not aggressive. To put it another way, I think that when women are encouraged to be competitive too many of them become disagreeable.

Dr. Benjamin M. Spock, DECENT AND INDECENT

When we selected these quotations from Robin Morgan's *Sisterhood Is Powerful,* we found ourselves laughing from time to time. When we showed the quotations to some of our friends, both men and women, we found that most of them would laugh, too. We expect that students who are reading this book will also laugh. Why do we laugh? Do we laugh because the quotations themselves seem absurd to us? Do we laugh because the men who said such things seem so silly to us? Do men laugh because they are happy that what they really think has already been said by historical celebrities? Do women laugh because they have been socially conditioned to think of their sisters as deserving of ridicule? And, finally, do we laugh because we are all simply nervous, both men and women, about the entire subject of women's liberation? Did you laugh? Why?

We believe that most of us who laugh at these sexist remarks are laughing at ourselves and at the collective cultural experiences of our ancestors and ourselves, which has led to such utterances. Ridicule can be a powerful social weapon for creating social change. If we interpret sexist remarks as being ridiculous in themselves, it is a socially healthy sign of the times that could mean that healthy social change is in the making.

ANDROGYNY AS A SOCIAL SYSTEM

I think what I would ideally like to see in our society is that . . . one is simply born a girl or a boy and that's it. And no worry about an activity de-feminizing or emasculating one.

(David Riesman)

Imagine a society in which the concept of masculinity and femininity would not be meaningful. That would be *androgyny*. Androgyny in society would mean that babies would not be committed at birth to specific adult roles based on whether they happened to be born female or male. Social roles would not be assigned on the basis of sex.

One of the celebrated books on sex roles is Caroline Bird's *Born Female*. Its publisher refers to *Born Female* as the "Source Book for the Women's Liberation Movement." Bird's thesis is that patriarchy is a social system that promotes inequality between the sexes. The liberation of women would also accomplish the liberation of men from sex roles that severely limit individual freedom of choice (Bird, 1970).

Republican convention, Kansas City, 1976.

Masters and Johnson also associate women's liberation with men's liberation. In *Redbook* magazine, Masters and Johnson, discussing sex and equality, said that

Any woman who has the will and the courage to break out of the cell that histori- cally has been considered appropriate for females, a cell comfortably padded with privileges, has something of value to offer a man — the key to his own prison door. For wherever equality of the sexes exists, and especially in the intimate world of marriage, liberation of the female liberates the male.

(Masters and Johnson, 1972)

In an androgynous society, the sexual drive would continue to be a significant factor in personal lives, but sexual identity would no longer be a decisive factor in public life. Men and women could see one another first as human beings who have interests, thoughts, feelings, life-styles, and hopes for the future. Their sexu- al differences could be stressed in personal relationships, but not in all the sec- ondary relationships that are characteristic of mass society. Men and women would tend to be more alike than they have seemed to be in patriarchal socie- ties. Similarities in social roles should have no serious consequences psychologi- cally or sociologically. Considering this, Alice Rossi said that

The physiological differences between male and female are sufficiently clear and so fundamental to self-definition that no change in the direction of greater similari- ty between male and female social roles is going to disturb the sex identity of chil- dren or adults. No one would be confused if men were more tender and expressive and women more aggressive and intellectual. If anything, greater similarity in fami- ly and occupational roles would add zest and vitality to the relations between men and women and minimize the social segregation of the sexes.

(Rossi, 1965)

Androgyny would permit an individual to select any mannerism, style, occupa- tion, and orientation without fear of being considered strange, unusual, or a dis- credit to one's sexual identity. That would be freedom. That would be consistent with the American dream.

Like Caroline Bird, we believe that after centuries of emphasizing the differ- ences between men and women things are changing. We may very well be head- ing into an androgynous world in which the most significant thing about a person will no longer be his or her sex. If this occurs, the traditional minority status of women in society will be a thing of the past.

Nine out of ten women will earn money at some time in their lives. Bird cites surveys reporting that half of the full-time homemakers say that they expect to work outside the home at some time in the future. One private social science re- search organization estimates that by the year 2000 most women will work be- tween the ages of 18 and 60, excluding those years required for childbearing. Simply because a woman is staying at home this year does not mean that she will stay at home indefinitely. See Diagram No. 12.

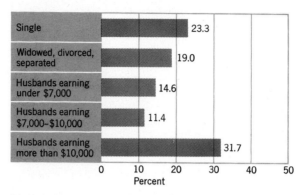

Diagram No. 12   Women at Work (Source. Newsweek—Harry Carter.)

"In 1970, 43 percent of adult American women worked outside the home. Today, a record 51 percent do—and for the first time in history, working wives outnumber housewives" (*Newsweek*, 1980). Many occupations in the United States continue to be thought of as either man's work or woman's work. A number of influences are doing away with this view of occupations. There is a growing number of *new* occupations that have not been sex-typed. When new types of jobs appear, they are most likely to be filled by the first qualified people to apply, regardless of sex. Even the old occupations are breaking away from the traditional sex typing. The trend is increasing in each decade. Indeed, there is now a determined effort being made to undo the damage of discriminatory hiring practices of the past. Both government agencies and business concerns are engaged in affirmative action on behalf of all minorities, including women.

Discounting any relationship between a job and a person's sex, Dr. Rebecca Sparling, of General Dynamics, declared:

There is nothing inherently feminine about mixing a given batch of materials, exposing it to a definite temperature for a definite time, and producing a cake. There is nothing inherently masculine in mixing a batch of materials, exposing it to a definite temperature for a given time, and producing iron castings. I have done both and find them satisfying occupations.

(Bird, 1970)

IN CONCLUSION?   Thus women's secrets I've surveyed
And let them see how curiously they're made,
And that, tho' they of different sexes be,
Yet in the whole they are the same as we.

For those that have the strictest searchers been,
Find women are but men turned outside in;
And men, if they but cast their eyes about,
May find they're women with their inside out.
                                                    ARISTOTLE

KEY TERMS AND
NAMES FROM
SECTION 21

femininity reconsidered

masculinity reconsidered

patriarchalism

women as a minority group

the double standard

domestic confinement of women

sexism and sexists

androgyny

Evelyne Sullerot

Margaret Mead

Robin Morgan

Caroline Bird

STUDY GUIDE FOR SECTION 21

1. Almost all national constitutions assure equality for citizens of both sexes. WHICH PEOPLE CONTINUE TO RESIST *REAL* LEGAL EQUALITY?

2. Biological factors influence everyone's life. We also emphasize how personalities are shaped by socialization. HOW ARE FEMININITY AND MASCULINITY ACQUIRED? EXPLAIN YOUR ANSWER.

3. DESCRIBE THE OPPORTUNITIES FOR MEN AND WOMEN THAT EXIST WITHIN A PATRIARCHAL SOCIAL SYSTEM.

4. A sampling of sexist quotations appears in this section. WHAT CONCLUSION CAN BE DRAWN ABOUT SEXISM BASED ON THE ORIGINS OF THESE QUOTATIONS?

5. Caroline Bird wrote *Born Female*. WHAT IS BIRD'S THESIS ABOUT PATRIARCHY AND ABOUT WHAT COULD BE ACCOMPLISHED WITH THE LIBERATION OF WOMEN?

6. With androgyny, the sexual drive would still be a significant factor in personal relationships, but sexual identity would not be an important factor in public life. EXPLAIN WHAT THIS STATEMENT MEANS.

7. Most occupations in the United States continue to be thought of as either a man's work or woman's work. HOW ARE THE NEW OCCUPATIONS AFFECTING THIS POINT OF VIEW?

8. In 1980, 51 percent of adult American women worked outside the home. WERE THERE MORE MARRIED WOMEN ACTING AS HOUSEWIVES OR MORE MARRIED WOMEN WORKING OUTSIDE THE HOME?

9. Aristotle said that the "strictest searchers" for knowledge about men and women agree in their conclusions. WHAT IS THE MESSAGE IN ARISTOTLE'S EIGHT LINES CONCLUDING THIS SECTION ABOUT MEN AND WOMEN?

PRACTICE TEST FOR SECTION 21

Select the best answer.

1. According to Margaret Mead, masculinity and femininity are
A. The result of natural selection.
B. Genetically determined.
C. Culturally determined.
D. Biologically determined.

2. A social system in which women are treated as a minority group is known as a(an)
A. Patriarchal society.
B. Androgynous society.
C. Equalitarian society.
D. Matriarchal society.

3. It was stated in the text that "for the first time in history, working wives outnumber . . ."
A. Working men.
B. All ethnic workers.
C. Single women.
D. Housewives.

4. "Suffer women once to arrive at an equality with you, and they will from that moment become your superiors." Which of the following does this statement *not* reflect?
A. Androgyny.
B. Patriarchy.
C. Sexism.
D. Ethnocentrism.

5. Almost every national constitution proclaims
A. The superiority of the male of the species.
B. Unique rights and responsibilities for women.
C. Equality of rights and responsibilities for men and women.

D. Unique rights and responsibilities for men.

6. The "double standard" in reference to adultery means that
A. Adultery is acceptable for both men and women.
B. Adultery is an equally serious offense for men and women.
C. A man's adultery is a more serious offense than a woman's.
D. A woman's adultery is a more serious offense than a man's.

7. A system in which the man, as husband and father, tends to rule with unchallenged authority the lives of women and children is known as
A. Androgyny.
B. Patriarchy.
C. Capitalism.
D. Totalitarianism.

8. According to Caroline Bird, the liberation of women could
A. Limit freedom of choice for men.
B. Result in reversal of sex roles.
C. Require men to accept a lower status.
D. Liberate men.

9. In an androgynous society, social roles would be assigned on the basis of
A. Sexual identity.
B. Ascribed status.
C. Achieved status.
D. Chance.

10. In an androgynous society, the sexual drive would be
A. Weakened.
B. Restrained by the superego.

C. Repressed.

D. A significant factor in the personal lives of men and women.

11. In an androgynous society, men and women would

A. Relate to one another primarily as sexual beings.

B. Stress their sexual differences in secondary relationships.

C. Tend to be more alike than they have been in patriarchy.

D. Look more favorably upon homosexual relations.

12. According to Masters and Johnson, the liberation of women would

A. Create serious psychological problems for men.

B. Jeopardize the proper raising of children.

C. Be of significant value to men.

D. Provide women with an occupational advantage over men.

Answer Key

1.	C	**7.**	B
2.	A	**8.**	D
3.	D	**9.**	C
4.	A	**10.**	D
5.	C	**11.**	C
6.	D	**12.**	C

CHAPTER SUMMARY

1. William Graham Sumner introduced the terms *in-group* and *out-group* to sociology. Each of us belongs to various in-groups. All of those who do not belong to one of our in-groups are considered to be members of the out-groups.

2. People are conscious of their own kind and of those whom they consider different. The concept of consciousness of kind was introduced to sociology by Franklin H. Giddings. He said that similarities that people see in one another encourage them to join together. Each group then becomes an in-group and an out-group, depending on whose point of view is being considered.

3. William Graham Sumner also introduced the term *ethnocentrism* to sociology. He defined it as a "view of things in which one's own group is the center of everything, and all others are scaled and rated with reference to it." Not all members of any group are equally ethnocentric. Ethnocentrism can be interpreted to be functional or dysfunctional for various groups.

4. Members of groups do experience consciousness of kind and consciousness of difference. As a result, social distance is maintained between a dominant group and a minority group. Social distance is a feeling of separation or actual social separation between or among groups.

5. One group may dominate and exploit another group. The dominant group will use methods to maintain social distance between itself and the minority group. Mechanisms designed to keep social distance between such groups include ethnic and racial slurs, stereotypes, prejudice, discrimination, and physical violence.

6.   Sociologists define the term *minority group* to mean a group that is discriminated against, resulting in social inequality. A minority group can be many or few in number. The important point is that the group is in a subordinate position because of prejudice and discrimination. In the United States, Latinos, American Indians, black-Americans, and women are examples of minority groups.

7.   For many years in American history, each immigrant group either chose or was forced to remain apart from the general American culture. This is pluralism. In a pluralist society, language and other minority-group values and behaviors are maintained.

8.   Assimilation occurs when a minority group gives up its separate identity and cultural traits and adopts those of the dominant group or general culture. This view maintains that all Americans should give up their old languages, customs, and identities. Both pluralism and assimilation can result from ethnocentric expressions of consciousness of kind and consciousness of difference.

9.   Racism is the belief that one racial group is superior or inferior to other races. It is a unique form of ethnocentrism. Racists believe that intelligence, character, and personality traits are inherited from one generation to the next.

10.   James Baldwin has said that black-Americans have had a unique experience in history. All oppressed groups share the common bonds of oppression and inequities. But as Baldwin said, black-Americans have had to face circumstances far more complex than any encountered by European immigrants.

11.   Throughout history, the cultures of most human societies have clearly defined specific social roles for women and other specific roles for men. Historically and cross-culturally, women have experienced the kinds of social inequalities associated with other minority groups.

12.   Feminine and masculine characteristics are defined by culture. They are acquired by those who participate in a society's culture. Socialization, not human nature, accounts for masculine and feminine characteristics.

13.   In patriarchal societies, men have access to far greater privilege, power, and prestige than do women. Patriarchy is a social system in which women are treated as a minority group. In such a system, the man usually rules with unchallenged authority the lives of his women and children.

14.   Sexism is a form of prejudice and discrimination that is the basis for any patriarchal system. Even in modern America, women are overrepresented in low-status, low-paying jobs. Sexism is a form of social inequality that is presently being challenged in many countries around the world.

15.   In an androgynous society the concepts of masculinity and femininity would be meaningless. Social roles would not be assigned on the basis of being male or female. Androgyny would permit one to select any mannerism, occupation, and orientation without fear of being a discredit to one's sexual identity. If androgyny should prevail, the traditional minority status of women in society will be a thing of the past. Men would also have more freedom of choice in reference to social roles.

SUGGESTIONS
FOR FURTHER
READING
RELATING TO
CHAPTER 7

Adorno, T. W., Else Frenkel-Brunswick, Daniel J. Levinson, and R. Nevitt Sanford, *The Authoritarian Personality* (New York: Harper, 1950). This is a renowned multidisciplined study of a highly ethnocentric personality type. It is an empirical study using attitudinal scales, projective tests, and clinical interviews.

Coles, Robert, *Eskimos, Chicanos, Indians* (Boston: Little, Brown and Co., 1977). This is a serious and beautifully written description of the present circumstances of Eskimo children, Mexican-American children, and North American Indian children.

Dorn, Edwin, *Rules and Racial Equality* (New Haven: Yale University Press, 1980). The thesis is that "if equal opportunity is to produce . . . racial equality, blacks must experience a period of compensatory treatment in order to overcome the effects of past discrimination."—Ronald L. Taylor

Fitzpatrick, Joseph P., *Puerto Rican Americans: The Meaning of Migration to the Mainland* (Englewood Cliffs, N.J.: Prentice-Hall, 1971). With a special focus on those in New York City, this book describes the constantly changing circumstances of the Puerto Rican experience.

Freud, Sigmund, "The Psychology of Women: Biology as Destiny," *New Introductory Lectures on Psychoanalysis* (New York: W. W. Norton, 1933). This is the lecture that is so vehemently rejected by the women's movement. In presenting his theory of female sexuality, Freud contends that women are biologically inferior to men.

Genovese, Eugene D., *Roll, Jordan, Roll* (New York: Pantheon Books, 1974). In his truly remarkable book, Genovese presents the American experience with slavery, "using as his main source plantation records, family papers, slave narratives, and travelers' accounts."

Greer, Germaine, *The Female Eunuch* (New York: McGraw-Hill, 1971). This book considers women's cultural legacy and their psychological conditioning within patriarchal societies.

Gutman, Herbert G., *The Black Family in Slavery and Freedom, 1750–1925* (New York: Pantheon Books, 1976). This is a scholarly challenge to the idea that the black-American family could not survive the oppressions of slavery. It is a study that should not be ignored by any means!

Haley, Alex, *Roots: The Saga of an American Family* (Garden City, N. Y.: Doubleday and Co., Inc., 1976). "As the first black American writer to trace his origins back to their roots, he has told the story of 25,000,000 Americans of African descent." Every American should read this book.

Harris, Middleton, *The Black Book* (New York: Random House, 1974). "A folk journey of Black America . . . beautiful, haunting, curious, informative and human."— From the Introduction by Bill Cosby.

Hertzberg, Hazel W., *The Search for an American Indian Identity* (Syracuse, N. Y.: Syracuse University Press, 1971). This work provides a historical view of the American Indian experience in reference both to the assimilationist view and the view of cultural pluralism.

Hraba, Joseph, *American Ethnicity* (Itasca, Ill.: F. E. Peacock, 1979). This is a good source of further information on assimilationism and pluralism in reference to American Indians, Mexican-Americans, black-Americans, Chinese-Americans, and Japanese-Americans.

Jensen, Arthur R., "How Much Can We Boost IQ and Scholastic Achievement?" *Harvard Educational Review* (Winter 1969), pp. 1–123. Jensen maintains that racial differences in IQ are genetic as well as environmental. This article evoked an avalanche of criticism. It contradicts the UNESCO statement on race and Montagu's "Challenge to the Ideology of Racism." This is a difficult article. Students should also read the series of answers to Jensen and Jensen's responses in the two subsequent issues of the *Harvard Educational Review* (Spring, 1970).

Mailer, Norman, *The Prisoner of Sex* (New York: Signet, 1971). On the cover of this edition is: "The most blistering sexual memoir of the decade! Mailer takes on Millet, Greer, Friedan, Steinem, Women's Liberation, and the politics of sex." The student who reads this should read Germaine Greer, too.

Millet, Kate, *Sexual Politics* (New York: Avon Equinox Books, 1971). "*Sexual Politics* is a remarkable document because it analyzes the need and nature of sexual liberation while itself displaying the virtues of intellectual and emotional openness and lovingness."—Barbara Hardy, *The New York Times Book Review.*

Morgan, Robin, editor, *Sisterhood is Powerful: An Anthology of Writings from the Women's Liberation Movement* (New York: Random House Vintage Books, 1970). We consider this to be *the book to read* if one is to select only one work from the women's movement.

Morse, Dean W., *Pride Against Prejudice: Work in the Lives of Older Blacks and Young Puerto Ricans* (Montclair, N.J.: Allanheld, Osmun, 1980). A description of the day-by-day existence of people who have been subjected to discrimination but who have exhibited a sense of pride, self-worth, and survival.

Nilsen, A. P., B. Haig, H. L. Gershuny, and J. P. Stanley, *Sexism and Language* (Urbana, Ill.: National Council of Teachers of English, 1977). "This book is about . . . female and male stereotypes as they are codified in language, more specifically in American English. . . . it provides a great deal of useful information on how and why sexist language is employed in our society."—Dan Dieterich.

Rose, Peter I., editor, *Nation of Nations: The Ethnic Experience and the Racial Crisis* (New York: Random House, 1971). This is a rewarding collection of excerpts from newspapers, novels, periodicals, and plays touching upon minority relations in the United States.

Rossi, Alice, editor, *The Feminist Papers: From Adams to de Beauvoir* (New York: Bantam Books, 1973). An anthology of historically significant feminist writings reflecting a wide range of women's concerns—politics, maternity, domestic life, entrapment, education, sexual standards, work, and wages. Rossi's prefatory essay provides biographical sketches of the contributors along with some sociocultural background information.

U.S. Government, *Report on Urban and Rural Non-Reservation Indians* (Washington, D.C.: U.S. Government Printing Office, 1976). This report describes the status and needs of urban and rural Indians who do not live on reservations.

Chapter 8
The Basic Social Institutions

SECTION 22 SOCIOLOGICAL VIEWS OF SOCIAL INSTITUTIONS

- ORIGINS AND UNIVERSALITY OF SOCIAL INSTITUTIONS
- INSTITUTIONAL TRAITS
- MANIFEST AND LATENT FUNCTIONS OF SOCIAL INSTITUTIONS
- INTERACTION OF SOCIAL INSTITUTIONS

Objectives

After completing this section, the student should be able to:

1. Define the term *social institution.*
2. Explain and challenge the state-of-nature thesis and social-contract thesis.
3. Indicate in what way institutional traits are functional.
4. Distinguish between manifest and latent functions of institutions.
5. Cite examples of how institutions can affect the functioning of other institutions.

Social institutions are the activities and organizations by which the basic needs of society are met. Each institution involves certain social norms and social relationships. Within social institutions, people observe customs and organized patterns of behavior. In this chapter we describe the functions of the five basic social institutions found in every society. They are marriage and family, economics, politics, religion, and education.

ORIGINS AND UNIVERSALITY OF SOCIAL INSTITUTIONS

Perhaps for millions of years *Homo sapiens* have been social beings, grouping themselves into clans, tribes, cities, and nations. Each social grouping developed unique beliefs, customs, arts, laws, and values that constituted its culture. As indicated in Chapter 3, there have been many different cultures.

Philosophers have speculated about the origins of life on Earth, about the origins of our species, and about the origins of social life among our species. At one time, because of the influences of Hobbes, Locke, and Rousseau, it was believed that humankind had lived in a *state of nature* without social organization and with total individual freedom. In this view, prehistoric human beings were pictured as free individuals roaming through forests and fields, collecting nuts and berries for food and sometimes meeting other humans with whom they might interact. In a state of nature, free from rules and regulations, people, it was thought, existed without the need for other people. The philosophic theory went on to suggest that at some time in the forgotten past humankind discovered the advantages of uniting with one another for protection from the elements, from other species, and from one another. Then, the story goes, a social contract was made, leading to social cooperation and organization. Each person sacrificed certain individual freedoms in order to assure collective security. Thus, a mythical social contract has been referred to—the agreement of people to establish societies with rules and regulations.

Such theories are romantic fantasies. We can no longer take social contract theories seriously. Instead, today's social scientists say that human society began when humankind appeared. In fact, it is now believed that family organization and other institutions existed for other species *before* humankind appeared. The isolated human in a state of nature could not have survived at all. This is the sociological perspective (Bensman and Rosenberg, 1963). Since the appearance of humans on Earth, there have been many societies with different cultures. Still, all human societies have had to deal with economic survival, government, sex and reproduction, education, and religion. In other words all societies have had some form of each basic social institution. This applies both to traditional folk societies and to dynamic mass societies.

C. Wright Mills recognized the importance of social institutions in a person's life when he wrote the following passage:

The life of an individual cannot be adequately understood without references to the institutions with which [one's] biography is enacted. For this biography records the acquiring, dropping, modifying, and in a very intimate way, the moving from one role to another. One is a child in a certain kind of family, one is a playmate in a certain kind of child's group, a student, a workman, a foreman, a general, a mother. Much of human life consists of playing such roles within specific institutions. To understand the biography of an individual, we must understand the significance and meaning of the roles [one] has played and does play; to understand these roles we must understand the institutions of which they are a part.

(Mills, 1959)

INSTITUTIONAL TRAITS

This subsection is based on material found in *Sociology*, 3rd edition, by Horton and Hunt. They say that each institution is likely to include what might be called *institutional traits*. Institutional traits include cultural symbols, codes of behavior, and ideologies that are associated with each social institution.

Cultural Symbols as a Trait of Institutions

Each institution has its significant symbols. Each government has a flag or banner that citizens are encouraged to respect and to recognize as a symbol of authority, unity, and dignity. The crucifix, crescent, and the star of David are symbols representing religious communities. The wedding ring is a symbol of marriage.

The school song and colors are symbols of educational institutions. The White House, the Kremlin, and Buckingham Palace are buildings *and* symbols of government. Even business concerns can have symbols with which they are associated. Brand names are an obvious example. In Baltimore, the Alex Brown & Sons brokerage, established in 1800, stresses the durability and reliability of the firm by advertising the fact that their building at 135 East Baltimore Street is one of the few buildings in the city to withstand the devastating Baltimore fire of 1904. Employers and employees of Alex Brown point out the chipped stone and dark stains that remain on the sturdy building to this day. To them the building is a source of pride and a symbol of the company's strength and endurance.

Codes of Behavior as a Trait of Institutions

People involved in institutional activities discover themselves in predefined situations requiring them to play certain roles. Whether one participates in a marriage, a jury trial, military service, or the medical or education professions, a code of ethics and behavior surrounds the appropriate role. Such codes of behavior can be both formal and informal. Marital vows, religious ceremonies, and oaths of allegiance are formal efforts to establish role playing within institutions. However, the informal traditions, expectations, and routines that accompany institutional roles also tend to reinforce the likelihood that role behavior will match role expectations.

Ideologies as a Trait of Institutions

Codes of behavior and social norms define *how* people are expected to behave. Ideologies explain *why* people should behave in a certain way. An ideology is a system of ideas shared by a human group. The ideology of an institution includes the main beliefs held by the people participating in the institution. An ideology explains the rest of the world in a way that is acceptable to the participants in the institution.

For example, juvenile delinquency is a problem in mass societies. All institutions develop explanations for this problem. Juvenile delinquency could be explained by socialists as a direct result of the capitalist system. Conservative members of the business world could blame delinquency on a government that is too permissive. As a Christian evangelist, Billy Graham has said the problem results from the neglect of religious training. Professional educators see the problem resulting from inadequate school systems. Finally, people who fear the family is losing influence will insist that juvenile delinquency is a symptom of the breakdown of family life and the declining influence of the home.

Both political and religious movements that become established as institutions guard against any challenges to their established ideologies. Communists who wander from the party line have been condemned as social deviants. Christians who go astray from church dogma have been condemned as heretics. An institutional ideology is an institution's explanation for its existence.

MANIFEST AND LATENT FUNCTIONS OF SOCIAL INSTITUTIONS

All societies hope and expect to survive throughout all time to come. Social institutions, with their symbols, codes of behavior, and ideologies, are supposed to provide the means for survival by performing certain vital functions. What must be understood, however, is that social institutions perform functions that *are not* intended in addition to functions that *are* intended. Robert K. Merton has written that *manifest functions* are both intended and recognized by participants in a system. *Latent functions* are consequences of a system that were neither intended nor readily recognized (Merton, 1968). When sociologists study the functions of social institutions, they attempt to distinguish between consequences that are intended and consequences that are not intended but that do occur as spinoffs of the institutions in action. The following observations are consistent with this approach:

The manifest functions of our military institutions are national defense and implementation of our foreign policy: their latent functions include educating youth, providing jobs and profits, stimulating some kinds of scientific research, spreading venereal disease, and exercising a disputed degree of influence upon foreign policy and domestic politics. Our health institutions have the manifest function of reducing illness and death; their latent function has been to create the population explosion. . . . The manifest function of the corporation was to organize resources efficiently for large-scale business enterprise; the latent functions include promoting the growth of labor unions — a development unintended and certainly not desired by the incorporators.

(Horton and Horton, 1972)

INTERACTION OF SOCIAL INSTITUTIONS

Social institutions collectively contribute to the cultural fabric of society. Actually, there is a complex network of interrelationships that exist between institutions. For a society to survive, its basic institutions must cooperate with and relate to one another. If one institution should fail to meet the needs of the population, its failure can affect the functioning of other institutions in various ways. After all, most people participate in all of the basic social institutions — family, religion, education, government, and economics. To support these views, we should point out that economic disruptions can affect family life and the government. Religion provides values and behavior expectations that are observed, ideally, in the marketplace and in politics. Political decisions can affect family life, businesses, and educational opportunities. Further examples of this interdependence of social institutions interacting within society follow. The government exerts numerous controls over the economic institution by setting minimum wage scales, collecting taxes, preventing monopolies, regulating money and credit, and arbitrating labor–management disputes. On the other hand, the economic institution affects the political institution through the success or failure of the national economy resulting from recessions, depressions, or economic booms. The government affects the institution of family when it issues licenses to wed, determines which marriages can be legally dissolved, and protects the rights of parents and children in relation to one another. In turn, the institution of family can influence the political and economic institutions through birth rates, voting patterns, and forms of family disorganization that require social welfare programs (Vander Zanden, 1970).

KEY TERMS AND NAMES FROM SECTION 22

the five basic social institutions

state-of-nature thesis

social-contract theory

institutional traits

cultural symbols

codes of behavior

institutional ideologies

manifest and latent functions of institutions

interaction among social institutions

C. Wright Mills

Robert K. Merton

STUDY GUIDE FOR SECTION 22

1.   DEFINE THE TERM *SOCIAL INSTITUTION.*

2.   It was once thought that prehistoric humans lived in what was called a state of nature. According to this theory, WHAT WAS LIFE SUPPOSED TO BE LIKE IN A STATE OF NATURE?

3.   WHY WAS A SOCIAL CONTRACT SUPPOSED TO HAVE BEEN MADE AND WHAT WERE TO BE ITS CONDITIONS?

4.   All societies have some form of each basic social institution. LIST FIVE BASIC INSTITUTIONS FOUND IN ALL SOCIETIES.

5.   Each institution is likely to include institutional traits. LIST THREE INSTITUTIONAL TRAITS.

6.   Each social institution has certain symbols. IDENTIFY ONE SYMBOL FOR EACH OF THE FIVE BASIC SOCIAL INSTITUTIONS FOUND IN THE UNITED STATES.

7. From ideological points of view, HOW WOULD JUVENILE DELINQUENCY BE EXPLAINED BY THE FOLLOWING: SOCIALISTS, CONSERVATIVES, RELIGIONISTS, EDUCATORS, AND FAMILY-ORIENTED PEOPLE.

8. Sociologists identify both manifest and latent functions of social institutions. HOW ARE MANIFEST AND LATENT FUNCTIONS DIFFERENT?

9. Social institutions do not exist in isolation from one another. CITE EXAMPLES IN WHICH ONE INSTITUTION OBVIOUSLY AFFECTS THE FUNCTIONING OF ANOTHER INSTITUTION.

PRACTICE TEST FOR SECTION 22

Select the best answer.

1. Which of the following phrases is essential to an understanding of social institutions?
A. Organized system of social reforms.
B. Special clusters of interpersonal expectations.
C. Designed to meet basic needs of society.
D. Any established pattern of interaction.

2. Which of the following is not considered to be a universal basic social institution?
A. Religion.
B. Education.
C. Libraries.
D. Government.

3. To assume there once existed a human epoch free from constraint and without social organization is most consistent with
A. The state-of-nature thesis.
B. The social-contract theory.
C. The contemporary sociological perspective.

4. Which of the following is most consistent with the social-contract theory?

A. Society began with the origin of humans.
B. Total individual freedom once existed.
C. Individual freedom was sacrificed for collective security.
D. People once existed without the need for others.

5. Manifest functions of institutions
A. Occur as spinoffs of institutional activity.
B. Are both intended and recognized.
C. Are neither intended nor recognized.
D. Are found in some but not all institutions.

6. Marital vows, religious ceremonies, and oaths of allegiance are examples of which institutional trait?
A. Ideologies.
B. Material objects.
C. Codes of behavior.
D. Cultural symbols.

7. Which institutional trait allows virtually anything to be explained differently from the point of view of each institution?
A. Ideologies.

B. Material objects.
C. Codes of behavior.
D. Cultural symbols.
8. Which of the following is not an institutional trait?
A. Cultural symbols.
B. Material objects.
C. Codes of behavior.
D. Ideologies.

9. Which of the following people introduced the concepts of manifest and latent functions into the sociological literature?
A. Henry Pratt Fairchild.
B. Robert Merton.
C. C. Wright Mills.
D. Paul Horton.

Answer Key

1.	C	**6.**	C
2.	C	**7.**	A
3.	A	**8.**	B
4.	C	**9.**	B
5.	B		

SECTION 23   MARRIAGE AND FAMILY AS A SOCIAL INSTITUTION

- THE VARIETY OF FAMILY FORMS AND CUSTOMS
- THE NEED FOR PAIRED RELATIONS IN MASS SOCIETY
- FIVE LIFE-STYLES IN AMERICAN MARRIAGES
- SOCIAL FUNCTIONS OF THE FAMILY

Objectives

After completing this section, the student should be able to:

1. Define various terms relating to the variety of family forms and customs.
2. Name and describe five marital life-styles in modern American society.
3. Identify three manifest functions of families.
4. Identify some latent functions that could occur in a family.

No society exists without some form of the family. Only in literature are societies portrayed without families. Plato's *Republic*, Aldous Huxley's *Brave New World*, and Ira Levin's *This Perfect Day* describe societies in which marriage and family do not exist, but these are fictional and philosophical, not historical, accounts of human societies.

THE VARIETY OF FAMILY FORMS AND CUSTOMS

So much material has been accumulated as a result of anthropological and sociological studies of marriage and family in various cultures that it is difficult to capture even a fraction of this knowledge in one brief section. Most introductory sociology courses attempt to identify certain forms and customs that have existed in the world, and there seems to be an infinite variety to identify. We choose to define and briefly to describe the following forms and customs that have been found in various cultures. The basic source for our discussion is George P. Murdock's *Social Structure* (1949).

Orientation, Procreation, Nuclear, and Extended Families

The *family of orientation* is the family into which one is born. It consists of one's parents and siblings (brothers and sisters). This is the family circle that orients the child to the culture in which the family is located. The *family of procreation* is the family that one forms by getting married and having children of one's own. It consists of one's mate (or mates) and any offspring of the marriage.

In either case described above, the family unit is called a *nuclear family*. We refer to an *extended family* when we refer to a family that also includes grandparents, aunts and uncles, cousins, and their spouses and children.

Endogamy and Exogamy

Every society tends to stress some form of both endogamy and exogamy. *Endogamy* is the practice of marrying within one's group. *Exogamy* is the practice of marrying outside one's group. Criteria used for either endogamy or exogamy depend on the norms of the society. Historically, Americans stress endogamy in reference to social class, race, and religion, while stressing exogamy in reference to close relatives and in male–female unions.

Authority Within the Family

Patriarchy is the term used to describe authority within the family unit held by the husband or male head. *Matriarchy* is used to describe the authority within the family unit held by the wife or female head. There are probably no clear-cut examples of societies in which the woman is obviously and admittedly the "head of the house," although there are occasions in many societies when the woman does exercise control over the family, including control over a man or men. In the United States we have traditionally paid lip service to having a patriarchal family form. The degree of male authority differs considerably from family to family. Indeed, it would seem that the American ideals of equality and democracy have found their way into family life. Many families tend to give somewhat equal credence to the views and preferences of all family members—adult and child, male and female. This has come to be known as *equalitarianism*. "Children raise their voices so clamorously in the contemporary American family that Philip Wylie, a satirist of some distinction, has whimsically suggested that what we now have is a pediarchy—or rule by children" (Bensman and Rosenberg, 1963).

Family Residence

When newlyweds establish residence with the husband's family of orientation, it is called a *patrilocal* arrangement. On the other hand, when the couple establish residence with the wife's family of orientation, it is called a *matrilocal* arrangement. In the United States an arrangement called *neolocal* is practiced more often than not. This means that most newly married couples establish an independent residence away from both families of orientation.

Tracing Family Lineage

When descent is traced through the father's family, it is called a *patrilineal* arrangement. When it is traced through the mother's family, it is called *matrilineal*. In some societies descent is traced through both the father's and mother's families—a *bilineal* arrangement.

Monogamy and Polygamy

Monogamy is a form of marriage in which one woman is married to one man at one time. *Polygamy* is a marriage that allows for multiple mates. Actually, there are three possible forms of polygamy: polygyny, polyandry, and group marriages. In his book entitled *The Family in Social Context*, Gerald R. Leslie discusses these three forms of polygamy, and our discussion draws heavily from his writing (Leslie, 1979).

Polygyny is the marital arrangement that permits one man to have two or more wives at the same time. It has been estimated that 75 percent of 554 societies examined have practiced polygyny (Murdock, 1957). Yet even where it has been preferred, it has been practiced by a small segment of the population. In some societies, having more than one wife has been limited to men of special privilege, power, and prestige. Even where there are no status restrictions on practicing polygyny, most people form monogamous marriages. Leslie points out that polygyny is limited because of economic factors and because of the sex ratio.

Economics becomes a factor because one man must enjoy a rather high standard of living in order to support at least two women and the children of each. Therefore, economic necessity has just about dictated that most men in polygynous societies have only one wife. The sex ratio is a simple matter of biological distribution of the sexes. There are approximately equal numbers of men and women in each society. All societies provide the opportunity for regular sexual intercourse through marriage. Too much polygyny would leave too many men without wives.

Polyandry is a marital arrangement in which one woman has two or more husbands. It is a rare form of marriage. The Todas, a tribe numbering between five and six hundred members living in small villages in southern India, provide one example of polyandry (Queen and Haberstein, 1967). The Toda woman marries one man and then automatically becomes the wife of his brothers, even those brothers born after the marriage. Since only brothers share a wife, this type of union is more precisely called fraternal polyandry. There is little friction, discord, or jealousy experienced by those in such a union. The practice of female infanticide existed among the Todas until the 20th century, causing a surplus of men.

It would be unscientific to say . . . female infanticide caused polyandry among the Todas. However, once given a surplus of males over females, polyandry becomes a cultural innovation to insure heterosexual unions for all or nearly all male members of the tribe.

(Queen and Haberstein, 1967)

A special problem is created by polyandry that is not present in polygyny. How does one determine which husband is the father of a child? Gerald Leslie explains that there is no deep emotional attachment of Toda men to the idea of having one's own child. The "chip-off-the-old-block" feeling would be meaningless among Toda men. For legal and ceremonial purposes, a husband would be recognized as father of a forthcoming child by giving a pregnant wife a toy bow and arrow. When other pregnancies occur, the rite might be repeated by other husbands who wish to be recognized as fathers. The social status of father has no literal relation to the biological fact of having sired a child.

Group marriage would be an arrangement in which several men and several women share a marital relationship.

Murdock says that group marriage "appears never to exist as a cultural norm." He acknowledges, however, that among the Kaingang of Brazil, 8 percent of all recorded marriages over a period of 100 years were group marriages. Linton describes the Marquesan Islanders as practicing group marriage. The Dieri of Australia and the Chukchee of Siberia also have [been] reported to practice group marriage.

(Leslie, 1979)

There seems to be some evidence that a relationship exists between types of marital arrangements and economic circumstances prevailing in a society. While admitting that the following is a very tentative generalization, Leslie suggests that in those societies where large families are advantageous and in which one man might support several women, polygyny may be favored. "In pastoral societies, keeping herds and flocks, one man and his sons may be able to shepherd enough animals to keep several women busy processing meat, hides, and milk, and operating the household" (Leslie, 1979). On the other hand, where extreme poverty exists so that the population must exist at a minimum subsistence level, polyandry may be favored. Several men could provide better for one woman and her children and the population would not increase and create further demand on limited resources. Finally, where small family units are as efficient as large ones, monogamy may be favored as well as practiced.

In conclusion, although a majority of the world's societies throughout history have allowed polygamy, the overwhelming majority of marriages have been monogamous. Monogamy may not be simply a social adaptation brought about because of economics, the sex ratio, or religious convictions.

Accumulating evidence from the rather new science of ethology, the study of the biology of behavior, is providing a rather impressive case for the possibility that the need to form a relatively permanent paired relation . . . may be one of the most basic of all needs, which comes to us through our evolution from lower forms.

(Saxton, 1979)

This is the subject of our next subsection.

THE NEED FOR PAIRED RELATIONS IN MASS SOCIETY

Lloyd Saxton says that "Very persistent paired relations have been observed as characteristic of many animals which have social organization., These relations are usually . . . heterosexual; they form a mating pair and—with offspring—the nucleus of the family." We are not suggesting that the behavior of other species is particularly pertinent to the subject of sociology. But it is difficult to ignore the fact that studies cited by Saxton indicate that many species, including *Homo sapiens*, practice one-to-one paired relations. Saxton cites herring, gulls, geese, beavers, tigers, wolves, whales, foxes, porpoises, and Calicebus monkeys as creatures who form paired relations.

We know that most people in any society form monogamous marriages. Of particular interest to us is whether such an arrangement is still relevant and viable for present-day mass societies. Some organs of popular culture have suggested that pairing off for life is an outdated carry-over from uptight, religiously oriented societies that tended to repress the "natural" human urge to go from person to person to still another person. Saxton rejects this thesis by addressing himself to the human condition in present-day mass society. Instead, he stresses the *need* for paired relations in urban, mass society.

He cites how much of the average person's time and energy and attention are occupied with dehumanized and dehumanizing secondary institutions and relations. Saxton says that it is not surprising that modern Americans place such a high value on the relatively few primary institutions and relations available to them. Primary relations established through dating and marriage provide physical and emotional gratification that are reinforced by intimacy and humanistic values. Such relationships act as a counterbalance to the formalized and impersonal behavior required of most people most of the time. Saxton says that this is what makes marriage in our society so desirable. Much more is now expected from marriage than in prior generations; in fact, the high incidence of marital failure can be attributed to high expectations held by those who marry, not to the undesirability of marriage itself.

Of course, paired relations can exist between people other than heterosexual couples who marry. For example, a homosexual couple can establish a primary relationship that is as enduring, responsible, and loving as heterosexual relations. However, at this time in history the homosexual couples are not held together—in fact, they are discouraged—by the conventions of society. Then, too, American society has become increasingly permissive and less rigid regarding sexual mores and role expectations. Many heterosexual couples now choose to live together without entering into a formal marriage (Saxton, 1979).

FIVE LIFE-STYLES IN AMERICAN MARRIAGES*

Monogamy is actually a formal paired relationship. Most Americans do attempt to establish successful marriages. They expect to get both emotional and material satisfaction from marriage. Sociologists have made many studies of American marriages and families. One such study was published in 1965 by John F. Cuber

*All quotations in the subsection entitled "Five Life-Styles in American Marriages" are reprinted by permission of Hawthorn Books, Inc., from *The Significant Americans*. Copyright 1965 by John F. Cuber. All rights reserved.

and Peggy B. Harroff as a book entitled *The Significant Americans*. The people interviewed in this study are highly educated and hold important positions in American institutions. See Diagrams Nos. 13, 14, and 15 to get an idea of the interviewees' marital status, religion, sex, and occupation. The people interviewed in this study are obviously members of the upper-middle class.

A study of upper-middle class marital experiences may seem to have little to do with the majority of American marriages, but we believe, like Cuber and Harroff, "that a study of other classes of American society would find that problems, the successes, and the failures of the Significant Americans are not unique." We believe that the five life-styles identified in this study can be applied to most American marriages in the late 20th century. The significant Americans are more able to express themselves verbally than are most Americans. However, their feelings of fulfillment and disappointment accompanying marriage are probably representative of paired relations in marriage up and down the social strata.

The following five types of contemporary American marriages were identified by Cuber and Harroff after carrying out in-depth interviews with people between the ages of 35 and 55 whose present marriages had already lasted 10 or more years and who said that they had never *seriously* considered divorce. Cuber and Harroff chose this age group because they were interested in the experiences and reflections of mature people. The minimum 10 years of marriage allows enough time for serious problems or outstanding success in marriage to develop.

The Conflict-Habituated Marriage

The conflict-habituated marriage is characterized by continual tension between the couple and within the family circle. It would seem that the couple are incompatible in almost all areas of their interaction, yet the ever-potential conflict is

Present Marital Status of Persons Interviewed

Married:		406
First marriages	313	
Second marriages	76	
Third marriages	17	
Unmarried:		31
Divorced	15	
Widowed	4	
Never married	12	
	437	437

Diagram No. 13   Marital Status of Persons Interviewed

Religious Classification of Interviewees

Protestant	213
Catholic	130
Jewish	27
"Nominal" (i.e. now totally inactive but once active in some religious organization)	46
No organized religious connection ever	21
	437

Diagram No. 14   Religious Classification of Interviewees

Interviewees, by Sex and Occupation

Occupation	Men	Women	Total
Artists (10)	9	1	10

Business Executives (81)
  "Organization men and women"
  "Small business" owners or top managers
	
	36
	27
		
		9
		9
			
			45
			36

Clergymen (17)	17	0	17

Government Officials (55)
  Appointed
  Elected
	
	17
	23
		
		12
		3
			
			29
			26

Housewives (i.e., not otherwise employed) (123)	0	123	123

Lawyers (43)
  Judges
  Practicing Attorneys
Military Officers (22)
	
	19
	18
	22
		
		0
		6
		0
			
			19
			24
			22

Physicians (29)	18	11	29
University Professors and Administrators (29)	16	13	29
Writers, Journalists, Editors (28)	13	15	28
	235	202	437

Diagram No. 15   Interviewees, by Sex and Occupation

not so terrible that the couple cannot and do not want to remain together. Although they may argue and fight, those who share the conflict-habituated marriage have a paired relation which, for one reason or another, is important enough to maintain. Cuber and Harroff say that "Some psychiatrists have gone so far as to suggest that it is precisely the deep need to do psychological battle with one another which constitutes the cohesive factor insuring continuity of the marriage." Although this life-style of marriage represents a minority of American marriages, most of us probably can identify a couple who seem to be sharing such a marriage.

An example of such a marriage is presented in the following remarks made by a 50-year-old man who has been married to the same woman for 25 years and who has two college-graduate children who are now themselves professional people.

You know, it's funny; we have fought from the time we were in high school togeth-er. As I look back at it, I can't remember specific quarrels; it's more like a running guerrilla fight with intermediate periods, sometimes quite long, of pretty good fun and some damn good sex. In fact, if it hadn't been for the sex, we wouldn't have been married so quickly. Well, anyway, this has been going on ever since. . . . It's hard to know what it is we fight about most of the time. You name it and we'll fight about it. It's sometimes something I've said that she remembers differently, some-times a decision—like what kind of car to buy or what to give the kids for Christ-mas. With regard to politics, and religion, and morals—oh, boy! You know, out-side of the welfare of the kids—and that's just abstract—we don't really agree about anything. . . . At different times we take opposite sides—not deliberately; it just comes out that way.

Now these fights get pretty damned colorful. You called them arguments a little while ago—I have to correct you—they're brawls. There's never a bit of physical violence—at least not directed to each other—but the verbal gunfire gets pretty thick. Why, we've said things to each other that neither of us would think of saying in the hearing of anybody else. . . .

Of course, we don't settle any of the issues. It's sort of a matter of principle not to. Because somebody would have to give in then and lose face for the next en-counter. . . .

When I tell you this in this way, I feel a little foolish about it. I wouldn't tolerate such a condition in any other relationship in my life—and yet here I do and always have. . . .

No—we never have considered divorce or separation or anything so clear cut. I realize that other people do, and I can't say that it has never occurred to either of us, but we've never considered it seriously.

A number of times there has been a crisis, like the time I was in the automobile accident, and the time she almost died in childbirth, and then I guess we really showed that we do care about each other. But as soon as the crisis is over, it's busi-ness as usual.

The Devitalized Marriage

To people who are presently involved in the "I'll love you and only you forever and ever" state of mind—known as having fallen in love—the prospect of a devi-talized relationship or marriage must seem very remote. However, if one of these five life-styles of marriage is to be acknowledged as the *real norm* for American marriages, it has to be the devitalized marriage.

A devitalized marriage is one that started out with the couple feeling that their relationship was the one most important factor in their lives. At the beginning of such a marriage, each person received fulfillment simply from being with the other person. People now in devitalized marriages describe themselves as having once been deeply in love. They spent most of their time together. They enjoyed sex. They had a close identification with one another. All this was in the early years of their marriage. Observing their marriage some years later, we find that they spend little time together, share few interests and activities, and find sex to be less satisfying both qualitatively and quantitatively. Interests and activities are not shared in the meaningful way they once were. Instead, most of their time spent together now is "duty time"—time spent with their children and time spent participating in various activities with mutual friends or acquaintances.

Cuber and Harroff point out that the devitalized marriage can cause some people to feel frustrated. Other people seem simply to accept their marriage as being what is to be expected when one reaches the middle years of life.

The two examples that follow are comments made by women in their late forties. Each describes her marriage as devitalized. The first woman sees a "cycle to life" that requires people to relinquish the vitality of a marriage as they relinquish their youth and acquire children and other responsibilities.

Judging by the way it was when we first married—say the first five years or so— things are pretty matter-of-fact now—even dull. They're dull between us, I mean. The children are a lot of fun, keep us pretty busy, and there are lots of outside things—you know, like Little League and the P.T.A. and the Swim Club, and even the company parties aren't always so bad. But I mean where Bob and I are concerned—if you followed us around, you'd wonder why we ever got married. We take each other for granted. We laugh at the same things, sometimes, but we don't really laugh together—the way we used to. . . .

Now I don't say this to complain, not in the least. There's a cycle to life. There are things you do in high school. And different things you do in college. Then you're a young adult. And then you're middle aged. That's where we are now. . . . I'll admit that I do yearn for the old days when sex was a big thing and going out was fun and I hung on to everything he said about his work and his ideas as if they were coming from a genius or something. But then you get the children and other responsibilities. I have the home and Bob has a tremendous burden of responsibility at the office. . . . You have to adjust to these things and we both try to gracefully. . . . Anniversaries though do sometimes remind you kind of hard. . . .

The second woman involved in a devitalized marriage cannot seem to adjust so gracefully to the differences between what is now and what used to be characteristic of her marriage.

I know I'm fighting it. I ought to accept that it has to be like this, but I don't like it, and I'd do almost anything to bring back the exciting way of living we had at first. Most of my friends think I'm some kind of a sentimental romantic or something— they tell me to act my age—but I do know some people—not very darn many— who are our age and even older, who still have the same kind of excitement about them and each other that we had when we were all in college. I've seen some of them at parties and other places—the way they look at each other, the little touches as they go by. One couple has grandchildren and you'd think they were honeymooners. I don't think it's just sex either—I think they are just part of each other's lives—and then when I think of us and the numb way we sort of stagger through the weekly routine, I could scream. And I've even thought of doing some pretty desperate things to try to build some joy and excitement into my life. I've given up on Phil. He's too content with his balance sheets and the kids' report cards and the new house we're going to build next year. He keeps saying he has everything in life that any man could want. What do you do?

These two examples are typical of the comments made by many people in the Cuber–Harroff study. The devitalized marriage remains a paired relation in which each person continues to care about the marital partner, but the quality of the relationship has changed so that the original zest is gone. One person used the term *habit cage* to describe this life-style of marriage. Cuber and Harroff say, "There is typically little overt tension or conflict, but the interplay between the pair has become apathetic, lifeless." This is not to say, however, that each mate is not a significant other to the other mate. It is not to say that they no longer love each other. We believe that it would be a mistake to make assumptions like that. We can conclude only that the intimate, personal aspect of their relationship has been eroded with the passing of time and with mounting responsibilities, which almost inescapably are the lot of mature adults, married or single.

The Passive-Congenial Marriage

People become involved in passive-congenial marriages in two ways. Some simply drift into marriage with each other because everyone else seems to be marrying and because they have been spending most of their time together, and they ask, "Why *not* get married?" Others deliberately choose to become involved in such a low-intensity marriage. They have interests and creative energies that they want to direct into something other than a paired relation, yet they want the comforts of the "habit cage" that a paired relation can offer. This type of marriage resembles the devitalized one. The difference is that passive-congenials do not suffer from the pain and disappointment that accompanies devitalization of their relationship. The following remarks by a physician seem to express both the passivity and the congeniality typical of such marriages.

I don't know why everyone seems to make so much about men and women and marriage. Of course, I'm married and if anything happened to my wife, I'd get married again. I think it's the proper way to live. It's convenient, orderly, and solves a lot of problems. But there are other things in life. I spent nearly ten years preparing for the practice of my profession. The biggest thing to me is the practice of that profession, to be of assistance to my patients and their families. I spend twelve hours a day at it. And I'll bet if you talked with my wife, you wouldn't get any of that "trapped housewife" stuff from her either. Now that the children are grown, she finds a lot of useful and necessary work to do in this community. She works as hard as I do.

The Vital Marriage

The vital marriage is the type of marriage that most people say they would like to have. In a sense, it can be seen as the *idealized norm* for American marriages, while the devitalized one is the *real norm*. Most young people in love, planning to be married, expect and hope to have a vital marriage. This marital life-style is rare after the first few years of marriage, yet it does exist. Actually, the vital pair are not necessarily obvious in their strong attachment to each other. Like other couples, they are concerned with their work, recreation, and family activities. For the most part, they do the same things and say the same things as everyone else who is married—publicly. Closer study of such marriages reveals that the vital paired relation is one in which the mates are psychologically bound together in important areas of their lives. They share things and activities together with a zest and vitality that is lacking in most marriages. Like young love, the vital marriage provides the life essence for the couple—the relationship is more important than anything else in their lives. For example:

The things we do together aren't fun intrinsically—the ecstasy comes from being together in the doing. Take her out of the picture and I wouldn't give a damn for the boat, the lake, or any of the fun that goes on out there.

It is not unusual for other matters of potential value to be sacrificed by either partner if such matters might interfere with the relationship of the vital pair. For example:

I cheerfully, and that's putting it mildly, passed up two good promotions because one of them would have required some traveling and the other would have taken evening and weekend time—and that's when Pat and I live. The hours with her (after twenty-two years of marriage) are what I live for. . . .

Another example:

I'll admit I'd rather have run for elective office. But my wife isn't comfortable with all the campaign dishonesty. . . . And a full life together is more important to me than being Senator. It's no sacrifice really. I just don't want to jeopardize or weaken the major satisfaction of my life for a minor one, even if it is important too. What would it profit me to try for a Senate seat and make it, if afterwards, I found that our close and deeply sustaining life had been damaged in the process? How can any success be worth that?

Although such marriages are in a distinct minority, Cuber and Harroff talked with dozens of couples who found their central satisfaction in life to stem from their living with and through each other. Although such couples may have conflicts from time to time, such strains usually result from matters that are of significance to them. Furthermore, vital couples tend to settle their disagreements quickly. A career woman married to a career man—and both in their second marriage—made the following unusual observation about a vital marriage.

Well, we've got a marriage-type marriage. Do you know what I mean? So many people—and me in my first marriage—just sort of touch on the edges of existence—don't really marry. It's funny, but my cookbook distinguishes between marinating and marrying of flavors. You know—the marinated flavors retain their identity—just mix a little—or the one predominates strongly over the other. But the married ones blend into something really new and the specific identities are lost. Well, a lot of people that I know aren't married at all—just marinated.

Cuber and Harroff point out that people in vital relationships are usually aware of being in a minority as far as married life-styles are concerned. It would seem that vital pairs realize that those around them simply do not believe or do not understand two people enjoying such a relationship. For example:

You know, if I told my neighbors or my husband's work associates at any of our parties how I really feel about him, and these other things I've told you, and what we do together, they'd laugh us out of the group. Well—not all of them, I suspect there are one or two couples who are a lot like us, but I'm not sure, because they don't say much either.

Another example:

Most of our friends think we moved out to the country for the kids; well—the kids are crazy about it, but the fact of the matter is, we moved out for ourselves—just to get away from all the annoyances and interferences of other people—our friends actually. We like this kind of life—where we can have almost all of our time together. . . . We've been married for over twenty years and the most enjoyable thing either of us does—well, outside of the intimate things—is to sit and talk by the hour. That's why we built that imposing fireplace—and the hi-fi in the corner.

. . . Now that Ed is getting older, that twenty-seven mile drive morning and night from the office is a real burden, but he does it cheerfully so we can have our long uninterrupted hours together. . . . The children respect this too. They don't invade our privacy any more than they can help—the same as we vacate the living room when Ellen brings in a date, she tries not to intrude on us. . . . Being the specialized kind of lawyer he is, I can't share much in his work, but that doesn't bother either of us. The big part of our life is completely mutual.

The Total Marriage

The total marriage is simply a vital marriage in which the couple's common interests are more numerous than in a regular vital marriage. In one marriage cited by Cuber and Harroff, the husband is an internationally known scientist. He has been married to the same woman for 30 years and refers to her as his friend, mistress, and partner. He goes home for lunch and a conversational hour or so with his wife whenever possible. They refer to these conversations as "our little seminars." This couple has four grown children who say that they enjoy visits with their parents as much as they do with friends of their own age. This indicates something positive about the vitality of this married relationship.

Another example of the total marriage is that of a consulting engineer who frequently is sent abroad by his company. In speaking of his wife he said:

She keeps my files and scrapbooks up to date. . . . I invariably take her with me to conferences around the world. Her femininity, easy charm and wit are invaluable assets to me. I know it's conventional to say that a man's wife is responsible for his success and I also know that it's often not true. But in my case I gladly acknowl-

edge that it's not only true, but she's indispensable to me. But she'd go along with me even if there was nothing for her to do because we just enjoy each other's company—deeply. You know, the best part of a vacation is not what we do, but that we do it together. We plan it and reminisce about it and weave it into our work and other play all the time.

Cuber and Harroff say that they occasionally found marital relations that were so total that all aspects of life were mutually and enthusiastically participated in. The total marriage is the type in which neither spouse has a truly private existence. No doubt there are people who would not choose to share such a close relationship. Like the vital marriage that is not quite total in scope, the total marriage is extremely rare. It is neither the *real norm* nor the *ideal norm* for American marriages at this time.

Five Marital Life-Styles: Some Cautions and Conclusions

We believe that the Cuber and Harroff study is a valuable contribution to the area of research on American marriages. It should be understood that each life-style of marriage is a typology. It would be wrong to assume that all marriages can be neatly pigeonholed into one type or another. Some marriages must be considered borderline cases or marriages in transition.

Furthermore, it should be understood that this study concerns relationships, not personalities. To describe a devitalized marriage is not to describe devitalized personalities. "A clearly vital person may be living in a passive-congenial or devitalized relationship and expressing his vitality in some other aspect of his life . . ."

And finally, the five types should not be interpreted as *degrees* of marital happiness or adjustment. "Persons in all five are currently adjusted and most say that they are content, if not happy. . . . The five types represent *different kinds of adjustment* and *different conceptions of marriage.*" Cuber and Harroff stress that "This is an important concept which must be emphasized if one is to understand the personal meanings which these people attach to the conditions of their marital experience."

SOCIAL FUNCTIONS OF THE FAMILY

To conclude this section, we return to the idea that the family is one of the basic social institutions of all societies. Marriage is the conjugal aspect of family. When the family is seen as a social institution, its historical importance in any culture becomes readily apparent. Certain functions are universally performed by the family. Other functions are relevant to the society in which the family is located. The modern American family's basic functions remain much the same as they have always been, but some of the family's past functions—economic, protective, recreational, and religious—have been taken over by other social institutions. In this subsection we consider only those functions that seem to be universal to families in all societies including modern American society.

Socialization

As we have stated before, the family is the first agent of socialization. It is the family that is responsible for transforming the "prehuman" infant into a "civilized" adult. The family introduces the child to attitudes, beliefs, and behavior expectations that prevail in the larger world in which the family is located. Concepts such as loving, loyalty, generosity, authority, and property are first introduced to children within the family circle. With some exceptions, basic personality is built during the formative years that a child spends in the family. Since the family provides for one's social status, one's very identity depends on the social location of the family into which one is born.

Biological Functions

Although most societies provide official or unofficial outlets other than marriage for sexual expression, marriage remains the principal institution in which sexual desires are satisfied. Some say that marriage is society's way of regularizing a potentially disruptive force—the sexual drive. Linked with providing fulfillment of the sexual drive has been the function of reproduction. All societies provide clear and strong social controls in reference to the circumstances under which children are to be brought into the world and nurtured. Thus, family, more often than not, is the means by which society recognizes the biological needs of sexuality and reproduction of the species.

Maintenance

Someone has said that home is a place where, if you go there, they have to take you in. The family is supposed to provide for the affectional and material needs of its members, up to a point. Again, we are reminded of the people-need-people theme. Good mental health is related to experiences of being loved and being able to love in return. Good physical health is related to one's receiving the basic necessities of food, clothing, and shelter. To varying degrees within a society and to varying degrees from one society to another, the family is expected to nourish the emotional and material needs of the individual.

Latent Functions of the Family

We have referred to three manifest functions of the family, but there are latent functions that are present within family experience too. In the United States, for example, mate selection is a private matter of those who engage in dating and courtship. But since it is the parents who decide where the family lives, the family of orientation has much to say about the pool of potential mates for those

A nuclear family, U.S.A.

who engage in dating. Then, too, because of family neglect, a child can become an emotionally disturbed adult. Sometimes, because of pressing family responsibilities, a potential warrior might avoid military service. These are latent functions of the family. All social institutions have such unintended functions that often are not recognized by those who participate in the institutions.

KEY TERMS AND NAMES FROM SECTION 23

family of orientation

family of procreation

nuclear family and extended family

endogamy and exogamy

patriarchy, matriarcy, pediarchy

equalitarianism

matrilocal, patrilocal, neolocal

matrilineal, patrilineal, bilineal

monogamy and polygamy

polygyny, polyandry, group marriage

sex ratio

female infanticide

need for paired relationships

conflict-habituated marriage

devitalized marriage

duty time

habit cage

passive-congenial marriage

vital marriage

total marriage

social functions of the family

George P. Murdock

Gerald R. Leslie

Lloyd Saxton

John F. Cuber

Peggy B. Harroff

STUDY GUIDE FOR SECTION 23

1. Almost everyone during a lifetime belongs to a family of orientation and a family of procreation. WHAT DOES EACH TYPE OF FAMILY CONSIST OF? WHAT ARE NUCLEAR AND EXTENDED FAMILIES?

2. Every society tends to stress some form of both endogamy and exogamy. DEFINE EACH TERM AND GIVE ONE EXAMPLE IN WHICH AMERICANS STRESS ENDOGAMY AND ONE EXAMPLE IN WHICH AMERICANS STRESS EXOGAMY.

3. Depending upon the culture—and even upon a family within a culture—authority within the family is distributed in several possible ways. WHERE DOES FAMILY AUTHORITY RESIDE IN REFERENCE TO EACH OF THE FOLLOWING TERMS: MATRIARCHY, PATRIARCHY, PEDIARCHY, EQUALITARIANISM?

4. There are a number of ways by which family residence is determined. In the United States, an arrangement called neolocal is practiced more often than not. DESCRIBE EACH OF THE FOLLOWING ARRANGEMENTS FOR FAMILY RESIDENCE: PATRILOCAL, MATRILOCAL, AND NEOLOCAL.

5. There are several ways by which societies can trace family lineage. DESCRIBE THREE WAYS BY WHICH DESCENT IS TRACED AND GIVE THE TERM USED FOR EACH ARRANGEMENT.

6. Monogamy is a form of marriage in which one woman is married to one man at one time. Polygamy is marriage that allows for multiple mates. NAME AND DESCRIBE THREE POSSIBLE FORMS OF POLYGAMY.

7. It has been estimated that 75 percent of 554 societies studied have practiced polygyny. Even where it has been preferred, it has been practiced by only a small segment of the population. GIVE THREE REASONS WHY MOST MARRIAGES IN POLYGYNOUS SOCIETIES ARE MONOGAMOUS.

8. Polyandry is a very rare form of marriage. A special problem is created by polyandry which is not present in polygyny. WHAT IS THE PROBLEM AND HOW HAVE THE TODAS OF SOUTHERN INDIA ADJUSTED TO THE SITUATION?

9. There seems to be some evidence that a relationship exists between types of marital arrangements and economic circumstances prevailing in a society. HOW MIGHT THIS TENTATIVE GENERALIZATION BE EXPLAINED?

10. NAME THE FIVE LIFE-STYLES OF CONTEMPORARY AMERICAN MARRIAGES AS IDENTIFIED BY CUBER AND HARROFF IN *THE SIGNIFICANT AMERICANS*.

11. Some people simply drift into marriage with each other because everyone else seems to be marrying and because they have been spending most of their time together, and they ask, "Why *not* get married?" WHICH MARITAL LIFE-STYLE DOES THIS DESCRIBE?

12. Most people who are in love and who expect to get married hope to have a marriage in which they will share things and activities together with a zest and vitality that is lacking in most marriages. WHICH MARITAL LIFE-STYLE ARE THEY HOPING FOR?

13. Some people describe themselves as having once been deeply in love, as having spent most of their time together. This was during the early years of their marriage. Now they spend little time together, share few interests, and put in what they call "duty time." WHICH MARITAL LIFE-STYLE DOES THIS DESCRIBE?

14. Some marriages are characterized by continual tension between the couple and within the family circle, yet the ever-potential conflict is not so terrible that the couple cannot and do not want to remain together. WHICH MARITAL LIFE-STYLE DOES THIS DESCRIBE?

15. Some marital relationships are so close that all aspects of life are mutually and enthusiastically shared. In such a marriage neither spouse can be said to have a truly private existence. WHICH MARITAL LIFE-STYLE DOES THIS DESCRIBE?

16. Certain functions are universally performed by the family. NAME THREE MANIFEST FUNCTIONS THAT SEEM TO BE UNIVERSAL TO FAMILIES IN ALL SOCIETIES, INCLUDING MODERN AMERICAN SOCIETY.

17. There are latent as well as manifest functions of the family. NAME TWO LATENT FUNCTIONS THAT MIGHT OCCUR WITHIN A FAMILY.

PRACTICE TEST FOR SECTION 23

Select the best answer.

1. The family that one forms by getting married and having children of one's own is known as
A. The extended family.
B. The family of procreation.
C. A patriarchal family.
D. The family of orientation.

2. The practice of marrying within one's group is known as
A. Endogamy.
B. Exogamy.
C. Patriarchy.
D. Matriarchy.

3. Authority within the family unit

held by the wife or female head is known as
A. Patriarchy.
B. Pediarchy.
C. Matriarchy.
D. Matrilocal.

4. Americans have stressed exogamy in reference to
A. Social class.
B. Race.
C. Religion.
D. Close relatives.

5. The most prevalent patterns in contemporary American society include
A. Patrilocal, patrilineal, polygamy.
B. Bilineal, matrilocal, monogamy.
C. Monogamy, neolocal, and patriarchy.
D. Polygyny, patrilocal, patriarchy.

6. Which of the following is not a form of polygamy?
A. Polygyny.
B. Monogamy.
C. Polyandry.
D. Group marriages.

7. Throughout history, the most favored form of marriage has been
A. Polyandry.
B. Polygyny.
C. Group marriage.
D. Monogamy.

8. The family is supposed to nourish the emotional and material needs of its members. Which family function is this?
A. Protection.
B. Socialization.
C. Maintenance.
D. Economic security.

9. Which of the following statements would be made by someone in a devitalized marriage?
A. "At different times we take opposite sides—not deliberately; it just comes out that way."

B. "I'd do almost anything to bring back the exciting way of living we had at first."
C. "I don't know why everyone seems to make so much about men and women and marriage."

10. The total marriage
A. Is the idealized norm for American marriages.
B. Represents a majority of modern American marriages.
C. Is best characterized by the term *habit cage*.
D. Is one in which neither spouse has a truly private existence.

11. Which of the following could be described as a manifest function of the family?
A. Reproduction of the species.
B. Producing emotionally disturbed adults.
C. Providing a mechanism for avoiding military service.

12. The vital marriage is characterized by which of the following?
A. The quality of the relationship has changed from the earlier years of marriage.
B. Disagreements are rarely settled.
C. There is continual tension.
D. The central satisfaction in life stems from the marital relationship.

13. Major family functions that are universal include all of the following except one. Which one?
A. Socialization.
B. Regulation and expression of sexuality.
C. Recreation.
D. Maintenance.

14. The Todas, a pastoral tride in southern India, are an example of
A. Polygyny.
B. Monogamy.

C. Polyandry.

D. Group marriage.

15. According to George Murdock, this "appears never to exist as a cultural norm." What is it?

A. Endogamy.

B. Group marriage.

C. Devitalized marriage.

D. Patriarchy.

16. The ideal norm is to the vital marriage as the real norm is to the

A. Passive-congenial marriage.

B. Conflict-habituated marriage.

C. Devitalized marriage.

D. Total marriage.

17. According to Lloyd Saxton, one of the most basic of all human needs is

A. To form a relatively permanent paired relation.

B. To be married.

C. To have satisfying work.

D. To have sexual gratification.

Answer Key

1.	B	**7.**	D	**13.**	C
2.	A	**8.**	C	**14.**	C
3.	C	**9.**	B	**15.**	B
4.	D	**10.**	D	**16.**	C
5.	C	**11.**	A	**17.**	A
6.	B	**12.**	D		

SECTION 24 ECONOMICS, POLITICS, RELIGION, AND EDUCATION

- ECONOMICS AS A SOCIAL INSTITUTION
- POLITICS AS A SOCIAL INSTITUTION
- RELIGION AS A SOCIAL INSTITUTION
- EDUCATION AS A SOCIAL INSTITUTION

Objectives

After completing this section, the student should be able to:

1. Identify two universal manifest characteristics of economic systems.
2. Describe economies run by tradition, by command, and by the market.
3. Identify latent functions associated with each of the three types of economic systems.
4. Describe traditional, legal-rational, and charismatic authority.
5. Explain how the routinization of charisma can lead to either traditional or legal-rational authority.
6. Describe three latent functions of American government.
7. Identify social functions of religion.
8. Identify the primary function and describe additional manifest and latent functions of American education.

In the previous section we described marriage and family as one of the basic social institutions. Four other basic social institutions are economics, politics, religion, and education. Such social institutions exist in both folk and mass societies. The economic institution provides the production and distribution of goods and services that meet human needs for survival plus some luxuries. Government (politics) is concerned with organizing and using power that is accepted as authority by the population. Religion directs human thought, feeling, and action to things that people believe to be above the ordinary experiences among people, within oneself, and in reference to the world in general (Nottingham, 1954). Education serves to socialize people so that they can participate in and understand their cultural heritage. Now let us look at these four basic institutions in more detail.

ECONOMICS AS A SOCIAL INSTITUTION

Economic systems differ widely from society to society. They also have certain features in common. Robert L. Heilbroner (1962) has identified two universal characteristics of economic systems:

1. "A society must organize a system for producing the goods and services it needs for its own perpetuation."

2. "It must arrange a distribution of the fruits of its production among its own members so that more production can take place."

Production and distribution have been important problems faced by every society. Robert Heilbroner has said that:

within the enormous diversity of the actual social institutions which guide and shape the economic process, the economist divines but three overarching types of systems which separately or in combination enable humankind to solve its economic challenge. These great systemic types can be called economies run by Tradition, economies run by Command, and economies run by the Market.

(Heilbroner, 1962)

We should like to describe the three typologies of economic systems as identified by Heilbroner.

Economies Run by Tradition

The oldest type of economic system is the economy based on traditional behaviors. It is the economics of folk societies. In traditional folk societies, production and distribution of goods are based on procedures developed in the distant past. The people experienced a long process of historic trial and error in reference to economic survival. Their methods became sacred and became based on strong customs and beliefs.

Traditional folk societies solve the production problem rather simply. An individual takes on the work that her mother or grandmother did and the work that his father or grandfather did. Certain skills and crafts are passed on from one generation to the next. Century after century, production methods are repeated in exactly the same ways. The longer certain methods have been used, the more sacred these methods become for the people. There is no interest in nor efforts made for economic progress.

Traditional folk societies also pass down from generation to generation the means of distributing the fruits of production. For example, the Bushmen of the Kalahari Desert in South Africa use hunting as their means of production. Elizabeth Marshall Thomas describes their methods of distributing the parts of an animal caught in a hunt:

The gensbok has vanished. . . . Gai owned two hind legs and a front leg. Tsetch had meat from the back, Ukwane had the other front leg, his wife one of the feet and the stomach, the young boys had lengths of intestine. Twikwe had received the head and Dasina the udder.

It seems very unequal when you watch Bushmen divide the kill, yet it is their system, and in the end no person eats more than any other. That day Ukwane gave Gai still another piece because Gai was his relation, Gai gave meat to Dasina because she was his wife's mother. . . . No one, of course, contested Gai's large share, because he had been the hunter and by their law that much belonged to him. No one doubted that he would share his large amount with others, and they were not wrong, of course; he did.

(Thomas, 1959)

Certainly, economics run by tradition have worked,

but we must note one very important consequence of the mechanism of tradition. Its solution to production and distribution is a static one. A society which follows the path of tradition in its regulation of economic affairs does so while sacrificing large-scale rapid social change and economic change. The bulk of the peoples living in tradition-bound societies repeat, in the daily patterns of their economic life, much of the routines which characterized them in the distant past. . . . Tradition solves the economic problem, but it does so at the cost of economic progress.

(Heilbroner, 1962)

And if progress does not occur, a society is apt to be at the mercy of the impersonal elements that make up the environment. On the other hand, progress-oriented societies have discovered that when economic progress *does* take place, polluted water and air and numerous other problems can accompany it.

Economies Run by Command

A command economy is a planned economy. How it is planned, by whom, and for whose benefit depends on the time and the place being considered. Both democratic and totalitarian societies have had occasion to run economies by command. In time of crisis, a society might have to resort to command in order to organize its resources for production and its energies for distribution of goods and services. One great advantage of command is its ability to bring about rapid and significant economic and social change. When Western Europe began moving from medieval to modern times, the new nations used a form of command economics called *mercantilism.*

Mercantilism is the name given to that group of ideas and practices particularly characteristic of the period 1500 to 1800 by which the national state acting in the economic sphere sought by methods of control to secure its own unity and power. . . . The national governments sought to take over the economic functions formerly carried on by the Church, the town, the province, the feudal lord, the gild. They sought to regulate industry and commerce, to handle poor relief and taxation, to set the interest rate and make laws on economic matters, to build up a national administration of economic life.

(Clough and Cole, 1952)

Adam Smith's *Wealth of Nations*, published in 1776, was an attack upon the restrictions of economic command as manifested in the national economic policies of his time. In the next century, Karl Marx's *Capital* was an attack upon the excesses of a market economy that had replaced the command economy of mercantilism.

Unlike traditional economies, command economies do not slow down economic change. In fact, as we have suggested, "the exercise of authority is the most powerful instrument society has for *enforcing economic change.*" Today, the socialist nations rely more upon economies of command than upon any other method. Much the same can be said of the nations of Africa. Heilbroner offers as one example, "the radical alterations in the systems of production and distribution which authority has effected in modern China and Russia." Command is an ancient technique that has captured the imagination of modern planners for economic progress. At the same time, command economies are rejected by those who believe that individual freedom can flourish best within a market economy.

Economies Run by the Market

When we speak of an economy run by the market, we refer to the economic system known as capitalism. A market economy is based on the private ownership of the means of production and distribution. Its basic assumption is that when an individual pursues personal interests, the interests of the entire society are

Laws of supply and demand at work in the New York Stock Exchange.

enhanced. The pursuit of self-interest is encouraged in a market economy. The element of competition is supposed to encourage reasonable prices and adequate goods and services. Furthermore, the quantity of goods and services is regulated by what Adam Smith called the "laws of the market place." These are the laws of supply and demand. The difficulty in explaining exactly how a market economy operates is obvious enough in the following passage.

Because we live in a market-run society, we are apt to take for granted the puzzling—indeed, almost paradoxical—nature of the market solution to the economic problem. But assume for a moment that we could act as economic advisers to a society which had not yet decided on its mode of economic organization. Suppose, for instance, that we were called on to act as consultants to one of the new nations emerging from the continent of Africa.

We could imagine the leaders of such a nation saying, "We have always experienced a highly tradition-bound way of life. Our men hunt and cultivate the fields and perform their tasks as they are brought up to do by the force of example and the instruction of their elders. We know, too, something of what can be done by economic command. We are prepared, if necessary, to sign an edict making it compulsory for many of our men to work on community projects for our national development. Tell us, is there any other way we can organize our society so that it will function successfully—or better yet, more successfully?"

Suppose we answered, "Yes, there is another way. Organize your society along the lines of a market economy."

"Very well," say the leaders. "What do we then tell people to do? How do we assign them to various tasks?"

"That's the very point," we would answer. "In a market economy no one is assigned to any task. The very idea of a market society is that each person is allowed to decide for himself what to do."

There is consternation among the leaders. "You mean there is no assignment of some men to mining and others to cattle raising? No manner of selecting some for transportation and others for cloth weaving? You leave this to people to decide for themselves? But what happens if they do not decide correctly? What happens if no one volunteers to go into the mines, or if no one offers himself as a railway engineer?"

"You may rest assured," we tell the leaders, "none of that will happen. In a market society, all the jobs will be filled because it will be to people's advantage to fill them."

Our respondents accept this with uncertain expressions. "Now look," one of them finally says, "let us suppose that we take your advice and let our people do as they please. Now let's talk about something important, like cloth production. Just how do we fix the right level of cloth output in this 'market society' of yours?"

"But you don't" we reply.

"We don't! Then how do we know there will be enough cloth produced?"

"There will be," we tell him. "The market will see to that."

"Then how do we know there won't be too much cloth produced?" he asks triumphantly.

"Ah, but the market will see to that too!"

"But what is this market that will do all these wonderful things? Who runs it?"

"Oh, nobody runs the market," we answer. "It runs itself. In fact there really isn't any such thing as 'the market.' It's just a word we use to describe the way people behave."

"But I thought people behaved the way they wanted to!"

"And so they do," we say. "But never fear. They will want to behave the way you want them to behave."

"I am afraid," says the chief of the delegation, "that we are wasting our time. We thought you had in mind a serious proposal. But what you suggest is madness. It is inconceivable. Good day, sir." And with great dignity the delegation takes its leave. *

In Summary: Tradition, Command, and Market

No matter which of the three types of economic systems is used, the basic needs of production and distribution are attended to. Whether the system be tradition, command, or market, there will be certain role expectations, folkways, and mores associated with the activities therein. We believe that Heilbroner's three typologies present a useful description of economic behavior. It should be understood that combinations of these types have existed in history and that some characteristics of each type exist in the United States today.

Latent Functions of Economics

The manifest functions of any economic system are to produce and to distribute a society's resources. Then the society is able to maintain and continue itself. Depending on the type of economic system established, certain latent functions occur also. A tradition-run economy that produces and distributes in exactly the same ways from century to century can function as a brake upon progress in other areas such as medicine, technology, and art. Both command and market economies can function as accelerators of ecological tragedy when industrial growth is accompanied by environmental destruction. Concern is being expressed in both command and market societies today about air and water pollution and the need to conserve the Earth's resources.

POLITICS AS A SOCIAL INSTITUTION

All societies have governmental systems. The form of these political entities varies widely, depending upon each people's history, value systems, and population size. A government is an ultimate power that is recognized as legitimate. No government can long remain in power and exercise authority without some general

*Robert L. Heilbroner, *The Making of Economic Society*, Copyright © 1962 pp. 15–16. Reprinted by permission of Prentice-Hall, Inc. Englewoods Cliffs, N. J.

recognition by the governed that the government has the right to rule. This is true whether the government is headed by a tribal chieftain, a dictator, or a president. This is true whether the government is democratic or totalitarian.

Types of Authority

Every government has as its ultimate social control the use of force. Force is seldom more than merely a threat. The majority of populations consent to being governed according to the established order. Max Weber identified three types of authority. They are traditional authority, legal-rational authority, and charismatic authority. Each type provides a basis for the legitimate use of power (Weber, 1947).

Traditional Authority.　The oldest type of political system known is based on traditional authority. The leader or leaders assume power because of traditional laws of succession that have been handed down from the past. No one questions the right of those who rule. Many times it is believed that those who rule were granted their authority by the gods. Both the population and the rulers are guided by an unwritten set of rules or laws. The rulers are expected to act within traditional definitions of the positions of authority. Traditional rulers are not expected to seek progress by changing the social order. Sometimes changes do occur because of new challenges from the environment. Sometimes changes occur because of contact with other cultures. Then the traditional rulers must explain and justify why the changes are acceptable. Traditional leaders are honored for their wisdom. Their decisions are seldom questioned by the governed. In such traditional societies, the social order would be based upon kinship, clanship, or tribal organization.

Legal-Rational Authority.　In modern, mass societies the outstanding characteristic of legal-rational authority is its bureaucratic organization. Those who have positions of authority must play roles that are rigidly defined. "Rights, duties, privileges, and procedures are specified by the organization and its internal laws." In principle, the person is held strictly responsible for performing the requirements of the position. One should not do more than is expected of the position; one should not neglect one's duties. To do too much or to do too little are both major offenses (Bensman and Rosenberg, 1963). More often than not, leaders are said to be

servants of the people even though high prestige may be accorded to their offices. Their loyalty is to the laws or regulations, and their main observable trait is efficiency in carrying them out. The laws are not sacred, however, as they are not traditional, and so the bureaucratic leaders may advocate changes in them if they think the public's purposes can be more effectively served by new laws. In this sense bureaucratic top leadership is "dynamic" and "liberal." The Western democracies have been moving toward a bureaucratic type of top leadership for several centu-

The flag is a symbol of authority and unity.

ries, although they still have certain elements of traditional leadership and some of them have occasionally experienced brief periods of charismatic leadership.

(Rose and Rose, 1969)

Peter and Brigitt Berger declare legal-rational authority to be the most common type of authority in the modern world and agree that its most appropriate form is bureaucracy. They say the legal-rational authority:

is based upon law and rationally explicable procedures. Question: By what right can the governor collect this tax? Answer: He has the right by virtue of a law passed by the state legislature on such and such a date . . . this form of authority does not cloak itself in mystery. Each exercise of power is, as it were, backed up by specific legal provisions. At least in principle, these provisions can be rationally explained, and so can the social purposes behind them.

(Berger and Berger, 1972)

Charismatic Authority.   The term *charisma* refers to a quality of leadership that inspires people to follow the charismatic person with enthusiasm and loyalty. Max Weber defined charisma as a "certain quality of an individual personality by virtue of which he is set apart from ordinary men and treated as endowed with supernatural, superhuman or at least specifically exceptional powers or qualities" (Weber, 1947). Max Weber considered charisma to be one of the potent forces in history. It affects matters in such a way that society is never again quite as it was before the charismatic person's influence appeared. Charisma "substitutes new meanings for old and radically redefines the assumptions of human existence" (Berger, 1963). In the 20th century, one might identify a number of people as having possessed charisma: Nikolai Lenin, Mao Tse-tung, Adolf Hitler, Mohandas Gandhi, Eva Peron, and Martin Luther King, Jr.

Charismatic authority does not retain its original excitement and does not remain a revolutionary force for very long. Its success means it becomes established. It must then take up the ordinary routines of everyday life. Consequently, charisma brings change to established society but it is changed itself when it replaces the established older order with itself. As the Bergers put it,

something which once broke the structures of everyday life now has become itself one of the structures. When this happens, charismatic authority inevitably loses its old legitimacy and must find new ways to maintain the institutional structures it has created. With this change, the revolutionary impulse of the charismatic movement begins to die.

(Berger and Berger, 1972)

This *routinization of charisma* then leads either to traditional authority or to legal-rational authority. We discuss charisma as a cause of social change in more detail in Section 30.

In this brief treatment of political institutions we have pointed out the three *types* of authority that can govern. We must also identify the major *functions* of government, which are seemingly universal. These functions of government are performed in various ways, depending upon the complexity of the society's social structure and the political ideology of the population.

Manifest Functions of Government (Bertrand, 1967)

Making Laws. This function may occur as a result of following traditions. Laws also can be made by absolute dictators or by legislative bodies. In democratic societies, legislators are given the responsibility and duty to pass laws to guide the population's behavior.

Enforcing Laws. We have said that every government can use force as its ultimate social control. Of course, the mere threat of govermental force is usually enough to enforce the established laws. Modern societies have police and military forces. Under the direction of political leaders, the police and military function to enforce the social norms codified into laws.

Resolving Conflicts. Governments must do more than make and enforce the laws. They must judge the population's behavior in reference to the laws. Most societies have a judicial system of courts. The courts must make judgments when there are disagreements or conflicts among the population. Some folk societies have less formal means for settling conflicts, but all societies expect the government to settle disagreements among the population.

Promoting the General Welfare.   Modern societies have become increasingly complex in organization, advanced in technology, and larger in populations. This has increased the role of government as promoter of the people's welfare.

Included under this general function are the establishment and control of school systems, the provisions for health care, regulations designed to improve communications and other public services, the promotion of certain types of social change, and broad welfare functions. The specific activity of this type varies with political ideology. In . . . socialistic countries, governments assume many more such functions than is normally true elsewhere.

(Bertrand, 1967)

Protecting Against External Attacks.   Throughout history societies have had to defend themselves against attacks from outsiders. From tribal chieftains to bureaucratic governments, political leaders must make decisions that assure the protection of their peoples from outsiders. Whether real or imaginary, external danger to a nation strengthens the ties that bind a society together. This often reinforces the established position already held by those in authority—the government.

Latent Functions of Government

We have listed five manifest functions of government that are seemingly universal despite a society's political ideology, and despite the simplicity or complexity of its social structure. It is far more difficult to identify latent functions of government that all societies have in common, since each society has a unique history. In this subsection we concentrate on latent functions of the American political system.

Legislation Changes Social Norms.   It is true that American mores can undergo change before American laws catch up with them and reflect the changes. It is also true that certain local, state, and national laws have had the effect of changing people's attitudes as well as their behavior. Laws are enacted to require certain behavior. Laws restricting child labor, racial segregation, and sexual repression have been passed because certain pressure groups have succeeded in achieving social change when the majority of the population actually opposed the changes. Once enacted, the law can become a powerful instrument of moral persuasion. As new generations grow up under the new laws, they tend to accept the attitudes and beliefs upon which the laws were originally based. It can be said, then, that morality *can* be legislated. Lawfully required behavior, over a period of time, can bring about changes in people's attitudes and beliefs.

Political Machines Provide Services.   Most Americans say that political machines and political bosses are contrary to the moral assumptions of democratic government. Nevertheless, political machines have functioned in a number of ways that have proved beneficial to many generations of Americans. James W. Vander Zanden has pointed out that political machines historically served the interests of urban populations alienated from the mainstream of American life. In earlier years, political machines

did not look upon the electorate as an amorphous, undifferentiated mass of voters. Through the precinct captain, it took a direct interest in every man; the precinct captain was forever a friend in need. He humanized and personalized government. He provided jobs, rendered legal and extra-legal advice, "fixed" cases involving minor scrapes with the law, got college scholarships for the bright poor boy, looked after the bereaved—in general was a friend who knew the score when crisis struck.

(Vander Zanden, 1970)

Government Agencies Provide Employment. Government in the United States was never intended to be a big business that would account for about 25 percent of the nation's economic activity, but this is what has happened.

We might . . . note the actual extent of work that is now accounted for by government. A large portion of that economic activity involves meeting a payroll of 3 million federal civilian workers (1.3 million in the Department of Defense alone), 3.5 million military personnel, and over 8.5 million state and local employees. Excluding military personnel, public employment has more than doubled since 1947, with state and local levels growing the most rapidly (owing greatly to the over 4 million employed in public schools). The some 15 million Americans on government payrolls compose about 20 percent of the entire labor force. Another 25 million privately employed workers are dependent in whole or in part on state contracts and facilities. In sum, government has generated the vast majority of new jobs that have been created over the past 15 years. And only government can be expected to avert an unemployment catastrophe.

(Anderson, 1971)

There are other latent functions performed by the American political system, but the three mentioned have probably had the greatest impact upon the evolving American scene.

RELIGION AS A SOCIAL INSTITUTION

Features of Institutionalized Religion (Dressler, 1969).

Beliefs. Each religion has some kind of belief system. As examples, most Judeo-Christian beliefs are related in some way to the Bible, Moslem beliefs are based on the Koran, and Mormon beliefs are related to the Book of Mormon. Many religions have beliefs that are not committed to written form. In nonliterate societies, beliefs are relayed from generation to generation by word of mouth. Religious dogma is presented as truth, which need not be proved by empirical means but must be accepted as a condition of faith. However, most religions refer to past miracles and revelations as special historical proofs of the validity of dogma.

Hierarchy.   Many religions are structured so that there is a hierarchical chain of authority. Each position within the hierarchy has certain privileges, powers, and prestige. Each position performs both religious and administrative functions. For example, the Church of Rome has a pope, cardinals, archbishops, bishops, and priests.

Symbols.   Most religions have symbols that encourage believers to identify strongly with the faith. The crucifix, the crescent, and the star of David are symbols representing religious communities.

Rituals.   All religions have special ceremonies and specific rituals to perform. Among Christians the Communion is a sacred ritual that observes the sacrifice made by Jesus so that his followers might be forgiven for their sins and attain eternal life.

Some religions seem to require little more than an individual believing in the dogma, obeying the hierarchy, respecting the symbols, and correctly practicing the rituals.

Social Functions of Religions (Dressler, 1969)

Religion Serves as a Socialization Force and as a Means for Social Control. Whether it be priests, ministers, rabbis, or medicine men, those who claim to possess the sacred knowledge instruct the people as to what the deity wants and how the deity expects people to behave. Since religionists usually define what is moral and immoral, it might be said that religion "creates" a moral order that recognizes a good way of life and its rewards, while also recognizing an evil way of life and its punishments.

Religion Supports Other Social Institutions by Providing Guidelines for Approved Behavior.   There is no question about religion's influence on behavior in other sectors of society. Both the form and the behavior of families have been influenced by religion. A slogan used by institutionalized religion in the United States is "The family that prays together stays together." Ethics in the economics of the marketplace are influenced by religion. So are some of the philosophies and practices in the institution of education. In some societies religion and government are one and the same. In most societies religion at least influences the behavior of those who occupy political positions.

Religion Attempts to Improve the Conditions of Contemporary Human Life.   In the latter 20th century, many religions advocate solving social problems that have been accepted in the past as part of the natural burden of human life. Religious leaders have addressed themselves to such matters as world peace, equal justice for all people, and the elimination of poverty.

Religion Tends to Promote Social Change.   In recent years it has become commonplace to see clergy involved in social issues. Religious activists have been associated with movements seeking social justice, equality for all before God and the courts, civil rights, amendment of abortion and birth control laws, and alterations in foreign policy. This involvement of religion in social causes is not entirely new. David Dressler reminds us that:

The humanitarianism of the 19th century stemmed from Protestant teachings in England and the United States. These teachings fostered attitudes that led to the abolition of slavery, better treatment of the indigent, prison reform, the introduction of probation and parole, factory legislation, the growth of the charities movement, and other programs for human welfare.

(Dressler, 1969)

Religion Tends to Retard Social Change.   Just as religion tends to promote change in some areas, it also tends to maintain the status quo in other areas. Religion, once established, tends more to support the social norms and institutions of society than to introduce or support changes in the basic system. Established religions are usually conservative. That is, most religions tend to conserve both the structure and the value system of society.

Religion Tends Both to Promote and to Diminish Conflict.   Certain religions have encouraged their believers to conquer and enslave nonbelievers. Both verbal and physical encounters have occurred between religions and between internal factions of religions. Religious ethnocentrism is among the strongest prejudices experienced by humans. At the same time, religions have functioned to reduce conflict between peoples. We are familiar with the saying "Peace on Earth, good will to men." Religions have encouraged the loving of one's neighbors as one would love oneself.

Latent Functions of Religion

Most religions perform certain functions that are neither intended nor recognized by those who are true believers. Religious congregations can provide individuals with professional and business contacts, marital partners, and other aspects of sociability. Less subtle are the examples provided by David Dressler:

The ancient Chinese boiled their drinking water to drive out the demons. This manifest function was purely religious in nature, but the latent function of this custom was to prevent the spread of cholera and other diseases. Similarly, the Jewish people traditionally considered it morally intolerable to eat the flesh of swine, and thus . . . they avoided contracting trichinosis, a disease that plagued their gentile neighbors.

(Dressler, 1969)

EDUCATION AS A SOCIAL INSTITUTION

Most children born today—of any nationality—will receive some amount of formal schooling. In the United States about 8 million students are enrolled in colleges and universities. Another 16 million attend secondary schools, and about 36 million are in elementary schools. The nations of Western Europe match our total enrollment of some 60 million students. The Soviet Union also has about the same number in schools. Between 250 and 300 million students attend schools and colleges in other countries of the world (Hodges, 1971). Prior to the Industrial Revolution, formal education was a luxury afforded only by the wealthy and privileged. With the rise of dynamic, urban industrial societies, the casual and informal education provided by parents and peers no longer was enough to provide an adequately prepared citizen for the modern state. The institution of education, once formalized, has come to provide certain functions that serve the needs of most societies to one degree or another.

Manifest Functions of Education

No matter how much is said about the virtue of seeking knowledge or the love of learning, the primary function of education in the United States and in other industrial nations is that of preparing people for occupational roles. Almost all occupational roles demand some literacy and some kind of specialized training. Unskilled labor is decreasingly in demand. Professionals, paraprofessionals, and technicians fill most employment positions that are available. It is a fact, then, that the primary function of American schooling is occupational preparation. However, it is also true that there are many additional manifest functions *attempted* by educational institutions in the United States today. Among them are:

1. To preserve the culture by passing it from one generation to another

2. To encourage democratic participation by teaching students to think rationally and independently.

3. To enrich the student's life by expanding intellectual and esthetic horizons.

4. To improve personal adjustment through personal counseling and through offering courses in psychology, sociology, family living, drug abuse, and sex education.

5. To provide physical exercise and courses in hygiene in order to maintain and improve the health of the population.

6. To produce citizens who understand their nation's history and who are dedicated to its future.

7. To build "character," however that may be interpreted in a given time and place.

These are the manifest functions of education as *attempted* in the United States today. Obviously, they tend to be somewhat idealistic and considerably unfulfilled as often as they are fulfilled. In a sense, they provide us with an unofficial ideology of American society (Horton and Hunt, 1980).

Latent Functions of Education

Like other social institutions in American society, education performs a number of latent functions in addition to the intended manifest functions. Some of these can be identified as follows.

1.   Schools have a custodial function—in essence, they provide a babysitting service that keeps children out from under the feet of adults and from under the wheels of automobiles.

2.   Schools function as a marriage market—they afford the opportunity for selective mating on the basis of similar class and educational status.

3.   Schools widen the individual's circle of acquaintances and facilitate various alignments that help him [or her] in launching a subsequent career—that is, he [or she] makes "contacts."

4.   Colleges expose students to a bureaucratic organization, preparing them for their immersion in postcollege, large-scale business organizations.

5.   The network of extracurricular political, fraternal, dormitory, and religious organizations that characterize most large universities gives at least some students experience in managerial posts.

6.   Formal compulsory education keeps younger children out of the labor market and thus out of competition with adults for jobs, and it further protects children against economic exploitation.

(Vander Zanden, 1970)

KEY TERMS AND NAMES FROM SECTION 24

economic production and distribution

traditional economy

command economy

market economy

mercantilism, capitalism, socialism

Smith's *Wealth of Nations*

Marx's *Capital*

pursuit of self-interest

laws of supply and demand

traditional authority

legal-rational authority

charismatic authority

charisma

routinization of charisma

manifest and latent functions of government and economics

institutionalized religion

formal education

manifest and latent functions of religion and education

Robert L. Heilbroner

Adam Smith

Max Weber

Karl Marx

STUDY GUIDE FOR SECTION 24

1. Economic systems have certain features in common. IDENTIFY TWO UNIVERSAL CHARACTERISTICS OF ECONOMIC SYSTEMS.

2. Robert Heilbroner identified three types of economic systems that enable humankind to solve its economic challenge. NAME THEM.

3. There is a hereditary chain that assures that certain skills and crafts will be passed on from one generation to the next. As for the means of distributing the fruits of production, they too are passed down from one geneation to another with little change. WHICH TYPE OF ECONOMIC SYSTEM DOES THIS DESCRIBE?

4. When Western Europe moved from medieval to modern times, the nations embraced a form of economics that became known as "mercantilism." WHICH TYPE OF ECONOMIC SYSTEM WAS REPRESENTED BY MERCANTILISM?

5. WHICH ECONOMIC SYSTEM MANAGES TO SOLVE ECONOMIC PROBLEMS BUT AT THE COST OF LARGE-SCALE RAPID SOCIAL CHANGE AND ECONOMIC PROGRESS?

6. WHICH ECONOMIC SYSTEM'S BASIC ASSUMPTION IS THAT WHEN AN INDIVIDUAL PURSUES ONE'S OWN INTERESTS, THE INTERESTS OF THE ENTIRE SOCIETY ARE ENHANCED?

7. Adam Smith in the 18th century attacked the restrictions of one economic system, while in the 19th century Karl Marx attacked the excesses of another economic system. WHICH SYSTEM DID ADAM SMITH'S *WEALTH OF NATIONS* DENOUNCE? WHICH SYSTEM DID KARL MARX'S *CAPITAL* DENOUNCE?

8. WHICH TYPE OF ECONOMIC SYSTEM DO SOCIALIST NATIONS RELY UPON PRIMARILY?

9. WHICH TYPE OF ECONOMIC SYSTEM DO CAPITALIST NATIONS RELY UPON PRIMARILY?

10. The manifest functions of economic systems are to produce and distribute resources so that societies can maintain and continue themselves. Certain latent functions also occur. NAME ONE LATENT FUNCTION OF A TRADITIONAL ECONOMY. NAME ONE LATENT FUNCTION THAT BOTH COMMAND AND MARKET ECONOMIES HAVE HAD IN COMMON IN MODERN TIMES.

11. No government can remain in power and exercise authority for very long without one specific condition. WHAT MUST BE NECESSARY FOR A GOVERNMENT TO REMAIN IN POWER?

12. Max Weber identified three types of authority, and each type provides a basis for the legitimate exercise of power. NAME THE THREE TYPES OF AUTHORITY IDENTIFIED BY MAX WEBER.

13. WHICH TYPE OF AUTHORITY IS IDENTIFIED WITH LEADERS WHO ARE DEFINED AS SERVANTS OF THE PEOPLE EVEN THOUGH HIGH PRESTIGE MAY BE ASSOCIATED WITH THEIR OFFICES?

14. WHICH TYPE OF AUTHORITY IS BASED ON A SET OF UNWRITTEN RULES OR LAWS?

15. The term *charisma* refers to a person's quality of leadership that inspires people to follow the charismatic person with enthusiasm and loyalty. NAME AT LEAST THREE 20th-CENTURY FIGURES WHO HAVE BEEN IDENTIFIED AS HAVING POSSESSED CHARISMA.

16. Charismatic authority does not retain its original excitement. The revolutionary impulses of the charismatic movement begin to fade, and success leads to establishment. WHAT DOES THIS ROUTINIZATION OF CHARISMA LEAD TO AS FAR AS AUTHORITY IS CONCERNED?

17. There seem to be at least five major universal functions of government. These functions are performed in various ways depending upon the complexity of the society's social structure. NAME THE FIVE UNIVERSAL MANIFEST FUNCTIONS OF GOVERNMENT.

18. Laws are enacted to require or forbid certain behavior. It is also true that certain laws can have the effect of changing people's attitudes as well as their behavior. EXPLAIN HOW THIS CAN OCCUR.

19. Political machines have functioned in ways that have proved beneficial to many generations of Americans. HOW HAVE PRECINCT CAPTAINS OF POLITICAL MACHINES SERVED THE INTERESTS OF URBAN POPULATIONS?

20. Government has generated the majority of new jobs that have been created in the United States over the past 15 years or so. DOES THIS GIVE EVIDENCE OF A MANIFEST OR LATENT FUNCTION OF GOVERNMENT IN THE UNITED STATES? WHY?

21. LIST FOUR FEATURES OF INSTITUTIONALIZED RELIGIONS.

22. In our description of the social functions of religion, we state that one function of religion is to support other social institutions. CITE AT LEAST TWO EXAMPLES IN WHICH RELIGION INFLUENCES HUMAN BEHAVIOR IN OTHER SOCIAL INSTITUTIONS.

23. Religion tends to promote conflict in some instances and to reduce conflict in other instances. CITE ONE OTHER EXAMPLE IN WHICH RELIGION'S SOCIAL FUNCTIONS TEND TO BE CONTRADICTORY.

24. No matter how much is said about the virtue of seeking knowledge or the love of learning, WHAT IS THE PRIMARY MANIFEST FUNCTION OF EDUCATION IN THE UNITED STATES TODAY?

25. Despite the fact that the function of American education mentioned above is the primary function of American schooling, LIST AT LEAST TWO ADDITIONAL MANIFEST FUNCTIONS ATTEMPTED IN UNITED STATES SCHOOLS.

26. Like the other social institutions in American society, education performs a number of latent functions. NAME AT LEAST THREE LATENT FUNCTIONS OF AMERICAN EDUCATION.

PRACTICE TEST FOR SECTION 24

Select the best answer.

1. The institution that provides the means for the production and distribution of goods and services is the
A. Economy.
B. Government.
C. Polity.
D. Bureaucracy.

2. Power is associated with which institution?
A. Religion.
B. Government.
C. Education.
D. Economics.

3. According to Robert Heilbroner, crucial problems faced by society are
A. Organizing and exercising power.
B. Socialization and education.
C. Inflation and recession.
D. Production and distribution of goods and services.

4. Societies based on this type of economy solve the production problems rather simply: an individual takes on the job that his father and his father's father had. Which type of economy does this decribe?
A. Command.
B. Tradition.
C. Market.

5. One great advantage of this type of economy is its ability to bring about rapid and significant economic and social change. Which one?
A. Command.
B. Tradition.
C. Market.

6. Mercantilism is a form of
A. Command economics.
B. Tradition economics.
C. Market economics.

7. Adam Smith's *Wealth of Nations* was an attack upon which economic system?
A. Command.

B. Tradition.

C. Market.

8. Karl Marx's *Capital* was an attack upon which economic system?

A. Command.

B. Tradition.

C. Market.

9. Socialist nations tend to rely upon which type of economy?

A. Command.

B. Tradition.

C. Market.

10. A latent function of command and market economies is

A. Production of goods and services.

B. Distribution of goods and services.

C. Industrial growth.

D. Environmental destruction.

11. In order for a government to remain in power, there must be

A. The consent of the governed.

B. An educated electorate.

C. Regularly held elections.

D. Charismatic leadership.

12. The oldest political system known is based on

A. Traditional authority.

B. Legal-rational authority.

C. Charismatic authority.

13. The statement, "It is being done this way because this is the way it has always been done" is suggestive of which type of authority?

A. Traditional.

B. Legal-rational.

C. Charismatic.

14. The outstanding characteristic of legal-rational authority is its

A. Sacred quality.

B. Unwritten rules.

C. Bureaucratic organization.

D. Laws of succession.

15. Max Weber described it as a "certain quality of an individual personality by virtue of which he is set apart from ordinary men and treated as endowed with supernatural qualities." What is it?

A. Clairvoyance.

B. Character.

C. Divinity.

D. Charisma.

16. The vast majority of new jobs that have been created over the past 15 years have been generated by

A. Business.

B. The private sector.

C. Government.

D. Industry.

17. Which of the following is a latent function of government?

A. Institutionalization of norms.

B. Providing employment.

C. Adjudication of conflict.

D. Protection from external attack.

18. Which of the following is correct?

A. Morality cannot be legislated.

B. Laws are a powerful instrument of moral persuasion.

C. Laws cannot alter attitudes and behavior.

19. Most religions offer special historical proofs of the validity of their dogmas through reference to

A. Logic.

B. Empirical evidence.

C. Past miracles and revelations.

20. Institutionalized religions are characterized by

A. Belief systems in written form.

B. Special ceremonies and rituals.

C. Empirical verification of dogma.

D. A lack of hierarchical chain of authority.

21. Latent functions of American education include all of the following except one. Which one?
A. Affording opportunities for mate selection.
B. Preserving the culture by passing it from one generation to another.
C. Protecting children from economic exploitation.
D. Widening a person's circle of acquaintances.

22. Traditional authority is
A. Dominant in Western democracies.
B. Based on leaders defined as servants of the people.
C. Characterized by a sacred quality.
D. Characterized by a charismatic quality.

Answer Key

1.	A	**9.**	A	**17.**	B
2.	B	**10.**	D	**18.**	B
3.	D	**11.**	A	**19.**	C
4.	B	**12.**	A	**20.**	B
5.	A	**13.**	A	**21.**	B
6.	A	**14.**	C	**22.**	C
7.	A	**15.**	D		
8.	C	**16.**	C		

CHAPTER SUMMARY

1. Social institutions are the activities and organizations by which the basic needs of society are met. Five basic social institutions exist in every society: marriage and family; economics; politics; religion; and education.

2. At one time it was believed that humankind had lived in a state of nature without social organization and with total individual freedom. Then, supposedly, a social contract was made, leading to social cooperation and organization. We can no longer take social-contract theories seriously. Now, social scientists say that human society began when humankind appeared on Earth.

3. Each social institution is likely to include institutional traits such as cultural symbols, a code of behavior, and an ideology.

4. Social institutions perform both manifest and latent functions. Manifest functions are intended and recognized by participants in a system. Latent functions are consequences neither intended nor readily recognized.

5. As an institution, the family has many forms and customs. Distinctions have been made between the family of orientation and the family of procreation and between the nuclear family and the extended family. Endogamy is the practice of marrying within one's own group. Exogamy occurs when one marries outside one's own group.

6. A variety of family forms and customs have been present in the many human societies through history. A patriarchal family has a man as the head. A ma-

triarchal family has a woman as the head. Equalitarianism exists when a man, a woman, and any children each can express views and preferences regarding family matters. Family descent can be traced through either a patrilineal, matrilineal, or bilineal arrangement. Patterns of residence include patrilocal, matrilocal, and neolocal arrangements.

7.   Monogamy is a form of marriage in which one woman is married to one man at one time. Polygamy is marriage that allows for multiple mates. There are three types of polygamy: Polygyny exists if one man has two or more wives at the same time. Polyandry exists if one woman has two or more husbands at one time. Group marriage exists if several men and several women share a marital relationship. It has been estimated that 75 pecent of 554 societies throughout history have practiced polygyny.

8.   Cuber and Harroff identify five American marital life-styles. They are the conflict-habituated, the devitalized, the passive-congenial, the vital, and the total marriage. The five types represent different kinds of adjustment and different conceptions of marriage. Most of those involved in each of these marital life-styles say that they are content, if not always very happy.

9.   Certain social functions are universally performed by the family. The family is the first agent of socialization and provides for one's social status. Both sexual satisfaction and reproduction are biological functions of the family. The family also is expected to nourish the emotional and the material needs of its members.

10.   In addition to marriage and family, other basic social institutions are economics, government, religion, and education. Economics provides the production and distribution of goods and services. Government (politics) is concerned with organizing and using power that is accepted as authority. Religion directs human thoughts, feelings, and actions to matters believed to be above ordinary experience. Education socializes people to participate in and to understand their cultural heritage.

11.   Robert Heilbroner identifies three typologies of economic systems. The tradition economy produces and distributes by procedures originated in the distant past. The concept of progress is meaningless. A command economy is a planned economy. Socialist nations rely more upon economies of command than on any other method. A market economy is based on the private ownership of the means of production. Capitalist nations rely more upon economies of marketing (supply and demand) than on any other method.

12.   Max Weber identified three types of authority. Traditional authority exists when leaders assume power through hereditary succession. Their orders and decisions are not questioned by the governed. Legal-rational authority is characterized by a formal system of laws and by bureaucratic organization. Charismatic authority inspires people to follow the charismatic leader with enthusiasm and unquestioning loyalty.

13.   Manifest functions of government include the making and enforcing of laws, resolving conflicts, promoting the general welfare, and protecting against external attack. Latent functions of government in United States history have included the changing of social norms through legislation, the provision of special

services by political machines, and the employment of many people in large government bureaucracies.

14. Religion as a social institution consists of a belief system called dogma, a hierarchical chain of authority, symbols to encourage believers to identify with the faith, and special ceremonies and rituals to perform. Many religions serve as a socialization force and as a means for social control.

15. The predominant function of education as a social institution in America today is that of preparing people for occupational roles. Of course, education also is concerned with passing on the cultural heritage in general.

SUGGESTIONS FOR FURTHER READING RELATING TO CHAPTER 8

Bane, Mary Jo, *Here to Stay: American Families in the 20th Century* (New York: Basic Books, 1976). Bane writes that "The facts—as opposed to the myths—about marriage, child rearing and family ties provide convincing evidence that family commitments are likely to persist in our society." Very good reading.

Becker, Howard S., Blanche Geer, and Everett Hughes, *Making the Grade* (New York: John Wiley, 1968). This is a good academic case study of ways in which college students achieve their desired grade point averages while participating in a life-style that is not academic. Participant observer techniques are used.

Bendix, Reinhard, *Max Weber: An Intellectual Portrait* (New York: Doubleday Anchor Books, 1962). This is a truly fine portrait of Max Weber's thoughts on the institutions of economics, politics, and religion. The thorough 28-page index enables one to use this as a handbook on Weber's writing.

Berger, Peter L., *A Rumor of Angels: Modern Society and the Re-Discovery of the Supernatural* (New York: Doubleday Anchor Books, 1970). "In this slim and gracefully written volume, Peter Berger continues his call for a many-sided conversation among sociologists, philosophical anthropologists and theologians."—Robert J. McNamara in *Sociological Analysis*.

Edwards, Harry, *The Sociology of Sport* (Homewood, Ill.: The Dorsey Press, 1973). Chapter 5 treats sport as a social institution.

Fromm, Erich, *Psychoanalysis and Religion* (New Haven: Yale University Press, 1950). Fromm analyzes traditional religion, pointing out its weaknesses and dangers, and stresses a need for a spiritual, humanistic reorientation of religious thought.

Kohl, Herbert R., *The Open Classroom: A Practical Guide to a New Way of Teaching* (New York: Random House Vintage Books, 1969). The author describes American schools as "authoritarian and oppressive." This is a forthright and provocative manifesto for teachers and students.

Lefebvre, Henri, *The Sociology of Marx* (New York: Random House Vintage Books, 1969). We especially recommend Chapter 1, "Marxian Thought and Sociology," and Chapter 5, "Political Sociology: Theory of the State." Highly motivated students should read both this and Bendix's book about Max Weber's thoughts.

Maher, Robert F., *The New Men of Papua: A Study of Culture Change* (Madison: University of Wisconsin Press, 1961). Maher provides an excellent description of cultural change within a nonliterate society that had been observed decades ago by anthropologists.

Mills, C. Wright, *The Power Elite* (New York: Oxford University Press, 1956). The thesis of this classic work is that the United States is actually ruled by a small power elite composed of people in top positions of industry, government, and the military, none holding elected positions.

O'Neill, Nena, and George O'Neill, *Open Marriage: A New Life Style for Couples* (New York: Avon Books, 1973). This book offers an intriguing description of a new type of monogamy. The guidelines for an open marriage include privacy, honest communication, equality, and trust.

Queen, Stuart A., and Robert W. Haberstein, *The Family in Various Cultures*, 3rd ed. (New York: J. B. Lippincott, 1967). This book offers invaluable insights to the variety of forms and customs experienced in marriage and family among diverse human groupings throughout history and up to the present time.

Scanzoni, John H., *The Black Family in Modern Society* (Boston: Allyn & Bacon, 1971). The author points out that "the majority (67%) of metropolitan black households in 1968 were headed by a *man* with his wife present." The focus of this book is on a sample of 400 black households, husband and wife present, in the city of Indianapolis.

Wilson, Bryan R., *The Noble Savages: The Primitive Origins of Charisma and Its Contemporary Survival* (Berkeley: University of California Press, 1975). This is a good recent consideration of how the concept of charisma has been corrupted by mass media and sociologists by reference to politicians and celebrities as examples.

Chapter 9
Working and Work Organizations

SECTION 25   THE CHANGING WORLD OF WORK
- HISTORICAL ATTITUDES TOWARD WORKING
- DEFINITIONS OF WORK
- THE FUNCTIONS OF WORK IN MODERN AMERICA
- THE INCREASING DIVISION OF LABOR
- CHANGES IN THE AMERICAN LABOR FORCE, 1900–1985

Objectives
After completing this section, the student should be able to:
1. Describe different historical attitudes toward working.
2. Define work in several ways.
3. Identify and describe the functions of work in modern America.
4. Explain how and why there has been an increased division of labor.
5. Describe broad changes in the American labor force.

Without work all life goes rotten. But when work is soulless, life stifles and dies.

(Albert Camus)

The quotation that begins this chapter expresses the view of a 20th-century Frenchman. His remark places great importance upon the value of work. Furthermore, he is saying that the work must be worthwhile and satisfying, not "soulless." These are typical views held by 20th-century scholars in the Western world. Like so many other things, attitudes about work are influenced by the times and the culture in which one participates. Not all people have thought of working as being very important.

HISTORICAL ATTITUDES TOWARD WORKING

In ancient Greece, working was looked upon as a curse. Those who had to work were considered lacking dignity. Ideally, the individual's role in life was to improve the mind in leisurely study and thinking. Slavery was practiced among the Greeks in order to allow citizens to reach full philosophic maturity. The ancient Hebrews looked upon working as punishment from God. The Hebrews believed that their need to work was the result of the disobedience of Adam and Eve. The earliest Christians adopted the Hebrew view of work, seeing it as both a curse and punishment from God. The early Christians especially disapproved of one's working for self-gain. As the centuries passed, however, Christianity interpreted working as a duty and as a way of serving God.

During the past few centuries, influenced by Christianity, many Europeans and Americans have been described as living according to the Protestant ethic. The

Protestant ethic was originally a system of beliefs about respect for God and the human obligation to work. It included an emphasis upon people being hard workers, thrifty, sober, and careful in providing for their futures. Such beliefs were taught in churches and schools. The Protestant ethic was associated with early capitalism. Work was thought to bring rewards such as a quiet, good feeling of a hard day's labor well done. The Protestant ethic emphasized the pleasures of working more than earning high wages or salaries. This high regard for work for the sake of work became known as the work ethic. Labor would be performed as a moral duty even if it had nothing to do with God's will. Karl Marx considered working to be a highly satisfying human experience, if the workers were freed from capitalist exploitation. Marx believed that working people could build a fulfilling and free society as they improved their environment through meaningful work.

DEFINITIONS OF WORK

Work can be defined as that which a person does in order to survive. At work a person may be happy or miserable. The person may work merely to receive money. The person may work because the work brings joy to his or her life. As long as the activities are in some way related to one's survival—either physical or social—then we can say that one is working (Braude, 1975). Another definition of work would be "an activity that produces something of value for other people. This definition broadens the scope of what we call work and places it within a social context." For example, we know that a housewife is really working, even though she receives no salary. She is being productive for other people. Of course, she may also be bringing joy to her own life as she pursues her work. Also, voluntary work without pay is still work. Finally, "work is the means by which we provide the goods and services needed and desired by ourselves and our society" (*Work in America*, 1973).

THE FUNCTIONS OF WORK IN MODERN AMERICA

During the 1970s a special task force on work in America reported to the Secretary of Health, Education and Welfare (*Work in America*, 1973). Using this report as a guide, we can identify six functions that work serves Americans here in the latter 20th century:

1. *Work provides money for goods and services.* The manifest function of working is that of providing an individual with the means to "make a living." The work that people do is expected to provide material comfort and economic security.

2. *Work also provides a place in which to meet people.* Although income may be the most significant reason for a person's going to work day after day, the social relationships that develop on the job are of value too. Primary relationships *do* develop within the secondary settings of factories, large offices, and most other types of working environments.

3. *Work provides a social status for the worker and probably for the workers's family.* In a family with children and two working parents, the types of work done by one or both working parents can determine the status of the family. The type of work and income received influences where people live, where children go to school, and with whom family members associate. Work definitely influences a family's life-style and life chances.

4. *Work contributes to self-esteem.* When a worker "achieves mastery in a job, he or she develops a feeling of competence and accomplishment. . . ." This leads to a feeling of self-confidence and high self-esteem (Scarpitti, 1980). Having a job to do is knowing that one has something to offer to the world at large day in and day out. Not having a job is not having something that is valued by one's fellow human beings. Having a job proves that one is needed by others. "Doing well or poorly, being a success or failure at work, is all too easily transformed into a measure of being a valuable or worthless human being" (*Work in America*, 1973).

5. *Work helps to shape a person's sense of identity.* People tend to think of themselves and to describe themselves in reference to the kind of work they do. If their work is held in high esteem by society, they feel a sense of well-being. On the other hand, people out of work or on welfare become "nobodies." Older people who have retired from regular work can suffer a severe loss of identity. People with low-status jobs either receive no sense of identity from their work or reject unfavorable identities forced upon them by others.

6. *Work satisfies the human desire to place an order or structure on the world.* In the first chapter we mentioned the "human rage for order." Without having a regular occupational social role, many people feel victimized by a sense of disorder. Without meaningful work to perform, people are apt to feel unable to plan or to predict their own day-to-day activities or overall lives. Work helps to "establish the regularity of life, its basic rhythms and cyclical patterns of day, week, month, and year" (Frankel, 1936). When one is out of work, one's life is disordered. Time patterns become confused or nonexistent. With no place to go and nothing to do, it does not matter what time of day it is.

THE INCREASING DIVISION OF LABOR

In modern societies production work, service work, and work on projects has been divided up so that each individual performs one small part of the entire task. This is what is meant by the division of labor. With the division of labor, each individual must perform some small, specific task that, in itself, has little to do with providing a sense of satisfaction. With the division of labor, work "is not the satisfaction of a need, but only a means for satisfying other needs" (Marx, 1964A).

Dividing labor so that each person performs one small task of some larger activity has helped modern societies to mass produce both goods and services. This has resulted in a higher standard of living for many people. In this way, the division of labor in modern societies has been functional. Nevertheless, there are also dysfunctional aspects of the increased division of labor. A person who does one small task over and over again for years is apt to suffer from a sense of isolation and meaninglessness. Although being productive, one feels nonproductive. The small task may in no way conform to an individual's personality and potentiality (Durkheim, 1933). Consider that "In the baking industry one can make a living as a cracker breaker, meringue spreader, a pie stripper, or pan dumper" (Wilensky, 1967). Even in making a pie, the labor can be divided into special tasks for different people.

The division of labor means dividing work into special tasks. This is *specialization*. We describe specialization in more detail in another section of this chapter. For now, consider George Ritzer's comments:

Although specialization is clearest among semi- and unskilled workers (in particular, assembly-line workers), it has occurred throughout the occupational hierarchy. In medicine we have witnessed the decline of the general practitioner and the increasing number of doctors in such specialties as pediatrics, surgery, psychiatry, and gynecology. . . . The secretary of the past who performed a variety of functions is being replaced with clerk-typists, typists, stenographers, and receptionists.

(Ritzer, 1977)

No individual is self-sufficient. Few individuals could perform all the tasks necessary for personal survival. It is reasonable to spread out these tasks throughout the population. This distribution of tasks is also division of labor. By different people taking on different responsibilities, production is more efficient and output per task is increased.

So we have farmers and letter carriers and tool-and-die makers, doctors, teachers and computer technologists—all sorts of people doing all sorts of things so that the work of the society might be accomplished efficiently and effectively. Think of all the people needed to see this book into print.

(Braude, 1975)

This is what we meant earlier when we said that the division of labor in modern societies has been functional.

CHANGES IN THE AMERICAN LABOR FORCE, 1900–1985

We have said earlier that people describe themselves in reference to the kind of work they do. Often, when asked what one does, people respond by naming the company or agency where they are employed. Here in the latter 20th century, only about 10 percent of the American labor force is self-employed. Each year there is a decreasing number of small-business owners. The corner grocery stores have given way to the large supermarkets. It is not easy for small businesses of any kind to compete successfully against the large corporations. The great change in the 20th century is away from self-employment and toward work in government agencies, large corporations, unions, and educational institutions from elementary to graduate schools. Now we shall briefly describe some of the changes in the American labor force taking place in farming, in the professions, and in the worlds of blue-collar and clerical workers.

Farming

One of the more remarkable changes in the American labor force relates to the number of people employed in agriculture. In the year 1900, 37.5 percent of the labor force engaged in farming. By 1974 the proportion of farm workers in the labor force was reduced to only 3.4 percent. It is believed that by 1985 only 1.6 percent of the labor force will be in farming (Rosenthal, 1973). There have been a number of factors causing the decline in the number of farm workers. George Ritzer cites the fact that technological advances have been so great that far fewer people are needed to produce much more food. He says, "Included in these advances are improved machinery such as mechanical harvesters and packing machines; better seeds, fertilizers, insecticides, and animal feed; and veterinary medicine" (Ritzer, 1977).

The Professions

What are known as the professions—medicine, law, education, communications, science, and public services—have been on the increase along with those working in such fields. In the year 1900, 4.3 percent of the labor force were considered professionals. By 1974 the proportion of professionals in the labor force had in-

Technological advances require fewer workers to produce food.

creased to 14.5 percent. It is believed that by 1985 almost 17 percent of the labor force will be in the professions (Rosenthal, 1973). "Professional recognition is a desirable goal for many occupations because it carries with it gains in power, economic position, and prestige" (Ritzer, 1977).

Clerical Work

In the year 1900 only 3 percent of the American labor force was engaged in clerical work. By 1974 clerical workers made up 17.5 percent of the work force. It has been estimated that by 1985 clerical workers will make up 19.4 percent of the labor force (Rosenthal, 1973). The main reason for the tremendous growth in clerical jobs is the steady increase in the number of large organizations that use bureaucratic administrations. Large bureaucracies employ many people to shuffle through papers and to feed the file cabinets that have come to symbolize our time. Paperwork is the lifeblood of bureaucratic administration. Such work requires many clerks (Ritzer, 1977).

We discuss ideal and real bureaucracy in another section of this chapter. Still, another reason why there has been such a growth in the number of clerical workers has to do with historical technological developments. First the typewriter and then other electric office machines have drawn many people into this field. For example, in 1960 there were less than 2000 operators of computers and computer-related equipment in the United States. In ten years that number had increased to almost 120,000 and is continuing to grow. From 1960 to 1970 keypunch operators increased from 160,000 to 270,000 (Ritzer, 1977). The computers do reduce the number of people needed to work in routine clerical jobs like filing and billing, George Ritzer has pointed out. But, he says, there has also been an increased need for people to prepare material for the computer. Ritzer suggests that technological changes will continue to *increase* the number of people needed to do clerical work.

Semi-Skilled and Unskilled Work

Semi-skilled and unskilled blue-collar workers made up 35.8 percent of the American labor force in the year 1900. By 1930 almost 40 percent of the labor force fit this occupational category. This increase was the result of rapid growth in industrialization during the early 20th century. By 1974 the semi- and unskilled workers made up 35.4 percent of the labor force. It has been estimated that by 1985 the proportion of such workers will decrease to 32.3 percent (Rosenthal, 1973).

Manual work has been in less demand primarily because of technological changes in factories, coal mining, and oil drilling. Automation can create jobs, but it also displaces workers who need little or no sophisticated skills to perform their work. George Ritzer mentions the loss of such jobs because of American industry's inability to compete with foreign manufacturers in some industries (electronics, automobiles, clothes, and shoes). Ritzer says that it is the least skilled blue-collar occupations that have suffered the greatest decline in job opportunities. This is because such work is the easiest to replace with machines. On the other hand, blue-collar workers who are highly skilled have suffered little decline in demand for their work.

Other Occupational Changes

There are many other occupational groups in addition to those we have cited. The proportion of people in sales work increased about 50 percent between 1900 and 1974. This increase has been leveling off due to such things as self-service stores and vending machines. The majority of salespeople are in retail outlets. However, that group is growing less rapidly than those in service occupations such as insurance and real estate sales (Ritzer, 1977). When we speak of service occupations we mean work that does not produce an actual product but does produce some specific service. The proportion of service workers in general has grown from 3.6 percent in 1900 to 12 percent in 1974. It has been estimated that by 1985 the labor force will include 12.9 percent of service workers (Rosenthal, 1973). There are many kinds of service jobs in the American economy. They include diaper service, chair-side assistants of dentists, physicians' aides, elevator operators, barbers, bus drivers, cab drivers, lawn-control service, and countless other activities that provide services rather than products. One very significant change in the American economic system is our shift from an emphasis on goods production to an emphasis on service offering (Ritzer, 1977).

KEY TERMS
FROM
SECTION 25

ancient attitudes toward work

Protestant ethic

work ethic

various definitions of work

functions of work in the United States

division of labor: functions and dysfunctions

specialization of jobs

technological advances

the professions

clerical work

blue-collar occupations

service workers

STUDY GUIDE FOR SECTION 25

1. Not all people have considered working to be rewarding. DESCRIBE ATTITUDES HELD BY ANCIENT GREEKS AND HEBREWS AND BY EARLY CHRISTIANS.

2. WHAT ATTITUDES TOWARD WORKING HAVE BEEN ASSOCIATED WITH THE PROTESTANT ETHIC (WORK ETHIC)?

3. We provide several definitions of work in this section. WHICH DEFINITION DO YOU PREFER?

4. WHAT IS THE MANIFEST FUNCTION OF WORKING IN THE UNITED STATES TODAY?

5. We have said that work provides social status. EXPLAIN HOW A FAMILY'S STATUS AND LIFE CHANCES ARE RELATED TO OCCUPATIONS.

6. We also have said that work helps to shape a person's sense of identity. GIVE EXAMPLES OF HOW THIS CAN OCCUR.

7. Working certainly provides people with more than goods and services. DESCRIBE SOME POTENTIAL RESULTS OF A PERSON HAVING NO MEANINGFUL WORK TO PERFORM.

8. There are functional and dysfunctional aspects to the increased division of labor in modern societies. EXPLAIN HOW THE DIVISION OF LABOR HAS BROUGHT FUNCTIONAL AND DYSFUNCTIONAL RESULTS.

9. Many changes have been occurring in the American labor force since the year 1900. DESCRIBE CHANGES THAT HAVE TAKEN PLACE IN FARMING, IN THE PROFESSIONS, IN CLERICAL WORK, AND IN BLUE-COLLAR WORK.

10. The service occupations do not produce an actual product. HOW HAS THE PROPORTION OF SERVICE WORKERS GROWN SINCE THE YEAR 1900?

PRACTICE TEST FOR SECTION 25

Select the best answer.

1. A characteristic view held by 20th-century scholars emphasizes that work is
A. Less important than philosophic maturity.
B. Worthwhile and satisfying.
C. Less important than leisurely study and thinking.
D. Punishment from God.

2. The Protestant ethic was associated with early
A. Socialism.
B. Communism.
C. Democracy.
D. Capitalism.

3. Work helps to establish the regularity of life, its basic rhythms and cyclical patterns of day, week, month, and year. Which function of work does this statement reflect?
A. Order and structure.
B. Social status.
C. Money for goods and services.
D. Sense of identity.

4. The division of work into small, individual tasks is known as
A. Mass production.
B. Routinization.
C. Specialization.
D. Sense of identity.

5. What percentage of the labor force is self-employed?
A. 20 percent.
B. 40 percent.
C. 10 percent.
D. 30 percent.

6. In 1974 the percentage of farm workers in the labor force was

A. 3.4 percent.
B. 6.2 percent.
C. 9.7 percent.
D. 11.3 percent.

7. In 1974 the percentage of professionals in the labor force was

A. 21 percent.
B. 14.5 percent.
C. 7 percent.
D. 28.5 percent.

8. In the period 1900–1974, there was a significant decrease in which type of work?

A. Clerical work.
B. Semi-skilled work.
C. Farming.
D. The professions.

9. In 1974 the semi- and unskilled workers made up what percentage of the labor force?

A. 8.3 percent.
B. 17.9 percent.
C. 27.6 percent.
D. 35.4 percent.

10. In 1974 service workers made up what percent of the labor force?

A. 6.3 percent.
B. 12.0 percent.
C. 17.1 percent.
D. 23.8 percent.

11. A very significant change in the American economic system has been a shift from

A. Goods production to service offering.
B. Capitalism to socialism.
C. The professions to the paraprofessions.
D. Capital gains to capital losses.

Answer Key

1.	B	**7.**	B
2.	D	**8.**	C
3.	A	**9.**	D
4.	C	**10.**	B
5.	C	**11.**	A
6.	A		

SECTION 26   BUREAUCRACY AS THE ADMINISTRATION OF MASS SOCIETY

- THE POPULAR VIEW OF BUREAUCRACY
- THE SOCIOLOGICAL VIEW OF BUREAUCACY
- THE BUREAUCRATIZATION OF MODERN SOCIETY
- CHARACTERISTICS OF IDEAL AND REAL BUREAUCRACY

Objectives

After completing this section, the student should be able to:

1. Explain the difference between the popular and sociological views of bureaucracy.
2. Explain what is meant by the bureaucratization of society.
3. Identify and describe characteristics of ideal bureaucracy.
4. Identify and describe characteristics of real bureaucracy.

THE POPULAR
VIEW OF
BUREAUCRACY

The term *bureaucracy* has come to be used by many people as a bad word. To many, bureaucracy is thought of as a system that should be eliminated. Bureaucracy is seen as simply a frustrating way in which government operates. People express disgust with "the bureaucracy." The workers in bureaucracy are seen as inefficient and bungling bureaucrats. It is said that all the red tape prevents any real work from getting done. These are the popular views of bureaucracy. Few people have not felt this way at one time or another. Most of us have experienced the runaround. We have been sent from one official to another without getting any satisfaction. Some of us, when we think of bureaucracy, can recall times when "lengthy forms we had to fill out in sextuplicate [were] returned to us because we forgot to cross a 't' or dot an 'i' " (Blau, 1956).

There is something wrong with this popular view of bureaucracy. It is true that many of us *have* sometimes been confused and frustrated by bureaucratic organizations. But this does not mean that bureaucratic administration is always inefficient and frustrating. Actually, not only government, but the entire social structure of modern society is dependent upon bureaucratic administration. "A large increasing proportion of the American people spend their working lives as small cogs in the complex mechanism of bureaucratic organizations" (Blau, 1956). Almost all the products that we consume and the services we receive are the results of bureaucratic efforts to meet our needs and desires. Without bureaucracy, the standard of living to which we are accustomed could not be maintained.

THE SOCIOLOGICAL VIEW OF BUREAUCRACY

Sociologists recognize bureaucracy as the administrative system that allows modern societies to function. To understand modern societies, one must understand the functions and structure of bureaucracy. Max Weber wrote that "however much people may complain about the evils of bureaucracy,' it would be sheer illusion to think for a moment that continuous administrative work can be carried out in any field except by means of officials working in offices. . . . For the needs of mass administration today, it is completely indispensible" (Weber, 1947).

Bureaucracy is the loom upon which modern, mass society is woven. It is not simply a way to run government in mass society. Bureaucracy is *the* way to run government of mass society. In fact, bureaucracy is the administrative system used in *any* large organization today. Let us cite examples. National, state, and local governments are bureaucratic. Large colleges and universities are bureaucratic. Organized religions are bureaucratic. All of the large businesses and industries that produce our goods and service are bureaucracies. As we have said, bureaucracy is the loom upon which modern society is woven.

THE BUREAU-CRATIZATION OF MODERN SOCIETY

As an administrative system, bureaucracy is not new to the human experience. To one degree or another, large organizations in the past were bureaucratized. Ancient Egypt used bureaucracy as a means to collect taxes and to assign irrigation rights. In ancient China, there were bureaucrats to administer dams, waterways, and irrigation systems. Even the Church of Rome in medieval times was a bureaucratic organization. We are saying, then, that bureaucracy is not unique to modern times. It is the *bureaucratization of society* that is unique to modern times. This phrase—bureaucratization of society—means that bureaucracy is everywhere all the time in our lives. We drive cars made by bureaucratic organizations on highways made by still other bureaucratic organizations. Our car radios play music recorded by bureaucratic organizations. The police officer who directs traffic works for a bureaucratic organization. And so it goes, on and on. In some way, everyday, most of us come in contact with bureaucracy. That is why we speak of the bureaucratization of modern society.

Since the Industrial Revolution, more and more people have discovered that to work, they must do so under an employer. In order to work, one must have tools and equipment. Tools and equipment are increasingly available only in bureaucracies, private or public, capitalist or socialist. Consequently, in order to have access to tools in order to work in order to live, one must find employment within a bureaucracy. The bureaucratization of society has separated workers from the instruments of production in both modern, capitalist enterprise and in modern, socialist enterprise. Generally, the worker no longer owns tools. In order

The boxes contain required federal government corporate paper-work. The people are additional employees hired by the corporation to process the paperwork for a period of one year.

to work, one must be employed. Whether blue collar, white collar, or stiff shirt, more and more people have become employed in bureaucracy. Even the physicist does not ordinarily own a cyclotron. To do research, the physicist must be employed by a bureaucracy with laboratory resources (Merton, 1968).

CHARACTER-ISTICS OF IDEAL AND REAL BUREAUCRACY

In Section 13 we explained that a typology is a sociological tool that is used to study society. Max Weber said that ideal types (typologies) are exaggerations that do not actually exist in reality. When Weber wrote about bureaucracy, he approached it as a typology of administration (Weber, 1947, 1958). Many other sociologists have followed with descriptions based upon or similar to Weber's writings (Blau, 1956; Bensman and Rosenberg, 1963; Ritzer, 1977). The following nine characteristics apply to both ideal and real bureaucracy. In each case we first describe what would exist in *ideal* bureaucracy. The second paragraph under each characteristic describes what does occur within *real* bureaucracy.

1. Financial Security

Both major and minor officials in bureaucracy are paid fixed salaries. Those employees who get paid wages by the hour are reasonably certain of steady income, fringe benefits, and pensions if they remain with the organization. One need not depend on individual initiative or good luck in order to survive financially. Most of all, one must fill the position regularly, which is to say that one must *be there*. Two people doing the same job make approximately the same income. Factors such as merit raises and seniority can account for slight differences in income.

In reality the extent to which the promise of financial security is fulfilled depends on several factors. For example, junior executives who wish to move up the hierarchical chain of command often have to move first from their present geographic location to a remote area with which they are unfamiliar. This movement of families has become rather commonplace in the United States. To retain financial security one must pay a nonfinancial price of dislocating one's family from familiar friends, activities, and one's extended family. Furthermore, bureaucracies have many branches throughout the country. It is not uncommon for them to close a branch. This terminates the employment of many lower-level employees. They are neither invited nor feel they can afford to move to a distant location of another branch of the company or agency.

2. Permanent Employment

Many people enter a bureaucracy expecting to remain with the organization for the duration of their active, preretirement lives. People are encouraged to think of themselves as part of the team. Ideally, those who remain with the organization through the years are rewarded with promotions, higher salaries or wages, and longer vacations. In turn, the bureaucracy is rewarded by officials and workers who believe that they have a vested interest in the success of the organization. This results in employees who grow increasingly skilled and increasingly devoted to the success and the stability of the organization. Supposedly, each employee develops a fund of specialized knowledge that makes that employee more valuable to the organization.

In reality we find that being assured of a position does not in any way assure the organization that an individual will become increasingly skilled and devoted to the success of the organization. It is not uncommon to find a person *decreasingly* identifying with objectives of the organization. Overwhelmed by the impersonality of their work—even the seeming meaninglessness of their activities

—many people give up the idea that they can get personal satisfaction out of performing their job well. Consequently, when they reject the significance of their work, they become less devoted and less efficient employees. As a result, the objectives of the bureaucracy are apt to be achieved less and less (Bensman and Rosenberg, 1963). This is an example of ritualism and also an example of what more recently has been called *burnout*.

3. Special Qualifications

Special qualifications are required for entry into the various bureaucratic positions. Sometimes competitive examinations are used to open the door to employment or to a higher position within the organization. Many jobs require specific educational certificates, diplomas, and degrees. Such educational requirements have caused people to flood the community colleges, state colleges, and universities "where they demand technical courses that will ultimately equip them with their passports to bureaucratic success" (Bensman and Rosenberg, 1963).

Still, neither entrance to nor promotion within a bureaucracy is guaranteed simply because a person does well on competitive examinations or because a person has acquired further formal education. Whom one knows and how well one gets along with others are important *unofficial* qualifications for acceptance or rejection. The fact is that one's chances for advancement often depend on whether one is liked and trusted by higher officials and by one's subordinates more than on one's qualifications and technical efficiency. This may not be the way in which the rules are written, but it is the way in which the game is played.

4. Role Expectations and Job Descriptions

Ideally, bureaucratic positions have rigid role expectations. The highest paid official and the lowest paid worker each knows the rights, duties, and privileges of the position being occupied. Each position has certain duties and certain authority. The individual occupying the position is expected neither to exceed his or her authority nor to neglect his or her duty. Whatever rights a person enjoys within the organization belong to the position, not to the individual occupying the position. In boot camp or basic training, military recruits are told that they must salute their officers because those officers occupy *positions* of authority, not because of *who* occupies the positions. Still another point to be made is this: personal whims must not play any part in the decisions or behavior of those who hold bureaucratic positions. The person occupying the position must play the role defined as appropriate for that position. This is why such phrases as "There's nothing I can do" and "I can't make an exception just for you" and "I'm only following orders" have become so familiar in bureaucratized mass society.

Despite all that is said in the paragraph above, the formal expectations of bureaucratic organizations are often not realized. An entire network of informal relationships and unofficial practices develop among the employees at every level

(Blau, 1956). Unofficial friendship groups—cliques—tend to form at all levels of large organizations, from executives to assembly-line workers. Cliques form as a result of close proximity, common interests, common ambitions, common resentments, or common ethnic or racial origins. As this process spreads, the bureaucracy is apt to be reorganized along informal and unofficial lines. Clique loyalty can be stressed above organizational loyalty. Some cliques have informal leaders with more influence than those individuals whose job descriptions indicate authority and prestige. In fact, it is not unusual to find that the informal network of cliques within an organization can get more done than the formal administrative machinery set up within the bureaucracy. "The uniformity, predictability, and precision built into [bureaucracy] are processed out of it by intervening social and emotional factors" (Bensman and Rosenberg, 1963).

5. Strict Accountability Versus Passing the Buck

Written accounts are kept of almost every action taken within a bureaucracy, leading one sociologist to say that "A large paper mountain hovers over the foothills of every bureau" and "the bulging file cabinets symbolize our age" (Bensman and Rosenberg, 1963). An official or clerk is expected to acknowledge receipt of a certain document by signing for it. A record is kept that it was received. Orders from executives are sent down to the lower ranks, acknowledged by signature or initials (in sextuplicate?) and then sent on to various filing cabinets. Practices like these have helped to give the red-tape reputation to bureaucracy. Nevertheless, people can be held responsible for what they do, and there usually is a way of pinning responsibility when necessary.

Because people know that they will be held accountable for their actions, there is a tendency *not* to make decisions whenever possible. Employees hesitate to take the initiative on innovations and changes in established procedures. Strict accountability might be responsible for producing timid employees. Some would rather pass the buck than make decisions that may be interpreted as wrong and then held against them later.

6. Specialization

Every bureaucrat is a specialist within an organization of specialists. There is an obvious *division of labor* in which each bureaucratic position is occupied by a specialist. Specialization is in evidence from the machine-run assembly line to the people-pushing public relations department. The duties of any one position tend to be narrow and specific. First through specialized training, then through constant repetition on the job, each individual becomes an expert in each of the organization's positions. This high degree of specialization is now so much a part of socioeconomic life that we tend to forget that it is a relatively recent innovation of modern bureaucracies (Blau, 1956). In modern, mass society, the factory worker's job is a mystery to the office clerk, the professional's work is a mystery to the farmer, with very few people really knowing what the others are doing.

However, this does not make any one person indispensable. Within the file cabinets are job descriptions for every bureaucratic position. It does not take long, first through specialized training, then through constant repetition on the job, for one expert to replace another expert in any one of the bureaucratic positions.

Real bureaucracies *do* stress the importance of specialization. In the higher levels of bureaucracy, this means that specialists are professionals. John Gardner said:

The loyalty of the professional man is to his profession and not to the organization that may house him at any given moment. Compare the chemist or electronic engineer in a local plant with the nonprofessional executives in the same plant. The men the chemist thinks of as his colleagues are not those who occupy neighboring offices, but his fellow professionals wherever they may be throughout the country, even throughout the world.

(quoted in Toffler, 1970)

This means that specialization at the higher levels of bureaucracy is decreasing the feelings of allegiance to the organization among professional engineers, scientists, psychologists, accountants, and sociologists. In a sense, these professionals are outsiders working within the system. On the other hand, the office clerks and blue-collar workers are specialists who remain more dependent on the organization.

7. A Hierarchy of Positions

Bureaucracy is characterized by a hierarchical chain of command. Each position within a bureaucratic organization is under the control and supervision of a higher position. In the military, chain of command is symbolized by rank. In the business world, the table of organization is symbolized by job titles. In the government, civil service ratings symbolize the chain of command. Each official is held accountable to the official immediately above for the decisions and actions of oneself and for the decisions and actions of those who are subordinate to oneself in the hierarchy. Each position grants rights to issue directives and give orders. Each position also presents duties and orders that come down from above. In an ideal setting, these circumstances create an orderly and efficient operation.

There are also nonofficial status symbols that can help one to recognize each position's status within the bureaucracy's hierarchy. A rug, a few extra feet of office space, an uncluttered desk, a longer lunch "hour," extra secretarial help, special assistants, a private lavatory, can indicate the authority of one position as contrasted with another. At one small college, the authors visited the mailroom and noticed that each instructor had one pigeonhole for receiving mail. The two deans and the president of the college each had two pigeonholes. There was no indication that the deans and the president received more incoming mail than the instructors. The clerk who had set up the mailbox arrangement had taken the initiative to recognize the superior status of the deans and president by the distribution of pigeonholes for mail.

The really BIG status symbol.

Real bureaucracy has been characterized by a hierarchy of power that extends from the top to the bottom. There is evidence of changes tending to alter the traditionally bureaucratic practice of separating those who make decisions from those who carry out the decisions (Toffler, 1970). The old bureaucratic arrangement was ideally suited to solving routine problems at a moderate pace. The acceleration of the pace of life both in bureaucracies and in society at large has increased the number of novel, unexpected problems. This increases the amount of information needed at a faster speed. The top managers of present-day organizations are losing their monopoly on decision making. There is no time for decisions to wend their way leisurely up and down the hierarchy. Many technological experts have stopped merely advising and have begun to make decisions themselves, often in direct consultation with workers and ground-level technicians. As a consequence, says a director of one great private corporation in the United States, "You no longer have the strict allegiance to hierarchy. You may have five or six different levels of the hierarchy represented in one meeting. You try to forget about salary level and hierarchy, and organize to get the job done" (Toffler, 1970). Nevertheless, it is extremely difficult to imagine a bureaucracy without a functioning hierarchy of some kind.

8. Depersonalization

Ideal bureaucracy stresses a depersonalization of relationships. We have mentioned the rigid role expectations of bureaucratic positions. Personal whims must not play any part in the decisions and behavior of those who occupy bureaucratic positions. In the ideal bureaucratic setting, a person is supposed to play the role of one's position without allowing personal feelings to interfere. Personal likes and dislikes regarding fellow workers or clients of the organization should in no way influence decision making. If a person should develop strong feelings about fellow workers, subordinates, or clients, those personal feelings are apt to interfere with the role expectations of the position. Then the person might be particularly lenient in evaluating the work of a subordinate or might discriminate against some clients and in favor of others. By maintaining an impersonal detachment while performing one's bureaucratic duties, one is more likely to extend equitable treatment to all people, thereby fostering a form of democracy within administration (Blau, 1956).

Still, we can see a trend from dehumanized and depersonalized bureaucracy. In attempts to be objective, real bureaucracy does expect employees to extend equitable treatment to everyone in order to promote a form of democracy within administration. However, public concern about indignities suffered at the hands of dehumanizing organizations has led many large organizations, both private and public, to strive for a more personal and individualized interaction with employees and clients.

9. Standardized Rules and Uniform Procedures

In ideal bureaucracy all cases that belong to a single category are treated identically. Those who occupy positions in a bureaucracy are governed neither by personal preference nor by passions, but by standardized rules and uniform procedures. In describing the ideal bureaucracy, Max Weber wrote:

The more the bureaucracy is "dehumanized ," the more completely it succeeds in eliminating from official business love, hatred, and all purely personal, irrational, and emotional elements which escape calculation. This is the specific nature of bureaucracy and it is appraised as its special virtue.

(Weber, 1958)

The standardized rules and uniform procedures define the responsibility of each member of the organization. There must be strict adherence to those general standards in deciding specific cases at all levels of the hierarchy, whether it be the level of a government filing clerk or the level of a Supreme Court Justice. When filing, the clerk must always file alphabetically. When interpreting the law of the land, the Justice must always consider its constitutionality. All cases that belong to a single category are treated identically. A specific set of procedures is established within each job description. These procedures guide everyone in determining how to categorize a case and then how to treat that particular category. This also leads to statements such as "I can't make an exception just for you" and "I'm only following orders." At the same time, this uniformity of rules allows the modern administrator to process thousands of cases. This would be impossible if each had to be considered on its individual merits.

Despite our comments in the preceding paragraph, in real bureaucracy all cases that belong to a specific category are not always treated identically for at least two reasons. First, personal relationships often dictate the direction of decisions made regarding both employees and clients of bureaucracies. Second, there is a general trend toward extending individualized considerations to employees and clients of large organizations. In a democratic culture, independent actions and equality of status are highly valued. Too many detailed rules and regulations and close supervision are causes for resentment among both bureaucratic employees and those outside the bureaucracy with whom the employees must interact (Blau, 1956). As a consequence, real bureaucracy in the latter 20th century is a far cry from the older rigid organizational structures "at which so many of our novelists and social critics are still, belatedly, hurling their rusty javelins" (Toffler, 1970).

KEY TERMS AND NAMES FROM SECTION 26

popular view of bureaucracy	passing the buck
sociological view of bureaucracy	specialized training
bureaucratization of society	constant repetition on the job
ideal and real bureaucracy	hierarchical chain of command
financial security	status symbols
permanent employment	depersonalization
special qualifications	standardized rules
unofficial qualifications	uniform procedures
job descriptions	trend toward individualized considerations
cliques and clique loyalty	Max Weber
strict accountability	John Gardner

STUDY GUIDE FOR SECTION 26

1. Many people see bureaucracy as little more than a frustrating way in which government agencies are run. They think of fumbling bureaucrats who are inefficient and preoccupied with red tape and passing the buck. WHAT IS A MORE SOUND AND A SOCIOLOGICAL WAY OF VIEWING BUREAUCRACY?

2. Bureaucracy can be considered as the loom upon which modern mass society is woven. CITE SEVERAL EXAMPLES OF BUREAUCRACIES IN THE UNITED STATES.

3. Bureaucracy is not unique to modern times, but there is something unique about the bureaucratization of modern society. HOW HAS BUREAUCRATIZATION AFFECTED THE RELATIONSHIP BETWEEN WORKERS AND THE TOOLS AND INSTRUMENTS OF PRODUCTION?

4. Employment in a bureaucracy should provide one with financial security. IN WHAT WAY DO GEOGRAPHIC MOVES RELATE TO FINANCIAL SECURITY?

5. The prospect of permanent employment should result in employees becoming increasingly skilled and devoted to the organization's success. Although this does happen in some cases, WHAT UNEXPECTED BEHAVIOR OCCURS IN THE CASE OF SOME LONGTIME EMPLOYEES?

6. Usually special qualifications are required for acquiring a bureaucratic position. WHY IS NEITHER ENTRANCE TO NOR PROMOTION WITHIN A BUREAUCRACY GUARANTEED EVEN THOUGH ONE QUALIFIES?

7. Ideally, each bureaucratic position has certain duties, privileges, and responsibilities. WHAT IS EXPECTED OF THOSE PEOPLE WHO FILL THE VARIOUS POSITIONS?

8. Describing bureaucracy, someone wrote: "A large paper mountain hovers over the foothills of every bureau," and "the bulging filing cabinets symbolize our age." WHY WOULD THIS BE CHARACTERISTIC OF BUREAUCRATIC ORGANIZATIONS?

9. Written accounts are kept of almost every action taken within a bureaucracy. HOW IS THE STRICT ACCOUNTABILITY RELATED TO THE BEHAVIOR OF PASSING THE BUCK?

10. Each position within a bureaucratic organization is under the control and supervision of a higher position. WHAT ARE SOME UNOFFICIAL STATUS SYMBOLS THAT CAN HELP ONE TO RECOGNIZE EACH POSITION'S STATUS WITHIN THE BUREAUCRATIC HIERARCHY?

11. Personal whims are not supposed to play any part in the decisions and behavior of those who occupy bureaucratic positions. WHY IS THE DEPERSONALIZATION OF HUMAN RELATIONSHIPS CONSIDERED DESIRABLE WITHIN IDEAL BUREAUCRACY?

12. In ideal bureaucracy, all cases that belong to a single category are treated identically. EXPLAIN WHAT THIS MEANS AND GIVE AT LEAST TWO EXAMPLES OF THIS STANDARD BEING APPLIED.

13. In bureaucracy there is an obvious division of labor in which each position is occupied by a specialist. Duties of any one position tend to be narrow and specific. IN WHAT TWO WAYS DOES AN INDIVIDUAL BECOME AN EXPERT AT A PARTICULAR JOB?

14. In ideal bureaucracy, positions have rigid role expectations so that personal feelings cannot interfere with the orderly performance of duty. HOW DO CLIQUES WITHIN REAL BUREAUCRACY AFFECT THE UNIFORMITY, PREDICTABILITY, AND PRECISION SUPPOSEDLY BUILT INTO IT?

15. Every bureaucrat is a specialist within an organization of specialists. In the higher levels of bureaucracy the specialists are professionals. WHAT DIFFERENCES EXIST BETWEEN THE LOYALTY AND DEPENDENCY OF THE PROFESSIONAL SPECIALISTS ON THE ONE HAND AND THE LOYALTY AND DEPENDENCY OF OFFICE CLERKS AND BLUE-COLLAR WORKERS ON THE OTHER HAND?

16. Although hierarchical chains of command persist as structural patterns within contemporary bureaucracies, there is evidence of changes in operational procedures. EXPLAIN WHY TOP MANAGERS OF PRESENT-DAY ORGANIZA-TIONS ARE LOSING THEIR MONOPOLY ON DECISION MAKING.

17. When considering ideal bureaucracy, an individual's personal detachment is supposed to insure equitable treatment to all people, thereby fostering a form of democracy within administration. WHAT TREND IS EVIDENCED IN INTER-ACTION WITH EMPLOYEES AND CLIENTS IN PRESENT-DAY BUREAUCRA-CIES WHICH RUNS COUNTER TO THE IDEAL OF DEPERSONALIZATION? WHY HAS THIS CHANGE COME ABOUT?

18. In real bureaucratic settings, all cases belonging to a specific category are *not* always treated identically. EXPLAIN WHY THIS CHARACTERISTIC OF IDEAL BUREAUCRACY IS NOT REALIZED AND OFTEN EVEN AVOIDED BY REAL BUREAUCRATIC ORGANIZATIONS OF TODAY.

PRACTICE TEST FOR SECTION 26

Select the best answer.

1. According to the text, the loom upon which mass society is woven is
A. Government.
B. The social structure.
C. An industrial economy.
D. Bureaucracy.

2. Which of the following is incorrect? Fundamentally, bureaucracy is a(n)
A. Administrative system.
B. Efficient way of carrying out societal functions.
C. Typology of administration.
D. Dispensable way in which mass society carries out its functions.

3. Unique to the modern era is
A. Bureaucracy.
B. Organizational structure.
C. The bureaucratization of society.
D. The disparity between ideal and real bureaucracy.

4. The bureaucratization of society has separated
A. The bourgeoisie from the proletariat.
B. Workers from the instruments of production.
C. Ideal culture from real culture.

D. Ideal bureaucracy from real bureaucracy.

5. Which of the following institutions is not bureaucratized?
A. The family.
B. Religion.
C. Education.
D. The economy.

6. In a bureaucracy, when people reject the significance of their work, they tend to become
A. More highly motivated employees.
B. Less efficient employees.
C. Less alienated employees.
D. More devoted employees.

7. Which of the following factors *unofficially* influences entrance to and promotion within bureaucracies?
A. Performance on competitive examinations.
B. Technical efficiency and knowledge.
C. How well one gets along with others.
D. Educational training and background.

8. It has been said that "A large paper mountain hovers over the foothills of every bureau," and "the bulging file cabinets symbolize our age." These statements are descriptive of which bureaucratic characteristic?

A. Role expectations and job descriptions.

B. Specialization.

C. Strict accountability.

D. Depersonalization.

9. The duties of any position within bureacracy tend to be

A. Narrow and specific.

B. Subject to wide interpretation.

C. Broad and comprehensive.

D. Generalized rather than specialized.

10. According to John Gardner, the loyalty of the professional person within bureaucracies is to

A. The organization.

B. One's family.

C. The bureaucracy.

D. The profession.

11. In the military, the chain of command is symbolized by rank. The term used to describe an organizational chain of command such as this is

A. Bureaucracy.

B. Social status.

C. Hierarchy.

D. Social stratification.

12. A major consequence of maintaining an impersonal detachment while performing bureaucratic duties is to

A. Provide equitable treatment to all.

B. Personalize interaction with clients.

C. Humanize relations between administrators and clients.

D. Heighten sensitivity to individual needs.

13. In ideal bureaucracy all cases that belong to a single category are treated identically. This is consistent with which characteristic of bureaucracy?

A. Specialization.

B. Standardized rules and uniform procedures.

C. Strict accountability.

D. Hierarchy of authority.

14. According to Max Weber, "For the needs of mass administration today, it is completely indispensable." What is it?

A. Industrialization.

B. A complex division of labor.

C. Bureaucracy.

D. Organizational loyalty.

Answer Key

1. D	**6.** B	**11.** C	
2. D	**7.** C	**12.** A	
3. C	**8.** C	**13.** B	
4. B	**9.** A	14. C	
5. A	**10.** D		

SECTION 27   THE IMPORTANCE OF WORK
- HUMAN MOTIVATION TO WORK
- JOB SATISFACTION AND DISSATISFACTION
- HUMAN DISTRESS CAUSED BY JOBLESSNESS

Objectives
After completing this section, the student should be able to:
1. Apply Maslow's theory to human needs in the work environment.
2. Explain how job dissatisfaction can be eliminated without achieving job satisfaction.
3. Describe how productive efficiency is affected by worker dissatisfaction.
4. Describe some of the circumstances of distress that are caused by joblessness.

The majority of adults in American society spend 40 years or more of their lives working eight hours a day, five days a week, fifty weeks a year, with two weeks for vacation and about six other paid holidays. The work people do influences many aspects of their lives. Work determines the material comforts available, the community in which people live, the schools their children attend, the quality of health care they receive, life expectancy, and self-esteem. One's life chances are closely related to one's working.

(Scarpitti, 1980)

HUMAN MOTIVATION TO WORK

We know that people work to earn a living. Another important reason why people work is because work provides them with a purpose in life. Many studies have proved this to be true. Over 50 years ago a nationwide sample of workers was asked, "If by some chance you inherited enough money to live comfortably without working, do you think you would work anyway or not?" About 80 percent of the sample said that they would continue to work. Those responding to the survey said such things as the following: Work keeps people occupied. Work gives people an interest. Work is enjoyable. Work keeps people healthy. Without work, we would not know what to do with ourselves. We would feel lost if we were not working. Work keeps our minds and hands busy. Work provides us a chance to contribute something to society.

The study did reveal that work has different meanings for different occupational groups, but the main point is that most people did emphasize the importance of work (Morse and Weiss, 1955).

Abraham Maslow suggested that there is a hierarchy of human needs that requires fulfillment. Maslow's theory suggests that human behavior is influenced by this set of needs. His hierarchy includes five steps toward human fulfillment. As a person fulfills a lower need, the next higher need becomes important in directing the person's behavior. Maslow's five steps were ranked in the following order of importance (Maslow, 1954):

1. Physiological needs such as air, water, food, sleep, and sex.

2. Safety and security needs such as shelter and economic security.

3. Companionship and affection needs such as family, friends, and group membership.

4. Self-esteem and status needs such as having self-respect, a feeling of accomplishment, and the recognition of others (ego needs).

5. Self-actualization needs such as becoming all that one is able to become by developing a unique self.

Maslow's theory is considered to be an important contribution to modern motivational theory. The needs identified by Maslow could be applied to all human beings. Motivation is concerned with how a person's behavior is started, kept going, directed, and halted (Jones, 1955). Applying Maslow's theory to human behavior and needs in the work environment, it would look something like this (Francis and Milbourn, 1980): Work should provide

1. Physiological needs such as wages or salary to pay for food, shelter, and clothing plus exercise and rest.

2. Safety needs such as job security, safe working conditions, and economic well-being provided by insurance, pensions, and other fringe benefits.

3. Social needs such as co-worker friendship, membership in a close-knit department, participation in departmental activities, and participation in organizational activities.

4. Ego needs such as praise and recognition from co-workers, supervisors, and managers, job competence, setting own goals, and making own decisions.

5. Self-actualization needs such as performing work for a sense of accomplishment, for a sense of challenge, and for fulfilling one's potential by doing excellent work and feeling good about oneself.

There are many opportunities for workers to have many of their needs fulfilled while performing their jobs. Modern workers spend much of their time in bureaucratic organizations. Those who manage the departments and agencies in which people work could and should create a work environment in which employees can satisfy their needs (Francis and Milbourn, 1980).

JOB SATISFACTION AND DISSATIS-FACTION

Frederick Herzberg has said that job satisfaction and job dissatisfaction are not really opposites. He says that they must be seen as two different ways of evaluating the working experience. For example, job dissatisfaction may be caused by inadequate pay, poor supervision, and undesirable conditions. Dissatisfaction caused by these circumstances can be reduced. Pay could be raised. Supervisors can be trained to be more efficient and more considerate of workers. Working conditions can be improved. But, Herzberg says, these actions alone will not produce worker *satisfaction*. Such actions would merely reduce dissatisfaction. Worker satisfaction depends more on opportunities for workers to have feelings of accomplishment, responsibility, challenge, and self-esteem. Worker satisfaction depends upon workers receiving recognition for their contributions on the job. Look at it this way: Dissatisfaction is related to the work environment. Satisfaction is related to the work's content and meaning. Improving the work environment may make work easier to put up with, but it does not always raise motivation or productivity. Studies indicate that making jobs seem more interesting and important *does* increase motivation and productivity (Herzberg, 1966).

In reference to job satisfaction, 1533 American workers at all occupational levels were asked to identify the most important factors in job satisfaction (Quinn et al., 1969). Through in-depth interviews, the workers revealed what were especially important factors contributing to work satisfaction. They said that they would want work to be interesting. They wanted enough help, equipment, information, and authority to get the job done. They wanted opportunities to develop their own special abilities. They wanted to see the results of their work. Then, too, they wanted good pay and job security. As the Report of a Special Task Force to the Secretary of HEW said:

What the workers want most, as more than 100 studies in the past 20 years show, is to become masters of their immediate environments and to feel that their work and they themselves are important—the twin ingredients of self-esteem. Workers recognize that some of the dirty jobs can be transformed only into the merely tolerable, but the most oppressive features of work are felt to be avoidable: constant supervision . . . , lack of variety, monotony, meaningless tasks, and isolation.

(*Work in America*, 1973)

During the past 40 years there have been thousands of articles published and studies done on job satisfaction (Lawler, 1973). One reliable indicator of job satisfaction has been responses to the question: "What type of work would you try to get into if you could start all over again?" One study using this question received the following responses. Of urban university professors, 93 percent said they would choose to do the same work. So did 83 percent of lawyers. Among a cross section of white-collar workers, only 43 percent said they would choose similar jobs. Among a cross section of blue-collar workers, a mere 24 percent would choose similar work again. Only 16 percent of unskilled autoworkers would choose to do the same work (Kahn, 1974).

In the long run, dissatisfaction of workers affects the productive efficiency of an organization. "Absenteeism, turnover, alcohol and drug abuse, sabotage, and theft were reported as being linked to job dissatisfaction." National surveys indicate that the more satisfied workers are college educated, white, middle-aged, and occupying a professional, technical, or manager's position (Francis and Milbourn, 1980). Young workers and blacks have been found to be the most dissatisfied segments of the population. Also, highly trained women in lower-level jobs are often extremely dissatisfied. But women and men with the same training in identical jobs were equally satisfied (*Work in America*, 1973).

It is particularly interesting to know that "job satisfaction affects life satisfaction more than life satisfaction affects job satisfaction. Individuals who are happy and content on the job are generally happy and content off the job as well" (Francis and Milbourn, 1980). This could indicate the importance of work in the human experience. We do not want to give up the material benefits that we have gained from mass production, specialization, and advanced technology. Still, to achieve the ideals of the American Republic, we must provide workers the satisfactions of significant work. Tens of millions of women and men deserve the attentions of every tool of government, education, and industry to improve the experience of work. Management must provide working conditions that can release the creativity of every worker's mind (Heron, 1948).

HUMAN DISTRESS CAUSED BY JOBLESSNESS

The first official study of joblessness was reported to the Massachusetts legislature in 1821. Little came from this other than the suggestion that jobless people be placed in workhouses where they would be forced to work. For the next 50 years, many of the "rootless out-of-work persons" were simply considered "pioneers." In the latter 19th century rapid industrialization and the waves of immi-

Unemployed and looking for work.

grants caused the subject to come to the fore again. In fact, it was in 1887 that the word *unemployment* was coined (Swartz, 1980).

The Bureau of Labor Statistics defines unemployment thus:

Unemployed persons comprise all persons who did not work during the survey week, who made specific efforts to find a job within the past four weeks, and who were available for work during the survey week (except for temporary illness). Also included as unemployed are those who did not work at all, were available for work and (a) were waiting to be called back to a job from which they had been laid off; or (b) were waiting to report to a new wage or salary job within thirty days.

(U.S. Department of Labor, 1978)

For an individual, being part of the unemployment statistics is to be jobless. To be jobless is, more often than not, to be distressed in any number of ways. A study was made of automobile workers who lost their jobs because their plant was permanently closed (Aiken et al., 1968). As their finances dwindled, many of the unemployed workers stopped seeing their friends and relatives. They felt awkward because they could not afford to return favors and meet mutual obligations. In a sense, they were avoiding the very people who might have helped them find new work. Furthermore, the unemployed workers missed their on-the-job friendships that had helped to provide meaning to their lives. They suffered from a sense of social isolation. They began to doubt whether they were of any real use to society. Without the personal identity provided by their former jobs, they were losing their own sense of self-esteem. The stress, anxiety, tension, and depression found among these jobless people indicate the importance of work to the lives of people in this society (Neubeck, 1979). "When work ties are cut, participation in community life declines and a sense of isolation grows. . . . the retired, the elderly, those who have been squeezed out of the labor market, and those who seldom get into it, are often isolated from their communities and American society" (Julian, 1980).

When the American economy suffers a severe economic downturn, individual workers suffer the worst consequences. "Unemployed workers run out of health insurance, put off visits to the doctor and eat poorly" (Seib, 1980). Both the unemployed and even the employed who fear for their jobs find it hard to make ends meet. This causes stress and pressure. Many turn to alcohol and drugs. "Illnesses of all kinds increase, and the death rate goes up. . . . More people die from various kinds of heart diseases and liver problems. Suicides rise. So do the infant-mortality rate, murders, and even the number of auto accidents" (Seib, 1980).

On Labor Day in the year 1980, an editorial in *The Evening Sun* commented on the connection between joblessness and health:

What makes it bad is that the rise in health problems comes just as many laid-off workers lose their company-paid health insurance. It is then that they begin putting off necessary health maintenance. They lower the quality of their diet, they put off visits to doctor and dentist and even stop getting eyeglasses.

It is not a pretty picture—surely not a happy picture to draw on a day devoted to celebrating labor's contribution to the nation. But it demonstrates why unem-

ployment, while it will never be eliminated entirely, can never be regarded as a necessary evil to be maintained at such-and-such a level for the sake of an economic equation or a political campaign. Jobs are precious. People who lose them suffer, and some die. That ought to be remembered on Labor Day.

(*The Evening Sun*, Sept. 1, 1980)

KEY TERMS AND NAMES FROM SECTION 27

life chances and working

Maslow's hierarchy of human needs

motivation in the work environment

social needs

ego needs

self-actualization

job satisfaction

worker satisfaction

job dissatisfaction

unemployment defined

economic downturn

joblessness and health

Abraham Maslow

Frederick Herzberg

STUDY GUIDE FOR SECTION 27

1. Studies prove that people work for reasons other than earning money. WHAT ARE SOME REASONS PEOPLE GIVE FOR WANTING TO WORK EVEN IF THEY COULD LIVE COMFORTABLY WITHOUT WORKING?

2. Maslow's theory on a hierarchy of human needs ranks them in the following order: Physiological, Safety and security, Companionship, Self-esteem and status, and Self-actualization. HOW CAN MASLOW'S THEORY BE APPLIED TO HUMAN NEEDS IN THE WORK ENVIRONMENT?

3. Herzberg says that job satisfaction and dissatisfaction are not really opposites. EXPLAIN HOW DISSATISFACTION CAN BE REDUCED WITHOUT ACHIEVING SATISFACTION.

4. Recall the survey of 1533 workers who were asked to identify the most important factors in job satisfaction. WHAT FACTORS DID THEY NAME?

5. "What type of work would you try to get into if you could start all over again?" WHO RESPONDED HOW TO THIS QUESTION?

6. IN WHAT WAYS CAN WORKER DISSATISFACTION AFFECT THE PRODUCTIVE EFFICIENCY OF AN ORGANIZATION?

7. WHAT RELATIONSHIP BETWEEN JOB SATISFACTION AND LIFE SATISFACTION IS DESCRIBED IN THIS SECTION?

8. To be jobless often means to be distressed in any number of ways. DESCRIBE SOME OF THE CIRCUMSTANCES OF DISTRESS THAT ACCOMPANY JOBLESSNESS.

PRACTICE TEST FOR SECTION 27

Select the best answer.

1. What percentage of a nationwide sample of workers indicated their desire to continue working even if they inherited enough money to live comfortably without working?
A. 20 percent.
B. 40 percent.
C. 60 percent.
D. 80 percent.

2. The theory of the hierarchy of human needs is associated with
A. Frederick Herzberg.
B. Abraham Maslow.
C. Francis and Milbourn.
D. The Secretary of HEW.

3. Which sequence correctly ranks Maslow's hierarchy of needs?
A. Self-esteem, safety, social, and ego.
B. Physiological, safety, companionship, self-esteem, and self-actualization.
C. Self-actualization, ego, physiological, and safety.
D. Physiological, ego, social, and companionship.

4. Becoming all that one is capable of becoming represents which need according to Maslow?
A. Self-actualization.
B. Self-esteem.
C. Ego needs.
D. Social needs.

5. The term for how a person's behavior is started, kept going, directed, and halted is
A. Behaviorism.
B. Self-concept.
C. Motivation.
D. Joblessness.

6. Frederick Herzberg has said that job satisfaction and job dissatisfaction are
A. Opposites.
B. Not opposites.
C. The same.
D. Inseparable.

7. According to Herzberg, the improvement of working conditions will likely
A. Increase work motivation.
B. Increase productivity.
C. Produce satisfaction.
D. Reduce dissatisfaction.

8. According to the Report of the Secretary of HEW, what workers want most is to
A. Have the work week reduced.
B. Become masters of their immediate environment.
C. Receive higher pay.
D. Receive better fringe and retirement benefits.

9. In response to the question, "What type of work would you try to get into if you could start over again?" the group most willing to remain in the same job was

A. University professors.
B. Lawyers.
C. White-collar workers.
D. Blue-collar workers.

10. Which statement is correct?

A. Job satisfaction affects life satisfaction more than life satisfaction affects job satisfaction.
B. Life satisfaction affects job satisfaction more than job satisfaction affects life satisfaction.

11. Absenteeism, turnover, alcohol and drug abuse, sabotage, and theft have been found to be related to

A. Low worker productivity.
B. Worker inefficiency.
C. Low self-esteem.
D. Job dissatisfaction.

12. Which of the following is *not* a factor in the Bureau of Labor Statistics' definition of unemployment?

A. People who were on a sabbatical leave of absence.
B. People who did not work during the survey week.
C. People who made specific efforts to find a job within the past four weeks.
D. People who were waiting to report to a new job within 30 days.

Answer Key

1.	D	**7.**	D
2.	B	**8.**	B
3.	B	**9.**	A
4.	A	**10.**	A
5.	C	**11.**	D
6.	B	**12.**	A

CHAPTER SUMMARY

1. Work has been interpreted differently by people through the years. In ancient Greece working was looked upon as a curse. The ancient Hebrews considered working to be punishment from God. Christianity interpreted working as a duty and as a way of serving God. Karl Marx considered working to be a highly satisfying human experience, if the workers were freed from capitalist exploitation.

2. Work can be defined as that which a person does in order to survive. Work is an activity that produces something of value to people. Also, work is the means by which goods and services are provided for society.

3. Six functions that work performs for Americans in the late 20th century are as follows: Work provides money for goods and services. Work provides a place in which to meet people. Work provides a social status for the worker and probably the worker's family. Work contributes to self-esteem. Work helps to shape a person's sense of identity. Work satisfies the human need to place an order or structure on the world.

4. In modern societies work is characterized by a division of labor. Each individual performs one small part of the entire task. Such specialization provides for mass production of both goods and services.

5. A great change in work in the 20th century is away from self-employment and toward work in large government agencies and in corporations. The Ameri-

can labor force has experienced changes in farming, in the professions, and in the worlds of blue-collar and clerical workers. In the American economic system, a significant change is the shift from an emphasis on goods production to an emphasis on service offerings.

6. Mass urban society is dependent upon bureaucratic administration. Bureaucracy is the administrative system used in any large organization today. Bureaucracy existed during ancient times. However, the bureaucratization of society is unique to modern times. This means that bureaucracy is everywhere all the time touching the lives of modern people.

7. Characteristics of ideal bureaucracy include the promise of financial security, permanent employment, and the requirement of special qualifications to acquire a position or to advance within the organization. There are rigid role expectations. Written accounts are kept of almost every action taken by workers in the bureaucracy. Every bureaucrat is a specialist within an organization of specialists. Each position within a bureaucracy is under the control and supervision of a higher position. In the ideal bureaucracy, one fulfills the role of one's position without allowing personal feelings to interfere with decision making. There are standardized rules and uniform procedures. This results in all cases that belong to a single category being treated identically. Real bureaucratic organizations fail to provide or to accomplish all that is ideally their missions and functions.

8. Abraham Maslow identified a hierarchy of human needs. As one fulfills a lower need, the next higher need becomes important in directing behavior. Ranked in order of importance, Maslow's five steps include physiological needs, security needs, affectional needs, self-esteem and status needs, and then self-actualization. Maslow's motivational theory has been applied to human behavior and needs in the work environment.

9. Frederick Herzberg has said that worker dissatisfaction is related to the work environment. Satisfaction is related to the work's content and meaning. Worker satisfaction depends on opportunities for workers to experience feelings of accomplishment, challenge, responsibility, and self-esteem through receiving recognition.

10. To be jobless is to be distressed in a number of ways. Many unemployed workers stop seeing their friends and relatives. They suffer from a sense of isolation. They doubt their value to society. And they lose the personal identity that had been provided by their former jobs. Self-esteem is lost. The stress, anxiety, tension, and depression experienced by the jobless indicate the significance of work to people today.

SUGGESTIONS FOR FURTHER READINGS RELATING TO CHAPTER 9

Blackburn, R. M., and Michael Mann, *The Working Class in the Labor Market* (Atlantic Highlands, N. J.: Humanities Press, 1979). This study is based on interviews with 951 workers occupying 275 different jobs. The intent is to indicate what degree of choice workers have regarding quality of jobs.

Blau, Peter M., *Bureaucracy in Modern Society* (New York: Random House, 1956). Blau sets forth the theory and actual operation of bureaucratic organizations.

Chapman, Elwood N., *Big Business: A Positive View* (Englewood Cliffs, N. J.: Prentice-Hall, 1972). This is an easy-to-read and interesting challenge to the view that big business is repressive and, for employees, a dull way of life.

Feldman, Roslyn L., and Evelyn Nakano Glenn, "Male and Female: Job Versus Gender Models in the Sociology of Work," *Social Problems*, Vol. 26, No. 5 (June, 1979). "Two case studies are examined in detail to illustrate the varying ways in which job and gender models have distorted investigation and interpretation" of work issues.

Goldstein, Bernard, and Jack Oldham, *Children and Work: A Study of Socialization* (New Brunswick, N. J.: Transaction Books, 1979). Children's views of work are presented based on interviews and questionnaires administered to about 900 school children from grades one through seven.

Hall, Francine S., and Douglas T. Hall, *The Two-Career Couple* (Reading, Mass.: Addison-Wesley, 1979). This book offers "commonsense advice" based on the results of new research, interviews, and questionnaires that focus on the major concerns of today's two-career couples.

Herzberg, Frederick, *Work and the Nature of Man* (Cleveland: World, 1966). In the preface, Herzberg writes, "Industry must realize that it is one of the despoilers of [our] efforts to achieve happiness. . . ."

LeMasters, E. E., *Blue-Collar Aristocrats: Life-Styles at a Working-Class Tavern* (Madison, Wisc.: University of Wisconsin Press, 1975). "LeMasters' book is a valuable and popularly written source of information on the attitudes of working class men and women." — *Library Journal*.

Nader, Ralph, and Mark J. Green, editors, *Corporate Power in America* (New York: Grossman, 1973). This is a collection of essays that reveals the degree of corporate power and influence existing in the United States.

O'Toole, James, "Thank God, It's Monday," *The Wilson Quarterly* Vol. IV, No. 1 (Winter, 1980). "Social science techniques may still be too primitive to measure the changes, but my guess is that young workers today really want some different things from work than did . . . their parents." — O'Toole.

Shannon, David A., *The Great Depression* (Englewood Cliffs, N. J.: Prentice-Hall, 1960). The worst experience with joblessness in American history occurred in the depression of the 1930s. This book describes the effects of joblessness on the victims of that economic disaster.

Sidel, Ruth, *Urban Survival: The World of Working-Class Women at Work* (Boston: Beacon Press, 1979). Open-ended interviews with eight working-class women reveal the frustrations, disappointments, and triumphs they have experienced with bureaucracy, prejudice, and crime.

Smith, Ralph E., editor, *The Subtle Revolution: Women at Work* (Washington, D.C.: The Urban Institute, 1979). "Based on original research, this book is comprehensive and well-documented . . . likely to emerge as the standard text on working women." — *Library Journal*.

Tentler, Leslie Woodcock, *Wage-Earning Women* (New York: Oxford University Press, 1979). This is a description of the work and life-styles of wage-earning women in manufacturing, sales, and nondomestic service in the early 20th century.

Terkel, Studs, *Working* (New York: Avon Books, 1975). This book is based on a collection of tape-recorded interviews with workers throughout the United States. "Work is the theme and we learn a lot about these trades, callings, crafts, professions, or ruts." — *The Wall Street Journal.*

Toffler, Alvin, *The Third Wave* (New York: Morrow, 1980). Toffler predicts that solar and geothermal power will replace present-day energies. He believes the future holds a demassified society characterized in the world of work by flexitime, nightwork replacing nine to five, and a place for creative child labor.

Whyte, William H., Jr., *The Organization Man* (New York: Simon and Schuster, A Clarion Book, 1972). Whyte describes the impact that large organizations have upon individual lives. He shows a relationship between the bureaucratic ethic and the social ethic in modern American life.

Chapter 10
Collective Behavior and Social Change

SECTION 28 A THEORY OF AND TYPES OF COLLECTIVE BEHAVIOR
- SMELSER'S THEORY OF COLLECTIVE BEHAVIOR
- TYPES OF COLLECTIVE BEHAVIOR

Objectives
After completing this section, the student should be able to:
1. Define the term *collective behavior.*
2. Explain Neil J. Smelser's theory of collective behavior.
3. Describe four types of crowds identified by Herbert Blumer.
4. Cite differences between mobs and riots.
5. Describe the impact of panic on human behavior.
6. Explain how rumors affect human behavior.
7. Define "special publics" and explain how they differ from the "general public."

Most social behavior is culturally structured. Most human interaction is patterned, recurrent, and predictable. Most social situations have been predefined. People simply observe the folkways, mores, and laws and fulfill the social roles expected of them. This is the way people behave within the social institutions of society. In modern society our institutions are highly structured (bureaucratized). People know what is expected of them. And, as we have said before, most people observe most of the norms most of the time. "A major portion of sociology is the examination of groups and group life in terms of social organization and the normative order, of the group and its culture. The emphasis is placed on the static, orderly, well-structured aspects of group life and on orderly change" (Turner and Killian, 1957).

Collective behavior has been defined by Turner and Killian as "the actions of groups that operate without clear-cut direction from their cultures." Collective behavior is unstructured and lacking in stability. It is not institutionalized behavior. It is behavior characteristic of riots, mobs, panic, mass hysteria, mass movement, and some social change. Collective behavior can occur only if there are certain preconditions present in society. Neil Smelser identified six basic conditions related to collective behavior. Let us consider his theory.

SMELSER'S THEORY OF COLLECTIVE BEHAVIOR

Neil J. Smelser's view is that people exhibit collective behavior when they experience conditions considered to be unpredictable and threatening. "These conditions may involve many factors, such as fear, boredom, or a sense of oppression, but people find them stressful and want to change them" (Robertson, 1977). The following six conditions must be present before norm-violating, hostile outbursts occur.

Structural Conduciveness

Smelser says that collective behavior is more likely to occur within mass society than folk society. In mass society there is mass communication among different groups. There is little emphasis upon traditional values and behaviors. Conflicting interest groups are apt to clash. "For example, one could not have a race riot if a community did not have two races in close proximity to one another. Or, police could not attack demonstrators where there are no people ready to demonstrate or police assigned to the task of controlling them" (Berk, 1974). Mass society "is open to collective behavior of all types, including riots, demonstrations, social movements, fads, and crazes. Structural conduciveness is only one factor that makes collective behavior possible; it does not make such behavior inevitable" (Stewart, 1978). Let us consider the other factors.

Structural Strain

Structural strain refers to the perception of contradictions or tension between basic elements in society. American society is supposed to provide equality of opportunity and equality before the law for all people. Often ideal expectations are not the real experience. "If cultural norms . . . call for equal opportunities but minority groups, poor people, and women feel excluded, then [a] source of strain develops" (Stewart, 1978). Both the civil rights movement and the women's movement are examples of collective behavior. Both movements came into existence because of the structural strain between the American creed of human equality and the American deed of racism and sexism.

A Generalized Belief About the Source of Strain

People will acquire a general belief about the source of their feelings of stress and strain. This belief "identifies the source of strain, attributes certain characteristics to this source, and specifies certain responses to the strain as possible or appropriate" (Smelser, 1963). "Such a belief need be nothing more complicated than . . . a minority group's agreement that its members are exploited by the local police or a belief by students at one high school that those attending another school are 'out to get them' " (Storer, 1980). More often than not, the generalized belief is an inaccurate and naive assumption. Still, a generalized belief can be taken seriously enough so that it motivates and determines collective behavior.

Precipitating Factors

An example of a precipitating factor would be "an incident in which a student from one high school is beaten up by a group from the other school" (Storer, 1980). Precipitating factors are incidents that touch off collective behavior. The urban riots of the 1960s had many causes. In Newark the precipitating factor was the arrest of a black taxi driver. In the Watts section of Los Angeles, the arrest of a black man on a drunk driving charge brought on riots. In both cases, the events were interpreted as examples of police brutality. And police brutality was interpreted by some members of the black community as evidence of general oppression by the white majority. So a generalized belief was supported by precipitating factors.

Mobilization for Action

Smelser does not use the term *mobilization* necessarily to mean military action. Mobilization refers to the hostile outburst. It involves the gathering of people at a certain location, often at the scene of the precipitating event. Mobilization includes a means of spreading propaganda, notifying potential activists, and attempting to gather community support. Often mobilization involves a leader or leaders who direct the behavior of other people as they express their discontent. Potential rioters, for example, have to learn about potentially rewarding activities. They must learn the location of the scene and be able to get to the scene without being sidetracked along the way (McPhail and Miller, 1973). Police raided a homosexual bar in Greenwich Village in New York City in 1969. Some of the patrons resisted arrest and fought the police. Their behavior mobilized other patrons and sympathetic onlookers. A serious riot followed. The event received national publicity that greatly stimulated the growth of the gay liberation movement (Robertson, 1977).

The Exercise of Social Control

Smelser says that the study of social control is the study of counter-actions that "prevent, interrupt, deflect, or inhibit the first five factors mentioned above" (Smelser, 1963). The social control mechanisms could be so effective that collective behavior is prevented or suppressed. If the social controls prove to be ineffective, they might even increase the intensity of the collective behavior.

Neil Smelser's theory has been useful to sociologists studying collective behavior. Fads, fashions, and crazes can be interpreted as responses to boredom. Panic can be seen as a reaction to threats. Riots can be interpreted as responses to social conditions of stress, strain, and resentment (Robertson, 1977). Now let us describe particular types of collective behavior, keeping Smelser's theory in mind.

TYPES OF COLLECTIVE BEHAVIOR

Crowds

A crowd is a large, temporary collection of people in a particular place who share a common interest or cause. In 1939 sociologist Herbert Blumer identified the following four types of crowds (Blumer, 1969):

Casual crowds are characterized as being loosely organized and having only a momentary existence. Its members come and go. People in a casual crowd bare-·ly relate to one another. There certainly is no emotional involvement among those in the crowd. They are there together simply because a certain object or event has temporarily drawn their attention.

Conventionalized crowds are somewhat like casual crowds except for the fact that their behavior is expressed in more established and regularized ways. People in a conventionalized crowd have planned in advance to become part of the crowd. Such crowds appear at sports events, at concerts, and in theaters. Blumer referred to such crowds as "conventional" because their behavior follows social norms that have been predefined in previous similar situations.

Expressive crowds have no particular goals or objectives. The reason for this type of crowd to form is to express feelings about something together. Situations that would draw an expressive crowd include religious meetings, rock festivals, and political rallies. Blumer said that the expressive crowd releases its tension on an objective and becomes united in its feelings and actions. For excample, if "a conventional crowd becomes particularly vocal in reacting to . . . a great opera performance or a referee's decision, it may be briefly transformed into an expres-sive crowd" (Storer, 1980).

Acting crowds, as described by Blumer, have no rules to guide their behavior. The acting crowd acts on impulse. It is "fickle, suggestible, and irresponsible" (Blumer, 1969). Acting crowds can become mobs. If the members of a crowd "be-gin to do more than express their feelings—to throw things, destroy property, or assault one another—it becomes an acting crowd. An acting crowd's members are *doing* something" (Storer, 1980).

Mobs

A *mob* is actually one form of the acting crowd. It is composed of people who are emotionally aroused and who intend to take violent and aggressive action. Usually, mobs have leaders. Strict conformity is demanded of those in the mob. "The mob has immediate and limited objectives." A mob is an especially tempo-rary and unstable form of collective behavior (Robertson, 1977). Generally, crowds do not become mobs until they acquire a generalized belief about who or what is responsible for their anger (Smelser, 1963). The hostility of the mob has to be directed toward a target. The target could be a business, a police station, a criminal suspect, or a foreign embassy. During the Civil War Baltimore became known as "mob town" because of the many mobs that formed from time to time to stone Union troops marching through the city.

Riots

Unlike mob behavior, a riot is not likely to have any clear leadership. Nor is a riot likely to have a specific target against which violence is directed. Riots are apt to spread out over different areas with the crowds' actions lacking unity of purpose or objectives. Once a riot has gotten out of hand, the only prevailing norm would be that of being violent for the sake of violence. When minority groups engage in rioting, it is usually because they believe they have been denied equal opportunities, economically or politically. Dominant group members may also riot and attack minority group members if the dominant group feels threatened by minority group behavior. In American history there have been many kinds of riots. Earlier we mentioned the mob actions in Baltimore during the Civil War. During that same period, antidraft riots occurred in New York City. Rioters looted businesses and homes, burned down buildings, and killed police, soldiers, and black civilians. These riots were as destructive as any in American history. Other riots during the late 19th century and early 20th century were expressions of discontent by workers against capitalists. Layoffs, low wages, poor working conditions, and union suppression were causes of the riots, but once begun, the riots had little structure and few, if any, recognizable leaders. Again, it was more a case of violence, once begun, continuing unchecked and without structure. During the 1960s there were many riots in American cities. Blacks who lived in economic poverty and who suffered many social injustices struck out against the areas in which they lived. The worst riots occurred in Watts, a section of Los Angeles, in 1965, in Newark and Detroit in 1967, and in Cleveland in 1968. Riots have occurred also at sporting events and in prisons in many parts of the world.

Panic

Smelser defines *panic* as "a collective flight based on a hysterical belief" (Smelser, 1963). Some kind of crisis creates confusion and fear in the crowd. People exhibit panic when they respond to a perceived threat without cooperation or normative behavior. Many sociologists refer to a situation in a theater where someone has called out, "Fire!" One such occasion of panic occurred in the Iroquois Theater fire of 1903 in Chicago. The draperies on the stage caught fire. Upon hearing the cry "Fire!" the audience surged toward the exits. Hundreds fell on the stairs or were crushed against the walls of the theater. The fire department responded quickly. The panic lasted no more than ten minutes. Still, the final death count totaled 602 people (Turner and Killian, 1957). The most dramatic panics occur in temporary situations of extreme danger. Not all panics are frantic and short-lived. "The stock market collapse of 1929 was a classic example of a financial panic. Fearing that the price of stocks would fall, investors rushed to sell their holdings, thus forcing the prices down even lower. As the panic spread, huge fortunes were wiped out in hours or even minutes, and many thousands of investors were ruined" (Robertson, 1977).

Rumors

A rumor is information passed from one person to another within a population without anyone checking its accuracy. Rumors should be recognized as one way in which people communicate about something about which there is little dependable information. Most rumors are spread orally, although some can be further dignified by appearing in printed form. More often than not, rumors are a kind of gossip. In themselves, rumors probably should not be thought of as collective action as we have been using the term. But rumors, accurate and inaccurate, can bring on collective behavior.

Fads, Crazes, and Fashions

Now we are talking about types of collective behavior that usually last longer than crowd behavior and which are usually experienced nationwide. At the same time, we are talking about matters that are generally recognizable as relatively unimportant. Earl R. Babbie reflects upon American fads and crazes when he writes:

Dance crazes are [an] example of this form of collective behavior, ranging from the lindy, the Charleston, the jitterbug, marathon dancing, the tango, the mambo, the twist, the frug, the monkey, Kung Fu dancing, disco dancing, and other things that people do with their bodies to music.

Even a partial listing of the various crazes that have swept America during this century alone may cause you to wonder how we survive as a society: goldfish swallowing, telephone-booth crowding, miniature golf, canasta, flagpole sitting, Monopoly, jogging, karate, barbecues, chain letters, grass, acid, pocket calculators, astrology, Mah-Jongg, massage, Hula-Hoops, drive-ins, topless dancers, and roller skating. . . .

Clothing fashions and hairstyles go in and out of vogue. Women's hemlines and the length of men's hair have gone up and down for generations. . . . Women curl their hair, then straighten it. Men grow beards, then shave them off.

(Babbie, 1980)

Babbie says that such fads and crazes and fashions provide a spirit of fun and break the monotony of our day-to-day experience. He says that the sense of excitement and identity with others that such behaviors provide gives individuals a feeling of belonging. We like the way in which Babbie describes these behaviors. These *are* matters relatively unimportant, yet they also are functional in their fashion!

Publics and Public Opinion

A *public* is a scattered group of people concerned about and in the process of discussing a certain issue. A public expects to register a collective opinion. This public opinion is then expected to affect the course of action of some group or individual (Turner and Killian, 1957). A crowd involves a number of people in close physical proximity, but a public does not gather in one place. Members of a crowd are united by a common purpose, whereas members of a public are still in the discussion stage as to what to do about what concerns them, if they do anything at all.

Rollerskating craze, 1979.

Each public has its own special language—often called *jargon* by those not belonging to the public. Members of a public use this special language when they communicate through special journals, newsletters, and bulletins. Wheat growers, dairy farmers, and other specific farming groups use terms known mostly only to themselves. The baseball public has information and uses language that is meaningless to those not interested in that sport. Publics agree upon the meaning and use of certain terms. One may wonder whether this use of jargon is a cause or effect of there being so many publics. Each of these "special" publics to which we are referring include people interested in a single issue. "The 'general' public refers to *all* the members of a particular society, who interact (however remotely) and who are expected to have an 'opinion' about certain general issues. . . . The people of the United States are, in this latter sense, a vast public" (Merrill, 1969).

Francis E. Merrill emphasized how collective behavior breaks institutional routines and provides for social dynamics in society. Merrill wrote:

In the crowd, the members work out new forms of behavior through their emotions. In the public, the emphasis is presumably upon discussion, although emo-

tion is not entirely ruled out. In either case, the result is a new form of behavior that departs from previous patterns. This departure may or may not be permanent, but in any event the traditional order has been broken and the old ways have been changed.

(Merrill, 1969)

KEY TERMS AND
NAMES FROM
SECTION 28

Smelser's collective behavior theory	acting crowds
structural conduciveness	mobs
structural strain	riots
generalized beliefs	panic
precipitating factors	rumors
mobilization for action	fads, crazes, and fashions
exercise of social control	publics
types of collective behavior	public opinion
casual crowds	Neil J. Smelser
conventionalized crowds	Herbert Blumer
expressive crowds	Earl R. Babbie

STUDY GUIDE FOR SECTION 28

1. Most social behavior is culturally structured. HOW DO TURNER AND KILLIAN DEFINE COLLECTIVE BEHAVIOR?

2. Neil J. Smelser says that six conditions must be present in society before norm-violating, hostile outbursts occur. EXPLAIN WHAT SMELSER MEANS WHEN HE REFERS TO STRUCTURAL CONDUCIVENESS.

3. IDENTIFY SOME EXAMPLES OF STRUCTURAL STRAIN THAT HAVE OCCURRED IN AMERICAN SOCIETY.

4. EXPLAIN HOW A GENERALIZED BELIEF ABOUT THE SOURCE OF STRAIN CAN CONTRIBUTE TO COLLECTIVE BEHAVIOR.

5. Precipitating factors are incidents that touch off collective behavior. EXPLAIN HOW A GENERALIZED BELIEF CAN BE SUPPORTED BY PRECIPITATING FACTORS. CITE EXAMPLES.

6. Mobilization for action refers to the hostile outburst. GIVE SOME EXAMPLES OF WHEN THIS HAS OCCURRED IN AMERICAN SOCIETY.

7. EXPLAIN HOW THE EXERCISE OF SOCIAL CONTROL CAN EITHER PREVENT OR INCREASE THE INTENSIFYING OF COLLECTIVE BEHAVIOR.

8. NAME AND DESCRIBE THE FOUR TYPES OF CROWDS IDENTIFIED BY BLUMER.

9. A mob is one form of the acting crowd. HOW DO CROWDS BECOME MOBS?

10. HOW DO RIOTS DIFFER FROM MOB ACTIONS? GIVE EXAMPLES OF CAUSES OF RIOTS IN THE UNITED STATES.

11. Panic occurs when a crowd experiences confusion and fear. HOW DO PEOPLE BEHAVE WHO EXPERIENCE PANIC? CITE EXAMPLES.

12. Rumors are part of social experiences. DESCRIBE WHAT RUMORS ARE AND HOW THEY AFFECT HUMAN BEHAVIOR.

13. Fads, crazes, and fashions are relatively unimportant. IDENTIFY SOME AMERICAN FADS, CRAZES, AND FASHIONS DISCUSSED BY EARL R. BABBIE.

14. A public is a scattered group of people concerned about a certain issue. HOW DOES A "SPECIAL PUBLIC" DIFFER FROM THE "GENERAL PUBLIC"? HOW ARE CROWDS AND PUBLICS DIFFERENT?

PRACTICE TEST FOR SECTION 28

Select the best answer.

1. Behavior that is unstructured, unpredictable, and lacking clear-cut direction is known as
A. Aberrant behavior.
B. Normative behavior.
C. Collective behavior.
D. Deviant behavior.

2. The perception of contradictions or tension between the basic elements of society is known as
A. Structural strain.
B. Cultural lag.
C. Cultural shock.
D. Structural functionalism.

3. Incidents that touch off acts of collective behavior are referred to as
A. Structural inconsistencies.
B. Latent functions.
C. Structural strains.
D. Precipitating factors.

4. A large temporary collection of people who share a common interest or cause is known as a
A. Mob.
B. Crowd.
C. Primary group.
D. Public.

5. Which type of crowd acts impulsively and is "fickle, suggestible, and irresponsible"?
A. Casual.
B. Acting.
C. Conventional.
D. Expressive.

6. Which type of crowd is characterized as being loosely organized and having only a momentary existence?
A. Casual.
B. Acting.
C. Conventional.
D. Expressive.

7. A group composed of people who are emotionally aroused and who intend to take violent and aggressive action is a(n)
A. Expressive crowd.
B. Riot.
C. Mob.
D. Acting crowd.

8. Being violent for the sake of violence is a characteristic of
A. A riot.
B. A public.
C. An expressive crowd.

D.   Collective behavior.
9.   A collective flight based on a hysterical belief is known as
A.   Rumor.
B.   Mass hysteria.
C.   Cultural frenzy.
D.   Panic.
10.   Unverified information passed from one person to another is known as
A.   Propaganda.

B.   Rumor.
C.   Knowledge.
D.   Scientific evidence.
11.   All members of a society who interact and who are expected to have an opinion about certain general issues are known as a
A.   Public.
B.   Generalized Other.
C.   Special public.
D.   Mass constituency.

Answer Key

1. C	**7.** C
2. A	**8.** A
3. D	**9.** D
4. B	**10.** B
5. B	**11.** A
6. A	

SECTION 29   SOCIAL MOVEMENTS
- IDEOLOGY WITHIN A SOCIAL MOVEMENT
- FOUR STAGES OF A SOCIAL MOVEMENT
- TYPES OF SOCIAL MOVEMENTS

Objectives
After completing this section, the student should be able to:
1. Define the term *social movement*.
2. Identify five functional aspects of a movement's ideology.
3. Describe the four stages through which a social movement might move.
4. Explain how the following types of social movements differ: reactionary, conservative, reformist, revolutionary, and escape movements.

A social movement can be defined as collective behavior in which efforts are made either to *prevent* social change or to *promote* social change. An informal collection of people who assemble only for their own enjoyment is not a social movement. A collection of people who assemble to improve their own conditions without making demands on society is not a social movement (Turner and Killian, 1957). Unlike other forms of collective behavior, social movements exist over a long period of time. Crowds and mobs do not exist for very long, once their goals have been achieved or the excitement has worn off. A social movement requires a long period of time to achieve its goals. Usually, the goals of a social movement involve major changes in the attitudes and behavior of the population of society at large (Merrill, 1969). The most significant characteristic of a social movement is that it seeks to change values and social structure and to redistribute the power of control within a society (Cameron, 1966).

In discussing modern social movements, William Bruce Cameron has said that "Social movements vary greatly as to the portion of the culture or the social order they attempt to change. . . . Some movements are concerned with altering the religious life, others with the economic, and still others with the political, the artistic, the dietary, the educational, or the recreational" (Cameron, 1966).

IDEOLOGY
WITHIN
A SOCIAL
MOVEMENT

A social movement's ideology consists of a system of beliefs and ideas that justify the particular goals of the movement. All social movements are motivated by an underlying ideological system. Herbert Blumer identified five functional aspects of a movement's ideological system (Blumer, 1969):

1. A statement of the objectives, purposes, and premises of the social movement.

2. A body of criticism and condemnation of the existing social order that the movement is attacking and seeking to change.

3. A collection of defense doctrines that serve to justify the objectives and methods of the movement.

4. A system of beliefs concerning policies, tactics, and practical operation of the movement.

5. The "myths" of the movement, which represent the significant concerns of humankind as interpreted by the movement.

Blumer said that a movement's ideology should be thought of as providing a movement with its philosophy and psychology. He said that the ideology gives a movement direction, justification, intellectual and emotional weapons of attack and defense, inspiration, and hope. Most importantly, the ideology should respond to the distress, wishes, and hopes of the people. It must have a popular appeal that reaches out beyond members of the movement to the general population of society.

FOUR STAGES OF A SOCIAL MOVEMENT

Each particular social movement in history has had its own special beliefs, objectives, and tactics. Still, it is possible to describe a general life cycle that applies to any social movement. Almost 50 years ago sociologists identified four stages in the life of a social movement (Dawson and Gettys, 1935):

1. *Social unrest* is the initial stage in which various groups express hostility toward other groups. The general population is uneasy, restless, and discontented. People in this stage are prepared to listen to appeals and suggestions that address their discontent. At this stage any leaders that appear are likely to be agitators. Their leadership roles would be that of agitating the already restless population. They encourage feelings of dissatisfaction.

2. *Popular excitement* is the second stage. During this period the discontented begin to share their complaints and realize that, through united action, they can bring about social change. In the stage of popular excitement, the type of leaders to appear are apt to be prophets or reformers. The prophet would offer a vision of a better future for all. The reformer would offer specific solutions for the causes of unrest and discontent.

3. *Formalization* occurs in the third stage of a social movement. The movement becomes obviously more unified, better organized, and characterized by formal rules, policies, tactics, and discipline. By better organized, we also mean that a set of leaders emerge who can guide the movement to reaching its goals and fulfilling its hopes. At this stage the most effective leader would be one who is experienced in government or who can exhibit wisdom and ability in dealing with the concerns of the people in the movement. This would be a statesman or stateswoman. It must be someone who can inspire those in the movement.

4. In this final stage of the movement, called *institutionalization*, the social movement becomes established as a permanent part of society. The old excitement is toned down. Decisions are made with careful routinized deliberation. Now the movement operates through a legal-rational leadership. At this stage, with things calmed down, the type of leader would be an administrator.

It should be understood that not all social movements go through all these stages. If certain objectives are achieved, the movement may then disband rather than become institutionalized. Certainly this is what happened to the peace movement in the United States that opposed American participation in the Vietnam conflict.

TYPES OF SOCIAL MOVEMENTS

Social movements occur when attempts are made to prevent or to promote social change. Sociologists have used numerous ways to classify social movements into types. "All sociologists agree that there are different types of social movements, but they disagree on what the types are" (Babbie, 1980). We have chosen to acknowledge the following types of social movements. Both our classifications and comments rely upon the writings of William Bruce Cameron (1966) and Earl R. Babbie (1980), with some additional intepretations of our own.

Reactionary Movements

Societies experience social change so that old values and behavior patterns fade away. Members of a reactionary movement *react* to these changes unfavorably. Their wish is to return to the "good old days" when people knew what was right and good and behaved accordingly. Reactionaries believe that all the changes in society have destroyed what had been a "grand and glorious heritage." They see present-day atitudes, values, and behaviors as immoral. To a reactionary, only a return to the cherished beliefs of the past will repair the damage done to society as a result of social change. The Moral Majority would be a recent example of such a movement.

Conservative Movements

A conservative movement seeks to *conserve* the present-day values and acceptable behaviors from the dangers of social change. Conservative movements are dedicated to preventing society from changing from what is presently thought to be good and right into what is bad and wrong. Put another way, conservatives seek to maintain the status quo. As Cameron says, ". . . conservative movements are most likely to spring up when there is a threat of change, and they are frequently organized specifically to combat the activities of some other movement which is making changes."

Reformist Movements

Reformist or revisionary movements accept much of the present structure and values of society. They do seek to change them for the better, however. Reformist movements usually are organized for the "improvement" of one thing or another. While the reformists desire *reform*, they do not desire to destroy the existing social order as a whole. In recent years examples of reformist movements would include those promoting birth control, civil rights, sound ecological living, gay liberation, women's equality, and elimination of the death penalty.

Revolutionary Movements

Revolutionary movements include those people described in Robert Merton's theory of deviance as exhibiting rebellion. They reject the existing social order and plan to replace it with something they believe to be superior. If a social revolutionary movement results in a total social revolution in society, little about the social institutions of the old society remains the same. Attitudes, values, and behavior are all drastically changed from the old to the new. China, Cuba, and many other nations have experienced the results of successful revolutionary movements in the 20th century.

Escape Movements

Social movements that are called "escape movements" are not attempting to deal with the present social order. Instead, the members of escape movements seek to remove themselves from society. Escape can occur either by physical isolation or by joining a sect or cult that is "in the world but not of it." Marcus Garvey's "Back to Africa" movement, the Mormon westward migration to the "promised land," and the movement of "The People's Temple" of Jim Jones to South America are examples of escape movements involving physical isolation from society. Examples of cults that have been "in the world but not of it" would include Hare Krishna (International Society for Krishna Consciousness), the Unification Church, the Children of God, The Divine Light Mission, and others (Conway and Siegelman, 1979). All of the aforementioned are examples of escape movements. Each movement sought to escape from the prevailing attitudes, values, and behaviors of American society. Escape movements are different from the other social movements since they do not seek to prevent or to promote social change. In the next section we discuss the subject of social change in more detail.

KEY TERMS AND NAMES FROM SECTION 29

social movement

ideology

social unrest

popular excitement

formalization

institutionalization

reactionary movements

conservative movements

reformist movements

revolutionary movements

escape movements

Herbert Blumer

Robert K. Merton

STUDY GUIDE FOR SECTION 29

1. An informal collection of people who assemble only for their own enjoyment is not a social movement. DEFINE AND IDENTIFY SOME CHARACTERISTICS OF A SOCIAL MOVEMENT.

2. All social movements are motivated by an underlying ideological system. HOW DID HERBERT BLUMER DESCRIBE THE IMPORTANCE OF IDEOLOGY TO SOCIAL MOVEMENTS?

3. Each social movement has a general life cycle. NAME AND DESCRIBE THE FOUR STAGES OF A SOCIAL MOVEMENT.

4. NAME AND DESCRIBE THE FIVE TYPES OF SOCIAL MOVEMENTS THAT WE DISCUSS IN THIS SECTION.

PRACTICE TEST FOR SECTION 29

Select the best answer.

1. Which of the following types of collective behavior is designed to prevent or to promote social change?
A. Crowd.
B. Social movement.
C. Mob.
D. Public opinion.

2. The initial stage in the life cycle of a social movement is known as
A. Popular excitement.
B. Formalization.
C. Institutionalization.
D. Social unrest.

3. In which stage of the life cycle of a social movement does a movement become more unified, better organized, and characterized by rules and policies?
A. Formalization.
B. Institutionalization.
C. Initial stage.
D. Transient stage.

4. In which stage of the life cycle of a social movement does the movement become established as a permanent part of society?

A. Institutionalization.
B. Termination.
C. Concretization.
D. Formalization.

5. The type of social movement that seeks a return to the cherished beliefs of the past is a
A. Conservative movement.
B. Reform movement.
C. Reactionary movement.
D. Escape movement.

6. Which type of social movement seeks to maintain the status quo?
A. Conservative.
B. Reactionary.
C. Revolutionary.
D. Reform.

7. Which type of social movement emerges when there is a threat of change and is organized to combat the activities of some other movement seeking change?
A. Reactionary.
B. Conservative.
C. Escape.
D. Reform.

8. Social movements that seek to promote birth control, civil rights, and gay liberation are examples of
A. Escape movements.
B. Revolutionary movements.
C. Reform movements.
D. Conservative movements.

9. What Robert Merton's theory of deviance refers to as rebellion is comparable to which type of social movement?
A. Conservative.
B. Reform.
C. Reactionary.
D. Revolutionary.

10. Which type of social movement seeks neither to promote nor to prevent social change?
A. Escape.
B. Reactionary.
C. Conservative.
D. Reform.

11. The People's Temple of Jim Jones represents which type of social movement?
A. Revolutionary.
B. Reform.
C. Escape.
D. Reactionary.

Answer Key

1.	B	**7.**	B
2.	D	**8.**	C
3.	A	**9.**	D
4.	A	**10.**	A
5.	C	**11.**	C
6.	A		

SECTION 30   **SOCIAL AND CULTURAL CHANGE**

- THEORIES OF SOCIAL CHANGE: KARL MARX AND MAX WEBER
- THREE CAUSES OF SOCIOCULTURAL CHANGE
- THE CONCEPT OF CULTURAL LAG
- SOURCES OF RESISTANCE TO SOCIOCULTURAL CHANGE

Objectives

After completing this section, the student should be able to:

1.   Explain how Karl Marx's theory of economic determinism can describe historical social change.

2.   Explain how Max Weber's theory of charisma and routinization can describe historical social change.

3.   Describe how discovery, invention, and diffusion contribute to sociocultural change.

4.   Explain how cultural lag relates to problems resulting from sociocultural change.

5.   Identify reasons why people tend to resist sociocultural change.

O̶ur times are characterized by rapid and pervasive change. It has been estimated that 90 percent of all the scientists who have lived are living today (Mack, 1967). Since modern science has contributed so much to social change, we can assume that never in history have people experienced as much change so rapidly as will the current generation. Over the course of the last 50,000 years, the human brain has not changed. In the same time span cultural changes have been staggering. Consider that agriculture developed about 10,000 years ago. The wheel was invented 5000 years ago. The steam engine appeared 200 years ago. The airplane, atomic energy, and space exploration are products of the 20th century. Projecting the discoveries of science into the year 2000, Stuart Chase suggests that scientific knowledge is doubling roughly every 10 years. This rapid advance in knowledge about the physical world has violently affected the human experience by creating new problems. "The college educated citizen of today, age 40, scarcely heard of, or imagined, during his years at school, any of the scientific-social problems he faces as an adult" (Chase, 1968).

THEORIES OF SOCIAL CHANGE: KARL MARX AND MAX WEBER

Two major concerns of sociologists are those of *social statics* (What is society?) and *social dynamics* (How does society *change*?). This section focuses on social dynamics. Most of us believe that there must be a cause for everything that happens. Some philosophers and scientists tell us that this cause-and-effect idea is not as formidable as it might seem. They say that we cannot *prove* that an event preceding another event causes the second event. Instead, they say, all that we can know is that one event is followed by the other event within a context called "time." For example, we may push a chair and then see the chair slide across the room. All we can know, they say, is that the chair slid across the room after we pushed it. The pushing and the sliding of the chair do not necessarily prove a principle of causation any more than a principle of succession—one event succeeding another. At first thought, this kind of reasoning may seem absurd, but consider this: how *do* we know that a push causes a slide, since all that we experience is the sensation of pushing and the observation of sliding? One occurrence follows the other in the context of time. That is all we can *know* about a simple matter such as pushing a chair and seeing the chair slide across the floor. What can we know, then, about the causes of broad social events that have occurred in human societies throughout the years?

What *caused* the Industrial Revolution? What *caused* the Western world's period of imperialism and colonialism? What *caused* the rise of an economic system called capitalism, and what *caused* socialism? And, in a narrower sense, what *caused* you to be reading this question at this moment in your life? In ancient Greece some people believed that all human affairs were caused by three goddesses known as the Fates. The Fates would spin the threads of human destiny, snipping and cutting whenever and wherever their whims might dictate. What *caused* people to believe in the existence of the Fates?

Sociologists cannot know what single factor or combination of factors explains the complexities of the human experience. We, like the scientists and philosophers who question the causal principle, cannot prove that the concept of cause and effect is valid. We ask our students to adopt a *temporary suspension of disbelief*. Without knowing whether anything caused anything, let us assume that the world we experience *is* a world of causes and effects.

Many efforts have been made to explain what circumstances caused various social and cultural changes through history. We have chosen to cite two theories of social change. We have selected those of Karl Marx and Max Weber because we are intrigued with the intellectual challenges in their theories and because of the historical significance of the thoughts of these two scholars. Students should bear in mind that these are two theories of social change selected from a body of many theories.

Karl Marx and the Theory of Economic Determinism

Marx and Engels wrote and published *The Communist Manifesto* in 1848. Just like the American *Declaration of Independence*, the *Manifesto* has had great impact on modern times. *The Communist Manifesto* was both a demand for social change and a description of social changes that had occurred and would continue to occur through economic changes because, Marx asserted, a society's economy determines all other cultural phenomena.

Marx's premise was this: before humans can engage in any other kind of cultural activity they must first provide the means for physical survival. Consequently, Marx would say that the so-called higher things in life have as their foundation the economic facts of life. The means by which a society produces and distributes its resources affect all other aspects of social life. Therefore, the forms and behavior of government, religion, education, and family as social institutions are determined by a society's economic system. This means that the social norms associated with other social institutions are somehow linked with the norms associated with property and with the production, distribution, and consumption of goods and services.

Great social upheavals resulting in radical social changes are motivated by economic interests. Marx identified numerous historical examples in which class struggles occurred because of conflicting economic interests. Indeed, the central theme of Marx's theory of social change is that of class conflict. In *The Communist Manifesto*, Marx and Engels wrote:

The history of all hitherto existing society is the history of class struggles.

Freeman and slave, patrician and plebeian, lord and serf, guild master and journeyman, in a word, oppressor and oppressed, stood in constant opposition to one another, carried on an uninterrupted, now hidden, now open fight, a fight that each time ended either in a revolutionary reconstitution of society at large, or in the common ruin of the contending classes.

In the earlier epochs of history, we find almost everywhere a complicated arrangement of society into various orders, a manifold gradation of social rank. In ancient Rome we have patricians, knights, plebeians, slaves; in the Middle Ages, feudal lords, vassals, guildmasters, journeymen, apprentices, serfs; in almost all of these classes, again, subordinate gradations.

The modern bourgeois society that has sprouted from the ruins of feudal society has not done away with class antagonisms. It has but established new classes, new conditions of oppression, new forms of struggle in place of the old ones.

Our epoch, the epoch of the bourgeoisie, possesses, however, this distinctive feature: it has simplified the class antagonisms. Society as a whole is more and more splitting up into two great hostile camps, into two great classes directly facing each other; Bourgeoisie and Proletariat.

(Marx and Engels, 1848)

With the exception of traditional, preliterate folk societies, Marx perceived the distribution of resources as inequitable in all the societies of history. According to Marx, social systems had been based on economies of scarcity rather than on economies of abundance. Consequently, privileges, power, and prestige would always be unequally distributed in such societies, and this inequality would lead to inevitable class struggle.

In the Marxist theory, the ownership of property and the forces of production can reach a stage in which they are controlled by one class at the expense of other classes. When this occurs, Marx said, the so-called productive forces are no longer what they should be, having developed in a way that "can only work mischief, and which are, therefore, no longer productive, but destructive forces (machinery and money)" (Marx, 1964B). Under these circumstances there emerges a class that must bear all the burdens of society while doing without any of the advantages enjoyed by others. This exploited class, said Marx, is excluded from the mainstream of society. It is forced into a position of opposition to the established system of society. Such a class would comprise the majority of society's population. Deprived and exploited, this majority develops a consciouness of the need for a fundamental revolution. The revolution has to be directed against the State, since those who control property and the means of production are also in control of the State (Marx, 1964B).

While recognizing sweeping social changes that had occurred throughout history because of economic factors, Marx devoted most of his attention to the social conditions of his own time. Believing that the modern epoch was ushering in a new *communist consciousness*, Marx anticipated that future social changes would come about through revolution that would abolish class rule and abolish classes themselves. Marx wrote:

For the creation on a mass scale of this communist consciousness, as well as for the success of the cause itself, it is necessary for men themselves to be changed on a large scale, and this change can only occur in a practical movement, in a revolution. Revolution is necessary not only because the ruling class cannot be overthrown in any other way, but also because only in a revolution can the class which overthrows it rid itself of the accumulated rubbish of the past and become capable of reconstructing society.

(Marx, 1964B)

Perhaps it would be a good idea for us to review for a moment. Remember that we are discussing theories of social change. Marx's theory has to do with economics being the basic factor behind all significant social change. While it is true that Marx often refers to the necessity of a violent overthrow of an established system in order to achieve social change, his references to violence do not preclude his recognition of social change occurring *without violent clashes*. Let us briefly explain what Erich Fromm calls "Marx's most complete formulation" of the concept of economic determinism.

Human beings, as social creatures, enter into definite relations, which are indispensable and independent of their will. These relations are based on the stage of economic development and the methods of production presently employed. These economic circumstances are the real foundation on which legal and political superstructures grow. "The mode of production of material life conditions the social, political and intellectual life process in general" (Fromm, 1961). Then, when new production methods challenge the old productive forces, the entrenched establishment, if it is not to collapse, will adapt itself to the new economics. Then, "With the change of the economic foundations the entire immense superstructure is more or less rapidly transformed" (Fromm, 1961). According to Marx, this is the stuff of which social change is made.

Students of American history know that Thomas Jefferson once anticipated an American society that would be primarily agricultural, happily depending upon the laboring masses of Europe to provide any of the frivolities and luxuries of life that manufacturing could produce. Jeffersonian society would have been characterized by individualistic citizens who would disdain the corrupting influence of crowded urban life as exemplified by Europe. This, of course, is not what happened. The productive forces of the Industrial Revolution soon challenged the early American establishment. This resulted in social change within the United States that created an urban industrial society whose social institutions and social norms reflected the new circumstances of economic industrialization. Perhaps this early American experience provides us with an illustration of the Marxist theory of social change *excluding* an organized, violent attack upon the State. Social change within the United States has not been without violence but, up to now, the State has accommodated itself to change, sometimes reluctantly, sometimes with fervor.

Some years after Karl Marx died, in 1883, Friedrich Engels wrote that the Marxist theory of social change

starts from the principle that production, and with production the exchange of its products, is the basis of every social order; that in every society which has appeared in history the distribution of the products, and with it the division of society into classes or estates, is determined by what is produced and how it is produced, and how the product is exchanged.

According to this conception, the ultimate causes of all social changes and political revolutions are to be sought, not in the minds of men, not in their increasing insight into eternal truth and justice, but in changes in the mode of production and exchange; they are to be sought not in the philosophy but in the economics of the epoch concerned.

(quoted in Heilbroner, 1967)

Thus did Engels sum up the theory of social change as it appears within the work of his friend and colleague, Karl Marx. The Marxist theory denies the importance or impact of ideological dedication or the especial significance of remarkable human beings who appear on the historical scene from time to time. Marx would say that the ultimate cause of all social change exists in the changes of economic production and distribution, not in inspirational ideas and actions of charismatic human beings or social movements. This, then, is the theory of economic determinism.

Max Weber and the Theory of Charisma and Routinization

In Section 24 we described three types of authority identified by Max Weber. One of them, charismatic authority, belongs to the individual with exceptional powers or qualities. "These are such as are not accessible to the ordinary person, but are regarded as of divine origin or as exemplary, and on the basis of them the individual concerned is treated as a leader" (Weber, 1947). As opposed to traditional or legal-rational authority, charismatic authority is based on extraordinary claims of an individual or group. Charismatic authority is revolutionary and innovative, seeking social changes that oppose established traditions and laws.

Whether we consider religion, politics, or any other type of institution, charisma can subvert and disrupt the institutional structures.

It is possible to suppress charismatic movements in order to preserve the status quo, but when charisma prevails there is a revolution of profound social change. Weber did not deny the possibility of other forces accomplishing social change. He recognized the potential impact of changes in technology and in economic relations, but he stressed that charisma was somewhere involved in the events bringing about significant change.

Weber's view of social change caused by charisma runs contrary to Marx's assertion that the ultimate causes of all social changes exist in economic phenomena and not in inspirational ideas and acts of individuals or movements. In order to understand Weber's theory of social change, we must examine his view of what happens to charisma after it has had its initial impact upon society., Weber said that charisma cannot retain its original power and zest forever, especially if it is successful and becomes established, for then it must become preoccupied with the routines of everyday life—this is called *the routinization of charisma.*

Weber said that as soon as charisma becomes established as authority it begins, through routinization, to change into something else. There are reasons for this change. Charismatic movements are usually organized in an informal and even haphazard manner. While the movement is new and dynamic and not firmly established in authority, a loose organization can be advantageous. "Authority is invested in the charismatic leader as an individual, or perhaps extended to a small group of lieutenants that surround him," and a more formal organization might rob the movement of the immediacy and dynamic quality of leadership (Berger and Berger, 1972). However, once the movement becomes the new establishment, the original free-wheeling organization must then tighten up so that it can cope with the basic problems of administration. This principle would apply to any charismatic movement, be it political, religious, or of any other variety. The old charismatic arrangements simply will not function to serve the population looking for established and orderly leadership. Relevant to this, Peter and Brigitte Berger observed that:

The history of twentieth-century revolutions is full of illustrations of this process. The Russian Revolution went through a period of intense charismatic fervor. It lasted, though probably with diminishing strength even then, while Lenin was alive. After Lenin's death, the revolution and its major organizational embodiment, the Communist party, "hardened" into the forms that subsequently came to be known as Stalinism.

Mao Tse-tung saw this process as a basic threat to his own revolution in China. He identified the threat with party bureaucracy. The so-called Cultural Revolution was Mao's attempt to revive the revolutionary charisma of an earlier period and to pit the enthusiasm of youth against the party bureaucrats.

In Cuba, Castro has continued to try to rule on the basis of a charisma born during the years of revolutionary struggle. As one (sympathetic) observer commented, 'Cuba has been ruled out of the pocket of Castro's fatigue jacket—the pocket into which he has the habit of stuffing the notes he takes while moving about the coun-

try by car or helicopter. Such habits of government have greatly endeared Castro to a large number of Cubans. But some (again, quite sympathetic) observers have wondered if some of Cuba's difficulties may not be related to this charismatic style of administration.

(Berger and Berger, 1972)

Max Weber suggested that the demise of charismatic authority can usually be detected when the first generation of followers has died. Charisma is extraordinary and extremely exciting. It can disrupt all the structures that once determined the day-to-day lives of people. Charismatic movements evoke intense emotions. Yet once established, how long can such celebration be associated with the new establishment? Eventually the original leader or leaders die. The new generation, which did not participate in the exciting beginnings of the movement, know of the earlier dramatic events only from history books and from stories told by their elders. What had been so extraordinary to the first generation becomes part of the orderly fabric of culture for the second generation. "For the second generation, the great events of the charismatic revolution are 'old hat', a more than slightly boring hangup of the parental generation" (Berger and Berger, 1972). This is exactly what is meant by routinization—it refers to those matters that once were extraordinary but, with the passing of time, becomes matters of routine. Weber said that routinization can take two distinct directions.

1. Routinization That Follows a Period of Charisma Can Lead to the Establishment of Traditional Authority. This has happened many times in history. A dynasty might be established in which the descendants of the charismatic leader or leaders retain the privileges, power, and prestige that were won during the charismatic period. If this occurs, a society can remain static under these conditions until a new challenge for social change comes along. An eminent American poet, Carl Sandburg, described the challenge to tradition as follows:

"Get off this estate."
"What for?"
"Because it's mine."
"Where did you get it?"
"From my father."
"Where did he get it?"
"From his father."
"And where did he get it?"
"He fought for it."
"Well, I'll fight you for it."*

2. Routinization That Follows a Period of Charisma Can Also Lead to the Establishment of a Legal-Rational System. Max Weber believed that the process of rationalization more typically follows charismatic movements in the modern world. He described the legal-rational system as one in which the *office* held by an individual is given the respect formally granted leaders within the charismatic

---

The People, Yes by Carl Sandburg, copyright ©1936, by Harcourt Brace Jovanovich, Inc.; copyright ©1964, by Carl Sandburg. Reprinted by permission of the publishers.

movement. In modern, mass society the bureaucratic administration of social institutions is efficient, predictable, objectively impersonal, and fast, Weber said. Privilege, power, and prestige belong to the office, and the individual occupying the office assumes its responsibilities and enjoys its rewards (Weber, 1958). In their interpretation of Weber's theory of social change, Peter and Brigitte Berger say that, in Weber's view, a legal-rational system provides the opportunity for constant change or "permanent revolution."

If charisma is for Weber the first great revolutionary force in history, the other is rationalization. . . . Like charisma, it is inimical to tradition; it subverts established institutional orders; it radically, and often abruptly, changes long-established patterns of social life. Unlike charisma, however, rationalization does not carry within it the seed of its own destruction. Rationality cannot be routinized. Indeed, rationalization is routinization. Thus, in Weber's view, the revolutionary transformations brought about by rationalization have an enduring character that charisma can never bring about. Put differently: Weber saw the revolution of modernity as a permanent one.

(Berger and Berger, 1972)

THREE CAUSES OF SOCIOCULTURAL CHANGE

As we have indicated earlier in this section, there are many different theories of social change. Sociologists refer to such factors as technology, charisma, economics, religion, ideology, and on and on. There are theories based on social evolution, on social conflict, and on historical cycles. Often the term *social process* is used to describe the events that embody social change. We presented two theories of social change in the previous section because we think the theories of Marx and Weber are especially challenging and because we acknowledge the historical importance of both the men and their ideas. Now we would like to be somewhat more specific by identifying three aspects of human experience that contribute to social change. We are not suggesting that these are the "real" causes of social change, as opposed to all the other possibilities. We are merely identifying three factors that we believe do significantly change social systems and cultural phenomena. Talcott Parsons might have been speaking for us when he said, ". . . we do *not* in the present state of knowledge possess a *general* theory of the processes of change in societies as a whole. . . . When such a theory is available the millennium for social science will have arrived. This will not come in our time and most probably never" (Parsons, 1951). But until the time that one comes along, we will string along with discoveries, inventions, and diffusion as causes of sociocultural change.

Discoveries

Parsons said that "We may define a discovery as any addition to knowledge. . . ." Discovery refers to such matters as the discovery of new astral bodies, new elements, and new treatments for disease. "For example, the great scientist Pasteur discovered the principle and technique of immunization only after he accidentally injected a stale bacterial culture of chicken cholera into some animals. When . . . they survived, it occurred to him that a weakened culture might immunize against the disease" (Lenski, 1970). Discoveries are additions to the human store of verified knowledge. Discoveries add something new to culture. People have discovered astral bodies, new elements, and cures for disease. These phenomena may always have existed, but they became part of culture only after their discoveries by human beings. Finally, discoveries become factors in social change only when they are actually put to use.

Inventions

Invention consists of combining existing elements of culture so that something new is produced. Actually, invention has two major sources. One source is the existing culture that represents all the ideas and materials available to the inventor. However, the popular conception of an individual inventor pursuing his or her own demon does not really apply very well in modern, mass societies.

Lonely men puttering in attics do not, for the most part, create the inventions of the modern day. It is rather in the research laboratories of large corporations, scientific foundations, universities, and government bureaus that new ideas are currently evolved. . . . The development of material invention today reflects the steady accumulation of thousands of able and trained laboratory scientists.

(Merrill, 1969)

The invention of computers has simplified data processing.

Certainly there can be no question about the significance for social changes in the invention of the wheel, the piston engine, and the telephone. These are material inventions. There are also social inventions. There also can be no question about the significance of such social inventions as the alphabet, constitutional government, social security programs, and economic corporations. Both material and nonmaterial inventions can cause radical social change. Diagram No. 16 offers a dramatic example of an invention's impact on American society.

Diffusion

When human groupings come into contact with one another, some exchange and cultural borrowing is apt to occur. The greatest amount of change in a culture comes from neither discovery nor invention. Most cultural changes result from diffusion—the exchanging of cultural traits among societies. With naive ethnocentrism, most people assume their cultures to be strictly "homegrown." This especially applies to those cultural traits that are considered desirable (Merrill, 1969). Ralph Linton said that "There is probably no culture extant today which owes more than 10 percent of its total elements to inventions made by members of its own society." (Linton, 1936). Because our modern age is characterized by rapid invention, people are apt to see their culture as largely self-created. In an attempt to indicate how much diffusion has affected the formation of present-day American culture, Ralph Linton described the beginning of one American's day. Keep in mind that the locations listed in the following passage written by Linton refer only to the origin points of various cultural elements and not to regions from which Americans now acquire materials through trade.

Our solid American citizen awakens in a bed built on a pattern which originated in the Near East but which was modified in Northern Europe before it was transmitted to America. He throws back covers made from cotton, domesticated in India, or linen, domesticated in the Near East, or wool from sheep, also domesticated in the Near East, or silk, the use of which was discovered in China. All of these materials have been spun and woven by processes invented in the Near East. He slips into his moccasins, invented by the Indians of the Eastern woodlands, and goes to the bathroom, whose fixtures are a mixture of European and American inventions, both of recent date. He takes off his pajamas, a garment invented in India, and washes with soap invented by the ancient Gauls. He then shaves, a masochistic rite which seems to have been derived from either Sumer or ancient Egypt.

Returning to the bedroom, he removes his clothes from a chair of southern European type and procedes to dress. He puts on garments whose form originally derived from the skin clothing of the nomads of the Asiatic steppes, puts on shoes made from skins tanned by a process invented in ancient Egypt and cut to a pattern derived from the classical civilizations of the Mediterranean, and ties around his neck a strip of bright-colored cloth which is a vestigial survival of the shoulder shawls worn by the seventeenth-century Croatians. Before going out for breakfast he glances through the window, made of glass invented in Egypt, and if it is raining puts on overshoes made of rubber discovered by the Central American Indians

THE AUTOMOBILE AS A
FACTOR IN SOCIAL CHANGE

Values
  Geographic mobility.
  Expansion of personal freedom.
  Prestige and material status derived from automobile
    ownership.
  Overevaluation of automobile as an extension of the self—
    an identity machine.
  Privacy—insulates from both environment and human
    contact.
  Consideration of automobile ownership as an essential
    part of normal living (household goods).
  Development of automobile cultists (group identification
    symbolized by type of automobile owned).

Environment
  Noise pollution.
  Automobile junkyards.
  Roadside litter.
  Land erosion from highway construction.
  Water pollution (oil in streams from road run—off).
  Unsightly billboards.
  Air pollution—lead, asbestos, hydrogen chloride, carbon
    monoxide, oxides of nitrogen, oxides of sulfur.

Economic
  Mainstay and prime mover of American economy in 20th
    century.
  Large number of the jobs directly related to automobile
    industry (one out of every six).
  Automobile industry the lifeblood of many other major
    industries.
  Rise of small businesses such as service stations and tourist
    accommodations.
  Suburban real estate boom.
  Drastic decline of horse, carriage, and wagon businesses.
  Depletion of fuel reserves.
  Stimulus to exploration for and drilling of new oil fields
    and development of new refining techniques, resulting
    in cheaper and more sophisticated methods.
  Increased expenditures for road expansion and inprove—
    ment.
  Increased Federal, state, and local revenues through auto—
    mobile and gasoline sales taxes.
  Decline of railroads (both passengers and freight).

Social
  Changes in patterns of courtship, socialization and train—
    ing of children, work habits, use of leisure time, and
    family patterns.
  Created broad American middle class and reduced class
    differences.
  Created new class of semiskilled industrial workers.
  Substitution of automobile for mass transit.
  Ready conversion of the heavy industrial capability of
    automobile factories during World War II to make
    weapons.
    Many impacts on crime.
  Increased tourism.
  Changes in education through bussing (consolidated
    school versus "one room country schoolhouse").
  Medical care and other emergency services more rapidly
    available.
  Traffic congestion.
  Annual loss of life from automobile accidents about 60,000.
  Increased incidence of respiratory ailments, heart disease,
    and cancer.
  Older, poorer neighborhood displacement through urban
    freeway construction.

Demography
  Population movement to suburbs.
  Shifts in geographic sites of principal U.S. manufacturers.
  Displacement of agricultural workers from rural to urban
    areas.
  Movement of business and industry to suburbs.
  Increased geographic mobility.

Institutional
  Automotive labor union activity set many precedents.
  Decentralized, multidivisional structure of the modern in—
    dustrial corporation evident throughout the auto industry.
  Modern management techniques.
  Consumer installment credit.
  Unparalleled standard of living.
  Emergence of U.S. as foremost commercial and military
    power in world.
  Expansion of field of insurance.
  Rise of entrepreneurship.
  Basis for an oligopolistic model for other sectors of the
    economy.
  Federal regulation of interstate highways and commerce
    as a pattern for other fields.
  Highway lobby—its powerful influence.

Diagram No. 16   The Automobile as a Factor in Social Change [Source. Taken from: The Mitre Corp. (Martin V.
Jones), A Technology Assessment Methodology (Some Basic Propositions), MTR 6009, Vol. 1, p. 79. Reproduced
by Permission.]

and takes an umbrella, invented in southeastern Asia. Upon his head he puts a hat made of felt, a material invented in the Asiatic steppes.

On his way to breakfast he stops to buy a paper, paying for it with coins, an ancient Lydian invention. At the restaurant a whole new series of borrowed elements confronts him. His plate is made of a form of pottery invented in China. His knife is of steel, an alloy first made in southern India, his fork a medieval Italian invention, and his spoon a derivative of a Roman original. He begins breakfast with an orange, from the eastern Mediterranean, a canteloupe from Persia, or perhaps a piece of African watermelon. With this he has coffee, an Abyssinian plant, with cream and sugar. Both the domestication of cows and the idea of milking them originated in the Near East, while sugar was first made in India. After his fruit and first coffee he goes on to waffles, cake made by a Scandanavian technique from wheat domesticated in Asia Minor. Over these he pours maple syrup, invented by the Indians of the Eastern woodlands. As a side dish he may have the egg of a species of bird domesticated in Indo-China, or thin strips of the flesh of an animal domesticated in Eastern Asia which have been salted and smoked by a process developed in northern Europe.

When our friend has finished eating he settles back to smoke, an American Indian habit, consuming a plant domesticated in Brazil in either a pipe, derived from the Indians of Virginia, or a cigarette, derived from Mexico. If he is hardy enough he may even attempt a cigar, transmitted to us from the Antilles by way of Spain. While smoking he reads the news of the day, imprinted in characters invented in Germany. As he absorbs the accounts of foreign troubles he will, if he is a good conservative citizen, thank a Hebrew deity in an Indo-European language that he is 100 percent American. *

(Linton, 1936)

THE CONCEPT OF CULTURAL LAG

Since this section is concerned with sociocultural change, it is fitting to mention here an interesting concept introduced by the American sociologist William F. Ogburn — the concept of cultural lag. Originally, Ogburn stated his hypothesis as follows:

The thesis is that the various parts of modern culture are not changing at the same rate, some parts are changing much more rapidly than others; and that since there is a correlation and interdependence of parts, a rapid change in one part of our culture requires readjustments through other changes in the various correlated parts of culture.

(Ogburn, 1922)

Cultural lag does not refer to differences between the cultures of two or more societies. It refers to different rates of change that occur within *one* society. Where cultural lag occurs, there are apt to be confusion and disharmony be-

---

*Copyright © 1936 by D. Appleton-Century Co. Inc., Ralph Linton, *The Study of Man*.

tween related aspects of a society's culture. This is likely to occur in a rapidly changing, dynamic culture. Ogburn contended that most changes occur first in the material aspects of culture. Then the nonmaterial aspects of culture have to accommodate themselves to the new material changes. Supporting this view of Ogburn's are all those people who, in recent years, have lamented that we live in an atomic age technologically and in a stone age moralistically and ideological-ly. They say that we have the means to destroy our entire planet without having the mores and values to bring ourselves totally to reject such a possibility.

We should point out that cultural lag can occur in reverse too. That is, a socie-ty can have the belief in and determination to achieve improved living condi-tions without having at its disposal the technical means to fulfill its aspirations. The tide of rising expectations that has appeared in many of the developing na-tions is frustrated by the cultural lag between social expectations and technolog-ical abilities. One further point should be made. It is really not possible for mate-rial advances to proceed very far ahead of nonmaterial aspects of culture, such as knowledge and desires. Material inventions result from the development of nonmaterial ideas. Human beings invent what they see as useful and consistent with their life-style.

A good example of cultural lag in which social behavior lagged far behind technological change is provided in the following passage by Robert A. Nisbet:

During World War II in Britain when armaments were becoming scarce and use of manpower critical, time and motion studies were made of gun crews in the artil-lery. It was hoped that the speed of operation of each gun could be increased. In one such study of a gun crew numbering five men, a peculiar act was noted. At a certain point, just before the firing of the gun, two of the men simply stood at at-tention for three seconds, then resumed the work necessary for the next firing. This was puzzling. The men themselves could not explain it; it was part of the tech-nique they had learned in gunnery school. Neither the officers nor the instructors at gunnery school could explain it either. All anyone knew was that the three-sec-ond standing at attention was a "necessary" part of the process of firing the highly mechanized piece of artilley. One day an old, long-retired artillery colonel was shown the time and motion picture again. Then his face cleared, "Ah," he said when the performance was over. "I have it. The two men are holding the horses."

Not for close to half a century had horses drawn artillery, but they once had—holding the horses while the gun fired was necessary. The horses disappeared from the artilley, but the way of behavior went on.

(Nisbet, 1970)

SOURCES OF RESISTANCE TO SOCIOCULTURAL CHANGE

One may wonder why people continue certain behavior long after that behavior has ceased to serve a useful purpose. So often changes that would provide more reasonable and practical means of achieving desired results are simply rejected out of hand. David Dressler identified what he called "four levels of conservatism" that partially account for so much resistance to sociocultural change (Dressler, 1969).

1. Change is sometimes resisted because it is easier to follow cultural paths already well established and learned than to learn and adapt to new modes of behavior.

2. There is sometimes vigorous opposition to proposed changes exerted by special interest groups.

3. There exist generally accepted beliefs that proposed changes constitute a threat to the basic values of an entire society.

4. Anything that stands in marked opposition to the cultural values of the given society may be thought of as to some extent "unnatural" and hence undesirable.

Many reasons have been advanced by sociologists attempting to explain what factors encourage people to resist sociocultural change. Economic costs, early imperfections in new inventions, simple inertia, and various psychological factors all contribute to the resistance to change (Vander Zanden, 1970). Finally, we must return to the subject of social institutions even when considering the social dynamics of human groupings. There is an unconscious conservatism associated with established social institutions. Institutional participants tend to reject institutional change. Whether we consider family, religion, education, economics, or government, those who participate in an institution perceive institutional change as a threat to themselves. Presenting established patterns of beliefs and expectations for behavior, social institutions, using both positive and negative sanctions, tend to conserve what is and to resist what might be as a result of social change.

KEY TERMS AND NAMES FROM SECTION 30

principle of causation

principle of succession

The Communist Manifesto

class conflict

exploited class

economic determinism

Jeffersonian society

charisma and social change

routinization of charisma

second-generation views of charismatic revolutions

traditional authority

legal-rational authority

process of rationalization

discoveries

material inventions

social inventions

diffusion

cultural lag

tide of rising expectations

resistance to sociocultural change

Karl Marx

Max Weber

William F. Ogburn

Ralph Linton

Talcott Parsons

STUDY GUIDE FOR SECTION 30

1. Karl Marx's *Communist Manifesto* was both a demand for social change and a description of social changes that had occurred in history. WHY IS MARX'S THEORY OF SOCIAL CHANGE CALLED ECONOMIC DETERMINISM?

2. In addition to Marx's stress on economic determinism, WHAT CAN BE IDENTIFIED AS THE CENTRAL THEME OF MARX'S THEORY OF SOCIAL CHANGE?

3. Marx believed that future social change would come about through revolutions abolishing social classes. WHAT TWO REASONS DID MARX GIVE FOR REVOLUTION BEING NECESSARY?

4. Marx often refers to the need to attack the State in order to achieve social change, but HOW CAN ECONOMICS DETERMINE SOCIAL CHANGE WITHOUT VIOLENT ATTACKS UPON THE STATE?

5. Early Jeffersonian America was considerably different in values and norms from modern America. APPLYING MARX'S THEORY OF SOCIAL CHANGE, WHAT HAPPENED TO BRING ABOUT SUCH RADICAL SOCIAL CHANGE?

6. Marx and Engels said that the ultimate cause of all social change exists in the changes of economic production and distribution. WHAT ASPECT OF THE HUMAN EXPERIENCE DID MARX AND ENGELS DENY AS BEING OF PARTICULAR IMPORTANCE IN CAUSING SOCIAL CHANGE?

7. Max Weber said that charismatic authority is revolutionary and innovative, seeking social changes that oppose established traditions and laws. WHAT CHARACTERISTICS ARE ASSOCIATED WITH CHARISMA?

8. Although it is possible to suppress charismatic movements, where charisma prevails there is a revolution of profound social change. WHY DID WEBER SAY THAT CHARISMA CANNOT RETAIN ITS POWER AND ZEST IF IT IS SUCCESSFUL AND BECOMES ESTABLISHED?

9. Routinization that follows a period of charisma can lead to the establishment of traditional authority. HOW DOES THIS OCCUR?

10. Routinization that follows a period of charisma can lead to the establishment of legal-rational authority. HOW DOES THIS OCCUR?

11. In their interpretation of Weber's theory of social change, the Bergers say that a legal-rational system provides opportunities for constant change or "permanent revolution." EXPLAIN THIS VIEW OF RATIONALIZATION. DO YOU AGREE WITH IT? WHY?

12. Parsons said that "We may define a discovery as any addition to knowledge." UNDER WHAT CIRCUMSTANCES DO DISCOVERIES ACTUALLY BECOME FACTORS IN SOCIAL CHANGE?

13. The popular conception of an individual inventor working alone and relying solely upon personal experience does not apply in modern, mass society. FROM WHERE DO MOST OF THE MATERIAL INVENTIONS OF TODAY COME?

14. Inventions make significant contributions to social change. There are material inventions and nonmaterial inventions, which might be called social inventions. NAME THREE MATERIAL INVENTIONS OF GREAT SIGNIFICANCE AND THREE SOCIAL INVENTIONS OF SIGNIFICANCE.

15. The greatest amount of sociocultural change in a society comes from neither discovery nor invention. Whenever human groupings interact, some exchange and cultural borrowing is apt to occur. WHAT TERM DESCRIBES THIS PHENOMENON?

16. William F. Ogburn introduced the concept of cultural lag. WHAT DOES CULTURAL LAG MEAN, AND HOW DOES CULTURAL LAG RELATE TO PROBLEMS THAT CAN RESULT FROM SOCIOCULTURAL CHANGE?

17. Ogburn contended that most changes occur first in the material aspects of culture and that the social aspects of culture lag behind. However, cultural lag can occur in reverse too, so too speak. CITE AN EXAMPLE OF EACH POSSIBILITY FOR CULTURAL LAG.

18. Changes that would provide more reasonable and practical means for achieving desired results are often rejected by people. LIST SOME FACTORS THAT ENCOURAGE PEOPLE TO RESIST SOCIOCULTURAL CHANGES.

PRACTICE TEST FOR SECTION 30

Select the best answer.

1. To maintain that we cannot prove that an event preceding another event causes the second event is consistent with the
A. Principle of succession.
B. Sociological perspective.
C. Principle of causation.

2. Throughout his life's work, Marx argued that social change had occurred and would continue to occur through
A. Charismatic leadership.
B. Cultural diffusion.
C. Economic changes.
D. Political upheaval.

3. According to Marx, all cultural phenomena are determined by a society's
A. History.
B. Politics.
C. Leadership.

D. Economy.

4. The central theme of Marx's theory of social change is that of
A. Violent overthrow of oppressive institutions.
B. Class conflict.
C. The economics of scarcity.
D. The economics of abundance.

5. According to Marx and Engels, the epoch of the bourgeoisie has
A. Simplified class antagonisms.
B. Complicated class antagonisms.
C. Created class antagonisms.
D. Done away with class antagonisms.

6. The theory of Charisma and Routinization is associated with
A. Frederick Engels.
B. Max Weber.
C. Karl Marx.
D. Erich Fromm.

7. Authority based on the extraordinary claims of an individual or groups is known as
A. Legal-rational authority.
B. Traditional authority.
C. Charismatic authority.

8. Weber said that charisma cannot retain its original power and becomes established with the routines of everyday life. This is called
A. The establishment of authority.
B. Legal-rational authority.
C. The normalization of charisma.
D. The routinization of charisma.

9. When a charismatic movement becomes the new establishment, it must cope with the basic problems of
A. Nonconformity.
B. Administration.
C. People's allegiance to the old normative structure.
D. Achieving its revolutionary goals.

10. Any addition to the human store of verified knowledge is a(n)
A. Invention.
B. Discovery.
C. Artifact.

11. When existing elements of a culture are combined so that something new is produced, what exists?
A. A discovery.
B. Diffusion.
C. An invention.
D. Cultural lag.

12. Major sources for inventions include
A. The existing culture.

B. Research laboratories.
C. The unique abilities of the inventor.
D. All of the above.

13. Whenever human groupings come into contact with one another, some exchange and borrowing are apt to occur. This process is known as
A. Diffusion.
B. Acculturation.
C. Cultural lag.
D. Sociocultural lag.

14. Most cultural changes result from
A. Inventions.
B. Discoveries.
C. Diffusion.

15. The concept of cultural lag was introduced into the sociological literature by
A. Robert A. Nisbet.
B. William F. Ogburn.
C. Ralph Linton.
D. Max Weber.

16. The disharmony between related parts of a culture is known as
A. Cultural lag.
B. Anomie.
C. Diffusion.
D. Cultural disequilibrium.

17. To say that we live in an atomic age technologically and in a stone age moralistically and ideologically would be an example of
A. Cultural lag.
B. Cultural shock.
C. Anomie.

Answer Key

1.	A	**7.**	C	**13.**	A
2.	C	**8.**	D	**14.**	C
3.	D	**9.**	B	**15.**	B
4.	B	**10.**	B	**16.**	A
5.	A	**11.**	C	**17.**	A
6.	B	**12.**	D		

CHAPTER
SUMMARY

1.   Collective behavior has been defined as the behavior of groups that operate without clear-cut direction. Collective behavior is unstructured and lacking in stability. It is behavior characteristic of riots, mobs, panic, mass hysteria, mass movements, and some social change.

2.   Neil Smelser has observed that people exhibit collective behavior when they experience conditions considered to be unpredictable and threatening. He identifies six conditions that give rise to collective behavior: structural conduciveness; structural strain; a generalized belief about the source of strain; precipitating factors; mobilization for action; and the exercise of social control.

3.   A crowd is a large, temporary collection of people in a particular place who share a common interest or cause. Herbert Blumer identified four types of crowds: casual crowds; conventionalized crowds; expressive crowds; and acting crowds.

4.   A mob is actually one form of the acting crowd. It is composed of people who are emotionally aroused and who intend to take violent and aggressive action. A mob is an especially temporary and unstable form of collective behavior. Usually, mobs have leaders.

5.   Unlike mob behavior, a riot is not likely to have any clear leadership. Nor is a riot likely to have a specific target against which violence is directed. Riots are apt to spread out over different areas. The actions of people in a riot lack a unity of purpose or objectives.

6.   Smelser defines panic as "a collective flight based on a hysterical belief." Some kind of crisis creates confusion and fear in the crowd. People exhibit panic when they respond to a perceived threat. Those who panic do not exhibit either cooperation or normative behavior.

7.   A rumor is information passed from person to person without anyone verifying its accuracy. Rumors are often a kind of gossip. Both accurate and inaccurate rumors can bring about collective behavior.

8.   Fads, crazes, and fashions are collective behavior that usually last longer than crowd behaviors. They are usually experienced nationwide.

9.   A public is a scattered group of people concerned about and in the process of discussing a certain issue. There are special publics interested in a single issue. General public opinion refers to *all* members of society who share an opinion about various general issues. In this sense, the whole population of the United States is a huge public.

10.   A social movement is collective behavior intended either to prevent or to promote social change. Social movements exist over a long period of time. The goals of a social movement involve major changes in the attitudes and behavior of society's population. A social movement's ideology attempts to respond to the distress, wishes, and hopes of the population.

11.   Four stages in the life cycle of a social movement are social unrest; popular excitement; formalization; and institutionalization. Types of social movements include the reactionary; conservative; reformist; revolutionary; and escape movements.

12. Karl Marx's theory of social change is based on economic determinism. Marx believed that people must first provide the means for physical survival before engaging in any other kind of cultural activity. The central theme of Marx's theory is that of class conflict. Still, Marx would say that the ultimate cause of all social change exists in the changes in the modes of economic production and distribution.

13. Max Weber's theory of social change is based on charisma and routinization. Weber believed that charismatic individuals have exceptional powers or qualities. Such people cause dramatic revolutionary changes to occur in society. Once successful, charismatic authority becomes routine. Then routinization leads to the establishment of either traditional or legal-rational authority.

14. Three causes of sociocultural change are discoveries, inventions, and diffusion. Diffusion is the exchanging of cultural traits among societies. Diffusion accounts for the greatest amount of change in a culture.

15. Cultural lag refers to different rates of change that occur within one society. Where cultural lag occurs, some confusion and disharmony are apt to be experienced between related parts of a single culture.

SUGGESTIONS FOR FURTHER READING RELATING TO CHAPTER 10

Canetti, Elias, *Crowds and Power* (New York: Viking Press, 1966). ". . . his analysis of the nature and behavior of crowds has given him the basis for a very comprehensive view of human affairs" — Arnold Toynbee.

Cantril, Hadley, *The Psychology of Social Movements* (New York: John Wiley, 1963). This book establishes a framework of interpreting social movements from a lynch mob to the Nazi movement in Germany.

Conway, Flo, and Jim Siegelman, *Snapping* (New York: Dell, 1979). A unique treatment of collective behavior as expressed in such movements as Hare Krishna, Scientology, People's Temple, est, and others. The subtitle is "America's Epidemic of Sudden Personality Change."

Curvin, Robert, and Bruce Porter, *Blackout Looting! New York City, July 13, 1977* (New York: Gardner Press, 1979). Collective behavior described in three looting stages during the blackout of New York City of July 13–14, 1977.

Kornhauser, William, *The Politics of Mass Society* (New York: The Free Press of Glencoe, 1959). This is a classic in social sciences literature that provides clues to the origin and nature of collective behavior.

LeBon, Gustave, *The Crowd* (New York; Viking Press, 1960). An often-challenged classic of sociology with an introduction by Robert K. Merton. The book was originally published in France in the year 1895.

Mandle, Joan D., *Women and Social Change in America* (Princeton, N.J.: Princeton Book Co., 1979). "The particular strength of this book is its linkage of women's role changes with general theories of social change . . ." — *Sociology*, Vol. 7, No. 1.

Nisbet, Robert, *Social Change and History* (New York: Oxford University Press, 1969). The author discusses the concepts of social change and progress during the history of the Western world.

Short, James F., Jr., and Marvin E. Wolfgang, editors, *Collective Violence* (Chicago: Aldine-Atherton, 1972). This is a close look at the political implications of collective violence as evidenced by racial and student unrest in the 1960s and 1970s.

Shupe, Anson D., Jr., Roger Spielmann, and Sam Stigall, "Cults of Anti-Cultism," *Society*, Vol. 17, No, 3 (March/April 1980). A discussion of the subject of "brainwashing" as a reaction to the collective behavior of cults.

Wehr, Paul, *Conflict Regulation* (Boulder, Col.: Westview Press, 1979). This work discusses nonviolent collective action. Cited are the environmental, peace, and equal-rights movements. Wehr's approach emphasizes the positive use of conflict of social movements.

Chapter 11
Ecology, Population, and Aging in the 1980s

SECTION 31   THE ECOLOGY OF PLANET EARTH

- THE ECOSPHERE ON PLANET EARTH
- HUMANOCENTRISM
- THE THREE LAWS OF ECOLOGY
- THE COLLAPSE OF THE MAYAN ECOSYSTEM
- GUIDE TO ECOLOGICAL LIVING

Objectives

After completing this section, the student should be able to:

1.   Compare and contrast "Spaceship Earth" with ordinary spaceships.
2.   Describe the Earth's ecosphere and explain how humans have broken out of the circle of life called the ecosystem.
3.   Define the term *humanocentrism* and give examples of humanocentric attitudes and behavior.
4.   Indicate an understanding of ecology by explaining how everything is connected to everything else, how everything must go somewhere, and why it would seem that nature knows best.
5.   Recognize means by which each individual can contibute to the future welfare of the Earth's ecosphere.

Let us again describe our planet Earth as one lonely lump of matter circling a star we call the sun. Our planet is located in a flat, wheel-shaped galaxy of a hundred billion stars. This galaxy is only one of perhaps ten or a hundred billion galaxies that come within reach of our measuring tools. In this vast universe there are more galaxies that even the most formidable tools of the future will not allow us to detect (Roberts, 1972). Astronauts who have traveled through space to the moon and back to Earth describe space as dark, lifeless, hostile, and desperately cold. Their spaceships have been complex life-support systems that have enabled them to survive their trips through the celestial desert. As the Apollo 8 capsule rounded the dry, barren face of the moon on Christmas Eve 1968, Captain James Lovell looked back at the entrancing bright blues and rich browns of our little planet glowing through the night and emptiness of space and exclaimed:

It's awe-inspiring. It makes you realize just how much you have back there on Earth. The Earth from here is a grand oasis in the blackness of space.

Scientists describe a spaceship as a craft with a closed system. This means that everything needed for a long trip must be carried on board. Nothing must be thrown away. On long voyages everything—even human wastes—must be recycled and used again. Our planet Earth is also a closed system. Our Spaceship Earth has everything on board the we will ever have—all the air, water, metal, soil, and fuel. Unlike the Apollo spaceships, however, our Spaceship Earth continues to take on more passengers all the time (Udall, 1972).

THE ECOSPHERE ON PLANET EARTH

As we said in the beginning of this book, no one knows for sure how it all began. For now, let us offer the explanation contained in the theory of organic evolution. This theory contends that several billion years ago life appeared and was nourished by the Earth's substance. With the passing of time, life evolved. Living things multiplied in number, variety, and habitat. Eventually they formed a global network in the environment they had themselves created through organic evolution. The home that life has built for itself on the outer surface of Earth is called the *ecosphere*. Any living thing that hopes to live on the Earth has to fit into the ecosphere or perish (Commoner, 1972).

It is difficult for the modern mind to comprehend the ecosphere. We are accustomed to think in terms of separate, singular events, each depending on a unique, single cause. In the ecosphere every effect is also a cause. For example, an animal's waste becomes food for soil bacteria. That which bacteria excrete nourishes plants. Animals eat plants. This is an ecological cycle. Ecological cycles are far removed, it would seem, from our experiences in the age of technology. We see Machine One always yielding Product One. Then, once Product One is used, it is thrown away, having no further meaning for the machine, the product, or the user. Barry Commoner says:

Here is the first great fault in the life of man in the ecosphere. We have broken out of the circle of life, converting its endless cycles into man-made, linear events: oil is taken from the ground, distilled into fuel, burned in an engine, converted thereby into noxious fumes, which are emitted into the air. At the end of the line is smog. Other man-made breaks in the ecosphere's cycles spew out toxic chemicals, sewage, heaps of rubbish—testimony to our power to tear the ecological fabric that has, for millions of years, sustained the planet's life.

(Commoner, 1972)

HUMANO-CENTRISM

There is a widespread belief on the part of many experts that human-made changes in the ecosphere now threaten the existence of the life-support system essential for the survival of human life. Throughout this book we have written about social phenomena—social institutions, social interaction, social location, social change, social-this and social-that. We have written about society, about culture, about the *human experience*. When we described the trend from *Gemeinschaft* to *Gesellschaft* we stressed human behavior and human organization within human societies. In our own way, like most social scientists, we have exhibited our own brand of ethnocentrism that we call *humanocentrism*. From folk to mass society, from subsistence economy to surplus economy, from humans huddling in small groups to humans soaring through space in the name of progress—these have been our expressions of humanocentrism. We have been humanocentric because we have ignored the fact that humanity, in all its cultural settings so various, so unique, is after all, only one form of life within this planet's ecosphere. Human technological accomplishments have not removed humanity from its place in the state of nature. We are social creatures, but *first* we are a species that participates within this planet's ecosystem. An *ecosystem* is "a community of organisms interacting with one another, plus the environment in which they live and with which they also interact" (*Penguin Dictionary of Biology*). The science that studies the relationships and processes linking each living thing and each form of life with each other and with the environment is *ecology*. In our next subsection we present an informal set of laws of ecology.

BARRY COMMONER'S THREE LAWS OF ECOLOGY

Human beings have broken out of the circle of life, driven not by biological need, but by the social organization which they have devised to "conquer" nature: means of gaining wealth that are governed by requirements conflicting with those which govern nature. The end result is the environmental crisis, a crisis of survival. Once more, to survive, we must close the circle. We must learn how to restore to nature the wealth that we borrow from it.

(Commoner, 1972)

Everything Is Connected to Everything Else

There is an elaborate network of interconnections in the ecosphere. These interconnections exist among different organisms and their physiochemical surroundings or environment. The ecosystems on this planet go through cycles of events. These cycles offer us evidence of how much everything is connected to everything else. For example, we know from trapping records in Canada that the population of rabbits and lynx follow ten-year fluctuations. When there are many rabbits in the area, the lynx multiply. Then, the increased population of lynx increasingly feeds on the rabbit population, reducing the number of rabbits. As rabbits become scarce, there is insufficient food to support the now numerous lynx. Then, as the lynx begin to die off, the rabbits are less fiercely hunted and they begin rapidly to multiply. This is a simple cycle within the ecosystem in which the lynx population is positively related to the number of rabbits, and the rabbit population is negatively related to the number of lynx.

In such a fluctuating system there is always the possibility that the whole system might collapse. Suppose, as an example, that in one particular swing of the rabbit–lynx cycle, the lynx manage to eat *all* the rabbits. As usual, the lynx begin to starve as the rabbits are consumed. In this supposition, however, the drop in the lynx population will not be followed by an increase in the number of rabbits. What will happen? The lynx will die off. The whole rabbit–lynx system will have collapsed. Suppose, as another example, that the lynx population were hunted down and wiped out by humans. This would leave the rabbits free to multiply to such an extent that they could further unbalance the ecosystem of their environment through their own eating habits.

The simple fact about any ecosystem is that everything is connected to everything else. A small disturbance of the balance of nature in one place may have large, distant, long-delayed effects elsewhere. Dumping industrial wastes into bodies of water or concentrating DDT in the soil can break down ecosystems. Environmental pollution is often a sign that ecological links have been cut and that the ecosystem has been made more vulnerable to stress and to final collapse. As a part of the Earth's total ecosystem, humankind is more than a social creature. Humanity has a *natural* role to play within the Earth's ecosystem. Everything is connected to everything else.

Everything Must Go Somewhere

This second law of ecology is simply another way to state a basic law of physics —that matter is indestructible. In nature there is no such thing as "waste." In every ecosystem, what is excreted by one organism as waste is taken up by another as food. For example, animals release carbon dioxide as a respiratory waste. Green plants use the carbon dioxide for nutrition. Plants excrete oxygen which, in turn, is used by animals. The organic wastes of animals nourish the bacteria of decay. Bacteria wastes such as nitrate, phosphate, and carbon dioxide all contribute to life forms.

One of the reasons for the present environmental crisis is that great amounts of materials have been taken from the ground, changed into new forms, and then discharged into the environment without considering the fact that everything has to go somewhere. This practice of discharging into the environment anything that we have "used and are finished with" has led to accumulations of harmful amounts of material in places where, in nature, they do not belong. Consider the following example. We might buy a dry-cell battery containing mercury, use it until it is no longer of value, and then throw it away. Where does it go when it gets "thrown away"? Let's say that we put it out in the trash container. The trash is collected and taken to an incinerator. Now the mercury is heated as the trash burns in the incinerator. Mercury vapor is then produced and emitted by the incinerator stack. Mercury vapor is toxic. It is carried by the wind, eventually coming down in rain or snow. Let's say that the mercury condenses and sinks to the bottom of a mountain lake. Here it is acted on by bacteria, dissolves, and is taken up by fish. The mercury accumulates in the organs and flesh of the fish. Then the fish are caught and eaten by human beings. Now the mercury is deposited in human organs where it can be harmful. The mercury in the battery was not "thrown away." Everything must go somewhere.

Nature Knows Best

This third law of ecology contends that any major change in a natural system brought on by humanocentric strivings for progress is likely to hurt the ecosystem. This law contradicts the modern conviction that our technological advances can now allow us to improve on nature. There are some two to three billion years of natural selection behind every living thing. In that time, we can

Everything must go somewhere.

assume that a staggering number of new individual living things have been produced. This has allowed nature to try out the suitability of various genetic changes. In this way, living things have accumulated a complex organization of compatible parts. Thus, this third law of ecology would suggest that the structure of a present living thing or the organization of a current natural ecosystem is likely to be "best," since it has undergone so many natural experimentations in the past.

This principle is particularly relevant to organic chemistry. The artificial introduction of an organic compound that does not occur in nature, one that is human-made, is likely to be harmful. When a new human-made organic substance is synthesized, one that is unlike anything that occurs in nature, it is not likely to be naturally recycled. The material will tend to accumulate. Who can know what side effects these human-made, organic chemicals might have? We have used detergents, insecticides, and herbicides without considering their potential danger to other forms of life. Billions of pounds of such substances have been produced and broadly scattered throughout ecosystems where they can reach and affect numerous organisms without our even knowing it (Ehrlich, Ehrlich, and Holdren, 1973).

Nature knows best. Without sacrificing our intellectual self-esteem, without denying the possibility of a glorious human destiny, we can still acknowledge that we are but part of the elaborate network of interconnections in Earth's ecosphere. We cannot think in terms of "conquering" nature because the human species and each single savage self is part of the Body Natural. We cannot afford to be humanocentric because, like *all* forms of life on this planet, we are products of and participants in the Earth's ecosphere.

THE COLLAPSE OF THE MAYAN ECOSYSTEM

About 1000 years ago the Mayan civilization of Central America was flourishing. The Maya were advanced in mathematics and astronomy and used an advanced form of writing. Their art and architecture, now in ruins, is still admired throughout the world. Mayan society was at its height 1000 years ago. Then, in the span of three or four generations, it fell into disrepair. Recently, a theory suggests that "environmental degradation, brought on by overpopulation and mounting pressures on the fragile tropical ecosystem may have been a major cause" (Norman, 1980). Scientists say that the growth of the Mayan population was slow, but that it did steadily increase. In time, much of the forests near Mayan settlements were cleared for farming. This exposed the soil to the heavy rainfall typical of that area. Soil erosion took place. Thus, a severe strain was placed on the region's agricultural resources. "Massive amounts of fertile soil were washed into lakes and streams, depleting the land of essential nutrients" (Norman, 1980). Colin Norman expresses concern for similar events in the present time throughout the developing world. Norman writes:

Extensive areas in Africa, Asia, and Latin America have been stripped of trees as more and more people need land to plant crops and require firewood for heating and cooking. And overgrazing on grasslands in arid regions is contributing to the malignant spread of deserts in many parts of the world..

(Norman, 1980)

Norman believes that just as Mayan civilization collapsed with little warning, gradual ecological deterioration might be experienced suddenly in parts of today's world. He mentions floods in India that have resulted from cutting forests in highlands, causing rapid runoff. Norman notes that "It is sobering . . . that some of the Mayan farmlands have not yet recovered their full productivity, 1000 years after the Mayan collapse." There has always been a delicate balance within the ecosphere. It would seem that most environmental crises result from human behavior.

GUIDE TO ECOLOGICAL LIVING

Concern about the ecosphere has been expressed nationally and internationally over the past 15 years. In 1971, a book sponsored by the Santa Barbara Underseas Foundation appeared entitled *Everyman's Guide to Ecological Living*. The subject matter of the book and the fact that it was published supports our contention about the increasing awareness of our planet's ecological plight. Included in the book are "General Rules to Live By." The rules were relevant and topical in 1971. They are just as relevant to the human condition today. Here are the rules for living as they appeared in *Everyman's Guide to Ecological Living* (Cailliet, Setzer, and Love, 1971):

1. *Be constantly aware of the interdependence of Humanity and Nature. Everything we do has an effect somewhere. Be alert to the ultimate fate of items you use. Before using, ask, "What will it do to the state of the environment?"*

2. *Use only those materials essential to your existence. Eliminate the "I WANT" philosophy of life. Eat to live, don't live to eat. Fight needless consumption; purchase only items that you really need.*

3. *Buy durable items, avoiding those designed for obsolescence. "Make what you can, bake what you can, grow what you can." Avoid "Take what you can."*

4. *Seek to recycle anything you "consume." Re-use products rather than discard them. Donate things that others can use.*

5. *Inform yourself about the activities of the Overt Despoilers of the Earth. Question everything!*

6. *Teach others ecologically sound concepts of living. Begin with your own family. Nature is the best teacher. Learn also from books, TV specials, and conservation meetings.*

7. *Support any political (or nonpolitical) action (or inaction) that tends to alleviate the problems facing our Earth. Vote, write letters, petition, boycott, testify.*

8. *Oppose the social myths of growth, progress. and development. There is nothing inevitable about "progress." Natural beauty and open spaces are the common heritage of all life and should be protected from "Improvements."*

9. *Fight the social pressures perpetuating the production of large families. The population bomb is your baby.*

10. *Set a good example yourself in your lifestyle, awareness of waste, consumption, reproduction, and communication with others. Nothing's going to change unless we're willing to live it ourselves!*

From Apollo 8, Captain James Lovell looked back at our Earth, describing it as "awe-inspiring" and seeing it as "a grand oasis in the blackness of space." If Earth has lost something, we need not search alone to restore the damage. There are many people today who are awakened and anxious to acknowledge one community of life on this planet. The following words from Thoreau's *Walden* seem to be an appropriate way to conclude this section:

I long ago lost a hound, a bay horse, and a turtledove, and am still on their trail. Many are the travelers I have spoken to concerning them, describing their tracks and what calls they answered to. I have met one or two who had heard the hound, and the tramp of the horse, and even seen the dove disappear behind a cloud, and they seem as anxious to recover them as if they had lost them themselves.

KEY TERMS AND NAMES FROM SECTION 31

Spaceship Earth

theory of organic evolution

ecosphere

ecological cycles

humanocentrism

organisms

ecosystem

ecology

balance of nature

environmental pollution

natural selection

collapse of Mayan ecosystem

Guide to Ecological Living

Barry Commoner

STUDY GUIDE FOR SECTION 31

1. The home that life has built for itself on Earth's outer surface is called the ecosphere. In the ecosphere every effect is also a cause. GIVE AN EXAMPLE OF AN ECOLOGICAL CYCLE.

2. Barry Commoner has said that we have broken out of the circle of life, converting its endless cycles into human-made, linear events. CITE ONE EXAMPLE COMMONER GIVES TO SUPPORT WHAT HE CALLS "OUR POWER TO TEAR THE ECOLOGICAL FABRIC THAT HAS . . . SUSTAINED THE PLANET'S LIFE."

3. Throughout the text we have written about society, culture, and the *human* experience. WHY, IN THIS SECTION, DO WE SAY THAT WE HAVE BEEN HUMANOCENTRIC IN OUR WRITING THROUGHOUT THE BOOK?

4. *Homo sapiens* is a species that participates within this planet's ecosystem. WHAT IS AN ECOSYSTEM?

5. DEFINE THE TERM *ECOLOGY*.

6. In this section we mention three "laws of ecology." WHAT ARE THEY?

7. A small disturbance in the balance of nature within an ecosystem can create stress within and even the collapse of the ecosystem. CITE AT LEAST TWO EXAMPLES OF HUMAN BEHAVIOR THAT MAY BE INTERPRETED AS DISTURBING THE BALANCE OF NATURE.

8. Industrial societies have removed great amounts of materials from the ground, changed them into new forms, and discharged them into the environment. HOW HAS THIS CONTRIBUTED TO THE PRESENT ENVIRONMENTAL CRISIS?

9. In modern industrial societies there is the conviction that our technological advances can allow us to improve upon nature. HOW IS THIS CONVICTION CONTRADICTED BY THE LAW OF ECOLOGY WHICH SAYS THAT "NATURE KNOWS BEST"? GIVE AN EXAMPLE THAT HAS TO DO WITH "RECYCLING."

10. Mayan civilization flourished 1000 years ago but fell into disrepair in the span of three or four generations. EXPLAIN WHAT MUST HAVE HAPPENED TO THE MAYAS FROM AN ECOLOGICAL VIEWPOINT.

11. HOW DOES THE FALL OF MAYAN CIVILIZATION APPLY TO CIRCUMSTANCES IN THE DEVELOPING NATIONS?

PRACTICE TEST FOR SECTION 31

Select the best answer.

1. The home that life has built for itself on the outer surface of Earth is called the
A. Ecosystem.
B. Ecosphere.
C. Ecological cycle.
D. Ecology.

2. In the ecosphere every effect is
A. A separate, singular event.
B. A linear event.
C. An end in itself.
D. Also a cause.

3. An animal's waste becomes food for soil bacteria. Bacteria excretion nourishes plants. Animals eat plants. This process is an example of a(n)
A. Ecological cycle.
B. Ecosystem.
C. Ecosphere.
D. Vicious cycle.

4. *Homo sapiens* have exhibited a unique form of ethnocentrism by ignoring the fact that humanity is, after all, only one form of life within the planet's ecosphere. We call this unique form of ethnocentrism
A. Homocentrism.

B. Humanocentrism.
C. Altruism.
D. Sociocentrism.

5. A community of organisms interacting with one another, plus the environment in which they live and with which they also interact is called a(n)
A. Ecosystem.
B. Closed system.
C. Ecosphere.
D. Ecological cycle.

6. Which law of ecology is synonymous with the basic law of physics which states that matter is indestructible?
A. Everything is connected to everything else.
B. Everything must go somewhere.
C. Nature knows best.
D. Everybody has to be someplace.

7. Which law of ecology contends that any major change in a natural system brought on by humanocentric strivings for progress is likely to be detrimental to the ecosystem?
A. Everything has its place.
B. Nature knows best.

C.   All is one.
D.   There is a communicative link be-
     tween all living organisms.
8.   The science that studies the relationship and processes linking each living thing and each form of life with
each other and with the environment is
A.   Sociology.
B.   Demography.
C.   Ecology.
D.   Environmental biology.
9.   Which of the following is a law of
ecology?
A.   Everything is beautiful in its own
     way.

B.   There is a communicative link be-
     tween all living organisms.
C.   Humanity is supreme in the uni-
     verse.
D.   Nature knows best.
10.   The collapse of Mayan civiliza-
tion 1000 years ago supports the view
that
A.   All societies must come to an
     end.
B.   The Maya were poor farmers.
C.   Most environmental crises result
     from human behavior.
D.   It is not possible to build cities in
     the jungle.

Answer Key

1.	B	6.	B
2.	D	7.	B
3.	A	8.	C
4.	B	9.	D
5.	A	10.	C

SECTION 32   THE INCREASING HUMAN POPULATION
- DOUBLING TIME IN THE PAST
- DOUBLING TIME IN THE FUTURE
- DEMOGRAPHY
- THE THEORY OF THE DEMOGRAPHIC TRANSITION
- LIMITING THE HUMAN POPULATION

Objectives

After completing this section, the student should be able to:

1.   Explain how the term *doubling time* can be applied to human population growth.

2.   Define the term *demography*.

3.   Identify four ways in which the number of people in a particular area can change.

4.   Describe the high potential growth, the transitional growth, and the incipient decline stages of the demographic transition theory.

5.   Explain why neither the maximum nor the minimum population for this planet could be the optimum population.

6.   Offer personal opinions favoring or opposing methods available for population control.

At the beginning of this book we spoke of planet Earth as one lonely lump of matter circling what seems to be a minor star that we call the sun. We spoke of the persistent human predicament that we all share. Not asking for birth, we are born. Not hoping for death, we die. We are children of humans, and most of us become parents of humans. Each generation has been born into a world that it did not make. And no one knows with certainty how it all began. At some time in the distant past our ancestors must have become aware of their own fragility, both as individuals and as a species. Few in number, with the planet as a gigantic residence, they huddled together in small groups, attempting to survive the challenges of the environment and the attrition of time. Little wonder, then, that the word went out to be fruitful and multiply.

DOUBLING TIME
IN THE PAST

It has been estimated that the total human population in 8000 B.C. was about 5 million people. During the time of Jesus, it is believed that the human population totaled about 200 million people, increasing to about 500 million (1/2 billion) by 1650. It doubled to 1000 million (1 billion) by 1850, then doubled again to 2 billion by 1930. The number of the Earth's human population has, with slight irregularities, increased continuously, and the *rate* of increase has also accelerated.

One authority has suggested that the best way to describe the human growth rate is in terms of "doubling time"—the time required for the population to double in size (Ehrlich and Ehrlich, 1973). From a population of 5 million in 8000 B.C. to a population of 500 million in 1650 means that the population of Earth increased a hundredfold. The population doubled about once every 1500 years from 8000 B.C. to 1650. Then the dramatic increases began. It took 200 years to double from 500 million to 1 billion. It took 80 years to double from 1 billion to 2 billion. Now, if the present rate of growth continues, the population will double again in about 35 years. Diagam No. 17 shows human population growth in these terms.

DOUBLING TIME IN THE FUTURE

Consider the implications of this growth rate in which the doubling time is now only about 35 years. The Earth's population could exceed a billion-billion people by 1000 years from now. This means that there would be 1700 people per square yard of the Earth's surface—both land and water (Ehrlich and Ehrlich, 1973). Such an increase would produce a human population whose weight would match that of the planet itself in about 1500 years! Something must change. Contemporary rates of population growth simply cannot continue for very long into the future. There would not be enough room on the planet with about 200 million square miles of surface, of which 50 million square miles is land surface. Sooner or later *any* rate of population increase will produce a saturation point. There will be no more room (Hauser, 1972).

Hunger is one result of overpopulation.

Date	Estimated World Population	Time Required for Population to Double
8000 B.C.	5 million	1500 years
1650 A.D.	500 million	200 years
1850 A.D.	1000 million (1 billion)	80 years
1930 A.D.	2000 million (2 billion)	45 years
1975 A.D.	4000 million (4 billion)	35 years

Diagram No. 17   Human Population Growth (Source. Newsweek—Fenga and Freyer.)

DEMOGRAPHY

All of the figures we have cited thus far are what might be called demographic arithmetic. They are not intended to be predictions of what lies ahead for the human race on Planet Earth. Demography is the science concerned with the statistical study of the human population. Demographers are concerned with both real figures of the past and projected figures of the future. Demographers seek to know how many people there are, where the people are distributed around the Earth, and what implications are present in demographic findings, as far as the human condition is concerned. Demographic information is provided by national and worldwide censuses made by governments and private organizations. In the broadest view, demography studies population composition and distribution. As vital statistics are analyzed, demographers consider such variables as births, deaths, age, sex, marriage, divorce, family size, race, education, illiteracy, unemployment, distribution of wealth, occupational distribution, crime rates, density of population, and migrations. The majority of demographers are sociologists by profession, although demography increasingly is viewed as a science in its own right. Demographers recognize four ways in which the *number* of people in an area can change.

1. Fertility: someone may be born in the area.

2. Mortality: an inhabitant may die.

3. Immigration: an outsider may move into the area.

4. Emigration: an inhabitant may move out of the area.

If the Earth faces a problem of overpopulation, we must recognize that the first two factors have contributed to the population explosion. In general, the population explosion has been the product of decreases in mortality, not of increases in fertility. Let us explain this in the next subsection.

THE THEORY OF THE DEMOGRAPHIC TRANSITION

Consider four possibilities that might relate to a society's population:

1. high birth rate, high death rate (high potential growth).
2. high birth rate, low death rate (transitional growth).
3. low birth rate, low death rate (incipient decline).
4. low birth rate, high death rate.

The fourth possibility—low birth rate, high death rate—is rare. It could not be maintained for many generations unless a large immigration of outsiders occurred in order to keep the society going. However, the first three possibilities have been grouped into a demographic typology known as the "transition theory." This theory holds that a historical transition has been made by some societies and might occur for other societies in the future. These stages of demographic evolution (these typologies) are identified as evolving from high potential growth to transitional growth to incipient decline. Let us describe each of the demographic stages.

High Potential Growth (High Birth Rate, High Death Rate)

This typology is similar to Heilbroner's economies run by tradition (discussed in Section 24), to *Gemeinschaft* and folk society (discussed in Section 14), and to any society that has not made the transition from subsistence to surplus. Throughout most of human existence, our control over environment has been negligible, resulting in a high death rate. Under such circumstances, a large supply of births is necessary if society is to balance the large number of deaths. In the 17th century, Thomas Hobbes characterized the natural state of human beings as one of "continual fear and danger of violent death, and the life of man solitary, poor, nasty, brutish, and short" (Hobbes, 1651). Describing a society at the stage of high potential growth Kingsley Davis wrote:

Under the old regime of high fertility and high mortality women experienced the drain and danger of pregnancy often to no purpose, because a large proportion of the offspring died before reaching maturity. Too much effort was spent in trying to bring each new generation to adulthood; too much energy was lost in sickness, malnutrition, and mourning; too much time was taken for mere sustenance.

(Davis, 1949)

In a society with high potential growth, both fertility and mortality are high. High fertility rates are rooted in strongly entrenched marriage customs and reproductive norms. High mortality rates are maintained by disease and chronic undernourishment. Deaths increase in response to recurring epidemics, famines, wars, and any other disasters not controllable by the skills of the culture. Births increase in times of good harvests and of political stability and in the absence of epidemics. Year-by-year fluctuations in these matters tend to cancel one another out over a period of time, resulting in a relatively stable condition of population growth.

This first stage of demographic evolution is described as having a potentially high growth rate for the population. The rapid increase in population is latent, because the high mortality rate keeps the increase from occurring. A rising standard of living can cause the population to enlarge rapidly if that rising standard of living includes the means to deal with natural disasters and the means to provide for more than basic needs. Lowering death rates tends to bring about rapid and possibly lengthy population increase. Many people in parts of Africa, Asia, and South America are presently living under conditions of high fertility and high mortality. However, a dramatic decline in mortality rates is occurring. A large proportion of the Earth's population is moving rapidly from a situation of high birth rates and high death rates to a situation of high birth rates and *low* death rates. This is resulting in sharply rising annual rates of population increase (Ehrlich and Ehrlich, 1973). This leads to the second stage of the demographic evolution — transitional growth.

Transitional Growth (High Birth Rate, Low Death Rate)

The one factor that has most affected the population increase is the decrease in mortality rates. For example, victory over malaria, yellow fever, smallpox, cholera, and other infectious diseases has contributed to the increasing population by decreasing the mortality rate, especially among children and young adults throughout the world (Ehrlich and Ehrlich, 1973). Improvements in medical care, agricultural techniques, social reforms, the ability to control temperature and humidity in homes and places of employment, improvements in public sanitation, better education regarding personal hygiene, and other technological changes have also contributed to decreasing the mortality rate (Thomlinson, 1965). The population increase that occurs during this transitional stage is usually interpreted by underpopulated nations as being a very hopeful sign. Underpopulated nations interpret such growth as helpful because they expect population growth to supply larger markets, more productive work forces, greater military potential, and increased national pride. Enthusiastic optimism has been associated with this transitional period as industrialization and urbanization occur. Some modern nations have room for such expansion, *but many are already crowded*, and expansion of population presents an obstacle to rising living standards. Now, more and more it is being said that controls must be placed upon the growth of the Earth's human population. For the first time in history, it is possible to keep mass populations alive, at least temporarily, while population growth accelerates much more rapidly than production rates. Population controls are said to be the only answer to the growing problem. Most people, it would seem, agree that the most humane means of achieving such controls is by reducing the birth rate. The other al-

ternative would be to permit the death rate to increase in those societies presently at the transitional growth stage of demographic evolution. There will be little
choice if humankind does not rationally limit its birth rate soon. Lowered fertility
rates are characteristic of what is called the incipient decline stage of demographic evolution.

Incipient Decline (Low Birth Rate, Low Death Rate)

Sociologist Ralph Thomlinson reminds us that:

*A few of the northwest European nations reached a condition of population de-
cline in the 1930s, but the name of this type must not be taken as a prediction of
population decrease. In fact, some of the areas in this class are now growing rather
rapidly. At the time the transition theory was formulated and disseminated, leaders
in many countries feared that population decline was imminent—and in the international depression of the 1930s, the fear was legitimate. But since then, the conditions of life and the fertility practices of the populace have changed, and few persons worry today about the prospect of an abidingly dwindling population.*

(Thomlinson, 1965)

Ideally, a society enjoying the stage of incipient decline would provide its population with a level of well-being unparalleled in human history. With fewer
deaths, less sickness, and fewer pregnancies, less effort is required to bring a generation to maturity. Agricultural and industrial commodities are more plentiful
because of the larger proportion of adults and the smaller percentage of people
who are chronically unfit to be productive. How can the people of the Earth
achieve such conditions? Is there still time? These questions lead us to our next
topic.

LIMITING THE HUMAN POPULATION

We have said that we believe most people would agree that the only humane
means of achieving a control over what has been called the population explosion
is through a worldwide reduction in the birth rate. Still, even if there is a consensus that limiting births is the preferred means to limit population, there are questions about how far and how fast limitation should proceed. Is there an optimum
population size for planet Earth? And how does one determine *what* the optimum population size might be, *if* there is such a thing?

The physical size of the Earth (200 million square miles of surface) is not the
only factor that will determine the *maximum* size the human population can attain. Other factors must be considered, such as land area, availability of mineral
resources, water, potential for food production, and the ability of biological systems to absorb mass society's wastes without breakdowns that deprive humankind of essential goods and services. No one knows exactly what the maximum
carrying capacity is. The capacity of the Earth to maintain a certain size population at a very high level for a short time may change as a result of rapid con-

sumption of nonrenewable resources. Even the accomplishments of technology in employing very common materials may ultimately fall short of what is needed to provide a living standard considered good today. At any rate, whatever the maximum sustainable population may be, the maximum and the optimum are certainly *not* the same as far as population size is concerned. When we think of a maximum population that the Earth can support, we are thinking of a bare level of subsistence for all. This is not what the worldwide tide of rising expectations has been anticipating. Unless we believe that the largest, most crowded population can achieve the ultimate good, the maximum population for Planet Earth simply is not the optimum population.

On the other hand, the *minimum* size of the human population would be that number of people who can reproduce themselves. The minimum size of population can hardly be said to approach being the optimum population size either. The minimum size would be too small to allow for the benefits of specialization and division of labor, too small to provide economies that could sustain a living standard considered good today. Somewhere between the minimum and maximum lies the optimum population size. Furthermore, the optimum population size may be one number at this time and another number at another time. Let us explain.

The optimum population size is a dynamic phenomenon, not a static one. Even the concepts of overpopulation and underpopulation are relative to circumstances and time. "Optimum," in this case, means the best population size under existing social and technological conditions. With the passing of time, both technological and cultural evolution can change the population sizes defined as optimum. Many people believe that in terms of *present* patterns of human behavior and the *present* level of technology, Planet Earth is overpopulated *today*. Consider the following point of view, which favors limiting the size of human population through governmental intervention:

. . . governments should be ready to encourage appropriate population trends, just as they now attempt to produce desired economic trends. In other words, the size of the human population must be brought under rational control, but not with the idea of establishing some sort of permanently frozen optimum. Actually arriving at population sizes regarded as optimum at any given time will involve extraordinary changes in human attitudes—attitudes that have been produced by eons of biological and cultural evolution.

These changes will inevitably trouble people's minds; limiting death goes with the grain of tradition, but limiting births goes against it.

(Ehrlich and Ehrlich, 1973)

Perhaps government intervention will not be necessary. Throughout the world there is evidence that people want to control their population growth. Voluntary sterilization has been chosen by many people in India, Japan, Latin America, and the Soviet Union. In Japan, in European nations, and in some parts of the United States legal abortions are available upon request. The birth rates of these countries have fallen dramatically (Cole, 1972). China is the world's most populous nation. According to the latest Chinese figures, China had 975 million people. Yet China had a remarkable drop in its birth rate during the 1970s. China seeks to reduce its population growth to zero by the year 2000. The Chinese hope to stabilize their population at 1.2 billion. An editorial in the *People's Daily* said that the best way to achieve zero population growth would be for each couple to have no more than one child (*The Evening Sun*, Feb. 11, 1980).

Humans have the intelligence to project themselves into the future. Disaster does not hide from the human imagination. It is clear that we must control our population size on Earth. Increasingly crowded situations and growing frustrations can explode in many violent and destructive ways. "Every one of the 125 million babies born each year is a bundle of aspirations. The drive to fulfill these will become the most dynamic and unpredictable force in world affairs in the years ahead" (Salas, 1980). Zero population growth has apparently become the objective of many of the industrially developed nations today. This cannot be said of the developing nations in the Third World. Rafael Salas, executive director of the U.N. Fund for Population Activities, says that 80 percent of all humankind will live in the Third World by the end of this century. Thus, the countries and regions of the world in which greatest population growth will occur are the poorest areas. Unless population growth can be checked, humankind is facing frustrations and dangers greater than any brought on by previous wars or natural disasters.

KEY TERMS FROM SECTION 32

doubling time in the past	theory of demographic transition
doubling time in the future	high potential growth stage
demography	transitional growth stage
demographic variables	incipient decline stage
fertility	population controls
mortality	optimum population size
immigration	zero population growth
emigration	Third World

STUDY GUIDE FOR SECTION 32

1.   It has been suggested that the best way to describe the human growth rate is in terms of "doubling time." The population doubled once about every 1500 years from 8000 B.C. to 1650. Then the dramatic increase began. IF THE PRESENT RATE OF GROWTH CONTINUES, HOW SOON WILL THE POPULATION DOUBLE AFTER 1975?

2.   Contemporary rates of population growth cannot continue for very long into the future because there would not be enough room on the Earth. AT THE PRES-

ENT RATE OF INCREASE HOW MANY PEOPLE WOULD THERE BE 1000 YEARS FROM NOW?

3. DEFINE THE TERM *DEMOGRAPHY*.

4. Demographers identify four ways in which the number of people in an area can change. LIST THE FOUR WAYS.

5. NAME THE THREE STAGES OF DEMOGRAPHIC EVOLUTION ACCORDING TO WHAT IS CALLED THE "TRANSITION THEORY."

6. DESCRIBE THE SOCIAL CIRCUMSTANCES AT EACH STAGE OF THE DEMOGRAPHIC EVOLUTION.

7. The phrase "population explosion" has been used to describe the rapidly growing human populaion. WHICH HAS BEEN MORE RESPONSIBLE FOR THIS EXPLOSION: THE DECREASE IN MORTALITY OR THE INCREASE IN FERTILITY?

8. The physical size of the Earth is not the only factor that will determine the *maximum* size the human population can attain. WHAT OTHER FACTORS MUST BE CONSIDERED?

9. The optimum population size is a dynamic phenomenon, not a static one. Even the concepts of overpopulation and underpopulation are relative to circumstances and time. EXPLAIN WHY THIS IS SO.

10. Arriving at population sizes regarded as optimum at any given time will involve extraordinary changes in human attitudes which will trouble people's minds. WHAT HAVE BEEN THE TRADITIONAL ATTITUDES TOWARD ACTIONS THAT LIMIT DEATHS AND ACTIONS THAT LIMIT BIRTHS?

11. China is the world's most populous nation. HOW DO THE CHINESE PLAN TO REDUCE POPULATION GROWTH TO ZERO BY THE YEAR 2000?

PRACTICE TEST FOR SECTION 32

Select the best answer.

1. During the time of Jesus, it is believed that the human population totaled about

A. 50 million.
B. 200 million.
C. 500 million.
D. 5 million.

2. The time required for the human population to double in size is termed

A. High potential growth.
B. Population squared.
C. Doubling time.
D. Transition time.

3. If the present rate of growth continues, the population will double in

A. 35 years.
B. 80 years.
C. 20 years.
D. 60 years.

4. At the present rate of growth, the human population 1000 years from now would be

A.   A hundred million people.
B.   A million million people.
C.   A thousand billion people.
D.   A billion billion people.

5.   The science concerned with the statistical study of the human population is
A.   Ecology.
B.   Human geography.
C.   Demography.
D.   Humanology.

6.   The majority of demographers are
A.   Sociologists.
B.   Economists.
C.   Political scientists.
D.   Geographers.

7.   The number of people in an area can change as a result of all of these except one. Which one?
A.   Fertility.
B.   Mortality.
C.   Immigration.
D.   Morality.

8.   Which of the following is the most rare for a society?
A.   High birth rate, high death rate.
B.   Low birth rate, high death rate.
C.   Low birth rate, low death rate.
D.   High birth rate, low death rate.

9.   Demographers are not concerned with which of these vital statistics?
A.   Birth and death rates.
B.   Density of the human population.
C.   Age, sex, and racial composition.
D.   Height and weight of the human population.

10.   High fertility and mortality rates characterize
A.   High potential growth.
B.   Incipient decline.
C.   Transitional growth.

11.   Many people in parts of Africa, Asia, and South America are in the stage of transition theory known as
A.   Transitional growth.

B.   High potential growth.
C.   Incipient growth.

12.   A high birth rate coupled with a low death rate is characteristic of
A.   Incipient decline.
B.   High potential growth.
C.   Transitional growth.

13.   Ideally a society in this stage would provide its population with a level of well-being unparalleled in human history. Which stage?
A.   Transitional growth.
B.   High potential growth.
C.   Incipient decline.

14.   A low birth rate coupled with a low death rate is characteristic of
A.   High potential growth.
B.   Incipient decline.
C.   Transitional growth.

15.   Regarding optimum human population size, which of the following is correct?
A.   Optimum population is absolute, since the Earth can sustain only a finite number of people.
B.   Technological and cultural evolution can change the population size defined as optimum.
C.   The optimum population size is a static phenomenon.

16.   In those nations in which legal abortions are available upon request, birth rates have
A.   Fallen dramatically.
B.   Increased significantly.
C.   Risen moderately.
D.   Stabilized.

17.   According to Rafael Salas, what percentage of the human population will live in the Third World by the end of the century?
A.   65 percent.
B.   73 percent.
C.   80 percent.
D.   87 percent.

Answer Key

1.	B	**7.**	D	**13.**	C
2.	C	**8.**	B	**14.**	B
3.	A	**9.**	D	**15.**	B
4.	D	**10.**	A	**16.**	A
5.	C	**11.**	B	**17.**	C
6.	A	**12.**	C		

SECTION 33   **THE AGING SYNDROME IN AMERICA**
- THE AGED AS A MINORITY
- AGEISM IN AMERICA
- SOCIAL PROBLEMS OF THE AGED
- HOW DEEPLY DO WE CARE?

Objectives
After completing this section, the student should be able to:
1. Describe the elderly as a minority or quasi-minority group.
2. Define ageism and cite examples.
3. Identify social problems associated with growing old in America.
4. Explain why the elderly attempt to prevent becoming dependent upon family or social agencies.

People who manage to survive to old age know that the present system is destroying them. They experience discrimination, intolerance and isolation based on the sole fact that they are old. Their oppression stems from an irreversible biological condition, as surely as the black person faces oppression because of color and a woman experiences oppression based on sex.

(Curtain, 1972)

THE AGED AS A MINORITY

Some sociologists say that old people in America should be viewed as a unique kind of minority. Like other minority groups, many of the elderly suffer from low incomes, unequal opportunities, and other discriminatory behavior that leads to low social status. D. Stanley Eitzen says that there are cultural reasons why the elderly are oppressed in modern American society. Americans seem to be obsessed with youth. Americans associate youth with beauty, health, sexual vigor, happiness, usefulness, and intelligence. These are all positive traits. On the other hand, the elderly are too often considered to be physically unattractive, sickly, sexless, nonproductive, and senile. Then too, Eitzen says, much of the knowledge and skill acquired by the elderly in their youth is now out of date. Old people whose educations and job skills have become obsolete are treated in much the same way as people who never got much education and who never acquired useful job skills (Eitzen, 1980). As Sharon Curtain has said, many old people suffer from ageism just as blacks have experienced racism and women have experienced sexism.

Other sociologists believe that the elderly cannot be considered a true minority group. Unlike blacks, Indians, and Latinos, the elderly are not really a specific subgroup. Everyone can grow old. Many of the elderly have their origins in the

The political power of the aged is growing.

majority group and many continue to live within families of the majority. Milton L. Barron says that it would be more accurate to consider the elderly as a *quasi-minority*. The term *quasi* means that something or someone seems to be or resembles but is not actually what is being described (Barron, 1971).

The political power of the aged as a quasi-minority is growing. The elderly are increasing in numbers. And the older population is changing in important ways. By today's standards, most of the present old people are poorly educated. As many as 50 percent did not go to school beyond elementary level. Only 5 percent are college graduates. As many as 20 percent were foreign born and remain unfamiliar with the American political system. The forthcoming population of "senior citizens" will be much better educated, mostly native-born, and well prepared to use the political system to their advantage. With their increase in numbers they will make a powerful and persuasive voting bloc (Julian, 1980).

AGEISM IN AMERICA

Perhaps only 25 percent or fewer of the American population is extremely ageist. Still, most people seem to have at least some degree of prejudice against aging and old people. Ageism occurs through negative prejudice and discrimination against people on the basis of age. If people are avoided or excluded from ordinary activities on the basis of age, that is ageism (Atchley, 1980). Newspapers, magazines, and television all too often present negative images of the elderly. On television, the elderly often are presented as "doddering old fools who cause problems for their relatives or as wise old ancients who are always ready with a pithy saying or a piece of warm gingerbread" (Jones, 1977).

The print media is as guilty of ageism as television. One study analyzed 265 articles on aging that were printed in a large Midwestern newspaper. For the most part, only negative images of aging and of old people were presented. The newspaper emphasized stories about "well-preserved physical culture addicts and 'old timers' reminiscing about the good old days" (Jones, 1977). Actually, the paper carried no more than two articles a day about old people or about aging. Half of these were merely human interest stories. Little or no realistic information about older people active in the community was printed. The realities of aging and of the activities of the elderly in the community were mostly ignored (Jones, 1977). Even school books have been guilty of stereotyping old people in much the same way that blacks and women have been stereotyped.

Our society has been described as having a throwaway culture: we have been socialized to think in terms of using something and then throwing it away. To some extent, this is how we have come to treat old people. Once they reach the age of 65 or retire from work, they are put on the shelf and forgotten. "The older a person gets the harder it is to get a bank loan, home mortgage, auto insurance, or a driver's license" (McVeigh and Shostak, 1978). Ageism results from too much emphasis on production values and too little concern about humanistic values. In conclusion we cite the view of David Popenoe on ageism:

Ageism encourages a stereotype of old people as being isolated, dependent, emotionally unstable, and physically unfit. Although this image is accurate in some cases, in many instances it is not. The stereotype reflects an unwillingness to confront the aging process as an experience common to all human beings. It further betrays a reluctance to acknowledge those aged people who succeed in living rich and complex lives despite a wide variety of hindrances.

(Popenoe, 1980)

SOCIAL PROBLEMS OF THE AGED

There are now about 25 million Americans who are over 65 years of age. Until recent years few sociology textbooks on social problems included any treatment of the personal troubles or public issues of an aging American population. Now just about every social-problems textbook considers the sociological implications of growing old in modern America. Let us cite and describe some of the experiences associated with the problems of aging.

Poverty and Income Deprivation

Most old people who had formerly worked for wages or salary and are now retired suffer from financial problems. Most retirees must learn to live on an income less than half of their previous earnings. Income is no longer tied directly to what one can earn. "Instead, income is now derived from the pension plans and social security benefits that workers have been contributing into during their working years" (Scarpitti, 1980). Many of the elderly find that they must supplement these small incomes. This means trying to find a part-time job that will itself pay very little money. And it is difficult for the elderly to find work. Therefore, many of the elderly live on fixed incomes and suffer from the erosion of inflation. They must lower the standard of living to which they had become accustomed for so many years. Because of lack of funds, a loss of personal independence occurs. Many older Americans become dependent on their children or on impersonal welfare agencies (Steglich and Snooks, 1980). In 1976, 15 percent of all persons 65 years or older were living below the government's established poverty line (Scarpitti, 1980).

Housing and Living Arrangements

Because so much of an elderly person's time is spent at home, housing is especially important. "Regardless of the type of home or location, the elderly in their own homes are more likely to be happy than those who do not own their residences" (Steglich and Snooks, 1980). Still, a large percentage of their homes are old and run-down. Many of the aged lived in neighborhoods that are high-crime areas. Also, because of property taxes and rising insurance and utility bills, economic problems increase each year. Nevertheless, many of the aged do not want to move from their homes. The home is the last link with old times, family, and friends. Others do not move simply because they cannot afford to. They feel trapped because there is no reasonable alternative residence.

Nursing homes for the elderly have increased in number since the government's Medicare law. Many such homes leave much to be desired. "Complaints

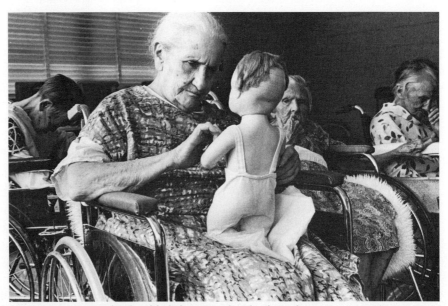

Many nursing homes for the elderly leave much to be desired.

against them include bad food, inadequate medical staffs, kickbacks and profiteering on food and housekeeping contracts, overcharges for medical services and drugs, and physical abuse" (Steglich and Snooks, 1980). There have been numerous exposés by newspapers and congressional investigators. Many such facilities have been improved. They are safer and better-staffed than they were. Yet, as Frank R. Scarpitti says, "since it is these better institutions that charge high fees, the poor elderly may again find themselves left out" (Scarpitti, 1980). In the late 1970s there were about 25,000 nursing homes in the United States. Almost 80 percent operated as commercial enterprises and made substantial profit (Hendricks and Hendricks, 1977).

Health Problems

Medical expenses for the aged are six times greater than those for young adults and three times greater than for the middle aged. Medicaid and Medicare programs help finance some costs, but many medical expenses must be paid by elderly patients themselves. Furthermore, older people have more difficulty traveling to and from doctors' offices, clinics, and hospitals.

Four out of five older people suffer from at least one chronic condition. Such long-lasting health problems considerably limit their activities. Ian Robertson says that many medical problems of the elderly are strongly influenced by factors other than simply aging. This is especially true in reference to mental illness among the aged. Of people aged 65 to 75, only about 5 to 10 percent actually suffer from senility. Senility is caused by loss of brain cells and affects mental functions such as memory and the ability to perform simple tasks. The proportion of senility does increase in the population past age 75 (Robertson, 1980), but many old people are labeled senile when they are not. They could be suffering from side effects of medication or from very poor nutrition. Undiagnosed heart or lung ailments that impede the flow of blood and oxygen to the brain can also cause behavior labeled senile (Butler, 1975). Some people are labeled senile when actually they suffer from severe depression that could have either social or psychological origins (Robertson, 1980). Certainly this much is true: ". . . as age increases, the probability of disease, illness, or disability becomes greater. . . . people age 65 and over are much more likely to suffer limitations of activity due to chronic conditions" (Atchley, 1980).

From Independence to Dependence

American society has always placed a high value upon individual independence. It should not be surprising that so many older people fear and resent the possibility of becoming dependent upon others. The elderly fear becoming dependent, either physically or financially. As Robert C. Atchley has said, Americans "are taught from birth that becoming independent and self-sufficient is a primary goal." Atchley says that older people first try to solve the problem of remaining independent themselves. They cut back on how much they spend, to maintain financial self-reliance. They cut back on how much they do, to maintain physical energy and independence. To compensate for failing memories, they keep notes. And in social relationships where they have no contributions to make, they simply drop out. For many, these personal solutions work out. For others, outside help eventually must be sought. As age increases, so does the need for outside help in most cases. "Illness, poverty, disability, declining energy, failing hearing or sight—all these roads lead to dependency" (Atchley, 1980).

Most older people first seek help from their families. This often places strains on family relationships. Nevertheless, Atchley says, most families manage to overcome the conflicts and feelings of guilt and resentment. When required, most families adjust and work out means to meet the needs of older family members. Of course, many families do attempt to avoid the situation by steering the older family member to community agencies and institutions.

Most old people try to avoid seeking help from community agencies. As Atchley says, the older person becomes particularly aware of his or her dependency when dealing with social services provided by community agencies. They must deal with rules, regulations, complicated forms, and the feeling that the bureaucratic organization is meddling far too much in their personal affairs. All this increases the dread of becoming dependent. Atchley says that becoming dependent is especially hard because a dependent status is accompanied by a set of expectations. In American society, any dependent people are expected to be thankful for what they get; they are expected to show that they are grateful for what they receive. Indeed, they are expected to surrender the right to lead their own lives. Such demands are made of our children, of the poor, or of any other dependent group. Little wonder that older people try to avoid the status of dependency, especially when many have spent as many as 50 years as independent adults! (Atchley, 1980).

HOW DEEPLY DO WE CARE?

In his social-problems textbook, D. Stanley Eitzen quotes Senator Charles Percy on the problems of elderly Americans. Percy said:

Somehow, we have to care more than we do now about the elderly dispossessed in America.

How deeply do we care when millions of our parents and grandparents die indirectly because of malnutrition or infectious diseases, both largely preventable and treatable?

How deeply do we care when as a nation we spend $14 million to build a single fighter airplane and the same amount for research into problems of aging?

How deeply do we care when we maintain demeaning, dehumanizing nursing homes on local, county and state levels for 1 million older Americans?

How deeply do we care when we permit highly qualified elderly workers to be forced out of jobs which they need?

Many of us in government, as in other fields, will continue to fight for the rights and the needs of the elderly in this country. We are fully committed to that strug-

gle. But we will neither secure those rights nor fulfill those needs without much broader and deeper support from vast numbers of our fellow citizens. Without that support, the pursuit of happiness will continue to come to an abrupt halt for millions at age sixty-five.

(Percy, 1974)

KEY TERMS FROM SECTION 33

the aged as a minority

the aged as a quasi-minority

senior citizens

ageism

media as ageist

problems of the aged

income deprivation

living arrangements

medical expenses

senility and medication

dependency

STUDY GUIDE FOR SECTION 33

1. Many old people suffer from prejudice and discrimination just as traditional minority groups have. WHY DO SOME SOCIOLOGISTS SAY THAT THE ELDERLY SHOULD BE VIEWED AS A UNIQUE KIND OF MINORITY?

2. Some sociologists believe that the elderly should be seen as a *quasi-minority*. HOW IS THIS DIFFERENT FROM A REGULAR MINORITY GROUP?

3. The elderly are increasing in numbers. WHY WILL FUTURE OLD PEOPLE BE ABLE TO HAVE MORE INFLUENCE IN SOCIETY?

4. Ageism results in behaviors that are similar to behaviors resulting from racism and sexism. DEFINE AGEISM.

5. HOW HAVE PRINT AND ELECTRONIC MEDIA CONTRIBUTED TO AGEISM?

6. ABOUT HOW MANY AMERICANS ARE OVER 65 YEARS OF AGE?

7. Many older people must lower the standard of living to which they had been accustomed. HOW ARE POVERTY AND OLD AGE RELATED IN AMERICA?

8. WHAT HAVE BEEN SOME OF THE PROBLEMS ASSOCIATED WITH HOUSING AND HEALTH IN REFERENCE TO THE ELDERLY?

9. Americans are taught from birth that becoming self-sufficient is an important achievement. WHY HAS THIS MADE AGING IN AMERICA PARTICULARLY DIFFICULT?

10. HOW ARE DEPENDENT PEOPLE IN AMERICAN SOCIETY EXPECTED TO BEHAVE?

PRACTICE TEST FOR SECTION 33

Select the best answer.

1. According to Milton Barron, the elderly constitute a
A. Minority group.
B. Contraculture.
C. Quasi-minority group.
D. Subculture.

2. According to current estimates, what percent of the American population is extremely ageist?
A. 25 percent.
B. 45 percent.
C. 35 percent.
D. 55 percent.

3. Prejudice and discrimination against people on the basis of age is known as
A. Ethnocentrism.
B. Humanocentrism.
C. Nationalism.
D. Ageism.

4. How many Americans are 65 years of age or older?
A. 25 million.
B. 15 million.
C. 35 million.
D. 45 million.

5. In 1976, what percent of all persons 65 years or older were living below the government's established poverty line?
A. 3 percent.
B. 21 percent.
C. 15 percent.
D. 32 percent.

6. Medical expenses for the aged are how many times greater than those of young adults?
A. Six times.
B. Three times.
C. Nine times.
D. Twice as great.

7. What percentage of people aged 65 to 75 actually suffer from senility?
A. 5–10 percent.
B. 10–15 percent.
C. 15–20 percent.
D. 30–35 percent.

8. The aged of future generations will be different from the aged of the 1980s. In which of the following ways will they *not* be different? The aged of the future will be
A. Mostly native-born.
B. Experiencing senility at earlier ages.
C. More likely to use the political system to their advantage.
D. Better educated.

9. What percent of nursing homes has made substantial profit from their elderly patients?
A. 20 percent.
B. 40 percent.
C. 60 percent.
D. 80 percent.

Answer Key

1.	C	**6.**	A
2.	A	**7.**	A
3.	D	**8.**	B
4.	A	**9.**	D
5.	C		

CHAPTER
SUMMARY

1. The ecosphere is the home that life has built for itself on the outer surface of the Earth. All living things must adapt to the ecosphere or perish. Within the ecosphere every effect is also a cause.

2. Humanocentrism refers to a unique form of ethnocentrism in which humanity views itself as the center of the universe. Humanocentrism ignores the fact that humankind is only one form of life within the ecosphere.

3. An ecosystem is a community of organisms that interact with one another, plus the environment in which they live and with which they also interact.

4. Ecology is the science that studies the relationships and processes that link each living thing and each form of life with the others and with the environment. The three laws of ecology state that everything is connected to everything else; everything must go somewhere; and nature knows best.

5. The human population has increased continuously. The rate of increase has accelerated. The term *doubling time* has been used to describe the time required for the population to double in size. If the present rate continues, the human population will double again in only 35 years.

6. Demography is the science concerned with the statistical study of the human population. Demographers study population composition and distribution. There are four ways in which the number of people in an area can change: fertility; mortality; immigration; and emigration.

7. The theory of demographic transition maintains that a historical transition has been made by some societies and might occur for other societies in the future. The three stages identified in the transition theory are high potential growth; transitional growth; and incipient decline.

8. Perhaps the only humane way to achieve control over the population explosion is through worldwide reduction in the birth rate. Many people believe that in terms of present patterns of human behavior and the present level of technology, the Earth is overpopulated today.

9. Old people in the United States should be viewed as a unique kind of minority. Like other minorities, many of the elderly suffer from low incomes, unequal opportunities, and other forms of discrimination. People are avoided or excluded from activities on the basis of age. This is called ageism.

10. Experiences associated with the problems of aging include poverty, income deprivation, poor housing and living arrangements, and poor health. There are

also problems related to the transition in status from being independent to dependent upon families or social agencies.

11.   The elderly are increasing in numbers. Future senior citizens will be well-educated and prepared to use the political system to their advantage. With their increase in numbers and with growing efforts at organization, the elderly will make a powerful and persuasive voting bloc in years to come.

SUGGESTIONS
FOR FURTHER
READING
RELATING TO
CHAPTER 11

Carson, Rachel, *Silent Spring* (New York: Crest, 1964). This has become a classic. "Carson's cry of warning is timely. If our species cannot police itself against overpopulation, nuclear weapons and pollution, it may become extinct." —*New York Times*.

Cottrell, Fred, *Aging and the Aged* (Dubuque, Iowa: Wm. C. Brown, 1974). Only 67 pages long, Cottrell's treatment of aging and the circumstances of being elderly is an excellent supplement to any textbook or chapter on the subject.

Fischer, David Hackett, *Growing Old in America* (New York: Oxford University Press, 1977). "Pointing to recent interest in and concern for the elderly, the author suggests we may be entering a new period characterized by partnership between young and old." —*Library Journal*.

Heilbroner, Robert, "Ecological Armageddon," *The New York Review of Books* (April 23, 1970). The author suggested in 1970 that perhaps all the concern about ecology might turn out to be a popular fad. These are stimulating views from the very beginning of the past decade.

Hess, Beth B., *Growing Old in America*, 2nd ed. (New Brunswick, N.J.: Transaction Books, 1980). This is a good collection of articles concerned with what it means to be old and how to improve the lives of the elderly.

McGraw, Eric, *Population Today* (London: Kaye and Ward, 1979). The origins of the population explosion and future effects on the ecosphere and social order are considered.

Ophuls, William, *Ecology and the Politics of Scarcity* (San Francisco: Freeman, 1977). Here is a serious and readable book about the human future in reference to scarcity of resources and limitation of human activities.

Quadagno, Jill S., editor, *Aging, the Individual and Society: Readings in Social Gerontology* (New York: St. Martin's Press, 1980). This includes numerous articles on all aspects of aging.

Schnaiberg, Allan, *The Environment: From Surplus to Scarcity* (New York: Oxford University Press, 1980). This is a scholarly book dealing with the environmental crisis. Suggestions are made to avoid ultimate disaster.

Smith, Joel, and Mark Evers, *Ecology and Demography* (Dubuque, Iowa: Wm. C. Brown, 1977). Here is a fine book only 88 pages long. It provides an excellent supplement to any discussion of ecology and population.

Stadler, John, editor, *Eco-Fiction* (New York: Washington Square Press, 1971). The need for people to accept their responsibility in maintaining the ecological balance is the connecting theme of all these short stories. Authors include Isaac Asimov, Ray Bradbury, Edgar Allen Poe, William Saroyan, and Kurt Vonnegut, Jr.

Chapter 12
The Human Experience: From Where? To Where?

SECTION 34   HUMANS AS UNIQUE PRIMATES
- PRIMATES AS MAMMALS
- ANIMALS INCLUDED IN THE ORDER OF PRIMATES
- DISTINCTIVE CHARACTERISTICS OF PRIMATES
- SOCIAL CHARACTERISTICS OF PRIMATES
- HUMANS AS THE MOST HIGHLY DEVELOPED PRIMATE
- NATURE VERSUS NURTURE . . . AGAIN

Objectives
After completing this section, the student should be able to:
1.   Identify three types of primates that most resemble humans.
2.   Describe characteristics of primates in reference to physical development, reproduction, and maturation.
3.   Describe some of the more obvious social characteristics of primates.
4.   Explain how the use of tools, the division of labor, sharing, and language make humans the most highly developed primates.

As we said in the beginning of this book, no one knows for sure how the world began nor how life appeared on Earth. We do know that there have been and are now many different forms of life. The theory of organic evolution contends that life appeared on Earth several billion years ago. With the passing of time, life evolved and multiplied in number, variety, and habitat. As we said in Chapter 11, any living thing has to fit into the Earth's ecosphere or perish. Humans belong to a class of life called *Mammalia*. Primates, which humans are, is one order of Mammalia.

PRIMATES AS
MAMMALS

Primates are members of the form of life called mammals. Primates include human beings and animals that most closely resemble humans. More than 200 species of mammals have been classified as primates. Mammals' bodies are covered with hair or fur that provides insulation. Humans have only fine hair on most parts of their bodies. Mammals are warm-blooded, meaning that their body temperature remains at a constant level.

Mammals give birth to living offspring. The newly born develop first to a considerable size within the mother. After birth, they are nourished by suckling from the mother's mammary glands. Young mammals must experience a rather long period of dependency on adults. During this early period of life, they have to learn many things in order to survive. Much of adult mammal behavior is learned, not instinctive. Playing is a way to learn that is typical of young mammals. It is especially important to primates (Ember and Ember, 1977). For humans, it is this early learning that makes it possible for one to participate in the culture of the society into which one is born.

ANIMALS INCLUDED IN THE ORDER OF PRIMATES

We have said that there are more than 200 species of mammals that have been classified as primates. Those that most resemble human beings (*Homo sapiens*) include the following:

Prosimians: This term means literally "pre-monkeys." They are small, large-eyed, tree-dwelling, nocturnal animals, such as tarsiers, lemurs, and lorises.

Monkeys: There are many species of monkeys.

Apes: This term includes gibbons, orangutans, gorillas, and chimpanzees. What makes these animals distinct from monkeys is their absence of tails, their chests and shoulders that are somewhat like those of humans, and their more developed brains. In fact, the brains of apes are greatly superior to those of all other animals, although inferior to humans in mental capacity and development (Hoebel and Weaver, 1979).

Hominids: The term *hominid* includes modern humans (*Homo sapiens*) and any earlier, now extinct, creatures who had characteristics similar to *Homo sapiens*.

DISTINCTIVE CHARACTER- ISTICS OF PRIMATES

Any one of the following traits might be found in nonprimates. However, only primates have *all* of these traits. These traits are least developed in the prosimians. The traits are progressively more developed as one's investigation moves on to monkeys to apes to hominids.

Hands and feet: There are five digits with flat nails on the top rather than claws. Most primates have opposable thumbs. Only humans do not have opposable big toes. The hands have strong grasping ability. This is also true of feet except in humans. Each digit has a soft, tactile pad on the underside of fingers and toes. With excellent sensory nerves, primates are able better to feel and to manipulate things.

Flattened face: There is no protruding snout and the jaw is small. The sense of smell is not as developed as in many other creatures.

Vision: Eyes are located in the front of the head instead of back and toward the sides. This allows the focusing of both eyes on an object at the same time, resulting in depth perception and more acute sight (stereoscopic vision). The higher primates also have color vision.

Brain: The brain is larger in proportion to body weight than in other mammals. It is more developed. The cerebral cortex is especially more developed. This allows for memory, perception, and, or course, learning.

Reproduction: Unlike other creatures, there is no mating season for most primates. Instead, mating and reproduction occur throughout the year. Females are fertile from time to time during the year and most ovulate about once every four weeks. Most primate females have two mammary glands. The uterus is constructed to hold a single fetus, and multiple births occur infrequently. "This reproductive system can be seen as emphasizing quality over quantity . . ." (Ember and Ember, 1977). Primate males have a pendulous penis that is not connected to the abdomen by skin, as is the case for most other animals.

Maturation period: Young primates are dependent on nurturing for a relatively long time. During this period of dependency on adults, much behavior is learned as it is passed on from the old to the young. For primates, much of behavior must be learned and is not governed by automatic instincts. Consequently, primates are very social creatures.

A prevailing theory is that gorillas and chimpanzees are the primates most similar to humans. For example, biochemical research indicates that hemoglobin and chromosomes of gorillas and chimps are very similar to those of humans. In fact, their hemoglobin and chromosomes are more like those of humans than like those of any other creatures.

The human, as the most highly developed primate, possesses many of the above characteristics in their most clearly distinguishable forms. This means that we have the largest and most complex brain, eyes set fully forward in completely enclosed sockets with the back walls of the orbit fully formed, the smallest jaw relative to the braincase, the most reduced snout, and the most upright posture of all primates.

(Hoebel and Weaver, 1979)

SOCIAL CHARACTERISTICS OF PRIMATES

With differences from species to species, primates *are* social creatures. Group life is necessary for the survival of most primates. Let us describe some of the more obvious social characteristics of primates.

Status and Hierarchy

Social systems of primates are not all alike. Some species consist of groupings with somewhat equal status. Others have strict dominance hierarchies. In dominance hierarchies, each individual has a ranking in reference to the other group members. Dominance has to do with one individual having more or less power in reference to the others. Males are usually dominant over females. Adults are dominant over the young. Older males are usually dominant over younger males. If the dominance hierarchy is clearly visible in the group, there may be one dominant male who is the group leader (Johnston and Selby, 1978). Such hierarchies seem "to reduce aggression somewhat by regulating which member [eats] first, or which male [mates] first with a female" (Ember and Ember, 1977).

At one time, scientists believed that primate societies were held together by a dominance hierarchy that was maintained by fighting. We now know that this isn't so. Dominance is species-specific. Where it exists, it is not maintained by fighting but is a feature implicitly recognized by the animals themselves and maintained by a set of subtle social mechanisms.

(Johnston and Selby, 1978).

Mother–Infant Bond

In primate societies, the mother–infant bond is one of the more significant social ties. The bond is based on the physical dependency of the young primate. Newborn primates are not left in nests at birth. Instead, the newborn accompanies its mother. Many studies indicate that this bond is intense, enduring, and actually necessary for the normal development of the young (Johnston and Selby, 1978). Anthropologist Thelma Rowell investigated the nature of the mother–infant bond among baboons:

In the course of some experiments she was doing with caged groups of baboons, she removed mothers from their infants when they were about six months old. The infants remained in their groups and were cared for by other females while their mothers were caged separately out of sight and hearing. Over half a year later the mothers were returned to their groups. As each mother was carried into sight of the cage, her infant, who had not seen her for over half its life, began to give "lost infant" calls and, when each mother was put into the cage, her infant rushed to her arms and their former relationship was resumed.

(Lancaster, 1975)

Anthropologist Jane B. Lancaster suggests that this persistence of the mother–infant bond indicates the existence of a *matrifocal* (mother-centered) core in primate societies (Johnston and Selby, 1978).

Male–Female Bond

In some primate species there is no real bond between males and females in a social sense. Monkeys, for example, mate promiscuously. Among the higher primates, however, males and females do stay together for longer periods of time. The attraction is said to be more than a sexual one. Among the apes called *gibbons*, the male–female bond is especially strong. Along with their offspring, the male and female gibbon will maintain a family-like grouping for over a year. Still, Johnston and Selby (1978) say that we cannot call this an actual family. Too many types of social interactions typical of family do not occur. For example, the adult male and female feed alone, without sharing food with each other.

Role Expections by Age

In primate societies, individuals of different ages are expected to play different roles. Since the young require a prolonged period for maturation, they are sheltered and protected. In such an environment, they are expected to learn adult roles through observation and experience. This is accomplished through play. Referring to the importance of play to young primates, anthropologists say that

Play provides practice for physical skills which are necessary or useful in adulthood. For example, young monkeys racing through the trees at top speed are gaining coordination which may save their lives if they are chased by predators later on. Play is also a way of learning social skills and social relationships. The experience gained in play seems very important in developing the ability to interact and communicate with other members of the group. Also, some dominance relationships seem to be partly established through the rough-and-tumble kind of game older juveniles play, where winning depends upon such factors as size, strength, and agility.

(Ember and Ember, 1977).

Role Expectations by Sex

How much social roles are based on gender varies from species to species. All primates show differences of role behavior based on sex other than simply the female taking the mother role. Some groups are characterized by the males remaining apart from the young. In such cases the expectation for the male is especially that of protector of the group. In other groups females join the males in protecting the group against predators. The greater the difference in bodily characteristics between the two sexes, the more distinctly different are their roles (Johnston and Selby, 1978).

HUMANS AS THE MOST HIGHLY DEVELOPED PRIMATE

Humans are unique among the primates for a number of reasons. For example, other primates, such as chimps, can stand upright and walk for short distances on two legs. Only humans walk erect on two feet as their normal way to move about. This leaves the upper limbs free for carrying and manipulating objects. Humans are able to do this because of the makeup of the human spinal column, pelvis, lower limbs, and feet. Among the primates, human thumbs are of greater length, stronger, and more flexible. Still, it is human behavioral abilities that rank them as the most highly developed primate.

Contrasted with other primates, much more of human behavior is learned and results from cultural patterns. Let us consider a few human behavioral abilities as discussed by Professor Monica E. Yost in an interview with the authors of this book (Yost, 1981).

Use of Tools

Humans make much greater use of and are far more dependent upon tools than any other creatures. Some primates, such as chimpanzees, are known to make and use a few simple tools. But humans have created many tools, and the tools are far more complex than any found in use by other primates. Indeed, human survival has come to depend upon the human use of tools. Humans are unique in that they have made tools whose only function is to make other tools!

Division of Labor and Sharing

Chimps in the wild have been observed sharing meat. However, eating of meat is a special menu that occurs only occasionally. Their principal foods are fruit and vegetation which each chimp gets on its own. "All nonhuman . . . primates subsist on leaves, shoots, berries, and possibly insects. Chimpanzees occasionally kill and eat the meat of young monkeys and antelopes, but the human is the only modern primate who is a habitual meat eater and hunter of large game" (Hoebel and Weaver, 1979). Of the primates, only humans regularly organize their food-

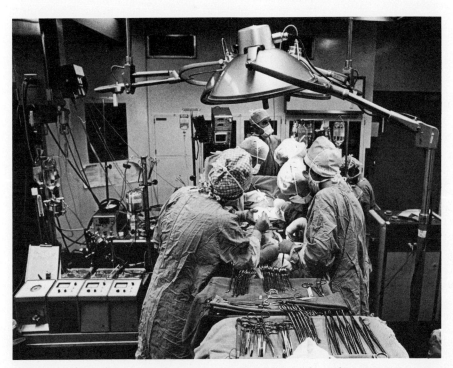

Humans use tools that are much more complex than tools used by other primates.

getting into patterns of cooperation that involve a division of labor and sharing. Among other primates, every adult individual is on its own in finding food. Human groups divide up the food-getting tasks. Some might gather plant foods, some might hunt, and others fish. For all such food producers, the objective is to obtain the food and then to return to the home-base and share it. The division of labor among humans has been by sex and age. Of course, technologically advanced societies have used other forms of labor division.

Use of Language

Only humans have created their own communication system consisting of symbols. Symbols are sounds or visual markings that are chosen and used by humans to represent phenomena about which they want to communicate. The use of symbols is learned by humans. Words and numbers are important symbols in the human experience. Word symbols can be used and understood in social interaction even when the *referent* (the object to which a symbol refers) is not immediately present or is abstract. Only humans are capable of abstract thought and symbol communication. Anthropologist Leslie White has said, "All culture (civilization) depends upon the symbol. It was the exercise of the symbolic faculty which brought culture into existence and it is the use of symbols that makes the perpetuation of culture possible" (White, 1949).

Research on the communication systems of other primates concludes that their communication does not use symbols. For them, the same sounds are always used for the same referent, and the referent must be present when the communication occurs. There have been experiments on teaching chimps and gorillas to use symbols to communicate. Even *if* these particular apes are really using symbols effectively, there is no evidence that any nonhuman primates use a language of symbols in their natural environment. In other words, any symbol manipulation done by particular apes has been the result of intensive teaching and conditioning of the apes by human beings. In such cases, the apes have learned far fewer symbols than a human child learns without the deliberate, systematic teaching given the apes.

It is the human's advanced ability to use language that has made the development of cultures possible. Language allows humans to share information about how to survive. Language also permits humans to reflect upon their experiences, to find meaning in their experiences, and to share those meanings with other human beings. Language can be thought of as both utility and poetry in the human experience.

NATURE VERSUS NURTURE ... AGAIN

Our readers may wonder why we have discussed the relationship of humans to other primates—animals—in this section. Throughout this book we have played down the significance of genetic inheritance. We have emphasized the significance of environment and socialization. Sociologists have always emphasized human nurture, not human nature. Nevertheless, the old nature versus nurture debate has come to the fore once again. Arguments favoring the great significance of heredity have been made by a new discipline called *sociobiology*. Sociobiology is the study of the *biological basis* of social behavior in all forms of life, including humankind. So you see, the similarities and differences between humans and other forms of life are again being examined. The subject for the next section of this chapter is the new discipline of sociobiology.

KEY TERMS FROM SECTION 34

mammals	matrifocal
primates	male–female bond
living offspring	roles based on age and sex
primates that most resemble humans	use of tools
primate reproduction	division of labor and sharing
primate maturation period	use of symbols
social characteristics of primates	referent
status and hierarchy	abstract thought
mother–infant bond	

STUDY GUIDE FOR SECTION 34

1. Primates are mammals. They include humans and animals that most closely resemble humans. NAME THREE GENERAL TYPES OF PRIMATES THAT MOST RESEMBLE HUMANS.

2. Distinctive characteristics of primates exist in the reference to hands and feet, faces, vision, brains, reproduction behavior, maturation time. WHAT IS TYPICAL OF PRIMATES IN REFERENCE TO EACH OF THESE VARIABLES?

3. There are some rather obvious social characteristics of primates. DESCRIBE HOW DOMINANCE HIERARCHIES OPERATE AMONG MANY PRIMATES.

4. DESCRIBE THE MOTHER–INFANT BOND AMONG PRIMATES.

5. DESCRIBE THE MALE–FEMALE BOND AMONG PRIMATES.

6. Among primates there are certain role expectations based on age. EXPLAIN WHY PLAYING IS SO IMPORTANT IN THE MATURATION OF YOUNG PRIMATES.

7. IN WHAT WAYS MIGHT ROLE EXPECTATIONS BASED ON GENDER INFLUENCE PRIMATE BEHAVIOR?

8. Humans are unique among the primates for a number of reasons. IDENTIFY AND DESCRIBE THE IMPORTANCE OF THREE HUMAN ABILITIES THAT

CAUSE US TO IDENTIFY HUMANS AS THE MOST HIGHLY DEVELOPED OF THE PRIMATES.

PRACTICE TEST FOR SECTION 34

Select the best answer.

1. The theory of organic evolution contends that life appeared on Earth
A. Several million years ago.
B. Several thousand years ago.
C. With the emergence of *Homo sapiens*.
D. Several billion years ago.

2. Much of adult mammal behavior is
A. Instinctive.
B. Learned.
C. Genetically determined.
D. Biologically determined.

3. Which of the following terms includes *Homo sapiens* and any earlier, now extinct creatures who had characteristics similar to *Homo sapiens*?
A. Hominids.
B. Prosimians.
C. Mammals.
D. Apes.

4. Which of the following is *not* a distinctive characteristic of primates?
A. Prolonged period of dependency.
B. Stereoscopic vision.
C. Sensory nerves.
D. A relatively short mating season.

5. The primates most similar to humans are
A. Gorillas and chimpanzees.
B. Prosimians.
C. Monkeys.
D. Gibbons and orangutans.

6. Which of the following is *not* a social characteristic of primates?
A. Instinctual behavioral patterns.
B. Status and hierarchy.

C. Mother–infant bond.
D. Male–female bonds.

7. Which of the following is *incorrect* regarding hierarchies?
A. Older males dominate younger males.
B. Males dominate females.
C. Adults dominate the young.
D. Females dominate males.

8. In primate societies, the mother–infant bond is
A. Matrilineal.
B. Patrifocal.
C. Bilineal.
D. Matrifocal.

9. The greater the difference in bodily characteristics between the sexes, the
A. More similar the roles.
B. More different the roles.
C. There is no relationship between bodily characteristics and sex role behavior.

10. In which way are humans unique among primates?
A. The existence of a maturation period.
B. Role expectations by age and sex.
C. Humans make tools to make other tools.
D. Humans have status and hierarchy.

11. Humans are unique among primates in that they
A. Possess language.
B. Use tools.
C. Have a hierarchy of status.

12. Humans are unique among primates in their ability to
A. Communicate.
B. Reproduce.
C. Grasp objects.
D. Think abstractly.

13. According to anthropologist Leslie White, all cultures depend upon
A. A division of labor.
B. Dominance hierarchies.

C. Symbolic communication.
D. Procreation and the rearing of offspring.

14. The study of the biological basis of social behavior is
A. Physical anthropology.
B. Sociobiology.
C. Cultural anthropology.
D. Physiological psychology.

Answer Key

1.	D	**6.**	A	**11.**	A
2.	B	**7.**	D	**12.**	D
3.	A	**8.**	D	**13.**	C
4.	D	**9.**	B	**14.**	B
5.	A	**10.**	C		

SECTION 35   SOCIOBIOLOGY
- GENERAL BELIEFS OF SOCIOBIOLOGY
- SPECIFIC VIEWS OF SOCIOBIOLOGY
- FURTHER REMARKS ON SOCIOBIOLOGY
- THE SOCIOBIOLOGY DEBATE

Objectives
After completing this section, the student should be able to:
1.   Define the term *sociobiology*.
2.   Explain the difference between instincts and genetic predispositions.
3.   Describe the sociobiological views on human aggression, love, altruism, homosexuality, and ideology.
4.   Cite criticisms made and concerns expressed in reference to sociobiology.

Which behavior a particular human being displays depends on the experience received within his [or her] own culture, but the total array of human possibilities, as opposed to baboon or termite possibilities, is inherited. It is the evolution of this pattern which sociobiology attempts to analyze.

(Edward O. Wilson, 1975)

Throughout this book we have emphasized the fact that humans think, feel, and behave as they do because of their cultures. We have noted that there are similarities between other primates and humans. But most of all we have emphasized the differences. The sociological perspective assumes that almost all human behavior is learned. The behavior of animals is, sociologists believe, mostly genetically inherited.

There is a great interest today in animal behavior and especially in relationships between animal and human behavior. A number of writers have addressed themselves to this subject in recent years. Robert Ardrey, a successful playwright, began to write about animal origins and the nature of humans over 20 years ago. His views fit into the sociobiology school. Readers interested in a popular treatment of the subject should read Ardrey's *African Genesis* (1961), *The Territorial Imperative* (1966), and *The Social Contract* (1970). Another book intended for a general audience is that of Desmond Morris, entitled *The Naked Ape* (1967). Three books by Konrad Lorenz would also be of interest. Lorenz wrote *On Aggression* (1963), *Evolution and Modification of Behavior* (1965), and *The Year of the Greylag Goose* (1979). All these writers claim that much social behavior is determined by genetically inherited characteristics.

GENERAL BELIEFS OF SOCIOBIOLOGY

The new discipline of sociobiology appeared as a challenge to historical social scientific thinking in 1975. In that year, Edward O. Wilson's *Sociobiology: The New Synthesis* was published. Wilson's book examined animal behavior. He wrote that behaviors such as aggression, altruism, dominance, parental care, and monogamy and polygamy were the result of genetically based evolutionary processes. In the final chapter Wilson suggested that biological principles applying to animals could also be useful in studying the social behavior of human beings (Wilson, 1975). This created quite a debate in the academic world. In 1978, Wilson's next book on sociobiology, entitled *On Human Nature*, was published. In this book Wilson emphasized the influence that genetic inheritance has on human behavior. Wilson wrote, "The question of interest is no longer whether human social behavior is genetically determined; it is to what extent" (Wilson, 1978).

Sociobiology is the study of the biological basis for the behavior of all forms of life, including humankind. This new discipline has not been well received by most social scientists. A debate continues. The debate is between those who emphasize the influence of nature versus those who emphasize the importance of nurture in the human experience. Genes can be described as units of heredity that determine the characteristics living things inherit from their parents. The belief of sociobiologists is that genes act as a leash on the social behavior of all creatures, including humans. Carried to its extreme, this view suggests that genes

Four generations in one family.

are the only units that fully control their own destiny. All larger forms of life, including insects, animals, and humans, are merely "throwaway survival machines" that the selfish genes use to ensure their own survival (Dawkins, 1976).

Edward O. Wilson says that the human brain exists only to promote the survival of human genes. In his view, human intellect has not developed in order to understand the mysteries of galaxies or of atoms or even of the human experience. Again, "the brain exists because it promotes the survival and multiplication of the genes that direct its assembly" (Wilson, 1978). We exist attached on the leash of our genes, the basic units of humankind. The genes can be said to program human behavior so that the genes can continue to exist on into the future.

Anyone, Wilson says, who reflects upon his or her experiences in life realizes that one is guided through a more or less fixed order of life stages. Wilson says that people sense "that with all the drive, wit, love, pride, anger, hope, and anxiety that characterize the species," in the end they can be sure only of helping to perpetuate the same cycle in the future of humankind (Wilson, 1978). We all share the human experience. Without asking, we are born children of parents. Most of us become parents. We live out our days in the social settings of the human experience. Generation after generation humankind has lived on the wheel of life. Now the sociobiologists contend that we do as we do because of genetic predispositions. It is a thought-provoking point of view.

SPECIFIC VIEWS OF SOCIOBIOLOGY

As we have indicated, sociobiologists believe that human behavior is shaped by inherited genetic controls in addition to cultural conditioning. Aggression, sex roles, and even ethical behavior are said to be shaped not only by culture but also by inherited genetic controls. Sociobiology attempts to combine the study of sociology and biology. It attempts to trace the biological basis of social behavior among animals and humans. Human behavior is said to be genetically based after millions of years of evolution.

Boyce Rensberger, writing in the *New York Times*, said that there has been a common misinterpretation of sociobiology. He contends that sociobiology does not suggest that human behavior is controlled by the same genes that control animal behavior, nor does it suggest that all human behavior is determined by genes. Instead, sociobiologists believe that *some* human behaviors are influenced by genes. It is believed that these genes evolved under similar pressures of natural selection that shaped both humans and animals.

Sociobiologists emphasize that human behavior is uniquely human, although it may share some features of other mammals. There is a wide variety of human social arrangements. But sociobiologists believe that they all are limited or confined to human distinctiveness. Genes shared throughout a species define and restrict behaviors. Some of the views of sociobiologists as presented by Edward O. Wilson in *On Human Nature* follow. Some of what follows we have paraphrased from the excellent summaries of these views by Boyce Rensberger (1978).

On Aggression

Humans do not seem to be instinctively aggressive in all circumstances. However, humans are genetically predisposed to experience a consciousness of kind and consciousness of difference. People categorize others as friends or aliens. When threatened by those considered alien, people respond with unreasoning hatred or violence.

On Men and Women

Men and women are born with predispositions to somewhat different temperaments. This permits them to participate in certain sex role specializations. Also, women are generally physically smaller and weaker than men. Sociobiologists do not say that these genetically controlled factors necessarily make men dominate women. Still, "cultural evolution in industrialized societies has exaggerated the expression of genetic factors into situations of extreme male dominance over females."

On Sex and Love

Sociobiologists say that the main biological purpose of sex among humans is *not* reproduction. Instead, it is love. Love serves to keep the parents together for the time it takes to raise children well. Continuous sexual attraction builds a mutual commitment and creates a bond between the couple. Wilson believes that love and sex are biologically linked.

On Altruistic Behavior

Altruism means putting the welfare of others above one's own. The tendency to make personal sacrifices for the good of others—even to give one's life—does not arise from some noble or divine motivation. Instead, sociobiologists say, altruism has been found to be genetically controlled among animals. At first, it might seem that the sacrifice of one's life would *eliminate* genes for altruism from a species and not favor that species' natural selection. But that is not the case. If the sacrifice is for one's close kin, who share many of the same genes, the chances of survival are actually improved. Genes *like* those of the altruist will more likely survive than had there been no sacrifice. Consider the following example:

. . . *When a bird gives up its life to alert the flock to danger, the bird is ensuring the survival of the other birds, some of whom are its relatives and therefore have some of the same genes it has. Over the course of evolution, birds who squawk when in danger (thereby alerting others) will survive better than those who don't. What appears to be heroism in the bird's actions sociobiologists attribute to the effect of mathematical chance over millions of years.*

(Federico, 1979)

Edward O. Wilson believes that human altruism is in some way related to bio-logical tendencies. These tendencies, he believes, have been developed through cultural evolution into broad, ethical guides for human social behavior. (In Section 36 we discuss the concept of altruism from the viewpoints of two other scholars.)

On Homosexuality

Wilson suggests that the genes that may predispose one to become homosexual under certain environmental conditions are linked to genes for altruism. Homo-sexuality might be a biologically influenced way of allowing individuals freed of family obligations better to serve society at large. Wilson writes:

How can genes predisposing their carriers toward homosexuality spread through the population if homosexuals have no children? One answer is that their close relatives could have had more children as a result of their presence. The homosexual members of primitive societies could have helped members of the same sex, either while hunting and gathering or in more domestic occupations at the dwelling sites. Freed from the special obligations of parental duties, they would have been in a position to operate with special efficiency in assisting close relatives. . . . If the relatives . . . were benefitted by higher survival and reproduction rates, the genes these individuals shared with the homosexual specialists would have increased. . . . Thus it is possible for homosexual genes to proliferate . . . , even if the homosexuals themselves do not have children.

(Wilson, 1978)

On Ideology, Sacred or Secular

Every society's culture includes the component of ideology (discussed in Section 7). A society's ideology justifies why people behave as they do. Wilson believes that whether sacred or secular, these bodies of beliefs are an expression of an in-born mechanism. Individuals are moved to subordinate their immediate self-interests to the interests of the group. Somehow, biologically, people are predis-posed to participate in group beliefs and rituals. They are bound together in unquestioning allegiance to the group. "To the extent that this group allegiance improves a person's chances of survival and procreation, the genetic propensity for [ideological] adherence will be propagated in the species" (Rensberger, 1978).

FURTHER REMARKS ON SOCIOBIOLOGY

In none of the views of sociobiology cited above does Wilson suggest that there are specific genes for aggression, sex roles, experiencing love and sex, altruism, homosexuality, or ideological dedication. Instead, he says that "Human genes . . . program the functioning of the nervous, sensory, and hormonal systems of the body, and thereby almost certainly influence the learning process" (Wilson, 1978). It should also be kept in mind that Wilson admits that much human behavior is the result of cultural conditioning. But the foremost sociobiological view of Wilson and others is that most human behavior also has strong genetic components.

THE SOCIOBIOLOGY DEBATE

Many criticisms have been made of the views of Wilson and of other sociobiologists. Opponents say that there is little evidence to support such views. Such critics believe that there is scientific evidence that genes might influence animal behavior, but applying this evidence to humans is, they say, not methodologically possible. Opponents to sociobiology are convinced that sociobiologists fail to consider the impact of cultural influences on human behavior. How, they ask, can the claims of sociobiology be proved? How can it be proved that human behavior is genetically based? Ashley Montagu has written that sociobiologists tend to write as if genes play a major role in determining human social behavior. Then he says, "I think there can be not the slightest doubt that a good deal of human social behavior has a genetic basis, but that it is a very different thing from claiming that such behavior is genetically determined" (Montagu, 1980). Other critics have expressed concern that sociobiology endorses the acceptance of the idea of genetically inferior and superior subdivisions of human beings. Still others have seen sociobiology as sexist in its orientation.

One sociologist has written that it cannot be concluded that one view is right and another view is wrong in the sociobiological debate. Reasonable conclusions cannot be drawn in such a limited discussion. The nature–nurture debate over the origins of human behavior continues. It can still arouse quite a bit of emotion, and it will probably continue to be a source of contention for a long time to come (Federico, 1979). We can only agree with Gerhard Lenski when he says that

What is needed is not a life-death struggle between sociology and sociobiology, but two disciplines that can begin to communicate and cooperate with one another and develop more sophisticated models of human societies and individual behavior than either alone can create.

(Lenski, 1977)

KEY TERMS AND NAMES FROM SECTION 35

sociobiology

aggression

altruism

dominance

genes

genetic predispositions

men, women, love, and sex

altruistic behavior: animal and human

genes and homosexuality

genes and ideology

criticisms of sociobiology

Robert Ardrey

Desmond Morris

Konrad Lorenz

Edward O. Wilson

Ashley Montagu

STUDY GUIDE FOR SECTION 35

1. At the present time there is a debate about the value of sociobiology. BRIEFLY DEFINE THE TERM *SOCIOBIOLOGY*.

2. In reference to human aggression, WHAT DOES WILSON SAY ABOUT INSTINCTS AND GENETIC PREDISPOSITIONS?

3. WHAT DO SOCIOBIOLOGISTS SAY ABOUT MEN AND WOMEN AND GENETIC INFLUENCES?

4. Sociobiologists say that reproduction is not the main biological purpose of sex among humans. WHAT IS, AND WHY, ACCORDING TO SOCIOBIOLOGY?

5. Altruism means putting the welfare of others above one's own. EXPLAIN THE SOCIOBIOLOGICAL GENETIC INTERPRETATION OF REASONS FOR ALTRUISTIC BEHAVIOR AMONG ANIMALS AND HUMANS.

6. Wilson suggests that genes may predispose one to become homosexual. HOW CAN GENES PREDISPOSING PEOPLE TOWARD HOMOSEXUALITY CONTINUE TO EXIST IF HOMOSEXUALS HAVE NO CHILDREN?

7. According to sociobiology, HOW DOES IDEOLOGY RELATE TO GENETIC PREDISPOSITIONS?

8. According to Edward O. Wilson, WHY DOES THE HUMAN INTELLECT EXIST?

9. Criticisms have been made of the views of Wilson and other sociobiologists. WHAT ARE SOME OF THESE CRITICISMS AND CONCERNS IN REFERENCE TO SOCIOBIOLOGY?

10. The nature–nurture debate continues. WHAT DOES GERHARD LENSKI SAY IS NEEDED IN REFERENCE TO THIS DEBATE?

PRACTICE TEST FOR SECTION 35

Select the best answer.

1. The discipline of sociobiology appeared as a challenge to
A. The biological basis of human behavior.
B. Social scientific thinking.
C. The biological basis of animal behavior.
D. Structural functionalism.

2. The study of the biological basis of human behavior is
A. Physiological sociology.
B. Biosociology.
C. Physiobiology.
D. Sociobiology.

3. The sociobiology debate centers on the respective roles of
A. Nature and nurture.
B. Genes and hormones.
C. Socialization and the environment.
D. Genes and behavior.

4. Units of heredity that determine the characteristics living things inherit from the parents are known as
A. Instincts.
B. Hormones.
C. Genes.
D. Drives.

5. According to Wilson, the function of the human brain is to

A. Promote the survival of human genes.

B. Define and act in reference to reality.

C. Insure the survival of the individual.

D. Enable abstract thought.

6. According to sociobiology, aggression, sex roles, and ethical behavior are said to be shaped by

A. Cultural conditioning.

B. Inherited genetic controls.

C. Both cultural conditioning and inherited genetic controls.

D. Society.

7. Sociobiology suggests that

A. All human behavior is influenced by genes.

B. All human behavior is determined by genes.

C. Some human behavior is determined by genes.

D. All human behavior is learned.

8. Sociobiologists believe that the main purpose of human sex is

A. Procreation.

B. Love.

C. To serve the pleasure principle.

D. Reproduction.

Answer Key

1. B
2. D
3. A
4. C
5. A
6. C
7. A
8. B

SECTION 36   THE OPTIMUM HUMAN CONDITION

- WHAT IS THE OPTIMUM HUMAN CONDITION?
- HUMANISTIC COMMUNITARIANISM: VIEWS OF ERICH FROMM
- OBJECTIVISM: PHILOSOPHY OF AYN RAND
- HUMAN BEHAVIORAL ENGINEERING: VIEWS OF B. F. SKINNER
- IN CONCLUSION: ONE WORLD AT A TIME

Objectives

After completing this section, the student should be able to:

1. Describe the philosophy and conditions that would prevail if Erich Fromm's humanistic communitarianism were achieved.
2. Explain Ayn Rand's reasons for rejecting humanistic communitarianism and describe her own philosophy of Objectivism.
3. Describe B. F. Skinner's philosophy of human behavioral engineering.
4. Speculate on the possibility of an optimum human condition and express his or her own views on how it might be achieved.

To see a world in a grain of sand
And build a Heaven in a wild flower
Hold Infinity in the palm of your hand
And Eternity in an hour
           (William Blake, 1757–1827)

WHAT IS THE OPTIMUM HUMAN CONDITION?

Stated simply, the word *optimum* means best. An optimum condition for anything is the best condition. On this planet there are many forms of life, from algae to zebra. For each life form there must be an optimum condition in which the form of life can flourish and fulfill itself. An optimum condition would include the most favorable conditions for the growth and reproduction of an organism.

Recall that Auguste Comte, in the 19th century, sought to establish a science of society that he called sociology. He believed that using the scientific method to study society would lead to the improvement of the human condition. Many people before and since Comte have sought to improve the quality of the human experience. In its quest for knowledge, the human race has searched for conditions that could provide both collective and individual fulfillment for human-

What is the optimum human condition?

kind. Seeking to improve the human condition has been a difficult and, at times, a divisive task. There have been and there are now many conflicting views on what is best for individual human beings and for the species in general. Still, it would seem that each social movement, whether it is political, religious, or scientific, has been dedicated to *its* concept of an optimum human condition. It would seem that most oracles, prophets, and geniuses throughout human history have been dedicated to the concept of an optimum human condition.

What *is* the optimum human condition? First, it is merely an idea. Second, we do not know *what* it is, beyond being an idea. Adrift among the suggestive pinpoints of energetic light dotting the quiet darkness of the universe, the *Homo sapiens* of planet Earth have had their children, fought their battles, and observed the various rites of passage from birth to death. With those who came before us and with those who shall come after us, we share the persistent human predicament. We are imprisoned within time and space and the tribe. We are imprisoned within our single savage selves. As Carl Sandburg put it, "In the darkness with a bundle of grief the people march. In the night, and overhead a shovel of stars for keeps, the people march: Where to? What next?" (Sandburg, 1950).

Now, in the late 20th century, there are debates all around us about matters pertaining to the human experience. Such debates address themselves to the possibility of an optimum human condition. Let us cite some examples of debates that are related to the search for an optimum human condition. Some say that humankind is the highest form of life on Earth. Others have suggested that the human race is little more than a dangerous virus that threatens to destroy the planet's ecosphere. Some say that we should return to a more simple life, close to the soil, in rhythm with the seasons, out in the air *under* the stars. Others say that human destiny lies not under the stars but in the vast reaches of the universe *among* the stars. Some say that the people should judge. Others say that the people should be subjected to enlightened guidance. The view that each person should seek personal salvation and individual fulfillment conflicts with the view that concern for others and collective fulfillment must come first. Some say that the optimum human condition is related to the condition of one's spiritual development. Others say that there is a relationship between the optimum human condition and an optimum population of humans within the Earth's ecosphere. Culture relativists describe right and wrong as matters related to specific cultures. The ethical absolutists say that right and wrong are as constant as the Northern Star. Some say that the human race is fettered by too many social restrictions. Others contend that people need more restrictions and prescribed restraints. Capitalism vies with socialism. Transcendentalism vies with existentialism. Where to? What next?

Recall that in Chapter 1 we wrote about the "microworld" and the "macroworld." The microworld consists of an individual's immediate experiences. The macroworld consists of the larger and more impersonal world of an individual's life. C. Wright Mills suggested that people must confront both personal troubles within the microworld and public issues within the macroworld. To resolve personal troubles, Mills said, we must concentrate on our individual selves. To resolve public issues, we must concentrate on the social structure in which we are located. Keeping this in mind, if there *is* an optimum human condition, where do we turn and what do we do to approach it? At this time in history there is no consensus among the world's intelligentsia. Shall we look into our single savage selves, or shall we look beyond ourselves into society for the optimum human condition?

We have selected three views that we believe are related to what we have called the search for the optimum human condition. Our treatment of these views is limited by space, but we hope that what is presented in the following passages might motivate students to investigate further the stimulating and provocative ideas of some of our more articulate and concerned contemporaries.

HUMANISTIC COMMUNITAR-IANISM: VIEWS OF ERICH FROMM

Erich Fromm rejects the assumptions of cultural relativists who would say that each society is normal if it functions to meet the recurring needs of its people. Without using the phrase "optimum human condition," Fromm's views certainly imply such a condition when he speaks of a "sane society" and of "normative humanism." Fromm has said that the concept of normative humanism is based on the assumption that there are right and wrong ways for people to live. He says that there are satisfactory and unsatisfactory solutions to the problems of the human experience. There is a "human nature" according to Fromm, and the nature of human beings requires them to "consult together and plan together" (Fromm, 1955). Like C. Wright Mills, Fromm says that the most important factor in developing an individual is the structure and values of the society in which one participates. Fromm contends that people can develop their human potential only in cooperation with others. Fromm has said that there is a human nature that must be fulfilled. He says that a society's goals should become identical with what is good for humankind. To Fromm, each person represents humanity. Although we may be different in intelligence, health, or talents, we are all one. As Fromm has said, "We are all saints and sinners, adults and children, and no one is anybody's superior or judge. We have all been awakened with the Buddha, we have all been crucified with Christ, and we have all killed and robbed with Genghis Khan, Stalin, and Hitler" (Fromm, 1962). Fromm's version of the optimum human condition is called *humanistic communitarianism*. This is the belief that all humans can share in sentiments, causes, and behaviors that uplift the human race and each individual. We must, Fromm has said, establish a society of humans in which loyalty to the human race is considered the most important loyalty that exists (Fromm, 1950). We must see ourselves as citizens of Earth, not of any one particular grouping of humanity.

Humanistic communitarianism upholds the principle that any individual has an inalienable right to live. Each human being has, Fromm says, "a right to which no conditions are attached and which implies the right to receive the basic commodities necessary for life, the right to education and to medical care" (Fromm, 1968). Following this principle, each child, woman, and man could be sure of freedom and a sense of community with others (Fromm, 1968). Fromm's dedication to humanistic communitarianism is a commitment to a cooperative search for a better life for all of humankind. We believe that Fromm's view of the "sane society" is one view of what we have called the optimum human condition. Fromm places a heavy emphasis upon altruistic behavior among people.

OBJECTIVISM: PHILOSOPHY OF AYN RAND

It was Auguste Comte who coined the term *altruism*, and it has been Ayn Rand (1905-) who has made a concerted effort to discredit the entire basis for motivating altruistic behavior. Altruism means placing other people before oneself. It means putting the interest of others above one's own. Those who subscribe to altruism believe that there is more satisfaction and self-fulfillment in providing nurture for others than in providing for one's own welfare. Emile Durkheim wrote:

Thus, altruism is not destined to become . . . a sort of agreeable ornament to social life, but it will forever be its fundamental basis. How can we ever really dispense

*with it? Men cannot live together without acknowledging, and consequently, mak-
ing mutual sacrifices, without tying themselves to one another with strong, durable
bonds. . . . Because the individual is not sufficient unto himself, it is from society
that he receives everything necessary to him, as it is for society that he works. . . . In
reality, cooperation . . . has its intrinsic morality.*

(Durkheim, 1933)

The humanistic communitarianism of Erich Fromm includes a strong emphasis
upon altruistic behavior. Ayn Rand deplores altruism. She considers altruism to
be a sentiment that "damns all those who achieve success or enjoyment" (Rand,
1961).

Ayn Rand's philosophy can be seen as yet another attempt to identify factors
that might contribute to an optimum human condition. Her emphasis is upon the
individualistic accomplishments of human beings. Rand says that the idea of social collectivism is dead and that no discussion, cooperation, agreement, or understanding is possible among people who choose the emotionalism of altruistic
communitarianism. In one of her novels, Rand has an architect express his feelings in behalf of individualists and in opposition to altruists:

*Altruism is the doctrine which demands that man live for others and place others
above self.*

*No man can live for another. He cannot share his spirit just as he cannot share
his body. . . .*

*The man who attempts to live for others is a dependent. He is a parasite in mo-
tive and makes parasites of those he serves. The relationship produces nothing but
mutual corruption . . . the man who enslaves himself voluntarily in the name of
love is the basest of creatures. He degrades the dignity of man and he degrades the
conception of love. But this is the essence of altruism.*

*Men have been taught that the highest virtue is not to achieve, but to give. Yet
one cannot give that which has not been created. Creation comes before
distribution — or there will be nothing to distribute.*

(Rand, 1943)

Here, then, is one way to express Rand's philosophy of objectivism. She believes
that the highest human achievement is to be productive and creative — not to be
charitable. Individual creative accomplishments are to be related to what we
have called the optimum human condition, if we consider the human condition
from Rand's point of view. Ayn Rand asserts that there are *objective facts* that
are available to active, reasoning minds of human beings. The objective must be
perceived by the individual acting as a productive, creative creature for no cause
other than the desire to produce and create. Rand's philosophy of objectivism rejects the concept of human rights without individual human effort. She rejects
Fromm's assertion that people have an inalienable right to receive the basic commodities necessary for life, education, and medical care. Addressing herself to
the communitarian view, Ayn Rand writes:

*They proclaim that every man is entitled to exist without labor and, the laws of re-
ality to the contrary notwithstanding, is entitled to receive his "minimum subsist-*

ence"—his food, his clothes, his shelter—with no effort on his part, as his due and his birthright. To receive it—from whom?

(Rand, 1957)

Throughout the writings of Ayn Rand is threaded the belief that a market economy (capitalism) provides human beings with the optimum challenge and opportunity and reward. Rand says that capitalism enables one's success to be based upon the *objective value* of one's work and upon the rationality of others who recognize the value of an individual's accomplishments. We believe that Rand's "objectivism" is another view of what we have been calling the optimum human condition. It is based on the premise that an individual seeking personal fulfillment through productive and creative acts will bring about—as a spinoff—circumstances that will contribute to a generally improved human condition.

HUMAN
BEHAVIORAL
ENGINEERING:
VIEWS OF
B. F. SKINNER

B. F. Skinner (1904-) has been associated with the psychological school of thought known as *behaviorism*. Behaviorism is a scientific effort to explain human behavior in terms of environmental controls. Skinner believes that humans are creatures subjected to environmental determinism (both ecological and social determinism). Skinner has said that a technology of human behavior is well advanced. He believes that knowledge acquired about human behavior will allow us to change the human condition in ways that would bring quick, dramatic, and beneficial results. Skinner does not believe that we should free people from social controls. He does believe that we must "analyze and change the kinds of control to which they are exposed." Skinner believes that a better human condition can result from a *planned* controlling of human behavior (Skinner, 1971). If there is an optimum human condition, Skinner would seek it through scientific planning and social conditioning.

Skinner's ideas have been debated for many years. He has written numerous articles and books that describe and explain what human behavioral engineering is and how it would work. To our readers, we especially recommend Skinner's utopian novel entitled *Walden Two*, first published in 1948. *Walden Two* is about a society in which there is food, clothing, shelter, and medical care for everyone. Each person can choose his or her own work and works only an average of four hours a day. Music and the arts flourish. Personal relationships develop under the most favorable conditions. Adequate education prepares each child for the social and intellectual life that lies ahead. The people are truly happy and self-fulfilled. They are secure, productive, creative, cooperative, and forward-looking human beings.

When the book was published, however, it was greeted with "wrathful violence" (Glass and Staude, 1972). Why? Skinner says that *Walden Two* was condemned because it was a planned society. He says that if the critics of *Walden Two* had come upon such a society in some remote part of the Earth, they would have jumped for joy. They would have hailed such a society as one that might set an example for all to follow. That is, they would have hailed it *if* the society was clearly the result of a "natural" process of cultural evolution. The fault found with *Walden Two* is that it resulted from intelligent planning and social conditioning. This, says Skinner, spoils it all for "the child of the democratic tradition" (Glass and Staude, 1972).

B. F. Skinner says that Henry David Thoreau's *Walden* championed principles that could be applied to the individualistic approach to what we are calling the optimum human condition. In his 1969 preface to *Walden Two*, Skinner says that Thoreau's *Walden* was for one, but "the problems of society call for something more than individualism. Other principles must be added." Skinner then offers the following five principles on which human behavioral engineering should be based (Skinner, 1969).

1. Build a way of life in which people live together without quarreling in a social climate of trust rather than suspicion, of love rather than jealousy, of cooperation rather than competition.

2. Maintain that world with gentle but pervasive ethical sanctions rather than a police or military force.

3. Transmit the culture effectively to new members through expert child care and a powerful educational technology.

4. Reduce compulsive labor to a minimum by arranging the kinds of incentives under which people enjoy working.

5. Regard no practice as immutable. Change and be ready to change again. Accept no eternal verity. Experiment.

Finally, regarding his views, Skinner says that a science of behavior is not yet prepared to solve all of the problems confronting humanity, for the science of human behavior is a science in progress: Its ultimate adequacy cannot be judged at this time. But, as Skinner asserts, "the analysis continues to develop and is in fact much further advanced than its critics usually realize" (Skinner, 1971). We believe that Skinner's proposals to design a culture with the help of a scientific analysis is another example of the human search for an optimum human condition.

IN CONCLUSION: ONE WORLD AT A TIME

We are now in the last quarter of what we call the 20th century. No one knows for sure how it all began. No one knows for sure what has been. We cannot be sure where we have been. We cannot be sure where we are going. We have said that a rage for order motivates the human quest for knowledge. Sociology is a fairly recent effort to add to knowledge about the human experience. In the first chapter of this book we said that sociology asks questions about the desirability of social stability. Sociologists want to know how people can experience social change without also suffering chaos and disasters. Sociologists seek to know what the real relationship is between one individual and that individual's society. The focal point of sociology is human interaction. The sociological perspective assumes that most, if not all, human behavior involves others, either directly or indirectly.

Despite our single savage selves, despite our unique individuation, each of us is inescapably bound to other people. Just as the tree and the forest are related, so are a human and society, biography and history, self and world. Each of us *is* involved in humankind. We believe that humankind can achieve something greater through a better understanding of itself. Perhaps there is an optimum human condition. Perhaps we can discover what it is. Perhaps we can achieve it.

You do what you must—
this world and then the next—
one world at a time . . .
And you take hold of a handle
by one hand or the other
by the better or worse hand
and you never know
maybe till long afterward
which was the better hand. . . .
In the darkness with a bundle of grief the people march.
In the night, and overhead a shovel of stars for keeps,
the people march.
                                            Where to? What next?*

KEY TERMS AND
NAMES FROM
SECTION 36

the optimum human condition	human behavioral engineering
persistent human predicament	behaviorism
microworld	scientifically planned social conditions
macroworld	*Walden Two*
humanistic communitarianism	Auguste Comte
Objectivism	C. Wright Mills
altruism	Erich Fromm
productivity versus charity	Ayn Rand
inalienable rights	B. F. Skinner

*From *The People, Yes,* by Carl Sandburg, copyright © 1936, by Harcourt Brace Jovanovich, Inc., copyright © 1964, by Carl Sandburg. Reprinted by permission of the publishers.

STUDY GUIDE FOR SECTION 36

1. This entire section is devoted to the concept of an optimum human condition. IN YOUR OWN WORDS, EXPLAIN WHAT IS MEANT BY THE PHRASE *OPTIMUM HUMAN CONDITION.*

2. Here, in the last quarter of the 20th century, there are debates about matters relating to the human experience. CITE AT LEAST THREE EXAMPLES OF CONFLICTING VIEWS THAT ARE RELATED TO THE SEARCH FOR AN OPTIMUM HUMAN CONDITION.

3. If there *is* an optimum human condition, there is no consensus among the world's intelligentsia as to how to achieve it. WHAT TWO BROAD QUESTIONS EXIST AS TO WHERE WE SHOULD LOOK FOR THE OPTIMUM HUMAN CONDITION?

4. Erich Fromm rejects the assumptions of cultural relativists. He speaks of a "sane society" and of "normative humanism" saying that there is a "human nature." WHAT IS NORMATIVE HUMANISM BASED ON, AND WHAT IS HUMAN NATURE ACCORDING TO FROMM?

5. Fromm's approach to the optimum human condition seems to be his commitment to what he calls "humanistic communitarianism." WHAT CONDITIONS DOES FROMM SAY WOULD PREVAIL IF HUMANISTIC COMMUNITARIANISM WERE PRACTICED?

6. HOW MUST PEOPLE SEE THEMSELVES AND TO WHAT SHOULD THEIR LOYALTIES BE DIRECTED IF HUMANISTIC COMMUNITARIANISM IS TO BE ACHIEVED?

7. It was Auguste Comte who coined the term *altruism*, and it has been Ayn Rand whose philosophy discredits altruistic behavior. WHAT DOES ALTRUISM MEAN?

8. Ayn Rand deplores altruism, believing that it "damns all those who achieve success or enjoyment" through efforts in their own behalf. WHAT DOES RAND SAY ABOUT COMMUNITARIANISM AND THE IDEA THAT A PERSON SHOULD ATTEMPT TO LIVE FOR OTHERS?

9. HOW DOES AYN RAND ADDRESS HERSELF TO ERICH FROMM'S ASSERTION THAT PEOPLE HAVE AN INALIENABLE RIGHT TO RECEIVE THE BASIC COMMODITIES NECESSARY FOR LIFE, EDUCATION, AND MEDICAL CARE?

10. Ayn Rand believes that a market economy (capitalism) provides people with the optimum challenge and opportunity and reward. UPON WHAT PREMISE DOES SHE BASE THIS VIEW?

11. WHICH VIEWS APPEAL TO YOU MORE—THOSE OF THE HUMANISTIC COMMUNITARIANISM OF FROMM OR THOSE OF THE OBJECTIVISM OF RAND? EXPLAIN WHY.

12 B. F. Skinner is associated with the psychological school of thought called "behaviorism." HOW DOES BEHAVIORISM VIEW HUMAN BEINGS AND THEIR BEHAVIOR?

13. The book *Walden Two* was, in Skinner's words, "greeted with wrathful violence." HOW DOES SKINNER ACCOUNT FOR THE ATTACKS ON *WALDEN TWO*? WHAT CIRCUMSTANCES DOES HE THINK WOULD MAKE A SOCIETY LIKE *WALDEN TWO* MORE ACCEPTABLE TO ITS CRITICS? WHY?

14. Skinner offers five principles on which human behavioral engineering should be based. WHAT IS YOUR REACTION TO THESE PRINCIPLES? DO YOU BELIEVE THAT IT IS POSSIBLE TO ACHIEVE A HUMAN CONDITION REFLECTING THESE PRINCIPLES? EXPLAIN YOUR ANSWER.

PRACTICE TEST FOR SECTION 36

Select the best answer.

1. Which of the following is inconsistent with humanistic communitarianism?
A. People can develop their human potential only through competition with others.
B. The most important factor in the development of the individual is the structure and values of the society in which one participates.
C. People can develop their human potential only through cooperation with others.

2. There is more satisfaction and fulfillment in providing nurture for others than in providing for one's own welfare. This statement is the foundation of
A. Egoism.
B. Objectivism.
C. Altruism.
D. Behavioral engineering.

3. According to the philosophy of objectivism, the highest human achievement is to be
A. Forgiving.
B. Productive.
C. Loving.
D. Charitable.

4. According to Ayn Rand and the philosophy of objectivism
A. A market economy provides human beings with the optimum challenge and the optimum opportunities and rewards.
B. People have an inalienable right to receive the basic commodities necessary to sustain life.
C. Altruistic communitarianism would approximate the optimum human condition.
D. Human rights have precedence over human efforts.

5. According to human behavioral engineering
A. Human beings should be held responsible for what they do and should be justly punished for offenses they commit.
B. A better human condition can result from a planned controlling of human behavior.

6. Which of the following is not a principle of human behavioral engineering?
A. Maintain society with ethical sanctions rather than a police or military force.

B. Transmit the culture through expert child care and a powerful educational technology.
C. Resist change and seek to preserve the status quo.
7. Associated with humanistic communitarianism is
A. Erich Fromm.
B. B. F. Skinner.
C. Ayn Rand.
8. People have an inalienable right to receive the basic necessities for survival. This statement reflects the views of
A. Objectivism.

B. Humanistic communitarianism.
C. Human behavioral engineering.
9. The term *optimum human condition* means
A. The most favorable condition for the growth and maintenance of the human organism.
B. The ideal physical, political, economic, and social conditions that provide individual and collective fulfillment to humankind.
C. Merely an idea.
D. All of the above.

Answer Key

1. A   6. C
2. C   7. A
3. B   8. B
4. A   9. D
5. B

CHAPTER SUMMARY

1. Primates are members of the form of life called mammals. Human beings and animals that most closely resemble humans are primates. More than 200 species of mammals have been classified as primates. Mammals give birth to living offspring. Much of adult mammal behavior is learned, not instinctive. Those primates that most resemble humans are prosimians, monkeys, apes, and hominids.
2. There are distinctive physical characteristics that primates share. They have five digits with flat nails on the hands and feet. Most primates have opposable thumbs. Primates are able better to feel and to manipulate things. The primate sense of smell is not as developed as in many other creatures. Both eyes can focus on an object at the same time. Primates have acute sight, and some have color vision. The brain is larger in proportion to body weight than in other mammals. Mating and reproduction occur throughout the year. Young primates are dependent on a relatively long time of nurturing.
3. Primates are social creatures. Group life is necessary for the survival of most primates. Both status and hierarchy are recognized among primates. Both a mother–infant bond and a male–female bond exist among the higher primates. All primates show differences of role behavior based on age and sex.
4. Humans are the highest developed of the primates. Tools used by humans are far more complex than any found in use by other primates. Only humans organize patterns of cooperation that involve a division of labor and sharing. Only humans seem capable of abstract throught and symbol communication as so-

phisticated as human language. The advanced use of language has made the development of human cultures possible.

5.　Sociobiology is the study of the biological basis for the behavior of all forms of life, including humankind. Sociobiologists believe that genes have some influence on the social behavior of all creatures, including humans. They believe that humans are genetically predisposed to experience of consciousness of kind and consciousness of difference. They believe that men and women are born with genetic predispositions to have different temperaments. According to sociobiologists, human aggression, sex roles, and ethical behavior are shaped both by cultural conditioning and by inherited genetic predispositions.

6.　Critics of sociobiology deny that human behavior is genetically determined. The old nature–nurture debate over the origins of human behavior is renewed. At this time, many criticisms have been made by social scientists of the views of sociobiologists.

7.　An optimum condition for anything is the best condition. The optimum human condition would be circumstances that would provide both individual and collective fulfillment for humankind. There is no consensus on what these circumstances should be.

8.　Erich Fromm's humanistic communitarianism offers the view that people can develop fully only in cooperation with others. Society's goals should be identical with what is best for humankind. Each person represents humanity. People must see themselves as citizens of the Earth, not as any one particular and special grouping of humankind.

9.　Ayn Rand's objectivism discredits the entire basis for altruism. She believes that the highest human fulfillment is achieved through being productive and creative—not being charitable and altruistic. The philosophy of objectivism rejects the concept of human rights without individual human effort.

10.　B. F. Skinner's human behavioral engineering offers the view that a better human condition can result from a planned controlling of human behavior. Skinner believes that a technology of human behavior is already well advanced. Socialization could be accomplished more successfully by means of better planning. He identified five principles on which human behavioral engineering should be based.

SUGGESTIONS FOR FURTHER READING RELATING TO CHAPTER 12

Campbell, Bernard G., editor, *Humankind Emerging*, 2nd ed. (Boston: Little, Brown and Co., 1979). This is a very good introductory textbook on anthropology. The editor says "through the book's eighteen chapters, the reader sees what we know of how, when, and where we came to exist."

Caplan, Arthur L., editor, *The Sociobiology Debate* (New York: Harper & Row, 1978). The editor expresses the hope that these many selections for and against sociobiology will "provide a basis for advancing a rational discussion of sociobiology." This is an excellent source book on the pros and cons.

Fromm, Erich, *The Revolution of Hope: Toward a Humanized Technology* (New York: Harper & Row, 1968). We especially recommend the chapters "Where Are We Now?", "Where Are We Headed?", and "Steps to the Humanization of Technological Society."

Kummer, H., *Primate Societies* (Chicago: Aldine-Atherton, 1971). This work examines the analogies that might be drawn between human and other primate social organizations.

Lancaster, J. B., *Primate Behavior and the Emergence of Human Culture* (New York: Holt, Rinehart and Winston, 1975). This is a brief introduction to human behavior, said to be the result of a long evolutionary history.

Lorenz, Konrad, and Paul Leyhausen, *Motivation of Human and Animal Behavior* (New York: Van Nostrand Reinhold Co., 1973). "The genetic programming within members of the human species must be taken into account and dealt with if human problems are to be solved."—Eckhard H. Hess.

Montagu, Ashley, editor, *Sociobiology Examined* (New York: Oxford University Press, 1980). "In this volume, Ashley Montagu and fifteen independent contributors . . . challenge Wilson's claims about the heredity basis of social behavior." Their conclusion is that sociobiology's views are scientifically unsound. All cons and no pros.

Skinner, B. F., *About Behaviorism* (New York: Alfred A. Knopf, 1974). This is an easily understood book in which Skinner defines, analyzes, and eloquently defends his philosophy.

Toffler, Alvin, *Future Shock* (New York: Random House, 1970). Future shock is what happens to people overwhelmed by change. The book discusses new subcultures, life-styles, and human relationships—all of which continue to be in transition.

Toffler, Alvin, *The Third Wave* (New York: Wm. Morrow, 1980). Toffler describes a new "demassified" society of the near future in which each individual will have significant control over his or her own destiny. The book presents what might be thought to be Toffler's conception of the optimum human condition.

REFERENCES

Aiken, Michael, et al. (1968) *Economic Failure, Alienation, and Extremism*. Ann Arbor: University of Michigan Press. Cited in Neubeck, 1979.

Allport, Gordon (1958) *The Nature of Prejudice*. New York: Doubleday.

Anderson, Charles H. (1971) *Toward a New Sociology*. Homewood, Ill.: Dorsey.

Anderson, Maxwell, and Weill, Kurt. Lyrics from the composition "Lost in the Stars." Copyright 1946 by Chappell and Co., Inc. Copyright renewed. Used by permission of Chappell and Co., Inc.

Annual Report (1975). New York: New York Stock Exchange, Inc.

Aronson, Elliot (1972) *The Social Animal*. San Francisco: W. H. Freeman.

Asimov, Isaac (1964) *Second Foundation*. New York: Avon.

Asimov, Isaac (1966) *Foundation*. New York: Avon.

Atchley, Robert C. (1980) *The Social Forces in Later Life*, 3rd ed. Belmont, Calif.: Wadsworth.

Babbie, Earl R. (1980) *Sociology: An Introduction*, 2nd ed. Belmont, Calif.: Wadsworth.

Baldwin, James (1963) *The Fire Next Time*. New York: Dial.

Barron, Milton L. (1971) "The Aged as a Quasi-Minority Group," in *The Other Minorities*, Edward Sagarin, editor. Lexington, Mass.: Ginn. Cited in Julian, 1980.

Becker, Howard S. (1963) *Outsiders: Studies in the Sociology of Deviance*. New York: The Free Press.

Becker, Howard S., and Geer, Blanche (1957) "Participant Observation and Interviewing: A Comparison." *Human Organization*, 16:28–32.

Bell, Robert R. (1971) *Social Deviance: A Substantive Analysis*. Homewood, Ill.: Dorsey Press.

Bensman, Joseph and Rosenberg, Bernard (1963) *Mass, Class and Bureaucracy*. Englewood Cliffs, N.J.: Prentice-Hall.

Berelson, Bernard, and Steiner, Gary (1967) *Human Behavior*. New York: Harcourt, Brace, and World.

Berger, Peter (1963) *Invitation to Sociology: A Humanistic Perspective*. New York: Doubleday Anchor Books. Excerpts paraphrased and used by permission of Doubleday and Co., Inc.

Berger, Peter L., and Berger, Brigitte (1972) *Sociology: A Biographical Approach*. New York: Basic Books.

Berk, Richard A. (1974) *Collective Behavior*. Dubuque, Iowa: Wm. C. Brown.

Bernard, Jessie (1966) *Marriage and Family Among Negroes*. Englewood Cliffs, N.J.: Prentice-Hall.

Berry, Brewton, and Tischler, Henry L. (1978) *Race and Ethnic Relations*, 4th ed. Boston: Houghton Mifflin.

Bertrand, Alvin L. (1967) *Sociology: An Introduction to Theory and Method.* New York: Appleton-Century-Crofts.

Bierstedt, Robert (1948) "The Limitations of Anthropological Methods in Sociology." *American Journal of Sociology*, 54:1.

Bierstedt, Robert (1970) *The Social Order*, 3rd ed. New York: McGraw-Hill.

Biesanz, John, and Biesanz, Mavis (1969) *Introduction to Sociology.* Englewood Cliffs, N.J.: Prentice-Hall.

Bird, Caroline (1970) *Born Female.* New York: David McKay.

Blau, Peter M. (1956) *Bureaucracy in Modern Society.* New York: Random House.

Blau, Peter M. (1965) "The Flow of Occupational Supply and Recruitment." *American Sociological Review*, 30.

Blau, Peter M. (1972) "Dialectical Sociology: Comments." *Sociological Inquiry*, Spring.

Blumer, Herbert (1969) "Elementary Collective Groupings," in *Principles of Sociology*, Alfred McClung Lee, editor. New York: Barnes and Noble.

Bottomore, T. B. (1966) *Classes in Modern Society.* New York: Random House.

Braude, Lee (1975) *Work and Workers: A Sociological Analysis.* New York: Praeger.

Broom, Leonard, and Selznick, Philip (1968) *Sociology*, 4th ed. New York: Harper and Row.

Burgess, E. W., Locke, H. J., and Thomas, M. M. (1963) *The Family*, 3rd ed. New York: American Book Co.

Butler, Robert N. (1975) *Why Survive? Being Old in America.* New York: Harper and Row. Cited in Robertson, 1980.

Byrd, Richard E. (1938) *Alone.* New York: G. P. Putnam's Sons.

Cailliet, G. M., Setzer, P. Y., and Love, M. S. (1971) *Everyman's Guide to Ecological Living.* New York: Macmillan. Reprinted with permission of Macmillan. Copyright © by the Santa Barbara Underseas Foundation, Inc.

Cameron, William Bruce (1966) *Modern Social Movements.* New York: Random House.

Carson, Gerald (1966) *The Polite Americans.* New York: Wm. Morrow.

Centers, Richard (1949) *The Psychology of Social Classes.* Princeton, N.J.: University Press.

Chase, Stuart (1968) *The Most Probable World.* New York: Harper and Row.

Clark, Kenneth (1965) *The Dark Ghetto.* New York: Harper and Row.

Clausen, John A. editor (1968) "Perspectives in Childhood Socialization," in *Socialization and Society.* Boston: Little, Brown.

Clinard, Marshall B. (1968) *Sociology of Deviant Behavior*, 3rd ed. New York: Holt, Rinehart and Winston.

Clough, Sheppard, and Cole, Charles W. (1952) *Economic History of Europe.* Boston: D.C. Heath.

Cohen, Albert K. (1955) *Delinquent Boys.* Glencoe, Ill.: The Free Press.

Cohen, Albert K. (1966) *Deviance and Control.* Englewood Cliffs, N.J.: Prentice-Hall.

Cole, Lamont C. (1972) "Can the World Be Saved?" in *Population Crisis*, S. T. Reid and D. L. Lyon, editors. Glenville, Ill.: Scott Foresman.

Commoner, Barry (1972) *The Closing Circle: Nature, Man, and Technology*. New York: Alfred Knopf.

Conway, Flo, and Siegelman, Jim (1979) *Snapping: America's Epidemic of Sudden Personality Change*. New York: Dell.

Cooley, Charles Horton (1909) *Social Organization*. New York: Charles Scribner's Sons.

Cooley, Charles Horton (1964) *Human Nature and the Social Order*. New York: Schocken.

Coser, Lewis (1957) "Social Conflict and the Theory of Social Change." *British Journal of Sociology*, Sept.

Cuber, John F., and Harroff, Peggy B. (1965) *The Significant Americans*. New York: Appleton-Century. All quotations are reprinted by permission of Hawthorne Books, Inc.

Current Population Reports (March, 1972) Table D, p. 6.

Curtain, Sharon R. (1972) *Nobody Ever Died of Old Age*. Boston: Atlantic Monthly Press. Cited in Eitzen (1980).

Cuzzort, R. P. (1969) *Humanity and Modern Sociological Thought*. New York: Holt, Rinehart and Winston.

Davis, F. James (1978) *Minority-Dominant Relations*. Arlington Heights, Ill.: AHM Publishing Corp.

Davis, Kingsley (January, 1940) "Extreme Isolation of a Child." *American Journal of Sociology*, 45.

Davis, Kingsley (March, 1947) "Final Note on a Case of Extreme Isolation." *American Journal of Sociology*, 52.

Davis, Kingsley (1949) *Human Society*. New York: Macmillan.

Dawkins, Richard (1976) *The Selfish Genes*. New York: Oxford University Press.

Dawson, C. A., and Gettys, W. E. (1935) *Introduction to Sociology*, revised edition. New York: Ronald.

Defleur, M. L., D'Antonio, W. B., and Defleur, L. B. (1971) *Sociology: Man in Society*. Glenview, Ill.: Scott Foresman.

de Lone, Richard H. (1979) *Small Futures: Children, Inequality and the Limits of Liberal Reform*. New York: Harcourt, Brace, Jovanovich.

Dinitz, Simon, Dynes, Russell R., and Clark, Alfred C. (1969) *Deviance: Studies in the Process of Stigmatization and Societal Reaction*. New York: Oxford University Press.

Dressler, David (1969) *Sociology: The Study of Human Interaction*. New York: Alfred A. Knopf.

Durkheim, Emile (1933) *The Division of Labor in Society*. Glencoe, Ill.: The Free Press.

Durkheim, Emile (1938) *The Rules of Sociological Method*. Chicago: University of Chicago Press, 1938.

Ehrlich, Paul R., Ehrlich, Anne H., and Holdren, John P. (1973) *Human Ecology: Problems and Solutions*. San Francisco: W. H. Freeman.

Eitzen, D. Stanley (1980) *Social Problems*. Boston: Allyn and Bacon.

Ember, Carol R., and Ember, Melvin (1977) *Anthropology*, 2nd ed. Englewood Cliffs, N.J.: Prentice-Hall.

Erikson, Kai T. (1962) "Notes on the Sociology of Deviance." *Social Problems*, 9:Spring.

Erikson, Kai T. (1965) "A Comment on Disguised Observation in Sociology," a paper read at the Annual Meeting of the Society for the Study of Social Problems.

The Evening Sun (Feb. 11, 1980). Baltimore: The A. S. Abell Co.

The Evening Sun (Sept. 1, 1980). Baltimore: The A. S. Abell Co.

Federico, Ronald C. (1979) *Sociology*, 2nd ed. Reading, Mass.: Addison-Wesley.

Feldman, Saul D., and Thielbar, Gerald W., editors (1972) *Life Styles: Diversity in American Society*. Boston: Little, Brown.

Festinger, Leon, Riecken, Henry, and Schachter, Stanley (1956) *When Prophecy Fails*. New York: Harper and Row.

Festinger, Leon, Schachter, Stanley, and Back, Kent (1950) *Social Pressures in Informal Groups*. New York: Harper and Row.

Fortune (Feb., 1940) "The People of the U.S.A.—a Self Portrait."

Francis, G. James, and Milbourn, Gene, Jr., (1980) *Human Behavior in the Work Environment*. Santa Monica, Calif.: Goodyear.

Frank, Roland G. (1981) Director of Programs for Deaf Adults, Catonsville Community College. Interview with authors.

Frankel, E. (1936) "Studies in Biographical Psychology." *Character and Personality*, 5. Cited in *Work in America*, 1973.

Fromm, Erich (1950) *Psychoanalysis and Religion*. New Haven: Yale Univerity Press.

Fromm, Erich (1955) *Sane Society*. New York: Holt, Rinehart and Winston.

Fromm, Erich (1961) *Marx's Concept of Man*. New York: Frederick Ungar.

Fromm, Erich (1962) *Beyond the Chains of Illusion*. New York: Simon and Schuster.

Fromm, Erich (1968) *The Revolution of Hope*. New York: Harper and Row.

Gabriel, Ralph Henry (1940) *The Course of American Democratic Thought*. New York: Ronald.

Gallup, George, and Rae, S. F. (1940) *The Pulse of Democracy*. New York: Simon and Schuster.

Gergen, David, and Schambra, William (1979) "Pollsters and Polling." *The Wilson Quarterly*, III:2:61–72.

Gibbs, Jack P. (1966) "Conceptions of Deviant Behavior: The Old and the New." *Pacific Sociological Review*, 9:Spring.

Glass, John F., and Staude, John R. (1972) *Humanistic Society*. Pacific Palisades, Calif: Goodyear.

Goffman, Erving (1961) *Asylums: Essays on the Social Situation of Mental Patients and Other Inmates*. Chicago: Aldine.

Haack, Robert W. (1971) *Annual Report*. New York: New York Stock Exchange, Inc.

Haley, Alex (1976) *Roots*. Garden City, N.Y.: Doubleday.

Hall, Susan, and Adelman, Bob (1972) *Gentleman of Leisure: A Year in the Life of a Pimp*. New York: New American Library.

Harrington, Michael (1963) *The Other America*. Baltimore: Penguin Books.

Hauser, Philip (1972) "The Emergence of the Population Problem," in *Population Crisis*, S. T. Reid and D. L. Lyon, editors. Glenville, Ill.: Scott Foresman.

Heilbroner, Robert L. (1962) *The Making of Economic Society*. Englewood Cliffs, N.J.: Prentice-Hall.

Heilbroner, Robert L. (1967) *The Worldly Philosophers*, 3rd ed. New York: Simon and Schuster.

Hendricks, Jon, and Hendricks, C. Davis (1977) *Aging in Mass Society: Myths and Realities*. Cambridge, Mass.: Winthrop.

Heron, A. R. (1948) *Why Men Work*. Stanford, Calif.: Stanford University Press.

Herzberg, Frederick (1966) *Work and the Nature of Man*. New York: World.

Hobbes, Thomas (1651) *Leviathan*.

Hodge, Robert W. (1964) "Occupational Prestige in the United States." *American Journal of Sociology*, 70:290–292.

Hodges, Harold M. (1971) *Conflict and Consensus*. New York: Harper and Row.

Hoebel, E. A., and Weaver, T. (1979) *Anthropology and the Human Experience*, 5th ed. New York: McGraw-Hill.

Horton, Paul B., and Horton, Robert L. (1972) *Programmed Learning Aid for Introductory Sociology*. Homewood, Ill.: Learning Systems.

Horton, Paul B., and Hunt, Chester L. (1980) *Sociology*, 5th ed. New York: McGraw-Hill.

Howells, William Dean (1928) *The Rise of Silas Lapham*. Boston: Houghton Mifflin.

Hraba, Joseph (1979) *American Ethnicity*. Itasca, Ill.: Peacock.

Humphreys, Laud (1970) *Tearoom Trade: Impersonal Sex in Public Places*. Chicago: Aldine.

Johnston, Francis E., and Selby, Henry (1978) *Anthropology: The Biocultural View*. Dubuque, Iowa: Wm. C. Brown.

Jones, James (1970) *The Merry Month of May*. New York: Dell.

Jones, M. R. (1955) *Nebraska Symposium on Motivation*. Lincoln: University of Nebraska Press. Cited in Francis and Milbourn, 1980.

Jones, Rochelle (1977) *The Other Generation: The New Power of Older Americans*. Englewood Cliffs, N.J.: Prentice-Hall. Cited in Julian, 1980.

Josephson, Erich, and Josephson, Mary (1962) *Man Alone: Alienation in Modern Society*. New York: Dell.

Julian, Joseph (1980) *Social Problems*, 3rd ed. Englewood Cliffs, N.J.: Prentice-Hall.

Kahn, Robert L. (1974) "The Work Module," in *Work and Quality of Life*, James O'Toole, editor. Cambridge, Mass.: The M.I.T. Press.

Keller, A. G., and Davie, M. R., editors (1924) *Selected Essays of William Graham Sumner*. New Haven: Yale University Press.

King, Martin Luther, Jr. (1964) "Letter from Birmingham Jail," in *Why We Can't Wait*. New York: New American Library.

Kluckhohn, Clyde, and Murray, Henry A. (1956) *Personality in Nature, Society, and Culture.* New York: Alfred A. Knopf.

Kolton, Paul (1971) *Annual Report.* New York: American Stock Exchange, Inc.

Ladd, Everett Carl, Jr. (1979) "What the Polls Tell Us." *The Wilson Quarterly,* III:2:73–83

Lancaster, Jane B. (1975) *Primate Behavior and the Emergence of Human Culture.* New York: Holt, Rinehart and Winston. Cited in Johnston and Selby, 1978

Landis, Judson R. (1980) *Sociology: Concepts and Characteristics,* 4th ed. Belmont, Calif.: Wadsworth.

LaPiere, Richard T. (1965) *Social Change.* New York: McGraw-Hill.

Lawler, Edward E., III (1973) *Motivation in Work Organizations.* Belmont, Calif.: Wadsworth.

Lenski, Gerhard (1977) "Sociology and Sociobiology: An Alternative View." *American Sociologist,* 12:2:May.

Lenski, Gerhard (1970) *Human Societies.* New York: McGraw-Hill.

Lerner, David (1958) *The Passing of Traditional Society.* Glencoe, Ill.: The Free Press.

Leslie, Gerald R. (1979) *The Family in Social Context,* 4th ed. New York: Oxford University Press.

Liebow, Elliot (1967) *Tally's Corner.* Boston: Little, Brown.

Lindsey, Robert (1979) "U.S. Hispanic Populace Growing Faster Than Any Other Minority." *New York Times,* Feb. 18.

Linton, Ralph (1936) *The Study of Man.* New York: D. Appleton-Century.

Little, Kenneth (1969) "Race and Society," in *Race and Science,* UNESCO. New York: Columbia University Press.

Loomis, Charles P. (1963) *Community and Society,* translated and edited by C. P. Loomis.

Lundberg, Ferdinand (1968) *The Rich and the Super-Rich.* New York: Lyle Stuart.

MacIver, Robert M. (1948) *The More Perfect Union.* New York: Macmillan.

McGee, Reece (1973) *Points of Departure: Basic Concepts in Sociology,* alternate edition. Hinsdale, Ill.: Dryden.

McKinney, John C., in collaboration with Loomis, Charles P. (1963) "The Application of *Gemeinschaft* and *Gesellschaft* as Related to Other Typologies." *Community and Society,* translated and edited by Charles P. Loomis. New York: Harper and Row.

McPhail, Clark, and Miller, David (1973) "The Assembling Process." *American Sociological Review,* Dec. Cited in Berk, 1974.

McVeigh, Frank J., and Shostak, Arthur B. (1978) *Modern Social Problems.* New York: Holt, Rinehart, and Winston.

Mace, David, and Mace, Vera (1960) *Marriage: East and West.* Garden City, N.Y. Doubleday Dolphin Books.

Mack, Raymond (1967) *Transforming America.* New York: Harper and Row.

Maine, Henry S. (1911) *Ancient Law: Its Connection with the Early History of Society, and Its Relation to Modern Ideas,* 10th ed. London: John Murray.

Marx, Karl (1961) *Capital*. Cited in Erich Fromm, *Marx's Concept of Man*. New York: Frederick Ungar.

Marx, Karl (1964a) *Economic and Philosophical Manuscripts of 1844*. New York: International Publishers.

Marx, Karl (1964b) *Selected Writings in Sociology and Social Philosophy*. New York: McGraw-Hill.

Marx, Karl, and Engels, Friedrich (1848) *The Communist Manifesto*.

Maslow, Abraham (1954) *Motivation and Personality*. New York: Harper and Row.

Masters, William H., and Johnson, Virginia E. (1972) "Sex and Equality." *Redbook*, March.

Merrill, Francis E. (1969) *Society and Culture*, 4th ed. Englewood Cliffs, N.J.: Prentice-Hall.

Merton, Robert K. (1946) *Mass Persuasion*. New York: Harper.

Merton, Robert K. (1968) *Social Theory and Social Structure*. New York: The Free Press.

Metropolitan Life (1975) "Work Disability by Occupation." *Statistical Bulletin*, 56. New York: Metropolitan Life Insurance.

Miller, Perry, editor (1954) *American Thought*. New York: Holt, Rinehart and Winston.

Mills, C. Wright (1959) *The Sociological Imagination*. New York: Oxford University Press.

Montagu, Ashley (1965) *Man's Most Dangerous Myth: The Fallacy of Race*. New York: World.

Montagu, Ashley (1966) *On Being Human*. New York: Hawthorne.

Montagu, Ashley (1980) *Sociobiology Examined*. New York: Oxford University Press.

Morse, Nancy C., and Weiss, Robert S. (1955) "The Function and Meaning of Work and the Job." *American Sociological Review*, 20:April. Cited in Steglich and Snooks, 1980.

Murdock, George P. (1949) *Social Structure*. New York: The Free Press.

Murdock, George P. (1957) "World Ethnographic Sample." *American Anthropologist*, 59:August.

Neubeck, Kenneth J. (1979) *Social Problems: A Critical Approach*. Glenview, Ill.: Scott Foresman.

Newfield, Jack (1969) *Robert Kennedy, A Memoir*. New York: E. P. Dutton.

Newsweek (November 29, 1971).

Newsweek (December 6, 1976).

Newsweek (May 19, 1980).

Newsweek (July 7, 1980).

Nisbet, Robert A. (1970) *The Social Bond*. New York: Alfred A. Knopf.

Norman, Colin (1980) "Lessons from the Mayan Collapse." *The Sun*, February 15. Baltimore: The A. S. Abell Co.

Nottingham, Elizabeth K. (1954) *Religion and Society*. New York: Random House.

Ogburn, William F. (1922) *Social Change*. New York: B. W. Huebsch.

Ogburn, William F., and Nimkoff, Meyer F. (1964) *Sociology*, 4th ed. Boston: Houghton-Mifflin.

Palmore, Erdman (1967) "Ethnophaulisms and Ethnocentrism," in *Minorities in a Changing World*, Milton Barron, editor. New York: Alfred A. Knopf.

Park, Robert E., and Burgess, Ernest W. (1921) *Introduction to the Science of Sociology*. Chicago: University of Chicago Press.

Parsons, Talcott (1951) *The Social System*. New York: The Free Press.

Percy, Charles (1974) *Growing Old in the Country of the Young*. New York: McGraw-Hill. Cited in Eitzen, 1980.

Perrucci, R., Knudsen, D., and Hamby, R. (1977) *Sociology: Basic Structures and Processes*. Dubuque, Iowa: Wm. C. Brown.

Peterson, W. Jack, and Maxwell, Milton A. (1958) "The Skid Road Wino." *Social Problems*, 5.

Pinkney, Alphonso (1969) *Black Americans*. Englewood Cliffs, N.J.: Prentice-Hall.

Polsky, Ned (1967) *Hustlers, Beats, and Others*. Chicago: Aldine.

Popenoe, David (1980) *Sociology*, 4th ed. Englewood Cliffs, N.J.: Prentice-Hall.

Queen, Stuart A. and Haberstein, Robert W. (1967) *The Family in Various Cultures*, 3rd ed. New York: J. B. Lippincott.

Quinn, Robert P., et al. (1969) *Survey of Working Conditions*. Ann Arbor: Survey Research Center, University of Michigan.

Rand, Ayn (1943) *The Fountainhead*. New York: Bobbs-Merrill.

Rand, Ayn (1957) *Atlas Shrugged*. New York: New American Library.

Rand, Ayn (1961) *For the New Intellectual: The Philosophy of Ayn Rand*. New York: Random House.

Redfield, Robert (1947) "The Folk Society." *American Journal of Sociology*, 52.

Redfield, Robert (1953) *The Primitive World and Its Transformation*. Ithaca, New York: Cornell University Press.

Reissman, Leonard (1959) *Class in American Society*. New York: The Free Press.

Rensberger, Boyce (1978) *New York Times*, September 28. Printed in *The Sun*, October 17, 1978. Baltimore: The A. S. Abell Co.

Reuter, E. B., and Hart, C. W. (1933) *Introduction to Sociology*. New York: McGraw-Hill.

Ritzer, George (1977) *Working: Conflict and Change*. Englewood Cliffs, N.J.: Prentice-Hall.

Roberts, Walter Orr (1972) "Man on a Changing Earth," in *Man and Society*, R. B. Guthrie and E. J. Barnes, editors. Palo Alto: James E. Freed and Associates.

Robertson, Ian (1977) *Sociology*. New York: Worth.

Robertson, Ian (1980) *Social Problems*, 2nd ed. New York: Random House.

Roethlisberger, F. J., and Dickson, William J. (1939) *Management and the Worker*. Cambridge, Mass.: Harvard University Press.

Rose, Arnold (1964) *The Negro in America*. New York: Harper and Row.

Rose, Arnold M., and Rose, Caroline B. (1969) *Sociology: The Study of Human Relations*, 3rd ed. New York: Alfred A. Knopf.

Rose, Jerry D. (1971) *Introduction to Sociology*. Chicago: Rand McNally.

Rosenthal, Neal H. (1973) "The United States Economy in 1985: Projected Changes in Occupations." *Monthly Labor Review*, 96. Cited in Ritzer, 1977.

Rossi, Alice (1965) "Women in Science: Why So Few?" *Science*, 148:3674.

Rottenberg, Dan (1978) "The Wealthiest Americans." *Town and Country*, May.

Salas, Rafael, Executive Director of the U.N. Fund for Population Activities. *The Sun* (June 16, 1980). Baltimore: The A. S. Abell Co.

Sandburg, Carl (1936) *The People, Yes*. New York: Harcourt Brace Jovanovich.

Sandburg, Carl (1950) "The People, Yes." *Complete Poems*. New York: Harcourt, Brace and World.

Sandoval, Moises (1980) "The Emergence of the Hispanics in America." *The Sunday Sun*, May 25. Baltimore: The A. S. Abell Co.

Saxton, Lloyd (1979) *The Individual, Marriage, and the Family*, 2nd ed. Belmont, Calif.: Wadsworth.

Scarpitti, Frank R. (1980) *Social Problems*, 3rd ed. New York: Holt, Rinehart and Winston.

Seib, Gerald F. (1980) "Recessions Cause Death Rate to Rise, As Pressures of Coping Take Hold." *The Wall Street Journal*, August 25.

Seligman, Edwin, editor (1957) *Encyclopedia of the Social Sciences*. New York: Macmillan.

Selltiz, Claire, and Jahoda, Marie, Deutsch, Morton, and Cook, Stuart (1962) *Research Methods in Social Relations*. New York: Holt, Rinehart and Winston.

Sherif, Muzafer (1966) *The Psychology of Social Norms*. New York: Harper and Row.

Silberman, Charles (1964) *Crisis in Black and White*. New York: Vintage Books.

Simmons, J. L., (1969) *Deviants*. Berkeley, Calif.: The Glendessary Press.

Skinner, B. F. (1969) *Walden Two*. London: The Macmillan Co.

Skinner, B. F. (1971) *Beyond Freedom and Dignity*. New York: Alfred Knopf.

Smelser, Neil J. (1963) *Theory of Collective Behavior*. New York: The Free Press of Glencoe.

Smith, Helen (1972) "They Love Me Not." *Village Voice*, October 19.

Spradley, James P. (1970) *You Owe Yourself a Drunk*. Boston: Little, Brown.

Spradley, James P. (1972) "Down and Out on Skid Row," in *Life Styles: Diversity in American Society*, S. D. Feldman and G. W. Thielbar editors. Boston: Little, Brown.

Spradley, James P., and McCurdy, David W. (1971) *Conformity and Conflict*. Boston: Little, Brown.

Srole, Leo, et al. (1962) *Mental Health in the Metropolis: The Midtown Manhattan Study*. New York: McGraw-Hill.

Steglich, W. G., and Snooks, M. K. (1980) *American Social Problems: An Institutional View*. Santa Monica, Calif.: Goodyear.

Stewart, Elbert W. (1978) *Sociology: The Human Science*. New York: McGraw-Hill.

Storer, Norman W. (1980) *Focus on Society: An Introduction to Sociology*, 2nd ed. Reading, Mass.: Addison-Wesley.

Sullerot, Evelyne (1971) *Women, Society and Change*. New York: McGraw-Hill.

Sumner, William Graham (1906) *Folkways*. Boston: Ginn.

The Sun (November 17, 1970). Baltimore: The A. S. Abell Co.

Swartz, Katherine (1980) "Helping the Jobless: Theories and Practice." *The Wilson Quarterly*, IV:1:Winter.

Theodorson, G. A., and Theodorson, A. G. (1969) *A Modern Dictionary of Sociology*. New York: Thomas A. Crowell.

Thomas, Elizabeth Marshall (1959) *The Harmless People*. New York: Alfred Knopf. Cited in Heilbroner, 1962.

Thomas, W. I. (1967) *The Unadjusted Girl*. New York: Harper and Row.

Thomlinson, Ralph (1965) *Population Dynamics: Causes and Consequences of World Demographic Change*. New York: Random House.

Thoreau, Henry David (1849) *Civil Disobedience*.

Thoreau, Henry David (1854) *Walden*.

Timasheff, Nicholas (1967) *Sociological Theory*. New York: Random House.

Toffler, Alvin (1970) *Future Shock*. New York: Random House.

Tonnies, Ferdinand (1963) *Gemeinschaft and Gesellschaft*, translated and edited by C. P. Loomis. New York: Harper and Row.

Tuckman, J., Youngman, W. F., and Kreizman, G. B. (1965) "Occupational Level and Mortality." *Social Forces*, 43.

Turner, Ralph H., Killian, Lewis M. (1957) *Collective Behavior*. Englewood Cliffs, N.J.: Prentice-Hall.

Tylor, E. B. (1872) *Primitive Culture*. London: John Murray.

Udall, Morris K. (1972) "Spaceship Earth—Standing Room Only." *Society and Environment*, R. R. Campbell and J. L. Wade, editors. Boston: Allyn and Bacon.

U.S. Bureau of the Census (1977) *Statistical Abstracts of the United States*. Washington, D.C.: U.S. Government Printing Office.

U.S. Bureau of the Census (1980) *Census of Population: Subject Reports, American Indians*. Washington, D.C.: U.S. Government Printing Office.

U.S. Department of Labor (1978) *Employment and Earnings*. Washington, D.C.: U.S. Government Printing Office.

Van den Berghe, Pierre (1967) *Race and Racism*. New York: John Wiley.

Van Gennep, Arnold (1960) *The Rites of Passage*, translated by Monika B. Vizedom and Gabrielle L. Caffee. Chicago: University of Chicago Press.

Vander Zanden, James W. (1966) *American Minority Relations*. New York: Ronald.

Vander Zanden, James W. (1970) *Sociology, A Systemic Approach*, 2nd ed. New York: Ronald.

Vanfossen, Beth Ensminger (1979) *The Structure of Social Inequality*. Boston: Little, Brown.

Veblen, Thorstein (1899) *The Theory of the Leisure Class*. New York: Macmillan.

Vernon, Glenn (1965) *Human Interaction*. New York: Ronald.

Volkart, Edmund H., editor (1951) *Social Behavior and Personality: Contributions of W. I. Thomas to Theory and Social Research*. New York: Social Sciences Research Council.

Von Hoffman, Nicholas, Horowitz, Irving, and Rainwater, Lee (1970) "Sociological Snoopers and Journalistic Moralizers." *Transaction*, 7:7.

Wallace, Samuel E. (1965) *Skid Row as a Way of Life*. Totowa, N.J.: Bedminster.

Wallechinsky, David, and Wallace, Irving (1975) *The People's Almanac*. Garden City, N.Y.: Doubleday.

Wambaugh, Joseph (1970) *The New Centurions*. Boston: Little, Brown.

Warner, W. L., and Lunt, Paul S. (1941) *The Social Life of a Modern Community*. New Haven, Conn.: Yale University Press.

Warner, W. Lloyd, et al. (1960) *Social Class in America*. New York: Harper and Row.

Warner, W. Lloyd (1962) *American Life: Dream and Reality*. Chicago: University of Chicago Press.

Warner, W. Lloyd, editor (1963) *Yankee City*, abridged edition. New Haven, Conn.: Yale University Press.

Weber, Max (1947) *The Theory of Social and Economic Organization*, translated by A. M. Henderson and Talcott Parsons. Glencoe, Ill.: The Free Press.

Weber, Max (1958) *Essays in Sociology*, translated and edited by H. H. Gerth and C. Wright Mills. New York: Oxford University Press, A Galaxy Book.

Weinberg, Alvin M. (1980) "Technological Optimism." *Society*, 17:3:March/April.

White, Leslie A. (1949) *The Science of Culture*. New York: Farrar.

Whitman, Walt (1855) "There Was a Child Went Forth." *Leaves of Grass*.

Wilensky, Harold (1967) "The Early Impact of Industrialization on Society." Readings in Industrial Sociology, W. A. Faunce, editor. New York: Appleton-Century-Crofts. Cited in Ritzer, 1977.

Wilson, Edward O. (1975) *Sociobiology: The New Synthesis*. Cambridge, Mass.: Harvard University Press.

Wilson, Edward O. (1978) *On Human Nature*. Cambridge, Mass.: Harvard University Press.

Work in America (1973) Report of a Special Task Force to the Secretary of Health, Education, and Welfare. Cambridge, Mass.: The M.I.T. Press.

Yinger, J. Milton (1960) "Contraculture and Subculture." *American Sociological Review* 25:October.

Yost, Monica E. (1981) Associate Professor of Anthropology and Sociology. Catonsville Community College. Interview with authors.

Young, Pauline V. (1966) *Scientific Surveys and Research*. Englewood Cliffs, N.J.: Prentice-Hall.

GLOSSARY

ACHIEVED STATUS

Any status or position that is acquired by an individual through his or her own effort, knowledge, and skill. Status that is based on factors over which the individual can exercise some control.

ACTING CROWD

This type of crowd acts on impulse. It is suggestible and irresponsible. Acting crowds can turn into mobs.

AGEISM

Ageism occurs through negative prejudice and discrimination against a person on the basis of age. A form of ethnocentrism.

ALCOHOLISM

This occurs when one develops a pattern of habitual heavy drinking that disrupts one's normal activities.

ALIENATION

A feeling of noninvolvement in and estrangement from society and culture. Alienation can be characterized by feelings of anxiety, apathy, loneliness, powerlessness, meaninglessness, and despair.

ALTRUISM

Behavior by an individual that places a higher premium on the welfare of others than on oneself. Those who subscribe to altruism believe that there is more satisfaction and self-fulfillment in providing nurture for others than in providing for one's own welfare.

ANATOMY IS DESTINY

A belief that biological and psychological traits are linked in such a way that we become "masculine" or "feminine" because of certain features and functions of our anatomies.

ANDROGYNY

A society in which concepts of "masculinity" and "feminity" would have no significance. An androgynous society would not assign social roles on the basis of sex.

ANOMIE

A condition characterized by the relative absence of or confusion about values in society. Anomie refers to circumstances wherein society has failed to provide individuals with opportunities to achieve the goals that have been set and honored by the population at large and by the social institutions of the society. As a consequence, there exists a clash between cultural goals and access to cultural goals through legitimate behavior.

ANOMIE THEORY OF DEVIANCE
The theory that deviant behavior occurs because society has failed to provide some people with opportunities to achieve goals defined as desirable by most of society's population.

ASCRIBED STATUS
Any status that is not acquired by effort, knowledge, and skill, but based on inheritance. Status that is based on factors such as age, sex, and race over which one has no control.

AUTHORITY
The legitimate exercise of power. Authority is of three types: traditional, legal-rational, and charismatic.

BEHAVIORISM
The scientific effort to explain human behavior in terms of environmental controls. A psychological school of thought associated with the ideas of B. F. Skinner.

BILINEAL MARRIAGE
Marriage in which descent or lineage is traced through both the father's and mother's families.

BOUNDARY MAINTENANCE
All those mechanisms used to create and maintain social distance between a dominant group and a subordinate group. Mechanisms include slurs, stereotypes, prejudice, discrimination, and physical violence.

BOURGEOISIE
According to Karl Marx, the owners of the means of production and distribution who, as a class, control and suppress the working class. The equivalent of middle class.

BUREAUCRACY
A large-scale formal organization that is designed to coordinate the activities of many individuals in the pursuit of administrative tasks. Bureaucracies are highly differentiated and efficiently organized by means of formal rules and a hierarchical chain of command.

CAPITALISM
An economic system based on private ownership of the means of production and distribution. It is less subject to government controls than to the laws of supply and demand. In theory all people are free to accumulate as many privileges and as much power as they can. See Market Economy.

CASE STUDY

An exhaustive, comprehensive study of some single social unit. A case study can be made of a person, group, social institution, or community. Sometimes called a case history.

CASTE SYSTEM

A system of rigid social stratification based on heredity and ascribed status. A pure caste system allows for no social mobility because positions of privilege, power, and prestige are determined at birth.

CASUAL CROWD

A large, temporary collection of people who are together simply because a certain object or event has temporarily drawn their attention.

CAUSATION

The concept that the occurrence of events is determined by cause-and-effect relationships. The assumption of causation is that events are associated in a one-way relationship so that the occurrence of one leads to the occurrence of the other.

CELEBRITY STATUS

Status that accrues not from such conventional criteria as income, education, and occupation but from one's "having made it." Possessed by people held in high public esteem because of their personal achievements as celebrities.

CENSUS

A periodic population survey that counts people and that also records data on age, occupation, sex, and a wealth of other information in statistical form.

CHARISMA

A certain quality of an individual personality by virtue of which he or she is set apart from others and treated as endowed with supernatural, superhuman, or at least exceptional powers.

CHARISMATIC AUTHORITY

A personal quality of leadership that inspires people to follow the charismatic person with enthusiasm and loyalty.

CLASS CONSCIOUSNESS

Awareness of belonging to and identifying with a given social class, accompanied by feeling that one's personal interests are dependent on the position and attainments of the social class as a whole.

CLIQUE

A small, exclusive group of people who relate to one another in such a way that a primary-like setting exists within large, bureaucratic organizations of industrial, mass society.

COLLECTIVE BEHAVIOR

The behavior of groups that have no clear direction from their cultures. Behavior that is unstructured. Noninstitutionalized behavior. Collective behavior occurs in riots, mob, panic, mass hysteria, and mass movements.

COMMAND ECONOMY

An economic system in which modes of production and distribution are planned. In time of crisis, a society might have to resort to this type of system in order to organize its resources for production and its energies for distribution of goods and services.

CONFLICT-HABITUATED MARRIAGE

A marital life-style characterized by continual tension between a couple and within the family unit. This type of marriage is one in which a couple is incompatible in most areas of their interaction, yet the ever-potential conflict is not so devastating that the couple cannot and do not want to remain together.

CONFLICT THEORY

The view that society should be thought of as a social experience of constant struggle and change. Changes resulting from conflict prevent society from becoming stagnant.

CONFORMITY

The process by which people adapt themselves to behavioral expectations that are peculiar to the social situations in which they find themselves, having been influenced either directly and formally, or subtly and informally by the social units into which they have been socialized.

CONSCIOUSNESS OF DIFFERENCE

A feeling of nonidentification with people who are perceived as being dissimilar from oneself. Consciousness of difference creates and maintains social distance.

CONSCIOUSNESS OF KIND

A feeling of identification with others who are similar to oneself. Consciousness of kind causes people to recognize others like themselves and want to associate with their own kind.

CONSERVATIVE MOVEMENT

A social movement dedicated to the conservation of present-day values and behaviors. Members seek to maintain the status quo.

CONSPICUOUS CONSUMPTION

The purchase and accumulation of material goods for the purpose of demonstrating one's wealth.

CONTINUUM

A continuous series of gradations acknowledging differences in degrees between the characteristics of two ideal types.

CONTRACULTURE

A subculture whose attitudes, values, and behaviors clash, contradict, and conflict with the attitudinal and behavioral norms of society at large. Some sociologists use the term *counterculture* synonymously.

CONTROL GROUP

In a planned experiment the people who are not exposed to the experimental conditions and the independent variables, thus allowing the experimenters to compare and contrast the control group's behavior with the behavior of the experimental group.

CONVENTIONALIZED CROWD
A crowd whose behavior follows social norms that have been predefined in previous similar situations. Examples would include crowds at sports events, concerts, and theaters.

COSMOGONY
A theory about the creation of the world and of human beings by some great god or gods. Also an attempt to explain the beginnings of time.

CROWD
A large, temporary collection of people in a particular place who share a common interest or cause.

CULTURAL ASSIMILATION
A subprocess of assimilation that refers to the extent to which an ethnic or minority group adopts and internalizes the cultural patterns of the larger society.

CULTURAL LAG
Applies to the differing rate of change within a society. Cultural lag describes the disharmony between related parts of a single culture, produced through unequal rates of change.

CULTURAL RELATIVISM
The principle that every culture must be judged by its own cultural criteria because standards of right and wrong and of good and bad are relative to the cultural context within which they appear. To argue that one life-style is superior or inferior to another is to violate the principle of cultural relativism. See Ethical Absolutism for an opposing view.

CULTURE
That complex whole that includes knowledge, beliefs, art, morals, laws, customs, and any other habits and capabilities acquired by human beings as members of society. Culture refers to all those ways of thinking, feeling, and behaving that are socially transmitted from one generation to the next.

CULTURE SHOCK
The bewilderment, frustration, and disorientation that immersion in a different culture has upon the unprepared visitor. Culture shock is evidence of the uniqueness of human groupings.

DEFINITION OF THE SITUATION
According to W. I. Thomas, "If men define situations as real, they are real in their consequences." The way that an individual perceives reality will determine the way the individual behaves.

DEMOGRAPHY
The science concerned with the statistical study of the human population. In its broadest view, demography studies population composition and distribution.

DEPENDENT VARIABLE

Any variable that is influenced or caused by another variable.

DEVIANT BEHAVIOR

Nonconformity to social norms. Behavior that represents a departure from social norms. Definitions of deviance are relative to time, culture, subculture, and circumstance.

DEVITALIZED MARRIAGE

A marital life-style in which a couple began with the feeling that their relationship was one of the most important factors in their lives, yet find over time that the quality of the relationship has changed so that the original zest is gone.

DIFFUSION

The exchanging of cultural traits from one society to another. Synonymous with "cultural borrowing." Diffusion accounts for the greatest amount of change in a culture.

DISCOVERY

Any addition to the human store of verified knowledge.

DISCRIMINATION

Overt behavior in which people are given differential and unfavorable treatment on the basis of their cultural, racial, or sexual membership. Any practice, policy, or procedure that denies equality of treatment to an individual or group.

DIVISION OF LABOR

The dividing of work into special tasks or activities. This is specialization. Different people carry out different jobs in order to complete a total product or total service.

DOGMA

A system of principles and beliefs that make up a doctrine. Usually associated with religions.

DOMINANCE HIERARCHY

Some species of primates have dominance hierarchies in which each individual has a ranking in reference to the other members of the group. Dominance has to do with one having more or less power in reference to the others.

DOMINANT GROUP

Any group that occupies a position of advantage in terms of access to privilege, power, and prestige within a society.

DOOMSDAY CULT

A small group of people who believe that the world is coming to an end or that some awful experience lies immediately in the future.

DOUBLING TIME

The time required for the human population to double in size. If the present rate of growth continues, the human population will double again in 35 years.

DYSFUNCTION

That which is harmful and prevents the fulfillment of a group's or society's objectives and goals. A negative consequence.

ECOLOGY
The science that studies the relationships and processes linking each living thing and each form of life with the others and with the environment.

ECONOMIC DETERMINISM
The doctrine that economic factors are the most crucial in explaining social behavior. A society's economy determines all other social and cultural phenomena.

ECOSPHERE
The "home" that organisms have built on the outer surface of the Earth. Any organism that has to live on the Earth must adapt to the ecosphere or perish. In the ecosphere, every effect is also a cause.

ECOSYSTEM
A community of organisms interacting with one another, plus the environment in which they live and with which they also interact.

EGALITARIANISM
The doctrine that equality of opportunity, rights, and privileges be available to all, irrespective of race, sex, religion, social standing, or any other discriminatory criteria.

EGO
According to Freudian theory, the aspect of human personality that attempts to reconcile the conflict between the impulsiveness of the id and the moral restraint dictated by the superego. The conscious self that operates on the reality principle.

EGOCENTRISM
The stage of development in which the human infant seeks complete and immediate gratification of its own needs and desires without taking others into account. Egocentrism is followed by the stage of development called sociocentrism.

ENDOGAMY
The practice of marrying within one's group. Historically, American society has stressed endogamy in reference to social class, race, and religion.

EQUALITARIANISM
Authority within the family unit is shared equally by all family members.

ESCAPE MOVEMENT
A social movement whose members seek to remove themselves from society. Escape movements are different from other social movements since they do not seek to prevent or promote social change.

ESTABLISHMENT
Positions of privilege, power, and prestige within the institutional framework of a society. Although the occupants of these positions can and do change, the positions themselves remain intact.

ETHICAL ABSOLUTISM
The principle that there may be universal circumstances that are always good and always bad for the human condition. If moral judgments are to be related to

human needs, and if there are basic needs common to all human beings, it seems to follow that there are standards that apply to all human beings. See Cultural Relativism for an opposing view.

ETHNIC GROUP
A subculture or group that is characterized by a common cultural tradition and a shared sense of identity. Ethnic groups are unique in terms of language, religion, customs, and national origin. Members may be spatially separated, yet retain a consciousness of kind.

ETHNOCENTRISM
That view of things in which one's own group is the center of everything and all others are scaled and rated with reference to it. A form of cultural conceit in which people assume the superiority of their way of life. Ethnocentrism involves an intense identification with the familiar and a devaluation of the foreign.

EXOGAMY
The practice of marrying outside one's group. Historically, Americans have stressed exogamy in reference to close relatives.

EXPRESSIVE CROWD
This type of crowd forms to express feelings about something together. Examples would be religious meetings and political rallies. Such a crowd releases its tension on an objective and becomes united in its feelings and actions.

EXTENDED FAMILY
This is a family that includes two or more nuclear families that are related. It could include grandparents, their unmarried children, their married children, and grandchildren.

EXPERIMENTAL GROUP
In a planned experiment the people who are exposed to the experimental conditions and the independent variables and whose behavior is observed and measured for comparing and contrasting with the control group.

EXTERNALLY ADAPTED LIFE-STYLE
Identified by Jessie Bernard as a subculture whose people have not really internalized the social norms of American culture and who live outside the so-called mainstream of American life. This subculture is essentially hedonistic, pleasure-loving, and consumption-oriented.

FADS, CRAZES, AND FASHIONS
Collective behavior that usually lasts longer than crowd behavior and is experienced nationwide. Such matters are generally considered as relatively unimportant.

FAMILY OF ORIENTATION
The family unit into which one is born and that orients the child to the culture. The family of orientation consists of one's parents and siblings.

FAMILY OF PROCREATION
The family unit that one forms through marriage. The family of procreation consists of one's mate (or mates) and any offspring of the union.

FELONIES
Codified mores that, if violated, evoke a severe formal penalty. Homicide is an example.

FOLK SOCIETY
A typology, created by Robert Redfield, that refers to a society that is small in population, culturally and physically isolated and homogeneous, with a simple division of labor. Stability and predictability are characteristic of life in folk society.

FOLKWAYS
Social norms that guide us through the ordinary social encounters of everyday life. Folkways are customs that are mildly enforced because their observance is not considered to be of great moral significance.

FUNCTIONAL
That which is useful and contributes to the goals and objectives of a group or society. A positive consequence.

GEMEINSCHAFT
A typology created by Ferdinand Tonnies, referring to a traditional, rural, agrarian society as well as to the particular type of human relationships that prevail in the society. Characterized by a profound sense of community. *Gemeinschaft* relations are primary relations.

GENERALIZED OTHER
The population of a society, past and present, who have contributed to an individual's internalization of attitudes, values, and behavior expectations.

GENES
Units of heredity that determine the characteristics that living things inherit from their ancestry. Sociobiologists believe that genes influence the social behavior of all creatures, including human beings.

GESELLSCHAFT
A typology created by Ferdinand Tonnies, referring to a dynamic, urban, industrial society as well as to the particular type of human relationships that prevail in the society. *Gesellschaft* relations are secondary relations.

GROUP
A collectivity of people who have a common identity, a feeling of unity, a degree of interdependence, and common goals and norms. Groups range in size and degree of intimacy from two people to an entire society.

GROUP MARRIAGE
A marital arrangement in which two or more men are married to two or more women at the same time. A form of polygamy.

GROUP-SUPPORT THEORY OF DEVIANCE
The theory that an individual receives support for his or her deviant behavior from members of a deviant group. A person conforms to the norms of a contraculture.

HAWTHORNE EFFECT

A phenomenon named after experiments at the Hawthorne branch of the Western Electric Company where researchers discovered that the findings of experiments may be due only to the attention the subjects of a study are receiving and not necessarily to the factors being tested.

HETEROGENEOUS

The quality characteristic of a human population when the individuals within it possess a marked difference in biological and cultural traits. Populations can be heterogeneous in terms of race, religion, customs, traditions, attitudes, values, beliefs, and behaviors.

HIDDEN CURRICULUM

Thoughts and behavior that are encouraged in school in addition to the formal or acknowledged curriculum. It includes learning to follow instructions in lining up, being quiet, waiting, and pleasing the teacher. Learning to do what the boss wants.

HIERARCHY

Refers to the rank ordering of positions within an institution, organization, or group and the relationship of the various positions to power.

HIERARCHY OF NEEDS

Maslow said that there is a hierarchy of human needs that requires fulfillment. Human behavior is influenced by this set of needs. As one fulfills a lower need, the next higher need becomes important and directs the person's behavior.

HIGH POTENTIAL GROWTH

A stage of demographic transition that is characterized by a high birth rate and a high death rate. In a society with high potential growth, high fertility rates are rooted in strongly entrenched marriage customs and reproductive norms, and high mortality rates are maintained by disease and chronic undernourishment.

HOMINID

This term applies to human beings (*Homo sapiens*) and to any possible earlier, now extinct, creatures who may have had characteristics similar to *Homo sapiens*.

HOMOGENEOUS

The quality characteristic of a human population when the individuals within it possess a marked similarity in biological and cultural traits. Populations can be homogeneous in terms of race, religion, customs, traditions, attitudes, values, beliefs, and behaviors.

HUMAN BEHAVIORAL ENGINEERING

An approach to the optimum human condition based on the ideas of B. F. Skinner. A technology of behavior, reflected in the utopian novel *Walden Two* is the basis for the development of planned societies that ideally are characterized by a climate of trust, love, and cooperation.

HUMAN NATURE

All those innate or hereditary characteristics that are biologically transmitted within the human organism.

HUMAN NURTURE
All those social, cultural, and environmental experiences to which the human organism is exposed as a result of the socialization process.

HUMANISTIC COMMUNITARIANISM
Erich Fromm's approach to the optimum human condition contending that people can develop their human potential only in cooperation with others. Humanistic communitarianism can be achieved only when there exists loyalty to the human race rather than to any particular grouping of humanity and when human beings view themselves as citizens of the Earth.

HUMANISTIC VALUES
A cluster of values emphasizing the virtues of knowing, caring, loving, being known, cared for, and loved.

HUMANOCENTRISM
A term we use to describe a unique form of ethnocentrism in which humanity views itself as the center of the universe. Humanocentrism ignores the fact that humanity is only one form of life within the ecosphere.

HUSTLING
Behavior intended to bring rewards without conforming to the social norms of the total American culture. Examples would be pimping, prostitution, drug pushing, and participation in any illegal rackets. See Externally Adapted.

HYPHENATED-AMERICANS
A phrase reflecting a dual ethnicity. Examples of hyphenated-Americans include Irish-Americans, Jewish-Americans, black-Americans, and the like.

HYPOTHESIS
A statement specifying a particular relationship between two or more variables.

ID
According to Freudian theory, that aspect of human personality consisting of biological drives that demand complete and immediate gratification. The id is the unconscious self activated by the pleasure principle.

IDEAL CULTURE
Those patterns of behavior that are formally approved and that members of a society are expected to observe.

IDEAL TYPE
A mental construct that can be used to compare and contrast the characteristics of two or more social phenomena. Ideal types are exaggerations or abstractions of social phenomena that do not literally exist in reality. Synonymous with "pure type."

IDENTIFICATION
According to Freudian theory, one of the two major mechanisms by which socialization takes place. By identifying with its parents, the child learns the socially approved channels through which its energies are allowed to flow.

IDENTIFICATIONAL ASSIMILATION
A subprocess of assimilation that refers to the extent to which members of an ethnic or minority group identify themselves with or are identified by the larger population.

IDEOLOGY
A system of interdependent ideas shared by some human grouping, reflecting and justifying particular social, moral, political, and economic interests. An institutional ideology is an institution's rationale for existence.

IDEOLOGICAL COMPONENT OF CULTURE
That portion of culture consisting of ideas, beliefs, and values shared by a human grouping. Also included are scientific facts, myths, legends, superstitions, and folklore, as well as definitions of worth, beauty, and achievement.

INDEPENDENT VARIABLE
Any variable that causes an effect or that influences another variable. Causation occurs when an independent variable influences another variable.

IN-GROUP
Any group whose membership has a strong sense of identification and loyalty accompanied by an attitude of exclusiveness toward nonmembers.

INCIPIENT DECLINE
A stage of demographic transition that is characterized by a low birth rate and a low death rate. Ideally, a society in this stage would provide its population with a level of well-being unparalleled in human history.

INDIVIDUAL DETERMINISM
A perspective that advocates an image of human beings as independent, active, free agents who make decisions and who act individually.

INNOVATION
An adaptation to anomie that involves the use of illegitimate means to achieve culturally approved goals. An individual conforming to the value of success but deviating from the norms for acquiring success, for example, is innovative.

INTERNALLY ACCULTURATED LIFE-STYLE
Identified by Jessie Bernard as a subculture whose people have internalized the social norms of American culture to the extent that the norms have become an intrinsic part of their personalities. This subculture is essentially puritanical, since its members seek to conform to standards of American ideal culture.

INVENTION
The creation of something new through combining existing elements of culture. Inventions are of two types, material and social.

LABELING THEORY OF DEVIANCE
The theory that whether or not an act is considered deviant depends upon how other people react to or label the act.

LATENT FUNCTIONS
Those consequences for a society or any of its segments that are neither intended nor recognized. Consequences that occur as spinoffs of institutions in action.

LAWS
Social norms that are designated, maintained, and enforced by the political authority within society. Laws are codified social norms which, if violated, evoke such legal punishments as fines and imprisonment.

LEGAL-RATIONAL AUTHORITY
Authority legitimized by a system of formal laws designated to regulate conduct and achieve designated goals. Primary characteristic is its bureaucratic organization.

LEVEL ABOVE THE COMMON PEOPLE
According to W. Lloyd Warner, the upper-upper, lower-upper, and upper-middle social classes.

LEVEL BENEATH THE COMMON PEOPLE
According to W. Lloyd Warner, the lower-lower social class.

LEVEL OF THE COMMON PEOPLE
According to W. Lloyd Warner, the lower-middle and upper-lower social classes.

LIFE CHANCES
The probability that an individual in a given status or social class will attain or fail to attain certain goals or experiences (a college education, for example) because of differential access to privileges and opportunities.

LIFE-STYLE
A distinctive way of life that centers around a major interest or activity. The life-style of a drug addict, for example, centers around the consumption of drugs.

LOOKING-GLASS SELF
According to Charles H. Cooley, an individual's perception of self as determined by the way one imagines one appears to others. We learn who we are by imagining how others perceive us.

MACROWORLD
The world that is abstract, impersonal, anonymous, and unfamiliar that surrounds and transcends the world of our immediate experiences. An essential part of our experiencing and understanding of society. The larger social reality. Associated with public issues.

MAMMALIA
A class of life to which humans belong. Mammals feed their young with milk from the female mammary glands. With few exceptions, they give birth to living offspring.

MANIFEST FUNCTIONS
Those consequences for a society or any of its segments that are intended and recognized by participants in the system.

MARKET ECONOMY
An economic system that is based on the private ownership of the means of production and distribution. Subject to the laws of supply and demand. See Capitalism.

MASS MEDIA
Agents of socialization that include television, radio, books, comics, magazines, movies, newspapers, and records and tapes. Mass media help make us all similar.

MATRIARCHY
Authority within the family unit held by the wife or female head.

MATRIFOCAL
A mother-centered relationship among members in primate societies.

MATRILINEAL MARRIAGE
Marriage in which descent or lineage is traced through the mother's family.

MATRILOCAL
Pattern of residence in which the husband and wife live with the wife's family of orientation.

MECHANICAL SOLIDARITY
A typology, created by Emile Durkheim, that refers to a traditional society characterized by a simple division of labor, a population that is mentally and morally homogeneous, and a high degree of unity and uniformity.

MICROWORLD
The world that consists of our immediate experiences with others in face-to-face interaction. It is a world that is personally meaningful, direct, immediate, and familiar. Associated with personal troubles.

MINORITY GROUP
Any racial, religious, or ethnic group that has less than equal access to positions of privilege, power, and prestige within a society. Any human grouping that experiences disadvantages because of prejudicial or discriminatory treatment.

MISDEMEANORS
Codified folkways that, if violated, evoke a mild but formal penalty. Routine traffic violations are an example.

MOB
An acting crowd composed of people who are emotionally aroused and who intend to take violent and aggressive action. Mobs are a temporary and unstable form of collective behavior.

MOBILIZATION
In Smelser's theory of collective behavior, this includes spreading propaganda, notifying potential activists, and attempting to gather community support.

MONOGAMY
A marital arrangement in which one man is married to one woman at one time.

MORALLY NEUTRAL LAWS
Laws that seek to establish dependable procedures for maintaining an ongoing society. Laws addressing themselves to such mundane and technical matters as traffic control, zoning practices, building permits, and the like are morally neutral.

MORES
Social norms invested with strong feelings of morality. Violation of mores evokes severe punishment because their observance is felt to be essential to the welfare of the group or society.

MOTIVATION
Concerned with how one's behavior is begun, kept going, directed, and stopped. That which causes a person to do and to act.

NEGATIVE SANCTIONS
A system of punishments (including threats of punishment) designed to discourage individuals from violating societal or group expectations. Negative sanctions are one type of social control.

NEOLOCAL
Pattern of residence in which a husband and wife establish an independent residence away from both families of orientation.

NOUVEAUX RICHES
The new rich. Families that have recently acquired their money so rapidly that they continue to exhibit class characteristics of their origins rather than those in upper-class positions.

NUCLEAR FAMILY
This is the basic family unit, which includes parents and their children, biological and adopted.

OBJECTIVE APPROACH
A method of stratifying populations based on an investigator's selection and determination of criteria that differentiate social-class levels. Income, education, and occupation are the most frequently used criteria in the objective approach.

OBJECTIVE REALITY
The version of reality that can be discovered and verified through the scientific method and scientific techniques of investigation.

OBJECTIVISM
The philosophy of Ayn Rand, based on the premise that an individual seeking personal fulfillment through productive and creative acts will bring about circumstances that will contribute to a generally improved human condition. The philosophy of objectivism rejects the concept of human rights without individual effort.

OBJECTIVITY
Objectivity exists when an observation is uninfluenced by one's personal biases, prejudices, beliefs or values. Objectivity requires a detached, impersonal, dispassionate view toward the phenomenon being observed.

OPTIMUM HUMAN CONDITION
The optimum human condition refers to the most favorable conditions for the growth and reproduction of the human organism. Those ideal physical, psycho-

logical, political, economic, and social conditions that provide both collective and individual fulfillment to humankind.

ORGANIC SOLIDARITY

A typology, created by Emile Durkheim, that refers to a modern society characterized by a complex division of labor, a population that is mentally and morally heterogeneous, and a low degree of unity and uniformity.

ORGANIZATION MAN

A typology that is subservient to the organization, hierarchy-conscious, and fearful of risk; one who subordinates his individuality to "play ball on the team." Organization man is tied to bureaucracies.

ORGANIZATIONAL COMPONENT OF CULTURE

The portion of culture that consists of the means by which members of a society coordinate their behavior and interact with one another. More specifically, an extensive network of rules, roles, and relationships that function to create a patterned, regulated social order.

OSTRACISM

Imposed separation or isolation of an individual from established social contacts. One mechanism of social control.

OUT-GROUP

Members of any group who are considered as being excluded from an in-group. All nonmembers of an in-group.

PANIC

Panic occurs when people flee because of hysterical beliefs. Something creates fear and confusion in the crowd. People respond in fear without cooperating or observing normative behavior.

PARTICIPANT OBSERVATION

A method of observation in which an investigator participates as a member of the phenomenon being studied. The goal of the participant observation is to accumulate knowledge about human behavior without distorting the behavior observed.

PASSIVE-CONGENIAL MARRIAGE

A marital life-style into which people simply drift because everyone seems to be marrying and because they have been spending most of their time together, and they ask, "Why *not* get married?" A low-intensity marriage.

PATHOLOGY

The term implies a biological analogy in which societies and individuals are seen as organisms that can be either sick or healthy. The assumption is that, just as human organs are subject to infection, disease, and impaired function, so also is social behavior subject to unhealthy or impaired functioning. Often the concept of pathology is used synonymously with deviant behavior.

PATRIARCHY

Authority within the family unit held by the husband or male head. A patriarchal social system is one in which a polarization of the sexes exists. Men occupy positions of dominance and control over women. Men, as husbands and fathers, tend to rule with unchallenged authority the lives of their women and children. In a pure patriarchal society sexual differentiation pervades virtually all life activities, experiences, and opportunities.

PATRILINEAL MARRIAGE
Marriage in which descent or lineage is traced through the father's family.

PATRILOCAL
Pattern of residence in which the husband and wife live with the husband's family of orientation.

PEER GROUP
A close, intimate group composed of individuals usually of the same age who have relatively equal status. Children's play groups as well as adult groups are examples.

PERSISTENT HUMAN PREDICAMENT
Refers to those aspects of the human experience that all people share. We are all subject to natural disasters. We are all finite beings in a universe that is infinite and eternal. We are all imprisoned within our five senses and the physical composition of our brains. We are all social beings who must adjust to one another.

PERSONAL REALITY
That version of reality that consists of those ideas and beliefs that an individual holds to be true. Reality is as one defines it. Personal reality is synonymous with unique reality.

PERSONAL TROUBLES
According to C. Wright Mills, personal troubles occur within the character of the individual and his or her immediate social setting. To resolve troubles, one must look to the individual.

PLANNED EXPERIMENT
A technique of sociological investigation that is designed to isolate and manipulate some variable and test its influence on some other variable or variables. Planned experiments consist of an experimental group and a control group and two sets of observations.

PLURALISM
The view that groups with different cultures and identities should remain apart from the general American culture. It is a view that opposes that of assimilation.

POLYANDRY
A marital arrangement in which one woman has two or more husbands at the same time.

POLYGAMY
A marital arrangement in which there are multiple mates. Polygamy is of three forms: polygyny, polyandry, and group marriages.

POLYGYNY
A marital arrangement in which one man has two or more wives at the same time.

POSITIVE SANCTIONS
A system of rewards designed to encourage individuals to act in accordance with societal or group expectations. Positive sanctions are one type of social control.

PRECIPITATING FACTOR
An event or incident that causes collective behavior to occur.

PREJUDICE
A rigid set of negative conceptions, feelings, and action-orientations toward members of a particular group. Prejudice is a state of mind.

PRIMARY GROUP
An intimate social group with frequent, direct, personal interaction among its members.

PRIMARY RELATIONSHIPS
Social relations that are durable, based on frequent and direct personal interaction and characterized by intimacy and emotional involvement. A person-oriented relationship that involves whole personalities rather than segments.

PRIMATES
Primates are members of the form of life called mammals. Primates include human beings and animals that most closely resemble humans. Mammals give birth to living offspring.

PRODUCTION VALUES
A cluster of values that emphasizes the virtues of doing, achieving, producing, efficiency, and success.

PROLETARIAT
According to Karl Marx, the working class that consists of wage earners who are exploited and thus forced into a position of opposition to the established system of society.

PROTESTANT ETHIC
A belief system combining respect for the Christian God and for the virtues of diligence, thrift, sobriety, prudence, and moderation in all things as standards by which one should conduct one's life. Beginning as a sacred orientation, the Protestant ethic evolved into a secular work ethic associated with capitalism.

PSEUDOCUSTOMS
Social norms of a transitory nature that are subject to rapid change. Popular music, hair styles, clothing styles, and the like are pseudocustoms.

PSEUDO-GEMEINSCHAFT
A utilitarian relationship that is characterized by pretending to have personal concern for another individual for the purpose of manipulation. Members of *Gesellschaft* often exhibit pseudo-*Gemeinschaft* behavior.

PUBLIC
A public is a scattered group of people concerned about and in the process of discussing a certain issue. Members of a public do not gather together in one place. They are united by a common purpose.

PUBLIC ISSUES

According to C. Wright Mills, public issues transcend the individual and are located in the larger social reality. To resolve issues, one must look to the social structure.

PUBLIC OPINION POLL

A random sampling of the opinions of at least 1500 people. Such a survey should produce results within a margin of error of plus or minus 3 percent.

RACIAL GROUP

An anthropological classification dividing humankind into at least three major racial stocks: Mongoloid, Negroid, and Caucasoid. Criteria for labeling various races are based on such physical characteristics as skin color, hair texture, size and shape of the head, etc.

RACISM

A form of ethnocentrism proclaiming that racial groups are inherently superior and inferior to one another. The central premise is that something called "race" —something fixed and unchangeable that is biologically transmitted from one generation to the next—is the exclusive determinant of character, of personality, and of entire civilizations.

RAGE FOR ORDER

The efforts by humanity to seek explanations and to put into order the mysteries of the universe and the complexities of human behavior.

RANDOM SAMPLE

In this process of selection every member of the population being studied has an equal chance of being chosen, thus minimizing experimenter bias.

REACTIONARY MOVEMENT

A social movement dedicated to the return of the good old behaviors and values. Members *react* to social changes unfavorably. They see present-day values and behaviors as immoral.

REAL CULTURE

Those patterns of behavior that members of society actually observe.

REBELLION

An adaptation to anomie in which the individual rejects conventional cultural goals and seeks to establish a new or radically altered social structure.

REFERENT

The object to which a symbol refers. For example, the word symbol "dog" can be spoken or written and understood by others without any actual dog being present.

REFORMIST MOVEMENT

A social movement dedicated to the reforming of the present structure and values of society. Reformist movements seek to *reform*. They do not desire to destroy the existing social order as a whole.

REPRESSION
According to Freudian theory, one of the major mechanisms by which socialization takes place. Socialization occurs most directly through parental repression of the child's antisocial and anticultural drives.

REPUTATIONAL APPROACH
A method of stratifying populations based on the way in which people perceive one another. Members of a community are placed in a class or stratum depending upon their reputations as perceived by other members of the community.

RESEARCH DESIGN
A strategy or plan that is developed in order to verify a hypothesis.

RESPONSE BIAS
This might occur if a person being interviewed is influenced by any particular social characteristics of the person doing the questioning.

RETREATISM
An adaptation to anomie in which an individual abandons both the cultural goals and the socially accepted means for achieving those goals. Retreatists are "true aliens" because they seek to escape from the requirements of society.

REVOLUTIONARY MOVEMENT
A social movement dedicated to rejecting the present social order and to replacing it with something believed to be superior. If a revolutionary movement succeeds, little about the social institutions of the old society remains the same.

RIOT
A riot is aggressive and destructive collective behavior that has no specific target against which violence is directed. The only prevailing norm is violence for the sake of violence.

RITES OF PASSAGE
Rituals and ceremonies that observe significant changes in the lives of individuals from one phase of the life cycle to another. Rites of passage serve to reinforce the socialization process as well as to support and intensify group loyalties.

RITUALISM
An adaptation to anomie in which an individual simply goes through the motions on a day-to-day basis. Life's activities become routine and lack incentives.

ROLE CONFLICT
Incompatibility between two or more roles that an individual is expected to perform simultaneously. The existence of mutually exclusive expectations for behavior.

ROLE EXPECTATION
All the expectations that specify proper and improper behavior for an individual occupying a given position. What one is expected to do while playing a specific role.

ROLE PERFORMANCE

The degree to which an individual acts in accordance with the expectations for a given role. Role performance is overt behavior that more or less fulfills role expectations.

ROUTINIZATION OF CHARISMA

A process of transition in which charismatic authority, once established and successful, undergoes a transformation to either traditional authority or legal-rational authority.

RUMOR

Information passed from person to person without anyone verifying its accuracy.

SACRED SOCIETY

A typology, created by Howard P. Becker, that refers to a society that is isolated geographically, socially, and psychologically from the rest of the world. Characterized by strong in-group and out-group sentiments, strong and durable kinship ties, the predominance of supernaturalism, powerful allegiance to tradition, and primary relations between members of the society.

SAMPLE SURVEY

A technique of sociological investigation that allows researchers to examine the views of a portion of a population (called the "sample") and then to generalize about the views of the population.

SANCTIONS

A system of rewards and punishments used by groups and societies to encourage conformity and discourage nonconformity.

SCIENTIFIC METHOD

A procedure used for building a body of scientific knowledge through observation, experimentation, and verification. A guide to the logic of scientific inquiry.

SECONDARY GROUP

An impersonal social group that involves only a segment of the members' lives and personalities. Secondary groups are usually united by the special interests of their members and usually perform specialized functions.

SECULAR SOCIETY

A typology, created by Howard P. Becker, that refers to a society that is geographically, socially, and psychologically accessible to the rest of the world. Characterized by the predominance of rationality and science, rapid social change, the existence of formal laws and legal contracts, a high value placed on individualism, and secondary relations between members of the society.

SECONDARY RELATIONSHIPS

Social relations that are impersonal, rational, calculating, and utilitarian. Secondary relations are role-oriented, goal-oriented, and usually devoid of emotional involvement. Secondary relationships are often contractual relationships.

SELF-ACTUALIZATION
According to Maslow, this is becoming all that one is able to become by developing a unique self. In the world of work, it means fulfilling one's potential by excellent work and feeling good about oneself.

SELF-CONCEPT
The aspect of human personality that consists of the individual's conception of self. The self-concept consists of self-awareness, self-identity, and self-esteem.

SENILITY
A decrease in the ability to perform simple tasks; a loss of memory; caused by a loss of brain cells, particularly in a small segment of the population past age 75.

SEXISM
Sexism occurs through negative prejudice and discrimination against a person on the basis of gender. A form of ethnocentrism.

SIGNIFICANT OTHERS
Significant others are individuals with whom we share a relationship that is intimate and that usually conveys expectations of permanency. Parents, siblings, and close friends are significant others.

SINGLE SAVAGE SELF
A term we use to describe the unique individuation of each human being. An intangible.

SKID ROW
An area that attracts the homeless who have no commitment to the work ethic and who are involved in a life-style in which drinking alcohol is the major motivation for living.

SOCIAL BEHAVIOR
Behavior that has incorporated in it the behavior of others. Any overt action that influences or is influenced by the behavior of others. From the perspective of sociology, human behavior is social behavior.

SOCIAL CLASS
A category of people within a system of social stratification who have a similar socioeconomic status and a similar life-style because of their life chances and social location.

SOCIAL-CONTRACT THESIS
A view that humankind emerged from a state of nature upon discovering the advantages of uniting with others. Thus, a social contract was made between people and led to social cooperation and organization. A view incompatible with the sociological perspective.

SOCIAL CONTROL
All those mechanisms that are designed to insure conformity to behavioral patterns that are considered essential to the smooth functioning of human societies and social groups. Positive and negative sanctions are types of social control.

SOCIAL DETERMINISM

A perspective that advocates an image of human beings as dependent, passive agents who are the objects of collective will and who are "rubber stamp" products of their societies.

SOCIAL DISTANCE

A feeling or an actual separation between or among segments of a society's population. Social classes, races, ethnic and religious groups can experience social distance.

SOCIAL DYNAMICS

As defined by Auguste Comte, the study of how human societies develop and change through time.

SOCIAL INSTITUTION

An organized system of social relationships that embodies certain common values and procedures and meets certain basic needs of society. Universal institutions include the family, politics, religion, and economy.

SOCIAL INTERACTION

The process of acting in awareness of others and adjusting responses to the way others respond. Any exchange between two or more individuals that involves a mutual or reciprocal influence.

SOCIAL ISOLATES

Children who have been kept in virtual isolation from significant human contact. Typically deprived of emotional and social interaction, these children manifest nonhuman behaviors.

SOCIAL LOCATION

The level, stratum, or social class into which one is born or socialized. The social location grants or denies certain privileges, power, and prestige to individuals who occupy the various social classes in the society.

SOCIAL MOBILITY

The movement of an individual or group from one social class to another. Social mobility refers to movement up or down a system of stratification.

SOCIAL MOVEMENT

Collective behavior in which efforts are made either to prevent or to promote social change. Social movements exist over a long period.

SOCIAL NORMS

Any standard or rule applying to expectations for human behavior. As behavioral expectations, social norms serve as guideposts that specify what one should, ought, and must do, as well as what one should not, ought not, and must not do. Folkways, mores, and laws are types of social norms.

SOCIAL REALITY

That version of reality consisting of those ideas and beliefs that a number of individuals hold to be true. The social reality is achieved through a consensual validation and is synonymous with the shared reality.

SOCIAL ROLE
A pattern of behavior associated with a distinctive social position. A social role consists of role expectation and role performance.

SOCIAL STATICS
As defined by Auguste Comte, the study of the interrelationships between the various parts of human societies. Social structure.

SOCIAL STRATIFICATION
The system of ranking individuals, families, and populations into different levels according to the distribution of privilege, power, and prestige. The process of stratification creates a social system of unequals and inequities.

SOCIALISM
An economic system based on government ownership of the means of production and distribution. Little free enterprise is allowed, and the people are, in theory, provided with any goods and services judged to be in the interest of the people. The government can be democratic or totalitarian. See Command Economy.

SOCIALIZATION
The process of social interaction in which the individual acquires those characteristic ways of thinking, feeling, and acting that are essential for effective participation within society.

SOCIETY
A large-scale human grouping that shares a common culture and that possesses a comprehensive social system including all of those social institutions required to meet basic human needs.

SOCIOBIOLOGY
The study of the biological basis of social behavior in all forms of life. Sociobiologists believe that humans, for example, behave as they do because of genetic predispositions.

SOCIOCENTRISM
The stage of development in which the child orients its behavior to the behavior of others. The child learns to take into account the wishes and expectations of others. This is the stage of development beyond egocentrism.

SOCIOLOGICAL PERSPECTIVE
The "world view" of sociology that is sensitive to social interaction as the supreme fact of human life. The sociological perspective views human beings as social beings and human behavior as social behavior.

SOCIOLOGY
The scientific study of social interaction. One of the social sciences that seeks to investigate, describe, and analyze the origins, nature, and consequences of social interaction.

SOCIOLOGICAL THEORY
An attempt to organize facts and ideas so that we are able to explain certain patterns of social interaction and social structure.

SPACESHIP EARTH
A phrase likening Earth to a spaceship as a craft with "closed systems." Spaceship Earth has everything on board that it will ever have—all the air, water, metal, soil, and fuel. Unlike a spaceship, however, planet Earth continues to take on more passengers all the time.

SPECIALIZATION
The division of work into special tasks. The duties of any one position tend to be narrow and specific. The bureaucratization of society has increased occupational specialization.

STATE-OF-NATURE THESIS
A view that humankind once lived in a state of nature without social organization and with total individual freedom. In such a state, free from constraint, people, it was thought, existed without the need for other people. A view incompatible with the sociological perspective.

STATUS
A defined position in the social structure that is distinguished from and at the same time related to other positions. Each status is linked to a social role, that is, a pattern of behavior expected of one who occupies a status.

STEREOTYPES
An exaggerated idea, image, or belief associated with some category. The fallacy of stereotyping is the assumption that the alleged attributes of the category apply to all of its members. Allows for no individual differences.

STIMULUS-DEFINITION-RESPONSE
A scheme for explaining behavior based on the existence of an intervening variable between a stimulus and a response. Through the ability to define stimuli, human beings are able to attach meaning and significance to stimuli and consequently alter and exercise some degree of control over their responses.

STIMULUS-RESPONSE
A scheme for explaining behavior based on the assumption of a one-to-one relationship between a particular stimulus and a particular response. A useful scheme for explaining reflex actions in human organisms and the behavior of animals in general.

STRUCTURAL CONDUCIVENESS
In reference to collective behavior, this is a condition in society in which conflicting interest groups are apt to clash.

STRUCTURAL FUNCTIONALISM
The view that society should be thought of as a living thing with parts that assist one another to keep the system alive and functioning. Concerned with an overview or an emphasis upon large segments of society.

STRUCTURAL STRAIN
This occurs when people are aware of contradictions or tensions in society. An example would be the structural strain because of the difference between the American creed of human equality and the American deed of racism and sexism.

SUBCULTURE
A distinctive set of attitudes, values, and behaviors characteristic of a particular group within the larger society. A life-style within the total culture that not only shares in the society's total culture but also has unique patterns that differ in varying degrees from other life-styles.

SUBJECTIVE APPROACH
A method of stratifying populations based on self-identification. The subjective approach relies upon how people perceive and classify themselves.

SUCCESSION
The concept that the occurrence of events is determined by cause-and-effect relationships cannot be *proved*. The assumption of succession is that all one can know is that one event was followed by the other event within a context called "time."

SUPEREGO
According to Freudian theory, the aspect of human personality that consists of internalized parental and cultural attitudes, values, and expectations. Created through socialization during the formative years, the superego is similar to the concept of conscience.

SYMBOLIC INTERACTION THEORY
The view that society should be thought of as a process of interaction among people using symbols. Society exists if people agree upon the meaning of language, facial expressions, and movements. Concerned with day-to-day interpretations that people make of the human experience.

TAKING THE ROLE OF THE OTHER
Coined by George Herbert Mead, this phrase suggests that we can view our thoughts, feelings, and behaviors from the perspective of people other than ourselves. It refers to our ability to see ourselves as others see us.

TECHNOLOGICAL COMPONENT OF CULTURE
That portion of culture consisting of all the material items that members of a society have and use. It also includes such nonmaterial phenomena as skills, crafts, and arts that enable people to produce material goods.

TEMPOROCENTRISM
The unexamined, largely unconscious acceptance of one's own era and lifetime as the center of sociological significance. A form of ethnocentrism that emphasizes the superiority of age groupings.

TOTAL MARRIAGE
A marital life-style differing from a "vital marriage" only because common interests are more numerous. Neither partner has a truly private existence.

TRADITION ECONOMY
An economic system in which modes of production and distribution are based on procedures originated in the distant past. There exists a hereditary chain assuring that certain skills and crafts will be passed on from one generation to the next. The concept of progress is meaningless in a tradition economy.

TRADITIONAL AUTHORITY
Authority in which the leader or leaders assume power by virtue of certain traditional laws of succession that have been handed down from the past. Having a sacred quality, their decisions are usually above reproach by the governed.

TRANSITIONAL GROWTH
A stage of demographic transition that is characterized by a high birth rate and a low death rate. Improvements in medical care, agricultural techniques, public sanitation, better education regarding personal hygiene, and other technological changes contribute to the decreasing mortality rate. Characterized by optimism, industrialization, and urbanization.

TRANSITION THEORY
A theory of demographic evolution that seeks to explain population growth in terms of the relationship between birth rates and death rates. Demographic transition theory consists of three stages: high potential growth, transitional growth, and incipient decline.

URBAN SOCIETY
An ideal type referring to a society that is the polar extreme of the folk society. Urban society is dynamic and complex with the bulk of human interaction based on secondary relations.

URBANIZATION
A growth in the number of cities and in the spread of urban areas and urban attitudes and behavior throughout society.

VARIABLE
This could be any attitude or behavior or action or condition that might change or bring about change as a result of experimentation.

VICIOUS CYCLE
A process in which two or more variables are so related that a change in one results in a change in the second, which in turn leads to a further change in the first. Useful in understanding the relationship between prejudice and discrimination.

VISIBILITY
The degree to which a human grouping is identifiable. Customs, accents, mannerisms, skin color, and other factors contribute to the visibility of human groupings and individuals.

VITAL MARRIAGE
A marital life-style that most Americans say they would like to have. Partners are psychologically bound together in important areas of their lives. They share experiences and activities together with zest and vitality.

WORK
That which a person does to survive. Work is the means by which people provide the goods and services needed and desired by society.

ZERO POPULATION GROWTH
If the births per thousand people during a given period of time equal the deaths per thousand people, the population neither increases nor decreases. Being stable, it is then at zero population growth.

PICTURE CREDITS

Chapter 1

Chapter Opener: © Sherry Suris/Rapho-Photo Researchers.
Page 4: Culver Pictures.
Page 5: © 1976 Joel Gordon.
Page 14: © Richard Wood 1980/The Picture Cube.
Page 28: © Sepp Seitz 1980/Woodfin Camp.

Chapter 2

Chapter Opener: © Harvey Stein 1980.
Page 44: Peter Buckley/Photo Researchers.
Page 54: Peter Menzel.
Page 64: © Barbara Alper /Stock, Boston.

Chapter 3

Chapter Opener: Arthur Tress/Photo Researchers.
Page 81: Ellis Herwig/Stock, Boston.
Page 82: © J. Allen Cash/Rapho-Photo Researchers.
Page 87: F. Miller/TIME-LIFE Picture Agency.
Page 97: Tom Korody/Sygma.
Page 112: Robert V. Eckert, Jr./EKM-Nepenthe.
Page 114: © Joel Gordon, 1978.

Chapter 4

Chapter Opener: © Joan Liftin 1980/Woodfin Camp.
Page 125: Chris Steele Perkins/Magnum.
Page 133: Jan Halaska © 1979/Photo Researchers.
Page 146: Mathias T. Oppersdorff/Photo Researchers.

Chapter 5

Chapter Opener: © Mark Chester 1974/Photo Researchers.
Page 156: Tim Graham/Sygma.
Page 166: © Marc & Evelyn Bernheim 1980/Woodfin Camp.
Page 175: © Russell Abraham 1976/Stock, Boston.

Chapter 6

Chapter Opener: © Sepp Seitz 1980/Woodfin Camp.
Page 192: Harry Riddle/The Stockmarket-The Burton Holmes Collection.
Page 209: Burt Glinn/Magnum.
Page 221: © Richard Kalvar/Magnum.
Page 225: © Anne Sager 1979/Photo Researchers.

Chapter 7

Chapter Opener: © Harvey Stein 1980.
Page 242: © Jim Anderson 1980/Woodfin Camp.
Page 249: Arthur Grace/Sygma.
Page 255: Library of Congress.
Page 257: Courtesy The New York Historical Society.
Page 266: Joel Gordon © 1978.
Page 270: © Jim Anderson 1978/Woodfin Camp.

Chapter 8

Chapter Opener: © Geoffrey Gove/Rapho-Photo Researchers.
Page 303: © Vicki Lawrence 1975/Stock, Boston.
Page 311: © Paolo Koch/Photo Researchers.
Page 315: © Joe Portogallo 1972/Photo Researchers.

Chapter 9

Chapter Opener: Pierre Berger/Photo Researchers.
Page 338: International Harvester.
Page 345: © John Marmaras 1980/Woodfin Camp.
Page 350: New York Public Library Picture Collection.
Page 359: Ellis Herwig/Stock, Boston.

Chapter 10

Chapter Opener: Christopher Brown/Stock, Boston.
Page 376: Mike Norcia/Sygma.
Page 394: Susan berkowitz, Courtesy C.U.N.Y./University Computer Center.

Chapter 11

Chapter Opener: Arthur Tress/Photo Researchers.
Page 412: Hugh Rogers/Monkmeyer.
Page 419: © Jason Laure 1980/Woodfin Camp.
Page 430: © Bettye Lane/Photo Researchers.
Page 432: B.D. Vidibor/Photo Researchers.

Chapter 12

Chapter Opener: Arthur Tress/Photo Researchers.
Page 447: Will McIntyre/Photo Researchers.
Page 453: Kathy Bendo/Photo Researchers.
Page 461: © Arthur Tress/Photo Researchers.

Name Index

Subject Index